UNLOCKING

LAND LAW

6th edition

Judith Bray

UNLOCKINGTHELAW

Routledge
Taylor & Francis Group

LONDON AND NEW YORK

First published 2019
by Routledge
2 Park Square, Milton Park, Abingdon, Oxon OX14 4RN

and by Routledge
52 Vanderbilt Avenue, New York, NY 10017

Routledge is an imprint of the Taylor & Francis Group, an informa business

British Library Cataloguing-in-Publication Data
A catalogue record for this book is available from the British Library

Library of Congress Cataloging-in-Publication Data
Names: Bray, Judith, 1954- author.
Title: Unlocking land law / by Judith Bray.
Description: 6th edition. | Abingdon, Oxon ; New York, NY : Routledge, 2019. |
Series: Unlocking the law | Includes bibliographical references and index.
Identifiers: LCCN 2018052270| ISBN 9780367183677 (hardback) | ISBN 9781138301054 (pbk.)
Subjects: LCSH: Real property–England.
Classification: LCC KD829 .B735 2019 | DDC 343.42/025–dc23
LC record available at https://lccn.loc.gov/2018052270

ISBN: 978-0-367-18367-7 (hbk)
ISBN: 978-1-138-30105-4 (pbk)
ISBN: 978-0-203-73288-5 (ebk)

Typeset in Palatino
by Wearset Ltd, Boldon, Tyne and Wear

Printed by CPI Group (UK) Ltd, Croydon CR0 4YY

Contents

4 THE TRANSFER AND CREATION OF PROPERTY INTERESTS — 95

Acknowledgements

I would like to thank Chloe James, Alexandra Buckley, Emily Kindleysides, Hannah Malkin and everyone at Routledge and Wearset for their enthusiastic approach to this new edition. I dedicate the book to my husband Richard, who, over the last fourteen years, has burnt almost as much midnight oil as myself and provided constant support, a sense of humour and invaluable advice. I also dedicate this edition to William, Alice, Emily and Alasdair, a whole new generation who I hope will one day enjoy the fascinating world of land law as much as I have done.

Judith Bray

Guide to the book

In the *Unlocking the Law* books all the essential elements that make up the law are clearly defined to bring the law alive and make it memorable. In addition, the books are enhanced with learning features to reinforce learning and test your knowledge as you study. Follow this guide to make sure you get the most from reading this book.

AIMS AND OBJECTIVES

Defines what you will learn in each chapter.

definition
Find key legal terminology at a glance

SECTION

Highlights sections from Acts.

CASE EXAMPLE

Illustrates the law in action.

JUDGMENT

Provides extracts from judgments on cases.

ACTIVITY

Enables you to test yourself as you progress through the chapter.

SAMPLE ESSAY QUESTIONS

Provide you with real-life sample essays and show you the best way to plan your answer.

SUMMARY

Concludes each chapter to reinforce learning.

Preface

The *Unlocking the Law* series is an entirely new style of undergraduate law textbooks. Many student texts are very prose dense and have little in the way of interactive materials to help a student feel his or her way through the course of study on a given module.

The purpose of this series, then, is to try to make learning each subject area more accessible by focusing on actual learning needs, and by providing a range of different supporting materials and features.

All topic areas are broken up into 'bite size' sections with a logical progression and extensive use of headings and numerous sub-headings. Each book in the series will also contain a variety of charts, diagrams and key fact summaries to reinforce the information in the body of the text. Diagrams and flow charts are particularly useful because they can provide a quick and easy understanding of the key points, especially when revising for examinations. Key facts charts not only provide a quick visual guide through the subject but are useful for revision purposes also.

The books have a number of common features in the layout. Important cases are separated out for easy access and have full citation in the text as well as the table of cases for ease of reference. The emphasis of the series is on depth of understanding much more than breadth. For this reason each text also includes key extracts from judgments where appropriate. Extracts from academic comment from journal articles and leading texts are also included to give some insight into the academic debate on complex or controversial areas.

Finally, the books also include much formative 'self-testing', with a variety of activities ranging through subject specific comprehension, application of the law and a range of other activities to help the student gain a good idea of his or her progress in the course.

Note also that all incidental references to 'he', 'him', his, etc., are intended to be gender neutral.

Many students regard Land Law as a difficult and uninviting subject to study but Land Law is not a dry academic subject; it covers issues that affect all our lives such as the buying and selling of houses, the letting or renting of flats, disputes between neighbours, rights of way across land and the inheritance of property under a will. It even covers lost and found objects, the discovery of treasure and valuable minerals in the ground. I hope you will find the layout of this book helpful and stimulating. The aim is to combine explanations of the law with short summaries of cases and some practical exercises. This latest edition has been extensively rewritten and updated and it includes references to a number of recent decisions including *Davies v Davies, Marr v Collie, Regency Villas v Diamond Resorts, Smith v Molyneaux* and *McDonald v McDonalds*. The law is as stated on 31 December 2018.

Judith Bray

Figures

Tables

Table of cases

EUROPE

European Court of Human Rights

AUSTRALIA

CANADA

NEW ZEALAND

SINGAPORE

Table of statutes and statutory instruments

TABLE OF STATUTES AND STATUTORY INSTRUMENTS

TABLE OF STATUTES AND STATUTORY INSTRUMENTS

1

Introduction

AIMS AND OBJECTIVES

After reading this chapter, you should be able to:

- Understand the different aspects of the definition of land
- Explain what is meant by an estate in land
- Explain what rights a landowner will have over the surface area of the land
- Explain what rights a landowner has over items found in the land or on the land
- Understand the difference between a fixture and a chattel
- Explain what rights a landowner has over the airspace above his land

1.1 Introduction

Land is central to everyone's lives. We all have to live somewhere, even if it is not a permanent home. Land law is the study of the relationship between land and the owner of that land. However, when we speak of owners of land we include not only the owner in law, who has the right to buy and sell the land, but also others who have lesser rights, such as the right to walk on the land. Many different people can be said to be owners of rights in respect of the same piece of land. These rights may also extend to having rights of control over your neighbour's land: if they try to develop their garden and build another house or build an extension, you may be able to stop them. It is the way all these rights overlap that causes many of the problems in land law.

> 'The name "land law" suggests a simple contextual category: all the law about land.... Every business needs premises, every factory needs a site. For most of us as private individuals our home is the centre of our lives. Functionally, this core of land law has the task of providing the structure within which people and businesses can safely acquire and exploit land for daily use, to live and to work. To discharge that function, it has to have its own conceptual apparatus.... There is a recurrent problem. Property rights in land have roots a millennium deep in a pre-commercial society in which land and wealth were virtually synonymous.

The structuring of land and the power that went with it was then land law's principal mission…'

P Birks, 'Before We Begin: Five Keys to Land Law' in S Bright and J Dewar (eds), *Land Law: Themes and Perspectives* (Oxford University Press, 1998), p. 457

1.2 The definition of 'land'

The definition of 'land' has long troubled lawyers. There have been several attempts at a statutory definition but none have been wholly satisfactory. We can start by looking at the statutory definition. 'Land' is defined in the Law of Property Act 1925 (LPA 1925) at s 205(1)(ix):

SECTION

2

INTRODUCTION

corporeal hereditaments
These are rights that have some real or tangible quality

incorporeal hereditaments
These are intangible rights in land

mortgages
A mortgage is security for money lent usually in the form of land

leases
A lease is one of two legal estates in land which gives the tenant exclusive possession of the property but for a limited time

's 205(1)(ix) Land includes land of any tenure, and mines and minerals, whether or not held apart from the surface, buildings or parts of buildings (whether the division is horizontal, vertical or made in any other way) and other corporeal hereditaments also a manor, an advowson, a rent and other incorporeal hereditaments; and an easement, right, privilege, or benefit in, over or derived from land…. And mines and minerals include any strata or seam of minerals or substances in or under any land, and power of working and getting the same.'

It is a long and complex definition and shows that land can include many different aspects and rights.

1.2.1 Corporeal and incorporeal hereditaments

Within the definition in s 205, two types of rights are identified: **corporeal** and **incorporeal hereditaments**.

1. **Corporeal hereditaments**: these are rights that have some real or tangible quality. They could include buildings or anything growing on the land, such as shrubs and trees, or anything which is found under the ground, such as minerals. These are as much part of the land as the physical plot of land itself.

2. **Incorporeal hereditaments**: these are intangible rights in land. Incorporeal hereditaments cannot physically be seen but they affect the landowner's enjoyment of the land and in many cases the enjoyment of the owner of the adjoining property as well. An example of an incorporeal hereditament would be the right to use a path crossing your neighbour's garden as a short cut [an easement]. This will affect your neighbour's enjoyment of his land. These rights, which include **mortgages** and **leases**, as well as **restrictive covenants** and **easements** will also affect the exact nature of your neighbour's rights over his plot of land.

ACTIVITY

Quick quiz

Consider the following rights over land: are they corporeal or incorporeal hereditaments?

1. You have agreed with your neighbour that you will not use your land for business purposes.
2. You allow your friend to rent your garage for £50 per week.
3. You plant several rose bushes in your garden.
4. You find some gold in the stream which runs through your garden.
5. The property that you agree to buy has a large stable block.

restrictive covenants

A covenant is an agreement in a deed between the covenantor and the covenantee imposing positive or negative obligations on the covenantor

easements

An easement is the right to enjoy land owned by another person

tenure

The exchange of rights in land for the performances of services to the superior

Note here that the first two rights over land are incorporeal rights (a restrictive covenant and a weekly lease) whereas the other rights are all corporeal (plants and shrubs; the gold and the buildings including the stable block).

Land also has a three-dimensional quality – a surface area, the airspace above it and the ground below – and also a possible fourth dimension which is made up of rights and interests in the land and, more importantly, the length of time that you can enjoy the land. We shall start by looking at the way these rights and interests have developed over hundreds of years to leave us with the system that we know today.

1.3 Tenures and estates in land

1.3.1 Tenure

After 1066 it was held that all land was owned by the king, and his subjects were then granted rights in that land. The rights that they held were really as rights as tenants of the king. In return for the right to enjoy the land each tenant agreed to carry out certain duties for the king. This was called **tenure**. Tenure was similar to paying rent but instead of paying money the tenants agreed to do something that the king wanted to be done. Tenure took several different forms – spiritual, military or agricultural.

Examples of tenure: agreement by the tenant to pray for the soul of the grantor (frankalmoign), the provision of armed horsemen for battle (knight's service) and the performance of agricultural services (socage).

The doctrine of tenure today

By around 1350, many of the tenants who held the tenure of knight's service preferred to make a money payment (scutage) rather than provide armed knights. By the end of the Middle Ages the decline in the value of money meant that it was not worth collecting scutage. The spiritual tenures experienced a similar demise, although frankalmoign continued until it was abolished by the Administration of Estates Act 1925.

Socage tenures were also largely commuted to monetary payments during the Middle Ages, and these payments had generally ceased to be made by the end of the medieval period.

Today, all of the early tenures have ceased to exist with the exception of common socage. All freehold tenures are therefore equivalent to socage tenure. This explains why there is still some truth in saying that all freehold land is owned by the Crown.

1.3.2 Estates

In law an estate in land means that you have a right of possession to that land. Historically, it was referred to as a right of **seisin**. When we speak of 'estates' we are talking about how long a person is allowed to enjoy the plot of land.

JUDGMENT

'The land itself is one thing, and the estate in the land is another thing, for an estate in the land is a time in the land, or land for a time, and there are diversities of estates, which are no more than diversities of time.'

Walsingham's Case (1573) 75 ER 805

The law would protect the tenant's right to the land against anyone unless they could prove that they had a better right to the land than the tenant.

Today there are only **two ways** that you can be said to own land in law:

1. a **freehold estate** which is regarded as absolute ownership, or

2. a **leasehold estate** which is absolute ownership but only for a defined period of time, for example example a lease of a flat for two years.

1.3.3 Legal estates in land before 1925

The position was very different in 1066. There were several legal estates in land which were all regarded as absolute ownership but, unlike freehold and leasehold ownership, they had some limiting feature.

1. **Fee simple**: this could last as long as the original grantee or his heirs survived. In practical terms this meant that it could last indefinitely. Until the fourteenth century the land had to pass through the family but this rule changed allowing the land to be sold in the owner's lifetime to anyone including a stranger or left by will to anyone, including someone outside the family.

2. **Fee tail**: this is not recognised as a legal estate today. It was a grant of land that could only pass to a certain class of descendant, usually the descendants of the original grantee and lasted as long as the original grantee or his descendants survived. If no descendant survived, the land passed to the Crown.

3. **Life estate**: this was recognised as a freehold estate although it was limited in length. It would end on the death of the holder of the life estate. It could be transferred during the original owner's lifetime but it would end when the original owner died. If someone purchased a life estate it was always dependent on the life of a third party so the purchaser was taking a risk on the length of the original owner's life.

Today, only the first of the three estates in land is recognised. The others will be less than a legal estate. They take effect **in equity**, which means rights in the land where the owner has only limited control over decision-making over the land itself, for example he has no right to sell the legal estate. The ownership of the land lies with third parties called trustees.

1.3.4 Estates in land from and after 1925

Section 1 of the LPA 1925 reduced the number of legal estates in land to two:

1. an estate in fee simple absolute in possession (the freehold estate);

2. an estate for a term of years absolute (the leasehold estate).

So the freehold estate in land is also called a **fee simple absolute in possession**. This can be broken down into three different parts:

1. **Fee simple**: meaning freehold ownership giving absolute rights over the property during someone's lifetime but also the chance to leave it to someone else on your death. (You may recall from above that, the life estate was a legal estate before 1925 but the property would revert back to the grantor when the grantee died.)

2. **Absolute**: meaning no limits on ownership, for example 'to Y until he leaves school' would not give Y absolute ownership and control over the property so this could not be a freehold estate.

3. **In possession**: meaning immediate occupation and enjoyment of the land. There would be no question of anyone else having a prior claim.

INTRODUCTION

grant
The transfer of property by written document where the property itself is not immediately transferred

grantor
The person who owns the land but is passing it to someone else. This would have been the person who had received it from the king. He became grantor of the land when he passed it on to someone else

grantee
The person who receives the land from the grantor

1.4 Ownership of the surface of the land: boundaries

'Whoever owns the soil owns everything up to the heavens and down to the depth of the Earth' (attributed to Accursius of Bologna in *Glossa Ordinaria on Corpus Iuris* (thirteenth century).

Any landowner will want to be quite clear about the extent of rights that he may have over a plot of land that he has purchased. He will start by finding out where the boundaries are. This will tell him how far his land extends. It will sometimes depend on the site of the land; in particular, does it border the sea or a river?

1.4.1 Land bordering the coast or a river

Land is often seen as permanent and unchanging but the processes of coastal erosion and deposition challenge this. Over a period of time, where land borders a river or the sea, soil may be removed by erosion and it appears to cease to belong to the owner and will transfer to the land of another. The effect of this is that one person's land will increase at the expense of the other. The law has to determine how these changes affect the ownership of the land.

1.4.2 The doctrine of accretion

alluvion
Additions to land bordering water

The doctrine of **accretion** is the legal mechanism employed to resolve disputes arising through changes in land bordering water. The doctrine of **accretion** says that any naturally occurring additions of soil to the waterside land (alluvion) become the property of the owner of the land which is increased and any reduction in the area of land (diluvion) must be borne by the landowner losing the land.

diluvion
Reductions to land bordering water

According to Lord Wilberforce in *Southern Centre of Theosophy Inc v State of South Australia* [1982] 1 All ER 283 the changes must take place very slowly, gradually and by imperceptible movements. He added: 'In the lottery of life the landowner may lose as well as gain from changes in the water boundary or level.'

This case concerned an inland lake in Australia which was reduced in size by 20 acres through deposits of sand over 60 years. The lake was owned by the Crown but it was held that it lost title to the 20 acres. This was added to the title held by the owners of the area gaining the land because the changes had taken place so gradually.

If there are any sudden changes as a result of flooding then the rules do not apply and the boundaries remain the same. For example, X and Y both own land on either side of a river. Suppose there is a storm which results in X's land losing considerable amounts of soil and so Y's land is considerably increased. Y cannot then claim the change in boundary under the doctrine of accretion and X's boundary will be changed to adapt to the sudden change.

Compare the situation where X is convinced that his land is receding. He measures the boundary and after five years there is a change of one-third of a metre – the doctrine will probably apply and X cannot do anything about the loss to his land.

When will the doctrine be applied?

The modern law stops short of applying the doctrine of accretion to all cases. It has to be decided whether the interest in land which is the subject of **accretion** is fixed or moveable and this is only made clear by looking at the wording of the conveyance. So if you know that the boundaries are subject to change and the conveyance refers to this then the landowner with an increased area of land cannot claim that for himself.

The doctrine of accretion can be excluded by clear words in the conveyance.

The Land Registration Act 2002, s 61 expressly states that a registered estate in land as shown in the Register as having a particular boundary does not affect the operation of the doctrine of **accretion**.

The doctrine of accretion shows us that not only does land extend upwards and downwards, it can grow or shrink in surface area.

1.4.3 Other boundaries

Even where boundaries do not border the sea and inland waterways, there may be uncertainty. The Land Registration Rules 2003 accept that maps and plans are imprecise and a filed plan or general map relevant to any registered title is normally 'deemed to indicate the general boundaries only' and the exact line of the boundary is left undetermined. So a map lodged at the Land Registry does not prove the location of the boundary. This general principle has been preserved in the Land Registration Act 2002 (LRA 2002). There is provision under s 60 LRA 2002 for rules to make provision for boundaries to be fixed exactly and under the Land Registration Rules 2003, r 122 the Registrar is allowed to determine an exact boundary line himself. Once this has been done, the boundary as shown on the map at the Land Registry will be conclusive.

SECTION

's 60(3) Rules may make provision enabling or requiring the exact line of the boundary of a registered estate to be determined and may, in particular, make provision about –

(a) the circumstances in which the exact line of a boundary may or must be determined;

(b) how the exact line of a boundary may be determined;

(c) procedure in relation to applications for determination.'

Unless such an application is made, then older, more general, common law rules will apply. These are some of the presumptions which can be used to decide the issue.

The 'hedge and ditch' rule

Wibberley (Alan) Building Ltd v Insley [1999] 1 WLR 894 applied the hedge and ditch rule which suggests that where land has a boundary consisting of a hedge and a ditch then the boundary lies along the edge of the ditch on the far side of the hedge. This assumes that when the owner of the land first dug the ditch he deposited the earth on his own land rather than the land of his neighbour. Without this rule, the more natural boundary would be the hedge.

JUDGMENT

'Boundary disputes are a particularly painful form of litigation. Feelings can run high and disproportionate amounts of money are spent. Claims to small and valueless pieces of land are pursued with the zeal of Fortinbras's army. It it therefore important that the law on boundaries are as clear as possible.'

Lord Hoffmann

The 'ad medium filum' rule

This applies to land which abuts a highway or non-tidal river. The rule says that the boundary between properties on opposite sides of the road is a line drawn down the middle of the road. The owners of land adjoining the highway are presumed to own the sub-soil as far as the middle of the road and the airspace above the soil. The owner cannot use the sub-soil so as to interfere with the use of the highway, for example if the sub-soil contained a mineral such as Fuller's Earth or alternatively gravel, you could not extract it in such a way as to cause subsidence to the road.

1.4.4 Natural rights of support for the land

Landowners have certain rights which are incidental to ownership and could give rise to an action in tort if they are interfered with. It is accepted that every landowner has the right to enjoy his land in its natural state and this means it must not be put at risk by a neighbour who undermines the foundations.

A landowner may be able to sue if his neighbour starts extensive mining operations and as a result his house is affected by subsidence. In order to be successful he would have to prove that his land has been affected. No case would succeed in court if the owner merely had proof that mining operations were going on and could affect his house.

It is important to note that the right affects only the land itself and not the buildings on the land. This can be criticised. It should extend to buildings as well. However, the land-owner may have a remedy for damage to buildings because the right of support for buildings may be recognised as an easement. The problem is that the claimant must first satisfy the rules relevant to easements and cannot claim the right of support automatically.

CASE EXAMPLE

Dalton v Henry Angus & Co (1881) 6 App Cas 740

The court upheld an easement of support acquired under the rules of **prescription or long use**, to be enjoyed by one landowner as against another. There was disagreement in court as to whether this was a negative or positive easement. The House of Lords held it to be a positive easement. The neighbour had removed his house which had affected the neighbouring building and although he could not claim for the damage to the building he could rely on the right of support.

prescription

Acquisition of an easement by a claimant through long use

1.5 Ownership of the surface of the land: items found in or on the surface of the land, including minerals

1.5.1 Fixtures and fittings

A fixture is a chattel which under the law becomes part of the land itself and belongs to the landowner.

Section 205(1)(ix) of the LPA 1925 specifically mentions buildings and parts of buildings within the statutory definition as forming part of the land. This is further developed because any item affixed to the land becomes land itself. There is an old maxim '*quicquid plantatur solo, solo cedit*' which, translated, means 'whatever is attached to the soil becomes part of it'. Any **fixture** also passes automatically to a purchaser under s 62, LPA 1925.

If the item has not become a fixture then it will be a mere chattel and so will not pass with the property to the purchaser and the seller can legally take it as his own on the sale of the property. For example, the clothes of the seller will always remain chattels and will not pass to the purchaser, but what of the fitted wardrobe that they are in? Some fitted wardrobes are attached to the wall but some can be free-standing. Specific forms

fixture

Any chattel that has become so attached to the land that it forms part of the land are used in conveyancing that deal with the ownership of movable items on the sale of property. These forms can usually solve any uncertainty about ownership of items as between the parties themselves. Where these forms are silent on an issue or are ambiguous, then the common law will apply. The common law will resolve the question of whether the purchaser can claim the fitted wardrobe and any other item that is not clearly a fixture or a chattel.

The law applies two tests:

1. the degree of annexation;

2. the purpose of annexation.

CASE EXAMPLE

Holland v Hodgson (1872) LR 7 CP 328

Spinning looms were nailed to the floor of a factory and the mortgagees of the factory claimed them as fixtures.

Blackburn J said:

'There is no doubt that the general maxim of the law is, that what is annexed to the land becomes part of the land; but it is very difficult, if not impossible to say with precision what constitutes annexation sufficient for this purpose. It is a question which must depend on the circumstances of each case, and mainly on two circumstances, as indicating the intention viz. the degree of annexation and the object of the annexation. When the article in question is no further attached to the land, than by its own weight it is generally to be considered a mere chattel ... but even in such a case, if the intention is apparent to make the articles part of the land, they do become part of the land ... Thus blocks of stone placed one on top of another without any mortar or cement for the purpose of forming a dry stone wall would become part of the land, though the same stones, if deposited in a builder's yard and for convenience sake stacked on the top of each other in the form of a wall, would remain chattels.'

Blackburn J is highlighting the importance of the method of annexation of the object to the land. This was a crucial issue at the time when this case was decided. He suggests that even if an object is very heavy, if it never becomes fixed to the land then it remains a chattel, whereas an item that is firmly fixed will become a fixture.

He then goes on to introduce the idea that what matters is the intention when the item is fixed. This later became a more significant issue than the practical question of how the item was attached to the ground.

'On the other hand, an article may be very firmly fixed to the land, and yet the circumstances may be such as to shew that it was never intended to be part of the land, and then it does not become part of the land ... Perhaps the true rule is, that articles not otherwise attached to the land than by their own weight are not to be considered as part of the land, unless the circumstances are such that they were intended to be part of the land, the onus of showing that they were so intended lying on those who assert that they have ceased to be chattels, and that, on the contrary, an article which is affixed to the land even slightly is to be considered as part of the land, unless the circumstances are such as to shew that it was intended all along to continue a chattel, the onus lying on those who contend that it is a chattel.'

Blackburn J regarded these items as part of the building because they were affixed to the floor and therefore they were fixtures. However, they were fixed by a single nail and could be removed easily without damage to the building and so it is harder to explain why they were regarded as fixtures.

Today the degree of annexation is less important and no longer conclusive. The second test of purpose of annexation has become far more significant.

The degree of annexation

This depends on whether the item is resting on the land by its own weight or whether it has been fixed. Traditionally, if an object rested on the ground by its own weight it was regarded as a chattel. So a Dutch barn resting on timber on the ground would be a chattel and could be removed by the seller in spite of its size and the difficulties posed by its removal.

CASE EXAMPLE

Hamp v Bygrave (1983) 266 EG 720

A number of items were removed by the seller and the purchasers argued that they were fixtures and should remain at the property. The items included patio lights fixed to the wall with screws, six urns resting on their own weight, a stone Chinese ornament resting on its own weight, several statues and their plinths and a lead trough.

> 'The first question is, therefore, were the items or any of them, fixtures? It is accepted that the answer to that question depends upon the application of two tests. First what was the degree of annexation? There is no doubt that none of the items was fixed or attached to the land or to any structure which was itself attached to the land. Each rested by its own weight either on the land itself or on some sort of plinth, and only in the case of the Chinese figure was the plinth fixed or attached to the land. Judged by this test therefore they were all prima facie chattels.'

However in spite of the fact that the items were not fixed permanently to the land the judge held that they were fixtures because under the second test they were intended to be 'part and parcel of the garden' and had been added in order to improve the property.

It is clear that the way the item is fixed is not conclusive, particularly today when technological advances have allowed items to be removed easily, even after semi-permanent fixing.

In *Holland v Hodgson* (1872) it was held that there were two questions to ask:

1. whether the annexation was intended to increase the value or enjoyment of the property;
2. whether it was for the better enjoyment of the item.

What happens if there is no annexation at all? This may be because the item is very heavy and so rests on its own weight.

CASE EXAMPLE

Elitestone Ltd v Morris [1997] 1 WLR 687

A wooden bungalow rested on its own weight on concrete pillars. As pointed out in the judgment, the materials used to construct the building, such as the chipboard ceilings, had all started life as chattels.

> 'A house which is constructed in such a way so as to be removable, whether as a unit, or in sections, may well remain a chattel, even though it is connected temporarily to mains services such as water and electricity. But a house which is constructed in such a way that it cannot be removed at all, save by destruction, cannot have been intended to remain as a chattel. It must have been intended to form part of the realty ... Applying the dry stone wall analogy to the present case, I do not doubt that when Mr Morris's bungalow was built, and as each of the timber frame walls were placed in position, they all became part of the structure, which was itself part and parcel of the land.'
>
> Lloyd LJ

The issue in this case was whether the occupiers of the bungalow occupied as tenants, which depended on the property being found to be a fixture. If it was a chattel then they would have been mere licensees and would have been unprotected when the owner of the land tried to evict them. The claimants sought protection under the Rent Acts which protect the rights of tenants, but not licensees, and this was dependent on the bungalow being part of the land. The court found that the bungalow was a fixture. Removal would only have been possible if it was demolished and then rebuilt elsewhere. A different conclusion was drawn in *HE Dibble v Moore* [1970] 2 QB 181 where greenhouses were deemed to be chattels. Lord Lloyd referred to this case in his judgment in *Elitestone v Morris* commenting '... I note that ... Megaw LJ, at p. 187G, drew attention to some evidence "that it was customary to move such greenhouses every few years to a fresh site." It is obvious that a greenhouse which can be moved from site to site is a long way removed from a two bedroom bungalow which cannot be moved at all without being demolished'. More recently in *Mew v Tristmire* [2011] EWCA Civ 912 a houseboat was held to be a chattel. The claimants lived on houseboats which rested on wooden platforms around the harbour. As in the case of *Elitestone* they wanted to claim Rent Act protection and this depended on proof that the houseboats were fixtures. The court held that the houseboats could easily be moved away from the harbour and so distinguished *Elitestone* because in this case the houseboats could be moved without having first to be demolished unlike the bungalow in *Elitestone*. The court also placed emphasis on the original intention of the parties which had always been that the houseboats would not be permanent. The Land Tribunal came to a similar conclusion in *Caddick v Whitsand Bay Holiday Park Ltd* [2015] UKUT 63 (LC) when it found that a holiday bungalow was not a fixture. In *Environment Agency v Gibbs* [2016] EWHC 843, a criminal case heard on appeal in the Divisional Court, a defendant had been prosecuted for failing to register his boat as required by law. The court held that the structures referred to as houseboats and moored on a river were not vessels requiring registration because they had no means of navigation on the water. They were constructed as 'homes' for people to live on the water and therefore did not require registration as boats.

Where chattels are not affixed to the land but stand on their own weight, the court looks closely at the second test, i.e. the intention of the owner of the chattel. In *D'Eyncourt v Gregory* (1866) LR 3 Eq 382 a number of stone statues were arranged in the garden of a large house, standing on their own weight. The purchaser argued that they were fixtures and should be left with the property. The court applied the second test (the purpose of annexation) and concluded that the statues were intended to become an integral part of the garden and so could not be removed by the seller. You could say that they were not just arranged in the garden: they had become part of the garden itself. The case also concerned items within the house. A number of tapestries had been affixed to the walls in the drawing room and it was successfully claimed by the purchaser that they were fixtures. They were an integral part of the decoration of the room.

Compare this decision with the later case of *Leigh v Taylor* [1902] AC 157 where a different result was achieved. Very valuable tapestries had been hung on the walls in the main drawing room. They were attached by tacking them to strips of wood which were then fixed to the wall. The House of Lords held that the tapestries had never been intended to become part of the property. The degree of annexation was all that was necessary to display the tapestries and for the owner to enjoy them.

We can account for the different approach in *Leigh v Taylor* by the difference in the intentions of the parties. The judge, Lord Halsbury, also drew attention to the change in attitude to styles in ornamentation over the years since the decision in *D'Eyncourt v Gregory*.

Lord Scarman pointed out in the later case of *Berkley v Poulett* (1977) 241 EG 911, that a degree of annexation which earlier the law would have treated as conclusive may now prove nothing. So the degree of annexation is less important today, although it will show where the burden of proof lies if an item is **securely** fixed. In these cases the burden shifts to those arguing that it is not a fixture. In other words, the burden of proof will shift to the seller, as he will want to prove that the items are chattels, so enabling him to take items away after sale. For example, if a wardrobe has been fastened to the wall then the burden will shift to the seller to argue that this was for convenience only and that the wardrobe remained a chattel even after annexation.

The purpose of annexation

This test is far more decisive in deciding whether an item is a fixture. This is principally because the technical skills of affixing and removing objects to land or buildings have improved significantly over the years.

Even where items have been attached to the land, making them appear to be part of that land the question of whether they are fixtures or not will depend on whether they were put there for the better enjoyment of the property or for the better enjoyment of the item.

Consider these cases: in *Re Whaley* [1908] 1 Ch 615 tapestries and portraits had all been fixed to the wall to form an Elizabethan room. They were held to be part of the general architectural design of the room and were held to be fixtures. In *Berkley v Poulett* (1977) the seller had taken a number of items from the premises including a white marble statue of a Greek athlete weighing about half a ton, a sundial and some pictures fixed into recesses in the walls of the property. The purchaser claimed that they were fixtures. The Court of Appeal held that none of these items could be fixtures; they were all chattels.

Scarman LJ looked at each in turn:

1. He found that the statue and the sundial had never been fixed to the property. They had not become fixtures because they had never formed part of an architectural design. The plinth on which the statue stood was a fixture but the owner of the property had changed the item which went on top of the plinth from time to time. This meant that the actual location of the plinth was important but the items which were fixed to it were not part of some grand design for the garden.

2. The pictures were in recesses in a panelled room. They were not considered to be a part of a composite design. In other words, it was a matter of choice which particular pictures were put there and so they remained chattels.

1.5.2 Everyday objects in a house

When property is sold, certain everyday domestic items which are found in most people's homes are presumed to be fixtures but some will also be presumed to be chattels.

CASE EXAMPLE

TSB v Botham [1996] EGCS 149

Mr Botham had failed to keep up with mortgage repayments on the flat he was purchasing and the bank was granted an order for possession and proceeded to sell the flat. Any fixtures would pass to the purchaser but all chattels would have to be returned to Mr Botham. The case concerned such items as fitted cupboards in the kitchen, 'white goods' consisting of the main electrical appliances in the kitchen, light fittings throughout the house, fitted carpets and also curtains.

The judge at first instance held most of the items to be fixtures. Mr Botham appealed the decision.

The Court of Appeal held:

> 1. The bathroom fittings and kitchen units, work surfaces and the fitted sink were all fixtures. The court thought it was misleading to apply the same tests to domestic items as were applied to ornamental items or machinery in factories. Roch LJ: 'They are not there . . . to be enjoyed for themselves, but they are there as accessories which enable the room to be used and enjoyed as a bathroom. Viewed objectively, they were intended to be permanent and to afford a lasting improvement to the property.'

> 2. The light fittings were chattels, except those that had been specially fitted in recesses.

> 3. The carpets, curtains and blinds were chattels and could all be removed because, although they had been cut to fit the rooms and the windows, they were attached to the building in an insubstantial way. 'The methods of keeping fitted carpets in place and keeping curtains hung are no more than is required for enjoyment of those items as curtains and carpets' (Roch LJ).

> 4. The white goods, i.e. the washing machine, dishwasher and refrigerator, were all chattels. Roch LJ distinguished the reasoning of the judge at first instance who had held these items to be fixtures. He based his judgment on the fact that the items probably remained in position by their own weight and not by virtue of the manner in which they had been attached to the building. He found that they were designed to last for a limited period of years. The degree of annexation was slight and they could be removed without damage to the fabric of the building and normally without difficulty.

Figure 1.1 Court of Appeal decision in *TSB v Botham*

Roch LJ made one further observation about ownership of domestic items or chattels. He suggested that items that had been installed by a builder will be more likely to be a fixture but where it has been affixed by a householder then it is more likely to be a chattel.

1.5.3 Items bought under hire purchase

The court in *TSB v Botham* (1996) also looked at items being purchased under a hire-purchase agreement and which continued to be owned by the hire-purchase company. The existence of the agreement will not prevent the item from becoming a fixture. In *Botham* some of the items had been purchased under hire purchase but the court held that this did not influence the decision as to whether they were fixtures or fittings. However, the owner under the agreement may have a right to enter and remove the item even when it has become a fixture.

This right of the former owner to enter and take the item away is a form of equitable interest giving the right to enter the premises and sever and remove chattels under the hire-purchase agreement which have become fixtures.

1.5.4 Intention of the parties

The intention of the parties is only relevant to the extent that it can be part of the tests which look at the degree and object of the annexation. The subjective intention of the parties cannot affect the question whether the chattel has in law become part of the freehold.

CASE EXAMPLE

Melluish (Inspector of Taxes) v BMI (No 3) Ltd [1996] 1 AC 454

A number of items were leased to a council including central heating installed in council flats, lifts in car parks and the filtration system in swimming pools. They were recorded in the agreement as remaining in the ownership of the suppliers to the council. However, the court held that simply to include a provision in the contract that these items remained in the ownership of the suppliers did not prevent them from taking effect as fixtures, so passing ownership to the council. The issue would be resolved by the tests of annexation.

If the seller says 'I thought the fitted wardrobes were always chattels' then the court will look at how they were fixed to the wall and the purpose of fixing them. This is similar to the approach the courts might take in other areas of law, such as contract, where a condition of a contract cannot become a warranty merely because the parties call it a warranty. A lease of land will not become a licence in land just because the agreement says it is a licence.

The issue will always depend on the two tests mentioned earlier as laid down in *Holland v Hodgson* (1872):

1. degree of annexation; and
2. purpose of annexation.

ACTIVITY

Quick quiz

Consider the following items and decide whether they are fixtures or chattels and can be removed by the seller:

1. Long velvet curtains and pelmets fitted above the curtains.
2. A fitted stair carpet.
3. A fridge in the kitchen.

4. Pine kitchen cupboards which have been designed for the kitchen by a local builder.
5. Four recessed lights which have been attached to the dining room ceiling.
6. A greenhouse and a garden shed. The garden shed was put up two years ago by the seller but the greenhouse was there when he arrived.
7. A statue of Persephone which is firmly attached to a concrete pillar which is placed in the middle of the garden.
8. A car bought a year ago which has not passed its MOT and is sitting in the garage.
9. A gas fire in the living room in regular use in the winter.
10. A freezer kept in the utility room.

The first five items can be resolved by applying the case of *Botham*. The greenhouse and garden shed can be resolved by applying *Elitestone*. The statue will be a fixture if it was part of a grand design for the garden applying *Berkeley v Poulett*. The car will be a chattel. The gas fire has been fitted for the better enjoyment of the item and will be a fixture and the freezer will be decided by applying Roch's judgment in *Botham*.

KEY FACTS

Annexation		Fixture or chattel	Case
Degree of annexation	Resting on its own weight	Fixture	*Eliteson v Morris* (1997)
		Chattel	*Berkley v Poulett* (1977)
How firmly was the object fixed?	Insubstantially fixed	Chattel	*Leigh v Taylor* (1902)
	Substantially fixed	Fixture	*TSB v Botham* (1996) (fitted kitchen)
Purpose of annexation	For the improvement of the land	Fixture	*TSB v Botham* (1996) (light fittings)
	For the use and enjoyment of the item	Chattel	*Berkley v Poulett* (1977)
	Part of an architectural design	Fixture	*Re Whaley* (1908) *D'Eyncourt v Gregory* (1866) *Hamp v Bygrave* (1983)

1.5.5 The tenant's right to remove fixtures

The general rule was that the tenant had to leave any fixture that he had affixed to the premises during the tenancy. They became the property of the landlord. However, there are several exceptions:

Trade fixtures

A tenant has always been able to remove trade fixtures that he has installed during the term of his lease. He must show that they were necessary for his trade or business.

CASE EXAMPLE

Mancetter Developments v Garmanson Ltd [1986] QB 1212

Tenants who ran a chemical business were allowed to remove an extractor fan from the wall of their premises after their lease had expired.

Even where, under the ordinary rules, items have become fixtures, the law will allow tenants of business premises to remove them.

CASE EXAMPLE

Young v Dalgety plc [1987] 1 EGLR 116

Tenants were allowed to remove light fittings and a carpet which they had fitted during their tenancy.

Ornamental and domestic fixtures

Any item added to the premises purely for ornamental or domestic purposes can always be removed by the tenant. It will depend on the way that it has been attached. If an item can be removed without substantial damage to the structure of the building then it will be seen as a chattel.

CASE EXAMPLE

Spyer v Phillipson [1931] 2 Ch 183

A tenant of domestic premises had installed valuable antique wood panelling and other ornamental items. It was held that these were domestic or ornamental fixtures and he was entitled to remove them. They did not belong to the landlord.

Agricultural fixtures

The general law prevented the agricultural tenant from removing certain items that he had fixed to the property from premises that he had rented. However, under the Agricultural Holdings Act 1986, some items can be removed by an agricultural tenant if certain conditions apply:

1. the tenant must give one month's notice to the landlord;

2. all rent due must have been paid; and

3. there must be no damage to the premises when the item is removed, unless this is unavoidable. If the landlord offers to buy the items and the price is fair then he is entitled to keep them.

The exercise of the tenant's right to remove fixtures

Under all these exceptions the tenant must normally remove the items during the tenancy but he continues to have the right even after it has ended if either:

1. he has the right to remain in possession; or

2. he did not have time to remove these items (in which case he must be given a reasonable time to remove them).

The tenant must make good any damage which occurs when he removes the items from the property. In *Mancetter v Garmanson* (1986) the large hole left by the extractor fan had to be filled in by the tenant.

1.5.6 Express reference in the contract for sale
The seller and the purchaser
Where the ownership of items is expressly referred to in the contract then the rules concerning fixtures and fittings are displaced. So, if the seller tells the purchaser that an item is going to be removed, even if it is firmly fixed to the property and under the tests of annexation would be held to be a fixture, the purchaser cannot challenge its removal.

Any other fixture is assumed to pass with the land, even if the contract does not mention an item, and the purchaser can challenge its removal by the seller.

CASE EXAMPLE

Taylor v Hamer [2002] EWCA Civ 1130

A seller removed a large quantity of old stone flagstones from a property she had just sold in Worcestershire and took them to another house on the Isle of Wight. The particulars of sale had not mentioned them. The Court of Appeal held that they must be returned. The purchaser relied on two clauses in the conditions of sale which said:

1. the buyer accepts the property in the physical state as it is in at the date of the contract;
2. the seller will transfer the property in the same condition as it was at the date of contract. The important issue here was: what was 'the property'? The court held that it meant 'what a reasonable person who knows what the parties know when they contracted would have taken it to mean'. In this case the facts indicated that they would have meant a garden with flagstones unless it was specifically mentioned that they were going to be removed. Sedley LJ pointed out in this case 'that simple morality would suggest that the seller cannot remove fixtures without telling the buyer that they are no longer for sale'.

The mortgagor and the mortgagee
Since fixtures are assumed to be part of the land then they will become part of the property subject to the mortgage. In *TSB v Botham* (1996) the mortgagee argued that many expensive items had become part of the land and so would pass with the land when it was repossessed. The court held that this would depend on whether they were found to be fixtures.

1.6 Objects found 'in or on' the surface of the land

If an object is found in or attached to the ground then the owner of the land has the best claim to it after the true owner of the object. The position will be different where the object is resting on the ground, because the finder of the object then has a good claim. Everyone is familiar with the saying 'finders keepers'. It has some truth in land law, but only in some cases, and that will depend on where the item was found.

For example, if you are out walking and you find a gold ring resting on the ground then you may have a claim as the finder, but if the ring is buried in the soil and you have to dig it up then the claim will be between the owner of the land and the owner of the ring. The finder does not have a claim unless you have been given express permission to dig the soil and also permission to keep any objects found in the process. If the ring was very old then the Crown may also have a claim.

CASE EXAMPLE

Armory v Delamirie [1722] 1 Strange 505

A jewel was found by a chimney sweeper's boy who claimed ownership as finder of the item. He took it to a jeweller to be valued. A dishonest employee of a jeweller took the jewel and when the finder, the chimney sweeper's boy discovered this, he claimed ownership. It was held 'the finder of a jewel, though he does not by such finding acquire an absolute property or ownership, yet he has such a property as will enable him to keep it against all but the true rightful owner'.

In cases of lost objects there are several different people who may have a good claim to the object:

1. the true owner of the object;
2. the finder of the object;
3. the owner of the land;
4. an employee of the owner of the land.

The claim to ownership often depends on where the object was found and the extent to which the object was attached to the ground.

1.6.1 Objects found in the ground

At common law, where an object is found in the ground, the landowner in possession of the land is usually entitled to it if the true owner cannot be found.

CASE EXAMPLE

Elwes v Brigg Gas Company (1886) 33 Ch D 562

A leaseholder could not claim possession of a pre historic boat which he found buried in the ground of his property whilst carrying out building works. The finder of the object could not claim it for himself. It was held to belong to the freehold owner of the land.

'He was in possession of the ground, not merely of the surface, but of everything that lay beneath the surface down to the centre of the Earth, and consequently in possession of the boat.... The plaintiff then, being thus in possession of the chattel, it follows that the property in the chattel was vested in him. Obviously the right of the original owner could not be established.'

Chitty J

In this case the leaseholder may have had a claim if he could prove the object had come on to the land during his tenancy but in view of its age it was clear that it came on to the land many years, indeed centuries, before the tenancy began.

ACTIVITY

Applying the law

Consider the following examples and decide who can claim the items:

1. Alfie owns a cottage in Brackley. He let it to a friend Bola on a five-year lease in 2014. Bola is working in the garden when she finds several two-pound coins. They were each dated 2015.

2. Bola is decorating one of the bedrooms. She removes the carpet and then lifts one of the floor boards which is loose. Under the floor board is an envelope with a number of bank notes in it. It is uncertain how long they have been under the floorboards but the notes are not plastic coated and carry old designs.

Bola may have a claim to the two-pound coins as it is clear that they came on to the land after the start of the tenancy. It will be difficult for her to claim the bank notes as they are unlikely to have come on to the land after the tenancy began.

CASE EXAMPLE

South Staffordshire Water Co v Sharman [1896] 2 QB 44

It was held that employees of the landowner could not keep rings found in the mud of an old pond. The rings were held to be the property of the landowner. The finders were employed by the landowner to remove the mud. The landowner and employer had a clear right to direct how the mud and anything in it should be dealt with.

In *Parker v British Airways Board* [1982] QB 1004 (see below) Donaldson LJ explained why the owner of items found in the ground should belong to the owner of the ground: 'the rationale of this rule is probably that the chattel is to be treated as an integral part of the realty as against all but the true owner and so incapable of being lost'.

Where an object is found under the floorboards in a property, there is some doubt as to whether the object is on or in the ground. This is at issue in a case decided in *Tamworth Industries Ltd v Att-General* [1991] 3 NZLR 616 where it was held that money bags found embedded under the floorboards were 'on' the land as opposed to 'in' the land.

1.6.2 Minerals found in the ground

Minerals found in the ground are part of the land and as a general principle belong to the landowner. Over the years, many exceptions have developed. Ownership of all coal and natural gas is vested exclusively in various privatised corporations under statute, for example the Coal Industry Act 1994 and the Gas Act 1986. The Petroleum Act 1998 gives to the Crown the exclusive right of 'searching and boring for' and getting petroleum. 'Petroleum' is defined as 'any mineral, oil or relative hydrocarbon and natural gas existing in its natural condition'. The Crown has had a prerogative right to gold and silver for centuries.

CASE EXAMPLE

The Case of Mines (1567) 1 Plowd 310

It was stated that any mine, whether of gold, silver or other metals containing in them gold or silver of even the smallest of quantities, was a Royal mine.

The ownership of mines under land can be severed from the ownership of the surface. The presumption that the landowner of the surface owns the land beneath can be rebutted by proof of long and continuous use of the mine or land beneath. In this way, land really does become three-dimensional. The Infrastructure Act 2015 allows fracking companies to access shale gas beneath privately owned land. This Act challenges the principle that freehold landowners not only own the land at the surface but also down to the Earth's core because it allows fracking companies to drill underneath privately owned land (usually at depths of approximately 1.5 km) without first obtaining the landowners' consent. There are certain safeguards and conditions which must be met before shale gas extraction can take place but local residents do not have to give consent.

1.6.3 Objects found on the surface of the ground

Where an object is found on the ground rather than in the ground ownership is far more difficult to determine.

In *Elwes v Brigg Gas Company* (1886) it was held that if the object had been found resting on the ground the finder may have had a good claim. However, more recently the law has more clearly defined this rule, and today the owner of the land may also have a good claim if he could prove that he intended to exercise control over the land and anything found on it.

CASE EXAMPLE

Parker v British Airways Board [1982] QB 1004

A passenger found a gold bracelet on the floor of an executive lounge at Heathrow Airport. He handed it to the owners of the land (British Airways Board) so that they could attempt to find the true owner. He left his name and address, claiming the object for himself if the true owner could not be found. He challenged British Airways' claim to keep the bracelet for itself. The court upheld the finder's claim.

> 'The plaintiff's claim is founded on the ancient common law rule the act of finding a chattel which has been lost and taking control of it gives the finder rights with respect to that chattel.... The defendant's claim is based upon the proposition that at common law an occupier of land has such rights over all lost chattels which are on that land, whether or not the occupier knows of their existence. The common law right asserted by the plaintiff has been recognised for centuries.
>
> Donaldson LJ

Donaldson LJ laid down the following rules on the rights and obligations of the finder:

1. The finder of a chattel acquires no rights unless (a) it has been abandoned or lost and (b) he takes it into his care.

2. If the finder is trespassing or acting with dishonest intent then he acquires very few rights.

3. The finder of a chattel acquires ownership against all but the true owner if he was on the land lawfully.

4. An employee working in the course of his employment who finds an object finds that object on behalf of his employer.

5. The finder is under an obligation to take measures to find the owner of the object.

Figure 1.2 Donaldson LJ's rules on the rights and obligations of the finder in *Parker v British Airways Board*

Donaldson LJ then discussed the rights of the occupier, which he said depended on whether the occupier had manifested a desire to control the property. This had not previously been raised in cases on finding.

CASE EXAMPLE

Bridges v Hawkesworth (1851) 21 LJ QB 75

A commercial traveller found a parcel when he was in the defendant's shop. Later he found that it contained some bank notes and he claimed them for himself. It was held that if he had found them in the street he could have claimed them. However, as the shop was open to the public who were invited to come in at any time and since the notes were dropped in the public part of the shop, they were never in the custody of the shopkeeper.

Did the owner of the land manifest control over the land?

The general principle from *Parker* is that where a person has possession of a house or land he must show that he intends to control it if he is to claim any lost objects found on the land. If it can be proved that he does control the land then there is a presumption that anything found, either by an employee of the owner or by a stranger, will be the property of the landowner.

So the issue all depends on what the law views as 'control'.

What constitutes 'control'?

Donaldson LJ held in *Parker* that a bank would be deemed to exercise sufficient control over a bank vault if an object was found there. This was because it would be closed to the general public and only limited people would have access. He contrasted areas such as a park where the public has unlimited access during the day. Between these two extremes he highlighted those areas where the public have limited rights of access, such as a petrol filling station forecourt or the unfenced front gardens of private houses.

In *Parker*, British Airways exercised some control over the airport lounge by checking tickets and allowing only certain people to enter; but, it was held that this was not sufficient to allow it to argue that it had superior rights to items found there.

So the question rests not only on the requirement that the owner of the land has manifested any intention to control the land but also on the degree of that control.

> 'In *Parker*, British Airways failed to satisfy the Court of Appeal that it had discharged this requirement, despite the existence of a company policy on found goods. There the Board had prepared and circulated to its staff members a document containing instructions and explaining the procedure to be followed in the event that lost goods were found and handed over to staff members in circumstances such as those of Mr Parker. The Court of Appeal thought that the mere existence of this document, and its communication to the Board's staff was not enough.'
>
> R Hickey, 'Stealing Abandoned Goods: Possessory Title in Proceedings for Theft' (2006) 26 *LS* 584

What if the finder was trespassing?

CASE EXAMPLE

Waverley B C v Fletcher [1996] QB 334

The defendant used a metal detector in a public park owned by the claimants, Waverley Borough Council. He found a medieval gold brooch nine inches below the surface. It was held that the council had a better claim than the finder. The object was beneath the surface and the finder became a trespasser when he began to dig the ground. He had permission to walk in the public park but he did not have permission to use a metal detector or to dig in the ground.

In *Parker* Donaldson LJ explained that the reason that it would be rare for an object found in or attached to the ground to be treated as the property of the finder was because the 'finder' would have to do something to the realty in order to detach the chattel and if he was not thereby to become a trespasser, he would have to justify his actions by reference to some form of licence from the occupier.

Rights of the true owner

If the finder or the landowner claims the object then he is under a duty to take reasonable steps to trace the true owner who will still own the goods. The finder will have a duty to advertise the find and follow up any advertisements about lost objects. It is only when the owner cannot be found that the finder can exert his rights.

CASE EXAMPLE

Moffat v Kazana [1969] 2 QB 152

Mr Russell hid a biscuit tin, containing cash, in the roof of his house. After his death, the house was sold to the defendant, who discovered the tin three years later. The deceased had simply forgotten about the money, and his relatives claimed it. They were successful because Mr Russell remained the true owner and had not abandoned the money. The purchaser could not claim that the tin containing the money passed to him as part of the land because it remained a chattel.

'If Mr Russell never got rid of the notes, that is to say, never got rid of the ownership of the notes, he continued to be owner of them and, if he continued to be the owner of them, he had a title to those notes which nobody else, whether the owner of the land in which they were found, or the finders, or anybody else would have.'

Wrangham J

This shows that a finder can never claim an object unless it has been abandoned by the true owner. This is why Donaldson LJ emphasised that the true owner continues to have rights over a lost object unless it can be shown that he had either lost or abandoned it.

KEY FACTS

Objects found in or on the land
1. Objects found in or on the ground *prima facie* belong to the true owner of the object.
2. If the true owner cannot be found then ownership lies with the owner of the land if the object is found buried in the land (*Elwes v Brigg Gas Company* (1886)).
3. If the true owner cannot be found and the object is resting on the surface, the object is the property of either the finder or the landowner.
4. Ownership then depends on whether the landowner has shown that he intends to exercise a sufficient degree of control over the land (*Parker v British Airways* (1982)).
5. If the landowner has sufficient control over the land then he can claim any objects found.
6. If the finder is trespassing then objects found belong to the landowner (*Waverley B C v Fletcher* (1996)).
7. The finder can be trespassing either because he has no right to be on the land or because he is using the land in a way not permitted by the landowner (*Waverley B C v Fletcher*).

ACTIVITY

Applying the law

Mrs Turner enjoyed visiting National Trust houses. One hot summer's day, she went to see a famous garden. She took her lunch and ate it in the garden. She was interested in the plants and when no one was looking she took the spoon that she had been using for her lunch and dug up one of the plants. She then noticed something in the ground, shining brightly. She put it into her pocket and looked at it when she got home. It was a gold bracelet.

Mrs Turner would like to keep the bracelet but she does not know what to do about it. Advise her whether or not she can keep it for herself.

Would it make any difference if the bracelet was resting on the ground when she found it?

Several questions must be addressed:
- Where was the object found? Was it in a public or private place?
- Did the owner of the land manifest control over the land?
- Was the finder trespassing?

Where was the object found? Was it in a public or private place?
If the object is in a **public place** then the finder has a good claim.

Figure 1.3 Donaldson LJ's rights of the occupier in *Parker v British Airways Board*

1.7 Treasure

If an item is found that comes within the definition of 'treasure' then it will be the property of the Crown. The definition of 'treasure' is in s1, Treasure Act 1996. This Act was passed to replace the common law of treasure trove which had a number of difficulties, not least a very narrow definition of 'treasure'. The old law excluded from the definition of treasure trove many ancient items which had little or no gold or silver content but were often very valuable. The emphasis was always on whether or not the object had a precious metal content but the circumstances of the loss was also relevant. The Act allows some antiquities without a high metal content to come within the definition but only in limited circumstances, such as when an object is found with an object within the definition. More objects will be preserved for the national heritage under the Act as the question of concealment is no longer relevant, but the Treasure Act itself has many limitations, such as the emphasis on precious metal content which excludes objects of bronze and other non-precious metals.

There is provision for rewards to be paid to anyone who finds an object that comes within the definition of 'treasure'. It is now a criminal offence to fail to report a relevant find to the Coroner within 14 days.

1.7.1 The Treasure Act 1996

SECTION

'Meaning of "treasure"

s 1(1)   "treasure" is:

(a)   Any object at least 300 years old when found which –

    (i)   is not a coin but has metallic content of which at least 10 per cent by weight is precious metal;

    (ii)   when found, is one of at least two coins in the same find which are at least 300 years old at that time and have that percentage of precious metal; or

    (iii)   when found, is one of at least ten coins in the same find which are at least 300 years old at that time;

(b)   Any object at least 200 years old when found which belongs to a class designated under section 2(1);

(c)   Any object which would have been treasure trove if found before the commencement of section 4;

(d)   Any object which when found, is part of the same find as –

    (i)   An object within paragraph (a) (b) or (c) found at the same time or earlier; or

    (ii)   An object found earlier which would be within paragraph (a) or (b) if it had been found at the same time.

s 1(2)   Treasure does not include objects which are –

(a)   unworked natural objects, or

(b)   minerals as extracted from a natural deposit, or which belong to a class designated under section 2(2).

. . .

s 2   The Secretary of State may by order, for the purposes of section 1(1)(b) designate any class of object which he considers to be of outstanding historical, archaeological or cultural importance.

. . .

s 3(3)   "Precious metal" means gold or silver.

. . .

s 8(1)   A person who finds an object which he believes or has reasonable grounds for believing is treasure must notify the Coroner for the district in which the object was found before the end of the notice period...

(3)   Any person who fails to comply with subsection (1) is guilty of an offence.'

A Code of Practice accompanied the Treasure Act, giving guidelines for the payment of rewards (Treasure Act 1996: Code of Practice) which depends on whether the finder has permission from the occupier to be on the premises and he has complied with the obligation to report the find to the coroner and there is no damage to the premises.

The finder will generally receive half of whatever reward is paid by the Coroner and the landowner will receive the other half. Even if he did not have permission to be on the premises then the guidelines allow for a possible reward to be divided between the landowner and the finder.

'Of course, objects of recent vintage may be treasure by virtue of having been found in circumstances which clearly associate them with objects which are otherwise treasure within section 1. Always assuming that the true owner cannot be ascertained, suppose a hoard of 18th century coins contains say, two or more gold coins which are at least 300 years old. The two or more gold coins aged 300 years or more will be treasure (section 1(1)(a)(ii)). Section 1(1)(d) of the Act will operate so as to engage the balance of coins, and their container together with any other contents such as books or papers, and transform them into treasure irrespective of the proof of an *animus recuperandi* or their precious metal content, if any. The point may well be of practical significance, not only for the purposes of the grant of a reward, but also because, were the coins or other objects not to be treasure then the ordinary law of "finders keepers" would fall to be applied.'

J Marston and L Ross, 'Treasure and Portable Antiquities in the 1990s still chained to the Ghosts of the Past: The Treasure Act 1996' [1997] 61 *Conv* 273

There has only been one case to date of a criminal prosecution for failure to report a find to the coroner. The defendant found a piedfort (a rare silver coin which was never used as currency) in her garden. She approached the local museum to value it and she was advised to report it to the coroner and when she ignored the advice a prosecution was brought. She was given a conditional discharge and ordered to hand over the coin to the coroner.

ACTIVITY

Applying the law

Your friend Terry is walking one summer's afternoon along a right of way over his neighbour's land with his dog, Fedora, who starts digging furiously in the ground. Fedora uncovers what looks to Terry like a number of coins and a pottery vase which looks very old and valuable to him. He takes the coins and vase home and shows them to his wife who is a history teacher and she recognises that the coins are Roman. He wants to keep them in his own coin collection but is unsure whether he can do so. He would like to give the vase to his mother as a present.

Advise Terry.

Would it make any difference to your answer if the coin was found on a public right of way?

1.8 Ownership of airspace above the land

'He who owns the land owns everything reaching up to the very heavens and down to the depth of the Earth' (attributed to Accursius of Bologna in *Glossa Ordinaria on Corpus Iuris* (thirteenth century).

Land must include part of the airspace above the ground, otherwise building above ground level would be a trespass. However, it cannot be an unlimited part of that airspace; it cannot be 'to the heavens above' because every time an aircraft flew over a house it would constitute a trespass.

The law has tried to define how much of the airspace is owned by a landowner. Airspace has been split into two levels: the higher stratum and the lower stratum.

1.8.1 The higher stratum

Until the advent of air travel, no one could pass through the higher part of the atmosphere, so ownership was never an issue. It was assumed that the landowner had ownership of the airspace. Air travel transformed the idea of ownership of the higher stratum of airspace. Planes now regularly fly through that part of the airspace above people's houses and gardens. However, the courts are unwilling to allow ownership in the higher stratum.

CASE EXAMPLE

Re the Queen in Right of Manitoba and Air Canada (1978) 86 DLR (3d) 631

Attempts by the province of Manitoba to argue that sales of goods on board commercial aircraft whilst flying over the airspace of the province of Manitoba could be taxed, failed on the basis that no one could claim ownership of that part of the airspace.

CASE EXAMPLE

Bernstein of Leigh (Baron) v Skyviews & General Ltd [1978] QB 479

The claimant claimed trespass because the defendant flew over his land without permission and took aerial photographs and tried to sell him the photographs. The claim was unsuccessful.

'The [claimant] claims that as owner of the land he is also owner of the airspace above the land, or at least has the right to exclude any entry into the air space above his land.... That an owner has certain rights in the air space above his land is well established by authority. He has the right to lop the branches of trees that may overhang his boundary, although this right seems to be founded in nuisance rather than trespass.... In *Wandsworth Board of Works v United Telephone Company* (1884) 13 QBD 904 the Court of Appeal did not doubt that the owner of land would have the right to cut a wire placed over his land.... I can find no support in authority for the view that a landowner's rights in the air space above his property extend to an unlimited height. In the same case Bowen LJ described the maxim, *usque ad coelum*, as a fanciful phrase, to which I would add that if applied literally it is a fanciful notion leading to the absurdity of a trespass at common law being committed by a satellite every time it passes over a suburban garden.... The problem is to balance the rights of an owner to enjoy the use of his land against the rights of the general public to take advantage of all that science now offers in the use of air space. This balance in my view is best struck in our present society by restricting the rights of an owner in the air space above his land to such a height as is necessary for the ordinary use and enjoyment of his land and the structures upon it, and declaring that above that height he has no greater rights in the air space than any other member of the public.'

Griffiths J

The main principles to consider from this judgment are:

1. The owner has rights in airspace above his property.
2. The owner does not own unlimited rights over airspace, otherwise there would be a trespass every time a satellite flew over someone's garden.
3. The owner owns as much of the airspace as he needs for the ordinary use and enjoyment of his land.

This area of law is now mainly governed by legislation such as the Civil Aviation Act 1982.

SECTION

's 76(1) No action shall lie in respect of trespass or in respect of nuisance, by reason only of the flight of an aircraft over any property at a height above the ground which, having regard to wind, weather and all circumstances of the case is reasonable.'

So this Act prevents actions in nuisance or trespass against aircraft flying over houses unless the aircraft fails to comply with any relevant regulations. In more recent years homeowners have an alternative potential claim under the Human Rights Act 1998 Sched 1 Part 1 The Convention Rights and Freedoms:

SECTION

'Article 8 Right to respect for private and family life

1. Everyone has the right to respect for his private and family life, his home and his correspondence.
2. There shall be no interference by a public authority with the exercise of this right except such as is in accordance with the law and is necessary in a democratic society in the interests of national security, public safety or the economic well-being of the country, for the prevention of disorder or crime, for the protection of health or morals, or for the protection of the rights and freedoms of others.'

CASE EXAMPLE

Hatton v United Kingdom (2003) 37 EHRR 28

An application was made before the European Court of Human Rights by an individual who lived near Heathrow airport that the court should declare night flying to be in breach of Article 8.

It was held by the Grand Chamber of the European Court of Human Rights that on the facts presented on night flying that Article 8 was not infringed but the Court did criticise the approach of English law to such complaints. It was commented by the court that H had no private law remedy available to her and further the narrow scope of judicial review meant that it was not capable of determining whether increased night flights amounted to a justifiable restriction on H's Article 8 rights.

The judgment of the European Court of Human Rights suggests that a further challenge to the European Court on this point may still be possible.

With the increase of air travel and the potential building of a third runway at Heathrow Airport it is likely that a further application will be made by those living around Heathrow based on violation of Article 8 particularly if night flying is allowed.

1.8.2 The lower stratum

The law accepts that the landowner has rights over the airspace immediately above his property. 'You own as much as is necessary for the reasonable enjoyment of your property' (Griffiths J in *Bernstein of Leigh v Skyviews and General Ltd* (1978)). So this will vary according to the type of property that you own.

It probably stops short of the altitude over which aircraft can legally fly. Under the Rules of the Air Regulations 1996 it is held to be no lower than 200 metres above roof level. There are a number of exceptions to this, including where an aircraft is taking off and landing and also where it is necessary to fly lower in order to save life.

One of the first cases on rights over airspace was *Pickering v Rudd* (1815) Camp 219, where the judge, Lord Ellenborough, did not think that there would be an invasion of airspace by a balloon passing over one's property and no action for trespass could be taken.

This view was criticised and overturned in a number of following cases including *Gifford v Dent* [1926] WN 336, where an overhead sign which was erected on the wall above the ground-floor premises which had been bought by the claimant was held to constitute a trespass.

In *Wandsworth District Board of Works v United Telephone Co Ltd* (1884) 13 QBD 904, a telephone line running across a street could constitute a trespass, although not on the particular facts of that case.

In *Kelsen v Imperial Tobacco* [1957] 2 QB 334, the claimant sought an injunction to stop the defendants from using an advertising sign. The sign projected into the airspace immediately above the claimant's shop. However, although it projected over the land, it did not interfere with his enjoyment of the airspace so an action in nuisance would not be successful. For an action in trespass to succeed, the owner must show that he owned that portion of airspace rather than prove he had suffered damage. The judge found that the sign did amount to a trespass to the airspace above the land and awarded damages to the claimant.

It is important to note that trespass is actionable per se: it is not necessary to prove actual damage.

CASE EXAMPLE

Laiqat v Majid [2005] EWHC 1305 (QB)

An extractor fan which projected over the claimant's land by 750 millimetres at a height of 4.5 metres constituted a trespass.

It was held that an interference with airspace above another person's land constituted a trespass except where the interference was at such a great height that it did not interfere with the claimant's airspace. The claimant did not have to prove that the offending activity interfered with the normal activity of the garden.

JUDGMENT

'If the overhanging by a defendant occurs four metres above the ground, it would be regarded as interference with the claimant's airspace and so would amount to trespass.'

Silber J

Several cases have been brought where property developers have used cranes which have swung through the airspace above adjoining buildings. If you apply the principles from *Bernstein of Leigh v Skyviews* that a landowner is entitled to as much airspace as is necessary for the ordinary use and enjoyment of his land and the structures upon it, then the owner of a high-rise block may be able to claim a much more extensive ownership of airspace than someone who lives in a bungalow or low-rise building. So an injunction was granted against the use of a crane which swung over the claimant's land in *Woollerton and Wilson Ltd v Richard Costain Ltd* [1970] 1 WLR 411 (although the defendant offered substantial sums in compensation which led to the suspension of the injunction) and again later in *Anchor Brewhouse Developments Ltd v Berkeley House (Docklands Developments) Ltd* (1987) 38 BLR 82.

KEY FACTS

Rights over airspace
1. Airspace is split between the upper stratum and the lower stratum.
2. There can never be ownership of the upper stratum (Civil Aviation Act 1949 and *Bernstein of Leigh v Skyviews and General Ltd* (1978)).
3. Ownership of the lower stratum depends on what can be said is reasonable for the use and enjoyment of the property (*Kelsen v Imperial Tobacco Co* (1957)).
4. 'Reasonable for use and enjoyment of the property' will vary according to the height and type of the building.

SUMMARY

1. Land comprises of three dimensions: the surface area, the airspace above it and the ground beneath it.
2. There is a fourth dimension of land which comprises the estate held in land or the length of time over which a person can have rights over the land.
3. A boundary of land may be uncertain even where there is a map at the Land Registry.
4. Uncertainties in boundaries can be clarified by using common law rules or by employing surveyors to agree the boundary.
5. Ownership of land includes any building attached to it and any item which is regarded as a fixture.
6. The tests for determining whether an item is a fixture is the degree of annexation and the purpose of annexation.
7. Tenants have the right to remove tenant's fixtures which include trade fixtures, ornamental or domestic fixtures and agricultural fixtures.
8. Objects found buried in the land generally belong to the owner of the land.
9. Minerals found in the ground are generally regarded as the property of the land-owner unless the Crown can lay claim to them.
10. Objects found on the surface of the land belong to the finder if the true owner cannot be found unless the landowner can show he has manifested an intention to control the land.
11. Treasure as defined by the Treasure Act 1996 is owned by the Crown but a finder may be able to claim a reward.
12. Ownership of the airspace is determined by deciding if the airspace is the upper stratum (which cannot be owned) or the lower stratum (which can be owned) if it is as much as is necessary for the reasonable enjoyment of your property.

SAMPLE ESSAY QUESTION

To what extent has the decision in *Parker v British Airways* (1982) clarified the law on ownership of lost chattels?

Brief explanation on the issues that arise in deciding ownership of lost chattels: (i) where found – 'in' or 'on' the land; (ii) whether found in a public or private place; (iii) whether found by a landowner or trespasser or licensee; (iv) lack of clarity in the law prior to *Parker*.

The issues arising when an object is found 'in' the land:

- s 205, LPA 1925;
- presumption that the object belongs to the landowner irrespective of whether he knows the object is there *Elwes v Brigg Gas Corporation* (1866);
- if found by employee whilst at work item belongs to employer *South Staffs Water Co v Sharman* (1896);
- if found 'in' the land by a trespassing 'finder' the landowner has a better claim *Waverley B C v Fletcher* (1996).

The issues arising when an object is found 'on' the ground:

- presumption that the finder has the better claim subject to the true owner's rights. Use of maxim 'finders keepers' *Armory v Delamirie* (1722);
- the owner of the land will have a better claim if he can demonstrate that he had an intention to exercise control over the land and things attached to it *Parker v British Airways Board* (1982);
- intention to exercise control over land will depend on whether the land is 'public' or 'private';
- issues of trespassing finders and whether they have any rights.

Discussion of the case of *Parker v British Airways Board*:

- facts of case;
- analysis of Donaldson LJ's judgment;
- the difference between the various places where an object can be found (a bank vault; a supermarket carpark; a public park);
- the points arising;
- the high standard expected in order to show 'control' by the landowner in areas accessible by the public.

What issues remain outstanding after *Parker* and how far has it clarified the law?

What constitutes 'control' by the landowner?

The issues surrounding trespassing 'finders'.

Is it clearer and easier to apply since the decision in *Parker*?

CONCLUSION

Further reading

Book

Birks, P, 'Before We Begin: Five Keys to Land Law' in S Bright and J Dewar (eds), *Land Law: Themes and Perspectives* (Oxford University Press, 1998), pp. 457–460.

Articles

Bray, J, 'The Law on Treasure from a Land Lawyer's Perspective' [2013] 77 *Conv* 265.

Bridge, S, 'Part and Parcel: Fixtures in the House of Lords' [1997] *CLJ* 498.

Crozier, R, 'Upwardly Mobile: Can a Mobile Home be a Dwelling?' [2011] 15(5) *L & TR* 174.

De Silva, J, 'Treasures or Theft?' [2014] 178(8) *CL J*107.

Gray, K, 'Property in Thin Air' [1991] 50 *CLJ* 252.

Haley, M, 'The Law of Fixtures: An Unprincipled Metamorphosis' [1998] *Conv* 137.

Hickey, R, 'Stealing Abandoned Goods: Possessory Title in Proceedings for Theft' (2006) 26 *LS* 584.

Luther, P, 'The Foundations of Elitestone' (2008) 28 *LS* 574.

Macmillan, C, 'Finders Keepers, Losers Weepers: But Who are the Losers?' (1995) 58 *MLR* 101.

Marston, J and Ross, L, 'Treasure and Portable Antiquities in the 1990s still Chained to the Ghosts of the Past' The Treasure Act 1996 [1997] *Conv* 273.

Murdoch, S, 'Hard Landings on Bembridge Bay' [2012] 1205 *EG* 81.

Stevens, J, 'Finders Weepers: Landowners Keepers' [1996] 216.

Wu, Tang Hang, 'The Right of Lateral Support of Buildings from Adjoining Land' [2002] *Conv* 237.

2

Common law and equity

AIMS AND OBJECTIVES

After reading this chapter, you should be able to:

- Describe the development of common law in England
- Explain the reasons for the growth of equity
- Describe the contribution made to law by equity
- Understand the nature of a trust
- Distinguish between rights in law and rights in equity
- Explain the doctrine of notice
- Describe the reasons why land law was reformed in 1925 and describe the main changes made by the legislation

2.1 Common law and equity

common law

The system of law in England after the Norman Conquest, which was a combination of law initiated centrally and local laws

Historically, England has had two systems of law. Initially, **common law** which was applied universally and was very successful as it brought consistency and some measure of fairness. Later it was also found to be defective in a number of ways and a new system of law called 'equity' grew to supplement common law.

The growth of common law

Before 1066, local law had been the main source of law but it varied from region to region and people could be treated differently according to which area they came from. After 1066 William the Conqueror gradually introduced a system of law that was uniform to all England. This system became known as the **common law** and it was administered by the Royal Courts.

writ

A formal document without which a claimant had no access to the courts if he wished to claim a remedy

2.1.1 Defects in the common law system

1. An action in court could only be started by a **writ** and there were only a certain number of writs available. After 1215 and the passage of the Provisions of Oxford in 1258 it was not possible for the courts to extend the circumstances for new

writs and so a claimant had to bring his action within the narrow circumstances of the existing writs. If there was no writ suitable for his claim, he had no right to bring an action in the courts.

2. The common law had only a limited range of remedies available.

3. The common law did not recognise certain types of right such as the rights of the mortgagor or the rights of a beneficiary behind a trust.

4. The dissatisfied litigant had nowhere to go except to take his case directly to the king and to ask the king to exercise his discretion in the litigant's favour.

2.1.2 The growth of equity

It was recognised that there were many defects in common law. Some of the litigants whom the common law had failed appealed directly to the king. The cases were decided individually and as the king could act on his discretion some found that they were successful in their claim. Others followed suit, hoping the king would also find in their favour. Eventually, the king found that there were too many appeals for him to deal with on his own and cases were passed to his adviser, the Lord Chancellor. He was a man of the Church and so came to his decisions through applying principles of fairness and conscience. This contrasted with common law where the law was strictly applied.

Eventually, a separate court grew up called the Court of Chancery, which was recognised as a court of conscience. It later developed its own principles and rights.

The differences between the two courts were significant:

1. The Court of Chancery would decide cases according to what seemed **just** and **equitable** whereas the common law courts were concerned with the strict enforcement of **legal rights**.

2. The Court of Chancery was prepared to grant a **range of remedies** including injunctions to restrain actions and also specific performance of a contract. These remedies were often more appropriate in the circumstances. The remedies available in the common law courts consisted only of damages which did not always fully compensate the wrong suffered.

3. The Court of Chancery was willing to recognise **new rights** such as the mortgage and the trust, which the common law courts had refused to recognise.

By the sixteenth century, the position of Lord Chancellor was no longer given to a religious person but to a lawyer. The court gradually became bound by strict rules and was far less flexible. Cases were no longer decided according to their particular circumstances and facts.

Problems arose in the administration of both the courts and there grew considerable rivalry as to which court was superior. It was also possible to bring an action on the same facts in both courts if the claimant sought different remedies. So if he were seeking damages he would pursue the case in the common law courts but if he were seeking an injunction he would pursue his case in the courts of equity. Pursuing two actions in two different courts was costly and time-consuming because of duplication.

Imagine that Edmund has promised to supply 50 sheep to Edward on the first Tuesday in March. He fails to do so. Edward wants the sheep and no one else can supply them. He can sue at common law for the breach of contract and claim the value of the sheep and he can also bring an action in equity in the Chancery court for specific performance of the contract. There would be two separate actions and two sets of lawyers.

2.1.3 The Judicature Acts 1873–75

Two separate courts and two systems of law were wasteful and ineffective. Litigants had to wait months, even years, for a judgment. There was also a conflict between the two systems. Reform came in the shape of the Judicature Acts in 1873–75 which combined the two systems of law and equity. It also combined the two courts, forming the Supreme Court which could hear cases both in common law and in equity. There was now effectively one system to govern all cases. However, the law expressly laid down that where there was any conflict between the rules of common law and the rules of equity then the rules of equity were to prevail: now s 49(1) Senior Courts Act 1981 (previously Supreme Court Act 1981 and the Supreme Court of Judicature (Consolidation) Act 1925).

2.1.4 Are common law and equity totally fused?

Some lawyers are not convinced that the two systems ever fused. It is true that in some ways equity and common law do remain distinct although they are both administered in the same court.

The two arguments for and against are:

1. 'The two streams of jurisdiction though they run in the same channel run side by side and do not mingle their waters' (W Ashburner, *Principles of Equity* (2nd edn, Butterworths, 1933). Ashburner was arguing here that although the systems run side by side, they have not combined.

2. Others have disagreed. Lord Diplock in *United Scientific Holdings Ltd v Burnley Borough Council* [1978] AC 904 said: 'The innate conservatism of English lawyers may have made them slow to recognise that by the Judicature Act 1873 the two systems of substantive and adjectival law formerly administered by Courts of Law and Courts of Chancery were fused.'

What we have to look at here is how the two systems affect our study of land law. Although the systems of law and equity have merged, there can still be both legal and equitable rights in property, in particular in land. These can exist over the same piece of property.

If you own land at law or have legal rights in land you can claim a legal remedy which takes effect in common law and, most importantly, your claim is good against the whole world. Your rights cannot be defeated by anyone. If you have an equitable right which takes effect in equity then your right does not bind the world. It is good against everyone unless you can prove that you have a better title than them. So equitable rights will never defeat legal rights, but they may affect the legal title so the legal owner may take the land subject to your rights. Equitable rights strictly give rise to an equitable remedy but legislation has now allowed damages to be granted instead of the equitable remedy (s 50 Senior Courts Act 1981; previously Supreme Court Act 1981).

2.2 The development of the trust

We have seen that equity contributed to the law in several different ways. Possibly the most significant contribution of equity was the recognition of new rights, the trust and the mortgage.

2.2.1 The historical development of the trust

Trusts were first used in the time of the crusades, although their form was rather different from the modern trust of today.

Picture the scene:

Many landowners were recruited to fight in the crusades. This involved leaving their lands and family for months, probably years. Someone needed to be in charge while they were away. The solution was to ask a friend to take over. The friend needed some control over the land and this was achieved by transferring the land to the friend while the crusader was away, but on the strict understanding that all income was to be for the benefit of their family and the property would be returned when they returned from fighting.

So imagine Thomas leaves for the crusades, asking Edward to take charge of his land on behalf of his two sons, Adam and Ben. Thomas transfers his property to Edward. For two years, Edward runs the property and makes a considerable sum of money but he keeps it for himself. Thomas returns and Edward refuses to hand over the money or return the property which is now in his name.

Thomas goes to the common law courts and it is held that he has no right to bring the claim since, in common law, Edward is now the owner. What does Thomas do? The only path left open is to go to the king and to ask him to intervene and to force Edward to return his land and to give all the profits to Adam and Ben, recognising that the transfer to Edward was only temporary. The king is prepared to act. This is the first recognition of a trust by the courts. You may read that at first it was not called a trust but a 'use'. The reason for this was that the land was conveyed 'for the use of the third party'. This distinguished the transfer from being one for his own benefit. The development of the 'use' into the trust was a result of refusal by the Crown to recognise uses, so a second use was employed to allow the same effect and the second use was the forerunner of the trust today.

trust
Transfer of property to a trustee who holds the legal title for the benefit of a third party

The reason that the common law courts were so reluctant to recognise the trust was because the property was put into the name of the trustee. In our example it was Edward. The trustee was the owner at law. Legally, he had control over the property. The rights of the beneficiaries were based on conscience and were recognised because the Lord Chancellor thought it would be unconscionable to ignore their rights.

ACTIVITY

Applying the law

Hereward creates a trust in favour of Edmund and transfers his property to Harold. Harold holds the property in his name and decides to give it to his friend, John, and not to preserve it for Edmund. What could Edmund do? Consider the defects in law which limited Edmund's rights.

2.2.2 The trust today

The trust involves three sets of interests. It has been called the 'magic triangle' by Alastair Hudson in *Equity and Trusts* (8th edn, Routledge, 2014, p. 51). (See Figure 2.1.)

1. Initially the **settlor** has absolute ownership of his property. If he decides that he wants someone to benefit eventually from all or some of his property, but not immediately, he could transfer the legal title to his property to another called the trustee who gets absolute ownership of the property, but not to enjoy for himself. Once the legal title has been transferred the settlor no longer owns the property at law.

2. The **trustee** receives the property but holds it on trust for the benefit of the beneficiaries. The trustee now holds the legal title to the property. So if the trust property comprised land and included a house he would have the title in his name and today he would be registered at the Land Registry as the owner. However, the trustee cannot claim the land for himself. He must keep the trust property separately from his other property.

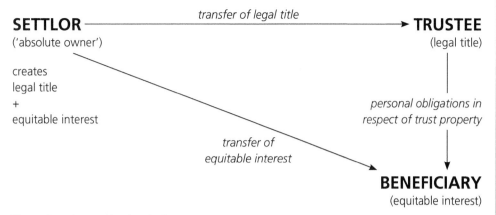

Figure 2.1 The 'magic triangle' in trusts

beneficiary
A person who has an interest in the trust property in equity but does not own the legal title

express trust
A trust which is expressly created by the settlor

Inter vivos
A trust created during a lifetime, as opposed to one created in a will, taking effect on death

3. The **beneficiary** has a personal right to force the trustees to act on his behalf if they refuse to act. He does not own a legal interest in the property but only an equitable interest. He cannot deal with the legal title so he cannot create a lease or a legal mortgage over the property; only the trustees can do this but he can deal in the equitable interest, e.g. he can take out an equitable mortgage of his equitable interest.

Once a trust has been created and is fully constituted, the settlor loses all control over the property unless he is also a beneficiary or he acts as trustee himself. The important fact to remember is that once the trust is constituted, the settlor cannot change his mind and try to recover his property. In many cases in land law the settlor may be the same person as the trustee but he fulfils different roles and owes different duties.

Some trusts arise **expressly** because the settlor wants to create a trust over his property but some trusts arise by **implication**.

2.2.3 The express trust

Express trusts arise by a deliberate act of the owner of the property. The settlor must appoint a trustee who could either be himself or a third party known to the settlor who agrees to act as trustee. Whenever there is an express declaration of trust in land *inter vivos* it must be evidenced in writing. According to:

SECTION

STATUTE
s 53(1)(b) of the Law of Property Act 1925: 'a declaration of trust respecting land or any interest therein must be manifested and proved by some writing signed by some person who is able to declare such trust or by his will'.

implied trust
A trust which arises because of circumstances and not through the express intention of the settlor

2.2.4 Implied trusts

Implied trusts can be split into two categories: resulting trusts and constructive trusts.

These trusts are not deliberately imposed by the settlor but arise by implication of law [constructive trusts] or on the presumed intention of the settlor [resulting trusts]. The parties may not even be aware that a trust has been created. Under s 53(2) LPA 1925, these trusts do not require writing or any formality for their creation.

- **Resulting trusts** of land are trusts imposed because of the circumstances of purchase, such as where a partner to a relationship contributes to the purchase but is not registered as joint owner; the law will give that person a share in equity. The owner of the legal estate is said to hold the property on trust for them both. The trust is said to give effect to the presumed intentions of the parties. Unlike express trusts, there is no requirement for a formal record of the trust.

- **Constructive trusts** are trusts that are imposed by the court because it would be 'unconscionable' for the owner of the property to hold that property for themselves. An example would be where the legal owner agrees that the non-legal owner is to have a share of the property if she carries out some work on the property. It would be unconscionable to later deny her an interest.

ACTIVITY

Applying the law

Consider the following situations and decide whether a resulting or constructive trust arises:

1. Janet and John both contribute to the purchase of Windy Hollow, a cottage in Malvern. Janet contributes £10,000 from her savings and John contributes £50,000 from the sale of another property and the rest is raised by a mortgage. The property is registered in John's name. He owns the legal estate. He could decide to try to raise some extra cash by taking out a second mortgage and he would be able to do this without consulting Janet. He could also put the house on the market without consulting her.
2. Mary and Mark move into Windy Hollow and the house is registered in Mark's name. Mark has provided most of the purchase money while the rest has been raised on mortgage. The house is in a very poor state. Mark tells Mary that he is holding the house on trust for them both. Mary carries out work on the property and supervises the builders while Mark is at work.

Under the trust we see the possibility of property being owned by one or more persons on behalf of themselves and/or several different people. They will all have rights but the nature of the rights will vary according to whether the rights are legal or equitable in nature. Trusts are often used where the beneficiary is unable to own property at law because of a disability. This could be because they are under age or because they are under a mental disability. No one can own land at law until he/she reaches the age of 18 (s 1(6) LPA 1925; s 1 Family Reform Act 1969). The land must be held under a trust until their eighteenth birthday.

ACTIVITY

Applying the law

Consider this example and decide who is the settlor, who is the trustee and who is the beneficiary.

Sean wants to give his seaside holiday house, Cliff View, to his grandson Ben, aged 12. As Ben is too young to own land, Sean asks his old friend, Richard, to look after it for him until Ben is old enough to hold it in his own name. He puts this into writing and signs it and later transfers the Cliff View to Richard.

What would happen if Richard refused to hand over the house when Ben reaches 18?

2.3 The difference between legal and equitable interests in property

The trustee (Richard) owns the legal estate of Cliff View and the beneficiary (Ben) owns the equitable estate. Sean is the settlor. Once the title is transferred to Richard, Sean no longer has any interest in the property. So, in a single piece of property there are two sets of interests shared between the trustee and the beneficiary. Whenever property is shared between two or more persons a trust is said to arise, splitting the legal and equitable ownership.

In many cases the trustees and beneficiaries are the same people. This is because the law will always impose a trust where property is co-owned.

Traditionally, equitable rights arose because they were rights in property not recognised by common law. Sometimes equitable rights arose because formalities had not been complied with when rights in property had been either transferred or created. Equity would still recognise the interest and would enforce the rights of the claimant.

Today, legal rights are distinguishable from equitable rights because the owner of a legal estate can deal with the estate at law and the owner of an equitable estate only has rights to deal in the equitable estate.

2.3.1 Rights *in rem* and rights in *personam*

The law draws an important distinction between rights which are said to be proprietary in nature and rights which are said to be purely personal. If you have a proprietary right then you can claim rights in the property itself. These rights will endure when the property passes into the hands of a third party. By way of contrast, a personal right is only good against another individual. The right cannot be enforced against anyone else.

If you have a proprietary right then the right will be good against the property even if it is later sold to someone else, since the right is not against the owner but a right in the property itself. This difference can be traced back to the first division between legal and equitable rights.

Historically, legal rights were enforceable only in the common law courts of the king. Equitable rights were only enforceable in the Courts of Chancery but at the discretion of the king and later the Lord Chancellor.

Another difference lay in the fact that legal rights are rights *in rem*, giving rise to real actions, and equitable rights are rights in *personam*, giving rise to personal actions.

realty
Real property or another name for land

personalty
Personal property such as money, cars or jewellery

'Realty and Personalty

...There is an almost perfect match between the category of real property and land. If a lay person hears "real property", or "real estate", or "realty", what will come to mind will be an image of land. For most lawyers the effect will be the same. Some lawyers may just manage to remind themselves that they should be thinking more abstractly, not of the land itself, but of interests in land. "Personal property" or "personalty" similarly evoke cars, cows, televisions, crockery, pictures, money, and a host of other **moveable** things. In fact the correlation is not quite perfect. A lease of land, however long, is technically personalty, and some moveable things are heirlooms and fall within the category of realty.... A judgment in money can be called personal because it gives the victorious plaintiff no right in or to any particular thing but merely a right that a person, the defeated defendant, pay the sum in question, a right backed by the law's machinery for executing judgments.... In some actions you could recover the thing itself. Those actions came to be called "real actions", "real" meaning "thing-related" in the simple sense that the person claiming would recover the very thing claimed. The subject matter of real actions then became real property or realty, the especial thing-relatedness of such assets being their specific recoverability: if it came to litigation, you would get back the thing itself.'

P Birks, 'Before We Begin: Five Keys to Land Law' in S Bright and J Dewar (eds), *Land Law: Themes and Perspectives* (Oxford University Press, 1998), pp. 470–471

Birks was highlighting the difficulties in trying to put all property into categories. In particular, the lease was traditionally considered to be personal property which could only give rise to a personal action. It did not give rise to a right *in rem* and so was not a claim to the land itself but only a personal claim against the landlord.

Leases are still classified as personalty but it makes little difference because under s 1 LPA 1925 they give rise to a legal estate in land.

One confusing aspect of land law is that equitable rights in land may give rise to proprietary rights which may be binding on the owner of the legal estate. It depends on the nature of the right.

2.3.2 The effect of equitable rights on third parties

Another important difference between legal and equitable rights is the way such rights are enforceable against a third party. It used to depend on whether the land was unregistered or registered. The difference between the two was that ownership of unregistered land depended on possession of documents called deeds which proved that the property was yours. In registered land, ownership is proved by entry of the landowner's name at the Land Registry by the Registrar. There are also different ways of proving that someone owns an interest in unregistered land or registered land, such as an easement.

If you have a legal easement in unregistered land then that would be a right in the land itself and anyone who acquired the land would be bound by that right even if they did not know about it. If you have a legal easement in registered land then the right has to be registered at the Land Registry if it is to be binding on the land.

Equity would only enforce rights against certain persons. When the trust was first recognised by the courts of equity, the beneficiary could only enforce the trust against the trustee. Later the trust was enforceable against third parties who purchased the land knowing that there were third-party rights in that land.

As we will see below, only the *bona fide* purchaser without notice of rights will be able to take land without being subject to rights in equity.

2.3.3 The *bona fide* purchaser for value without notice

A purchaser could acquire a legal estate without being subject to equitable rights in the land if he could claim to be a ***bona fide*** purchaser without notice of the rights.

If someone purchases property honestly, not knowing that there are any other rights in the land then he will not be bound by those rights. Once the purchaser could establish that he was a *bona fide* purchaser for value then he had what James LJ described in *Pilcher v Rawlins* (1872) 7 Ch App 259 as an 'absolute, unqualified, unanswerable defence' against an equitable right. This was because the effect of the claim was that it destroyed the equitable interest involved and it could not be revived. It makes no difference that a later purchaser had notice of these rights.

Consider the earlier example where Hereward creates the trust in favour of Edmund and transfers it to Harold as trustee. Harold holds the property in his name and then gives it to his friend, John. John will take the land subject to Edmund's rights.

COMMON LAW AND EQUITY

bona fide
Means 'in good faith'

Contrast the situation where John pays Harold £200 for the land instead of receiving it as a gift. Then it would be treated differently and the law would have allowed John to keep the land. He would not be subject to Edmund's rights.

In the second example, John is called a '*bona fide* purchaser for value of a legal interest without notice'. The *bona fide* purchaser is also called 'equity's darling' because the courts of equity were prepared to look more favourably on someone who had paid for property. However, he could only take free of someone's rights if he was unaware of them. Originally notice depended on actually knowing of the right. If John had been told by Harold that he had the right to transfer the property to him and John did not know of Edmund's rights then John would be 'without notice of Edmund's rights'. Suppose that John was told by a neighbour that Edmund had rights, then he would lose the protection and he would be bound by his rights.

CASE EXAMPLE

Wilkes v Spooner [1911] 2 KB 473

A landlord granted two leases of two properties to Spooner. Spooner assigned one lease to Wilkes and Spooner covenanted within the lease not to compete with Wilkes' own business as a butcher. Spooner surrendered his lease to the landlord who then granted a fresh lease to Spooner's son and he started a business as a butcher, knowing of the covenant with Wilkes. The landlord did not have notice of the covenant and so it was destroyed when the lease was surrendered to the landlord and therefore Spooner's son was not bound by the covenant.

2.3.4 What does '*bona fide* purchaser for value' mean?

1. *Bona fide*: this means 'to act in good faith'.

2. Purchaser for value: this means that something of value must have been given. It does not have to be money, it could be 'in kind' and it does not have to be what the property is worth. The word 'purchaser' goes beyond the purchaser of the fee simple and includes mortgagees and also lessees.

3. Of a legal estate: the purchaser must have purchased a legal estate in the land rather than an equitable estate.

2.3.5 Notice

The *bona fide* purchase must be without notice of the equitable rights. There were three different forms of notice:

1. **Actual notice**: a purchaser had actual notice if he knew of any rights affecting the land because he had been told of the rights or had found out for himself. Later, when rights were capable of registration, it meant rights which the purchaser knows about because they were registered and the purchaser has checked and found out about them. There is a duty to check and below we will see that it is no excuse to say you have not had time to check the Register for rights.

2. **Constructive notice**: a purchaser had constructive notice if he would have been aware of the estate if he had checked for himself. Checking would include all those enquiries and inspections which he ought reasonably to have made. This would be either by visiting the property or by checking whether registrable rights had been registered. The purchaser should always visit the property because he may be bound by rights that can only be discovered by physical inspection of the property. Under s 199 LPA 1925 the purchaser is prejudicially affected by notice of those matters which would have come to his knowledge if such enquiries and inspections had been made as ought reasonably to have been made by him.

3. **Imputed notice**: a purchaser would have imputed notice if his legal agent (usually his solicitor or his adviser) had made investigations. They would check on his behalf and even if they had not told him of the rights, the law would say he had notice of the rights.

The doctrine plays a very minor role in the law today.

> 'The equitable doctrine of notice is nowadays marginal. Nevertheless there remain a few entitlements in unregistered land which are neither overreached nor capable of registration as land charges and whose priority against a purchaser therefore turns on the traditional doctrine. These rights tend to be both anomalous and awkward, presenting conveyancing difficulties wholly disproportionate to their number.'
>
> K Gray and S F Gray, *Elements of Land Law* (5th edn, Oxford University Press, 2009) p. 1155

The main examples are the rights of beneficiaries under some trusts of unregistered land and rights in unregistered land that were created before 1926, for example a restrictive covenant or an equitable easement.

ACTIVITY

Applying the law

Consider the following:

Hereward owns a large property in Warwickshire, called Windy Heath. He transfers it to his friend, Harold, to be held in trust for his three grandchildren, Edmund, William and Gerald, who are all students. Consider the effect of Harold's actions in each of the following situations:

1. Harold decides to give Windy Heath to his friend, John.
2. Harold decides to sell Windy Heath to his friend, James.
3. Harold decides to sell Windy Heath to James but he knows about the three grandchildren because he has been told that they were staying there for the summer.
4. Harold decides to sell Windy Heath to Joan who never visits the property but her solicitor, Frank, does and he finds the three children have been staying there.

2.3.6 Overreaching

Definition

Overreaching can be described as the substitution of the subject matter of the trust so that whereas before overreaching the beneficiaries enjoyed the equitable ownership of land after overreaching they only enjoy the equitable ownership of money.

Overreaching arises on the sale of property which is held under a trust. So it can apply to any jointly held property. Where overreaching applies equitable rights arising under a trust which attach to the land are transferred from the land to the capital monies. It allows land under a trust to be sold free of certain rights. The purchaser may have notice of the rights of the beneficiaries but will still be held to take free of these rights. The rights may have been entered on the Register against the title of the property. Overreaching can apply to all land held in trust, whether it has registered or unregistered title.

Purpose of overreaching

Overreaching allows land to be disposed of free of equitable rights affecting the land. It allows the rights of the beneficiaries to be safeguarded by making the trustee statutorily obliged to transfer the capital money to them.

Conditions for overreaching

Under s27(2) LPA 1925, overreaching will apply where there is a sale of a legal estate in land to a purchaser and purchase monies are paid over to two or more trustees or a trust corporation by the purchaser and the rights are capable of being overreached. What constitutes a legal estate in land capable of triggering overreaching was revisited in *Baker v Craggs* [2018] EWCA Civ 1126. A couple had been granted a legal easement over land and they argued that the grant of the easement triggered the overreaching provisions and thus overreached equitable rights subsisting in the land. This was accepted in the High Court but rejected in the Court of Appeal where the orthodoxy of the interpretation of s2(1) Law of Property Act 1925 was reinstated. Section 2.1(1) requires the conveyance of a legal estate in land to two or more trustees and under s1 Law of Property Act such legal estate in land are limited to just two estates the term of years absolute [leasehold] and the fee simple absolute [freehold].

Overreaching can still occur even where the purchaser has notice of the equitable rights such as where the rights have been entered as a restriction on the proprietorship register at the Land Registry. (See Figure 2.2.)

Figure 2.2 Overreaching

Overreaching will not apply where the capital money is paid over to a single trustee. See also *HSBC Bank Plc v Dyche & Anor* [2009] EWHC 2954 (Ch) below, where an overriding interest was not overreached because the purchaser was not a purchaser 'in good faith'.

CASE EXAMPLE

Williams & Glyn's Bank v Boland [1981] AC 487

A husband owned the legal title to the matrimonial home. The wife had an equitable interest in the land because she had made contributions to the purchase. The husband took out a loan with Williams & Glyn's Bank who executed a charge over the property. The wife was not aware of the loan and had not given her consent. When the husband failed to make the agreed repayments the bank claimed the right to sell the property. The rights of the wife were not overreached because the 'sale', i.e. the loan from the bank, had been made to a sole trustee, i.e. the husband. The wife's right to remain in the property was upheld.

Overreaching will only apply where the purchase money is paid over to two trustees. The rule does not depend on good faith or on the circumstances of the transfer of the money. Under s27(2) LPA 1925 the key issues are whether the capital money has been transferred to two trustees. This was the important feature in the case below and distinguishes the facts from the case of *Boland*.

CASE EXAMPLE

City of London Building Society v Flegg [1988] AC 54

A son-in-law, his wife and her parents joined together to purchase property. The son-in-law and daughter were registered as owners. They owned the legal estate as trustees for themselves and the son's parents-in-law and all four were in occupation of the property. The son-in-law took out a second mortgage with his wife and the money was paid over to them by the building society. The parents-in-law were not aware of the second mortgage but were in occupation of the property. When the loan was not repaid the building society exercised its power of sale. The parents-in-law claimed the right to remain in the property but the House of Lords held that their rights were overreached because the purchase money had been paid to two trustees the daughter and son-in-law.

The rights of the parents-in-law should have been protected because their rights were transferred from the property to the capital money. However, on the sale of the property the building society had first claim on the purchase money and there was nothing left after the loan had been repaid. It suggests that overreaching will not necessarily protect the beneficiaries of the trust and much will depend on whether there are two trustees of the land. Where the trustees exceed their powers then overreaching will not apply. This is because it would be an *ultra vires* transaction.

Only specified interests in land can be overreached. There are many that are excluded under statute see s 2(3) LPA 1925, e.g. easements, restrictive covenants and estate contracts, which we know as the contract before conveyance of the property which confers rights in the property to the purchaser. None of these rights can be overreached.

The effect of this section is that the main right capable of being overreached is equitable ownership of property arising behind a trust. For example, the rights of Mrs Boland and Mr and Mrs Flegg and anyone who makes a contribution towards the purchase of property but is not registered as owner.

The decision in the following case appeared to challenge the principles of overreaching but the facts are unusual and the case was decided on those facts and the main principles of overreaching still apply.

CASE EXAMPLE

HSBC Bank Plc v Dyche [2009] EWHC 2954

Mr C transferred the title of a property that he owned to his daughter Mrs Dyche and her husband. It was agreed that they held it on constructive trust for him. When Mrs Dyche later divorced her husband the title of the property was transferred into Mrs Dyche's sole name as part of the divorce settlement. This constituted a transfer for value as Mrs Dyche gave consideration. The consideration was 'received' by two trustees Mrs Dyche and her husband. Mrs Dyche immediately took out a mortgage and when she defaulted the bank took proceedings to repossess the property. Mr C claimed that he had the right to remain in the property but the bank argued that his rights had been overreached on the transfer to Mrs Dyche. The judge upheld Mr C's claim because he considered the transfer on the divorce not to be 'in good faith' and so she could not be 'a purchaser' for the purposes of overreaching. He decided that Mr C's rights had not been overreached.

This decision can be criticised because there is nothing in the LPA 1925 s 27 about the transaction having to be 'in good faith'. It focuses purely on the transfer of value by a purchaser to two trustees. The LPA 1925 intended to simplify conveyancing and the transfer of property. However if the sale by the daughter is seen as a sale to perpetrate fraud then the decision can be justified because where fraud is present overreaching will not apply. This is not the same as 'bad faith'.

CASE EXAMPLE

First National Securities Ltd v Hegerty [1984] 3 WLR 769

Here, it was held that where the transaction was fraudulent because the husband had forged his wife's signature then there could be no overreaching of the wife's share.

Compare:

CASE EXAMPLE

State Bank of India v Sood [1997] Ch 276

Two trustees mortgaged trust land which they owned. They did not receive the capital money because the complicated transaction meant the purchase money was not paid over to them (the mortgage being taken out to back an earlier loan). The claimants argued that their rights in the property were not overreached because the purchase money had not actually been advanced to the two trustees. However, the Court of Appeal held that their rights had been overreached because there had been payment to two trustees albeit in a very circuitous way.

This decision can be criticised because it undermines the protection granted to the beneficiaries which is that they will have a share in the purchase monies. This will be denied in this case.

1. There must be a '**purchase**' of the legal estate. A 'purchaser' is given a very wide definition here and will include a mortgagee or chargee, as in the cases of *Boland* and *Flegg*.

2. There must be a **conveyance** of rights to the purchaser.

3. The interest itself must be **capable of being overreached**. Certain equitable rights will continue to attach to land, for example restrictive covenants, equitable easements and estate contracts even after the property has been transferred to a purchaser and the money has been paid to two trustees.

4. Under s 27 of the Law of Property Act 1925, the purchase money must be paid over to at **least two trustees** or a trust corporation (*City of London Building Society v Flegg* (1988)).

5. Overreaching can still occur even where the capital monies are **not paid over contemporaneously** with the conveyance (*State Bank of India v Sood* (1997)).

6. Overreaching can still occur **where the purchaser has notice of the equitable rights**. This could be notice of an interest that overrides or an entry of a restriction on the proprietorship register at the Land Registry.

Figure 2.3 When will overreaching occur?

Overreaching cannot take place unless certain conditions apply: we can see this from the case law above.

The key requirements for overreaching: there must be a 'purchase' of a legal estate and this must be conveyed to a purchaser who must pay the purchase money to two trustees. It is not necessary for the purchase money to be paid contemporaneously with the conveyance. Overreaching can still take place even where the purchaser has notice of the equitable rights but it cannot take place unless the interest is capable of being overreached.

ACTIVITY

Applying the law

Consider the following examples and decide whether the rights of the beneficiaries are capable of being overreached or not:

1. Hattie and Emily and their parents, Jean and Peter, decide to move to the country and buy a country cottage together. The two girls each contribute £10,000 and their mother, Jean, contributes £120,000. The rest of the purchase money is provided by Peter. The legal estate is registered in Peter's name alone. Peter takes out a second loan with the Doubtful Bank Ltd. He fails to repay the money and runs away with Flora. The daughters and their mother want to remain in the house.

2. Jean and Peter buy a country cottage in Kent. They both contribute towards the purchase money and are registered as joint owners. Peter takes out a second loan by fraudulently using Jean's signature on the form, which the building society did not check. Jean likes the house in Kent and wants to remain there.

3. Jean and Peter live together in Number 4 Magnificent Mansions. Peter purchased the property in his sole name, with a contribution of £150,000 from Jean. He takes out a second loan on the property when he runs into financial difficulties in his new business. He appoints his brother as a second trustee. He is unable to repay the loan and the bank wants to sell the property to recover the money. Jean says she has nowhere else to live.

2.4 The historical background to the property legislation of 1925

Before 1925 there were a number of pitfalls for the potential purchaser of land. There could be equitable rights affecting his land which could be binding and he might not have had an opportunity to find out about them. Purchasers of land would buy land subject to an equitable estate if they had notice of the estate. As seen above, notice could take different forms and much would depend on actual knowledge. The purchaser could find himself bound by unknown rights of third parties if he was held to have notice.

The purchase itself was also a lengthy and difficult procedure because the title required proof that the seller owned the property and initially there were several legal estates in land. As you had to investigate each seller's right to sell the land, this could be time-consuming, expensive and prone to mistakes. If there was another sale within a relatively short space of time then the whole procedure had to be repeated; you could not rely on the investigations of title in the earlier sale.

So the two main problems in the transfer of land were:

1. the complication of proving title to the land you were buying;
2. finding out whether other people had rights in the land you were buying.

Under (1) the purchaser had to check that each owner of a legal estate in the land had rights and this involved proof for each separate estate. Also, the purchaser had to check that no one else had hidden rights in the legal estate.

Under (2) the purchaser had to check whether anyone had a right in equity that could affect his enjoyment of the land. Such rights would not be immediately obvious.

These were just two of the problems for the purchaser of property in the nineteenth and early twentieth centuries. The problems prompted the passage of a whole range of property legislation in 1925, the most significant in land law being the Law of Property Act, the Land Registration Act and the Land Charges Act. These have all been supplemented and replaced by subsequent legislation but the main principles behind the legislation remain the same.

2.4.1 Legal estates under the Law of Property Act 1925

Under s 1(1) of the Law of Property Act 1925, the only legal estates that could exist in land were reduced to two:

1. the term of years absolute in possession; and
2. the fee simple absolute.

However, apart from the two legal estates, there were lesser rights which could be created and were enforceable at law.

2.4.2 Legal interests under the Law of Property Act 1925

Under s 1(2) of the Law of Property Act 1925 the following interests could exist at law:

- an easement, right or privilege in or over land for an interest equivalent to an estate in the fee simple absolute in possession or a term of years absolute (s 1(2)(a));
- a rentcharge in possession issuing out of or charged on land being either perpetual or for a term of years absolute (s 1(2)(b));
- a charge by way of legal mortgage (s 1(2)(c));
- any other similar charge on land which is not created by an instrument (of very little importance today) (s 1(2)(d));
- rights of re-entry exercisable over a legal term of years absolute (this right reserved to the owner of the rentcharge to enter the land if the owner of the estate fails to pay the sum due) (s 1(2)(e)).

Under the LPA 1925 s 1(3) all other estates and interests were therefore equitable.

2.4.3 Equitable interests

Other proprietary rights in land therefore are said to be equitable only under s 1(3) of the 1925 Act. These include:

1. The rights of a beneficiary under a trust of land.
2. An interest under a contract to create a legal estate or interest in land. The purchaser is treated as owning an equitable estate from the date the contract is exchanged. The legal estate remains with the seller.
3. Restrictive covenants.
4. Interests that become equitable as a result of statutory reform. These would include any interest that is not within s 1(1) or s 1(2) of the Law of Property Act 1925, for example life estates will only exist in equity.

5. Interests that have not conformed with the requisite formalities in their creation, for example a deed is needed to convey an interest in land which must be signed, witnessed and delivered. If the required formalities are not complied with then the interest conveyed will be equitable only. This list would include leases, easements and profits à prendre and also mortgage charges. They are capable of existing at law if the formalities necessary for their creation have been complied with.

2.4.4 The 1925 property legislation

As noted above, there were some significant problems with the transfer of rights and estates in land in the nineteenth and early twentieth centuries. As a result, extensive reforms were introduced and six Acts were passed in 1925 which fundamentally changed the shape of land law in England and Wales.

> 'the structure of modern land law was put in place by the 1925 legislation, whose dominant policy was to facilitate the transfer of land by easing the burden on purchasers without defeating the interests of others unfairly. A fundamental principle underlying the legislation, but nowhere explicitly stated in it, was to distinguish between commercial interests and family interests. Examples of commercial interest are leases, rights of way and mortgages; such rights are almost invariably created for money or money's worth. Examples of family interest are rights of beneficiaries under a trust or settlement (this includes the beneficial rights of co-owners of land); such rights are not usually created for money or money's worth.... Broadly speaking, with some exceptions intentionally created in 1925 and a few further exceptions not envisaged by the 1925 legislation which have been created subsequently by both the courts and the legislature, it was intended that:
>
> (1) legal estates and interests should bind the successors in title of the person who created them; and
> (2) interests under a trust should upon sale or other disposition giving rise to the payment of a capital sum, be overreached, that is to say transferred from the land to that capital sum, and so should not bind the successors in title of the person who created them.'
>
> P Rainey, M Walsh, P Harrison and D Dovar (eds), *Megarry's Manual of the Law of Real Property* (9th edn, Sweet & Maxwell, 2014), pp. 71–72

The Land Registration Act 1925 (LRA 1925) introduced a system of registration of title to replace the unregistered system of conveyancing. There had been a limited system of registration of title prior to 1925 but the LRA 1925 was far more ambitious. This would go some way towards eliminating the problems that were created by making it necessary to prove title on each sale of the property.

The Acts passed in 1925 established a completely different approach to property law, although many of their main objectives have still not been fulfilled today, nearly 90 years later.

The main principle that was established was the idea that every title should be registered – so there would be no need to actually 'prove' good title each time the property changed hands. Registration of title, however, was not entirely new.

> **'The Emergence of Registration**
> ...In retrospect, the value of registration of title seems irresistibly obvious. Instead of having a system of archaeological proof, in which the task of the conveyancer was

to sift through many layers of paper title, establishing which interests were still relevant or effective, and ensuring that there was no danger of hidden documents surfacing in the future, one would have a much simpler scheme of tabular proof, in which all effective interests would be visible at a glance. The idea of registration, and the sort of administrative framework which it implied, had been familiar for many decades before the first effective scheme of registration of title was introduced by the Land Transfer Act 1897. During that period there were various attempts to implement a system of registration, and many inquiries into the failure of these tentative schemes. These moves were played out against the background of progress in other areas of property law.... There are a number of reasons why it took so long for these strands to be bound into an effective scheme of registration of title. First, a good deal of time was wasted on experiments with deeds registration. Secondly, there were some outstanding technological problems to be overcome, not least that of finding an effective method of identifying and indexing landholdings. Most contentious and most important, there is the question of economic self interest. The question is whether, or to what extent, the slow evolution and final configuration of registration should be attributed to the success of a campaign of resistance to reform, mounted by the conveyancing profession in the defence of its monopoly.'

A Pottage, 'Evidencing Ownership' in S Bright and J Dewar (eds), Land Law:
Themes and Perspectives (Oxford University Press, 1998), pp. 142–144

2.5 The Land Charges Act 1925

Where title remained unregistered because it was outside the area of compulsory registration, a system of registration of equitable interests in land was introduced in the Land Charges Act 1925. This replaced the different types of notice.

The Land Charges Act 1925 was replaced by the Land Charges Act 1972 but the same list of charges introduced under the 1925 Act remains with the addition of Class F land charges.

2.5.1 Classes of land charges

Land charges are divided into six classes (Classes A–F) with some further sub-division. Classes C, D and F are the most important:

- **Class A.** Charges that arise under statute but come into operation when the owner applies for registration, for example a landlord's right to receive compensation under the Agricultural Holdings Act 1986. They are very rare.

- **Class B.** Similarly, these are rights under statute which come into operation directly from the statute rather than on the application.

- **Class C.** These land charges are sub-divided into four groups:

  1. The **puisne mortgage**. This is a legal mortgage not protected by title deeds. In unregistered land this will always be a second mortgage. This is unusual because it is the only legal interest capable of being registered as a land charge under the Land Charges Act 1925. The Act was intended to cover equitable interests only.

  2. The **limited owner's charge**. This is a right in equity which can be registered against the estate, for example Gordon is a tenant for life in an existing settlement and from his own resources he pays for the inheritance tax on the whole estate under the settlement. He is entitled to register the charge and will be able to claim to have the sum discharged out of the estate and paid to him.

3. The **general equitable owner's charge**. This covers a number of rights which are not registrable under any other heading. A number of rights are excluded from this group, for example interests under trusts.

4. **Estate contracts**. These are important in conveyancing. An estate contract consists of any contract to convey or create a legal estate in land or any option to purchase a legal estate or any right of pre-emption in respect of a legal estate (this is a right of first refusal). When a purchaser of land exchanges contracts with the seller, the purchaser acquires an equitable estate in the land. This estate is capable of registration. Once registered it attaches to the land. If the seller tries to sell to anyone else the second purchaser will be bound by the rights of the first purchaser because he bought subject to their rights. In view of the relatively short period between exchange of contracts and completion, solicitors rarely register an estate contract for the purchaser, which is potentially taking a grave risk. However, where an option to purchase land is granted it is always advisable to register such a right. In *Midland Bank Trust Co Ltd v Green* [1981] 2 WLR 28, discussed below, the consequences of failure to register become apparent. Note that only the option to purchase was registrable under the 1925 legislation and the right of pre-emption could not be registered.

Class D. This group is further sub-divided into three sub-headings:

1. **Inland Revenue charges** for inheritance tax payable on death.

2. **Restrictive covenants**. This class covers any restrictive covenant created after 1926 but excluding any covenant that was created between lessor and lessee. Once the interest is registered then the purchaser is bound by the covenant. If the holder of the right fails to register the right then the fact that the purchaser knows about the right is irrelevant.

ACTIVITY

Applying the law

Catriona, owner of Happyland Cottage, enters into a covenant with her neighbour, Kirsty, that she will not use her land for business purpose. Kirsty fails to register the covenant against Catriona's name. Catriona sells Happyland Cottage to Hamish, who wants to run a small computer software company in the garage. He searches the Register for any rights registered against Catriona's name which restrict his use of the land, but none are registered. A neighbour of Catriona is talking to Hamish one day and she says that no one in the area is allowed to use their land as a business. Will Hamish be bound by the right?

Hamish will not be bound by a right that has not been entered on the Register.

3. **Equitable easements**. Any easement that has been created on or after 1 January 1926 and which is equitable only. A legal easement in unregistered land would not be registrable under this category since it would take effect in law and be binding on the world, irrespective of registration.

Class E. This class comprises annuities created before 1926, which are very rare indeed.

Class F. This is an important group which is referred to as 'matrimonial home rights'. They were first created by the Matrimonial Homes Act 1967, and are now contained in the Family Law Act 1996, and although much of the Act has never been adopted those sections covering rights to occupy the matrimonial home were preserved.

Rights of civil partners are also included under the Civil Partnership Act 2004. The right only extends to a spouse or civil partner who is not a legal owner of the matrimonial home. Once registered the spouse or civil partner has the right to occupy the family home. The significant fact is that the right is dependent on status and not on contributions made towards the purchase. The right is dependent on marriage or civil partnership and will be lost if the parties later divorce.

2.5.2 Registration of land charges

Registration under the Land Charges Act 1925 is made by the person claiming the right. Registration is made against the name of the owner of the property and not the name of the property. This has caused a number of problems in the past:

1. There may have been defective registration of the charge because the name used was wrong.
2. There may have been a defective search because the purchaser searched against the wrong name.
3. The purchaser may not know the full names of all the previous owners of the property because the seller has only to prove title for the previous 15 years. This means that the seller must prove that for the past 15 years, whether the land was in his hands or in the hands of another owner, that he had ownership of the land.

Each of these problems is discussed below:

1. **Registration in the wrong name.** If the registration was made in an incorrect name then the court is presented with a problem because a later purchaser may be given a clear certificate showing no land charges against the land itself. In *Oak Co-operative Building Society v Blackburn* [1968] Ch 730 the charge was registered against the name of 'Frank David Blackburn'. A search was made by a subsequent purchaser against the name of 'Francis Davis Blackburn'. The court upheld the earlier registered charge as it was made against a recognised form of 'Francis'. The court concluded that there should have been searches in all forms of the purchaser's name as the defendants would then have found the earlier charge. It was held in *Standard Property Investment Plc v British Plastics Federation* (1985) 53 P & CR 25 that the appropriate name for the purposes of registration was the name of the owner of the estate affected as found in the deeds of title.

2. **Search against incorrect name.** The general rule is that a purchaser who claims a search against an incorrect name will be bound by any charges that are registered against the correct version of the owner's name. Under s 198 of the Law of Property Act 1925

    'the registration of any instrument or matter ... shall be deemed to constitute actual notice of such instrument or matter and of the fact of registration to all persons and for all purposes connected with the land affected as from the date of registration'.

3. **The purchaser may not know the names of all previous owners of the land.** On any sale of property with unregistered title all charges properly registered will continue to be binding on the land. The problem for the purchaser is that if they do not know the names of all the previous owners then they have no way of discovering all the potential charges that have been registered against their names and could therefore be binding on the land.

Wade described the use of a name-based register as the equivalent of creating Frankenstein's monster, which, with the passing years, would become not only more dangerous but also more difficult to kill. He pointed out that as the years went by it would become impossible to successfully convert the Register from 'name-based' into 'title-based'. The time and costs involved would make it impossible (H W R Wade, 'Land Charges Required' [1956] 14 *CLJ* 216).

The problem has not been solved within the land charges system itself but by the introduction of compulsory registration of title which itself is title-based. Charges in the registered land system are registered against the name of the property. Gradually, with more and more properties being brought within the system of land registration, the problems with the land charges system is rapidly becoming less relevant.

2.5.3 The effect of registration

After 1925 all registrable interests were either registered, in which case the purchaser took subject to them, or were not registered, in which case the purchaser took free of them. The effect of non-registration of a charge depends on which class of charge was involved. In Classes C(iv) and D(i)–(iii) the purchaser of a legal estate in the land charged for money or money's worth can take free of the unregistered charge. It means that whereas under the other land charges a purchaser of an equitable estate can take free of the charge, only the purchaser of a legal estate can take free of the unregistered charge under Class C(iv) and D(i)–(iii). The purchaser of an equitable estate will therefore be bound by an unregistered estate contract in the land.

Once a search had been made at the Land Charges Registry a certificate would be produced and if a charge against the land had not been made, for whatever reason, then the charge would not be binding on the land.

It no longer mattered whether or not the purchaser actually knew about the existence of equitable rights in land. These rules could have very dramatic results because the court had no right to intervene, however unfair the result might seem.

CASE EXAMPLE

Midland Bank Trust Co Ltd v Green [1981] 2 WLR 28

A father owned a farm with unregistered title. He granted his son a ten-year option to purchase the farm at an agreed price but the son failed to register the option against the father's name. Later, the father sold the farm to his wife at undervalue, in order, principally, to avoid the option after a quarrel with the son. The son tried to register the option but it was held to be too late. Even though the mother was aware that the son had rights in the land, she still took free of his rights. She had purchased the farm for £500 when it was worth about £40,000.

1. Oliver J at first instance held that the option was not binding because it had not been registered before the 'purchase' by the wife.
2. The Court of Appeal reversed the finding of Oliver J. Lord Denning drew attention to the fact that the statutory immunity could only be claimed for unregistered options where payment had been for a fair and reasonable value in money and money's worth and not at undervalue. Lord Denning regarded the payment of £500 as a gross undervalue.
3. The House of Lords reversed the finding of the Court of Appeal. Lord Wilberforce held that the wife need only show that payment had been for 'money or money's worth'. He relied on the contractual rule which said that the court will not enquire into the adequacy of consideration as long as the consideration is real. She had paid £500 which was held to be valuable consideration. The House of Lords unanimously held that the unregistered land charge was unenforceable against the purchaser. The House of Lords held that good faith was irrelevant in this transaction. The wife had known that the transaction would affect the son's right to exercise the option but this did not affect the transaction because it had not been registered at the time of sale.

An option to purchase can be very valuable. It gives a right to demand the transfer of property at the agreed price at any time during the period of the option. Once registered, it will be binding on the land. It does not prevent a later sale to someone else but the person with the option has the right to claim the property at the agreed price, even from the third-party purchaser. Where property is rising in value it can be a very valuable right to own. In commercial transactions the option is usually granted for valuable consideration.

2.5.4 Rights that are incapable of registration under the Land Charges Acts 1925–72

Under unregistered conveyancing there are still some equitable rights that are incapable of registration. Even after the passage of the Land Registration Act 2002, they will continue to be relevant because there are still substantial numbers of properties with unregistered title.

There is no requirement compulsorily to register your land unless you carry out a transaction that acts as an 'event' which triggers registration.

One of the most important rights in unregistered land that cannot be registered is the right of a beneficiary under a trust of land. These are the rights of someone who has contributed to the purchase of land but does not have rights in law. These rights cannot be entered on the Land Charges Register. The old rules concerning the doctrine of notice govern whether these rights are binding on a purchaser.

CASE EXAMPLE

Kingsnorth Finance Co Ltd v Tizard [1986] 1 WLR 783

A husband held the legal title to the family home on trust for himself and his wife. The wife had an interest in the property because of contributions she had made towards the purchase. The marriage broke down and the wife lived apart from the husband who remained in the matrimonial home with the two children of the marriage. The wife continued to return to the property, often twice a day, to cook for the children and to carry out domestic chores. The husband secretly took out a loan with a finance company. It then obtained a charge over the house, giving it rights over the property if the husband defaulted on the repayments. He later left to go to America with one of the children. An agent from the finance company had visited the premises but the husband had arranged the visit when the wife was not visiting and had eliminated all traces of her existence, hiding photographs and all her remaining possessions in the house. The agent of the finance company failed to make sufficient enquiries. It was held that the finance company did not take free of the wife's rights as it had constructive notice of her rights.

This case suggests that any bank or building society would be bound in unregistered land by the rights of a wife or any holder of an equitable interest where there had not been proper enquiry. 'Proper enquiry' includes failure to ask questions about others who may have potential rights in the property. Mr Tizard had put 'single' as his status on his application for a loan. However, there were clearly children in the property and this should have alerted the agent to ask further questions about their mother and whether she had any potential rights in the property.

ACTIVITY

Self-assessment questions

1. List the problems with unregistered conveyancing prior to 1925.
2. How did the 1925 Land Charges Act address those problems?
3. Explain why properties with unregistered title remain today.

2.6 Unregistered land in the twenty-first century

Although the numbers of registered titles in the United Kingdom are well in excess of 90 per cent, unregistered land still remains a significant part of the total land ownership in the United Kingdom today. Major landowners such as the Crown, charities and many companies may not deal in their land in such a way so as to trigger first registration which we will discuss in the next chapter. The incentives under the Land Registration Act 2002 to encourage these landowners to register their titles to land have encouraged extensive voluntary registration of property with unregistered title.

The principles of unregistered land continue to be relevant because any transfer of property with unregistered title will be subject to the unregistered land rules and it is only when title is transferred to the purchaser that the purchaser then applies to have the title registered in his name. Ownership of land must be proved through title deeds and the purchaser satisfies himself that the title cannot be challenged. Further, the purchaser must investigate any equitable rights in the land by checking the Land Charges Register.

SUMMARY

1. Common law was introduced to bring in uniform laws across England.
2. Defects in the common law system led to the introduction of equity which was administered in a different court: the Court of Chancery.
3. Equity and common law were merged under the 1873–75 Judicature Acts but equity still remains a separate strand of law today.
4. Equity introduced a number of new rights and remedies.
5. There is a distinction between legal rights and equitable rights.
6. Legal rights in unregistered land are binding under the principle that legal rights bind the world.
7. Equitable rights in unregistered land will be binding under the doctrine of notice or if registered at the Land Charges Register.
8. Unregistered land is gradually being phased out and the rules are less relevant in land law today.

Further reading

Books

Birks, P, 'Before We Begin: Five Keys to Land Law' in S Bright and J Dewar (eds), *Land Law: Themes and Perspectives* (Oxford University Press, 1998), pp. 470–471.

Gray, K and Gray, S F, *Elements of Land Law* (5th edn, Oxford University Press, 2009), pp. 1143–1156.

Hudson, A, *Equity and Trusts* (8th edn, Routledge, 2014), ch. 2.

Pottage, A, 'Evidencing Ownership' in S Bright and J Dewar (eds), *Land Law: Themes and Perspectives* (Oxford University Press, 1998), pp. 142–144.

Rainey, P, Walsh, M, Harrison, P and Dovar, D (eds), *Megarry's Manual of the Law of Real Property* (9th edn, Sweet & Maxwell, 2014).

Articles

Coulter, J, 'Owners and Occupiers: The Dangers' [2012] 156(23) *SJ* 17.

Gravells, N, 'HSBC v Dyche: Getting your Priorities Right' [2010] *Conv* 169.

Harpum, C, 'Purchasers with Notice of Unregistered Land Charges' [1981] 40 *CLJ* 213.

Harpum, C, 'Overreaching, Trustees' Powers and the Reform of the 1925 Legislation' [1990] 49 *CLJ* 277.

Howell, J, 'Notice: A Broad View and a Narrow View' [1996] *Conv* 34.

Howell, J, 'The Doctrine of Notice: An Historical Perspective' [1997] *Conv* 341.

Owen, G, 'A New Paradigm for Overreaching: Some Inspiration from Down Under' [2013] *Conv* 377.

Thompson, M P, 'The Purchaser as Private Detective' [1986] *Conv* 283.

3

Registered land

AIMS AND OBJECTIVES

After reading this chapter, you should be able to:

▪ Explain the main features of the registered land system

▪ Understand the need for reform of the land registration system that was introduced in 1925 and describe the main features of the reforms of the Land Registration Act 2002

▪ Describe the transfer of legal title in registered land

▪ Explain how third-party rights are protected on the Register

▪ Understand the role of third-party rights that override the Register

▪ Describe the circumstances when the Register can be altered

In view of the significance of land, it is important to have some reliable system of recording transactions involving land ownership.

3.1 Introduction to registration of title

The traditional system of unregistered conveyancing had no national record of the ownership of the property other than the deeds themselves. Indeed, early transfers of property were not even required to be made in writing. The system was clearly open to fraud and misuse. Documentation could be lost or damaged. These problems were soon recognised and over a period of 300 years attempts were made to regulate the system of recording ownership of land in the UK. The first successful legislation introducing the principle of registered title was passed in 1862, but the first meaningful legislation was the Land Transfer Act of 1875 which introduced the idea of a single Land Register. The Land Register would be used to record ownership of land and those records could be relied on by subsequent purchasers. The idea was to have a system of registering title to land which had two features:

1. the title to land would be guaranteed by the state; and

2. it could be relied on by all prospective purchasers as proof of ownership of property.

As seen in the last chapter, the old system of unregistered land was based on the purchaser proving title by the possession of title deeds. On each purchase a purchaser had to undertake an investigation of the title deeds to prove the seller had a 'good root of title'. This had to be repeated on each sale of the property. It was wasteful and repetitive and there was always the risk that undiscovered rights attaching to the land would be found and would bind the purchaser.

The Land Registry Act 1862 and Land Transfer Act 1875 introduced the principle of registration of title but the system was voluntary and most titles remained unregistered. In 1897 compulsory registration was introduced on the sale of property in London. This was the beginning of the compulsory system of land registration which now affects all dealings in land which come within the Land Registration Act 2002. The land registration scheme in England has its roots in the Torrens registration scheme introduced in Australia in the nineteenth century.

3.1.1 Features of the land registration system

The scheme of registration of title aims to create a system in which one register will disclose all the relevant details concerning ownership of any piece of land and all the rights and interests that bind that land.

Registration allows registered estates in land, both freehold and leasehold, to be separately registered. Each has its own title on the Register. Once registered the state guarantees the title and the purchaser can accept the title without making his own separate investigations.

The Register is divided into separate sections which cover different aspects of ownership: the property itself, ownership of the property and rights affecting the property.

3.1.2 The aims behind the Land Registration Acts

The key feature of the land registration scheme is that when an application is made to enter a title on the Register the title is scrupulously investigated by the Land Registry staff. It will not be entered on the Register until they are satisfied that it has no defects. Once it is entered on the Register it is regarded as indefeasible and conclusive. Any subsequent purchaser will also receive a title that can be regarded as indefeasible and conclusive.

Against that title any further interests or rights are entered as burdens to the land and any rights that the land enjoys over neighbouring land.

> 'Each substantively registered title number effectively identifies a major interest around which are clustered register entries relating to a range of minor interests. The operative distinction is therefore between large forms of estate ownership (which are recorded substantively under unique title numbers) and all other kinds of interest in the land which enhance, diminish or qualify such ownership.'
>
> K Gray and S F Gray, *Elements of Land Law* (5th edn, Oxford University Press, 2009), p. 189

The Land Registration Act 1925 intended to introduce a system of land registration which would eventually extend to all land. Indeed, the aim was for the system to extend to all areas within 30 years. This proved to be overly optimistic. There were two main ways of extending the registration system:

1. **Voluntary registration**: the owner had the option of whether or not to register the title; as the advantages were not necessarily clear and it cost the owner to register a title he already owned, few took this option up.

2. **Compulsory registration**: the purchaser had to register as soon as an event triggering registration took place. Initially this was only on the sale of the property but it gradually extended to cover most dealings in property. The Land Registration Act 2002 includes a transfer by gift and a transfer under a court order as triggers for registration. There is no option for the purchaser but to register because otherwise he will lose the property. Today, the only way that land will continue to have an unregistered title will be if there are no transfers or dealings in the property and that will mainly apply where land is in the hands of a charity or a limited company or it is owned by the Crown.

For example, if Valentine owns Cedar Grange, which has unregistered title, he does not have to register his title until he deals in the land in a particular way. While he lives there, enjoying his property, the title remains unregistered. If he sells the land, the sale will act as a trigger for compulsory registration. The sale will take place under the rules governing unregistered conveyancing. If he gives the property away during his lifetime or on death registration will be triggered. However, after the completion of the sale, the new owner will have to take steps to register the title.

Gradually, areas of compulsory registration were extended across England and Wales. The last areas of voluntary registration were brought into the system in 1990. (This was introduced by the Registration of Title Order 1989.) However, even in 2013, according to the Land Registry Report of 2013 over 18 per cent of all land in England and Wales remained unregistered. There were new incentives to register land under the LRA 2002. These are mainly financial as it costs less to voluntarily register land than to register after a transaction has triggered registration but it is also a good way to ensure that squatters will not take over one's land.

3.1.3 The key features of the registration system

1. The mirror principle.
2. The insurance principle.
3. The curtain principle.

1. Under the **mirror principle** it is held that the Register is an accurate and conclusive reflection of ownership of title and also relevant interests affecting the land in question. The mirror principle relies on registration of all rights. If rights can exist in land that cannot or need not be registered then the Register does not give an accurate picture of the title to the land.

2. Under the **insurance principle** the accuracy of the Register is guaranteed and if the Register is found to be inaccurate it will be altered or rectified. Any persons affected by alteration/rectification are entitled to be paid a sum in compensation.

3. Under the **curtain principle** the purchaser of land is not concerned with matters behind the entries on the Register, for example trusts affecting the land. The purchaser is not concerned with whether the beneficiaries' interests in the land are satisfied after sale.

3.1.4 The Land Registry

The Land Registry consists of three registers:

> 1. The **Property Register**. This describes the property and will refer to a filed plan prepared from the Ordnance Survey map; this part of the Register may include details of any benefits attached to the land, such as any easements, rights or privileges. It also describes the status of the property, whether it is held with freehold or leasehold title. Where the boundary has been agreed under s 60 of the Land Registration Act 2002 then that will be referred to in this section. If the boundary has not been agreed then the entry on the register will explain that the boundary shown is for general purposes only.

incumbrance
A right that attaches to the title of land

> 2. The **Charges Register**. This shows details of any burdens or **incumbrances** or third-party rights registered against the estate. These are usually negative rights which exist in equity and restrict the rights of the owner, for example restrictive covenants, estate contracts or statutory home rights, as well as easements granted over the property. It also records any mortgage created by the registered proprietor of the property.

profit à prendre
A right to take something from land belonging to another produce or soil, e.g. the right to collect apples or timber

> 3. The **Proprietorship Register**. This shows the name and address of the registered proprietor of the relevant title, the date of registration and the nature of the title, for example, if it is an absolute title; it will also record any restrictions on the power of the proprietor to deal with the land, for example whether he is a trustee or has been declared bankrupt; there may be entries preventing any disposition of the land without the approval of the lender.

rentcharge
A right to claim a money payment from land that is neither a mortgage nor rent payable under a lease

For an example of a register, see Figure 3.1.

There is one central Land Registry which is now located in Croydon. There are also 13 other district land registries around the country each having an extensive geographical catchment area. The registration rules are common to all.

Entry of a title at the Land Registry

Under the Land Registration Act 2002 several different estates in land are capable of substantive registration. These include:

franchise
An estate in land which entitles the claimant to claim a privilege over the land such as the right to hold an annual fair on the land

- the fee simple absolute;
- the term of years absolute.

There are three other estates which are also capable of substantive registration in the Land Register under an independent title number and these include: *profits à prendre*, **rentcharges** and **franchises**.

Other estates in land cannot be substantively registered with an independent title number but can be entered on the Register against another title in one of the three registers.

OFFICIAL COPY OF REGISTER ENTRIES

This official copy shows the entries subsisting on the register on **9 December 2003** at **11:44:12**.
This date **must be quoted as the search from date in any official search** application based on this copy.
Under s.67 of the Land Registration Act 2002, this copy is admissible in evidence to the same extent as the original.
Issued on 9 December 2003.
This title is dealt with by **Land Registry, Maradon Office**.

Land Registry

Title Number: CS72510

Edition Date: 3 December 2003

A: Property Register

This register describes the land and estate comprised in the title.

CORNSHIRE : MARADON

1. (19 December 1989) The **Freehold** land shown edged with red on the plan of the above title filed at Land Registry and being 13 Augustine Way, Kerwick (PL14 3JP).
2. (19 December 1989) The mines and minerals are excluded.
3. (19 December 1989) The land has the benefit of a right of way on foot only over the passageway at the rear leading into Monks Mead.
4. (3 December 2003) The exact line of the boundary of the land in this title (between the points A - B in blue on the title plan) is determined under section 60 of the Land Registration Act 2002 as shown on the plan lodged with the application to determine the boundary dated 3 December 2003.

   Note: Plan filed.

B: Proprietorship Register

This register specifies the class of title and identifies the owner. It contains any entries that affect the right of disposal.

Title Absolute

1. (10 July 2000) **PROPRIETOR:** PAUL JOHN DAWKINS and ANGELA MARY DAWKINS both of 28 Nelson Way, Kerwick, Maradon, Cornshire PL14 5PQ and of pjdawkins662@ail.com
2. (10 July 2000) The price stated to have been paid on 2 June 2000 was £78,000.
3. (10 July 2000) **RESTRICTION:** No disposition by a sole proprietor of the land (not being a trust corporation) under which capital money arises is to be registered except under an order of the registrar or of the Court.
4. (5 October 2002) Caution in favour of Mary Gertrude Shelley of 18 Cambourne Street, Kerwick, Maradon, Cornshire, PL14 7AR and care of Messrs Swan & Co of 25 Trevisick Street, Kerwick, Maradon, Cornshire PL14 6RE.
5. (28 November 2003) **RESTRICTION:** No disposition of the registered estate by the proprietor of the registered estate is to be registered without a written consent signed by the proprietor for the time being of the charge dated 12 November 2003 in favour of Fast and Furious Building Society referred to in the charges register.

Page 1

Figure 3.1 Example of a register

Specimen Register

C: Charges Register

This register contains any changes and other matters that affect the land.

1. (19 December 1989) The passageway at the side included in the title is subject to rights of way on foot only.

2. (10 July 2000) A Transfer of the land in this title dated 2 June 2000 made between (1) John Charles Brown and (2) Paul John Dawkins and Angela Mary Dawkins contains restrictive covenants.

   NOTE: Original filed.

3. (1 August 2002) **REGISTERED CHARGE** dated 15 July 2002 to secure the moneys including the further advances therein mentioned.

4. (1 August 2002) **PROPRIETOR:** WEYFORD BUILDING SOCIETY of Society House, The Avenue, Weyford, Cornshire CN12 4BD.

5. (28 November 2003) **REGISTERED CHARGE** dated 12 November 2003.

6. (28 November 2003) **PROPRIETOR:** FAST AND FURIOUS BUILDING SOCIETY of Fast Plaza, The Quadrangle, Weyford, Cornshire CN14 3NW.

7. (3 December 2003) The parts of the land affected thereby are subject to the leases set out in the schedule of leases hereto.

****

Schedule of Notices of Leases

	Registration date and Plan ref.	Property description	Date of lease and Term	Lessee's Title
1.	3.12.2003	13 Augustine Way, Kerwick	12.11.2003 999 years from 10.10.2003	CS385372

END OF REGISTER

NOTE: A date at the beginning of an entry is the date on which the entry was made in the Register.

Figure 3.1 continued

3.1.5 How land registration works

First registration

This is governed by s4 LRA 2002 under which certain dealings 'trigger' compulsory registration of title.

1. If land has not been registered before, the purchaser buys the land subject to the old rules of unregistered conveyancing. Title is investigated under the traditional rules, e.g. the seller must show a 15-year good root of title.

2. The purchaser then has a duty to register his legal estate at the Land Registry. Failure to do so within a time limit will result in the purchaser losing his legal estate in land.

3. The Registry is responsible for investigating title before first registration; it will check the accuracy of all the documents of title and, if satisfied, it will then register the new owner as Proprietor on the Proprietorship Register.

4. Once registered, the Land Registry guarantees the accuracy of the registration of title on behalf of the state.

5. Before the Land Registration Act 2002 the Land Registry issued a document called a land certificate on registration of title. The 2002 Act has now abolished land certificates. Today, a 'title information document' is issued to the registered proprietor with an official copy of the Register and an official copy of the title plan and will be issued whenever there is a change to the register of title. These documents have no legal effect but serve only as evidence of the proprietor's title. It is the official entry on the Register that proves ownership of the land.

6. Previously where land was subject to a **mortgage** the Land Registry would issue a document called a charge certificate to the lenders. These have also been abolished under the 2002 Act.

7. However, registration is not simultaneous with the purchase. This takes place some weeks later and for a time the seller's name is on the Register although the purchaser has moved into the property and is now living there. This is called the 'registration gap' and can cause difficulties if new rights arise in the 'gap' between the conveyance and the registration of the new owner.

8. Where the land is subject to third-party rights most are recorded in the Charges Register. Some rights are not capable of registration. This means that it would not be possible to find out about them by checking with the Register. The only way that they can be discovered is by visiting the land itself. In this way the system of land registration is not a completely accurate record as to the state of the land.

	Comments
Step one: purchaser buys land subject to unregistered conveyancing rules.	The seller must show a good root of title of at least 15 years. The property is conveyed to the purchaser by deed.
Step two: the purchaser seeks registration of the title at the Land Registry. Failure to register within a time limit results in loss of property.	The Land Registry is responsible for checking the accuracy of all the documents and investigating the title. The new owner must register title within two months of the date of completion of the transaction (s 6(4) of the LRA 2002).
Step three: the Land Registry issues a title information document and official copies of the title and the plan.	The Land Registry once issued a land certificate on registration, which replaced documents of title, but land certificates have been abolished by the LRA 2002. Proof of ownership lies with the entry at the Register.

Table 3.1 Steps in first registration of title

Subsequent registration

1. Where registered land is sold then the new purchaser applies to the Land Registry to be registered as the new proprietor of the land.

2. Prior to sale, the purchaser investigates the land by visiting the land itself to find out if there are any rights not capable of registration and also by checking the Charges Register.

3. The title has already been investigated so this part would be straightforward; there does not have to be a fresh investigation into the state of the title. Any new incumbrances affecting title would have been added as they came into existence. An example would be an easement. It could not take effect in law unless it was entered on the Register. If your neighbour grants you a right to park your car in his driveway and it is granted in writing, it will not take effect until the easement has been entered on your neighbour's title at the Land Registry. The Land Registry would have checked the validity of this new right before adding it to the title under the Charges Register.

4. A title information document is issued which is evidence of the state of the Register at the time of issue of the document.

Land and charge certificates have now been abolished and instead it is the Register itself that represents proof of ownership. Land certificates will gradually be removed from circulation. When land is sold they must be submitted to the Land Registry with any application for registration and the Land Registry will not issue a replacement.

		Comments
Step one: buyer decides to purchase property. The purchase is completed.	The buyer checks the Register for information about the property.	The Land Registry guarantees the accuracy of the original registration.
Step two: buyer applies to be registered as the new proprietor of the land.	The Land Registry does not have to carry out checks of the title as this has already been done.	Registration must be carried out within two months. New proprietor is registered as owner.
Step three: the existing land certificate must be submitted to the Registry.	A title information document will be issued.	No fresh land certificate is issued.

Table 3.2 Steps in subsequent registration of title

3.2 The reform of the law on land registration

3.2.1 The need for reform

The expectation under the Land Registration Act 1925 for all titles to be entered on the Register within the 30-year period was not met. Compulsory registration for all areas of England and Wales was eventually introduced in 1990. The land registration system itself was found to have a number of problems. These were disclosed in the Report of the Law Commission called 'Land Registration for the Twenty-First Century: A Consultative Document' (Law Com No 254, 1998).

1. There had been considerable litigation over the status of overriding interests and it was agreed that they should be reduced in number or abolished completely. Overriding rights undermine the 'mirror principle' of land registration.

2. The 1925 legislation was very complicated, with too many rules affecting the registration of interests.

3. The gap between transfer and registration gave rise to uncertainty and should be closed by using modern technology.

4. There was no provision for the advance in modern technology in the current system of conveyancing.

5. The rules relating to adverse possession of land needed reform.

The 2002 Act repeals the entire Land Registration Act 1925 although many of the original principles and ideals are included in the 2002 Act.

3.2.2 The objectives of the 2002 Act

1. The Register should be a complete and accurate reflection of the state of title of land at any given time.

2. The number of overriding interests in land should be reduced or abolished altogether.

3. The law on adverse possession should be reformed.

4. The Act should reflect the advances in modern technology.

To a large extent the 2002 Act has achieved a greater degree of accuracy. The purchaser of land will only be bound by certain categories of rights provided the purchaser has provided valuable consideration. The rights that will be binding are those that enjoy priority because they are either:

- a registrable charge; or
- it is an interest which has been protected by the entry of a notice against the title; or
- it is an unregistered interest which will 'override' a registered disposition.

Under Scheds 1 and 3 of the Act the number of rights that override the Register has been reduced and the law on adverse possession has been reformed as set out in Sched 6 LRA 1925.

The final main objective, which was to reflect advances in technology, has still some way to go. Full electronic conveyancing has not been introduced yet by the Land Registry either at exchange of contracts or for the transfer of title although there have been advances. The Land Registry has trialled some of the principles of electronic conveyancing such as electronic signatures and also the use of the Chain matrix in exchange of contracts. A number of lenders and conveyancers are using e-charges. These require an electronic signature by the borrower to be legally valid. However the Land Registry announced in 2011 that it had dropped plans to introduce electronic transfers using e-signatures in spite of investing heavily in the scheme.

3.3 Registration under the Land Registration Act 2002

Only legal estates are capable of registration.

Under s 1 of the Law of Property Act 1925 there are two legal estates in land:

1. the fee simple absolute in possession (the freehold estate); and

2. the term of years absolute (the leasehold estate).

The 2002 Act has extended leasehold estates capable of registration from any lease in excess of 21 years to any lease in excess of seven years. Any lease which is to take effect more than three months after the grant of the lease (known as a 'future lease') must also be registered even if they are to last less than seven years.

There are three separate provisions covering registration of title under the 2002 Act:

1. Under **s 3**, which covers **first** registration of title, a title may be **voluntarily** registered. The owner takes the initiative for registration; it is not triggered by some event such as purchase. This incurs a lower fee (up to 25 per cent discount on the cost of registration) so it only applies in limited circumstances; it does not apply where there is a transfer of title. It would be tempting to use the cheaper fees for voluntary registration before a sale has been finalised.

2. Under **s 4**, which also covers **first** registration, there is provision for **compulsory** registration of title when an event triggers the need to register. These include a wide variety of circumstances such as a transfer for valuable consideration and a gift.

3. Under **s 27**, where there is a **disposition** of an estate or charge which is **already registered** then that must be registered before it can take effect.

3.3.1 Voluntary registration under s 3

In a new provision under the 2002 Act, certain other rights which take effect as legal interests can be voluntarily registered as legal estates with their own titles. In fact, they can only take effect as legal interests. These rights include the following:

1. *Profits à prendre*: these are rights to take something from another's land, for example the right to take fish from a river or the right to take wood for fuel. This right is quite independent of ownership of the land but is dependent on having a right to enter the other's land.

2. **Franchises**: these are rights or privileges which are granted by the Crown, for example the right to hold a market or a fair in their own right.

3. **Rentcharges**: this is a right to receive a periodic sum of money from the owner of land charged with that payment. It excludes rent payable under a lease or tenancy and any sum payable as interest.

SECTION

's 3(1) This section applies to any unregistered legal estate which is an interest of the following kinds –

    (a) an estate in land,
    (b) a rentcharge,
    (c) a franchise, and
    (d) a profit à prendre.

  (2) Subject to the following provisions, a person may apply to the registrar to be registered as the proprietor of an unregistered legal estate to which this section applies if –

    (a) the estate is vested in him, or
    (b) he is entitled to require the estate to be vested in him.'

So the person registering the right must show that it is held for an interest equivalent to a legal estate, either a fee simple absolute or, under s 3(3), a term of years absolute where the lease has at least seven years to run.

There is also a new provision for Crown land to be voluntarily registered. There are problems with this, discussed earlier. The Crown is the feudal landlord of all property held in the United Kingdom. It does not hold the land as freehold or under a fee simple absolute in possession, so the first step is for the Crown to grant itself a freehold estate.

Section 79 allows the Queen to grant a fee simple absolute to herself and then allows her to register this. The main advantage of this will be to prevent adverse possessory rights running against the Crown.

An example of this would be of land in Windsor Great Park. It is possible for the Queen to grant herself a freehold estate of a part of it. She can then approach the Registrar to register the title of the land. The Crown would then be entered on the Register as freehold owner of the land. The Crown would have all the rights of a freehold owner. If squatters took possession of the land under the reform of the rights of squatters to acquire adverse possessory rights, the Queen would have to be informed if any attempt was made for the squatters to register title.

3.3.2 Events which trigger compulsory registration under s 4

Today, any dealing in a legal estate which has an unregistered title will make it subject to compulsory registration. The 2002 Act refers to 'events' triggering compulsory registration. The only estates which can continue to have unregistered title are those estates which are not subject to any dealing at all in the title. However, the registration of a land charge in unregistered land will not trigger registration of title.

SECTION

's 4(1) The requirement of registration applies on the occurrence of any of the following events –
(a) the transfer of a qualifying estate –
(i) for valuable or other consideration, by way of gift or in pursuance of an order of any court, or
(ii) by means of an assent (including a vesting assent).'

Consideration can be money but it can include the exchange for assets or exchange for land. Gifts were included in compulsory registration in 1997 and cover both *inter vivos* gifts as well as assents giving effect to a gift under a will or on intestacy.

SECTION

's 4(1)(c) the grant out of a qualifying estate of an estate in land –
(i) for a term of years absolute of more than seven years from the date of the grant
(ii) for valuable consideration, by way of gift or in pursuance of an order of any court
. . .
(g) the creation of a protected first legal mortgage of a qualifying estate.'

The Land Registration Act 1997 included all first mortgages of an unregistered title as triggers for registration. Mortgages that escape registration are second mortgages of unregistered land which will be rare.

In the 2002 Act:

SECTION

's 4(2) For the purposes of subsection (1) a qualifying estate is an unregistered legal estate which is:

(a) a freehold estate in land, or

(b) a leasehold estate in land which, at the time of the transfer, grant or creation, has more than seven years to run

...

(7) In subsection (1)(a) and (c) references to transfer or grant by way of gift include transfer or grant for the purpose of –

(a) constituting a trust under which the settlor does not retain the whole of the beneficial interest

(b) uniting the bare title and the beneficial interest in property held under a trust under which the settlor did not, on constitution, retain the whole of the beneficial interest.

(8) For the purposes of subsection (1)(g)

(a) a legal mortgage is protected if it takes effect on its creation as a mortgage to be protected by the deposit of documents relating to the mortgaged estate, and

(b) a first legal mortgage is one which, on its creation ranks in priority ahead of any other mortgages then affecting the mortgaged estate.'

The 1925 Act made registration compulsory on **dispositions** of the estate. By way of contrast, the 2002 Act makes registration compulsory on any **event** concerning the estate. These include:

1. the transfer for valuable consideration of a freehold or leasehold estate in unregistered land;

2. a gift of an unregistered estate;

3. a transfer in pursuance of an order of the court;

4. the grant of a lease in excess of seven years to take effect immediately or to take effect in the future;

5. the creation of the protected first legal mortgage of a qualifying estate.

3.3.3 Events which do not require compulsory registration under the 2002 Act

Certain events specifically do not induce compulsory registration:

1. where land is transferred to trustees to hold the estate 'as nominees for [S]' will not induce compulsory registration;

2. the transfer of the legal estate by the operation of law which includes the transfer on death of someone's estate to his personal representatives;

3. a merger of a lease by assignment or surrender of a lease to the owner of the immediate reversion.

(S)

Figure 3.2 Transfer with no element of gift

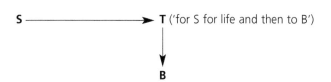

S ⟶ T ('for S for life and then to B')

↓

B

Figure 3.3 Transfer with gift as a triggering event

In Figure 3.2 there is no element of gift, S will eventually recover the property whereas in Figure 3.3 there is a gift of the property which will pass eventually to B. In Figure 3.3 there is a triggering event.

Since the aim of the 2002 Act is for 100 per cent compulsory registration of title to all land in the UK there is provision in the Act under s5 to permit the Lord Chancellor to add new events that will themselves trigger compulsory registration.

ACTIVITY

Quick quiz

Consider the following examples and decide whether they are capable of registration in their own right:

1. Rachael buys fishing rights over a stretch of the River Test which runs through her neighbour Rory's land.
2. Eleanor is granted a five-year lease of a flat in Newcastle.
3. Patrick is given a lifetime right to take wood from his neighbour Edward's land.
4. Henry sells the right to hold a mid-summer fair on his land to a friend, Tom. Henry's family was granted this right in 1386.
5. Zoe takes an eight-year lease over a large house in Dulwich.
6. Phoebe has a large garden which leads down to the River Yealm. She grants her neighbour, Rosalind, a right of way to the river over her land for the rest of her life.
7. William is left a large house by the sea in Sussex by his Aunt in her will. William is 19 years old.
8. Toby is 80 and he owns a house with unregistered title. He now lives abroad. He is worried about squatters taking over part of his land.

Where the right is capable of registration will it be compulsory or can it be made voluntarily?

The important issue here is whether there is a legal estate. In (3) Patrick is only given a lifetime right so this cannot be registered as a title, nor can the right granted to Rosalind in (6). The lease granted to Eleanor in (2) is less than seven years and appears to take effect immediately so that is not capable of registration. The others are capable of registration. Where the property is purchased it will act as a trigger and the registration will be compulsory, whereas in (8) Toby could register voluntarily.

3.3.4 The effect of the duty to register under the 2002 Act

When unregistered land triggers compulsory registration, the time starts to run in which registration must take place. Registration must take place within two months of the relevant period (s6(4) of the 2002 Act). The period can be extended by the Registrar if he is satisfied that there is good reason to do so.

Failure to register the fee simple absolute

Failure to register a fee simple absolute or freehold estate within the time limit will result in the transfer becoming void, which means that the transferor will hold the legal estate on bare trust for the transferee. The transferor is the seller of the land and the transferee is the purchaser.

Failure to register the term of years absolute

Failure to register a term of years absolute or leasehold estate or a protected mortgage of property will result in the interest becoming void and the transfer will take effect as a contract for valuable consideration to grant or create a lease or mortgage.

If the transferee wants the property, which is likely since valuable consideration will normally have been paid, then steps must again be taken to ensure that the property can be registered. It will be necessary to transfer the interest a second time. This will result in additional costs. The 2002 Act laid down that these costs should be borne by the transferee or grantee or possibly the mortgagor. They will also be liable for any other liability which has been reasonably incurred because the interest has not been registered.

SECTION

's 8 If a legal estate is retransferred, granted or recreated because of a failure to comply with the requirement of registration, the transferee, grantee or, as the case may be, the mortgagor –

(a) is liable to the other party for all the proper costs of and incidental to the retransfer, regrant or recreation of the legal estate, and

(b) is liable to indemnify the other party in respect of any other liability reasonably incurred by him because of the failure to comply with the requirement of registration.'

ACTIVITY

Applying the law

Thomas purchases Greenacre Cottage, which had an unregistered title, from Phillip on 1 June. He leaves for a long holiday in South America in mid-June. He did not register the title before he left. He stays away until late September because he loves the life in Argentina and cannot bear to leave.

Advise Thomas.

Under s 11(2) of the 2002 Act, once registration has taken place, the estate is vested in the proprietor.

Section 11(3) states that the estate is vested in the proprietor, together with all interests subsisting for the benefit of the estate.

3.3.5 Different classes of title

The Land Registry has a choice of seven classes of title to grant to a registered estate although in practice the absolute freehold and the absolute leasehold continue to be the most frequently used. The Registrar will not grant an absolute title unless he is completely satisfied about the title, in particular that there is no one who may come forward claiming rights in the property at a future date. If this occurred after the Registrar had granted absolute freehold or absolute leasehold title then the state would have to pay compensation to the claimant.

1. **Absolute freehold**: an absolute title guarantees that the estate registered is vested in the registered owner named in the Proprietorship Register, subject only to entries in the Register and any overriding interests that may affect it. In practice this is most likely to be the type of title registered and it is very unusual for the Registrar to register a freehold estate with any other title.

2. **Absolute leasehold**: this guarantees not only that the lease under which the land is held is vested in the owner but also that the lease itself was validly granted, so the Registrar can grant an absolute leasehold title once he is satisfied that there is good title to both the freehold and the lease itself.

3. **Qualified freehold**: in very rare cases where the Registrar thinks that either the title of the applicant has limitations in time or the title itself is not good, then a qualified title will be granted. An example might be that the title is subject to rights arising because the title has only been investigated for less than the required 15 years for good root of title, for example only 12 years. There may be practical reasons why the full 15 years were not covered but the title granted will still be less than absolute, to take account of the fact that someone with rights arising in the three years not investigated may claim rights to the property.

3.3.6 The transfer of a registered title

The transfer of the legal estate in unregistered land takes place on completion of the sale. The law immediately regards the purchaser as the new owner. He can deal in the land on the day of completion.

In **registered** land the position is slightly different. The transfer of the legal estate in the land does not take place until the name of the purchaser has been entered on the Register.

SECTION

'$s\,27(1)$ If a disposition of a registered estate or registered charge is required to be completed by registration, it does not operate at law until the relevant registration requirements are met.'

The section continues by listing all the types of disposition which require registration to take place.

SECTION

'$s\,27(2)$ In the case of a registered estate, the following are the dispositions which are required to be completed by registration –

(a) a transfer

(b) where the registered estate is an estate in land, the grant of a term of years absolute –

(i)   for a term of more than seven years from the date of the grant,

(ii) to take effect in possession after the end of the period of three months beginning with the date of the grant,

(iii) under which the right to possession is discontinuous.'

Section 27 first covers the transfer of the freehold estate. In the case of the transfer of a leasehold estate it depends whether the freehold estate is already registered. If the landlord's title is unregistered then, on the creation of a lease, registration should take place under $s\,4$ (see above). This covers first registration of title. If the title is registered then registration takes place under $s\,27$.

Other dealings with title which require registration in order to take effect include:

1. **Legal easements**: they cannot be registered with separate title but must instead be registered on the Charges Register of the land carrying the burden. They must also be entered on the Property Register of the land benefiting from the easement.

2. **Legal charges (mortgages)**: again, they cannot be registered with their own title but must be entered on the Charges Register of the land which carries the charge.

	Voluntary registration under s 3 LRA 2002	Compulsory registration under s 4 LRA 2002	Registration under s 27 LRA 2002
When the section applies	The applicant can decide to register where certain conditions apply.	Applies where a triggering event occurs.	Applies on a disposition requiring registration.
An estate in land: freehold or leasehold estate in land	Where the estate is vested in the applicant or he is **entitled** to have the estate vested in him.	The transfer of a qualifying estate either as a gift or through sale or any event triggering registration.	A disposition of a registered estate.
A rentcharge	Where an estate is vested in the applicant or he is **entitled** to have the estate vested in him.	–	The express grant or reservation of an interest under s 1(2)(b).
A franchise	Where the estate is vested in the applicant or the applicant is **entitled** to have the estate vested in him.	–	The grant of a lease of a franchise or manor which is itself a registered estate.
A *profit à prendre*	Where the estate is vested in the applicant or the applicant is **entitled** to have the estate vested in him.	–	The express grant or reservation of an interest under s 1(2)(a) LPA 1925.

Table 3.3 Registration of registrable interests under the Land Registration Act 2002

3.4 Interests in registered land

There are four types of rights that can exist over registered land:

1. **Registrable estates and interests**: these include the two legal estates in land under s 1 of the Law of Property Act 1925 and are registrable with their own title as well as other legal interests such as legal easements.

2. **Registrable charges** which will be registrable as a mortgage. The legal mortgage must be registered as a registered charge against the relevant title in order to ensure that it is a legal interest and will take priority over other interests. It is the entry of the charge on the Register that confers the legal nature on the interest.

3. **Registered incumbrances**: this is a residual category of interests which were referred to as minor interests under the 1925 legislation and do not fall into either of the two other categories. They include any interest which affects the registered title which cannot take effect as an overriding interest. The 2002 Act refers to them as 'burdens on the register'. However, they continue to be referred to as 'minor interests'.

4. **Overriding interests**: these are interests which 'override a disposition' or interests which override a registered disposition but which are not protected by an entry on the Register but which still bind the land. They have been retained by the

Land Registration Act 2002 in Scheds 1 and 3 in spite of the many problems they present. They are not protected by an entry on the Register, so the only way that a purchaser can discover their existence is by making enquiries and visiting the property.

3.4.1 Methods of protection for registered burdens on registered land

Under the 2002 Act there are now only two methods of protection for registered incumbrances or burdens on registered land:

1. the notice; and
2. the restriction.

Two of the previous four methods of protection – the caution and the inhibition – have been abolished. They may be referred to in earlier case law and remain on the Register during the transition to the new system and will therefore be briefly mentioned here. Cautions are now used in a different context as cautions against first registration of title.

3.4.2 Old methods of protecting burdens on registered land

1. The **notice**: this was entered in the Charges Register and was dependent on production of the relevant land certificate and so relied on the co-operation of the landowner and was not generally hostile when used to register interests.
2. The **caution**: by contrast, this was a hostile entry and did not require the production of the land certificate. It would restrict the way the proprietor dealt with the land. A caution is still used before first registration of title to protect certain persons interested in the land. They will be informed of any application for first registration of title under s 16 LRA 2002.
3. The **restriction**: this was an entry entered on the Proprietorship Register which limited the proprietor's power to dispose of the property.
4. The **inhibition**: an inhibition would be entered on the Proprietorship Register and prevented any registered dealing in the land.

3.4.3 New methods of protecting burdens on registered land

There are now only **two** ways of protecting a minor interest under the 2002 Act: notices and restrictions:

Notices

These are described as an entry in the Register in respect of the burden of an interest affecting a registered estate or charge under s 32 Land Registration Act 2002. These replace old notices and cautions under the Land Registration Act 1925. Once a notice is entered in the Charges Register a purchaser will be bound by the interest. Most interests can be protected by notice but there is no exhaustive list of rights that can be protected in this way. It is the reverse that is true and some interests are expressly excluded by the 2002 Act:

's 33 **Excluded interests**

No notice may be entered in the register in respect of any of the following:

(i) a trust of land; or

(ii) a settlement under the Settled Land Act 1925;

(iii) a lease granted for a term of years of three years or less from the date of the grant, and which is not required to be registered;

(iv) a restrictive covenant made between lessor and lessee, so far as related to the property leased;

(v) an interest which is capable of being registered under the Commons Registration Act 1965; and

(vi) an interest in coal or any coal mine and any rights attaching under the Coal Industry Act 1994.'

Interests under a trust cannot be entered as a notice on the Register; they are protected by the use of a restriction. This is a much more effective entry on the Register, since it means that anyone entering a restriction will be notified of any dealings in the land by the Registrar. Rights that cannot be protected by notice also include leases of less than three years, leaving leases of between three and seven years capable of being entered on the Register by way of notice. Leases over seven years are registrable interests and are entered on the Register with their own title. A major criticism of the 2002 Act is that leases are now left with three different sets of rules which vary according to the length of the lease. Some would argue that all short leases should be capable of entry on the Register rather than leaving them as rights that override the Register with all the potential problems that such rights may incur.

A notice can be either:

a. agreed; or

b. unilateral.

a. An **agreed notice**: this must fall within one of three circumstances under s 34 LRA 2002:

1. the applicant must be either the registered proprietor or the person entitled to be registered as proprietor of the estate or charge that is burdened by the interest to be noted; or

2. consent is given by the registered proprietor of the estate or charge who consents to the entry of the notice; or

3. the Registrar is satisfied as to the validity of the applicant's claim.

In the first two situations the parties are agreed about the entry of the notice. In the last situation the entry of the notice will be with the Registrar's consent. Certain types of rights must be protected by an agreed notice and cannot be subject to a unilateral notice. This group is rather varied and includes the matrimonial home right under the Family Law Act 1996 and also the entry of a notice under the Access to Neighbouring Land Act 1992.

The applicant must provide evidence to the Registrar that the notice should be entered. An example would be to give the Registrar a copy of the written agreement that created the right. The entry of the notice is not proof of the validity of the claim. There is however an advantage for a claimant of entering such a notice on the Register and that is the priority that the entry may give later. Without such an entry the right may lose priority.

The agreed notice is not usually challenged since its entry is usually with the agreement of the proprietor. There is a fallback procedure for exceptional cases allowing cancellation.

b. A **unilateral notice** can be entered **without** the consent of the proprietor of the legal estate. It is used where there is hostility between the parties. If the Registrar enters a unilateral notice in the Register, the proprietor of the registered legal title or charge to which the entry relates must be notified of the entry. When the notice is entered on the Register, two key features must be shown; it must identify itself as a unilateral notice and it must also indicate who is the beneficiary of the notice. The unilateral notice is similar to the old caution but is more effective as protecting the rights of the person making the entry. It is more effective because it actually protects the interest lodged on the Register. It differs from the old caution because the caution only allowed the cautioner the right to be informed of any dealings in the title. Today, it provides priority for the right it protects. Once the unilateral notice is entered, the proprietor has the right to be informed and under s 36 LRA 2002 can apply to the Registrar to have the notice cancelled; this is called 'warning-off'. If a dispute arises then this must be referred to the adjudicator for settlement and if the proprietor applies for cancellation and the beneficiary of the notice does not object, then the notice will be cancelled. If the proprietor can prove that the right protected does not exist, then removal will be ordered. Under s 35 LRA 2002 the beneficiary of the notice can apply for removal of the notice and this is a straightforward process.

Restrictions

These replace inhibitions and old restrictions. They are defined under s 40 of the 2002 Act as 'an entry in the register regulating the circumstances in which a disposition of a registered estate or charge may be the subject of an entry in the register'. They will restrict any dealing with the registered estate or charge.

The most common situation for their use is when the land sold is held under a trust. If there is a restriction on the Register then the purchaser will insist on compliance with the restriction. The terms of the restriction will be that the purchase money is paid to two trustees, so overreaching the equitable interest arising under the trust. Another significant use of a restriction is in bankruptcy where it may be used to prevent dealings in the land intended to defeat the interests of the creditors.

ACTIVITY

Applying the law

Peter has split up with his girlfriend, Josie. He decides to sell his house in London so that he can work in the country. Josie made financial contributions to the purchase of the London property but was never registered as co-owner of the property. However, on advice from a friend who was a lawyer, she registered a restriction to protect her interest in the property. Max visits the house and decides he wants to buy it immediately.

Advise Shelagh who is a solicitor acting on his behalf.

Another situation when the use of a restriction is appropriate is where land is managed by a management company and there is a restriction in the Register which indicates that no registration of a transfer may be made without the consent of an officer of the management company.

Restrictions can be registered without the consent of the registered proprietor, for example where a right is claimed under an implied trust but the registered proprietor denies the existence of the right.

3.4.4 Removal of old forms of entry on the Register

Inhibitions and cautions have been abolished by the 2002 Act but existing inhibitions and cautions remained on the Register during the transitional arrangements. Cautions can still be entered against first registration and these are held in a new Cautions Register. The effect of such a caution will be that the cautioner will be notified of any application to register the property.

The Cautions Register

Cautions are recorded in the new Cautions Register. Any person having an interest in unregistered land can lodge a caution against first registration. This is to ensure that the registration will take account of any existing rights in the land.

There are special rules which prevent registration of a caution against one's own estate where it is registrable. This is to prevent someone from using the system of cautions as a substitute for first registration. It is also intended to persuade people who own unregistered title to register their land voluntarily. This is not the first time that the legislation has tried to encourage voluntary registration of title but the incentives are greater under the 2002 Act.

Effect of a caution against first registration

Under s 16(1) of the Land Registration Act 1925:

SECTION

> 's 16(1) Where an application for registration under this part relates to a legal estate which is the subject of a caution against first registration, the registrar must give the cautioner notice of the application and of his right to object to it.'

The registration of this type of caution does not give priority but merely gives the cautioner the right to be notified of a later transaction.

Cancellations

Certain persons can apply to the Registrar to cancel a caution against first registration.

Who can apply for cancellation of a caution against first registration?

1. the owner of the legal estate to which the caution applies;
2. a mortgagee of the land;
3. a receiver appointed to deal with the estate of the legal estate owner.

On receipt of the application for cancellation the Registrar must then notify the cautioner and notify him that he will cancel the caution unless the cautioner objects within a specified time.

The matter must be referred to the adjudicator unless agreement can be reached or it is shown that the objection is groundless.

Where the estate owner has consented to the lodging of the caution, it is unlikely that he will then be allowed to object to it. There is a duty to act reasonably when entering a caution, so damages can be awarded for any loss caused by an entry which is groundless.

3.4.5 The effect of registration of a burden on registered land

If the burden or incumbrance is not registered then a purchaser will take free of the third-party interest and the question of notice is quite irrelevant.

Where a disposition is made without valuable consideration then an unprotected burden will remain binding on the transferee.

SECTION
....

's29(1) If a registrable disposition of a registered estate is made for valuable consideration, completion of the disposition by registration has the effect of postponing to the interest under the disposition any interest affecting the estate immediately before the disposition whose priority is not protected at the time of registration.'

ACTIVITY
....

Applying the law

Annie and Stuart have seen a beautiful house in Somerset which they decide to buy. They visit the house and a neighbour tells them that there is a covenant attached to the land that prevents them from using the property for the purposes of running a business. Annie wants to start an organic jam and chutney business which she intends to run from home. The Charges Register does not show a covenant relating to use of the premises.

They note that on the Charges Register there is a second mortgage for £20,000. Nothing has been discussed about this loan.

Advise Annie and Stuart about the possibility of starting the business and whether they will be bound by the mortgage.

3.5 Unregistered interests which override a registered disposition under Sched 3 of the Land Registration Act 2002 (overriding interests)

JUDGMENT
....

'It is vital to the working of the Land Registration system that notice of something which is not on the register should not affect a transferee unless it is an overriding interest.'

Strand Securities v Caswell [1965] Ch 958

3.5.1 Introduction

The system of registration of title is supposed to ensure that the purchaser is able to see the exact state of the title of the land he is buying. This is the true meaning of the 'mirror' principle. An accurate register of title will show the purchaser what rights and encumbrances attach to the land. However, there remain some rights which are not discoverable by searching the Register. These were called **overriding interests** under the 1925 Land Registration Act. They are called 'overriding' because in law they override the sale and remain binding on the purchaser irrespective of the fact that they are not discoverable by searching the Land Register. Under the LRA 2002 overriding interests are renamed 'unregistered interests which override a first disposition' and unregistered interests which override registered dispositions. Although these rights have been renamed they continue to be referred to as overriding interests. These rights are potentially very dangerous for purchasers because unwittingly they may find that the land is bound by some right which affects their enjoyment to such an extent that they would never have contemplated purchasing the land if they had known about it. So, overriding interests are interests which are binding on the registered proprietor despite not being on the Register. The categories of right were listed in s70 of the Land Registration Act 1925. In 1925 there were many different classes of right, covering many different aspects of land ownership.

These have caused considerable problems in the system of registration of land. Since the Register does not reflect the existence of overriding interests, the only way that the purchaser can find out about their existence is by visiting the property. The purchaser must inspect the property and of course this can create problems if he does not discover the overriding interest when he visits, as in most cases he will still be bound by it.

Under s70(1) of the Land Registration Act 1925 the list of overriding interests was extremely long. The list included easements both legal and equitable, and rights of squatters under the Limitation Acts, but the most significant group of all were rights of a person in actual occupation of property, under s70(1)(g). There was considerable litigation covering this subsection alone. The rights under s70(1)(g) have been retained as overriding rights under the Land Registration Act 2002. When the Law Commission reviewed land registration, this area was discussed in detail and many argued that all overriding interests should be abolished, making the Register a more reliable reflection of the true nature of the land but it was felt that certain rights should continue to be protected in this way.

3.5.2 Reform of overriding interests under the Land Registration Act 2002

The Law Commission wanted to reform this aspect of land registration but had to accept that there were reasons why overriding interests could not be abolished altogether.

> 'The way in which the law on overriding interests has developed over the last seventy-two years has demonstrated that overriding interests are by no means only "minor liabilities".... Most overriding interests do appear to have one shared characteristic, however, that is related to the orthodox explanation of them, namely that it is unreasonable to expect the person who has the benefit of the right to register it as a means of securing its protection.'
>
> Law Commission, 'Land Registration for the Twenty-First Century: A Conveyancing Revolution' (Law Com No 271, 2001)

Some of the reasons why overriding interests should be retained are as follows:

1. Overriding interests provide a means of accommodating rights which can be created informally and where it is unrealistic to expect registration at the time of creation, for example rights of persons in actual occupation.

2. Some rights are either pointless or inconvenient to register. The Law Commission specifically mentioned short leases.

3. There are some rights which are otherwise protected and it would therefore be unrealistic to expect them to be registered. An example of such rights would be local land charges which are registered at the Local Land Charges Register.

'Thus the rationale that underpins the informal acquisition of interests in land would be defeated by a prescriptive method of ensuring their priority against a purchaser. Accordingly, the 2002 Act retains the idea that certain interests should be given priority over the estate of a subsequent registered proprietor even though that interest has not been entered on the land register. However the principal means by which the 2002 Act aims to improve the accuracy of the register is to narrow the scope for unregistered interests to have overriding effect.'

N Jackson, 'Title by Registration and Concealed Overriding Interests:
The Cause and Effect of Antipathy to Documentary Proof'
(2003) 119 *LQR* 660

The retention of overriding rights also attracted criticism because of the effect they have on the mirror principle. They seem to be unfair on the purchaser. Even if a purchaser makes an attempt to discover whether there are overriding interests but continues to be unaware of their existence, he will still be bound by them and there is no provision for compensation to be paid.

The Law Commission concluded that it was neither desirable nor feasible to abolish such rights totally but the Land Registration Act 2002 includes a number of different provisions which together minimise their effect.

1. The number of rights have been **reduced in number**; for example, the rights acquired by squatters under adverse possession no longer bind as an overriding right at all.

2. A number of overriding interests which existed under the Land Registration Act 1925 were **phased out after ten years** from the entry into force of the Land Registration Act 2002; for example, the ancient right of franchises, manorial rights, Crown rents and rights concerning embankments and sea walls and payments in lieu of title (also called 'corn rents').

3. Some rights have retained their status as overriding interests but their **scope has been narrowed down and clarified**; for example, easements and profits under s 70(1)(a) of the 1925 Act and also rights of persons in actual occupation under s 70(1)(g) of the 1925 Act.

4. A requirement that when an overriding interest is discovered it will be entered on the Register; any person applying for registration now has **a duty to disclose any overriding interests** known to him.

Figure 3.4 Provisions of the Land Registration Act 2002

3.5.3 Overriding interests under the Land Registration Act 2002

The 2002 Act distinguishes between those overriding rights which come within **Sched 1** (interests which override a first disposition) and **Sched 3** (interests which override registered dispositions). The law gives greater recognition to those rights coming within Sched 1 as opposed to those rights coming within Sched 3. This is logical since it would be unfair for the owner of such a right to be prejudiced simply because the title to the land was unregistered and is now being placed on the Register.

The 2002 Act allowed 15 overriding interests to continue but five were removed from the Register in October 2013: a franchise, a manorial right, a right to rent which was reserved to the Crown on the granting of any freehold estate (whether or not the right is still vested in the Crown), a non-statutory right in respect of an embankment or sea or river wall, a right to the payment in lieu of a tithe and a right in respect of the repair of a church chancel. The five interests that have been removed can still be registered as minor interests but unless they are entered on the Register they will not bind a purchaser. The registration of such rights in advance of the deadline by a number of landowners, in particular manorial rights, in October 2013 prompted considerable opposition from the landowners over whose property the registration was made. In January 2014 the Justice Committee recommended that the Law Commission should review this area of law. This will be undertaken as part of a wider project to review the protection of third-party interests.

Overriding interests abolished by the 2002 Act

One of the intentions of the 2002 Act was to **reduce overriding interests**. The following categories of right have been abolished:

1. Rights acquired or in the course of being acquired under the **Limitation Act 1980**. These were overriding under s 70(1)(f) of the Land Registration Act 1925. They are conventionally referred to as 'squatters' rights'. (These rights will be considered in detail in Chapter 14.)

2. Rights of **persons in receipt of rent and profits** under s 70(1)(g) save where enquiry is made of such persons and the rights are not disclosed. This allowed someone who was a landlord but not in occupation to claim an overriding right. It was particularly difficult for a purchaser to discover such a right.

Rights taking effect under Sched 1

When any person becomes the first registered proprietor of a freehold estate in land on first registration, they take the legal estate subject to certain interests.

Schedule 1 includes the following:

- **para 1**: leasehold estates not exceeding seven years;
- **para 2**: interests of persons in actual occupation;
- **para 3**: easements and *profits à prendre*;
- **para 4**: customary rights;
- **para 5**: public rights;
- **para 6**: local land charges.

Other rights included in the Schedule include a right to coal and coal mines and also the right to certain minerals.

Interests of persons under a settlement under the Settled Land Act 1925 are excluded. The 2002 Act has been more generous in relation to overriding interests under Sched 1 on first registration. The reason for this is that it would be wrong for a landowner bound by a right under registered land simply to avoid the right by applying for registration. The rules are not intended to assist a landowner to avoid a right simply by registering the title.

There are some slight differences between the provisions of Sched 1 and Sched 3.

Rights taking effect under Sched 3

The rights under Sched 3 are very similar but there are some limits in this Schedule on which rights can be overriding:

Schedule 3 includes the following:

- **para 1**: short leases not exceeding seven years;
- **para 2**: interests of persons in actual occupation;
- **para 3**: easements and *profits à prendre*;
- **para 4**: customary rights;
- **para 5**: public rights;
- **para 6**: local land charges.

So the list of rights in Sched 1 is almost the same as the list in Sched 3.

ACTIVITY

Quick quiz

Consider the following rights and decide whether they will take effect as overriding rights or not:

- A lease of eight years granted to Ian.
- The right to take fish from the stream belonging to your neighbour Jack.
- A covenant against your neighbour Keith's land preventing him from using the land as a business which you have forgotten to register against his title.
- Sue has contributed to the purchase of a flat with her partner, registered in his name but since the breakdown of the relationship she now lives in Ireland. She failed to register her right as a restriction on the Register.

There are some important observations to be made about the rights coming under the Schedules:

3.5.4 Overriding rights under para 1: short leases

Legal leases were overriding rights under the LRA 1925 and continue to be so under the 2002 Act although the length of the lease has been reduced from 21 years to seven years. Leases of 21 years or under which were in existence in 2002 continue to be overriding under the old rules and do not require registration.

1. Short leases, i.e. under seven years, are overriding. They will bind any purchaser and it is irrelevant whether the tenant is in occupation or not. Note it is likely that a tenant of a short lease will be in occupation so the purchaser will usually be protected.

2. The exception to this rule is **future leases**, of whatever length, as they will not be overriding. These are leases which take effect more than three months after the date of grant. These are registrable and must be entered on the register in order to bind a purchaser. The grant of a lease under 'the right to buy' provisions both under the Housing Act and in the private sector must also be registered and not protected as overriding rights.

3. Leases are not dependent on actual occupation to qualify as overriding interests but a lease which is to take effect over three months in advance could not be discovered by a purchaser and it seems fairer that such a lease is only binding if placed on the Register.

4. Only legal leases are mentioned in the Act. An equitable lease will not be overriding but the lessee may be protected as a person having an interest in land and in actual occupation of the land.

3.5.5 Overriding rights under para 2: actual occupation

It is this category of right that has caused the most litigation and was subject to the most discussion both in Parliament and amongst interested parties before the passage of the 2002 Act. The right is not limited to rights under a trust of land but has extended to rights such as where the claimant is seeking to alter the Register or the right to have a transaction set aside for undue influence. The most problematic aspect of this right is what constitutes 'actual occupation'.

1. Some interests which appear to qualify under this paragraph are expressly excluded.

2. One of the main exceptions is where the purchaser has tried to discover whether someone in actual occupation has rights but the holder of the right has not disclosed it when he could reasonably have been expected to do so.

3. Any interest which the purchaser could not have discovered when visiting the property and of which the purchaser does not have actual knowledge. The law therefore restricts overriding rights to those that a purchaser must have been able to see if he had visited the property. It would be unfair if such rights were binding where they were not visible.

4. There is a similarity with s 70(1)(g) of the 1925 Act, as that section holds that the right will be overriding except when inquiry has been made and the person has not disclosed the right when they could reasonably have been expected to do so.

5. However, it is new to exclude rights that are not apparent and not actually known and will have the effect of restricting rights that can be binding. This increases the need to inspect the property and the purchaser who takes adequate steps to visit the property and inspect it will be protected.

6. The nature of the physical presence necessary may vary according to the type of property. It may be fairly limited if the property itself is derelict. In *Malory v Cheshire Homes (UK)* [2002] Ch 216 the claimant established actual occupation through minimal use because the land was derelict and putting a fence around the land was seen as sufficient proof of actual occupation.

3.5.6 Overriding rights under para 3: easements

1. All legal easements and profits created before the Land Registration Act 2002 came into force took effect as overriding interests. It did not matter how they had been created.

2. Legal easements created before the Act came into force continue to have overriding status.

3. All easements that have been expressly created since the Act came into force must be registered in order to take effect. This means that these easements can no longer be automatically binding as overriding interests. It is their entry on the Register that confers on them their legal status. If they are not registered then they will not bind the purchaser.

4. Some implied easements will continue to be binding as overriding interests if they are created under s 62 Law of Property Act 1925 or under the rule in *Wheeldon v Burrows* (1879).

5. There are quite significant differences between the treatment of easements and *profits à prendre* under Sched 1 and Sched 3.

6. Under Sched 1 an existing legal easement will override on first registration. This clearly excludes equitable easements. Both implied and express easements appear to be covered under this Schedule. However, Sched 3 restricts the number of legal easements. Under s 27(2) of the 2002 Act, the disposition of a legal interest including an easement requires completion by registration. It seems that the only easements which can be overriding under Sched 3 are those that arise under prescription or implied grant.

3.5.7 Interests of persons in actual occupation

Although in the 1925 Act the interests of persons in actual occupation were regarded as unimportant and indeed were only assigned to a subsection of a subsection, these rights have always been the subject of considerable litigation. After lengthy discussion by the Law Commission, they were retained within the Land Registration Act 2002 but have been reduced in significance. The interest is still based on two criteria which were introduced in the 1925 Land Registration Act.

Section 70(1)(g) required proof of two elements:

1. an interest in the land;
2. actual occupation of the land.

1. *An interest in the land*

The right is based on proof of a proprietary right in land. A claim cannot be based on a purely personal right such as a licence to remain on the land or a right based on status such as the matrimonial home right claimed by a spouse under the Family Law Act 1996 (initially granted under the Matrimonial Homes Act 1967). Under the Land Registration Act 2002 for an interest to take effect as a burden that overrides the register it still requires both an interest in land and also actual occupation.

Note the following cases which were both decided under the LRA 1925 but the issues in both cases apply under the LRA 2002.

CASE EXAMPLE

Williams & Glyn's Bank v Boland [1981] AC 487

A husband and wife purchased property together. The property had registered title and although they both made contributions it was registered in the husband's sole name. The husband held the legal estate on trust for himself and his wife in equal shares. The husband then mortgaged the property to Williams & Glyn's Bank by way of legal mortgage. He could do this on his own without consulting the wife because she did not have an interest in the legal estate. He defaulted on the repayments and Williams & Glyn's Bank sought possession of the property. The issue was whether the bank was subject to Mrs Boland's interest. She had the right to register the equitable interest as a minor interest but she had failed to do so. She was in occupation of the property and was found to have an overriding interest under s 70(1)(g) of the 1925 Act. Her husband was the sole trustee so her rights were not transferred to the capital under the doctrine of 'overreaching' but were rights in the land and were good even against a legal mortgagee.

One aspect of the decision that caused unease was the fact that her rights were capable of registration but it was held that she also had an overriding interest. She was therefore protected in two ways. She could register but if she failed to do so she could also claim an overriding interest. Usually the system would give only one type of protection.

Compare this case where the right claimed was not a proprietary right but was based on a purely personal right to be on the property.

CASE EXAMPLE

National Provincial Bank Ltd v Ainsworth [1965] AC 1175

The right claimed was the right of the wife to occupy property because she was a wife. This claim was based on status and not on contributions as in the case of *Williams & Glyns Bank v Boland* (1981). Lord Denning argued strongly that the wife should be protected in this case. He argued that she had 'a deserted wife's equity', but his argument was rejected. The House of Lords held that her right was purely personal and could not constitute an overriding interest. However, Lord Denning was later vindicated when legislation was passed giving a wife the right to register her rights based on her status under the Matrimonial Homes Act 1967; this is now incorporated into the Family Law Act 1996.

2. *Actual occupation of the land*

The concept of what constitutes 'actual occupation' has troubled the courts over the years. At one extreme, it is obvious that it includes someone living in property as their sole residence. Mrs Boland is an example of someone clearly in actual occupation. At the other extreme, there are cases where someone may live away from home and so will not be in actual occupation for all of the time or a person may claim to be in actual occupation of derelict land where occupation will not be continuous.

It has been held that 'actual occupation' should be determined according to the ordinary meaning of the term. There was no definition in the 1925 Act and it has not been expressly defined in the 2002 Act. This is not surprising, since it can vary on the facts.

Actual occupation or acts preparatory to occupation: when does actual occupation begin?

Actual occupation should be distinguished from acts preparatory to occupation. In *Abbey National v Cann* [1991] 1 AC 56, a purchaser could not be said to be in actual occupation where only a few items of furniture were in the property prior to occupation. The court drew a distinction here between preparatory acts and acts consistent with occupation. It accepted that often this will be a matter of degree.

CASE EXAMPLE

Abbey National Building Society v Cann [1991] 1 AC 56

A mother acquired rights in property owned by her son, through her rights under the 'right to buy' legislation. She was on holiday on the day that her son moved into the property. However, her belongings were moved in by removal men and some of her furniture was moved into the premises 35 minutes before completion. The courts decided that this was insufficient for her to claim that she was in actual occupation at the time of completion thereby giving her priority over the mortgagees.

Minor children

Minor children cannot be in actual occupation in their own right. Their rights are dependent on their parents' rights in the property. This raises some interesting issues about the nature of the rights of the claimant. It is possible for one person to be in actual occupation of another, for example a builder on behalf of the client.

CASE EXAMPLE

Hypo-Mortgage Service v Robinson [1997] 2 FLR 71

It was held that infant children could not be in actual occupation of property. 'The minor children are there because their parent is there. They have no right of occupation of their own. As Templeman J put it in *Bird v Syme-Thomson* [1979] 1 WLR 440 "... they are there as shadows of occupation of their parent"' (Nourse LJ). It makes no difference that they are often in the property on their own.

Occupation by a third party

CASE EXAMPLE

Lloyds Bank v Rosset [1989] Ch 350

A husband and wife, recently married, decided to purchase a semi-derelict property. The property was registered in the sole name of the husband. They could not move in until a certain amount of renovation work had been done and much of it was supervised by the wife. The work was still in progress after the transfer but the issue was whether the wife could be in actual occupation when she was not in permanent occupation. She had spent a considerable amount of time at the property but could not be said to be in permanent occupation. The builders were working at the premises permanently. Although the wife was not successful in her claim in this case because the court held that she did not have an interest in the property the court accepted that it was possible for a builder to be in actual occupation of property on behalf of his client. This has been supported by the later case of *Thomas v Clydesdale Bank* (2010).

CASE EXAMPLE

Thomas v Clydesdale Bank plc [2010] EWHC 2755

T had contributed to the purchase of a house in the name of her partner X. Builders and interior designers were employed to carry out work before the couple and their children moved into the property. A representative of the respondent bank had visited the property and saw the builders at work. The question before the court was whether the presence of the builders constituted 'actual occupation' under the requirements of the Act. The court held that this was 'occupation' under the Act and it would have been obvious on a reasonably careful inspection of the property. As a result the bank had the requisite knowledge of T's interest and was bound by her interest.

The nature of overriding interests was explored fully in the complex case of *Scott v Southern Pacific Mortgages Ltd* [2014] UKSC 52. Mrs Scott was in financial difficulties. She had taken out a mortgage over her home which she jointly owned with her husband who had left her. She was introduced to North East Property Buyers who agreed to pay off her mortgage and give her a sum in cash and allow her to remain in her home on condition that they took over the property. The purchaser took out a mortgage herself with Southern Pacific Mortgages Ltd but the mortgagees were unaware of Mrs Scott's presence. Mrs Scott remained in the property for several years after the sale and then she received notice of a possession action brought by Southern Pacific. She argued that her right in the house was an overriding interest and any purchase was subject to her interest. This depended on proof that she had an overriding interest but the Supreme Court held that her rights could not be overriding. The purchaser had relied on a mortgage in order to fund the sale and therefore her rights could not have priority to the mortgage as argued in the case of *Abbey National v Cann* (1991): this case concerned both the timing of rights as well as the priority of rights. The court found that Mrs Scott did not have an interest that was binding on the lenders but there has been academic discussion following the case as to how the court would deal with the case if the priorities were seen to be equal as was a possibility in this case.

Could the rights have been discovered on a reasonable inspection of the property?

Some of the unregistered land cases may be relevant in assessing this aspect of actual occupation, in particular the case of *Kingsnorth Finance Co Ltd v Tizard* (1986). The wording of Sched 3 suggests that a purchaser will not be bound if the rights could not have been discovered on reasonable inspection of the property.

CASE EXAMPLE

Kingsnorth Finance Co Ltd v Tizard [1986] 1 WLR 783

This case concerned a house with unregistered title. A married couple split up. They had lived in a house owned by the husband but the wife had an equitable interest having made contributions towards the purchase. Mrs Tizard continued to return to the property to care for the children and to carry out household chores. She also stayed in the property when her husband was away. Mr Tizard took out a mortgage over the property and he did not disclose that his wife had rights in the property. Someone on behalf of the mortgagees visited the property but failed to make proper inquiries although it was obvious that the owner had children. It was held that the mortgagees took subject to her rights.

Temporary absences from the property

A temporary absence from the property will not defeat actual occupation. The key issue is not whether the claimant was actually present at the time of inspection but whether he had a continuing intention to occupy the property. This means that holidays away from the property even for extended periods would not defeat a claim, nor would a business trip abroad or a stay in hospital.

CASE EXAMPLE

Chhokar v Chhokar [1984] FLR 313

A married couple split up. The wife, who had an interest in the property, remained in the house but had to leave temporarily when she went into hospital to have a baby. It was held that the stay in hospital did not constitute a break in actual occupation. The case suggests that brief absences will not interfere with actual occupation of land.

Recently the court has addressed the question of whether a claimant can be in 'actual occupation' where he or she is detained in hospital long-term under the Mental Health Act. The key issue was held to be whether the claimant had a continuing intention to return to the property.

CASE EXAMPLE

Link Lending v Bustard [2010] EWCA Civ 424.

Mrs Bustard owned property but spent long periods of time in hospital as she suffered from mental illness. She returned to her house occasionally for brief visits and also had all post delivered to her house. She had all her belongings and furniture in the house. In November 2004 she transferred the title of her property to Mrs Hussain. It was likely that this was done under undue influence and was therefore open to challenge. Whilst Mrs Bustard spent a year in hospital as a result of mental illness, Mrs Hussain took out a loan with Link Lending and when Mrs Hussain fell behind with the payments the mortgagees sought possession. The key issue was that Mrs Bustard always intended to return to the home to live after she had made a full recovery. The court held that she was still in 'actual occupation' within the terms of the Act.

Actual occupation where the property is not used as residential property

Where property is not used as residential property the rules concerning actual occupation may vary according to the use. If permanent residence is not feasible then some other evidence of physical presence will be proof of actual occupation.

CASE EXAMPLE

Malory Enterprises v Cheshire Homes (UK) [2002] Ch 216

Malory was the registered proprietor of land. A third party had forged a transfer to Cheshire Homes. As Malory had remained in actual occupation by virtue of storage of goods, the changing of locks on the land and fencing of the property, the Court of Appeal held that he was in actual occupation of the land and therefore had an overriding interest which was binding on Cheshire Homes.

'What constitutes actual occupation of property depends on the nature and state of the property in question, and the judge adopted that approach. If a site is uninhabitable, as the rear land was, residence is not required, but there must be some physical presence, with some degree of permanence and continuity.... Moreover no-one visiting the rear land at the time of the sale to Cheshire could have drawn the conclusion that the land and buildings on the rear land had been abandoned; the evidence of activity on the site clearly indicated that someone claimed to be entitled to it.'

Arden LJ

Actual occupation is not simply use. It must amount to occupation of the property. Certain uses of property could not be deemed to be occupation.

In *Chaudhary v Yavuz* [2011] EWCA 1314 a claimant argued that he was in actual occupation of a staircase. It was held that the claimant was claiming the exercise of an easement which would not amount to actual occupation of the servient land so it fell short of what was required in order to prove actual occupation.

The date on which actual occupation must be established

After *Abbey National v Cann* the courts held that actual occupation must be established on the date at which the transaction was completed. Schedule 3 para 2 LRA 2002 passed after *Cann* lays down that the relevant time of the actual occupation is the 'time of the disposition'. The LRA 2002 determines the time of disposition as the date of registration. The court had to consider this in *Thompson v Foy* [2009] EWHC 1076 and Lewison J held that the time of execution was the time of disposition but it is not clear whether the actual occupation was necessary at the time of transfer also. The Act was passed when it was anticipated that electronic conveyancing would be adopted within a short period and so a 'registration gap' between transfer and registration would no longer apply. Until electronic conveyancing is fully adopted, the timing when the actual occupation has to be established may still be uncertain.

> 'However while much attention is rightly given to the considerable impact it will have on those every day principles of land registration that currently regulate over £2000 billion worth of property. As has been said already, most of these substantive changes are designed to facilitate the new conveyancing processes and to ensure that we move from registration of title to a system where it "will be the fact of registration and registration alone that confers title".'
>
> M Dixon, 'The Reform of Property Law and the Land Registration Act 2002: A Risk Assessment' [2003] 67 *Conv* 136

Occupation of the property preparatory to moving in cannot be held to be actual occupation.	*Abbey National v Cann* (1991)
Children cannot be said to be in actual occupation on their own behalf in property owned by their parents.	*Hypo-Mortgage Service v Robinson* (1997)
Occupation by builders working on property can constitute actual occupation.	*Lloyds Bank v Rosset* (1989) *Thomas v Clydesdale Bank* (2010)
Occupational rights in unregistered land are subject to the doctrine of notice.	*Kingsnorth Finance v Tizard* (1986)
A short visit away from the property, e.g. a visit to hospital, will not prevent actual occupation from continuing.	*Chhokar v Chhokar* (1984) *Link Lending v Bustard* (2010)
Actual occupation will vary according to the type of property, e.g. there will be actual occupation where the owner uses the property for storage, keeps it locked and ensures it is securely fenced.	*Malory Enterprises v Cheshire Homes* (2002)

Table 3.4 What constitutes actual occupation?

ACTIVITY

Consider the following examples and decide whether these give rise to an overriding interest for the claimants.

1. Alice has bought a new flat. She is allowed into the flat one day before completion, to put up some curtains. She decides to sleep there overnight.
2. Tom and Henry are twin boys aged 17. Both their parents travel in their work so the boys often live in their family home on their own.
3. Annie and Ian buy a dilapidated barn. They fall in love with it but it is not habitable and they cannot live there, however Annie visits daily, to oversee the builders who work every day and sometimes at weekends.

4. Carmel, who is pregnant, has recently split up with her husband, Gerry. While she is in hospital having the baby, Gerry comes into the property and changes all the locks and sells the property to a friend.
5. Mr Singh owns a large area of land which could be used for development. He used the land for storage of his goods and he boarded it up, changing the locks. The title was fraudulently transferred to Mr Tan by a third party and Mr Tan subsequently registered the title in his name.

3.5.8 The duty to disclose rights under the Land Registration Act 2002

Under s 71 LRA 2002 any applicant for registration has a duty to disclose any overriding right of which he/she is aware. The right will however be preserved if the applicant fails to do so. This section has its exceptions and preserves the overriding status of certain rights such as a lease which could have been entered on the Register because it is in excess of three years but has less than a year to run.

ACTIVITY

Applying the law

Consider the facts of this problem:

Leah purchased freehold title to a property with registered title called Runaway House. Sometime later, Tom married Leah and he moved into the house. Tom was often away and she had to deal in the affairs of the house on her own. Her neighbour, Joan, asked to enter into a restrictive covenant, with her, not to use the house for any business purposes. She paid Leah for this. Leah granted David a legal lease for six years, over a cottage attached to the house. Leah also granted Isaac the right to park his car in the driveway of Runaway House. This was put into writing but not registered. Leah now thinks she would like to sell the property but is concerned as to the status of the rights that she has granted over the property.

Advise Leah what these rights are and whether they are binding on the property.

3.6 Alteration and indemnity

Under the Land Registration Act 1925 there was provision for rectification of the Register in cases where there was an error on the face of the Register. There was also a scheme of statutory indemnity for any purchaser who suffered loss by reason of the conclusive nature of the Register. There is still provision for changes to the Register in the 2002 Act under Sched 4 but referred to as an 'alteration' which includes two categories of changes: those that prejudicially affect the title of proprietor and those that do not. Rectification continues, but as just one way of altering the Register. There continues to be provision for the payment of an indemnity where the Register is rectified because a mistake has occurred and a person suffers loss.

The change in terminology was made as a result of recommendations of the Law Commission. It thought it was misleading to describe all changes as rectification and that it would be better if they were described as alterations, saving the term 'rectification' for those entries which required to be actually rectified. It gave examples of minor changes which are often made, such as the removal of obsolete entries which differ vastly from errors on the Register. 'Alteration' is the term used to describe any abnormal change in the Register which did not proceed from an application.

3.6 ALTERATION AND INDEMNITY

Alteration can now be made under s 65 of the 2002 Act but the details are contained in Sched 4.

3.6.1 Alteration of the Register under the Land Registration Act 2002

SECTION

'Schedule 4
1. In this Schedule, references to rectification, in relation to alteration of the register, are to alteration which –

   (a) involves the correction of a mistake, and
   (b) prejudicially affects the title of a registered proprietor.

2. (1) The court may make an order for alteration of the register for the purpose of –

   (a) correcting a mistake,
   (b) bringing the register up to date, or
   (c) giving effect to any estate, right or interest excepted from the effect of registration.

3. (2) If alteration affects the title of the proprietor of a registered estate in land, no order may be made under paragraph 2 without the proprietor's consent in relation to land in his possession unless –

   (a) he has by fraud or lack of proper care caused or substantially contributed to the mistake, or
   (b) it would for any other reason be unjust for the alteration not to be made.'

There is also provision for altering the Register without a court order in certain cases under Section 5. The 2002 Act is governed by principle rather than covering specific circumstances when the Register can be altered.

SECTION

'5. The registrar may alter the register for the purpose of –

   (a) correcting a mistake,
   (b) bringing the register up to date,
   (c) giving effect to any estate, right or interest excepted from the effect of registration, or
   (d) removing a superfluous entry.'

The 2002 Act envisages administrative **alterations** where no one is prejudiced by the change in the Register. These are usually a purely administrative procedure and are unlikely to be prejudicial to the proprietor. By way of contrast there are prejudicial alterations which are referred to as **'rectifications of the Register'**. In the second category the problem for the Registrar is that the change will prejudicially affect the title of a registered proprietor. In some cases there may be two claimants over one piece of property and the issue is which party can claim the title. Special rules apply where the registered proprietor is in possession of the property. The fundamental rule under the 2002 Act is that the register must be seen as conclusive and the title of registered proprietors should be preserved.

The Court of Appeal overturned the judgment of the judge at first instance who had found against a registered proprietor who was in possession of a disputed strip of land. The court did not order rectification in favour of the claimant, however an indemnity payment was ordered.

Although the 2002 Act laid down that the Register will not be rectified against an innocent proprietor, the court will order rectification against a proprietor in possession where:

1. the registered proprietor consents;

2. the registered proprietor has caused or substantially contributed to the mistake by fraud or lack of proper care;

3. it would be unjust not to make the alteration.

In *Pinto v Lim* [2005] EWHC 630 (Ch) the court refused to rectify the Register to reflect the claimant's beneficial ownership of a property where the current registered owner was an innocent proprietor who had been in possession of a property for over four years. An important factor in this case was the claimant's beneficial interest at the time the property was sold to the innocent proprietor was fairly small.

The Register will only be rectified where there has been a 'mistake' and this is given a broad interpretation.

In *Baxter v Mannion* [2011] EWCA Civ 120 it was held that an owner of property was entitled to have the Register rectified in his favour as against a squatter who had wrongly been registered as owner of property because he had not been in adverse possession of land. The true owner had failed to object to the application for registration within the required period of time but as the judge quoted at first instance 'it would be strange if a registered proprietor could be at risk of losing his land to a squatter who had never been in adverse possession'.

Cases concerning a fraudulent transaction are problematic as shown in *Fitzwilliam v Richall Holdings Services Ltd* [2013] EWHC 86 (Ch). In this case property owned by Mr Fitzwilliam was fraudulently transferred to Mr Richall by a third party who had fraudulently forged a power of attorney. The judge decided in Mr Fitzwilliam's favour on the basis that although Mr Richall had the legal title the equitable title remained with Mr Fitzwilliam. This decision can be criticised because it appears to undermine the status of the Register which 'guarantees' title. Perhaps it would have been better to have upheld Mr Richall's claim and then allow Mr Fitzwilliam to apply to have the Register rectified in his favour. As the judge in this case decided that Mr Richall never held title he was not entitled to have the Register rectified in his favour.

3.6.2 Human rights

It could be argued that refusal to register in favour of someone who has lost his title to land as a result of an error in the registration process may lead to a claim under the Human Rights Act 1998. Their argument would be founded on contravention of Article 1 of the First Protocol of the European Convention on Human Rights. This issue was argued unsuccessfully in *Kingsalton v Thames Water Developments Ltd* (2002). The court rejected the human rights claim and held that it was a legitimate aim in the public interest to enhance the security of the land registration system. The court also felt that the payment of an indemnity under Sched 8 to the 2002 Act would ensure that the unsuccessful claimant would be compensated.

3.6.3 The payment of an indemnity

The Land Registration Act 1925 provided for the payment of an indemnity where loss had been caused by rectification or refusal to rectify.

There is provision under Sched 8 to the 2002 Act for the payment of an indemnity by the Registrar in a number of situations, including:

1. to anyone who suffers loss by reason of rectification of the Register;

2. refusal to correct a mistake;

3. removal of title from an innocent victim of forgery;

4. a mistake in an official search.

This mirrors the circumstances for payment of compensation under the old rules. The grounds for the payment of compensation had been extended under the Land Registration Act 1997. An indemnity is not payable where the Register is merely altered.

The claimant loses the right to an indemnity in certain circumstances:

i. if any part of his loss has been caused by his own fraud;

ii. if his own lack of proper care caused his loss;

iii. the indemnity may be reduced if the claimant has partly contributed to his loss by lack of proper care.

A claim for indemnity must be brought within six years from the time that the claimant knows or ought to have known of his claim.

How much will be paid? In cases of rectification an indemnity representing the full value of the estate or interest then lost will be paid. Where rectification is refused, the amount paid will be the equivalent of the value of the interest at the time of the error. This can be unfair where the error occurred at a time when the value of the property was much lower.

The following recent case highlights the problems that can arise when property is transferred from A to B (possibly by lease or by mortgage) by a forged transfer where both A and B are innocent parties. The law must decide which of the two parties should have the land and which party is to get an indemnity.

CASE EXAMPLE

Swift 1st Ltd v Chief Land Registrar [2015] EWCA Civ 330

Mrs R was registered owner of property. Without her knowledge a charge was taken out over her home to Swift 1st Ltd by a forged document. When the payments were not made Swift took possession proceedings against her. The court held that the charge should be removed from the Register. Swift 1st Ltd then sought an indemnity from the Registrar as it had lost a sum in excess of £65,000. The problem for Swift lay in the wording of Scheds 4 and 8 (see the wording of Sched 8, above). The Registrar relied on the fact that the Register had been altered merely to remove the forged transfer and the title of the registered proprietor was not prejudicially affected. If there was no rectification of the Register no indemnity could be paid. The Court of Appeal upheld the claim notwithstanding the fact that the charge was forged and the occupier Mrs R had always had an overriding interest in the form of a right to have the charge set aside. The court had to construe rectification in a very wide way and by that means Swift was entitled to an indemnity. This has been subject to criticism.

Law Commission Review

The Law Commission has included a review of the Land Registration Act 2002 in its twelfth programme of reform and this issue will form part of its overall review.

SUMMARY

1. The main features of registered land are the mirror principle, the insurance principle and the curtain principle.

2. The Land Registry consists of three registers: the Property Register, the Proprietorship Register and the Charges Register.

3. Entry on the Register constitutes conclusive proof of the ownership of the legal title to land.

4. Third party rights must be entered on the Register in order to be binding on land unless they take effect as rights that override the Register.

5. Rights that override the Register do not require entry on the Register but require the purchaser to visit the property in order to discover them.

6. The Register can be rectified within certain prescribed rules.

7. An indemnity will usually be paid to anyone who can demonstrate that he has suffered loss through rectification of the Register. An indemnity may also be claimed where the claimant can prove a mistake has been made by the Land Registry.

SAMPLE ESSAY QUESTION

The Land Registration Act 2002 represents a failure to fully reassert the 'mirror principle' in property law in England and Wales. Discuss.

> Define the mirror principle: the Register should reflect the totality of rights and interests concerning any title of registered land. Why?

> Discuss the aims of the LRA 2002: to protect both (i) purchasers and (ii) those with interests in land and to balance their needs.

> Discuss the failure of the LRA 2002 to reassert the mirror principle, the 'crack' in the mirror.
>
> Define rights that override and their importance under the LRA 1925.
>
> Explain how they constitute a 'crack in the mirror'.
>
> Discuss the Law Com Report 254/271.
>
> Discuss the difference between rights under Sched 1 and rights under Sched 3.

Explain how these rights were retained in the LRA 2002.

Explain why the LRA 2002 could not put into effect the mirror principle fully:

Discuss what rights can still override: (i) short leases; (ii) those with an interest in land in actual occupation of the land; (iii) legal easements and profits which are impliedly granted after October 2003 or arise through prescription if such rights satisfy certain conditions; (iv) other rights in a miscellaneous group. Discuss why these rights were not made registrable, e.g. very short leases would clutter the Register and the work involved would be disproportionate to the benefit. Rights of persons in actual occupation thought to be wrong in principle for an individual to lose a proprietary right through failure to register. Discuss whether these reasons are valid.

Discuss the safeguards to the principle and the way the law under the LRA 2002 protects the purchaser:

(i) rights were reduced in number, e.g. equitable easements no longer overriding; (ii) rights operate in a different way when entered on first registration to subsequent registration; (iii) some rights must be put on to the Register after ten years; (iv) an applicant for registration must disclose the right of which he is aware with some notable exceptions.

CONCLUSION

Further reading

Book

Gray, K and Gray, S F, *Elements of Land Law* (5th edn, Oxford University Press, 2009), p. 189.

Articles

Bevan, C, 'Overriding and Over-Extended? Actual Occupation: A Call to Orthodoxy' [2016] *Conv* 104.

Bogusz, B, 'Defining the Scope of Actual Occupation under the LRA 2002: Some Recent Judicial Clarification' [2011] *Conv* 268.

Cooke, E and O'Connor, P, 'Purchaser Liability to Third Parties in the English Land Registration System: A Cooperative Perspective' (2004) 120 *LQR* 640.

Cooke, E, 'Chickens coming Home to Roost' [2014] *Conv* 444.

Cooper, S, 'Regulating Fallibility in Registered Land Titles' [2013] 72(2) *CLJ* 341.

Dixon, M, 'The Reform of Property Law and the Land Registration Act 2002: A Risk Assessment' [2003] 67 *Conv* 136.

Dixon, M, 'Priorities under the Land Registration Act 2002' (2009) *LQR* 401.

Dixon, M, 'The Boland Requiem' [2015] *Conv* 285.

Dixon, M, 'Updating the Land Registration Act: Title Guarantee, Rectification and Indefeasibility' [2016] *Conv* 423.

Elkins, J and McGinley, K, 'How to tackle Property Fraud' [2015] 330 *PLJ* 2.

Ferris, G and Battersby, G, 'The General Principles of Overreaching and the Modern Legislative Reforms 1996–2002' (2003) 119 *LQR* 94.

Goymour, A, 'Mistaken Registrations of Land: Exploding the Myth of "Title by Registration"' [2013] 72 *CLJ* 617.

Jackson, N, 'Title by Registration and Concealed Overriding Interests: The Cause and Effect of Antipathy to Documentary Proof' (2003) 119 *LQR* 660.

Lees, E, 'Title by Registration: Rectification, Indemnity and Mistake and the Land Registration Act 2002' (2013) 76(1) *MLR* 62.

Pearce, R, 'Can I Sell my House but Continue Living in It? The North-East Property Buyers Litigation' [2015] *DLJ178.*

Sparkes, P, 'Reserving a Slice of Cake' [2015] *Conv* 301.

Tee, L, 'The Rights of Every Person in Actual Occupation: An Enquiry into Section 70(1)(g) Land Registration Act 1925' [1998] *CLJ* 328.

Websites

Land Registry e-Conveyancing: www.landregistry.gov.uk/e-conveyancing.

Law Commission reports

'Land Registration for the Twenty-First Century: A Consultative Document' (Law Com Report No 254, 1998).

'Land Registration for the Twenty-First Century: A Conveyancing Revolution' (Law Com Report No 271, 2001).

4

The transfer and creation of property interests

AIMS AND OBJECTIVES

After reading this chapter, you should be able to:

- Understand the importance of formalities in the transfer of land and property interests
- Identify the key stages in the transfer of property
- Explain the formalities necessary for each stage in the transfer of land
- Describe the documents used for the transfer of land
- Understand the basic principles involved in e-conveyancing

4.1 The importance of formalities in the transfer and creation of property interests

Land has a special significance and so special formalities are required for a transfer of an interest in land. Land has always been treated differently from other interests and rights. If personalty – a piece of jewellery or a car – is transferred then the law allows a purely oral transfer, but if land is transferred then the law insists that it must be in a special written form. This is called a deed and it is a particularly formal document. Deeds can be used to transfer other interests, and are compulsory in some circumstances, but a deed must be used for the transfer of an interest in land. Formalities are also important when contracts are drawn up to sell land. There are many reasons for imposing strict formalities for the sale of land. The principal reason is to ensure that there is evidence of the sale so that there can be no later dispute about who owns the land or whether there is a contract to sell the land.

> 'Quite apart from the evidentiary benefit to third parties the parties to the transaction may themselves need evidence of the existence of terms of the transaction, to forestall or settle disputes at some future point, when memories have become unreliable. This is important for transactions involving property rights, since they tend to be of longer duration than purely personal rights ... and it is particularly important relating to land, because one of the notable features of real (as compared

with personal) property is its sheer durability. The most effective type of formality for this purpose is one requiring some permanent record – writing, registering, and the like – which in fact all current English land law formalities prescribe. However, even a requirement that a transaction be completed in front of witnesses is better in this respect than total informality, since it increases the stock of (impartial) oral evidence and thus the chance that the transaction can be reconstructed accurately.'

P Critchley, 'Taking Formalities Seriously' in S Bright and J Dewar (eds), *Land Law: Themes and Perspectives* (Oxford University Press, 1998), pp. 515–516

4.1.1 Reasons for formalities being used for the sale of land

We can point to the following reasons for formalities having been relied on for the sale and disposition of interests in land:

1. It provides **written evidence** of a transaction. There is an element of risk in relying on purely oral evidence because it can easily be challenged.

2. It gives those entering a transaction **a warning that the transaction will have a legal effect**. The parties will treat such transactions with more care than a transaction which they do not believe is enforceable in the courts.

3. It means that the **terms themselves will be clear**. In a purely oral transaction there could be some dispute about the exact terms of sale, for example the cost of the property, the date for completion.

There are **disadvantages** in the use of formalities:

1. The **cost** of forms or registration and possibly the cost of legal advice can unjustly penalise some people and force them to withdraw from the transaction.

2. Making formalities compulsory means that any **informal transaction will become unenforceable**, which seems unjust where non-compliance is as a result of ignorance.

However, most people would argue that the advantages in the use of formalities far outweigh the disadvantages.

4.2 Contracts for sale and dispositions of interests in land: the steps leading to a conveyance of property

The purchase of land takes certain **defined steps** before the legal estate can pass from one person to another. When land is sold there are four distinct stages.

Stage one: the **preliminary negotiations**. These will not have any effect in law. If someone views a house and likes it enough to make an offer which is accepted by the seller, this will not be enforceable until contracts have been exchanged.

ACTIVITY

Applying the law

Consider the following situations:

1. Ellen decides to sell her house. She puts it on the market and several people visit her. Gerald offers her the full purchase price if she agrees to a quick sale. They shake hands. He writes a letter to her, saying 'I love your house and I am contacting my solicitor immediately.' Ellen hears nothing more from him. Advise Ellen.

2. Bill decides to sell his bungalow. He puts it on the market and several people visit the property. Mary makes an offer £1,000 below the asking price. Bill accepts and they agree a sale with a celebratory cup of tea. Mary contacts her surveyor and solicitor about the sale. The surveyor conducts a survey of the property and sends this to Mary. Three weeks later, Bill has a further offer from Jill, who offers the full asking price which is accepted by Bill.

Will Ellen in question (1) and Bill in question (2) be bound by their agreements?

Stage two: the **exchange of contracts** between the seller and the purchaser. This is the stage after preliminary negotiations where the parties sign contracts which have been drawn up, usually by their legal advisers. The contract constitutes a binding agreement to sell and transfer the land in return for the payment of an agreed price. The contract will become binding once it has been exchanged with the other side. If the transaction is not pursued then either side can go to court for a remedy.

Stage three: this involves the **transfer of ownership** from the seller to the purchaser. In unregistered land this is done by the transfer of the important documents of ownership (called the deeds) to the purchaser. This is called a conveyance. Under the system of registration of title this is done by the transfer of title from one party to the other.

The exchange of contracts does not give effect to the transfer of the land from the seller to the purchaser; this depends on a further stage. Up until contracts are exchanged, the parties are free to withdraw from the agreement without fear of legal action being taken against them. The agreement may be made 'subject to contract' which is often interpreted as leading to legal consequences, but in spite of attempts over the years to argue that this is binding, such an agreement will not be binding in law.

Stage four: registration of the purchaser's name at the Land Registry.

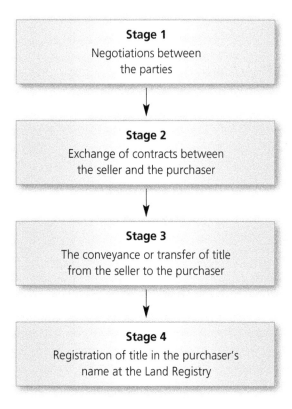

Stage 1
Negotiations between
the parties

Stage 2
Exchange of contracts between
the seller and the purchaser

Stage 3
The conveyance or transfer of title
from the seller to the purchaser

Stage 4
Registration of title in the purchaser's
name at the Land Registry

4.3 Stage one: pre-contract stage

At this stage the parties are still negotiating the sale of the property. The negotiations may reach the stage where the purchaser makes an offer to the seller who accepts the offer. The agreement may be made 'subject to contract'. However, they are not contractually bound.

The preliminary negotiations have the effect of a 'gentleman's agreement' which is not binding in law. In the words of Sachs LJ, in reality, both parties act in the mutual hope that 'the other will act like a gentleman' in circumstances where neither 'intends to act if it is against his material interests' (*Goding v Frazer* [1967] 1 WLR 286).

The fact that there is no legally binding agreement at this stage can cause problems for the purchaser who then finds that the seller has sold to someone else, as he is legally entitled to do.

4.3.1 'Gazumping' and 'gazundering'

There have been attempts to try to make the early stage of negotiations enforceable in the courts. The purchaser of property is always at risk that another purchaser will come along and offer more money which will be accepted by the seller and the first would-be purchaser will have no remedy in the courts. The acceptance of the higher price is called **gazumping** and in a rising property market such as was experienced in the UK in the 1980s, hundreds of purchasers of property were affected by it. The alternative – **gazundering** – will affect sellers in a falling property market. They agree a sale with a purchaser and then, as the property market falls, the purchaser decides to reduce his offer or withdraw altogether.

Gazumping has a far greater impact than gazundering because the purchaser may have incurred considerable costs over the property which will then be lost.

JUDGMENT

'After a series of futile visits to unsuitable houses [the purchaser] eventually finds the house of his dreams. He makes an offer, perhaps at the asking price, perhaps at what the agent tells him the vendor is likely to accept. The offer is accepted. A deal is done. The purchaser instructs solicitors to act. He perhaps commissions an architect to plan alterations. He makes arrangements to borrow money. He puts his own house on the market. He makes arrangements to move. He then learns that the vendor has decided to sell to someone else, perhaps for the price already offered and accepted, perhaps for an increased price achieved by a covert, unofficial auction … no explanation, no apology. The vendor is able to indulge his self-interest, even his whims, without exposing himself to any legal penalty.'

Sir Thomas Bingham in *Pitt v PHH Asset Management Ltd* [1994] 1 WLR 327

The main reason why there is no legally binding agreement until the exchange of contracts is to give the parties a chance to make enquiries and searches before committing themselves to the sale or purchase. However, other systems (e.g. the Scottish system of conveyancing) build in commitment from the parties at a much earlier stage.

4.3.2 Home Information Packs

Over the years, the fact that preliminary oral agreements in house purchases are not binding in law has been criticised by many, including lawyers and judges as seen above in the judgment of Sir Thomas Bingham. There may be expenditure of time and money on the negotiations. If the sale does not go ahead then this is lost and cannot be recovered.

PROPERTY INTERESTS: TRANSFER AND CREATION

gazumping

The acceptance of a higher price by the seller from a new purchaser having accepted an offer from another purchaser before contracts have been exchanged

gazundering

The withdrawal of an offer to purchase property by the purchaser and substituted with an offer of a lower price

Over the years, the government tried to introduce proposals to address the problems created by gazumping including compulsory seller's packs (Home Information Packs) which were information packs about the property, provided by the seller giving prospective purchasers information about the property.

Under the Housing Act 2004, the proposals were fully in force in 2008 but in the face of considerable criticism suspended in 2010. Although they had some merit in giving the purchaser important information about the property pre-exchange of contracts such information could be out of date and could be costly for the seller to continually update and the purchaser was not always prepared to rely on the information provided by the seller. The only aspect of the pack that remains is the need for the seller to provide the buyer with an energy efficiency certificate.

4.3.3 The lock-out agreement

One way that gazumping can be addressed although not prevented is the use of a 'lock-out' agreement.

In *Pitt v PHH Asset Management Ltd* (1994) it was held that it is possible to overcome the limitations of the 'subject to contract' rule by drawing up a 'lock-out' agreement or 'exclusivity' agreement. A lock-out agreement is a prior collateral contract for valuable consideration that, during a stipulated period, the seller will not negotiate with anyone else. It is important to note that this agreement does not give the purchaser the right to require that the land be sold to him but merely entitles the purchaser to recover damages for breach of the agreement.

It is not a contract for the sale of land, so it is not subject to the same formalities. It need not be in writing, although generally it will be put in writing. It goes some way towards solving the problems of gazumping, as it prevents the seller for a period of time from negotiating with third parties. The purchaser has time to deal with preliminary issues and, so at the end of the lock-out period may be ready to proceed.

JUDGMENT

'B, by agreeing not to negotiate for this fixed period with a third party, locks himself out of such negotiations. He has in no legal sense locked himself into such negotiations with A. What A has achieved is an exclusive opportunity, for a fixed period, to try and come to terms with B, an opportunity for which he has, unless he makes his agreement under seal, to give good consideration.'

Lord Ackner in *Walford v Miles* [1992] 2 AC 128

The period preceding contract allows the parties to proceed towards sale by negotiating important issues such as sale price and terms of the contract and the date for completion. Surveys of the land and searches of the title will be carried out by the purchaser and his/ her agents. He will make enquiries of the seller but the principle of *caveat emptor* still applies to transfers of land. The seller is under a duty to disclose all latent defects of title. If the seller is asked questions directly about the state of the property or other matters associated with the property, he/she must answer truthfully. In *McMeekin v Long* (2003) 29 EG 120 the purchaser successfully sued the seller for damages where he stated that there were no disputes with neighbours and that there had been no complaints when he had lived at the property. This was untrue. However, there is no duty of care to disclose matters to the purchaser. In *Sykes v Taylor-Rose* [2004] 2 P & CR 30 the Court of Appeal refused to award damages to a purchaser who had argued that the seller was under a duty to disclose that the property purchased was once the scene of a horrific murder which could have an adverse effect on the value of the property.

4.4 Stage two: the exchange of contracts

The contract for a sale of land today is in a standard form which has been drawn up by the Law Society but which can be varied by the parties themselves. In theory, the parties could draw up their own contract but this is rarely done.

4.4.1 The Law of Property (Miscellaneous Provisions) Act 1989

Any contract for the sale or other disposition of an interest in land created after 27 September 1989 must comply with the Law of Property (Miscellaneous Provisions) Act 1989:

SECTION

's 2(1) A contract for sale or other disposition of an interest in land can only be made in writing and only by incorporating all the terms which the parties have expressly agreed in one document or, where contracts are exchanged, in each.
(2) The terms may be incorporated in a document either by being set out in it or by reference to some other document.
(3) The documents incorporating the terms or, where contracts are exchanged, one of the documents incorporating them (but not necessarily the same one) must be signed by or on behalf of each party to the contract.'

An 'interest' in land means any estate, interest or charge in or over land. Essentials for the contract for sale:

1. the contract for sale of land must be in writing;

2. it must contain all the terms of the agreement;

3. it must be signed by both the parties. Note that under s 2(3) both parties must sign, not just the party to be charged. Where contracts are exchanged both copies must be signed – one by the seller and the other by the purchaser.

4.4.2 What is the position if any one of these provisions is not complied with?

The contract is void. The law does not regard it as an unenforceable contract but as a void contract.

Compare the previous relevant section, s 40 of the Law of Property Act 1925: under this section a contract for the sale of land merely had to be **evidenced** in writing so the law was less stringent with regard to formalities of contract. If there was no evidence in writing then the contract could still be saved if there were sufficient acts of part performance. An example would be allowing the purchaser into possession as soon as there was an agreement to sell. This would be seen as a sufficient act of part performance relying on the previously agreed terms. This doctrine was abolished under the 1989 Act.

ACTIVITY

Quick quiz

Consider these examples and decide whether the contracts will be enforceable under the 1989 Act:

1. Alex wants to sell some land. A contract for the sale of land is drawn up between Alex and Max. The contract is in writing and both parties sign the agreement.

2. Alex wants to sell some land to Max. A contract is drawn up in writing but only Max signs. Alex changes his mind and wants to withdraw from the sale.
3. Alex wants to sell some land but he wants the date of sale to be delayed for two months. The contract is in writing but this term is not put into the contract. Again, he changes his mind and no longer wants to sell.
4. Alex wants to sell the same land but does not put the contract into writing but merely shakes hands with Max who is allowed to move some possessions into the barn on the land. He terminates a lease on a lock-up garage where he has been storing the possessions. Later, Alex decides not to sell to Max.

The document incorporating the terms of the contract agreed by the parties must be signed not simply by 'the party to be charged' but by or on behalf of all the parties to the contract. Further, the signature itself must be a signature by hand and not merely a stamp or a typed name.

CASE EXAMPLE

Firstpost Homes Ltd v Johnson [1995] 1 WLR 1567

In this case the purchaser had prepared a letter for the seller to sign: the purchaser's name was typed at the top of the letter. The purchaser had signed the plan mentioned in the letter but not the actual letter itself and it was held that there was no contract because the plan did not refer to the letter. If two documents are to be used then the first must refer to the second document. It was held that the contract must be contained in one document or two documents joined together. All the terms of the contract must be signed by all the parties to the contract. A signature must be a real signature by hand and is not constituted by the printing or typing of a party's name as the addressee of a supposedly contractual undertaking.

The move towards electronic exchange and transfer will have to take notice of the fact that an electronic signature may be used. The courts have indicated that an electronic signature may be acceptable in order to comply with s 2(1) of the Law of Property (Miscellanous Provisions) Act 1989.

Once electronic exchange is introduced then there will no longer be exchange in the traditional sense, the Land Registry will simply receive notification that the parties now intend to be bound and the Registry will record this by an entry on the Register.

4.4.3 Options to purchase

option to purchase

The right given to a purchaser to call on the seller to sell the land within the stipulated period at a pre-agreed price

Options to purchase are a useful mechanism to allow a purchaser the right to purchase property at a future date at an agreed price when they may not be ready to proceed immediately. Usually, the holder of the option will have given consideration. The purchaser may wait until the value of the property goes up and then he/she may exercise the option at a lower price. The seller must sell to him and if he sells to anyone else, the right of the purchaser is binding on the new purchaser so long as he has notice of the existence of the option.

The rules concerning formalities for options to purchase land are slightly different from formalities generally concerning the disposition of an interest in land.

The agreement conferring the option must conform with s 2(1) of the Law of Property (Miscellaneous Provisions) Act 1989 but the exercise of the option is not a contract for sale of an interest in land and so does not have to conform with the section.

CASE EXAMPLE

Spiro v Glencrown Properties Ltd [1991] Ch 537

It was held that the notice given by the parties exercising the option does not have to comply with the requirement for writing under s2 of the 1989 Act. So it will still be an effective notice even if it has been signed by only one of two option holders and indeed it need not be signed by the option holder at all in order to be binding.

'Apart from authority, it seems plain enough that section 2 was intended to apply to the agreement which created the option and not to the notice by which it was exercised. Section 2, which replaced section 40 of the Law of Property Act 1925, was intended to prevent disputes over terms they had agreed. It prescribes the formalities for recording their mutual consent. But only the grant of the option depends upon consent. The exercise of the option is a unilateral act. It would destroy the very purpose of the option if the purchaser had to obtain the seller's countersignature to the notice by which it was exercised.'

Hoffmann J

4.4.4 Collateral contracts

collateral contract

A separate contract that is not part of the substantive contract, enforceable as a separate agreement

If the parties agree other conditions in a separate agreement then that is a **collateral contract** and that is enforceable as a separate agreement so long as the terms are not at the heart of the contract. The collateral contract does not need to be evidenced in writing if it can be interpreted as not being one for the disposition of an interest in land. For example, an agreement that the seller will sell an item of furniture to the purchaser will be regarded as a collateral contract.

CASE EXAMPLE

Record v Bell [1991] 1 WLR 853

In this case the collateral contract was a promise by the seller to the purchaser as to the state of the seller's title. There was no writing to support this promise which would satisfy the requirements of s2(1) of the 1989 Act. This was held to be collateral to the main contract and did not require writing. It was held that the term did not comprise part of the main contract and it did not undermine the validity of the main contract.

4.4.5 The contract: 'one document' rule

Section 2(1) of the 1989 Act envisages that there will be one document rather than two, meaning that one single document will contain all the terms of the contract. However, under s2(2) there can be limited joinder of documents. This had been allowed under pre-1989 law. This means that some of the terms could be in another document but they must be expressly referred to in the primary contractual document, which must be signed.

Exchange of contracts will always involve two contracts and each party will sign one copy. The next stage is for the contracts to be 'exchanged' so that each party sends the copy that they have signed to the other and then the contracts are effective.

The 1989 Act specifically deals with this under s2(3):

SECTION

's2(3) The document incorporating the terms or, where contracts are exchanged, one of the documents incorporating them (but not necessarily the same one) must be signed by or on behalf of each party to the contract.'

Can letters represent two documents?

The courts have considered whether the two documents mentioned in s2(3) of the 1989 Act can be two letters exchanged by the parties.

CASE EXAMPLE

Commission for New Towns v Cooper (Great Britain) Ltd [1995] Ch 259

It was concluded that the exchange of letters cannot usually constitute a contract although if the letters expressly refer to an agreement that is already in existence then the letters will be enforceable.

The postal exchange has been superseded by telephone exchange. Today, electronic exchange is possible, which opens up the question of what constitutes a signature for the purposes of s2 of the Law of Property (Miscellaneous Provisions) Act 1989.

> 'Under s2 LP (MP) Act 1989, a contract for the sale of land must be agreed in writing and it must be contained in a document (or documents) that sets out the terms agreed and is signed by the parties. It has been assumed that these requirements could not be met online. However, both the Law Commission and the High Court have suggested that this assumption is misguided.... The Interpretation Act 1978 defines "writing" as typing, printing, lithography, photography and "other modes of representing ... words in visual form". The Law Commission considers that this definition also covers the natural meaning of "writing", and that this will include any updating of its construction, for example because of technological developments. The question whether an e-mail can constitute writing has been hotly debated. The argument against states that the digital information: (i) is held as a series of on and off switches in a chip, or in some other type of recording medium, and does not form a visible representation of words; and (ii) will represent the words only after a coding convention has been applied. The data is not visible because computer language is not directly accessible to humans. The Commission disagrees. It argues that although the digital information may not constitute "writing" its on-screen representation does. Thus an e-mail will generally satisfy the Interpretation Act definition and the functions of writing.'
>
> E Newton and M Dowden, 'The Perpetual Advance of Technology'
> [2006] 630 *EG* 97

Here, Newton and Dowden examine the increasing use of e-mail and its place in exchange of contracts. They point out that the signature in commercial contracts focuses not so much on form but instead function. So if an electronic form of signature is used then it is the purpose of the signature which is all-important. In their words, 'if the "authenticating intention" is the determining factor, the Commission may well be correct in saying that a confirmatory mouse click can now be regarded as a functioning "signature"'.

If the contract is held by the solicitors then the contract may be signed but it will not be effective until there is agreement that it is to be acted on.

4.4.6 A variation in the terms of the contract

Where the terms are subsequently varied then they will not be effective unless both parties sign them.

To conform with s 2 of the 1989 Act, the contract must be in writing and all the terms must be included in the contract. This is subject to the possibility that a term has been omitted by a genuine mistake, in which case the court may rectify the agreement. This means that the contract will take effect with the omitted term included. The rectified document must be signed by both parties or the earlier signatures must be acknowledged. However, it does not give the parties the chance to include fresh terms which they had not previously discussed.

If the parties informally vary the terms of the contract then the informal variation will not take effect and the original contract will stand in these cases.

CASE EXAMPLE

McCausland v Duncan Lawrie [1997] 1 WLR 38

It was held that an informal variation to the terms of the contract will not affect the previous formally agreed contract. In this case the completion date, a Sunday, had been stipulated in the original enforceable contract. The parties informally rearranged the completion date for another day. The solicitors for the two parties exchanged letters varying the completion date. The Court of Appeal held that this did not amount to an effective variation of contract because it did not satisfy s 2 and the requirement that both parties had to sign the contract. The court enforced the original contract and upheld the date agreed.

If the parties had failed to stipulate a completion date at all then the contract would have been rendered void as all the terms were not in the contract as laid down in the 1989 Act. Here, there was a completion date in the formal contract, so that contract was enforceable.

4.4.7 Exceptions to the requirements of s 2 of the Law of Property (Miscellaneous Provisions) Act 1989

1. The 1989 Act expressly excludes contracts to **grant leases** of less than three years in length at full market rent (s 2(5)(a)) – such contracts can be created orally.

2. The 1989 Act also expressly excludes a contract made in the course of a **public auction** (s 2(5)(b)) and a contract regulated under the **Financial Services Act 1986** (s 2(5)(c)).

3. It will not apply to **collateral contracts** if they are not considered to be a disposition of an interest in land (*Record v Bell* (1991)).

4. **Proprietary estoppel**. The Law Commission anticipated that the doctrine of part performance might be replaced by proprietary estoppel. It was thought that once part performance had been abolished, its role in the enforcement of rights rendered unenforceable by the lack of formalities would be taken over by the doctrine of proprietary estoppel.

In *Lim Teng Huan v Ang Swee Chuan* [1992] 1 WLR 113, a case decided by the Privy Council, an agreement that did not comply with s 2 was upheld on the basis of proprietary estoppel. It held that it would be unconscionable for the claimant to go back on an agreement made with the defendant that he could go into occupation of property that he had built on jointly owned land.

The doctrine of proprietary estoppel was expressly endorsed by Robert Walker LJ in *Yaxley v Gotts* [2000] 1 All ER 711:

> 'The circumstances in which s 2 has to be complied with are so various, and the scope of the doctrine of estoppel is so flexible, that any general assertion of s 2 as a "no-go area" for estoppel would be unsustainable.'

In this case (as discussed below) the Court of Appeal upheld the oral agreement on the basis of a constructive trust in spite of its own endorsement of proprietary estoppel as a way of circumventing the lack of formalities as required under s 2(1) of the Law of Property (Miscellaneous Provisions) Act 1989. However, the use of proprietary estoppel as a way to uphold oral agreements that do not conform with s 2 has been restricted by the case of *Cobbe v Yeoman's Row Management Ltd* [2008] 1 WLR 1752. An owner of a building and a developer reached an oral agreement in principle under which the developer would obtain planning permission to develop the property and the property would be transferred to him for development and later sale and distribution of the profits between the parties. The developer obtained the planning permission and sought to enforce the agreement even though it had never been put into writing. The House of Lords refused the developer's claim. The House of Lords was reluctant to uphold a claim based on proprietary estoppel in the context of commercial negotiations since it could introduce an element of uncertainty in an area where certainty was important. Although the claim was based on an expectation it was not an expectation of an interest in the property but rather an expectation that a contract would be drawn up. Proprietary estoppel has traditionally been based on an expectation of an interest in property.

JUDGMENT

'Proprietary estoppel requires, in my opinion, clarity as to what it is that the object of the estoppel is to be estopped from denying, or asserting, and clarity as to the interest in the property in question that that denial, or assertion, would otherwise defeat. If these requirements are not recognised, proprietary estoppel will lose contact with its roots and risk becoming unprincipled and therefore unpredictable.'

Scott LJ

JUDGMENT

'In the commercial context, the claimant is typically a business person with access to legal advice and what he or she is expecting to get is a *contract*. In the domestic or family context, the typical claimant is not a business person and is not receiving legal advice. What he or she wants and expects to get is an *interest* in immovable property, often for long-term occupation as a home.... *Crabb v Arun District Council* is a difficult case, not least because of different views taken by different members of the Court. The situation was that a commercial negotiation in which both sides expected formal legal documents to be agreed and executed ... In my opinion none of these cases casts any doubt on the general principle laid down by this House in *Ramsden v Dyson*, that conscious reliance alone will not give rise to an estoppel. Nor do they cast doubt on the general principle that the court should be slow to introduce uncertainty into commercial transactions by over-ready use of equitable concepts such as fiduciary obligations and equitable estoppel.'

Walker LJ

The judgment in *Cobbe v Yeomans Row Management* raised again the question of whether there can be exceptions to the strict requirement for adherence to formalities in the sale of land.

Other cases have revisited the question whether proprietary estoppel has survived s 2 of the Law of Property (Miscellaneous Provisions) Act 1989. The problem lies in the discretionary nature of proprietary estoppel which conflicts with the prescriptive nature of the statutory section, s 2 Law of Property (Miscellaneous Provisions) Act 1989. Proprietary estoppel as shown later in Chapter 7 is an informal doctrine based on unconscionability where a party has relied on an assurance or promise from another who later refuses to carry out the terms of the promise. The problem with the use of proprietary estoppel in the sale and purchase of land is that a seller cannot through an informal promise 'contract out' of the need to follow the formal requirements. However this has not prevented the court from taking a different and more liberal view of the effects of s 2 LP (MP) Act 1989 in some cases as shown below.

CASE EXAMPLE

Whittaker v Kinnear [2011] EWHC 1479

Mrs Whittaker owned a large property which she sold to a developer at undervalue. It was orally agreed that she would be able to remain in the property after the sale. The developer took out a mortgage over the property and defaulted on the repayments and the bank obtained a possession order against him. Mrs Whittaker claimed that she had the right to continue to live in the property on the basis of an equitable interest arising under the doctrine of proprietary estoppel. She claimed that a promise had been made to her on which she had relied to her detriment which was the selling of her property at undervalue. The County Court dismissed her claim on the basis that proprietary estoppel could not be a defence to the possession action brought by the mortgagees because it had been defeated by s 2 of the Law of Property (Miscellaneous Provisions) Act 1989. It held that although s 2 of the 1989 Act had preserved the constructive trust as a way of avoiding the statutory formalities that arose on the transfer of an interest it did not expressly preserve an interest that arose by proprietary estoppel. The High Court overturned the decision of the County Court and held that proprietary estoppel has survived the enactment of the 1989 Act and can be claimed as a defence to the lack of formalities.

This case suggests that estoppel can still be pleaded in cases where the parties contemplated a formal contract. In the words of Bean J 'notwithstanding Lord Scott's dicta in *Cobbe*, proprietary estoppel in a case involving land has survived the enactment of s 2 of the 1989 Act.'

5. **Constructive trusts**. A constructive trust may be imposed by the court where it believes that the conduct of the defendant has been unconscionable. The 1989 Act expressly preserves the operation of constructive trusts in connection with contracts which do not comply with the need for writing under s 2(5)(c) 'and nothing in the section affects the creation or operation of resulting, implied or constructive trusts'. It was held expressly in *Yaxley v Gotts* (2000) that where a constructive trust can be pleaded then the non-compliance with s 2 will not be fatal. In this case the courts upheld an oral agreement by an owner of some property to grant a builder the ground floor of premises in exchange for labour, materials and services supplied for work on other parts of the property. This decision raises one significant difficulty, as it allows contracts to be upheld which would otherwise be void for lack of formality and can cause uncertainty.

In an article in 2002 Griffiths suggested that there are problems in using constructive trusts and also estoppel as exceptions to s 2(1) LP (MP) Act 1989 because they are both unclear as to what the remedy will be if the court finds in favour of the claimant. This is particularly true in cases of estoppel. He considers whether these doctrines bear any resemblance to the old doctrine of part performance which was an exception to s 40 LPA 1925, the predecessor of s 2(1) LP (MP) Act 1989.

> 'The finding of a constructive trust will mean that the claimant has a right which in addition to being undoubtedly proprietary in nature is, according to a considerable body of authority, capable of binding third parties. In these respects, it is, at the very

least a comparable alternative to part performance. Furthermore, as with the latter, there is no discretion as to the remedy awarded.'

G L H Griffiths, 'Part Performance: Still Trying to Replace the
Irreplaceable' [2002] Conv 216

Griffiths continues his article by considering whether or not estoppel goes some way towards replacing the old doctrine of part performance.

'The position in estoppel – and indeed its case for replacing part performance – may be much less clear cut for although there are strong indications that a right so based may bind a third party acquiring land to which it relates, this cannot at present be regarded as being beyond doubt ... However, it is clear that ... the courts have one clear aim. This is as Scarman LJ observed in *Crabb v Arun DC* to give the "minimum equity to do justice" to the claimant, a task approached "in a cautious way".

What form this minimum justice will take may be greatly influenced by whether estoppel is seen as satisfying only the claimant's reliance upon the representation or the legitimate expectations engendered by it.'

Griffiths highlights how the law has adapted since the passage of the 1989 Act removing the doctrine of part-performance, and shows that the result achieved may not be as predictable but the contract which fails to conform to the necessary formalities may still be enforceable either under proprietary estoppel or under a constructive trust.

One case where the claimant relied on a constructive trust assists in showing how it is likely to develop as an exception to s 2(1). In *Herbert v Doyle* [2010] EWCA Civ 1095 negotiations had been entered into by two neighbours. H rented property to D which included a number of parking spaces. H wanted to develop his property and requested the return of some of the parking spaces which D orally agreed. The agreement was not put into writing. H started the development and when the parties later fell out D refused to transfer the parking places. It was held that a constructive trust could give rise to a successful claim where the formalities had not been complied with but there were exceptions. The main exceptions were: (1) where the parties still intended to make a formal agreement setting out the terms on which one or more of the parties was to acquire an interest; (2) where further terms remained to be agreed between them; or (3) if the parties did not expect their agreement to be immediately binding.

KEY FACTS

The contract
1. The parties are not bound until there has been exchange of contracts.
2. The seller may be bound before exchange not to negotiate with anyone else for a limited period of time by a lock-out agreement.
3. The contract must conform with s 2(1) of the Law of Property (Miscellaneous Provisions) Act 1989. It must be in writing and signed by both the parties. It must incorporate all the terms which the parties have expressly agreed.
4. Two documents can make up the contract but must be joined by each expressly referring to the other.
5. A collateral contract does not have to conform with the requirements of s 2 of the 1989 Act.
6. Any variation in the terms of the contract will not be effective unless both parties sign them.
7. A contract which does not comply with s 2 of the 1989 Act may still be upheld on the grounds of either estoppel or a constructive trust.

4.5 Enforcement of agreements for sale of land

specific performance

An equitable remedy granted by the court ordering one side of a bargain to carry out his obligations

Once contracts have been exchanged, there is a binding contract between the parties. This means that neither party can then withdraw from the sale without committing a breach of contract and the other will be able to seek a remedy from the courts. Since the property involves land, which is regarded in law as unique, an order for **specific performance** is available.

Specific performance is an equitable remedy and so, like all equitable remedies, it is discretionary and may be unavailable in the following circumstances:

1. if the party seeking it has acted **unconscionably**;
2. if the award would **prejudice the interests of third parties**; or
3. if it would cause **hardship** amounting to an injustice.

In *Patel v Ali* [1984] Ch 283 a catalogue of disasters beset the sellers after the exchange of contracts including the husband becoming bankrupt and as a result being sent to prison and the wife suffering from severe ill-health and the eventual amputation of a leg. The wife cared for the parties' three children and relied on the support of her family and friends who lived near the house. These facts together persuaded the judge not to make an order for specific performance of the contract.

If specific performance is refused or not sought by the parties then damages can be claimed for the loss of the bargain if either party refuses to perform the contract.

Rescission may be available if it is possible to return the parties to the position they were in before contracts were exchanged. Where this is impossible then damages will be the appropriate remedy.

If there has been an error in the contract then rectification can be claimed. The contracts can then be relied on in their altered state and the sale can proceed.

The contract itself is regarded as a type of interest in land, which is known as an **estate contract**. Since it does not fall within either of the legal estates mentioned in s 1(2) of the Law of Property Act 1925, it is only capable of being an equitable interest. If the land is wrongly conveyed to someone other than the purchaser by the seller before the purchaser completes the sale, it is possible that the third person will be bound by the purchaser's estate contract.

This will depend on whether the contract has been properly protected by registration. In registered land this will be by the entry of a burden on the Charges Register. Registration is essential in case the seller accepts a further offer for the property. The second purchaser will realise that there has been another earlier agreement when he sees the registered estate contract.

If no estate contract is entered then the second purchaser has no way of knowing about the earlier negotiations.

ACTIVITY

Quick quiz

Consider these situations. In each case, is there an enforceable contract?

1. Mark decides to sell his house. He puts it on the market and Sally offers him the full asking price. Contracts are prepared by both solicitors. Sally's signature is typed in by the secretary because Sally is away at the time. When she comes back, Sally initials the signature.

2. Tim has agreed to sell his house to Jane. His solicitor writes to say that Tim wants to delay the completion date. Jane's solicitor writes back to agree. Would it make any difference if the change in completion date is changed after exchange of contracts?

3. Anne agrees to sell her house to Neil. Contracts are exchanged. Neil registers his estate contract. Les offers Anne £30,000 more and behind Neil's back she agrees to sell to Les. How does that affect Neil's rights? Would it make any difference if Neil's rights were not registered and Les simply knew that Neil had offered to buy the house?

Note in case (3) that once the estate contract is registered it will be binding on a subsequent purchaser. Failure to register means that the subsequent purchaser will not be bound and in this example Neil's only remedy will be to sue Anne.

A typed signature is not acceptable under the 1989 Act but clearly the law must change to accommodate moves towards the electronic exchange of contracts.

The entering into a binding contract does not transfer the legal title to the purchaser. However, because 'equity treats as done that which ought to be done' and the contract to transfer the land is specifically enforceable, the equitable ownership of the land passes to the purchaser as soon as the contract is entered. This has the consequence that from the moment of exchange of contracts the seller becomes a trustee and holds the property **on trust for the purchaser**. The obligation to show good title was the central term of a contract for the sale of land, *Lysaght v Edwards* (1876) 2 Ch D 499. If the contract is silent, the obligation is a matter of legal implication.

JUDGMENT

'[T]he moment you have a valid contract for sale the seller becomes in equity a trustee for the purchaser of the estate sold.'

Jessel MR in *Lysaght v Edwards* (1876) 2 Ch D 499

One of the consequences of this is that from the moment of contract the purchaser is required to insure the land, since under common law the risk passes to him when he obtains the equitable ownership of the land. So if there is a fire which destroys the house between contract and completion, the purchaser must still pay the full asking price as the risk has now passed to the purchaser. The purchaser should insure the property as soon as possible after exchange of contracts.

The Law Commission has criticised this because 'it is fundamentally unsatisfactory and unfair'. It thought it was unfair because it imposed a responsibility on the purchaser to protect his property at a time when he has no physical control over it.

The Standard Conditions of Sale used in the purchase of property allow for the seller to retain the risk until completion; he will not be under an obligation to insure the property. The purchaser may have the right to rescind the contract if the physical state of the property has made it unsuitable for its purpose at the date of the contract as a result of damage which is outside the purchaser's insurance contract. These conditions of sale go some way towards redressing the imbalance between the position of the purchaser and the seller after the exchange of contracts.

4.6 Transfer of interests in land and other property

4.6.1 Stage three: completion of the sale

The third stage in the transfer of land is completion. This is the formal transfer of the legal title from the seller to the purchaser. It was traditionally six weeks after exchange of contracts but it is now far shorter and can be on the same day but is most likely to be about three weeks after exchange.

In order to convey, transfer or create a legal estate or interest in land it has traditionally been necessary to use a deed.

SECTION

Deeds prior to July 1990

deed
A document which has been drawn up to satisfy certain prescribed formalities. These formalities depend on the date at which the deed was executed

Before July 1990 all **deeds** had to be **signed, sealed and delivered.** There was no express requirement for the deed to be witnessed, although it was usual practice to do so. The most important factor was the seal, which was once a genuine sealing wax seal melted on to the paper and then impressed with a special mark. Long before 1990, this had ceased to be usual practice and a standard seal was stuck on to the deed. Delivery ceased to mean physical delivery of the document several centuries ago. Today delivery means that the document is now regarded as binding and it cannot be reversed.

Deeds after July 1990

SECTION

KEY FACTS

What is a deed?
• A deed must make it clear on its face that it is intended to be a deed.
• It must be signed by the grantor or by both of them if there is more than one.
• The signature must be witnessed.
• It must be delivered as a deed by the grantor or someone authorised to do so on his behalf.

The purchaser has the responsibility of drawing up the draft transfer of sale. Completion differs between unregistered and registered land.

The eventual introduction of e-conveyancing will result in the demise of the deed. Under s 91 Land Registration Act 2002 once certain formalities have been complied with the electronic disposition of estates and interests in registered land will be deemed to satisfy the formality requirements for a written document or deed. The deed will no longer be necessary because the documents will be created online and signed with an electronic signature. Once the transaction becomes electronic then the requirements of s 52 LPA 1925 and s 1 LP (MP) Act 1989 will largely become redundant. There will no longer be a need for a witness and the old concept of delivery will cease to be important.

The introduction of full electronic conveyancing in England and Wales at completion is still some way off.

4.6.2 Completion of sale in unregistered land

In unregistered land the interest vests as soon as the formalities have been completed. There must be a formal conveyance using a deed and the title deeds of the property must be handed over to the purchaser.

Once the purchase monies have been paid then the purchaser is deemed to be owner of the property. However, since 1990 any sale of land will act as one of the 'triggers' for registration of title and the property will then need to be registered by the purchaser. All new owners of property acquired under the unregistered system of conveyancing have to apply to the Land Registry for first registration as registered proprietor.

Registration must be made within two months of purchase (s 6 of the Land Registration Act 2002). If registration is not made within two months then the conveyance is void and the legal estate reverts back to the seller who will hold it on a bare trust for the purchaser in the case of a freehold estate (s 7(2) LRA 2002) or in the case of a lease of more than seven years in duration, as a contract to grant or create a lease (s 7(2), (6) LRA 2002).

In some cases of non-registration of a disposition, for example the grant of a new estate such as a new lease, the grant will become void and the disposition will take effect simply as an estate contract.

4.6.3 Completion of sale in registered land

In registered land there are no documents of title to transfer to the purchaser, so on receipt of the purchase monies the seller's solicitor will complete the transaction by sending the form of transfer to the purchaser's solicitors. The transfer is by a Land Registry Form which takes effect as a deed (but it differs from the deed of conveyance in unregistered land). It must be 'signed and delivered' to the other party's solicitors. It must also be witnessed.

The transfer is not final until the purchaser has been registered in the Proprietorship Register at the Land Registry. That is the moment when legal title passes. Traditionally, this has taken several weeks to complete so there has arisen what is known as a 'registration gap'.

'The defects in the present system
The "registration gap"
… The fact that there is a period of time between the execution of a transfer or other disposition and its subsequent registration gives rise to a number of difficulties. We have mentioned one of these above, namely that it is necessary to have in place a system of official searches which offer priority protection. It is in practice not uncommon for applications to register a disposition to be made long after the period of

protection has passed thereby placing the transferee at risk. In any event, the official search procedure applies only to a purchaser, who is defined as "any person (including a lessee or chargee) who in good faith and for valuable consideration acquires or intends to acquire a legal estate in land". There is no equivalent protection available, at least at present, for those who are intending to acquire some lesser interest in the property, such as an equitable chargee or the grantee of an option.'

Law Commission and HM Land Registry, 'Land Registration for the Twenty-First Century: A Consultation Document' (Law Com 254, 1998)

This gap will be removed under e-conveyancing, as completion and registration will all be one computerised process which will be carried out at the Land Registry. Transfer still involves the transfer of paper-based written deeds. Transfer of title will be simply a matter of updating the Register with the new owner's name and details. This will then be instantly accessible electronically to the general public. The new owner will not receive a land certificate noting the change in ownership. One of the advantages is that it will avoid duplication of effort and also the risk of error. However, it also risks new types of crime in the transfer of property. The problems will arise with electronic signatures. They will have to be kept safe and public registers will have to be under sufficient degree of security to prevent possible theft. It could always be possible that someone could steal the key giving access to the signature and then misuse it in some way, using the signature to sign documents fraudulently.

Property visited and liked, offer made to the seller. Seller accepts offer. Lock-out agreement may be negotiated.	Effect not binding in law.	*Pitt v PHH Asset Management Ltd* (1994)
Contracts exchanged. Must comply with the requirements of the LP (MP) Act 1989: writing; all terms included; signed by both parties.	Parties now bound, cannot change mind without incurring penalties.	*Firstpost Homes Ltd v Johnson* (1995) *Spiro v Glencrown Properties* (1991)
Completion, mortgage finalised and money paid.	The seller holds as trustee for the purchaser who has an equitable estate but the seller's name is still registered at the Land Registry.	
Registration of the purchaser's name at the Land Registry.	The purchaser is now the owner at law of the property.	s27 LRA 2002

Table 4.1 Stages in the conveyancing process in registered land

ACTIVITY

Applying the law

Mercia agrees to buy 55 Grange Road from Joan. She particularly likes the way that Joan has decorated the property. They draw up an agreement which they both sign but it does not mention the carpets and curtains that Mercia had agreed to buy and which were to be included in the sale at a price to be agreed. The agreement also omits other important points such as the date when the sale will be completed and the exact amount to be paid by way of deposit. Mercia later has second thoughts about the property and wants to withdraw from the purchase.

Advise Mercia whether she is bound by the purchase and what remedy would be appropriate if she is so bound.

What would be the position if Joan decided not to sell to Mercia but Mercia was still keen to purchase the property?

4.7 E-conveyancing

Much of the law on exchange of contracts and completion will be transformed by the advent of electronic conveyancing or 'e-conveyancing'. One of the reasons for the passage of the 2002 Act was to facilitate electronic conveyancing. It has long been recognised that computerisation of conveyancing will have several advantages. It will speed up the whole process of house purchase and also minimise mistakes. There are provisions in the 2002 Act and also in the Electronic Communications Act 2000 for the introduction of e-conveyancing.

Under s 93 of the 2002 Act the Lord Chancellor has the power to make the system compulsory. It will be available both to legal practitioners and to members of the general public who wish to carry out their own conveyancing.

'The aims of electronic conveyancing are quite clear, namely to remove the traditional paper requirements normally associated with the conveyancing transactions and replace them with a system allowing the transfer of property interests between parties to be conducted via a computer. This will include not only the final stages of conveyancing such as the exchange and completion of land transactions but all associated communications beforehand, including those concerned with the drafting of contracts and the exchange of the lists of fixtures and fittings.'

D Capps, 'Conveyancing in the 21st Century: An Outline of Electronic Conveyancing and Electronic Signatures' [2002] *Conv* 443

4.7.1 How will the system work?

Conveyancers will have to use specific software which, once installed, will give them access to a secure system. It will not be accessible through the Internet. The secure system will give conveyancers the right to access each other and exchange all relevant information and documentation. When the purchaser and seller have agreed the terms of the contract they will send a copy in electronic form to the Land Registry where it will be checked electronically to find any inconsistencies. The purchaser and seller will have first agreed the terms of the contract in an on-line secure deal room. The contract will then be made in electronic form and signed using a digital signature which will be carried out electronically. The electronic signature will have the same force of law as a signature on a paper conveyance.

SECTION

's 91(4) A document to which this system applies is to be regarded as –

(a) in writing, and

(b) signed by each individual, and sealed by each corporation, whose electronic signature it has.'

One of the main advantages with such a system will be the ease with which searches can be made into the land. There is often considerable delay for the purchaser of property before these are all completed. The new system will allow all of these to be carried out electronically. The rules will allow an electronic contract to replace a paper contract.

The contracts will then be binding but must be registered in the same way as before if they are to bind the land in the event of another sale.

Completion and registration will be done electronically. The same process will be carried out for the completion of sale and for registration. The main advantage at this stage will be the removal of the 'registration gap' between completion and the entry on the Register of the new owner, so minimising any risk of rights arising in that gap. The registration gap arises because at the time of sale of registered land the seller remains registered as owner of the property until the purchaser's name has been entered on the Register and it is often several weeks before the purchaser's name appears at the Registry. This will not happen with electronic conveyancing because the registration of the new owner will take place at the same time as completion.

4.7.2 The electronic document

Under s 91(3) of the 2002 Act, the documents must satisfy certain conditions:

1. The date and time of the transaction must be included in the document.
2. The electronic signatures of all the parties involved must be added to the document.
3. Each electronic signature must be certified.
4. Such other conditions as rules may provide must be met.

4.7.3 The effect of e-conveyancing

At the moment it is not clear which rights will be subject to the system of e-conveyancing. It is clear that not all rights will be subject to the system. However, there are several likely effects on the transfer and nature of rights of such a system:

1. It will no longer be relevant whether the transfer of the legal estate has been by deed.
2. It will also no longer be relevant whether the right is equitable or legal in nature.

4.7.4 Comment

It is anticipated that only those who are authorised to do so will be able to use the system of e-conveyancing, so some could argue that it will now be subject to state control.

There are some risks involved with digital signatures because they can be misused. The risks of fraud if interested parties gain access to the Register are great and although the system may become more certain, it will not be without potential problems.

> 'The secrecy of the signature key, and the nature of the assurance that it is accessible only to its owner, is critical to the usefulness of digital signatures. The verification procedure can say no more than that the text was signed with a specified signature key. It cannot say who made or authorised the running of the signature algorithm and the supply to it of the necessary inputs, namely the text to be signed and the signature key. The security of the signature key, and the trustworthiness of the computer on which the signature algorithm is run, are the basis for inferring from a successful signature verification that the apparent signatory is bound by what was signed.'
>
> S Mason and N Bohm, 'The Signature in Electronic Conveyancing: An Unresolved Issue?' [2003] 67 *Conv* 460

Mason and Bohm discuss the security of computers, citing a number of examples of how computers can be insecure, for example the user fails to log off and leaves the computer unattended; the user uses a password that is easy to guess. More sophisticated possibilities include installation of software which can record the user's keystrokes which would include a password and could be subsequently retrieved. They also point out that the possibilities are enhanced where the user's computer is connected to the Internet.

The main problem that could arise is a possible fraudulent sale by someone who has access to the electronic signature key, for example Jon purports to be the seller, Ken, and sells Ken's property to an innocent purchaser, Les. Will this sale be upheld by the Land Registry, since it has used a valid electronic signature? There is no means of deciphering whether the signature is forged where it is signed electronically.

The case of *Malory Enterprises Ltd v Cheshire Homes (UK) Ltd* [2002] Ch 216 suggests that where a conveyance is based on a forgery then this cannot be a disposition giving legal rights to the innocent purchaser. In this case the subsequent registration could be rectified by the Registrar since the true owner had sufficient standing to sue for trespass. Perhaps this reasoning will be applied to electronic signatures where they are used illegally.

The proposed system is not without its critics and many think that the provisions will bring with them a number of problems.

Provision for e-conveyancing was made in the Land Registration Act 2002 but despite consultation and a desire for this to proceed it has not been adopted within the ten-year period envisaged in 2002 indeed. In 2013 the Land Registry stated that it had abandoned plans to move to a fully on-line conveyancing service instead deciding to rely on a variety of on-line services instead. By contrast Scotland has embarked on a programme to adopt electronic conveyancing for transfers of land. The Electronic Documents (Scotland) Regulations 2014 allows certain legal documents that must be in writing to take an electronic form and to be legally valid. The legal documents affected by this change are listed in the Requirements of Writing (Scotland) Act 1995 and expressly excludes wills. England and Wales are now lagging behind other jurisdictions such as Australia, Canada and New Zealand in the move towards electronic conveyancing. There have been piecemeal attempts by the Law Society to introduce an electronic portal for some stages in conveyancing but this falls short of the plans envisaged under the Land Registration Act 2002.

SUMMARY

1. Formalities are used in the transfer of land because they provide written evidence of a transaction.

2. Formalities also put the parties on notice that the transaction will have legal effect and can clarify any terms for the parties.

3. There are some disadvantages of formalities because they can penalise parties in terms of cost.

4. The transfer of land involves four definite stages.

5. The parties are not bound until exchange of contracts, which is the second stage, so the purchaser may be open to gazumping.

6. A contract for the sale of land must comply with s 2 Law of Property (Miscellaneous Provisions) Act 1989.

7. Once contracts have been exchanged both parties are bound and will be liable for breach of contract if they do not proceed.

8. The formal transfer of title is made on completion by using a deed.

9. The final stage in transfer of property in both registered and unregistered land is the entering on the Register of the purchaser's name.

SAMPLE ESSAY QUESTION

The rules for the purchase and sale of land are unnecessarily complex. Discuss.

Discuss the general requirement for certainty in transactions involving land. The special nature of land.

Summarise the stages of a purchase of land:

i. pre-contract stage; no formalities necessary;

ii. exchange of contracts: must comply with s 1 LP (MP) Act 1989;

iii. completion: must use a deed under s 52 LPA 1925. The deed must comply with s 1 LP (MP) Act 1989;

iv. entry on the Register of the name of the purchaser, identify where there is unnecessary complexity at each stage of the transaction.

Consider exceptions to the formalities in exchange of contract, e.g. proprietary estoppel and discussion in *Cobbe v Yeomans Row*; constructive trusts in *Yaxley v Gott;* certain types of property such as short leases. Consider the decision in *Whittaker v Kinnear*. Discuss whether the exceptions undermine the principle that formalities lead to certainty in locating the title.

Discuss alternatives: purely oral transactions could lead to uncertainty and constant litigation.

Compare other types of transaction, e.g. the purchase of a car where formalities are at a lower level.

Discuss the advantages of electronic conveyancing.

Discuss the effect of s 91 LRA 2002.

List key advantages: may speed up the process as all documents at the Land Registry; will remove need for witnesses at completion.

List key disadvantages: potential lack of security; may slow process down because of need for security checks.

CONCLUSION

Further reading

Articles

Brymer, S, 'Secure Digital Signatures' [2014] *PLB* 3.

Capps, D, 'Conveyancing in the 21st Century: An Outline of Electronic Conveyancing and Electronic Signatures' [2002] *Conv* 443.

Dixon, M, 'What Sort of Land Registration System?' [2012] *Conv* 349.

Elkins, J and McGinley, K, 'How to Tackle Property Fraud' [2015] *PLJ* 330.

Griffiths, G L H, 'Part Performance: Still Trying to Replace the Irreplaceable?' [2002] *Conv* 216.

Hatfield, E, 'The e-Conveyancing Re-Revolution' [2015] (2) *Conv* 148.

Mackie, B and Higbee, J, 'The e-Conveyancing Jigsaw' [2006] 156 *NLJ* 222.

Mason, S and Bohm, N, 'The Signature in Electronic Conveyancing: An Unresolved Issue?' [2003] 67 *Conv* 460.

Moore, I, 'Proprietary Estoppel, Constructive Trusts and s 2 of the Law of Property (Miscellaneous Provisions) Act 1989' (2000) *MLR* 912.

Murali, M, 'Electric Dreams' [2010] *SJ* 19.

Newton, E and Dowden, M, 'The Perpetual Advance of Technology' [2006] 630 *EG* 97.

Owen, G and Rees, O, 'Section 2(5) of the Law of Property (Miscellaneous Provisions) Act 1989: A Misconceived Approach?' [2011] 6 *Conv* 495.

Perry, R, 'e-Conveyancing: Problems Ahead?' [2003] 67 *Conv* 215.

Rennie, R and Brymer, S, 'e-Missives: What Now?' [2014] *JLSS* 18.

Slessinger, E, 'Conveyancing: Preliminary Enquiries; Seller's Power's and Duties' [2004] 68 *Conv* 433.

Thornton, R, 'How to Lock Out a Gazumper' [1993] *CLJ* 392.

Wu, Tang Hang, 'An Unjust Enrichment Claim for the Mistaken Improver of Land' [2011] *Conv* 8.

Websites

Land registration: www.gov.uk/topic/land-registration.

Land Registry e-Conveyancing: www.landregistry.gov.uk/e-conveyancing.

5

Equitable rights in land

AIMS AND OBJECTIVES

After reading this chapter, you should be able to:

- Explain the nature of equitable rights in land
- Describe the different types of trust of land
- Explain when a resulting trust of land will arise
- Explain how the courts assess the shares in a resulting trust
- Describe a constructive trust and understand when it will be imposed by the courts
- Explain how the courts will quantify shares under a constructive trust

5.1 The nature of equitable rights in land

Equitable rights in land may arise in several different ways:

(a) Failure of formalities: the creation and transfer of legal rights in land is subject to certain formalities. If the formalities are not complied with, rights cannot be transferred in law. Common law has traditionally been very strict on this, but in some circumstances equity may step in and recognise these rights as equitable rights. Such rights may affect the legal owner's enjoyment of the property and also his right to transfer the property to a third party.

(b) Equitable rights arise under a trust imposed by law: in some situations the law may impose a trust because of the circumstances, in which case equitable interests and rights will be created, for example, where the courts believe that it would be unconscionable for the owner to deny the claimant rights in the land.

We have already considered the fact that wherever there are two or more owners of property the law will automatically impose a trust even where they both have a legal title.

The legal owner is said to own as **trustee** on behalf of another called a **beneficiary**.

5.1.1 The definition of a 'trust'

A trust allows ownership in property to be split between legal and equitable ownership:

- The **legal title** to property is held by one or more persons (the trustee(s)).
- The **equitable title** is owned by the beneficiary or beneficiaries.

The trustee holds the legal title on behalf of the beneficiaries who take the benefit of the trust. In land, where a trust is frequently implied because property is owned by more than one person, the trustees and beneficiaries are often the same people.

5.1.2 Types of trust

Trusts are split into two categories:

1. The **express trust**: based on the declared intentions of the parties. This is created by the settlor who wishes his property to be held under a trust.

2. The **implied trust**: generally based on the presumed intentions of the parties. The legal owner may not have consciously thought about his property being held under a trust but the law imposes a trust.

The Trusts of Land and Appointment of Trustees Act 1996 introduced the trust of land replacing a complex set of rules concerning trusts set in place in 1925. The trust of land is a statutory trust imposed whenever two or more people have an interest in one piece of land. (See Chapter 9, Trusts of land.)

5.2 The express trust

In an express trust the settlor **either** asks the trustees expressly to hold on trust for the beneficiaries on the terms named by the settlor, **or** the owner of the property declares himself to be trustee of the land on behalf of the beneficiary.

An express trust can also arise under a will. The main point is that a will takes effect on death, which distinguishes wills from *inter vivos* transfers.

Under the Wills Act 1837, no will shall be valid unless:

SECTION

's 9(a) it is in writing, and signed by the testator, or by some other person in his presence and by his direction; and

(b) it appears that the testator intended by his signature to give effect to the will; and

(c) the signature is made or acknowledged by the testator in the presence of two or more witnesses present at the same time; and

(d) each witness either –

(i) attests and signs the will; or

(ii) acknowledges his signature,

in the presence of the testator (but not necessarily in the presence of any other witness), but no form of attestation shall be necessary.'

Unless a will complies with this section, it shall not take effect and any provision under the will cannot take effect. This would include any trust created under the will.

The creation of an express trust in land *inter vivos* must comply with s 53(1)(b) of the Law of Property Act 1925 which requires evidence of the trust in writing. The trust will be unenforceable unless there is written evidence that complies with the statute. This does not mean that the trust will always be void. The effect of this is that the beneficiary can seek to enforce the trust, but if the action is defended by the legal owners and the claim is based on the fact that there is no written evidence this will make it unenforceable.

So if Flora tells her nephew, Donald, that she will hold her flat in London on trust for him, but does not put it into writing, even if she gives him the rent she receives from the property every year Donald cannot force her to transfer the equitable title of the flat to him.

There are exceptions to s 53(1)(b) LPA 1925:

1. Resulting, implied or constructive trusts are expressly excluded under s 53(2) of the 1925 Act. No written proof is necessary for these types of trust to come into existence.

2. The court makes an exception in cases of fraud. It was laid down in *Rochefoucauld v Boustead* [1897] 1 Ch 196 that where someone receives property knowing that they are to hold as a trustee then they cannot deny the existence of the trust:

JUDGMENT

'It is fraud on the part of a person to whom land is conveyed as a trustee, and who knows it was so conveyed, to deny the trust and claim the land for himself. Consequently, notwithstanding the statute, it is competent for a person claiming land conveyed to another to prove by parol evidence that it was so conveyed upon trust for the claimant, and that the grantee, knowing the facts, is denying the trust and relying upon the form of conveyance and the statute, in order to keep the land for himself.'

Lindley J

This means that although in law the property has been transferred to someone else, if he/she knows that the transfer is not a gift even if there is no writing to comply with (s 53(1)(b)), equity will say he/she does not enjoy it for him/herself but for the person named as beneficiary.

ACTIVITY

Applying the law

Tim transfers his house to his brother, Chris, telling him he is to hold as trustee for Tim's twin boys until they are 18. Tim should put this into writing but because Chris and the boys are members of the family, he may not think he should do so. In law, Chris owns the house for himself absolutely. Can the boys force Chris to convey the house to them when they reach 18?

The trustees of an express trust of land are under a duty both at common law and also under the Trustee Acts 1925 and 2000 to act in the best interests of the beneficiaries and according to the settlor's instructions. The beneficiaries have the right to compel the trustees to carry out the terms of the trust under the rule in *Rochefoucauld v Boustead*. If the court finds the trustee to be in breach of his duties then he must compensate the trust for any loss.

5.3 Implied trusts

Trusts can arise where the parties involved have not thought about creating a trust and have not taken any express steps to do so. The law imposes a trust because it is appropriate to do so.

As suggested earlier, where one person owns land but two or more persons own equitable interests in the land, a trust of land will arise. These rights will take effect in the form of an implied, a resulting or a constructive trust. It has traditionally been quite difficult to distinguish between these types of trust.

JUDGMENT

'A resulting, implied or constructive trust – and it is unnecessary for the present purposes to distinguish between these three classes of trust – is created by a transaction between the trustee and the **cestui que trust** in connection with the acquisition by the trustee of a legal estate in land, whenever the trustee has so conducted himself that it would be inequitable to allow him to deny to the *cestui que trust* a beneficial interest in the land acquired. And he will be held so to have conducted himself if by his words or conduct he has induced the *cestui que trust* to act to his own detriment in the reasonable belief that by so acting he was acquiring a beneficial interest in the land.'

Lord Diplock in *Gissing v Gissing* [1971] AC 886

> **cestui que trust**
> A beneficiary under a trust

Although Lord Diplock is here referring to three types of trust, we tend to refer to resulting and constructive trusts as implied trusts so under the law there are two types of trust: a resulting trust and a constructive trust. There has long been a debate amongst lawyers as to whether or not there is a difference between the two but current thinking suggests that there is a distinction.

5.4 Resulting trusts

5.4.1 The definition of a 'resulting trust'

A resulting trust gives effect to the presumed intentions of the parties. It arises where the parties have not declared any express intention to create a trust but the law will imply a trust because of particular circumstances. In land this is because there has been a contribution of money towards the purchase of the property. The law will hold that the owner of the land does not own absolutely for himself but owns on behalf of another or others. The ownership then is said to 'result' back to the person providing the money, rather than remaining with the person who owns the property at law.

JUDGMENT

'Under existing law a resulting trust arises in two sets of circumstances:

(A) where A makes a voluntary payment to B or pays (wholly or in part) for the purchase of property which is vested either in B alone or in joint names of A and B, there is a presumption that A did not intend to make a gift to B: the money or property is held on trust for A (if he is sole provider of the money) or in the case of joint purchase by A and B in shares proportionate to their contributions. It is important to stress that this is only a *presumption*, which presumption is easily rebutted either by the counter-presumption of advancement or by direct evidence of A's intention to make an outright transfer.

(B) Where A transfers property to B on express trusts, but the trusts declared do not exhaust the whole beneficial interest.... Both types of resulting trust are traditionally regarded as examples of trusts giving effect to the common intention of the parties.'

Lord Browne-Wilkinson in *Westdeutsche Landesbank Girozentrale v Islington BC* [1996] AC 669

The best example of a resulting trust in land law is where property is bought in the name of someone but the purchase money is provided by another.

For example: John buys Windy Ridge for £300,000. He asks Janet to come and live with him. Janet contributes £45,000 towards the purchase price but John is registered as sole owner. The law says that Janet would assume that she would get an interest in Windy Ridge. This is because the law does not think that people intend to make gifts to each other. John owns the property absolutely in law but he owns as resulting trustee of the equitable interest in Windy Ridge for himself and Janet.

If Janet had provided **all** the purchase money then John will hold as trustee for Janet absolutely.

There will also be a resulting trust where there has been a purchase in two names, for example in both Janet's and John's names but the money has been provided by one person, for example Janet.

5.4.2 Presumed intention
The resulting trust then depends upon the presumed intention of the transferor for its operation.

JUDGMENT

'A trust of a legal estate ... results to the man who advances the purchase money.'
Eyre CB in *Dyer v Dyer* (1788) 2 Cox Eq Cas 92

If both parties make contributions then the courts will presume a resulting trust for both. This is because it would be **unconscionable** for the legal owner to keep the property for himself absolutely. This is a presumed intention because, unlike an express trust, the parties do not have to expressly intend that a trust be created. It is also irrelevant whether or not they know that a trust has arisen. The law simply presumes that that would be the intention of anyone who advances money to another for the purchase of property. The key word here is 'unconscionable'.

ACTIVITY

Quick quiz
Consider the following situations and decide whether there is a resulting trust and, if so, for whom.

1. Alex purchases a flat in his name, with money provided by him and by Alice.
2. John purchases a farm in his name, with money provided solely by his Aunt Jamila.
3. Hanna purchases a cottage in the country in her name and that of her friend Polly. The purchase money is provided solely by Polly.

Where Alex owns the flat in his sole name but Alice has provided part of the purchase money then he will own on resulting trust for himself and Alice. Compare the purchase by John on behalf of Jamila. John will hold on resulting trust for Jamila. Unless other circumstances come to light she will own the entire beneficial interest. If Polly provides the purchase money then Hanna and Polly will hold as joint resulting trustees for Polly.

5.4.3 Rebuttal of the presumption of resulting trust

Gifts

The resulting trust is based on the presumed intentions of the parties and this presumption is **rebuttable**. Each of the parties is free to come to court with evidence to show that the transferor intended to make a gift or perhaps a loan.

In the example at section 5.4.1, John can come to court and say that Janet intended to make him an outright gift towards the purchase of Windy Ridge, and as a result there is no resulting trust in Janet's favour. Then the law says that the presumption of a resulting trust in Janet's favour is **rebutted**.

Loans

A resulting trust will not be inferred where there is proof that the money advanced was by way of a loan. In this case the money is not referable to acquiring as a purchaser and so the lender cannot argue that they can take an interest in the property. The loan is personal to the borrower. It will be enforceable in contract and under common law rules but the lender does not get an equitable interest in the property.

CASE EXAMPLE

Re Sharpe (a bankrupt) [1980] 1 WLR 219

The purchaser's aunt had contributed towards the purchase of a house. The purchaser was declared bankrupt and the aunt tried to argue that her nephew held the property on resulting trust for her. This would give her rights in the property which would be satisfied in full ahead of the other creditors. The court held that she had made him a loan and the property therefore was not held on resulting trust for her. Although the court did not find evidence of a resulting trust, the aunt was given the right to remain in the property under a constructive trust which is the alternative type of implied trust discussed below.

Presumption of advancement

The presumption of advancement can also rebut the presumption of a resulting trust. It has traditionally arisen in certain relationships, usually where the donor has an obligation to provide for the donee, for example father and child; husband and wife. It also arose where someone acts in *loco parentis*. This means that someone, either a woman or a man has taken on the responsibility of maintaining another. It has never arisen between mother and child or between wife and husband.

There has been considerable criticism in relation to the presumption of advancement particularly where it arises between husband and wife. The presumption of advancement was abolished by s 199 of the Equality Act 2010 but this section has not yet been brought into force and it is possible that it will never be brought into force. So where a transfer is made from husband to wife and father to child the law still applies a presumption of an outright gift but once this section is in force no such presumption will apply. There is some doubt today whether this section will ever be brought into force. Note also that all transfers made before the section has been brought into force will still have the presumption applied to them.

Although the presumption has remained for so long in spite of increasing criticism, it has played a limited role in deciding the beneficial entitlement to property. Even if it was acted on there could be a potential challenge under the European Convention on Human Rights based on Article 1 Protocol 1 and also Article 14.

CASE EXAMPLE

Sekhon v Alissa [1989] 2 FLR 94

A mother transferred the whole of her savings to her daughter so the daughter could purchase some property. There could be no presumption of advancement because it was a transfer from mother to daughter. The transfer was carried out in order to gain a tax advantage and the savings were held under a resulting trust for the mother.

In a case like this, where the presumption of advancement does not apply, it does not prevent the presumption of resulting trust from being rebutted by evidence of a gift.

Imagine Caroline is 18 years old. After her 'gap year' she goes to university in Cardiff. Her father Danny buys her a flat and it is registered in Caroline's name.

Who owns the flat?

Applying the resulting trust principles, the flat would be held for Danny by Caroline because one person provided all the purchase money but the property was registered in the name of another.

But as this was a purchase by a father for his daughter, there is a **presumption of advancement** and this rebuts the presumption of resulting trust. An important detail is that Caroline is already 18, if she were under 18 the property must be held under a trust, as children cannot hold property in their own name until the age of 18.

The position would be different if Caroline's mother Margaret purchased the flat, as there is no presumption of advancement between mother and child.

This presumption can itself be rebutted. In the example above, if Danny wanted to retain an interest in the flat then he could rebut the presumption of advancement by showing that he did not intend to make an outright gift of the flat. Consider the case below where there was clear evidence that the father never intended his daughter to benefit from the presumption of advancement.

CASE EXAMPLE

Warren v Gurney [1944] 2 All ER 472

A father purchased a house and put it into his daughter's name. The presumption of advancement was rebutted because it was clear that he did not intend to make a gift to his daughter but always intended to loan the money to her. The father retained the title deeds until his death so the daughter held the house on resulting trust for her father.

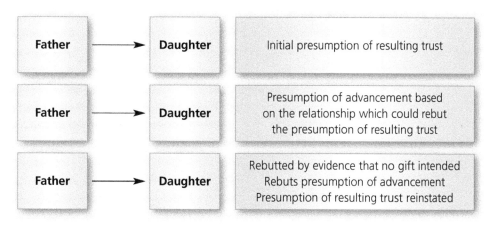

Figure 5.1 The transfer in *Warren v Gurney*

5.4.4 Improper motive in transfer of property

In some cases there may be an improper or illegal motive for the transfer of the property, for example, to defeat creditors, in which case the court will look carefully at the motive of the party making the transfer.

CASE EXAMPLE

Gascoigne v Gascoigne [1918] 1 KB 223

A husband put the title to a house into the name of his wife. It was done purely to avoid creditors from taking his house. It was held that he could not give evidence in court that the house belonged to him because he would be using his own dishonesty to support his own claim.

CASE EXAMPLE

Tinker v Tinker [1970] P 136

A husband purchased a house in the name of his wife. This was done solely as a precaution against the property being taken by the man's creditors.

'I am quite clear that the husband cannot have it both ways. So he is on the horns of a dilemma. He cannot say that the house is his own and, at one and the same time, say that it is his wife's. As against his wife, he wants to say that it belongs to him. As against the creditors, that it belongs to her. That simply will not do. Either it was conveyed to her for her own use absolutely: or it was conveyed to her as trustee for her husband. It must be one or the other. The presumption is that it was conveyed to her for her own use: and he does not rebut that presumption by saying that he only did it to defeat his creditors. I think that it belongs to her.'

Lord Denning

By way of contrast, in cases where there has been an illegal motive but it has not been acted on or it is not material to the claim as in the case below, the law will allow the ordinary presumptions to apply.

CASE EXAMPLE

Tinsley v Milligan [1994] 1 AC 340

Miss Milligan and her lover, Miss Tinsley, bought a house together, both providing purchase money. It was put into Miss Tinsley's name, for the sole reason that Miss Milligan wanted to claim social security benefits which would be denied to her if she owned an interest in the property. Miss Tinsley claimed that the property was held by her absolutely because of the illegal motive of Miss Milligan, arguing that the illegal motive tainted the entire claim. The House of Lords did not accept this and held that the property was held on resulting trust for Miss Milligan. The illegal motive was irrelevant and was not relied on by Miss Milligan in support of her claim that a resulting trust had arisen.

CASE EXAMPLE

Tribe v Tribe [1996] Ch 107

The above principle was supported in this case, where a father had transferred his house into his son's name on the basis that it would defeat his creditors. However the creditors did not lose any money as he had sufficient funds to pay them all. The son refused to return the property, relying on the presumption of advancement. The court upheld the father's claim as he was not relying on an illegal motive that had been carried out but merely on a reason to rebut the presumption of advancement. If the creditors had been wrongly deprived of their money then the father would not have been able to reclaim his property from his son.

The case of *O'Kelly v Davies* [2014] EWCA Civ 1606 revisited the effect of illegality on implied trusts, in this case a constructive trust which is discussed later in the chapter. A couple had been together for over 20 years. They purchased two properties; one of which was in joint names and later transferred into Ms O'Kelly's sole name. The purpose of this was to enable the woman to make fraudulent claims for social security benefits as a single woman living alone. When the relationship broke down Mr Davies claimed a share in the property. Ms O'Kelly argued that his claim should not succeed because it would be based on a fraudulent intent. The court held that on the facts it was not necessary for the man to advance his unlawful agreement in order to make good his claim.

The reason for the purchase in the woman's sole name had been unlawful but the acquisition of a beneficial interest had not arisen from the illegal purpose but from the parties' common intention inferred from their continuing course of dealing, that the man should have an interest.

The intervention of public policy was avoided. Although 'the benefits obtained fraudulently represented part of the family income', Mr Davies had paid the mortgage from his legitimate earnings.

Miss O'Kelly took her case to the Court of Appeal and in dismissing her appeal, Lord Justice Pitchford said it had been their 'common intention' that he should have half of the property.

He concluded: 'Their common intention was to be inferred from his consistent financial contributions to the purchase of the properties, and the parties' conduct in remaining a cohabiting family when work commitments permitted, and not from the unlawful agreement.'

So Miss O'Kelly held the property on trust for Mr Davies. The issue of the effects of illegality was further raised in *Patel v Mirza* [2016] UKSC 42. Although not about the family home, the decision affects those cases where there is an illegal motive and would therefore include those cases where the family home had been registered in the name of one party for an illegal purpose. The Supreme Court held that a claimant who satisfied the ordinary requirements of a claim for unjust enrichment should not be debarred from enforcing his claim simply because he was seeking to recover money paid pursuant to a contract to carry out an illegal activity. In a dissenting judgment Lord Sumption argued that the *Tinsley* approach should be retained so that a claimant should be prevented from bringing evidence of illegal activity. The Supreme Court decision is broadly in line with the recommendations of the Law Commission which were that a beneficiary under a trust should be able to retain his/her interest and enforce a trust despite the illegality other than in exceptional circumstance.

Gifts	Based on evidence that a gift was intended.	
Loans	No resulting trust where it is proved that a loan was made as a loan and was not referable to rights in the property.	*Re Sharpe (a bankrupt)* (1980)
Advancement to members of one's family, either father to child or husband to wife	Outright gift presumed on basis of presumption of advancement until s 199 Equality Act 2010 has been brought into force.	*Warren v Gurney* (1944) (rebutted) *Sekhon v Alissa* (1989) (no presumption of advancement)
Improper motive for transfer of property	Will not rebut presumption of resulting trust unless improper motive was not carried out.	*Tinker v Tinker* (1970) *Tribe v Tribe* (1996) *Gascoigne v Gascoigne* (1918) *Tinsley v Milligan* (1994) *O'Kelly v Davies* (2014) (constructive trust)

Table 5.1 Rebuttal of presumption of resulting trust

KEY FACTS

Presumptions of resulting trusts and advancement
1. A resulting trust will be presumed where property is transferred into the name of one person but all or part of the purchase money has been provided by another.
2. The presumption of a resulting trust can be rebutted by the presumption of advancement. This arises in certain relationships, for example father and child, husband and wife but not mother and child.
3. Both presumptions can be rebutted by evidence of a gift or a loan.
4. An illegal motive cannot normally be relied on to rebut either presumption.
5. Where it can be shown that the illegal purpose has not been carried into effect, the illegal purpose can be used as evidence in court to support or rebut a presumption.

5.4.5 The effect of s 60(3) of the Law of Property Act 1925

The operation of a resulting trust rests on the fact that the legal title to land is held in the name of A but the capital is provided by B or by A and B together. If property is simply transferred voluntarily from B to A, a gift is assumed and A will be able to claim absolute ownership without the inference of a resulting trust although the property was originally owned by B.

SECTION

's 60(3) LPA 1925 In a voluntary conveyance a resulting trust for the grantor shall not be implied merely by reason that the property is not expressed to be conveyed for the use or benefit of the grantee.'

This does not mean that you could never have a resulting trust where land is subject to a voluntary transfer. It depends on whether there is evidence that the transferee was to hold on resulting trust for the transferor.

CASE EXAMPLE

Hodgson v Marks [1971] Ch 892

The claimant transferred property into the name of her lodger in circumstances where it was clearly not intended that the lodger should be the beneficial owner. The court looked at the effect of s 60(3) of the 1925 Act and concluded that it was 'a debatable question' whether a resulting trust arose on a voluntary transfer by A to stranger B. This was revisited in the later case of *Lohia v Lohia* [2001] WTLR 101.

CASE EXAMPLE

Lohia v Lohia [2001] WTLR 101

The Court of Appeal considered whether the presumption of resulting trust applies on a voluntary transfer of land and concluded that s 60(3) abolished the presumption of a resulting trust and there would have to be evidence that the transferor intended to retain an interest in order for a resulting trust to apply on a voluntary conveyance of property.

However, this subsection remains confusing as normally when there is a change in the law it is expressly referred to as a change to existing rules but the wording of s 60(3) does not expressly refer to such a change.

ACTIVITY

Applying the law

Noah has just won a large sum of money on the lottery and he decides to benefit his father Joshua. Noah transfers one of his two houses to his father. There is no consideration and nothing is discussed at the time. According to s 60(3) LPA 1925 as interpreted by *Hodgson v Marks* (1971) Noah will continue to have an interest in the property. If the views of the Court of Appeal in *Lohia v Lohia* (2001) are applied then Joshua will be able to claim the property belongs to him absolutely and Noah no longer has an interest because nothing was discussed between the parties at the time of the transfer.

5.4.6 Types of contributions that give rise to a resulting trust

A resulting trust will arise on the basis of different types of contributions towards the purchase of property. The key feature of them all is whether they are referable to the purchase of the property.

Direct contributions to the purchase price

If Gillian gives her boyfriend, Jack, a cheque for £60,000 towards the purchase of a flat costing £180,000 which is put into Jack's name, then Gillian will be presumed to have a share in the property. Her contribution was one-third of the purchase price, so she can claim a one-third share in the property. It is irrelevant that there is no written evidence of the transaction as it is an implied trust (s 53(2) of the Law of Property Act 1925).

According to *Burns v Burns* [1984] Ch 317, a direct cash payment is sufficiently referable to the acquisition of title to generate a trust and the contributor will be presumed to have intended that he should acquire a beneficial share in the property. However in *Burns v Burns* although Mrs Burns contributed to household expenses she did not make a direct cash payment towards the purchase of the property owned by her partner Mr Burns so no resulting trust arose.

Contribution to the deposit or legal expenses

If Gillian gives her boyfriend a cheque for £3,000 towards the deposit, or even the legal expenses arising on, the purchase of a flat put into Jack's name, there is a presumption that the property is held on resulting trust for Gillian.

CASE EXAMPLE

Midland Bank v Cooke [1995] 4 All ER 562

Property was purchased by a husband and wife with the intention that it should become the family home. It was partly financed by a cheque for £1,100 given to the parties as a wedding gift from the husband's parents. This was used towards the deposit on a house and gave the wife a share in the property. Her share by way of resulting trust should have amounted to the same fraction as her contribution to the purchase price (approximately 6.74 per cent). The courts found that she was entitled to more, by imposing a constructive trust on the proceeds of sale.

Contribution to mortgage repayments

There has been considerable debate as to whether mortgage repayments will constitute a contribution to the purchase price.

In *Gissing v Gissing* (1971), Lord Diplock related the payment of the mortgage instalments to the acquisition of the property in this way:

JUDGMENT

'The economic reality which lies behind the conveyance of the fee simple to a purchaser in return for a purchase price the greater part of which is advanced to the purchaser upon a mortgage repayable by instalments over a number of years, is that the new freeholder is purchasing the matrimonial home upon credit and that the purchase price is represented by instalments by which the mortgage is repaid in addition to the initial payment in cash. The conduct of the spouses in relation to the payment of the mortgage instalments may be no less relevant to their common intention as to the beneficial interests in a matrimonial home acquired in this way than their conduct in relation to the payment of the cash deposit.'

In *Curley v Parks* [2004] EWCA Civ 1515 the claimant Mr Curley was denied a share in the property under a resulting trust based on mortgage repayments because the contributions were deemed to be made after the acquisition of the property. This view has been criticised strongly by academics as taking a very narrow view of the status of mortgage repayments in claims for rights under a resulting trust.

'It takes only a little imagination to regard the mortgagee as the agent of the purchasers, paying at the time of the purchase, with the mortgagee being repaid as agent with interest by the contributors. Indeed cases before *Curley* have rather assumed that payment of mortgage instalments would suffice.'

M Dixon, *Modern Land Law* (11th edn, Routledge, 2018), p. 173

The law takes a different view of contributions towards mortgage instalments where the property purchased is an investment property. Mortgage instalments were held by the Court of Appeal to be contributions towards the purchase price in *Laskar v Laskar* [2008] EWCA Civ 347. Here a mother and daughter purchased property together but did not intend to live in the property as a family home. The Court of Appeal regarded contributions towards the mortgage to be contributions towards the purchase price.

The rejection of mortgage repayments as contributions under a resulting trust in *Curley v Parkes* appears to have been rejected in *Wodzicki v Wodzicki* [2017] EWCA Civ 95 where a range of contributions including those towards a mortgage were accepted as sufficient to base a claim under a resulting trust.

Household expenses

There have been attempts in several cases to argue that contributions to the general household expenses can give rise to a resulting trust. A particularly forceful argument is that these contributions will release funds from the other party to pay the mortgage. However, unless there is an express agreement that this arrangement will give rise to rights in the property, the courts have refused to recognise these contributions. The problem is that they cannot automatically be linked to the acquisition of the property.

> 'It is widely recognised nowadays that the mere sharing of family living expenses is not intrinsically referable to the acquisition of family property. Accordingly economic contributions of this kind are best regarded, not as generating some strained form of resulting trust, but rather as evidence of a relevant detriment or "change of position" for the purpose of founding a constructive trust. In this way the resulting trust is confined more narrowly to money payments which serve directly to finance the purchase of a legal estate.'
>
> K Gray and S F Gray, *Elements of Land Law* (5th edn, Oxford University Press, 2009), p. 848

CASE EXAMPLE

Burns v Burns [1984] Ch 317

The parties had been together for nearly 19 years and had two children. They never married. The woman stayed at home for much of the relationship, caring for the children. The property was registered in the name of the man. When the relationship broke down, the woman claimed a share of the property, based on her indirect contributions towards living expenses. Matrimonial law did not apply because the parties were never married. It was decided on property law principles and under the law the courts were not entitled to take domestic duties and contributions to household expenses into account when assessing shares in the property.

It can seem unfair to a party to a relationship that contributions in kind or the provision of domestic services do not lead to rights in property, especially in circumstances such as *Burns v Burns* (1984) where they take place over a long period of time. Such contributions may influence financial decisions in divorce proceedings but if the parties in a relationship cohabit and the relationship breaks down they cannot be used in support of a claim based on a resulting trust.

The right to buy under the Housing Act 1985

A tenant's right to buy under the Housing Act 1985 can represent a contribution to the purchase of property and so give rights under a resulting trust even where no cash contributions have been made.

It is difficult to quantify the contribution but it is best seen in terms of the actual reduction in the purchase price. If there were two joint occupiers then they may both have a right to buy the property and the courts have to decide how to quantify the shares in the property. This could be apportioned between the parties. It may depend on the length of time each party has lived in the property.

If there is a separate agreement as to how much each person is to receive, that will govern the apportionment. In *Savill v Goodall* [1993] 1 FLR 755 it was held that as the parties had agreed that they should share the beneficial interest equally, that agreement would govern the actual apportionment.

CASE EXAMPLE

Springette v Defoe [1992] 2 FLR 388

It was held by the Court of Appeal that a discount of 41 per cent of the market value of a council flat constituted a contribution to the purchase price. It was available because the claimant had been a tenant for 11 years.

Direct contributions to purchase price	*Burns v Burns* (1984) no resulting trust as no direct contributions found
Contributions to the deposit or legal expenses	*Midland Bank v Cooke* (1995)
Contributions to mortgage repayments	*Gissing v Gissing* (1971) mortgage repayments can give rise to a resulting trust but no resulting trust found *Curley v Parkes* (2004) mortgage repayments cannot give rise to a resulting trust *Laskar v Laskar* (2008) mortgage repayments allowed where property acquired for investment purposes *Wodzicki v Wodzicki* (2017) mortgage payments allowed where property acquired for a family home
Household expenses	*Burns v Burns* (1984) no resulting trust
Right to buy under Housing Act 1985	*Savill v Goodall* (1993) *Springette v Defoe* (1992)
Property purchased for investment purposes	*Laskar v Laskar* (2008) a resulting trust will normally be imposed where property is purchased not for residential purposes but as an investment. But see the decision in *Marr v Collie* discussed later in the chapter

Table 5.2 Types of contributions that may give rise to a resulting trust

5.4.7 Assessing the shares of the parties in a resulting trust

Where the property is held on resulting trust it is assumed that the shares will be proportionate to the contribution that has been made. These are said to crystallise at the date of acquisition. Generally the size of the share under a resulting trust will follow the size of contribution made. If at the date of acquisition of the property A pays one-third of the purchase price, B will hold one-third of the value of the property on resulting trust for A.

ACTIVITY

Applying the law

Robert and Penny decide to buy a new house together. It is registered in Robert's name but Penny makes a contribution of £50,000 from her savings. The house is purchased for £500,000.

If the house is sold in five years' time can Penny claim a share in the property and if so how much can she claim?

This approach, based on contributions may be rebutted where there is evidence that the parties intended to share in a different way. Perhaps they always shared their joint assets.

> 'In *Midland Bank v Cooke* [1995] 4 All ER 562 the Court of Appeal has examined whether, in the absence of any actual "agreement" as to the extent of the beneficial interest, the resulting interest must be proportional to the contribution to the purchase of the property by the non-legal title holder. In giving sole judgment of the court, Waite L.J. held that once Jane Cooke had shown some direct contribution it was open to the court to calculate the extent of her beneficial interest otherwise than in proportion to that direct initial contribution. In such a case the court must scrutinise the whole course of dealings between the parties.... The preponderance of previous English authority had indicated that the resulting trust is proportional to the cash sum contributed, as any other way would require the court to give an opinion as to what the property interest should be in all the circumstances rather than to make a finding on the evidence as to what it was. This limitation is one factor which has caused a shift in argument to the more flexible constructive trust, which permits the ultimate interest to differ from the money value contributed.'
>
> P O'Hagan, 'Quantifying Interests under Resulting Trusts'
> (1997) 60 *MLR* 3

What we learn from this analysis of *Midland v Cooke* (1995) is that where there is an initial contribution to the purchase price by the claimant, however small, a resulting trust is presumed but today in all cases of trusts of the family home the court leans in favour of a constructive trust which is decided on different principles.

KEY FACTS

Finding a resulting trust
1. Where direct contributions in money are made towards the purchase of property then this will raise the presumption of a resulting trust.
2. A contribution to the deposit will also raise the presumption of a resulting trust.
3. A contribution to mortgage instalments or even the release of money from the payment of household expenses for one party, in order that they may pay the mortgage repayments, may raise the inference of a resulting trust but it is not definitive.
4. The payment of household expenses and contributions in kind cannot raise the inference of a resulting trust.
5. The right to buy under the Housing Act 1985 is seen as a direct contribution towards payment towards the purchase of property and can also infer a resulting trust.

5.4.8 Resulting trusts: the modern position

In recent years the resulting trust has been shown to be inadequate as a way of dealing with property interests. One of the problems is that it focuses on the original purchase and the presumed intentions at the time. It therefore limits the situations in which a third party can acquire rights in the property. In cases such as *Oxley v Hiscock* [2005] Fam 211, where a resulting trust approach would have seemed appropriate, the court preferred the constructive trust as a way of resolving disputes over ownership of the shared property. The resulting trust was also categorically rejected in *Stack v Dowden* [2007] 2 AC 432 by a majority of the House of Lords where again the resulting trust was seen as inappropriate to resolve difficulties over shares in the family home. This case is discussed in detail later in the chapter but the judgment contains some important comments on the role of the resulting trust in the acquisition of property which are outlined here.

Ms Dowden and Mr Stack were an unmarried couple who purchased property together in joint names with Ms Dowden contributing 65 per cent towards the purchase. When registering the title they did not indicate whether they intended to own the property as joint tenants or tenants in common. After the relationship broke down Mr Stack claimed a 50 per cent share in the property. Ms Dowden argued that she should get a share equivalent to her contribution. The House of Lords rejected the presumption of a resulting trust but nevertheless decided that Ms Dowden should receive a larger share.

JUDGMENT

'The presumption of a resulting trust is not a rule of law. According to Lord Diplock in *Pettitt v Pettitt* [1970] AC 777 the equitable presumptions of intention are "no more than a consensus of judicial opinion disclosed by reported cases as to the most likely inference of fact to be drawn in the absence of any evidence to the contrary". Equity, being concerned with commercial realities, presumed against gifts and other windfalls (such as survivorship).... These days, the importance to be attached to who paid for what in a domestic context may be very different from its importance in other contexts or long ago. There is no need for me to rehearse all the developments in the case law since *Pettitt v Pettitt* and *Gissing v Gissing*. The law has indeed moved on in response to changing social and economic conditions. The search is to ascertain the parties' shared intentions, actual, inferred or imputed, with respect to the property in the light of their whole course of conduct in relation to it.'

Baroness Hale

By way of contrast Lord Neuberger in a dissenting judgment supported the use of resulting trusts in all cases including cases concerning the family home.

JUDGMENT

'Where the only additional relevant evidence to the fact that the property has been acquired in joint names is the extent of each party's contribution to the purchase price, the beneficial ownership at the time of acquisition will be held, in my view, in the same proportions as the contributions to the purchase price. That is the resulting trust solution. The only realistic alternative in such a case would be to adhere to the joint ownership solution. There is an argument to support the view that equal shares should still be the rule in cohabitation cases, on the basis that it may be what many parties may expect if they purchase a home in joint names, even with different contributions. However, I consider that the resulting trust solution is correct in such circumstances.'

He continued by arguing that the resulting trust is useful even in cases where title is not held jointly because of the clarity that the resulting trust solution brings to the quantification of the shares.

Consider the following case where the court was prepared to impose a resulting trust suggesting that it remains appropriate in cases where property is purchased by two members of a family purely as a business venture.

CASE EXAMPLE

Laskar v Laskar [2008] EWCA Civ 347

A mother and daughter purchased property which had become available to the mother under the 'right to buy' provisions. The daughter had provided some of the funds and had also been party to the mortgage application. The property was let to a tenant with the mother taking responsibility for this. The relationship between the mother and daughter broke down and the daughter instituted proceedings claiming a half-share of the property. The court held that where property had been purchased as a joint investment it would not be appropriate to apply the presumption of joint ownership. This was nothing more than a business venture. This was a resulting trust and each party was entitled to the value of her own contribution.

The rejection by the court in *Stack v Dowden* of the use of a resulting trust in the acquisition of an interest and quantification of shares in a family home was followed in *Jones v Kernott* [2009] EWHC 1713 (Ch). One can conclude that a resulting trust is now only relevant where property is purchased for an investment as in *Laskar v Laskar* and is no longer relevant in cases concerning the family home. However there continue to be cases concerning the family home where the courts have applied the resulting trust showing that it may still have a role in the acquisition and quantification of shares in the family home. In *Wodzicki v Wodzicki* [2017] EWCA Civ 95 the court returned to the resulting trust to resolve issues of rights in a property registered in the name of the deceased widow but claimed by the daughter of the deceased. The daughter lived in the property as her family home. The court held that the daughter had an interest assessed in proportion to her contributions.

The most significant of these recent cases is *Marr v Collie* [2017] UKPC 17, a Privy Council case on appeal from the Bahamas. The case concerned the breakdown in a same-sex relationship and the apportionment of the family assets. Over a period of 17 years the parties had acquired a large number of investment properties as well as a family home. All but one of the properties had been bought in the joint names of the parties although the purchase monies had been provided by one party, Mr Marr. He argued that having provided the purchase monies the properties were held on resulting trust for him absolutely. If *Laskar v Laskar* had been followed then Mr Collie would undoubtedly have lost his claim because apart from the family home the couple had purchased investment properties but the Privy Council chose to take a different approach because they viewed the properties as assets of the relationship. The court held that even in cases where property has been purchased as an investment the intentions of the parties remain relevant and it is the duty of the court to decide what the parties had intended at the time of purchase. This approach introduces the issue of intention into the purchase of any property as an investment where the parties are in a relationship. It is therefore no longer possible to always rely on the resulting trust where the property purchased was for commercial or investment purposes but to take as a first step the intentions of the parties. This may not be as wide reaching as it appears since the Privy Council held that it was unlikely that this approach would affect a case like *Laskar* as the property purchased was never intended to be anything other than an investment but nevertheless it introduces an extra layer of uncertainty into an area of property law which is already subject to criticism by the Judiciary, lawyers and academics for its lack of clarity.

> '... the decision in *Marr v Collie* is to be regretted because it takes the law one step back; commercial partners now find themselves tied up in litigation over what they had intended or not intended because one party is encouraged to chance their arm, in the hope they could take a higher proportion of the equity under the Stack framework and cohabiting couples could equally be faced with a submission that the presumption of joint beneficial ownership should not be used at all.'
>
> M George and B Sloan, 'Presuming too Little About Resulting and Constructive Trusts?' (2017) *Conv* 4, p. 303

5.5 Constructive trusts

5.5.1 The definition of a 'constructive trust'

It is difficult to define a constructive trust clearly, because it can arise in such a large number of diverse situations:

JUDGMENT

'English Law provides no clear and all-embracing definition of a constructive trust. Its boundaries have been left perhaps deliberately vague, so as not to restrict the court by technicalities in deciding what the justice of a particular case may demand.'

Carl Zeiss-Stiftung v Herbert Smith & Co (No. 2) [1969] 2 Ch 276

Constructive trusts arise by operation of law

A constructive trust arises in circumstances outlined by Lord Millett in *Paragon Finance plc v D B Thakerar & Co* [1999] 1 All ER 400 where it would be 'unconscionable for the owner of property (usually but not necessarily the legal estate) to assert his own beneficial interest in the property and deny the beneficial interest of another'.

Such trusts are imposed because it would be **unconscionable** for the owner at law to claim the legal estate wholly or in part for himself. They arise in many situations both in land law and also the law of trusts.

An example of where the court would impose a constructive trust is if an express trustee takes part of the trust property for himself then the trustee will hold the property and any profit he makes from it as constructive trustee.

If Anthony buys a house property, and Kate his girlfriend says she has no money to put towards the purchase but instead she will renovate the property, a trust will only arise if Anthony agrees that they will share the property between them. If the owner, Anthony, tries to deny any rights in the property to Kate, then the courts will impose a constructive trust and Anthony will hold the property on trust for Kate.

Constructive trusts are similar to resulting trusts but there are significant differences.

The similarities

1. They are both informal in nature.
2. Neither requires written evidence (s 53(2) of the Law of Property Act 1925).
3. They both rely on intention, although the role of intention in constructive trusts of land is more significant. The court must be satisfied that it was intended that the

non-legal owner would acquire an equitable interest in the property or it must be inferred from his conduct, before the court can impose a constructive trust. Note that since *Jones v Kernott* the court is now also able to impute intention from the circumstances of the purchase. In a resulting trust the intention is presumed and need not be express. The intention that the non-legal owner is to own a share can always be rebutted by evidence, for example that it was a gift.

The differences

1. Constructive trusts of land rely on a bargain between the parties normally based on express or implied intention, whereas the resulting trust historically relies on contributions of the parties. This key difference may now be less significant since the Privy Council decision in *Marr v Collie*.

2. The shares awarded under a constructive trust do not depend on the exact contributions of the parties, whereas in a resulting trust the shares are usually the equivalent of the amount contributed to the initial purchase.

> 'Whilst resulting trusts focus on **contributions** towards the purchase of realty, constructive trusts are more heavily concerned with **bargains** relating to beneficial ownership. Consistently with its disfavour of informal mechanisms of rights creation, English law generally denies effect to mere oral gifts, agreements or transactions relating to land. But once the repudiation of an informally promised beneficial entitlement crosses the threshold of unconscionable behaviour, equity is ultimately prepared to impose a special form of trust liability on the errant estate owner, thereby safeguarding the bargained interest notwithstanding its informality of origin.'
>
> K Gray and S F Gray, *Elements of Land Law* (5th edn, Oxford University Press, 2009), p. 863

A useful starting point for the law on constructive trusts is the decision of the House of Lords in *Gissing v Gissing* (1971), which concerned a claim by a former wife to a proprietary interest in the house owned by her husband and subject to a mortgage. The wife claimed that she had contributed substantially, though indirectly, to the payment by her husband of the original deposit and the subsequent instalments payable under the mortgage. The husband had paid for the house and had paid for all the mortgage payments. The wife had made indirect payments; she had purchased clothes for herself and their child; she had contributed towards the housekeeping; and had spent money on the garden and buying furniture.

Lord Diplock considered all these contributions and found that they were not referable to the house and held that the husband was absolutely entitled to the house and that the wife had no interest in it by way of trust. It was also significant that the House of Lords could find no conduct from which it could be inferred that the parties had a common intention that the wife was to be entitled to a share of the house.

JUDGMENT

'The picture presented by the evidence is one of husband and wife retaining their separate proprietary interests in the property whether real or personal purchased with their separate savings and is inconsistent with any common intention at the time of the purchase of the matrimonial home that the wife, who neither then nor thereafter contributed anything to its purchase price or assumed any liability for it, should nevertheless be entitled to a beneficial interest in it.'

Lord Diplock

5.5.2 Types of constructive trust

In *Gissing v Gissing* Lord Diplock held that a constructive trust of land was based on a 'common intention' between the parties that the claimant should have some interest in the land. It may arise when two people jointly purchase property or it may arise when property is purchased and the purchaser agrees to give effect to rights of a third party; alternatively it may arise after the acquisition of property although this has until recently been more controversial. The acquisition of rights are usually dependent on financial contributions but unlike resulting trusts where the parties agree that the claimant should have rights then non-capital contributions shall suffice.

However the courts are reluctant to uphold rights where non-capital contributions are made unless there is very clear evidence of an agreement and also some detriment suffered by the party who attempts to enforce it.

In *Bernard v Josephs* [1982] Ch 391 Griffiths LJ held that the mere fact that one party 'has spent time and money on improving the property' would not normally be sufficient ground to justify an inference of a constructive trust.

It is possible for rights to be acquired by a third party if the sale is made expressly subject to those rights.

CASE EXAMPLE

Lyus v Prowsa Developments Ltd [1982] 1 WLR 1044

A plot of land was owned by a company which subsequently went into liquidation. The claimants entered into a contract with the company to buy a plot of the land as well as a house to be built on it. The defendants purchased the entire plot including the claimant's estate and later sold it on to the second defendants. They were held to buy subject to the claimant's interest as they bought expressly subject to the claimant's rights.

It is important to note that the court will not impose a constructive trust unless it is satisfied that the conscience of the estate owner is affected. If land is simply expressed to be conveyed 'subject to contract' it does not necessarily mean that the purchaser will be bound. It is important that in *Lyus v Prowsa Developments* (1982) the purchaser bought the land expressly subject to an option to purchase the land at a later date.

CASE EXAMPLE

Hussey v Palmer [1972] 1 WLR 1286

A widow went to live with her daughter and son-in-law in a house owned by the son-in-law. She paid for an extension to the house, so that she could live with the family. They later argued and the relationship broke down and the widow left. She successfully claimed a share in the property.

JUDGMENT

'The trust may arise at the outset when the property is acquired or later on, as the circumstances, may require. It is an equitable remedy by which the court can enable an aggrieved party to obtain restitution.'

Lord Denning

This is a controversial approach and has been disapproved of in later cases where the courts have relied on the common intention of the parties before imposing a constructive trust of a family home.

Where a constructive trust is claimed it does not matter that the formalities usually associated with a trust of land are not complied with because implied trusts are excluded from s 53(1)(b) Law of Property Act 1925 which requires trusts of land to comply with certain formalities.

5.5.3 Elements in a constructive trust

The law on constructive trusts has been traditionally based on Lord Bridge's judgment in *Lloyds Bank v Rosset* (1991) although this has been challenged in recent cases it still remains the starting point in any analysis of cases on constructive trusts. Lord Bridge held a constructive trust depends on proof of **three** elements:

1. the common intention or a bargain between the parties;

2. a change of position by the claimant or the fact that he can show that he relied on the bargain and suffered to his detriment;

3. the fact that the legal owner has denied the rights of the claimant.

1. *The common intention*

A constructive trust of land depends on proof that both parties were to have an interest in the land.

> 'The role of bargain (express or implied) is both central and irreducible in the context of the classic constructive trust. For present purposes every constructive trust derives from some bargain which affects the conscience of the party who is eventually made liable as constructive trustee.'
>
> K Gray and S F Gray, *Elements of Land Law* (5th edn, Oxford University Press, 2009), p. 871

More recently the judgments in two joint ownership cases *Stack v Dowden* (mentioned above) and *Jones v Kernott* have both cast doubt as to whether this judgment continues to be binding even in sole ownership cases but, until there has been a Supreme Court decision on *Rosset* it continues to be the key case in this area of law. However it should be noted that *Stack v Dowden* and *Jones v Kernott* have been frequently referred to in sole ownership cases to ascertain whether rights have arisen.

Bridge LJ identified the need for proof of an agreement between the parties before a constructive trust case arose.

Under *Rosset* there are two alternative situations:

a. **Evidence of an agreement** between the parties that they are both to have a share in the property. The claimant must show that he relied on this and acted to his detriment.

b. **No evidence of an agreement** between the legal owner and the claimant to share the equitable interest. Only direct contributions to the purchase price will be enough to infer a constructive trust in these circumstances.

Evidence of an agreement or arrangement
The party seeking to establish rights in the land has to point to some agreement made between the parties prior to the purchase of the property. This was identified in *Lloyds*

Bank v Rosset (1991) by Lord Bridge. He said that there must be proof of an 'agreement, arrangement or understanding reached between them that the property is to be shared beneficially'. He went on to accept that such an arrangement might be imperfectly remembered and the discussion itself may be imperfect in terms. The problem in this area is that people in a relationship rarely have detailed discussions about property rights. It is only the very cynical, or perhaps two lawyers, who would sit and discuss such things at the start of a relationship.

JUDGMENT

'Spouses living in amity do not normally think it necessary to formulate or define their respective interests in property in any precise way. The expectation of parties to every happy marriage is that they will share the practical benefits of occupying the matrimonial home whoever owns it. But this is something quite distinct from sharing the beneficial interest in the property asset which the matrimonial home represents.'

Lord Bridge in *Lloyds Bank v Rosset* (1991)

CASE EXAMPLE

Lloyds Bank v Rosset [1991] 1 AC 107

This case concerned a couple who purchased a dilapidated house, in Mr Rosset's sole name, with funds wholly supplied by Mr Rosset partly through a mortgage with the bank. The house was uninhabitable, so Mrs Rosset took over the job of supervising the building work and carrying out much of the decorating herself. She had considerable expertise in this area and had undertaken such work professionally. The marriage broke down and Mr Rosset defaulted on repayments to the bank who sought possession of the property. The wife claimed that she had a beneficial interest in the house based on a constructive trust. If she had succeeded, her rights would have been binding on the bank. Her claim was unsuccessful.

Lord Bridge was reluctant to find in Mrs Rosset's favour because he felt that the kind of work that she carried out was work that any wife would carry out in similar circumstances:

'It would seem the most natural thing in the world for any wife, in the absence of her husband abroad, to spend all the time she could spare and to employ any skills she might have, such as the ability to decorate a room, in doing all she could to accelerate progress of the work quite irrespective of any expectation she might have of enjoying a beneficial interest in the property.'

It is possible that there is a genuine discussion when property is purchased, particularly where it is in one name only.

The courts have sometimes found the necessary **common intention** to infer a constructive trust.

Two cases were cited by Lord Bridge in *Lloyds Bank v Rosset* (1991): *Eves v Eves* [1975] 1 WLR 1338 and *Grant v Edwards* [1986] Ch 638 as examples of where a discussion of property interests has led to a finding that there was a common intention that the beneficial interest was to be shared between the parties.

CASE EXAMPLE

Eves v Eves [1975] 1 WLR 1338

An unmarried couple lived together in property vested in the man's name. The woman made no financial contribution but there was evidence that she had contributed towards the renovation of the property. The fact that distinguishes this case from *Rosset* (1991) is that the parties had discussed the possibility of the woman getting a share in the property, and the man had told her that she was too young to have a legal estate in property, which was incorrect but it was sufficient to show that she was intended to have some rights.

CASE EXAMPLE

Grant v Edwards [1986] Ch 638

The facts here were similar to those of *Eves v Eves* (1975) because in this case there was a discussion between the parties about the woman getting a beneficial interest in the property. Ms Grant was in the middle of divorce proceedings and her new partner thought it likely to affect the amount that she would be entitled to if she owned property in her own name so he decided not to enter her name on the Register. Nourse LJ held that she would be entitled to a share since there was a clear inference from the conversation about why the woman's name was not on the title that she was to get an interest in the property.

Although in these two cases the courts were able to find evidence of a common intention it is not always easy for a party claiming rights in property to show that there has been an express agreement to share the property.

Consider the approach of the courts in the following case:

CASE EXAMPLE

Oxley v Hiscock [2005] Fam 211

Contributions had been made by a woman in a new relationship towards the purchase of property, but the property was purchased in the sole name of the man on similar grounds to those in *Grant v Edwards* (1986), namely to avoid difficulties with her former husband. The relationship broke down and the woman claimed a share in the former family home, based on her financial contributions. The Court of Appeal had to address a number of issues, in particular whether the man held the property on trust for the woman. If the property was held on trust, was it a resulting or constructive trust and if a trust was found what were the sizes of the respective shares? The court held that in co-ownership cases it must first address the question of whether or not there was a common intention that each party should have a beneficial interest in the land. Once an agreement that the property will be shared between the parties has been proven, a constructive trust will arise. It does not matter that the parties have not agreed about the precise shares in the property.

The facts of this case would suggest a resulting trust because the woman made an initial contribution to the purchase price and this was argued by Mr Hiscock, the legal owner of the property. If a resulting trust had been found then the woman's share would have been limited to the size of her contribution which was 20 per cent. However, the facts also suggested a common intention to share the beneficial estate. In this case, the contributions by Ms Oxley were enough to show an intention to share under a constructive trust and there was no requirement that there be evidence of an express agreement.

It is often very difficult to point to an express discussion about the beneficial entitlement in property owned by one party. The cases are rare because the standard of proof is high and the court will only accept express intention and it does not allow itself to draw conclusions on the fairness of the claim.

JUDGMENT

'[T]he court does not as yet sit under a palm tree, to exercise a general discretion to do what the man in the street, on a general overview of the case, might regard as fair.'

Dillon LJ in *Springette v Defoe* [1992] 2 FLR 388

CASE EXAMPLE

James v Thomas [2007] EWCA Civ 1212

Ms James appealed to the Court of Appeal after her claim to a beneficial interest in a property had been dismissed by the High Court. Mr Thomas had been sole owner of the property for some years before they met. They had lived together for about 15 years and during that time Ms J had become his business partner. The property had been extensively modernised by their joint works.

During their relationship Mr T had said the following 'this will benefit us both' and also 'you will be well provided for'. It was held that both statements related to other things not a promise or an agreement that rights would arise in the property.

The Court of Appeal held that there was no evidence of express common intention and these promises were insufficiently specific to found a constructive trust. The assurances were not intended or understood as a promise of some property interest.

Implied common intention inferred from the conduct of the parties
Where there is no evidence of an express common intention, the court must establish that the claimant has made direct contributions towards the purchase price. These contributions could either be to the initial purchase price or to the payment of mortgage instalments.

In *Lloyds Bank v Rosset* (1991) Lord Bridge said that he doubted 'anything falling short of direct contributions would suffice'. These direct contributions could either be towards the purchase itself or towards the mortgage instalments. In these cases indirect contributions will never be sufficient.

This is similar to a resulting trust since the contributions usually arise at the initial purchase. The real difference lies in the role of intention. In a resulting trust intention is only relevant to rebut the existence of the trust, but in a constructive trust intention is the significant indicator of the fact that a trust has arisen.

In *Oxley v Hiscock* (2005) the fact that contributions had been made by a woman to the purchase of property in the name of her partner Mr Hiscock could have given rise to a resulting trust but in this case the Court of Appeal found a constructive trust. The constructive trust was inferred from the conduct of the parties and in this case the contribution of the woman to the purchase price. If the court finds there is a constructive trust then the court can decide the shares of the parties. A constructive trust can arise even where the parties have not previously agreed the size of the shares. In this case, Mr Hiscock and Mrs Oxley had not discussed either ownership of the property or the precise size of the shares in the property that each would own.

Lord Bridge limited a finding of an implied bargain constructive trust to those cases where the claimant can show contributions towards the purchase price. He emphasised the need for a financial contribution saying that direct contributions to the purchase price 'will readily justify the inference necessary to the creation of a constructive trust' adding that 'it is extremely doubtful whether anything less will do'.

The issue of when a court can infer common intention was discussed in the cases of *Stack v Dowden* and *Jones v Kernott* and although both these cases concern property registered in joint names the courts are beginning to rely on these cases where the property is in the sole name of one party.

CASE EXAMPLE

Stack v Dowden [2007] 2 AC 43 (see later under jointly owned property)

Ms Dowden and Mr Stack purchased property together with Ms Dowden paying 65 per cent towards the purchase price and Mr Stack paying 35 per cent. At the time of purchase there was no declaration of how the shares were to be held. When title was registered at the Land Registry the parties did not note on their form whether they intended to hold as joint tenants or tenants in common. After a relationship lasting 27 years the couple separated. Mr Stack claimed to be entitled to 50 per cent of the equity in the house based on the fact that the title was held in joint names. Ms Dowden argued that she should be awarded a share equivalent to her contribution to the purchase price namely 65 per cent. At first instance the judge upheld Mr Stack's claim for a 50 per cent share but the Court of Appeal and the House of Lords found in favour of Ms Dowden granting her a 65 per cent share. The leading judgment in the House of Lords was given by Baroness Hale who commented that in most cases where the legal title is co-owned the court would apply the principle that equity follows the law and so where there is no express declaration of shares the shares will be held to be equal.

JUDGMENT

'Just as the starting point where there is sole legal ownership is sole beneficial ownership, the starting point where there is joint legal ownership is joint beneficial ownership. The onus is upon the person seeking to show that the beneficial ownership is different from the legal ownership.'

Baroness Hale

However the court also held that where the **circumstances are exceptional** the courts would investigate the circumstances before deciding the size of each equitable estate. Baroness Hale drew up a long list of factors which would indicate that the circumstances are exceptional in a particular case.

For example:
any advice or discussion at the time of transfer which cast light upon their intentions then;
the reasons why the home was acquired in their joint names;
the purpose for which the home was acquired;
the nature of the parties' relationship;
whether they had children for whom they both had responsibility to provide a home;
how the purchase was financed both initially and subsequently;
how the parties arranged their finances, whether separately or together or a bit of both;
how they discharged the outgoings on the property and their other household expenses.

Ms Dowden successfully rebutted the strong presumption of joint beneficial ownership by showing that the couple had kept their finances rigidly separate throughout their relationship. An important issue here was the fact that the parties had separate bank accounts

This was a significant move forward in the resolution of property disputes where the legal title is jointly owned. Indeed Lord Walker suggested in his judgment that 'the law had moved on' since the days of Lord Bridge's formula set out in *Rosset* and he urged his fellow members of the House of Lords to 'move it a little more in the same direction'. It is the extent to which the court can consider matters such as general contributions towards the family finances in sole ownership cases that is of particular interest.

This case can be read in conjunction with *Jones v Kernott* which follows. Again this was a case where the parties jointly owned the property but the Supreme Court also considered the position of sole owned properties. The court introduced the idea of **imputing** the intention of the parties. It is a very interesting development although the courts have yet to impute intention at what is regarded as the acquisition stage of a constructive trust. This is where a non-legal owning party must prove to the court that he has an interest in the property. It is problematic as the court is tasked with looking for intention based on what the parties would have agreed had they thought about it.

CASE EXAMPLE

Jones v Kernott [2010] 3 All ER 423

Jones v Kernott gives the courts even greater flexibility in the way that they can draw conclusions about the intentions of the parties. In this case the Supreme Court upheld a decision of the High Court concerning the beneficial ownership of property co-owned by a couple, Mr Kernott and Ms Jones. The property was in their joint names but the contributions of the parties both initially and over the years had been unequal. There was no express declaration of trust. Ms Jones successfully contended in the Southend County Court that although their intention initially had been to have equal shares in the property the intentions of the parties had changed following their separation and therefore she should be entitled to a 90 per cent share of the property. Following *Stack v Dowden* (2005) it was accepted at the County Court and in the subsequent decision that the initial presumption where parties own the legal title jointly is for equal division of the property. However although the Court of Appeal then in the words of Lord Neuberger in *Stack v Dowden* 'trespassed into the forbidden territories of imputed intention and fairness' the Supreme Court was prepared to find that the intentions of the parties had changed after the initial purchase and so this should be reflected in the shares of the parties. Baroness Hale had expressed a view in *Stack* that 'the court should not override the intention of the parties, in so far as that appears from what they have said or from their conduct, in favour of what the court itself considers to be fair'. Nicholas Strauss QC held that the first instance judge was entitled to infer or to impute that the parties' intentions had changed following their separation. Mr Kernott had ceased to make any contribution towards the mortgage instalments or other outgoings of the house and a life insurance policy has been cashed in and the money had been divided between them allowing Mr Kernott to purchase his own house. The Court of Appeal found in favour of Mr Kernott and awarded the parties equal shares in the property. The Supreme Court reinstated the decision of the High Court and Ms Jones was awarded a 90 per cent share in the property. The Supreme Court agreed that the starting point in any decision should be the parties' express intentions. In many cases this can present a problem as the parties in cases concerning the family home rarely express clear intentions about the ownership of the equitable interest. So a key issue in *Jones v Kernott* was how the court should proceed in the absence of evidence of an express intention of the parties. It was held that a court cannot only infer the intention of the parties but it is also able to impute their intention.

The difference is subtle and was illustrated in *Jones v Kernott* by Lady Hale and Lord Walker in the following way:

JUDGMENT

'Whenever a judge concludes that an individual "intended, or must be taken to have intended, or knew, or must be taken to have known", there is an elision between what the judge can find as a fact (usually by inference) on consideration of the admissible evidence, and what the law may supply (to fill the evidential gap) by way of a presumption. The presumption of a resulting trust is a clear example of a rule by which the law *does* impute an intention, the rule based on a very broad generalization about human motivation.'

An analysis of cases following *Stack v Dowden* and *Jones v Kernott*

In the cases of sole ownership decided since *Stack v Dowden* and *Jones v Kernott* there appears to be some confusion as to whether or not the principles from these cases will apply.

However although a number of judges have applied the principles from these cases no case has yet found in favour of a claimant who can neither prove an express common agreement nor financial contributions towards the purchase price.

The most interesting question is to what extent the courts will **infer** or **impute** intention in either acquisition of rights or quantification of the shares following the guidance of the Supreme Court in *Kernott v Jones*.

Geary v Rankine (2012) was the first case decided in the Court of Appeal that adopted the *Kernott v Jones* approach. Lord Justice Lewison stated in the Court of Appeal that common intention has to be deduced objectively from the parties' conduct. In saying this he was adopting the approach of the court in *Jones v Kernott* and turning away from Lord Bridge's approach in *Rosset* but nevertheless the claimant was not successful.

Mr Rankine and Mrs Geary lived together from 1990, having one child in 1992. As a business venture Mr Rankine purchased a guest house in 1996 with his own money and he appointed a manager to run it. This arrangement did not work well and with the help of Mrs Geary he took over the management. She worked very hard for little reward and when the relationship broke down she claimed a share of the property. It was shown that he kept the business separate from her; her name never appeared in any of the accounts, there was no joint bank account. Although the judge accepted that the business was to be run together this never went as far as to accept that the business would belong to both parties and her claim failed.

In *Crown Prosecution Service v Piper* (2011) property registered in the sole name of the husband was subject to a confiscation order. In order for the wife to claim any share of the property she had to show that there was a common intention to share the equity. The court accepted that their common intention was to be deduced from their conduct and careful scrutiny of the evidence was required. The court referred to and applied principles from *Kernott v Jones*.

The judgment of Judge Behrens in *Aspden v Elvy* [2012] EWHC 1387 makes express reference to the fact that the law has 'moved on' and he applied the judgment of *Kernott v Jones* rather than referring back to *Rosset*. However in this case substantial contributions had been made by Mr A to improving property which could be seen to imply common intention. Mr Aspden and Ms Elvy had lived together for some years buying various properties in particular a barn later used by Ms Elvy as a cattery and kennels. There were no express discussions about ownership. The barn was later put into Ms Elvy's sole name and it was converted into living accommodation with contributions towards the work by Mr Aspden and when the relationship broke down he claimed a share. The courts held that there must be evidence of a common intention to share ownership of the barn and the fact that he had worked on the barn and had contributed money towards the improvements was sufficient to show that there was common intention to share.

By way of contrast the decisions in *Condappa v Slater* [2012] EWCA Civ 1506 and *Re Ali* [2012] EWHC 2302 both refer to *Rosset* as the authority for the first stage in showing whether a share has arisen or not.

More recently the decision in *Capehorn v Harris* [2015] EWCA Civ 955 suggests that the court still regards acquisition of rights and quantification of shares in sole ownership cases to be two distinct questions with two distinct approaches applying.

This case concerned a couple, Ms Capehorn and Mr Harris, who lived and worked together for some years. Mr Harris had been made bankrupt and Ms Capehorn had purchased the business and employed Mr Harris. They owned two properties both registered in the name of Ms Capehorn and when their relationship broke down the question before the court was to what extent Mr Harris could claim a share in either property. The Judge at first instance found that Mr Harris had acquired a share in the property by finding that Ms Capehorn would have imputed an intention that he should benefit based on his contributions to the business. This was rejected by the Court of Appeal who found that the court was not entitled to impute intention at the first stage in a sole ownership case but it could be done at the later stage of quantification.

The decisions since *Kernott v Jones* have been disappointing in that although the courts do seem to have grasped the opportunity to accept that 'the law has moved on' from *Rosset* the decisions themselves do not seem to reflect this. Nevertheless there is a body of opinion that there is now a third way of deciding acquisition in sole ownership cases:

> 'the essence of the matter is that it is permissible to infer a common intention as to ownership based on the parties' entire relationship with each other. It was not necessary to limit the enquiry to promises or payments ...'
>
> M Dixon, *Modern Land Law* (11th edn, Routledge, 2018), p. 180

Conclusion on proving a constructive trust in sole ownership cases

In sole ownership cases there is a two-stage process for any claimant to satisfy.

Stage one [acquisition stage]. First a claimant must show that there is a common intention that he or she has a share in the property. Under Lord Bridge's test in *Rosset* this can be either by showing that there is an express agreement that the equitable interest is to be shared or that an agreement is implied by reference to capital contributions towards the purchase price of the property. In a number of cases decided since *Jones v Kernott* the courts have gone beyond the strict confines of *Rosset* but *Capehorn v Harris* suggests that this cannot amount to imputation and the onus lies with the claimant to show that a share has arisen.

Stage two [quantification stage]. Once common intention is proved then the court can move on to the second stage which is the quantification of the shares of the parties. The court has always been less rigid in its approach to what can be adduced in evidence in the second stage of the process. Following *Capehorn v Harris* the court will allow imputation at this stage.

KEY FACTS

Finding a constructive trust
1. There must be evidence of an agreement from conversations between the parties in the past that the claimant is to have a share in the property.

2. This must be supported by evidence of detrimental reliance.

3. If there is no evidence of an express common intention then a common intention can be implied by the courts but the evidence needed in support must be contributions in money towards the purchase. Anything less will not be sufficient to infer a constructive trust.

4. Dicta in *Stack v Dowden* and *Jones v Kernott* (although both cases concern joint ownership) suggests that it is possible to infer or impute intention in cases of sole ownership.

2. Detrimental reliance

According to Lord Bridge in *Lloyds Bank v Rosset* (1991), it is not merely enough to show that there has been a common agreement but there must also be evidence that this has been relied on. It is necessary to show that you have altered your position in reliance on the agreement made.

ACTIVITY

Applying the law

Flora is promised by Sandy that she will get a share in the three-bedroomed house owned by him. She gives up her rent-protected tenancy to move in with him. She then starts to renovate the property and pays towards the mortgage instalments.

Can Flora claim a share of the property?

Some behaviour stops short of coming within the definition of 'detrimental behaviour' as there has not been sufficient sacrifice or detriment in the real sense.

If the claimant has simply relied on behaviour that has given him a benefit either because it is something he likes to do anyway or because he has saved money or he has been compensated in some other way then this will not support a claim for rights under a constructive trust.

CASE EXAMPLE

Layton v Martin [1986] 2 FLR 227

The claimant had provided housekeeping and other services. These were then relied on as acting to her detriment but the court held that she had already been compensated at least in part by the award of a regular salary.

CASE EXAMPLE

Wayling v Jones (1993) 69 P & CR 170

The claimant gave evidence that he would have acted in the same way even if he had not been promised a share in the property. This put the court in a difficult position because it had to decide whether the issue should be considered objectively or subjectively. If it was a subjective test then the claimant must fail even though the court thought it was the type of behaviour that was capable of giving rights in the property. In the event, the court found that there had been detriment.

'During the course of such relationships, the parties will inevitably change their positions in all sorts of ways and for all sorts of reasons. Allegations of detrimental reliance require judges to decide which of these changes of position would be factually disadvantageous to a claimant, should an assurance of ownership subsequently be denied, and to decide which of them were motivated by beliefs arising from that assurance. Not surprisingly, the results arrived at in the reported cases appear to be arbitrary and unrealistic.'

A Lawson, 'The Things We Do for Love: Detrimental Reliance in the Family Home' (1996) 16 *LS* 218

Detrimental reliance can take many forms:

1. Clearly, financial contributions will qualify but, as already noted, if made at the time the property was purchased then this will give rise to a resulting trust.

2. Improvement of the trust property will qualify. In *Eves v Eves* (1975) the woman undertook extensive work which even involved wielding a sledge hammer weighing 14 lbs, demolishing a shed and preparing the garden for the laying of turf.

3. 'In my judgment it must be conduct on which the woman could not reasonably have been expected to embark unless she was to have an interest in the house' (Nourse LJ in *Grant v Edwards*).

'Some of the arbitrariness caused by the operation of the detrimental reliance requirement, in this context, would be avoided if the approach advocated by Browne-Wilkinson VC in *Grant v Edwards* (1986) were adopted. He believed that acts which could easily be attributed to love and affection, such as setting up house together or having a baby, should be regarded as capable of amounting to detrimental reliance requirement. What is needed is an entirely new method for the determination of the property rights of unmarried couples. It should, perhaps, also be used to determine such rights as between people standing in other relationships to one another, eg parents and children, who disagree about the ownership of a home they used to share.'

A Lawson, 'The Things We Do for Love: Detrimental Reliance in the Family Home' (1996) 16 *LS* 218

ACTIVITY

Applying the law

Assuming there is evidence of express common intention, could any of the following be considered to be detrimental reliance?

1. Sally moves in with John and decorates all the bedrooms in her spare time.
2. Sally moves in with Carl and later in the year gives birth to twins and stays at home to care for them and uses her savings to buy them clothes and curtains for their new bedroom.
3. Sally moves in with Sam and contributes £3,000 towards the purchase price of the property.
4. Sally moves in with Paul and pays all the household bills. This allows Paul to pay the mortgage.
5. Sally moves in with Alex and pays for a new kitchen and conservatory to be built on to the existing house.

There is proof of detrimental reliance in all these cases, even evidence of giving birth to twins. Lord Browne-Wilkinson found this to be acceptable in *Grant v Edwards*.

3. The conscience of the legal title owner must be affected

Finally, a constructive trust cannot be imposed unless there is evidence that the conscience of the legal owner is affected. In Lord Diplock's words in *Gissing v Gissing* (1971): 'a constructive trust will arise only where an owner has so conducted himself that it would be inequitable to allow him to deny to the claimant a beneficial interest in the land'.

5.5.4 Interests behind jointly owned legal titles

The decision in *Stack v Dowden* suggests that where a couple jointly own the legal title the law will now presume equal beneficial entitlement.

The judgments in this case show that it is for the claimant to prove that on the facts the parties either expressly or impliedly did not intend to share the property.

JUDGMENT

'For the reasons already stated, at least in the domestic consumer context, a conveyance into joint names indicates both legal and beneficial joint tenancy, unless and until the contrary is proved. But the questions in a joint names case are not simply "what is the extent of the parties' beneficial interests?" but "did the parties intend their beneficial interests to be different from their legal interests?" and "if they did, in what way and to what extent?" '

Baroness Hale

CASE EXAMPLE

Fowler v Barron [2008] 2 FLR 831

A couple lived together for over 22 years. They owned a house in joint names but Mr Barron had paid for the majority of the purchase price and most of the daily expenses.

The court applied *Stack v Dowden* and held that in the absence of exceptional circumstances equity will follow the law and the equitable interest will be held in equal shares. The Court distinguished Stack in finding that in this case the parties largely treated their incomes and assets as one pool from which household expenses will be paid.

CASE EXAMPLE

Barnes v Phillips [2016] EWCA Civ 463

A rather different approach was taken in this case indicating that in joint ownership cases there are a number of steps that the court should take before assessing the shares of the parties. The first step will always be to decide whether the presumption that 'equity should follow the law' had been rebutted.

As decided in *Kernott* this can arise at the initial purchase of the property or at a later date. The court is not restricted to evidence of an express agreement – this can arise by inference.

The second step is to consider what the shares in the property should be and at this stage the court may impute an intention to the parties as to the size of their respective shares. This couple had lived together in jointly owned property for nearly ten years. Mr Barnes had serious financial problems and this had resulted in a remortgage of the property. The Court of Appeal upheld the decision by the first instance judge which was based on imputing an intention as to shares which had changed over the years and resulted in the shares of the property being assessed as a 85 per cent share for Ms Phillips and a 15 per cent share for Mr Barnes.

5.6 Quantification of the shares in a constructive trust

Once a claimant has established an interest in either sole owned or jointly owned property he will be entitled to a share. It is for the court in cases of a constructive trust to determine the size of that share. The courts have struggled to find a consistent approach to quantifying the size of the share.

5.6.1 Comparison with a resulting trust

The shares in a resulting trust are assessed according to the contributions made to the initial purchase price although *Marr v Collie* does suggest that the courts may place weight now on the intentions of the parties as to how the property is to be shared between them. However, until that approach has been adopted by the courts the traditional view is that the courts do not have a discretion to decide how to apportion the shares in a resulting trust. In a constructive trust the courts try to assess contributions according to the intentions of the parties.

For example, Alison and Barney decide to set up home together and they find a small cottage in the Yorkshire Dales, valued at £220,000. They both contribute towards the purchase, with Alison contributing £20,000 but the house is registered in Barney's name. Suppose over a romantic dinner one evening, Barney says to Alison 'Everything we own, we share equally' and she agrees. Her share will be 50 per cent even though this will be well in excess of the actual amount that she has contributed.

This means that there will only be a half-share split if there is evidence of the common intention of the parties leading to the assumption that they intended the property to be divided into half shares.

The following cases illustrate the way the courts have quantified the shares where the property is held on constructive trust.

CASE EXAMPLE

Midland Bank v Cooke [1995] 4 All ER 562

This case has already been discussed in connection with resulting trusts. The contribution of the wife was a mere 6.74 per cent which came from a wedding present of the husband's parents towards the deposit on the property which became their matrimonial home. It was assumed that this was a case of resulting trust, but the judgment of Waite LJ shows that he based his calculations on the parties' common intention about the share, so he attributed to the parties 'an intention to share beneficial ownership equally, explicitly because such a conclusion was mirrored in the past pattern of their shared endeavour, their family life and their mutual commitment'.

The courts also considered quantification in *Drake v Whipp* [1996] 1 FLR 826 and the Court of Appeal found that where there was evidence of the parties' common intention as to the shares of each party then this would be the basis of apportionment of the shares; but where the parties had no clear intention then the courts were free to take a broad approach to quantification of the shares. So matters such as conduct would become relevant. The courts were then free to look at direct and non-direct financial contributions and also indirect contributions such as housework. These matters would not be relevant in looking at whether there was a constructive trust at all.

CASE EXAMPLE

Drake v Whipp [1996] 1 FLR 826

The claimant had contributed 40 per cent of the total purchase price and had made a small financial contribution of £13,000 towards the cost of conversion of a barn, but she had made an additional contribution of about £30,000 in labour on the actual conversion. The court found that there was unchallenged evidence of a common understanding between the parties that they would share the property beneficially; the only question then was: in what shares would they own the property? The courts held in this case that the woman was entitled to a one-third share of the property.

The court can rarely depart from the agreement once it has found that such an agreement exists.

It is clear from *Oxley v Hiscock* (2005) that where the parties have not agreed the exact quantification of the shares, the court can step in and decide the size of the shares. This is seen as the second stage in a two-stage approach.

There are four possible approaches to assessing the shares under a constructive trust:

1. The courts apply the size of share that the parties have **expressly agreed** upon.

2. They **will infer the size of the shares according to the course of dealing between the parties**. This is a purely objective approach, based on what the courts believe the parties would have agreed if they had considered it at all (*Midland Bank v Cooke* (1995)).

3. Or they decide what is **fair** in the light of the parties' whole course of dealing in relation to the land. There is a distinction between this approach and that adopted in *Midland Bank v Cooke*. The emphasis in *Oxley v Hiscock* (2005) is on what the court thinks is fair according to the facts whereas in *Midland Bank v Cooke* the court looks objectively at the whole course of dealing and infers what the parties would have intended if they had thought about the issue. So where the parties have always shared equally, then the property will be shared equally. This approach can be criticised as being highly artificial and based on a fiction. The court disapproved of the 'fairness' approach adopted by Lord Justice Chadwick in *Stack v Dowden* but later in *Jones v Kernott* this approach appeared to have received approval by the court.

4. The Supreme Court in *Jones v Kernott* advocated using a third way, '**imputation**' to discover the intention of the parties. This is similar to seeking 'fairness' as suggested in *Oxley*. An imputed intention as related to the actual size of the share of each party is an intention that the parties would have had were they to have thought about it. Such an approach is likely to produce a share that is 'fair' based on all the circumstances.

CASE EXAMPLE

Stack v Dowden [2007] UKHL 17

Ms Dowden and Mr Stack met in 1975 when she was 17 and he was 19. The parties never married. In 1983 Ms Dowden purchased a house at undervalue. Four children were born between 1983 and 1991. In 1991 the house was sold and another property was purchased this time in joint names. There was no declaration of trust on the form. The funding of the purchase was divided between the parties but a larger share was paid by Ms Dowden. The parties separated in 2002. Mr Stack sought a declaration that he owned a half share in the property based on the fact that they owned the legal title jointly therefore they would own the beneficial interest jointly. The judge in the county court found in favour of Mr Stack. Ms Dowden appealed and the Court of Appeal found in Ms Dowden's favour dividing the proceeds of sale 65 to 35 per cent in her favour. The property was eventually sold for £754,345. The extra 15 per cent claimed by Mr Stack amounted to nearly £112,000.

JUDGMENT

'[I]f the question is one of the parties' common intention, we believe that there is much to be said for adopting what has been called a holistic approach to quantification, undertaking a survey of the whole course of dealing between the parties and taking into account of all conduct which throws light on the question what shares were intended.

That may be the preferable way of expressing what is essentially the same thought, for two reasons. First it emphasises that the search is still for the result which reflects what the parties must in the light of their conduct, be taken to have intended. Second, therefore, it does not enable the court to abandon that search in favour of the result which the court itself considers fair.

Baroness Hale

The court also held that where the **circumstances are exceptional** then the presumption of equality could be rebutted. Baroness Hale drew up a long list of factors which would indicate that the circumstances are exceptional in a particular case, for example:

- any advice or discussion at the time of transfer which cast light upon their intentions then;
- the reasons why the home was acquired in their joint names;
- the purpose for which the home was acquired;
- the nature of the parties' relationship;
- whether they had children for whom they both had responsibility to provide a home;
- how the purchase was financed both initially and subsequently;
- how the parties arranged their finances, whether separately or together or a bit of both;
- how they discharged the outgoings on the property and their other household expenses.

Ms Dowden successfully rebutted the strong presumption of joint beneficial ownership by showing that the couple had kept their finances rigidly separate throughout their relationship. An important issue here was the fact that the parties had separate bank accounts.

Although the list drawn up by Baroness Hale seems to cover a wide number of issues which can be seen as exceptional and would indicate the intention to keep finances separate, cases decided since *Stack v Dowden* have shown that where the legal title is jointly owned it will not be easy to rebut the presumption that equity follows the law.

In a dissenting judgment, Lord Justice Neuberger sought simply to apply the ordinary principles of equity. He preferred to start by applying the principles of a resulting trust but accepted that these could be displaced where there was evidence of a constructive trust.

JUDGMENT

'There are practical reasons for rejecting equality and supporting the resulting trust solution. The property may be bought in joint names for reasons which cast no light on the parties' intentions with regard to beneficial ownership. It may be the solicitor's decision or assumption, the lender's preference for the security of two borrowers, or the happenstance of how the intial contact with the solicitor was made. As Baroness Hale ... indicates, parties in a loving relationship are often not anxious to discuss how they should divide the beneficial interest in the home they are about to buy.'

Neuberger LJ

However, Lord Justice Neuberger accepted that where the parties had contributed in unequal shares a resulting trust would be a better solution. He suggested that this conclusion can be rebutted with evidence of intention either express or inferred and normally supported by evidence of detriment. He explained that an inferred intention is one which is objectively deduced to be the subjective actual intention of the parties, in the light of their actions and statements.

On the facts of the case Lord Justice Neuberger concluded that there was no evidence to justify departing from using a resulting trust to apportion the beneficial interest in the property.

CASE EXAMPLE

Jones v Kernott [2011] UKSC 53

A property was purchased in the joint names of the parties Ms Jones and Mr Kernott but the contributions of the parties both initially and over the years had been unequal. There was no express declaration of trust. After 18 years together the parties separated and Mr Kernott left the property making no further contributions towards it and leaving Ms Jones to pay all the outgoings. An attempt was made to sell the property but when that proved to be unsuccessful Mr Kernott purchased another property for himself with the proceeds of an insurance policy. In 2008 after the parties had been apart for nearly 15 years Mr Kernott made a claim for a half share in the property. As seen above Ms Jones successfully contended in the Southend County Court that although their intention initially had been to have equal shares in the property the intentions of the parties had changed following their separation and therefore she should be entitled to a 90 per cent share of the property. Nicholas Strauss QC held that the first instance judge was entitled to infer or to impute that the parties' intentions had changed following their separation. Mr Kernott had ceased to make any contribution towards the mortgage instalments or other outgoings of the house and a life insurance policy has been cashed in and the money had been divided between them allowing Mr Kernott to purchase his own house. The Court of Appeal found in favour of Mr Kernott and awarded the parties equal shares in the property. The Supreme Court reinstated the decision of the High Court and Ms Jones was awarded a 90 per cent share in the property. The decision was based on inferences made about what would have been the parties' intentions at the time when they separated.

'... We accept that the search is primarily to ascertain the parties' actual intentions, whether expressed or to be inferred from their conduct. However, there are at least two exceptions. The first, which is not this case, is where the classic resulting trust presumption applies.... The second, is where it is clear that the beneficial interests are to be shared, but it is impossible to divine a common intention as to the proportions in which they are to be shared. In these two situations, the court is driven to impute an intention to the parties which they may never have had ...'

Lord Walker and Baroness Hale

Conclusion on quantification of shares in jointly owned property

In cases of jointly owned property it is presumed that 'equity will follow the law' so in the majority of cases the beneficial interest will be shared equally. If the presumption can be rebutted then the court is entitled to look at what the parties had actually intended the beneficial entitlement to be. Where there is no evidence of what the parties' actual intentions were then the court is able to look at a wide range of issues in order to infer or impute their intentions as to the size of shares.

KEY FACTS

Quantification in constructive trusts
1. If there is evidence of common intention as to the shares in the property then the shares will be in accordance with that agreement.
2. The court will quantify the shares according to the agreement unless there are exceptional reasons for departing from it.
3. If there is no agreement about exact shares but evidence of a common intention to share then the courts can look at many different factors.
4. The courts can apportion the property according to these other factors rather than according to the size of the actual contribution.
5. Following *Oxley v Hiscock* (2005), the court could take the approach that it will decide on the shares according to what it thinks is fair according to the facts of the case, later criticised in *Stack v Dowden* by the House of Lords. It held that the correct approach was not what was 'fair' but what was 'intended by the parties'. To allow the court to award a share of the beneficial interest what they thought was fair would be to allow the court too much discretion.
6. *Jones v Kernott* (2011) introduced a different approach where the parties have not expressed their intentions as to the size of their share and it is impossible for the courts to divine their share. In this instance, the court may 'impute' the intentions of the parties.
7. In cases where the parties jointly owned the legal estate the court would presume that the beneficial interest would be shared equally. Cases where the presumption of joint beneficial ownership would be rebutted would be unusual. This will depend on the facts of each case and a number of relevant factors.

ACTIVITY

Applying the law

Consider the following facts:

Lizzie, an art student, and John, an estate agent, decide to live together. John's parents say they will help them towards the cost of buying a home. They give them a cheque for £13,500. Lizzie and John find the perfect house, which costs £230,000, and they move in. It is registered in John's name alone as Lizzie, who does not think it will make any difference to what they each own, does not challenge this and John persuades her that it does not make any difference. They have three children. Lizzie qualifies as an art teacher and works part-time and contributes towards the family expenses. They have separate bank accounts but a joint account for the payment of some of the joint bills such as gas and electricity. After 18 years the relationship breaks down and they split up and Lizzie claims a share in the property. How much can she claim?

5.7 Constructive trusts in other jurisdictions

Other jurisdictions take a broader approach to the use of constructive trusts to resolve disputes over the ownership of property. It is useful to examine these other jurisdictions.

Canada

The Canadian courts have applied the notion of unjust enrichment to constructive trusts. This approach uses the remedial constructive trust to resolve ownership of the property. Under the remedial constructive trust the court looks at what the defendant has acquired through the contribution of the claimant rather than an agreement between the parties.

CASE EXAMPLE

Pettkus v Becker (1981) 117 DLR (3rd) 257

A woman who had contributed to a beekeeping business was able to claim a beneficial interest because the man had been unjustly enriched by her efforts and it was unjust to deny her rights.

CASE EXAMPLE

Peter v Beblow (1993) 101 DLR (4th) 621

This case focused on the contribution by the claimant as housekeeper, homemaker and step-mother and so gave rise to enrichment to the man who otherwise would have had to pay for these services.

This case is important because it struck new ground as to what constituted enrichment. In previous cases the contribution by the woman had linked to the business in order to give rise to an interest.

The Canadian courts have a wide discretion as to how it proceeds in these cases. The courts in Canada can consider purely domestic labour equally with direct financial contribution.

New Zealand

New Zealand has also taken a more realistic approach. Rather than concentrating on unjust enrichment it focuses on the concept of reasonable expectations. The judiciary has embraced the idea that cohabitation per se could generate expectations concerning property ownership. These expectations would automatically arise in any relationship and if the parties do not wish to share property then they must expressly assert their intention not to be bound in this way.

Lankow v Rose [1995] NZLR 277 laid down the elements necessary to found a claim as follows:

i. There must be contributions to the property; these can be direct or indirect.

ii. There must be the expectation of an interest by the claimant.

iii. The expectation must be reasonable.

The reasonable expectation is similar to the English courts granting rights under the agreement, but here it is unilateral because there is no requirement for there to be a consensus between the parties.

Australia

Australia has a similar approach but based on unconscionability rather than expectation or common intention. The courts can award an interest based on the nature of the parties' relationship and their intentions.

A brief survey of other jurisdictions highlights the problems with relying on common intention. Common intention can produce unfair results in several ways. If there is no evidence of an express common agreement then no interest can be awarded, if an implied agreement can be found but the contributions are indirect then no interest can be awarded and, finally, if there is a common agreement but the agreement itself is inherently unfair then the court must uphold it.

Scotland

Many of the problems encountered in the English courts have been avoided in Scotland since the introduction of legislation giving cohabitants the right to claim a share in the other cohabitants' property. Before making a claim for financial provision under the Family Law (Scotland) Act 2006 an applicant must first prove that the couple has lived together as if they were husband and wife or civil partners. There is no minimum time period for this although there is a maximum time period (one year) in which to bring a claim. Under s 28 a claim for a capital sum can be made by the applicant where cohabitants cease to cohabit otherwise than by reason of death. There is also provision for the making of an interim order. Under s 28(2)(b) the court can make an order requiring the defender to pay towards the burden of caring for a child of whom the cohabitants are the parents. The court has to have regard to certain matters listed under s 28(3) which are whether the defender has derived economic advantage from contributions made by the applicant and whether the applicant has suffered economic disadvantage in the interests of the defender or any relevant child. Further, the court has to have regard to matters listed under s 28(5). First, the extent to which any economic advantage derived by the defender from contributions made by the pursuer (the applicant) is offset by any economic disadvantage suffered by the defender in the interests of the applicant or any relevant child. Second, the extent to which any economic disadvantage suffered by the applicant in the interests of the defender or any relevant child is offset by any economic advantage the applicant has derived from contributions made by the defender. This section appears to involve the court in balancing what a party brings into a relationship and against what a party gains from that relationship in financial terms. The case law decided in the courts under the Act shows a measure of uncertainty as to how far such a balancing act should go and also what the courts are trying to achieve through the process. Economic advantage is defined in the Act as any gains in capital, income and earning capacity. Contributions are defined as including indirect and non-financial contributions. The importance of this definition is the contrast it presents with the much criticised constraints of Lord Bridge's judgment in *Lloyds Bank v Rosset* (1991) which only allows for a claim in property in England and Wales under an implied trust where direct financial contributions can be shown or where there is evidence of an express agreement between the parties to share the property.

CASE EXAMPLE

Gow v Grant [2012] UKSC 29

In this case the Supreme Court had an opportunity to consider the Scottish law. Mrs Gow cohabited with Mr Grant having sold her own property. The Court awarded her a sum just under £40,000 to compensate her for her economic disadvantage suffered when she sold her flat and moved into the property of Mr Grant. He had benefited from the proceeds of sale through holidays and other purchases and so in the eyes of the court he had derived an advantage at her expense. Lady Hale observed in her judgment 'The Act has undoubtedly achieved a lot for Scottish cohabitants and their children. English and Welsh cohabitants and their children deserve no less.'

The Law Commission has published a number of reports on the rights of cohabitants the most recent 'Cohabitation: The Financial Consequences of Relationship Breakdown' (Law Com No 307, 2007). It recommends a legislative approach to the breakdown of cohabitation but this has not been acted on by the government. The majority of cases that are heard before the courts on rights in the family home are cases concerning cohabitants and the breakdown of their relationship. In the absence of legislation outlining the rights of cohabiting couples, the burden falls on the courts, which have to determine rights under the complex law of trusts, usually implied trusts. Amongst practitioners, academics and the judiciary there are many supporters of the introduction of a legislative framework giving limited financial rights to the parties on the breakdown of cohabitation.

SUMMARY

1. Equitable rights in land are rights under a trust of land.

2. Equitable rights can either arise under an express or an implied trust of land.

3. Express trusts can only be created if certain formalities are complied with.

4. Implied trusts take two forms: resulting and constructive trusts.

5. Resulting trusts arise where one party makes a financial contribution to the purchase of land in the name of another. The law presumes that he should retain an interest in the land.

6. Constructive trusts of land depend on common intention or a bargain which can be proved either by an express agreement or an implied agreement based on financial contributions.

7. The quantification of the shares under a resulting trust is based on the size of the contribution.

8. The quantification of the shares under a constructive trust depends on the agreement of the parties either expressly agreed or an inferred agreement.

9. Where the legal title is jointly owned the court presumes that equity follows the law and the beneficial interest is shared equally, but this can be rebutted by evidence that the parties did not intend to share the benefical interest equally.

SAMPLE ESSAY QUESTION

In *Lloyds Bank v Rosset* [1991] 1 AC 107 Lord Bridge affirmed the principle that informal rights under a constructive trust of land should be based on proof of a common intention between the parties.

In the light of recent cases to what extent do you think that this principle still applies in relation both to establishing a share in property and the quantification of the shares of the parties?

> Discuss *Lloyds Bank v Rosset*:
>
> Lord Bridge: a constructive trust can only be established in two circumstances:
>
> i. express common intention; or
>
> ii. implied common intention.

Discuss express common intention:

Illustrate with case law: *Grant v Edwards*, *Eves v Eves* and *Lloyds Bank v Rosset*.

Criticise the limitations of the present law.

For example, does not take into account the failure of parties to discuss the ownership of the beneficial interest.

For example, where the parties have not discussed ownership of the beneficial interest but contributions in kind have been made no share can arise.

Discuss implied common intention:
What financial contributions will count as evidence of common intention, e.g. *Oxley v Hiscock*.

Quantification of the shares:

How can the courts approach quantification?

i. common agreement: explain that it is rare that the courts will find evidence of a common intention with regard to shares;

ii. inferring a common intention to share: explain the difficulties of this approach;

iii. the whole course of dealing in *Midland Bank v Cooke*;

iv. discuss the rejection of Lord Justice Chadwick's approach in *Oxley v Hiscock* in *Stack v Dowden*;

v. the approach in cases of joint ownership of the legal title and the approach in *Stack v Dowden*.

Critical analysis of various approaches:

Can *Stack v Dowden* be used as a universal approach in other cases?

Limitations of the decision, e.g. what approach can the court take to non-financial contributions in cases where the title is vested in one name?

CONCLUSION

Further reading

Books

Dixon, M, *Modern Land Law* (11th edn, Routledge, 2018, Chapter 4).

Gray, K and Gray, S F, *Elements of Land Law* (5th edn, Oxford University Press, 2009), p. 848.

Hayward, A, 'Finding a Home for Family Property: *Stack v Dowden* and *Jones v Kernott*' in N Gravells (ed.), *Landmark Cases in Land Law* (Hart, 2013), Chapter 10.

Articles

Allardice, M, 'Cohabitants and Constructive Trusts in 2015' [2015] *PCB* 105.

Battersby, G, 'How not to Judge the Quantum (and Priority) of a Share in the Family Home' (1996) 8 *CFLQ* 261.

Bray, J, 'The Financial Rights of Cohabiting Couples' [2009] *Fam Law* 1151.

Bray, J, 'Gow v Grant Leads the Way towards Financial Rights for Cohabitants' [2012] *Fam Law* 1505.

Dixon, M, 'The Never-Ending Story: Co-ownership after *Stack v Dowden*' [2007] *Conv* 456.

Dunn, A, 'Whipping up Resulting Trusts and Constructive Trusts' [1997] *Conv* 467.

Etherton, T, 'Constructive Trusts and Proprietory Estoppel: The Search for Clarity and Principle' [2009] *Conv* 104.

Gardner, S, 'Rethinking Family Property' (1993) 109 *LQR* 263.

George, M and Sloan, B, 'Presuming too Little About Resulting and Constructive Trusts?' [2017] *Conv* 4, 303–312.

Hayward, A, 'Common Intention Constructive Trusts and the Role of Imputation in Theory and Practice' [2016] *Conv* 227.

Lawson, A, 'The Things We Do for Love: Detrimental Reliance in the Family Home' (1996) 16 *LS* 218.

Lees, K, 'Geary v Rankine: Money isn't Everything' [2012] *Conv* 412.

Mee, J, 'Joint Ownership, Subjective Intention and the Common Intention Constructive Trust' [2007] *Conv* 14.

O'Hagan, P, 'Quantifying Interests under Resulting Trusts' (1997) 60 *MLR* 3.

Pawlowski, M, 'Imputing Intention and the Family Home' (2016) 46 *Family Law* 189.

Sawyer, C, 'Equity's Children: Constructive Trusts for the New Generation' [2004] *CFLQ* 31.

Sloan, B, 'Keeping Up with the *Jones* Case: Establishing Constructive Trusts in "Sole Legal Owner" Scenarios' (2015) *LS* 226.

6

Licences

AIMS AND OBJECTIVES

After reading this chapter, you should be able to:

- Define a licence in land
- Describe the different types of licences and the various methods of their creation
- Understand the effect of licences in land on third parties
- Describe how a licence can be revoked

6.1 The nature of a licence

Definition

A licence is permission given by the owner of land to a person to do something or to go on the land which would otherwise be a trespass, for example permission given to a neighbour's child to recover a football from your garden, the right of a hotel guest to occupy a room and the right to enter a cinema to watch a film. Ownership of the land remains with the owner but it is subject to the licensee's rights which, once granted, cannot be denied. However, it does not usually grant any rights in the land itself. The landowner can later withdraw that licence.

JUDGMENT

'A dispensation or licence properly passeth no interest, nor alters or transfers property in anything but only makes an action lawful, which without it had been unlawful.'

Thomas v Sorrell (1673) Vaug H 330

No formalities are required for the creation of a licence. The licence does not constitute an interest in land so it is outside the ambit of s 53(1)(b) Law of Property Act 1925. This contrasts with the creation of express rights in land which must be evidenced in writing. A licence can arise from a written document as well as from an oral grant. It can even arise by implication.

Sometimes a licence is coupled with an interest in land, in which case the grant of the interest must comply with any formalities necessary for the interest, for example a right to enter someone's land to hunt deer is called a *profit à prendre* and this type of right can only arise if it has been created by deed.

There are a number of issues to consider in relation to licences:

1. **Is the right claimed a licence or a lease?** This is an important issue because a tenant holds an estate in land and this carries with it a number of significant rights often denied to a licensee, for example rights to force the landlord to carry out repairs to the property.

2. **Can the licence bind a third-party purchaser?** Another way of looking at this would be to ask: is the licence a proprietary interest in land? The straightforward answer to that question is 'no' but licences may be binding if they are coupled with other rights.

3. **What rights can a licensee claim against the licensor?** This depends on what type of licence has been granted.

6.2 Types of licence

There are four main types of licences:

1. bare licences;
2. licences coupled with an interest;
3. contractual licences;
4. estoppel licences.

6.2.1 Bare licences

The bare licence is the simplest type of licence. It is permission given to the licensee to enter land belonging to the licensor without the payment of consideration. Any lawful visitor to your house comes with a bare licence.

Permission may be expressly given, for example to a guest to a party, or it may be impliedly given, for example to the postman delivering mail every day or the right under statute given to a police officer to enter premises under warrant.

JUDGMENT

'An entry charge of this sort can aptly be described as carrying with it an implied licence. The entrant who pays and the man on the gate who takes his money both know what the position is without the latter having to speak any words of permission (although he may qualify the permission by saying that no dogs, or bicycles, or radios are allowed). Similarly (especially in a small village community where people know their neighbours' habits) permission to enter land may be given by a nod or a wave, or by leaving open a gate or even a front door. All these acts could be described as amounting to implied consent, though I would prefer ... to describe them as the expression of consent by non-verbal means. In each instance there is a communication by some overt act which is intended to be understood, and is understood, as permission to do something which would otherwise be an act of trespass.'

Lord Walker of Gestingthorpe, *R (on the application of Beresford) v Sunderland CC* [2004] 1 AC 889

While the visitor remains within the terms of the invitation, he is a lawful visitor. If he goes beyond the invitation then he becomes a trespasser. For example, if the postman decides to sunbathe in your garden after a tiring morning delivering post, he becomes a trespasser because he has gone beyond the terms of his implied licence.

JUDGMENT

'When you invite a person into your house you do not invite him to slide down the banisters.'

Scrutton LJ in *The Calgarth* [1927] P 93 at 110

It is important to identify the exact terms on which the licensee enters the property. Once these are exceeded then the licensee becomes a trespasser. It is also important to note that the licensee must be given time to leave the property. He will not immediately become a trespasser on being told to leave.

CASE EXAMPLE

Robson v Hallet [1967] 2 QB 939

A police sergeant was told to leave by the owner of a house whose son had called the police. The court held that he would not become a trespasser until he had been given time to leave the property which in this case involved going out of the front door, down the steps and through the gate.

6.2.2 Licences coupled with an interest

This is a licence that is granted along with or coupled with the grant of an interest. For example, if you grant someone the right to hunt deer on your land or cut down trees, he/she must also have the right to go on the land because without such access he/she will not be able to exercise the right. The interest usually takes effect as a *profit à prendre* which can exist as a proprietary right in land if it is created correctly. However, in some earlier cases an interest in land has been very broadly interpreted to include a contractual right, such as the right to attend a play in the theatre or to see a film in the cinema. There is a problem with this approach because in this group of cases the interest claimed does not constitute a proprietary right in the land.

CASE EXAMPLE

Hurst v Picture Theatres Ltd [1915] 1 KB 1

Hurst was watching a film in a cinema, having bought a ticket. The defendant evicted him for breach of contract because he mistakenly thought that Hurst had entered without paying, and requested him to leave. The claimant, Hurst, then brought an action for assault and false imprisonment. His action was based on him having a lawful right to be there as he had bought a valid ticket. This argument was accepted by the Court of Appeal which held that he had a licence coupled with an interest:

'the right to go upon the premises, was only something granted him, namely the right to see. He could not see the performance unless he went into the building. His right to go into the building was something given to him in order to enable him to have the benefit of that which had been granted to him namely the right to hear the opera, or see the theatrical performance, or see the moving pictures as was the case here.'

Buckley LJ

Examples of types of interest which have been held to be coupled with the licence:

1. the right to see a film at the cinema (*Hurst v Picture Theatres Ltd* [1915] 1 KB 1);

2. the right to attend a creditors' meeting (*Vaughan v Hampson* (1875) 33 LT 15);

3. the right to take away game or timber (*James Jones & Sons Ltd v Earl of Tankerville* [1909] 2 Ch 440).

CASE EXAMPLE

Vaughan v Hampson (1875) 33 LT 15

A solicitor claimed that he had a right to be on premises when he attended a general meeting which had been held by a debtor. The solicitor was acting on behalf of a creditor. He had been forcibly ejected from the meeting. The Court of Appeal held this to be an assault because he had a right to be on the premises, coupled with his interest in attending the meeting on behalf of his client.

The idea that the licensee has an interest in the land when he has in fact got a contractual right to be there was further explored in *Hounslow LBC v Twickenham Garden Development Ltd* discussed below. The court questioned whether there was a right to be on the land independent of the rights under the contract as seen above in *Hurst*.

CASE EXAMPLE

Hounslow LBC v Twickenham Garden Developments Ltd [1971] Ch 233

This case considered whether the right of a contractor to do works on land constituted an interest for the duration of the contract. If this were so then the contractors could remain on the land even after the claimant had given notice to them to leave the ground.

'If for this purpose "interest" is not confined to an interest in land or in chattels on the land, what does it extend to? If a right to attend a creditors' meeting or to see a cinema performance suffices to constitute an interest, can it be said that the right and duty to do works on land falls short of being an interest? I cannot see why it should. Yet if this be so, it is not so easy to see any fair stopping place in what amounts to an interest, short of any legitimate reason for being on the land.'

Megarry J

In this judgment Megarry questions what can constitute an interest in land and suggests that there should be a limitation placed on what constitutes an interest and should include only those interests which grant proprietary rights in land.

The important thing to remember is that this type of licence cannot be revoked until the interest itself has come to an end.

This could affect a third party purchasing land because, as the interest can be in the form of a *profit à prendre*, the purchaser may buy subject to that right and the third party would be bound to allow them to come on to the land to exercise their rights.

6.2.3 Contractual licences

A contractual licence is a licence granted in exchange for valuable consideration. Examples of types of contractual licence:

1. a ticket for the theatre or cinema;

2. the right to park your car in a multi-storey car park;
3. the right of members to play golf at their golf club;
4. the right of a lodger to live on the land owned by the licensor.

The 'contractual terms'

The rules concerning contractual licences lie in the rules of contract as well as the rules of land law. There must be an intention to create legal relations. In informal arrangements between families this may cause difficulties as parties to a relationship or family members do not generally 'enter into legal relations'. In some cases the courts will imply a contract and its terms.

CASE EXAMPLE

Tanner v Tanner [1975] 1 WLR 1347

A married man entered into a relationship with a woman and she gave birth to twins. Later, the woman left a rent-controlled flat and went to live with the man in a house purchased in his name on the basis that this house would become their family home. In fact, he never lived there and after three years he asked her to leave so that he could sell the house. The Court of Appeal found that she had an implied contract and held under the contract she had an irrevocable contractual licence to occupy the house while the children were growing up. Since she had already been evicted by the man from the property she was awarded the sum of £2,000 for the loss of a contractual licence.

So, the terms of the contract can be agreed either expressly or impliedly. It was accepted by Lord Denning, who had found in favour of the woman in *Tanner v Tanner* (1975), that there was no express contract 'but circumstances are such that the court should imply a contract by the plaintiff – or, if need be, impose the equivalent of a contract by him'.

The contractual licence was argued in several cases on facts similar to *Tanner v Tanner*, but not always with the same degree of success.

In *Horrocks v Forray* [1976] 1 All ER 737 a woman unsuccessfully claimed a contractual licence to live in property owned by the man with whom she was now living. It was found to be a purely informal arrangement and she had not given any consideration. *Tanner v Tanner* could be distinguished since in that case the woman had given up a Rent Act-protected property.

However, two other cases decided after *Tanner v Tanner* were both decided on the basis of a contractual licence. In *Chandler v Kerley* [1978] 1 WLR 693 a former matrimonial home was purchased by a woman's new boyfriend after the marriage broke down, based on the understanding that the couple were going to live there. The new relationship also broke down and the court found that the woman had a right under an implied contractual licence to continue to live there. The right could not be terminated without reasonable notice. On the facts of the case, reasonable notice was deemed to be 12 months.

Hardwick v Johnson [1978] 1 WLR 683 concerned a married couple who lived as licensees in a house belonging to the wife's mother-in-law. The couple agreed to make payments towards the mortgage, which they occasionally made, but were unable to make regular payments because they were in a poor position financially. The marriage broke down and the husband left. The mother-in-law claimed possession of the house from her daughter-in-law. The Court of Appeal upheld the rights of the daughter-in-law on the basis of a contractual licence, although in this case Lord Denning was not convinced that the facts disclosed a contract because it was a family arrangement.

Most of the cases upholding contractual licences within family arrangements were decided by Lord Denning who used the contractual licence as a way of enforcing rights in property, but such an approach has not been supported in more recent cases and the contractual licence has given way to other more successful means of enforcing rights in property.

> 'The contractual licence approach adumbrated in *Tanner v Tanner* faded into the background and subsequent "family arrangement" decisions have focused, not on strained and scarcely credible implications of contract, but rather on more appropriate variants of equitable or irrevocable licence, proprietary estoppel and constructive trust.'
>
> K Gray and S F Gray, *Elements of Land Law*
> (5th edn, Oxford University Press, 2009), p. 1310

Some terms will be implied by the courts in the same way that the courts will imply a term into the agreement, for example a right to quiet enjoyment for licensees of residential premises.

If the terms are broken then a right to sue will arise. If the terms provide for the termination of the licence upon notice then the notice must be reasonable. This will vary according to the circumstances of the case.

CASE EXAMPLE

Winter Garden Theatre (London) Ltd v Millennium Productions Ltd [1948] AC 173

The licensee, Millennium Productions Ltd had a right to produce plays in the licensor's theatre for six months, with options to renew. The licensee exercised his right to renew several times until eventually the defendant (the licensor) revoked the licence. The House of Lords held that the contract was revocable but that reasonable notice of revocation of the licence would have to be given and in these circumstances that would be one month. Until the contract had been revoked the licensee had an implied right to remain on the premises under the contract. This is often referred to as the 'implied contract' theory. This will apply where the contract includes the right to occupy the land for a specific purpose such as the right to see a theatre production or to carry out building obligations. Once this term has been implied into the contract then the court can exercise its equitable jurisdiction and grant an equitable remedy such as specific performance or an injunction.

At one time the contractual licence was revocable at will by the licensor, even while the contract was in force.

CASE EXAMPLE

Wood v Leadbitter (1845) 13 M & W 838

The licensee purchased a ticket allowing him entrance to Doncaster racecourse for four days. The defendant acting on instructions from the clerk of the course evicted him, using reasonable force, on the basis that he was involved in an illegal betting ring at another racecourse. The licensee sued the defendant. The court held that the licence could be revoked at will and the defendant was entitled to use reasonable force to eject the licensee. The licensee was not protected under his contractual licence from being evicted at will by the licensor.

This principle of law remained for nearly 70 years and gave licensees even under contract little protection from eviction by the licensor.

In *Hurst v Picture Theatres* (1915) it was accepted that it would be a breach of contract to revoke the contract before it had been fulfilled. This approach was also accepted in *Hounslow LBC v Twickenham Garden Developments* (1971) that the right to carry out building works gave the contractors a contractual right to remain on the land after they were given notice to quit by the claimants. It was held that they could not be sued for trespass when they remained on the land, even though they had got behind with their schedule. These cases suggest that a contractual licence cannot be revocable at will.

If a licence has been given for a **particular purpose under contract** there is no right to revoke it while the purpose exists and the licensee remains within the terms of the licence. This only applies to the contracting parties and it would not bind successive owners because the contractual licence does not grant proprietary rights; e.g. the rights of a licensee of residential premises under a contractual licence will not be binding on a third-party purchaser.

6.2.4 Estoppel licences

proprietary estoppel

This is based on the principle that if a person acts to his detriment in reliance on a promise or assurance that he will get rights in land owned by another, the court will uphold his claim

A licence by estoppel is a licence that arises under the doctrine of **proprietary estoppel**.

According to *Taylor Fashions Ltd v Liverpool Victoria Trustees Co Ltd* [1982] QB 133 there are **three** elements in proprietary estoppel:

1. a **promise** or representation is made by the representor;
2. the claimant **relies** on that promise;
3. the claimant acts to his **detriment**.

These rules will be considered in detail in Chapter 7.

Where rights arise under estoppel a claimant will have a lawful right to be on land, which can take the form of an estoppel licence and prevents the claimant from becoming a trespasser.

The claimant must prove that a **promise or assurance of rights** in the land has been made to him.

If the claimant is successful in claiming estoppel then the court has a wide discretion in granting rights to the claimant. The right granted will vary according to the circumstances of each case. In some cases the court grants a licence which may be combined with some other right which will make it binding on a third party.

CASE EXAMPLE

Re Sharpe [1980] 1 WLR 219

An aunt lent her nephew £12,000 in order to buy a house. The aunt was promised a right to remain in the house for the rest of her life. The nephew went bankrupt and his trustee in bankruptcy ordered the aunt to leave. The court found that she had a right to remain in the house, based on an estoppel, and she was granted a licence that was irrevocable during her lifetime.

The key issue in estoppel cases is whether the promise made has been acted on by the claimant. The promise alone would not be enforceable without proof of detrimental reliance.

CASE EXAMPLE

Greasley v Cooke [1980] 1 WLR 1306

In this case Cooke was employed as a maid in Greasley's house. Greasley's son, Kenneth, and Cooke formed a relationship. Greasley died and Cooke continued to perform household duties in the house, including caring for a mentally ill sister of Kenneth, for no payment although she continued to live in the property. She was assured by Kenneth and his brother before they too died that she could live in the property rent-free for as long as she liked. The Court of Appeal held that she had a right to live in the property rent-free, based on an estoppel licence.

The law recognises four different types of licence: bare licences, licences coupled with a grant or interest, contractual licences and estoppel licences. In all but bare licences there is a separate component to the right which may make it enforceable against the licensor even after the licence has been withdrawn.

ACTIVITY

Applying the law

Consider the following and decide whether a licence is created in each case. If you decide that there is a licence, what type of licence is it?

1. You are asleep at home. You are awoken in the night by a policeman kicking in the front door who shows you a warrant to enter your premises and to look for stolen goods. You ask him to leave telling him that he is trespassing and has no right to be on your land.
2. You visit the Barbican Theatre in London to see *As You Like It*. At the interval, you go to the bar to have a drink. Accidentally, you lose your ticket and then find someone sitting in your seat. When you challenge the manager, he asks you to leave, believing you have not paid to enter.
3. You park your car in a multi-storey car park, paying for a monthly season ticket.
4. For ten years you have tended the garden of your employer, an elderly man aged 91, who has promised you the right to go on living in the flat above the garage for the rest of your life. On his death, his son asks you to leave.
5. Every year for five years you collect a Christmas tree from the wood owned by your neighbours. This year, they challenged you as you went on to their land but you prove that you have always had the right to take the Christmas tree from their land.

6.3 The creation of licences

Licences are usually informal grants allowing someone to have the lawful right to be on land. As they rarely confer proprietary rights formalities are kept to a minimum. Where there is an additional right such as a *profit à prendre* then there may be formalities to adhere to that are required for that type of right.

6.3.1 Bare licences

A bare licence may be expressly granted and need not adhere to any formalities. It can be impliedly granted, for example to people delivering goods to the premises. In *R (on the Application of Beresford) v Sunderland CC* (2004) it was accepted that a bare licence may arise by implication from circumstances or conduct.

6.3.2 Licences coupled with an interest

This type of licence is dependent on the type of interest that has been granted and so if the interest requires any formalities then these must be complied with in order for the licence to be valid. A *profit à prendre* can be created either by deed or through prescription. Prescription arises from long use of the right.

A *profit à prendre* must be created by a deed. If you are granted the right to cut down timber in a neighbouring wood owned by the defendant then that must be granted by deed. If there was no deed then the grant would be invalid and if you tried to enter the wood to cut down timber, you would be a trespasser.

6.3.3 Contractual licences

A contractual licence depends on whether there is a valid contract. The terms of the licence are governed by the terms of the contract. The formalities required will be governed by the type of contract.

ACTIVITY

Applying the law

If you purchase a ticket to attend a play in the theatre what rights do you have to enter the theatre and how long can you remain after the play is over?

Contrast between a contractual licence and a tenancy

The contrast between a right to occupy land under a licence and a right to occupy land under a tenancy highlights the status of a contractual licence. The contractual licence does not confer an interest in land so it does not have to follow the usual formalities, that is evidence in writing in accordance with s2 of the Law of Property (Miscellaneous Provisions) Act 1989 when conveying an interest in land. The rights of the licensee under the contract will depend on the express terms. Some terms may be implied into the contract, in particular where the land is let as residential premises.

CASE EXAMPLE

Smith v Nottinghamshire CC, The Times, 13 November 1981

The Court of Appeal upheld the claim of a number of students claiming that their right to quiet enjoyment had been infringed when workmen carrying out repairs in the halls of residence made excess noise. The claim was upheld even though the students were only contractual licensees of the premises. They had entered into an agreement with the university who were their licensors which included a term they should be able to work in their rooms without undue disturbance.

6.3.4 Estoppel licences

The creation of an estoppel licence arises only where the court believes that it would be unconscionable for the owner to deny an interest, and this depends on the proof of the three elements of estoppel, namely; the assurance, reliance on that assurance and proof of acting to your detriment. There are no other required formalities.

6.4 The effect of licences on third parties

Licences rarely confer rights that will be binding on a third party. This is because licences do not confer proprietary rights in land on the licensee. Where there is an additional right such as a *profit à prendre* or evidence of a constructive trust then the licensee may be able to argue that a proprietary right has arisen.

6.4.1 Bare licences

A bare licence is purely personal to the licensee and will not be binding on a purchaser from the licensor, even where he has notice of the licence. The bare licensee cannot transfer the licence to another, as it is a purely personal right against the licensor.

6.4.2 Licences coupled with an interest

Where a licence is coupled with an interest it will be binding on a third-party purchaser of land but only where he buys the land subject to that proprietary interest.

ACTIVITY

Applying the law

If Alex buys a house which has a wood adjoining it and he is aware that his neighbour, James, has the right to shoot in the wood and take away any game, can Alex deny James the right to come on to his land when he moves into the property?

6.4.3 Contractual licences

Licences have always been regarded as purely personal rights and so will only be binding on the licensor. The licensee may be liable to claim damages, if the licence is denied to the licensee. The effect of this is that a third-party purchaser will not be bound by a licence when he buys land, even where he had notice of the rights of the licensee.

CASE EXAMPLE

King v David Allen & Sons Billposting Ltd [1916] 2 AC 54

The defendant had agreed to give the claimant the right to put up posters on some of the walls in a cinema that he owned under a contract. The licence was to last for four years. Before the contract had expired, the cinema was sold. It was held that the purchasers took free of the rights of the claimant, who could only sue the defendant for breach of contract.

For a while this position was reversed, so that it was possible to claim that the contractual licence **did** create an interest in land.

Lord Denning found in *Errington v Errington & Woods* [1952] 1 KB 290 that contractual licences could be binding on successors in title. In that case a daughter-in-law had been allowed to remain in property which her mother-in-law had inherited from her father-in-law. The mother-in-law had sought to evict the daughter-in-law but the court held that her rights were good against the whole world, with the exception of the *bona fide* purchaser for value without notice of her rights.

Lord Denning continued to champion the rights of the licensee in further cases.

CASE EXAMPLE

Binions v Evans [1972] Ch 359

A widow had been given the right to remain in a cottage that her husband had been granted rent-free as part of his job. She had entered an agreement that 'if she kept the cottage in good repair and managed the garden then she could enjoy the property as tenant at will'. The property was subsequently sold to the claimants who bought at a reduced price because they were aware of the rights of the widow. They gave her notice to quit after the purchase. The Court of Appeal upheld her rights to remain in the property, although Lord Denning was the only judge who based his decision on a contractual licence.

> 'In my opinion, the defendant, by virtue of the agreement, had an equitable interest in the cottage which the court would protect by granting an injunction against the landlords restraining them from turning her out. When the landlords sold the cottage to a purchaser "subject to" her rights under the agreement, the purchaser took the cottage on a constructive trust to permit the defendant to reside there during her life, or as long as she might desire. The courts will not allow the purchaser to go back on that trust.'
>
> Lord Denning MR

Lord Denning placed emphasis on the fact that the third parties knew of the widow's rights and 'took subject to' her rights. He contrasted the position in earlier cases such as *Clore v Theatrical Properties Ltd and Westby & Co Ltd* (1936) where there was no express or implied agreement that the third party purchaser should take subject to the rights of the contractual licensee. However, this approach to contractual licences has been strongly criticised in subsequent cases and it is only where the third party gains an advantage, such as a reduction in price, that the courts are prepared to uphold the licence against a third party.

More recently the courts have only been prepared to uphold the rights of a contractual licensee where there is evidence of a constructive trust. A constructive trust confers proprietary rights in favour of the claimant and this approach prevents a licence from becoming a proprietary right in land and so distorting conventional orthodoxy about the status of a licence in land.

CASE EXAMPLE

Ashburn Anstalt v Arnold [1989] Ch 1

The claimants based their claim against third-party purchasers on a contractual licence. Fox LJ categorically denied that a contractual licence can bind purchasers, even where they have notice of the rights, and rejected the law as laid down in *Errington v Errington & Woods* (1952):

> 'A licence in connection with land while entitling the licensee to use the land for the purposes authorised by the licence does not create an estate in the land.... Before the *Errington* case the law appears to have been well understood. It rested on an important and intelligible distinction between contractual obligations which gave rise to no estate or interest in the land and proprietary rights which by definition, did. The far-reaching statement of principle in *Errington* was not supported by authority, not necessary for the decision of the case and *per incuriam* in the sense that it was made without reference to authorities which, if they would not have compelled, would surely have persuaded the court to adopt a different ratio as a response to the problems which had arisen, the *Errington* rule ... was neither practically necessary nor theoretically convincing.'
>
> Fox LJ

Although Fox's judgment is convincing on the facts of the case the claimants were allowed rights based on a lease rather than a licence so the comments were *obiter*.

The law today will not recognise a contractual licence as a binding interest in land unless it is accompanied by a **constructive trust**. This will be found by the court where it believes that the conscience of the successor in title is affected so that it would be inequitable to allow him to deny the claimant's interest in the property.

When will the court find a constructive trust?

In *Binions v Evans* (1972) the purchasers bought 'subject to' the widow's rights. This would not have been enough to establish a constructive trust. The **key factor** was that they bought at a reduced price, taking into account the fact that she was in occupation of the premises thereby conferring an advantage on the purchasers. It would have been unconscionable to deny the widow her right to remain. The courts will only uphold the constructive trust where the purchasers promise to uphold the licence rather than buy 'subject to the right' as a term of the agreement.

In *Lyus v Prowsa Developments Ltd* [1982] 1 WLR 1044 a development company took over an uncompleted development from a company in liquidation. It purchased expressly subject to the rights of the contractual licensees. This was included as a clause in the contract of sale and the court held that the development company held the property as constructive trustees for the licensees and could not seek to deny their rights after the purchase.

The basis of the constructive trust here was that the express terms of the agreement cannot be ignored when the agreement between the parties was based on such terms. Knowledge of a term would not be enough; it was the fact that the agreement was expressly based on the term that was significant in this case.

KEY FACTS

Contractual licences
1. Contractual licences depend on contractual principles.
2. The licensor will only be bound if a contract can be proved with all the essential features of a contract, for example consideration and an intention to create legal relations.
3. Contractual licences do not give rise to proprietary rights in land even when a third-party purchaser buys with notice and 'subject to' those rights.
4. If the purchaser holds as a constructive trustee then a contractual licence may give rise to a proprietary right in land.
5. A constructive trust is dependent on proof that it would be unconscionable for the owner of the land to deny the rights of the claimant. The fact that the purchaser bought at a reduced price may be sufficient to give rise to a constructive trust in favour of the licensee. Or that the agreement between the parties was based on an express term protecting the licensee's rights.

6.4.4 Estoppel licences

Originally, licences by estoppel developed as rights enforceable only against the licensor and were not therefore capable of binding a successor in title. However, there are several cases which have held that such a right will be binding on the land itself.

This would mean that someone purchasing the land would be bound by the licensee's rights and could not attempt to deny them.

ACTIVITY

Applying the law

Consider whether John will be bound by third party rights in these circumstances.

John purchases a large property called Richmond House. He knows that Shirley has a licence to remain in the two-bedroomed cottage adjoining the house for the rest of her life. Will her rights bind John? What difference will it make if he had paid a reduced price to the seller of the property?

Registered land

An estoppel licence is capable of registration in registered land. Under s 116 of the Land Registration Act 2002, estoppel licences are registrable and if properly entered on the Register will be binding on third parties. This has resolved any doubt about whether they will be binding on third-party purchasers.

SECTION

'**s 116** Proprietary estoppel and mere equities

It is hereby declared for the avoidance of any doubt that, in relation to registered land, each of the following –

(a) an equity by estoppel, and

(b) a mere equity

has the effect from the time the equity arises as an interest capable of binding successors in title (subject to the rules about the effect of dispositions on priority).'

This means that they will be binding from the time when the innocent party acted to his detriment in reliance on the promise. The estoppel requires protection on the Register unless the interest takes effect as an overriding interest by virtue of actual occupation of land.

Unregistered land

An estoppel licence is subject to the doctrine of notice in unregistered land. It cannot be registered under the Land Charges Act 1972. It will depend on whether the purchaser was aware of the rights of the licensee when he purchased the property. The right will be binding only if the purchaser has actual or constructive notice of the licence when he purchased the property.

CASE EXAMPLE

Inwards v Baker [1965] 2 WLR 212

The son of Mr Baker had built a bungalow on his father's land, with some financial help from his father. He had lived there for nearly 30 years when proceedings were brought against him by the successors in title of his father who were the children of his father by his second wife. Lord Denning upheld the son's rights to remain:

'All that is necessary is that the licensee should, at the request or with the encouragement of the landlord, have spent the money in the expectation of being allowed to stay there. If so, the court will not allow that expectation to be defeated where it would be inequitable so to do.'

Lord Denning

6.5 The revocation of a licence

As the creation of licences is usually fairly informal so the revocation of a licence does not generally have to follow strict formalities.

6.5.1 Bare licences

A bare licence can be withdrawn at will at any time. The licensor does not have to give any notice or any reason. Once a licence has been revoked, the licensor must give the licensee a reasonable time to pack up and leave the premises.

JUDGMENT

'[T]he sergeant had a reasonable time to leave the premises by the most appropriate route for doing so, namely, out of the front door, down the steps and out of the gate, and, provided that he did so with reasonable expedition, he would not be a trespasser while he was doing so.'

Diplock LJ in *Robson v Hallett* (1967)

A bare licence is always automatically revoked in the following circumstances:

1. on the death of the licensor;
2. when land is sold or disposed of in some other way by the licensor. There has never been any issue as to whether or not the licensee has any interest in the land.

The right to withdraw such a licence at will has been reviewed by Jonathan Hill:

'Since there are many cases (such as those involving occupational licences) in which it is not practicably possible for the licensee to vacate the land immediately on being informed that the licence has been revoked, there is no plausible alternative to the law's recognition of a period of grace in cases involving the termination of a bare licence. There is, of course, no hard and fast rule as to how long the packing-up period should be – as what is reasonable depends on the circumstances. In a case in which a door-to-door salesman is asked by the owner-occupier to leave, a reasonable period would, in most cases, be no more than a few seconds. At the other end of the spectrum, on the termination of a bare licence of residential or commercial premises, a reasonable period would normally be sufficient to allow the licensee to find alternative accommodation and may be as much as a year.'

J Hill, 'The Termination of Bare Licences' [2001] *CLJ* 89

Jonathan Hill is arguing that although it has long been held that the bare licence can be terminated at will, the law will protect the licensee by upholding his right to a period of grace in which he will be allowed time to leave and this will vary according to the type of property. However, Hill is not convinced that this has a basis in law but feels that it has merely arisen as a result of conflicting case law:

'Furthermore, there is no argument of principle in support of the proposition that a licensor should be under obligation to give the licensee a period of notice before revocation of a bare licence is to take effect ... When bare licences are located in the broader picture of rights in relation to land, the notion that a bare licensee is entitled to a period of notice is illogical. The bare licence's closest analogue is not the contractual licensee, but the rent-free tenancy at will. Given that, as regards a tenancy at will, there is no need for a notice to quit, the law would be incoherent if, in relation to a bare licensee the licensor were under an obligation to give the licensee a reasonable period of notice.'

J Hill, 'The Termination of Bare Licences' [2001] CLJ 89

6.5.2 Licences coupled with a grant

A licence coupled with a grant cannot be revoked unless the right or interest itself is withdrawn. The reason for this is that the interest may constitute a proprietary right in land itself, which cannot be withdrawn at will.

6.5.3 Contractual licences

Historically, contractual licences were capable of being withdrawn at will. The licensee would have a remedy in damages which would be calculated according to ordinary contractual principles, but the right to remain on the premises was not protected. So, in *Wood v Leadbitter* (1845) it was held that the racegoer who was ejected from the licensor's racecourse could only claim for damages, as the licensor had the right to exclude him at will.

The more modern approach is to uphold the rights of the licensee to remain on the property for the duration of the contract. Today, according to G P Selvam J:

JUDGMENT

'A contractual licence is irrevocable except as contemplated by the terms of the contract.'

Tan Hin Leong v Lee Teck Im [2000] 3 SLR 85

If the licensee is deprived of his right to live on the property then the court has a choice of whether or not to grant damages or to grant specific performance of the contract. The change in attitude was championed by Lord Denning and one of the first cases to reflect this was *Errington v Errington & Woods* (1952).

CASE EXAMPLE

Errington v Errington & Woods [1952] 1 KB 290

This concerned the right of a daughter-in-law to live in property bought by her father-in-law. The father-in-law promised his son and his wife that they could have the property transferred to them if they continued to live in the house and paid all the mortgage instalments. The father died and left all his property to his wife, including this house. The son left his wife and returned to live with his mother. His wife continued to pay the mortgage. The widow brought an action to evict her from the house, on the basis that the daughter-in-law had only a revocable licence. The Court of Appeal refused the action and upheld the right of the daughter-in-law to continue to live in the house, on the undertaking that she would continue to repay the mortgage instalments.

These rights were not rights in law but were rights in equity. The right was 'a contractual right, or at any rate, an equitable right to remain so long as they paid the instalments, which would grow into a good equitable title to the house as soon as the mortgage was paid'.

The decision has been criticised in later cases, in particular *Ashburn Anstalt v Arnold* (1989). Today a contractual licence can only be binding on third parties if there is evidence also of a constructive trust. As mentioned above, the contractual licence in *Binions v Evans* (1972) was not binding on the third-party purchasers even though the purchasers bought knowing of its existence, but the widow's rights were binding because the purchasers held as constructive trustees having purchased at undervalue. Where property is purchased at undervalue to take into account the rights of a third party the conscience of the purchaser must be effected.

A licence is a personal right only and so the licence can be revoked by someone other than the licensor. Such rights do not bind the third-party purchaser.

6.5.4 Estoppel licences

Revocation of an estoppel licence will depend on the terms of the licence. The court will usually determine the extent of the rights of the licensee under the estoppel. A licence will not be revocable if the licence is held to be perpetual. If the court holds that a licence can be determined on the occurrence of certain events then that is the only condition by which the licence can be revoked.

ACTIVITY

Applying the law

George builds a cottage on his grandfather's land and lives there for ten years. On the death of his grandfather George's uncle Ishmael takes over the land including his cottage. Can George continue to live in his cottage? Will his rights be binding on Ishmael?

6.6 Comparison of different types of licence

	How created	How terminated	Effect on third parties
Bare licences: permission to enter someone's land without payment of consideration.	Informally. Can be impliedly created.	Can be withdrawn at will although the licensee usually given time to leave (*Robson v Hallett* (1967)).	Cannot be binding on a third party.
Licences coupled with a grant: licences granted in order to enjoy an interest on the land.	Dependent on the nature of the interest; if it is a *profit à prendre* then requires a deed.	Cannot be revoked unless interest is revoked (*Hurst v Picture Theatres Ltd* (1915)).	Will be binding as long as the right to enjoy the interest exists.
Contractual licences: licences in exchange for valuable consideration.	Created informally (*Tanner v Tanner* (1975)) unless the contract requires any formalities.	Once could be withdrawn at will (*Wood v Leadbitter* (1845)) but now subject to the terms of the contract.	Third party will not be bound unless there is evidence of a constructive trust (*Binions v Evans* (1972); *Lyus v Prowsa Developments* (1982)).
Estoppel licences: licences arising under proprietary estoppel.	Arises informally once the requirements for estoppel are satisfied (*Greasley v Cooke* (1980)).	Depends on the terms of the licence granted by the court.	Can be binding where registered land and the right has been registered.

Table 6.1 Different types of licence

SUMMARY

1. A licence is permission given by the owner of land to a person to do something or go on to land which would otherwise constitute a trespass.

2. There are four types of licence: bare licences, licences coupled with a grant or interest, contractual licences and estoppel licences.

3. The creation of a licence will vary according to the type of licence.

4. The bare licence requires no formalities and can be impliedly created. A licence coupled with a grant will require a deed where the grant is of a *profit à prendre*.

5. Only a licence coupled with a grant and an estoppel licence binds a third party.

6. A contractual licence will bind a third party if a constructive trust can be found.

7. A bare licence can be revoked at will but revocation of a contractual licence or an estoppel licence or a licence coupled with a grant is subject to stricter rules.

SAMPLE ESSAY QUESTION

Many attempts have been made to argue that licences in land are capable of binding third parties. Critically assess the success of these attempts.

> Define a licence. A licence is permission from a landowner (the licensor) to the licensee to enjoy the licensor's land within the terms of the licence. It is not a proprietary right in land. Discuss the different types of licences:
>
> i. bare licences;
> ii. licences coupled with a grant;
> iii. contractual licences;
> iv. estoppel licences.
>
> Discuss their overlap with other rights in land, e.g. easements.

> Discuss whether licences can bind third parties. General rule: a licence can never bind a third party unless coupled with another right that can give rise to proprietary rights in land. See *Thomas v Sorrell* (1673).
>
> Consider licences coupled with a grant and estoppel licences and discuss why these licences can bind third parties.

> Distinguish bare licences and contractual licences.
> Discuss case law seeking to give licences proprietary status.

Discuss the tension in allowing licences to be binding on third parties: see *Errington v Errington & Woods*.

Discuss the difference between personal rights and proprietary rights and the importance of maintaining the distinction.

Consider cases where a licence has been enforced under a constructive trust and consider whether this is a useful approach: see *Lyus v Prowsa*; *Binions v Evans*.

Analyse the judgment of Fox LJ in *Ashburn Anstalt v Arnold* and discuss.

State current position: third parties are not bound by contractual licences unless there are circumstances which allow the court to impose a constructive trust.

Discuss those circumstances.

CONCLUSION

Further reading

Books

Dixon, M, 'Proprietary Estoppel and Formalities in Land Law and the Land Registration Act 2002: A Theory of Unconscionability' in E Cooke (ed.), *Modern Studies in Property Law* Vol 2 (Hart Publishing, 2013).

Gray, K and Gray, S F, *Elements of Land Law* (5th edn, Oxford University Press, 2009), p. 1310.

Gray, K and Gray, S F, 'The Idea of Property in Land' in S Bright and J Dewar (eds), *Land Law: Themes and Perspectives* (Oxford University Press, 1998).

Articles

Anderson, S, 'Of Licences and Similar Mysteries' (1979) 42 *MLR* 203.

Battersby, G, 'Informal Transactions in Land, Estoppel and Registration' (1995) 58 *MLR* 637.

Bright, S, 'The Third Party's Conscience in Land Law' [2000] *Conv* 368.

Dixon, M, 'An Everyday Story of Country Folk: Proprietary Estoppel and Licences' [2004] 41 *SL Rev* 52.

Dixon, M, 'Defining and Confining Estoppel' (2010) 30 *LS* 408.

Hill, J, 'The Termination of Bare Licences' [2001] *CLJ* 89.

Kerbel, T, 'Unreasonable Revocation of a Licence' [1996] *Conv* 63.

Thompson, M P, ' "My Home is Not my Castle": *Macclesfield v Parker* [2003] EWHC 1846' [2003] 67 *Conv* 516.

7

Proprietary estoppel

AIMS AND OBJECTIVES

After reading this chapter, you should be able to:

- Define what is meant by proprietary estoppel
- Describe the main elements of proprietary estoppel
- Understand what constitutes a representation
- Explain what is meant by detrimental reliance
- Describe the remedies that may be granted by the courts
- Explain how rights under proprietary estoppel may be lost

7.1 Background to proprietary estoppel

Proprietary estoppel is an informal way of acquiring rights in land. It has its roots firmly in the law of equity as it allows the claimant the right to claim land even where the strict formalities have not been complied with.

7.1.1 Introduction

The transfer of rights in land is subject to a number of strict formalities, such as evidence in writing or a particular formal document, e.g. a deed. By way of contrast, the law on proprietary estoppel is a way of establishing informal rights in property. It will generally only arise where the formalities of transfer of rights in property have been ignored. It is often considered in the context of the family home.

There is an overlap with constructive trusts but **note** the main difference between the two

1. proprietary estoppel is based on **representations**; whereas
2. constructive trusts rely upon **bargains** or **common intention**.

So the importance of proprietary estoppel is that it allows persons to claim that they have rights where the ordinary formalities associated with the transfer of land have been ignored. However, without formalities to guide us, it is particularly important to try to be clear about when such rights arise. It is important that it is not left to the

....

representation

A person who makes a representation to another that he has rights in property cannot later deny those rights where the representation has been acted upon. The person who relies on the representation must prove that he has acted to his detriment

....

discretion of the court. As Lord Walker declared in *Cobbe v Yeoman's Row Management* (2008) proprietary estoppel 'is not a sort of joker or wild card to be used whenever the Court disapproves of the conduct of a litigant who seems to have the law on his side'.

JUDGMENT

'Equity comes in ... to mitigate the rigours of strict law ... It will prevent a person insisting on his strict legal rights ... when it would be inequitable for him to do so having regard to the dealings which have taken place between the parties.'

Denning MR in *Crabb v Arun DC* [1976] 1 Ch 179

CASE EXAMPLE

Crabb v Arun DC [1976] 1 Ch 179

The Council agreed with Mr Crabb that he would have access to some of his land through the adjacent land owned by the Council. He intended to sell part of the land which would be inaccessible without this right of way. The Council later denied him rights of access, which resulted in his land becoming landlocked. The court upheld Crabb's claim based on the promise made to him by the Council. He had acted on the promise to his detriment by selling the land without reserving rights of access.

The introduction of the Land Registration Act 2002, with its objective of ensuring that as many rights and interests appear on the Register as possible including proprietary estoppel, has reinforced the significance of proprietary estoppel as a way of ensuring that informal rights will remain binding on the registered proprietor.

SECTION

's 116 (a) an equity by estoppel, and
     (b) a mere equity, has the effect from the time the equity arises as an interest capable of binding successors in title.'

7.1.2 Historical background

There are several nineteenth-century cases which show that interests in land could be passed from one to another without formal documentation but instead on the basis of conduct of one party.

An early example of the operation of the doctrine is:

CASE EXAMPLE

Dillwyn v Llewelyn (1862) 4 De GF & J 517

A son built a house at considerable expense in reliance on an informal memorandum that he would have rights in his father's land. The memorandum did not satisfy the necessary formal requirements to pass rights in land but nevertheless the son's rights were upheld, on the basis that he had incurred expenditure in reliance on a promise made to him by his father. Normally the law would regard this as an imperfect gift and the courts would not uphold it. The difference is the fact that a representation was made to the son and he acted on that representation.

This case was based on the express representation made by the father to the son, but estoppel has been held to extend further to include circumstances where there have been dealings between parties which suggest that one party has made an assumption and acted on that assumption. These cases could be identified as cases where the parties have a common expectation that one party will acquire rights in land held by another based on their dealings together in that land as shown in the two cases below.

CASE EXAMPLE

Plimmer v Mayor of Wellington (1884) 9 App Cas 699

A licensee of land spent a large sum of money on various alterations to the land including the extension of a jetty and the building of a warehouse, all at the licensor's request, but later had his licence withdrawn by the licensor. Normally a licence would not give the licensee any rights in that land but the Privy Council upheld the claim of the licensee that the licence had become irrevocable because of the large sums of money that had been spent on the land. The key feature here was the encouragement of the licensor to the licensee to carry out the work.

CASE EXAMPLE

Ramsden v Dyson (1866) LR 1 HL 129

A tenant built on his land, believing he would be entitled to a long lease. He claimed that he should be entitled to the lease because he had acted on the belief and built on the land. The House of Lords, by majority, decided he could not claim the lease but the case lays down the following important principle of law:

'if a stranger begins to build on my land supposing it to be his own, and I perceiving his mistake, abstain from setting him right, and leave him to persevere in his error, a court of equity will not allow me afterwards to assert my title to the land on which he had expended money on the supposition that the land was his own'.

Lord Cranworth LC

This is an important case in the development of the doctrine as it shows that simply staying silent when someone else tries to enjoy one's land will be enough for the law to accept acquiescence in the claim. The law would expect that a landowner would object in circumstances when another builds on your land or treats it as one's own. If the landowner stands by and does nothing the law holds that this is encouragement.

7.1.3 The *Willmott v Barber probanda*

We can trace the development of proprietary estoppel further to the case of *Willmott v Barber* (1880) 15 Ch D 96. This case laid down a formula for the informal acquisition of rights in property. According to Fry J, it involved satisfying five requirements, or *probanda* as they were known.

1. The claimant must have made a mistake about his legal rights over land belonging to another.
2. The claimant must have spent money or carried out some action relying on his mistaken belief.
3. The defendant must know of his own right which is inconsistent with the right claimed by the claimant.
4. The defendant must know of the claimant's mistaken belief.
5. The defendant must have encouraged the claimant when spending money in his mistaken belief, either actively or by abstaining from asserting his legal right.

7.1.4 The modern doctrine of proprietary estoppel

The five *probanda* were very prescriptive and proved difficult to apply. Today, as proprietary estoppel has grown in significance in property law the *probanda* have been replaced by a much simpler set of requirements. The leading authority is *Taylor Fashions Ltd v Liverpool Victoria Trustees Co Ltd* [1982] QB 133 which sets out three requirements for a successful claim in estoppel:

- a **representation**;
- **reliance** on that representation;
- **detriment**.

In circumstances that it would be **unconscionable** to deny a remedy to the claimant.

CASE EXAMPLE

Taylor Fashions Ltd v Liverpool Victoria Trustees Co Ltd [1982] QB 133

Liverpool Victoria Trustees had purchased land subject to a lease. The tenants had options to renew their leases but had failed to register them, believing that they were not registrable. This rendered them unenforceable. The tenants, however, spent money on the premises, expecting to exercise the options, but were still not aware of the need to register them. They attempted to renew the lease and were challenged by the landlords.

The judge dismissed part of the claim by the tenants because the defendants had not encouraged the tenants to act on the belief that the lease was renewable. This was required under the *Willmott v Barber* probanda.

'More recent cases indicate ... that proprietary estoppel ... requires a very much broader approach which is directed rather at ascertaining whether, in particular individual circumstances, it would be unconscionable for a party to be permitted to deny that which, knowingly, or unknowingly, he has allowed or encouraged another to assume to his detriment than to inquiring whether the circumstances can be fitted within the confines of some preconceived formula serving as a universal yardstick for every form of unconscionable behaviour.'

Oliver J

The distinction here lies in the fact that there does not have to be a mistake about rights and knowledge that the other party has made a mistake about their rights. Mr Justice Oliver also laid weight on the unconscionable behaviour of the defendant who tries to deny rights to the claimant when he has already encouraged the claimant in his beliefs.

However, in some cases following *Taylor Fashions* the older criteria have been used as a basis for the decision.

CASE EXAMPLE

Coombes v Smith [1986] 1 WLR 808

A woman in a relationship claimed the right to be able to continue living, with the child of the relationship, in a property owned by her partner as long as she wished after the relationship ended.

'The second element or requisite is that the plaintiff must have expended money, or otherwise prejudiced himself or acted to his detriment, on the faith of his mistaken belief in his legal rights.'

Deputy Judge Jonathan Parker QC

CASE EXAMPLE

Matharu v Matharu (1994) 2 FLR 597

A woman's father-in-law tried to recover possession of a house after the breakdown of her marriage and the death of her husband, his son. The daughter-in-law based her claim on her mistaken belief, which was known to her father-in-law, that the house belonged to her husband. She had worked on the house and so acted to her detriment on the basis of this belief. The court upheld her rights on the basis of estoppel, allowing her the right to remain in the property, but it did not grant her any proprietary rights. She was granted a licence to remain in the house 'for her life or such shorter period as she may decide'. This right was granted subject to her agreeing to pay for the outgoings on the property, including the mortgage repayments. The claim was based on establishing all five of the probanda under *Willmott v Barber* (1880).

The approach of the court in this case was surprising since it appears to have ignored the more straightforward requirements laid down in *Taylor Fashions* (1982). In both *Matharu* and *Coombes* the court reverts back to the basis of the claim resting on the problems of the mistaken belief of the claimant. In *Matharu* the court found in favour of the daughter-in-law because it accepted that she had satisfied the five *probanda* but the claim by Mrs Coombes failed as the court held that she had not satisfied the criteria.

7.1.5 The scope of proprietary estoppel

Proprietary estoppel has its limitations and it is not open to everyone who has failed to meet the strict formal requirements necessary for the transfer of rights in property. The key issue is whether it would be unconscionable for the landowner to deny the claimant rights.

CASE EXAMPLE

Cobbe v Yeoman's Row Management [2008] 1 WLR 1752

The owner of a building and a property developer reached an oral agreement in principle under which the developer would obtain planning permission to develop the property and the property would be transferred to him for development and later sale and distribution of the profits between the parties. The developer obtained the planning permission and sought to enforce the agreement even though it had never been put in writing as required under s 2(1) the Law of Property (Miscellaneous Provisions) Act 1989. The House of Lords held (reversing the Court of Appeal) that the claimant was not entitled to a share in the increase in value of the property under the doctrine of proprietary estoppel. Both parties knew that the deal had not been completed and that the contract had to be in writing in order for it to be enforceable and as a result the claimant had no expectation of rights in land.

This decision has limited the use of the doctrine in certain cases in particular where the parties are fully aware of the need for formalities to be followed before rights will arise. This is more likely in cases where two people who have business expertise are negotiating as in *Cobbe v Yeomans Row Management*. In such cases there cannot be an expectation of rights because the claimant would know that no rights could arise until contracts have been exchanged. This has been welcomed by a number of academics who had criticised the more flexible approach to proprietary estoppel embraced by the courts in recent cases such as *Gillett v Holt*.

'The law of real property places limits on the ability of persons to create property rights – usually, the parties must employ a degree of formality. The extent to which estoppel permits the claimant to obtain a property right without such formality necessarily contradicts the policy of certainty that is inherent in the statutory formality rules. It is perfectly reasonable to regard the current law of estoppel as going too far in this direction. In Yeoman's Row, Lord Scott makes the point that estoppel does not operate to remedy some general sense of unconscionability.'

M Dixon, 'Proprietary Estoppel: A Return to Principle?' [2009] 3 Conv 260

This case can be contrasted with another decision *Thorner v Major* (2009) where the House of Lords again reviewed the doctrine of proprietary estoppel and established that it still continues to have a use in enforcing informal rights in land if the right conditions are present.

CASE EXAMPLE

Thorner v Major [2009] UKHL 18

David Thorner made a claim against his deceased cousin's estate after his cousin had died intestate. The cousin, Peter Thorner, had made a will leaving his farm to David Thorner but he had asked his solicitor to revoke the will because he wanted to change a gift under the will. He did not make another will before he died. In this case the cousin David Thorner had an expectation of rights in the estate which were encouraged by the cousin who gave him assurances, albeit in rather vague terms, that he would inherit the farm after his death.

The House of Lords upheld his claim on the basis that it would be unconscionable for his rights to be denied.

'In the short term, the decision in *Thorner v Major*, by implicitly rejecting the limits suggested in *Cobbe v Yeoman's Row Management*, allows proprietary estoppel to continue to perform its vital role of protecting those who reasonably rely on assurances from another that they have, or will acquire, a right in relation to that other's land. That role may call for intervention in commercial as well as domestic cases, although of course the inquiry as to whether A has made an assurance and whether B's reliance is reasonable will have to be sensitive to the particular background of the case.'

B McFarlane and A Robertson, 'Apocalypse Averted: Proprietary
Estoppel in the House of Lords' (2009) 125 LQR 535

These two cases have tried to reset the parameters of proprietary estoppel but some uncertainty still remains. As McFarlane and Robertson point out

'In the longer term, the decision in *Thorner v Major* may force a re-examination of some of the more tricky questions relating to proprietary estoppel, such as the extent of the rights it gives rise to and the scope of its application beyond cases involving land.'

Although *Thorner* and *Cobbe* are very different in context and were decided on very different facts it is important not to fall into the trap of suggesting that the courts were looking at commercial cases and family cases in a different way. The context and facts will be relevant in every proprietary estoppel case and the courts will look to see if the elements of estoppel are present.

7.2 The elements of proprietary estoppel

In order to establish a claim under proprietary estoppel the claimant must prove the three elements from *Taylor Fashions Ltd v Liverpool Victoria Trustees Co Ltd* [1982] QB 133; a representation, reliance and detriment in circumstances in which it would be unconscionable to deny a remedy to the claimant.

7.2.1 The representation

The claimant must prove that some kind of representation or assurance or promise was made which encouraged him to believe that he would acquire rights over the land.

Different types of representation

1. Representations can be **positive** assurances; or
2. **mere silence leading** the claimant to believe that he had rights.

1. Positive assurances or representations

The assurance made must be an express promise of positive rights in the land.

CASE EXAMPLE

Cobbe v Yeoman's Row Management Ltd [2008] 1 WLR 1752

In this case (discussed earlier) the House of Lords held that there was no promise of rights in the property by the owner to the developer, they merely entered into negotiations over the purchase of the property. The owner of the property did not promise an interest in the land merely that he would enter into further negotiations concerning the sale of the property.

CASE EXAMPLE

Inwards v Baker [1965] 2 QB 929

A father encouraged his son to build a bungalow on his land. The son acted on this representation and built on the land as his father suggested. The son would not be contractually bound to build the bungalow on the father's land. However, as the father gave permission and encouragement then this amounted to a representation sufficient to raise estoppel.

If the father had later refused to offer the son the land before the building had started then the son could not force him to do so. Equally, if the son had gone back on his promise to build on the land he could not be forced to do so by his father.

ACTIVITY

Applying the law

Rachael lives in a large house surrounded by several fields which she owns. Her brother, Thomas, tells Rachael that the field adjoining her house would be a perfect location for a house and he asks her if he can build on her land. She agrees and assures him that the house will be his but the agreement is not recorded in writing as necessary for a transfer of an interest in land. Can she later try to evict him after the house has been built, and rely on the lack of written evidence?

Would the court uphold his rights on the basis of proprietary estoppel?

You will note here that the rights promised were rights in land so they should have been in writing. However the fact that Thomas goes ahead and builds on the land on the basis of the promise will make it difficult for Rachael then to refuse to allow him rights in the land. His claim would be supported by *Inwards v Baker* discussed above.

The promise made does not have to amount to an enforceable contract.

In *Thorner v Major* (2008) the Court of Appeal refused the claim of the representee partly because the extent of the land was uncertain and so neither the extent of the land nor the exact boundaries could be defined. However, the House of Lords took a different view. It was held that an assurance could generate an estoppel if when it was made it related to an identified parcel of land, but this does not preclude a claim still being successful where the boundaries and extent of land have changed since the original representation has changed.

A representation of future rights under a will

The representation can be held to be binding on the representor even where it is made within a will.

If a representation is made in a will then it will not necessarily be binding on the representor for the rest of his lifetime. If your grandmother tells you that she is going to leave her house to you in her will, she is not bound to do so. Everyone has the right to change his will at any time up until death. However, if you immediately act on your grandmother's promise it may then be held sufficient to raise an estoppel on her death if she has not left her house to you.

Can a representation made about rights arising under a will be relied on where it has been acted on and there is some evidence of detriment?

The courts were originally reluctant to uphold a claim of the promise of rights arising in a will even where it had been acted upon by the representee but recently the courts have revised that view.

Compare the following cases:

CASE EXAMPLE

Taylor v Dickens [1998] 3 FCR 455

An old lady had told her gardener that she would leave her estate to him in her will. He relied on this statement and carried on working for her without pay. On her death, she did not leave the property to him. The court did not uphold his claim since she had the right at any time to revoke her will and she had not led him to believe that she would not do so.

JUDGMENT

'Subject to specific statutory exceptions (such as for dependants) the right to decide, and change one's mind as to, the devolution of one's estate is a basic and well understood feature of English law. The law allows one to disappoint the expectations of those who have no more than a moral claim on one's affections, however strong. During the lifetime of the potential testator, that is a risk which anyone seeking to rely on such a representation necessarily faces.'

Carnwath J in *Gillett v Holt* [1998] 3 All ER 917 (judgment at first instance)

CASE EXAMPLE

Gillett v Holt [2001] Ch 210

Mr Gillett had worked for Mr Holt for over 30 years and had been promised, over a period of years on at least seven occasions, that Mr Holt would leave his farm to him. In the event, they fell out and Mr Holt left his property to someone else whom he had known for a very short period of time. Even though it is open to anyone to change their will up until death, estoppel can always be argued if a representation can be shown and in reponse the claimant has acted to his detriment. At first instance Mr Gillett's claim was refused on the basis that there had been no assurance from Holt that was capable of amounting to an irrevocable promise that the claimant would inherit his estate despite subsequent changes in circumstances. The court also held that there was insufficient evidence of detriment.

It was held in that case that there may be some circumstances where a representation that someone is to inherit property under the will of the representor on his death will be held to be binding.

> 'In the generality of cases it is no doubt correct [that one should not count one's chickens before they were hatched], and it is notorious that some elderly persons of means derive enjoyment from the possession of a testamentary power, and from dropping hints as to their intentions, without any question of an estoppel arising. But in this case Mr Holt's assurances were repeated over a long period, usually before the assembled company on special family occasions, and some of them … were completely unambiguous … Plainly some of the assurances were to be relied on.'
>
> Robert Walker LJ

The following factors from *Gillett v Holt* (1998) suggest that a representation may be acted on:

- repetition of representations made;
- representations made before witnesses;
- the nature of the representation was unambiguous.

Indeed the decision in *Taylor v Dickens* (1998) has been subject to considerable criticism from academics and the judiciary:

> 'This decision is clearly wrong, for the judge seemed to have forgotten that the whole point of estoppel claims is that they concern promises which, since they are unsupported by consideration, are initially revocable. What later makes them binding, and therefore irrevocable, is the promisee's detrimental reliance on them. Once that occurs, there is simply no question of the promisor changing his mind.'
>
> W Swadling, 'Restitutionary Claims: A Comparative Analysis' [1998] RLR 220

This point was raised again in the case of *Thorner v Major* [2009] UKHL 18. The deceased (Peter Thorner) owned a farm and other assets which were valued at around £3.6 million. He had no children or close family. He was much older than the claimant who treated him like an uncle. The claimant (David Thorner) was a first cousin who had gone to the deceased's farm in 1976 to help him and usually worked for no pay. He had other work and he helped his cousin mainly through family loyalty. His commitment to the farm increased over the years. At first the claimant had only a hope that the farm would be left but later he was promised albeit obliquely by the deceased Peter Thorner that he would inherit the farm.

In 1997 Peter made a will and under the terms he left the farm to the claimant. In 1998 Peter went to the solicitor to change his will. He wanted to change one of the legacies under the will, however he never made a new will but took the old will away and it was never found, so it was assumed he had destroyed it.

The unusual feature of this case was that although the two worked together on the farm for over 30 years they rarely spoke to each other directly about property rights although it was accepted in court that they were close and understood each other very well. David had considered moving away from the area but had remained and it was assumed that he remained because he had thought that the farm would be his. Peter died intestate and under the intestacy rules the claimant David would not benefit as his relationship with the deceased was too remote and the property would pass to Peter's brothers and sisters.

The judge at first instance found in favour of the claimant emphasising that the basis of estoppel is to prevent unconscionable conduct and to prevent the claimant from having an interest in the farm would be unconscionable.

This view was reversed in the Court of Appeal on the basis that the assurance given was too vague; the claim was rejected on the basis that it was not clear, express and unequivocal. The House of Lords reinstated the judgment at first instance and found in favour of David Thorner although his claim was based on a future interest under a will and although the nature of the promise was very vague. The House of Lords applied the principle that the case should be looked at in its entirety relying on a key expression that 'context is everything' rather than a single assurance given to the claimant. The fact that the older cousin never once expressly told the claimant that the farm and the house would be his was not important where there were implied promises made every day when the younger cousin worked on the farm for very little and often for no pay. The handing over of an insurance policy bonus by Peter Thorner and the statement 'this is for my death duties' was held to be a sufficient assurance in support of David's claim. The claimant argued that there was a mutual understanding that he would inherit the estate on his cousin's death.

Agents

The representation can be made by the agent of the owner of the land and this can be relied on. However, a tenant cannot make a representation on behalf of the landlord.

Generally worded representations do not raise proprietary estoppel

If a representation is made in very general terms, no estoppel can arise. So if a promise to support someone financially is made then this will not be directly linked to rights in property.

CASE EXAMPLE

Layton v Martin [1986] 2 FLR 227

Here, the claimant had been told that she would be provided for by the representor. There was no express reference to rights in land.

The problem with this representation was that it was very general and did not relate directly to the acquisition of rights in the property itself. It does not matter if the representation is general in terms if the promise concerns actual rights in land. More recently in *James v James* [2018] EWHC 43 (Ch) a claim under estoppel by a son who had not been included in the will made by his father was rejected because there was no evidence that the father had made a particular promise to the claimant son that he would be left any property under the will. The court accepted that that would not necessarily be fatal to his claim as the court must look at the totality of the evidence. Nevertheless there was not a sufficient degree of clarity to amount to such an assurance.

By way of contrast where the claimant can point to an express statement then this will amount to a representation.

CASE EXAMPLE

Pascoe v Turner [1979] 1 WLR 431

The defendant said to the claimant during their relationship together: 'The house is yours and everything in it.' This was a clear representation of rights in the property.

Statements made in the context of cohabitation may give rise to an assurance. Although general statements as made in *Coombes v Smith* discussed above did not amount to an assurance; today such statements may be taken in the context of a relationship, as in *Liden v Burton* [2016] EWCA Civ 275 and *Southwell v Blackburn* [2015] EWCA Civ 1347. In *Liden* the defendant had said to the claimant that regular monthly sums were 'towards the house' and 'were needed if the house was to be kept for the benefit of both of us'. In *Southwell* the Court of Appeal upheld a finding by the Judge at first instance that Ms Blackburn would have 'the sort of security that a wife would have, in terms of accommodation at the house, and income'. These cases are discussed further later in the chapter.

2. Mere silence
In *Ramsden v Dyson* (1866) LR 1 HL 129 Lord Cranworth referred to the silence of a landowner where someone starts building on his land. He suggested that equity would intervene if someone silently allows another to build on his land and does not interfere to prevent that and rights in the land may arise.

ACTIVITY

Applying the law
Edward and Gerald live next door to each other. Gerald says to Edward: 'You need somewhere to keep your vintage car – it will get very rusty if you leave it outside all winter.' Edward decides to build a shed to house his vintage car and he builds it on some land belonging to Gerald which adjoins his garden. The shed was finished earlier this year and he moved in his vintage car. Gerald has watched it being built and has said nothing about the fact that it is on his land. Gerald has suddenly become less friendly and told Edward last week that he expected him to move the car out as the shed was his property.

Has Edward a claim to the shed?

The important point here is that there must be some encouragement from the owner of the property. If the claimant simply moves on to the land and starts to build then the court would never hold that he has rights in the property. This is referred to as a legitimate expectation of rights and, even if it is reasonable, the claimant must be encouraged in his belief before the courts will uphold his rights.

The courts are careful not to allow mere silence to be legally significant unless it can be clearly linked to an acceptance or endorsement of rights in property.

Other jurisdictions
In other jurisdictions the courts have been prepared to grant rights in land to someone who has acted to their detriment in the absence of any representation or assurance. In Australia, the doctrine of unjust enrichment would allow a successful claim based on expenditure incurred where no representation about rights has been made. The Australian courts look at the issue from the point of view of the landowner and see the issue as one of unjust enrichment of the landowner at the expense of the claimant (see the discussion of the approach to implied trusts in other jurisdictions in Chapter 5).

KEY FACTS

Representations
1. A representation can be a positive statement or mere silence.
2. There must be some form of encouragement to the claimant that he has acquired rights in the property.
3. A representation of future rights under a will can be binding in some circumstances. These will be where the representor shows an intention to be bound and the representee has acted on the promise.
4. A representation can still be binding if it is made by an agent of the owner of the land.
5. A tenant cannot make a representation on behalf of his landlord.

ACTIVITY

Applying the law

Consider the following situations and decide whether they amount to a representation:

1. Mr Wells was getting older and had developed arthritis. When his son, Andrew, came to visit, he told him if he wanted to build a bungalow on the side of the garden where apple trees were growing at present, he could have the bungalow for himself. Nothing was put into writing. When the bungalow was built, Andrew moved in and lived there for five years until Mr Wells died. Mr Wells left no will. Andrew's sisters, to whom he had not spoken for ten years, contested Andrew's rights over the land and the bungalow.
2. Andrew visited his grandfather and found him to be gradually losing his eyesight. Andrew said he would move in to help him. He spent several weekends decorating the house.
3. Andrew's girlfriend, Sue, comes to live with him. Andrew tells her she has nothing to worry about as half the house and its contents will be hers from now on. Nothing is put into writing. She carries out repairs amounting to over £3,000 which amounted to one-quarter of the total capital that she had.

There is a clear representation in the first example but not in the second example. In example (3) Andrew makes a representation to Sue when he expressly tells her she has rights to half the house and its contents. This is similar to *Pascoe v Turner*. She could argue that she only carried out the repairs because of Andrew's promise that half the house was hers.

7.2.2 Reliance on the representation

The claimant must show that he relied on the repre sentation made to him and changed his position in reliance on that representation. Reliance is based on a change of position, so there must be a link between the representation made and the change of position. It must be shown that it was the assurance that persuaded the representee to act as he did. It is the reliance on the representation which would then make any denial of the right by the representor unconscionable. It does not have to be the sole inducement, as other factors may be shown to have had an influence.

ACTIVITY

Self-assessment questions

Consider the following situations and decide whether Katie and Moira have rights under proprietary estoppel if Kenneth does not leave either of them property in his will:

1. If an elderly uncle, Kenneth, promises his niece, Katie, rights in his house if she will come and live closer to him and the niece acts on this, would this be evidence of reliance?
2. Consider also the position of another niece, Moira, who moves closer to her elderly uncle Kenneth because her job changes and she would like to help him more. Kenneth does not make her any promises of rights in his house.

There is an overlap between reliance and acting to your detriment. Many of the factors that are relevant under this heading will be relevant under the next heading, but it is important that the claimant can show that he acted the way he did because he relied on an assurance made rather than acting to his detriment because he always intended to act in that way.

Consider the following case where there was evidence that although Mr Campbell had said in evidence that he would have cared for the couple even if the assurances had not been made. The court found in his favour because it accepted that the assurances were an inducement to Mr Campbell.

CASE EXAMPLE

Campbell v Griffin [2001] EWCA Civ 990

Mr Campbell replied to an advertisement offering accommodation and as a result had gone to live with an elderly couple, paying rent. After five years their relationship changed and he became like a son to them. They made promises that he would have a home for life. When they both died there was no will in existence and Mr Campbell made a claim that he could live in the house for the rest of his life. He produced evidence of ways that he had helped the couple over the years but the court did not place much reliance on this. It found that the expenditure was small and could not be taken as reliance on the assurances which Mr Campbell had been given with regard to the house. However, the court was prepared to uphold his claim in spite of the fact that he had said in evidence that he would have cared for them under any circumstances and even without promises concerning the property.

> 'This seems sensible and avoids carers who have a close personal relationship with the people being cared for, being in a potentially worse position than those who perform such tasks without the prior existence of such a bond.'
> M P Thompson, 'Estoppel: Reliance, Remedy and Priority' [2003] *Conv* 157

This considers the problem that can beset carers and close family members in estoppel cases. If they suggest that they would have looked after the family member in any event even without the promise of rights then the court may look unfavourably on their claims whereas if they suggest that their care was based solely on their belief that they would get an interest in land then they look hardhearted and uncaring.

CASE EXAMPLE

Re Basham [1986] 1 WLR 1498

The claimant and her husband had cared for her step-father and his home for a period of many years. The daughter had been led to believe by him that his entire estate would be left to her when he died. The couple had had a chance to move because her husband could have moved with his job but they had remained, partly relying on the promises made to the step-daughter that she was to inherit the property. Once, the step-father had asked the claimant to deal with a dispute over the boundary of the property because, in his words, she should sort it out herself because she was going to be entitled to the property when he died. However, he died intestate and she would not inherit absolutely under the intestacy rules. Her claim over the cottage was upheld based on proprietary estoppel.

This case also shows that detriment suffered by someone other than the representee can also be relevant.

CASE EXAMPLE

Greasley v Cooke [1980] 1 WLR 1306

A live-in maid, Cooke, had been assured of the right to remain in the property for her lifetime when she started to live with one of the members of the family. She continued to care for the property and also to look after a mentally ill member of the family. Her right to live in the property for her lifetime was upheld.

One issue in this case was whether Cooke could claim rights under proprietary estoppel when she had not spent any money on the property. Lord Denning found that she did not need to prove that she acted on the assurances; it could be assumed that she did so. There was no need to prove that she specifically acted to her detriment as it could be assumed from the fact that she stayed on to care for property without payment when she could go elsewhere to find another job.

'No one can say what she would have done if Kenneth and Hedley had not made those statements. It is quite possible that she would have said to herself, "I am not married to Kenneth. I am on my own. What will happen to me if anything happens to him? I had better look out for another job now: rather than stay here where I have no security." '

Denning MR

Expenditure of money

In most cases, reliance or change of position will be shown by expenditure of money: *Inwards v Baker* (1965) and *Dillwyn v Llewelyn* (1862). In both cases the claimants had spent money on improving the land of the defendant by building on that land.

Expenditure of money alone is not enough to raise an estoppel. If the claimant would have acted in this way without the assurance, then estoppel does not arise.

CASE EXAMPLE

Coombes v Smith [1986] 1 WLR 808

The claimant formed a relationship with the defendant and left her husband. A house was bought in the man's name and the intention was that they would live there together but at first only the woman lived there. They had a child but they never lived together in the house. She cared for the child and the house and carried out a number of improvements. The judge found no evidence of an assurance that she would have rights in the property so the acts of detriment could not be linked to any rights in property; the two were unrelated.

'The reality is that the plaintiff decided to move … because she preferred to have a relationship with, and a child by, the defendant rather than continuing to live with her husband. It seems to me to have been as simple as that. There is no evidence that she left her husband in reliance on the defendant's assurance that he would provide for her if and when their relationship came to and end: the idea of detriment or prejudice is only introduced *ex post facto*.'

Deputy Judge Jonathan Parker QC

The courts could not find the necessary link between the acts to the claimant's detriment and a promise made by the defendant. The judge saw all the acts such as the care of the child as the 'kind of conduct that you would expect of any woman in the same position'.

Compare this case:

CASE EXAMPLE

Pascoe v Turner [1979] 1 WLR 431

The defendant owned a house and the claimant moved in. He then made a promise to her that the house and everything in it belonged to her. In reliance on this promise she improved the property at her own expense. The court held that she was entitled to claim the legal estate. This case contrasts with *Coombes v Smith* (1986) where the court was not convinced that the claimant could rely on general assurances to imply that she would have rights in the house belonging to the father of her child. In *Pascoe v Turner* the representations were much more specific in relation to the house. However, there is considerable dispute about the way the two courts reached their decision in these cases.

'Jonathan Parker QC distinguished the case on the grounds that in *Pascoe v Turner* there had been a much clearer express representation that Mrs Turner was to "regard the house as belonging to her", but this alone would not have been sufficient to establish the equity in the absence of reliance. The acts of Mrs Turner, such as moving into the cohabited house, could also have been explained on the basis of her affection for Mr Pascoe rather than any expectation of gaining an interest in the land, but this did not prevent a finding that she was entitled to an equity. In reality the judgment in *Coombes v Smith* seems to draw too categorical a distinction between motives of love and affection and the desire to acquire a proprietary interest. People act with mixed motives, and in many cases where a claim by proprietary estoppel has succeeded it could be said that the claimant was motivated by emotional attachment to a relationship.'

J Stevens and R Pearce, *Land Law* (5th edn, Sweet & Maxwell, 2013), p. 727

CASE EXAMPLE

Wayling v Jones (1993) 69 P & CR 170

Here, two men had lived together in a relationship for over 16 years. Jones had promised to leave his business to the claimant, Wayling, and in reliance he had continued to work for very little pay. When cross-examined, the claimant had admitted that he would still have remained even if he had not been promised a share of the property. However, he also said in court that if Jones had said that he would not have kept his promise then he would have left. The Court of Appeal then found that this was sufficient to show the claimant's detriment in this case.

Other forms of reliance

There is no requirement that the reliance has to be confined to improvements on the property. There can be estoppel where there is reliance shown in other ways.

There are several cases where the claimant sells up his home and moves closer to the defendant and this act can be evidence of reliance on an assurance.

CASE EXAMPLE

Jones (A E) v Jones (F W) [1977] 1 WLR 438

The step-mother of the claimant tried to force him to pay rent for the use that he made of a house that he had jointly owned with his father, having failed in gaining an order for sale. The son had given up his existing job and home and had moved closer to his father, having been promised the right to live there for the rest of his life. The act of selling up and moving was sufficient evidence of reliance.

CASE EXAMPLE

Riches v Hogben [1986] 1 Qd R 315

This was an Australian case. A son's claim for rights under estoppel was based on the fact that he had sold his own home at a loss and left his job and emigrated to Australia in order to be closer to his mother as she got older. This was held to be sufficient reliance to establish estoppel.

Note that *Re Basham* the husband of the step-daughter gave up a chance of a much higher paid job in order that he and his wife could stay to care for her step-father.

The burden of proof in estoppel

The burden of proving detrimental reliance will be on the claimant, the representee. However, reliance can often be inferred from the circumstances, such as in *Greasley v Cooke* (1980). In that case working without payment was sufficient to raise an inference. The facts of *Gillett v Holt* (1998) show that working for the landowner could be sufficient proof of detrimental reliance where other factors are present.

The burden of proof does not remain with the claimant. Reliance by the representee can be presumed in circumstances where it can be shown that the representation was 'calculated to influence the judgment of a reasonable man' according to Lord Denning in *Greasley v Cooke*. So once the representation and reliance on that has been proved, the burden of proof then shifts to the representor who has to establish that the representee did not rely on the representation given.

ACTIVITY

Quick quiz

Consider the following factual situations and decide whether the claimants have relied on the representation or not.

1. The Browns have longed to move. One day, Mr Brown's widowed mother says to them: 'If you come and live near me then I will leave you my house.' The Browns move to a cottage near Mrs Brown's house. When she dies some four years later, she leaves her house to a charity in her will. Have the Browns any claim to her house?
2. The Whites want to live nearer Mrs White's father who has very bad arthritis. They move at Easter. He says: 'I am so glad you have come to be closer to me. I want you to have my house on my death.' When he dies suddenly later that year, they find that under the will his house has been left to the local branch of the Samaritans. Can the Whites claim his house?

In the first scenario consider whether the court will be influenced by the fact that the Browns have wanted to move in any event. Can they still claim rights under proprietary estoppel?

The problem for the Whites in the second scenario is that the promise is made after they have moved so it is difficult for them to show that they have relied on his promise. If he made subsequent promises such as if you help me in my house I will leave you my house in my will then the court may consider this to be reliance on his promise. In this case he is making a gratuitous promise to them about rights in his property after his death.

Estoppel claims under the Land Registration Act 2002

As the transfer of title becomes subject to more stringent formalities it will be even more important to define clearly what constitutes reliance and what is not included. Rights arising under proprietary estoppel can be binding not just on the representor but also a third-party purchaser.

7.2.3 Detriment

The claimant must show that they have suffered some detriment. The court will only award the claimant rights if they can show that the representation has left him unconscionably disadvantaged by his reliance on the relevant representation.

Inevitably reliance and detriment will be considered together. Detriment is evidence of reliance in the same way that consideration is a key element in proving the existence of a contract.

JUDGMENT

'There is no doubt that for proprietary estoppel to arise the person claiming must have incurred expenditure or otherwise have prejudiced himself or acted to his detriment.'

Dunn LJ in *Greasley v Cooke* (1980)

Lord Denning held in *Greasley v Cooke* (1980) that the burden of proof does not rest with the claimant to show that he has suffered detriment. In that case the maid had relied on the assurances given to her by the brothers that she would have a right to stay in the property. Lord Denning found that the burden of proof was on the brothers to prove that she did not rely on the assurances given.

The courts are asking the question: would it be unfair or unjust if the representor could now go back on the representation made to the claimant?

Detriment will be proved in a number of situations such as:

1. expenditure of money on the land of the representor;
2. acting to one's detriment, incurring financial loss;
3. suffering personal detriment by not taking advantage of opportunities or giving up time and effort to care for the representor.

As seen above, detriment is not restricted to expenditure of money on the land and it is not restricted to detriment only suffered by the claimant, as shown in *Re Basham*, the loss of a job opportunity for the husband of the claimant was admissible as evidence of detriment.

However, where there is no relationship between the person making the representation and the person who suffers the detriment this will not be admissible. This is illustrated by the unusual facts of *Lloyd v Dugdale* [2001] EWCA civ 1754 where a distinction was made between someone acting personally and someone acting as a managing director of a company. The court held that an assurance had been made to the claimant in his personal capacity and likewise the detriment had been suffered personally. It meant that the company was not entitled to rely on the claimant's personal detriment because it was a separate legal entity.

1. Expenditure of money

The claimant who starts to improve the land or builds on the land will be held to act to his detriment. The most obvious example would be *Inwards v Baker* (1965), where the son built a bungalow, at his own expense, on his father's land. This is clearly evidence of acting to one's detriment. The law assumes that no one would build on land belonging to someone else unless he genuinely believes that he has rights in the land.

Once a promisee has shown that he did something to his detriment then the burden of proof lies with the promisor to show that such acts were not done in reliance upon the promise.

The courts can look at other factors, but even where there is detrimental reliance they can still refuse to find that the owner is estopped from denying the claimant's rights. In the following case the court found that there had been detrimental reliance but it still refused to recognise the rights because there were other significant factors to consider.

CASE EXAMPLE

Sledmore v Dalby (1996) 72 P & CR 196

Mr Dalby and his wife had moved into a house owned by his parents-in-law. He had carried out a number of improvements to the house and was led to believe that the house would be given to him and his wife. However, after the death of his father-in-law the house was passed to the mother-in-law. After the death of his wife, Dalby continued to live at the property without paying rent. By now he had a job and also a new partner who had her own house and he went to live with her for much of the time. Although the Court of Appeal thought that an equity had been raised in his favour, it also felt that other factors should be considered. It did not think that Dalby should be able to claim his share through proprietary estoppel.

Factors which influenced the Court of Appeal:

1. Dalby was now in employment and did not need the rent-free accommodation.
2. The mother-in-law was elderly and was now in reduced financial circumstances.
3. The house was in disrepair and needed work carried out which the mother-in-law could not afford.
4. Mr Dalby's children were all grown up and did not need accommodation.

When these factors were all assessed, the court found that here it was no longer inequitable to deny the claimant the equity through change of circumstances so it could refuse to give a remedy to the claimant, Mr Dalby.

2. *Acting to one's detriment, incurring financial loss*

This will generally involve expenditure on the land itself. If you believe that a house will be yours one day, then you are going to ensure that the property is in good repair and to maintain a high standard of decoration. The logic of this is that someone would not spend money on improving land unless he genuinely believed that he had rights in that property. You do not simply paint another's house without believing that you will have rights in the land.

Cohabitants

Cases such as *Coombes v Smith* (1986) show that the claim will be defeated if there are other reasons why you have undertaken the work. So in that case the work carried out could be justified because of the relationship between the parties and not because the woman thought the work on the house would lead to her having rights in the land. This is a difficult area of law. Claimants may alternatively be able to claim rights under an implied trust, but in a constructive trust there must first be proof of a common intention and in proprietary estoppel there must be proof of a representation and the work must be carried out in reliance on that representation. By contrast a woman who gave up her secure tenancy to move into a house owned by her partner was entitled, on the breakdown of their relationship to a claim on the property based on proprietary estoppel, *Southwell v Blackburn* [2014] EWCA Civ 1347. He had made a promise to her that she would have a home for her life and she had relied on that promise and also a promise that he was making a long-term commitment to provide her with a secure home. In *Liden v Burton* [2016] EWCA Civ 275 the Court of Appeal had to decide whether statements made to the claimant showing payments that she made 'towards the house' were sufficiently clear to constitute an assurance in a claim under proprietary estoppel. It was accepted by the court following *Thorner v Major* that statements made must be seen in the context of the case and in particular their relationship. In this case the court held that it was fair to assume that Ms Liden believed that the statements related to rights in the family home and therefore could amount to an assurance.

3. Suffering other forms of detriment

There may be other forms of detriment suffered by the claimant. In *Crabb v Arun DC* (1976) the claimant had sold off part of his land in the belief that he had a right of way over the defendant's land. The fact that he had not reserved himself these rights was held to constitute detriment. A similar claim for an easement over land owned by Cromer Town Council was made in *Hoyl Group v Cromer Town Council* [2015] EWCA Civ 782 based on proprietary estoppel which was also successful.

The care of the house and family for no payment in *Greasley v Cooke* (1980) constituted detriment since, as the court pointed out, the maid could have left at any time to find another job. Similarly, in *Re Basham* (1986) the claimant's husband had given up opportunities to get a better job and also to move but had instead remained to care for the claimant's elderly step-father. This was held to be sufficient detriment although it was not expressly expenditure on the land itself.

More recently a claim by a son in *Suggitt v Suggitt* [2012] EWCA Civ 1140 who had been left out of a will by his father was upheld on the basis that he had believed that he would inherit a share in the family farm and thereby adjusted his life in order to take account of this. In fact the farmer left his farm to his daughter with a proviso that if the son at any time showed himself to be capable of managing farmland then the daughter was to transfer the farm to him. The Court of Appeal upheld the claim accepting that the claimant had acted to his detriment in reliance on his father's promises before his death.

This decision was applied in [2016] EWCA Civ 463, where a daughter was held to have a valid claim for rights in the family farm. She had worked for long hours for low wages over a long period of time in reliance upon her parents' assurances that the farm would be hers one day. She left the farm after an argument with her parents and claimed a share which she said had been promised to her. The court held that detrimental reliance was an evaluative judgment normally within the exclusive province of the trial judge and an appeal court could only interfere with the judge's assessment if it was perverse or clearly wrong. The court took into account the different forms of detriment suffered which were more than merely financial. She had expertise as an animal reproduction specialist and she could have secured other work elsewhere. She could have worked shorter hours in a working environment of her choosing and would have been free of the difficult working relationship with her parents.

The factors highlighted in *Davies* were similar to those in *Gillett v Holt* where detriment was seen to be more than just financial detriment but extended to the working environment enjoyed by the claimant.

Rosalyn Wells considered the different types of detriment that the Gilletts had suffered. In this case representations had been made over a period of time to Mr Gillett by Mr Holt that he would leave his farm to him. She writes:

> 'Robert Walker L.J. who delivered the judgment said that detriment is not a narrow or technical concept and need not consist of the expenditure of money or other quantifiable financial detriment so long as it is substantial. The requirement for detriment must be approached as part of the inquiry as to whether or not the repudiation of the assurances is unconscionable in all the circumstances.'
>
> R Wells, 'The Element of Detriment in Proprietary Estoppel' [2001] 65 *Conv* 13

In *Gillett v Holt* (2001) the following were all held to constitute detriment:

> **a. Mr Gillett had continued to work for his employer rather than to pursue opportunities of going into work on his own account**. In the words of the Court of Appeal, he had devoted the best years of his life to working for Mr Holt and his company, showing loyalty and devotion to his business interests. The facts are similar in *Wayling v Jones* (1993), where the claimant had remained working for little more than pocket money because he expected to inherit his partner's business.

> **b. Mr Gillett and his family had spent time with his employer, Mr Holt, beyond the normal scope of an employee's duty**. It was accepted that not only had Mr Gillett continued to work for Mr Holt but he had also spent considerable time with him outside his duties as an employee. Mr Gillett and the rest of his family spent time sharing normal family and social activities. This is a rather controversial aspect of detriment since Mr Gillett and the rest of his family undoubtedly also gained advantages from these social activities, but the Court of Appeal also accepted that Mr and Mrs Gillett and their sons had provided Mr Holt with a sort of 'surrogate family'. This aspect of detriment has been found in earlier cases. In *Coombes v Smith* (1986) it was said that 'the claimant's acts went far beyond what was called for by the natural love and affection for someone to whom she had no blood relationship'.

> **c. Loyalty and devotion to the defendant's wishes**. The most important factor here was the sending of the Gilletts' children to boarding school. They had to find the funds to send the second child to boarding school as the first child's fees had been funded by Mr Holt. He refused to fund the fees of the younger child. They did not wish to treat the two children differently. The judge thought that part of the detriment that they had suffered was the subordination of their wishes to those of Mr Holt. The judge found that they had adopted a higher standard of living than they would have envisaged and one higher than was appropriate to their income.

Where a claimant has suffered detriment but cannot show there has been a representation the court will not order a remedy. Compare the following cases:

CASE EXAMPLE

Hoyl Group Ltd v Cromer Town Council [2015] EWCA Civ 782

A company claimed a right of way over council land. The claimants had converted a basement property under lease. When access to the flat was discussed with the council it was indicated that it was acceptable to use a route over its land. There was an alternative route, but that later became unavailable. The court held that there had been representation that access would be available on which the claimants company had acted.

CASE EXAMPLE

Smyth-Tyrell v Bowden [2018] EWHC 106 (Ch)

A tenant had renovated buildings and cleared land for a holiday letting. The landlord served notice to quit and the tenant claimed that he should be granted a new business tenancy relying on proprietary estoppel. The tenant lost his claim as he was unable to point to any particular action or words of the landlord that demonstrated an assurance or shared understanding.

The above two cases are set in a commercial context. In *James v James* [2018] EWHC 43 (Ch), discussed earlier, an estoppel claim in a family case by a son who had not been included in the will of his father failed because there was no evidence that the father had made a particular promise to the claimant son that he would be left any property under the will. The courts will look at the whole course of conduct in such cases but without evidence of an assurance, express or implied estoppel cannot be found.

KEY FACTS

Detriment
1. A representation followed by expenditure on the land will constitute detriment (*Inwards v Baker* (1965)).
2. A representation followed by other forms of expenditure which can be linked to the belief that you have rights in the land can also constitute detriment (*Gillett v Holt* (1998)).
3. Detriment is not restricted to expenditure of money on the land.
4. Detriment need not be purely financial in nature but it must be linked to the belief that it will lead to rights in land (*Re Basham* (1986); *Crabb v Arun DC* (1976)).
5. Even where detriment has been proved, the claim may be defeated if there are other factors which show it would not be inequitable to do so (*Sledmore v Dalby* (1996)).

Representation	Positive assurance of rights or silence. Can be made within a will, can be made by an agent but not a tenant on behalf of a landlord.	*Inwards v Baker* (1965) (assurance of rights) *Taylor v Dickens* (1998) *Gillett v Holt* (1998) *Pascoe v Turner* (1979) (assurance of rights although in general terms) *Ramsden v Dyson* (1866) (mere silence)
Reliance	Genuine belief that rights will arise.	*Re Basham* (1986) *Greasley v Cooke* (1980) (provided care without pay) *Inwards v Baker* (1965) (expenditure of money) *Campbell v Griffin* (2001) *Coombes v Smith* (1986) (expenditure of money not referable to rights in the property) *Jones v Jones* (1977) (son sold house and moved closer to father) *Suggitt v Suggitt* (2012) (lifestyle choices based on the expectation that the farm would be his after his father's death)
Detriment	The representation has led to the claimant suffering some detriment.	*Sledmore v Dalby* (1996) (insufficient detriment shown for remedy) *Crabb v Arun DC* (1976) (failure to reserve rights of way over land was detriment) *Greasley v Cooke* (1980) (maid remained in house when she could have left at any time) *Re Basham* (1986) (claimant's husband had given up opportunities at work in order to live near the claimant's step-father) *Gillett v Holt* (1998) *Davies v Davies* (2014) (gave up opportunities to work shorter hours for a higher rate of pay in a better working environment) *James v James* [2018]; *Smith-Tyrrell v Bowden* [2018] (detriment without proof of an assurance will not lead to a remedy under proprietary estoppel)

Table 7.1 Key features of estoppel

Unconscionability

This is sometimes seen as a further element that must be satisfied in proprietary estoppel. According to Oliver J in *Taylor Fashions* where the landowner has made an assurance to the claimant that rights in land will arise and that assurance has been acted on by the claimant then it would be unconscionable for the landowner to deny him/her rights. In most cases then it is the retraction of that assurance or promise that is seen as unconscionable conduct. There is logic in including unconscionability because the basis of a claim in proprietary estoppel is that the legal title to property lies with another but because of his behaviour in promising the claimant rights it would now be **unconscionable** to enforce his strict legal rights. So the court in these cases is not remedying all unconscionable behaviour but that where the promisor has made a promise which is acted on by the claimant and the promisor then denies him rights.

It is not unconscionable to deny a purchaser of property rights when he/she has expended money and time on enquiries at the Land Registry and surveyor's fees before contracts have been exchanged; because in the majority of cases the parties are well aware that rights in land cannot pass until contracts satisfying s53(1)(b) have been exchanged. This was the basis of the House of Lords decision in *Cobbe*. There may still be cases where a claimant can argue that rights have passed under proprietary estoppel where formalities have not been complied with, e.g. *Ghazanni v Rowshan* [2015] but these cases should still be considered as exceptional.

7.3 Satisfying proprietary estoppel

Once the elements of proprietary estoppel have been satisfied, the claimant is entitled to a remedy. The court has a very wide discretion as to what kind of remedy to award. The interests have ranged from conveying the freehold to simply awarding an occupational licence or monetary compensation.

> 'When rights are claimed through the medium of estoppel, the relief sought is entirely equitable. This equitable jurisdiction is widely regarded as fluid. Thus Scarman L J approvingly described equitable estoppel as being "immensely flexible, yet perfectly clear…". With regard to the issue of flexibility, the general academic view of the court's role in an estoppel case is that it has the power to make such order as the justice of the case demands and this seems to be accepted by the courts themselves … In selecting the appropriate remedy, a court will have regard to various considerations: the nature of the expectation, the extent of reliance, the relative wealth of the parties, the existence of children and so on. Inequitable conduct by either party is then one factor amongst many to be taken into account. Only in the more extreme cases should someone be disentitled to equitable relief as a result of misconduct.'
>
> M P Thompson, 'Estoppel and Clean Hands' [1986] *Conv* 406

Traditionally the courts have taken one of two approaches when awarding a remedy to the claimant:

1. **compensating the loss** suffered as a consequence of relying on the assurance, i.e. making good the detriment suffered;

2. giving effect as far as possible to the **expectations of the claimant**.

Both approaches been adopted by the courts in various cases. If, as in *Pascoe v Turner* (1979), the defendant has made a representation that the claimant shall have legal rights in the land then that is the appropriate remedy if as in this case the court adopts the approach of giving effect to the reasonable expectations of the parties. However, if the representation falls short of this, then in a case on similar facts the remedy should be something less than the freehold estate. The recent case of *Habberfield v Habberfield* [2018] EWHC 317 (Ch) shows how the court can use both approaches when deciding on a remedy to award the claimant. In this case a daughter had worked for many years on her parent's farm. This involved long hours at low pay with very little time off and few holidays. Assurances had been made to the daughter that she would take over the farm when the father retired. The value of the farm was £2.5 million, whereas the value of her detriment was £250,000. The court sought a compromise and decided that merely compensating her for reliance losses would not be equitable and unless there were contrary reasons the amount awarded should be based on the promises made and therefore the court awarded her £1.2 million.

CASE EXAMPLE

Parker (9th Earl of Macclesfield) v Parker [2003] EWHC 1846 (Ch)

The 9th Earl of Macclesfield claimed the right to live in Shirburn Castle which had been in the family since 1716 – this was based on proprietary estoppel. Although the claim had been for a right of occupation for life, the judge held that a successful plea of estoppel was limited to the claimant's expectation. He found that the claimant had not expected to get a life interest and therefore he granted the 9th Earl a right to remain in the property until he was given two years' notice.

In more recent cases a third principle has also been applied, the principle of proportionality. This was first applied in *Commonwealth of Australia v Verwayen* (1990) 170 CLR 394 and echoed later in *Jennings v Rice* [2003] 1 P & CR 100. The principle of proportionality tries to balance the remedy with the detriment suffered. This was summed up by Robert Walker LJ in *Jennings v Rice* in this way: 'the essence of the doctrine of proprietary estoppel is to do what is necessary to avoid an unconscionable result, and a disproportionate remedy cannot be the right way of going about that.'

He also commented that:

> 'It cannot be doubted that in this as in every other area of law, the court must take a principled approach, and cannot exercise a completely unfettered discretion according to the individual judge's notion of what is fair in any particular case.'

CASE EXAMPLE

Jennings v Rice [2003] 1 P & CR 8 (Part 1)

A very wealthy widow died, leaving an estate worth over £1.2 million including her home and furniture valued at over £400,000. Before her death she employed a gardener, Mr Jennings, who had worked for many years and in later years without pay. When her health failed, he began to look after her as a carer and continued to do so until she died. During the time he had worked for her she had made a number of promises concerning the property but they were very vague in nature. She had told him that 'he would be alright' and she would 'see to it' and she had said to him on more than one occasion 'this will be yours one day'. The court at first instance found that she had clearly led him to believe that he would inherit all or part of the estate when she died and awarded him £200,000. Mr Jennings appealed to the Court of Appeal because although he had been granted a monetary remedy he claimed to be entitled to the property itself.

The problem for the claimant was that the representations made were vague in nature and it was possible to argue that the gardener had been unwise to rely on the assurances made. The Court of Appeal upheld the finding of the judge at first instance who held that he should be entitled to £200,000. This sum was roughly the equivalent to the value of the work as a carer carried out by the claimant. The court justified its decision in the following way.

'The task of the court is to do justice. The most essential requirement is that there must be proportionality between the expectation and the detriment.'

Aldous JL

The court rejected the claim on behalf of Jennings that he should be entitled to the whole of the estate although that was what he thought he had been promised.

The principle of proportionality has been widely adopted in recent cases although the decision in *Suggitt v Suggitt* (2012) discussed earlier in this chapter has attracted criticism. Arden LJ commented that the court must satisfy the expectations of the claimant and there does not have to be a relationship of proportionality between the level of detriment and the relief when asserting an interest in property through proprietary estoppel. This appears to contradict the principles in *Jennings v Rice*.

Transfer of the legal estate or legal interest in land

This is granted in a limited number of cases and relies on establishing that the assurance or representation promised the transfer of the freehold rights.

In *Dillwyn v Llewelyn* (1862) the transfer of freehold ownership was ordered because the father had gone as far as transferring the interest to the son by written memorandum but had not satisfied the formalities because he had failed to execute a deed. The son had acted on the promise by building a house on the land. The only remedy that would satisfy the expectation of the son would be to transfer the freehold to the son.

A similar decision was reached in *Pascoe v Turner* (1979) where the courts had a choice of remedies: either to transfer the fee simple or to grant the wife a licence to live in the property for the woman's life. They chose to transfer the freehold because it was felt that that was the only way that the equity was satisfied. The facts also indicate that the defendant was trying to evict the claimant and if she had only got a licence then he could have tried to sell to a third party, and as her rights were personal only he could sell leaving her without any remedy. This shows us that the remedy granted is firmly equity-based and the courts have a wide discretion when deciding what remedy to grant.

By way of contrast, when the son built his bungalow in *Inwards v Baker* (1965), there was some doubt as to what sort of interest the son believed that he was to gain. The courts did not transfer the full freehold estate, transferring instead the right for the son to enjoy the bungalow for his lifetime.

The key issue appears to be that there must be an express representation either orally or in writing that the claimant is to receive the freehold. It is only in these cases that the court is prepared to award the transfer of the legal estate. In these cases there is a much higher standard of proof of an assurance of rights in the freehold.

The claim for the transfer of the legal estate was accepted in these two recent cases:

CASE EXAMPLE

Bradbury v Taylor [2012] EWCA Civ 1208; [2012] EWCA Civ 1140

These cases suggest that the courts are prepared to grant a remedy that exceeds the detriment suffered by the claimants and does not sufficiently take into consideration the advantages that the claimants had received during the life of the deceased. In *Bradbury* the claimants were the nephew of the deceased and the nephew's wife. They had moved from their home in Sheffield in order to live with the deceased in his very substantial house in Cornwall. Whilst living there, relations between the parties deteriorated and the deceased had sought a declaration from the court that they were no more than licensees or tenants living in the house. They lived rent-free in the property and received income from their house in Sheffield as they were able to let it. In spite of the very vague nature of the representations made by the deceased to the nephew and his wife the Court of Appeal granted them the freehold of the property.

There were also very vague representations made in the case of *Suggitt* where property had been left by a father to his only daughter expressing a non-binding wish that 'if at any time Caroline [the daughter] felt that John [the son] had showed himself capable of working on and managing my farmland she shall transfer my farmland to him'. The son made a claim on the basis that he had acted to his detriment in reliance of that promise and the farmland should be transferred to him. The work on which he based his claim was very vague and included some work on the farm and agreeing to study at college in order to acquire the necessary skills. In comparison to the work undertaken in *Thorner v Major* by David Thorner it was much less substantial. Nevertheless the judge at first instance was prepared to accept that a representation had been made and the son had acted on it and this was upheld by the Court of Appeal. An appeal by the daughter Caroline was based partly on the fact that the award made was disproportionate to the detriment suffered by the claimant. The Court of Appeal held that the principle of *Jennings* did not mean that there had to be a relationship of proportionality between the level of detriment and the relief awarded. Instead it held that if the expectations were extravagant or out of all proportion to the detriment suffered the court should recognise the claimant's equity in another way.

Applying the principle of proportionality is a difficult issue for the courts. Dixon comments on its application in the recent case of *Davies v Davies* [2016] as follows:

'… *Davies v Davies* … suggests that the clearer the expectation and the longer the detriment is incurred, the more likely it is that the claimant will get what they were promised. There is, according to *Davies* a sliding scale where a remedy based on the expectation generated becomes less likely as the assurances become less certain or the detriment less meaningful …'

M Dixon, *Modern Land Law* (11th edn, Routledge, 2018) p. 396

The right to occupy

In *Inwards v Baker* (1965) the son was not granted a freehold estate but a lifetime right to occupy. The problem with this is that the right was one of enjoyment rather than a right of ownership which brings with it a chance to sell or deal in the land.

This remedy is based on a licence which may be deemed to be irrevocable and will give the claimant the right to remain in the property rent-free either for life or for a determined period.

So in *Greasley v Cooke* (1980) the claimant was granted the right to remain rent-free for the remainder of her life. It was held to be unjust and inequitable for the party making the representation to go back on it.

In *Campbell v Griffin* (2001) the court awarded Mr Campbell an interest in the property valued at £35,000 which would take effect as a charge on the property. He would be required to leave the property. The possibility of a lifetime right to occupy the property had been discussed as that was what he had expected and the remedy given usually reflects the expectations of the parties. However, the court considered the interests of the other parties and decided that a lump sum was more appropriate.

The lifetime right to occupy has one possible complication attached to it. This could be seen as giving the claimant a right similar to a tenant for life in a settlement under the Settled Land Act 1925. The tenant for life has all the rights of an owner and the effect was that a tenant for life had the right to sell the land. This was not the intention when the remedy was granted. Under the Trusts of Land and Appointment of Trustees Act 1996 settlements can no longer be created in land and have been replaced by trusts of land. They allow for rights of occupation and so do not create the same sort of problems.

Financial compensation

Monetary compensation has been ordered in several cases. This will be appropriate where the financial detriment is relatively small in relation to the full value of the property, as shown in the case of *Dodsworth v Dodsworth* (1973) 228 EG 1115, or where it would be impossible for the parties to live together because there has been a breakdown in relations (*Hussey v Palmer* (1972)) or in many cases where it is not possible or inappropriate for the claimant to have rights in the property. It may not be possible where the property has been sold as in *Wayling v Jones* (1993).

CASE EXAMPLE

Dodsworth v Dodsworth (1973) 228 EG 1115

A sister invited her brother and sister-in-law to come and live with her when they returned from Australia. She said they could live in her bungalow for as long as they liked. In reliance on this promise, they set about carrying out improvements to the property which amounted to over £700. On her death, the administrator brought a successful action against them both, requesting that they should leave but ordering that they should be awarded the costs of the improvements to the property.

There was a similar problem in the following case. The court could not order that the mother had a right to remain in the property because there had been a breakdown in relations.

CASE EXAMPLE

Hussey v Palmer [1972] 1 WLR 1286

Here, a mother-in-law paid £607 for an extension to her son's house, as he had told her that she could then make her home with him and his wife. The mother and son argued and she was granted a share in the property. In this case the court imposed a constructive trust. It is arguable that her rights arose by virtue of estoppel and she could claim that she had the right to continue to live there. The problem in this case was that it was impossible for both the son and the mother to live there together because of the breakdown of relations.

CASE EXAMPLE

Re Sharpe [1980] 1 WLR 219

An aunt claimed the right to remain in a property purchased by her nephew who had been declared bankrupt. She based this right on the large contributions that she had made to the purchase of the property. The house had cost £17,000 and the aunt had contributed £12,000. The court held that she should be awarded her contribution to the purchase under the terms of the loan but it refused her a proprietary right in the property. However, she could remain until the loan was repaid, based on an estoppel licence.

It seems from the previous cases that the courts will be prevented from awarding a right to occupy property where relationships between the parties would make it impossible.

In *Gillett v Holt* (2001) the court ordered the transfer of part of the property including some land as well as a sum in monetary compensation.

Quantification of the compensation

Where improvements have been made to the land the courts have a choice between simply assessing the value of the improvements themselves or assessing the increase in value of the property itself. The latter option could be much higher than the cost of the improvements themselves. In *Dodsworth v Dodsworth* (1973) the court ordered the cost of the improvements rather than the enhanced value of the property.

A more problematic question is to what extent the court should offset any advantages that the claimant may have gained from the defendant, e.g. rent-free accommodation or costs of living. In many cases, e.g. *Greasley* and *Davies* it is possible to argue that the claimant has been in receipt of quantifiable benefits which should then offset any detriment suffered by the claimant. In *Inwards v Baker* (1965) the son had lived for a long period of time on his father's land without paying rent and this constituted a considerable advantage for him and was relevant in the remedy awarded.

There is an argument that this alone would be sufficient to satisfy the claim. In *Gillett v Holt* (2001) the defendant had given the claimant a number of benefits such as help with the school fees for the claimant's son and other help with such things as pension contributions.

'There are a number of authorities in which the court has considered that the benefits received by the claimant have reduced the detriment to such an extent that it is insufficient to support the claim in proprietary estoppel. In other cases the court finds that although an equity has arisen it would not be appropriate to award any remedy in view of the reciprocal benefits received. In each of these categories the claimant is unsuccessful because he has not persuaded the court that it would be unconscionable for the promisor to be allowed to resile from his promises. For the Court of Appeal to dismiss the High Court's approach as too narrow is mistaken because it has thrown into doubt the use of the concept of advantage and disadvantage. It is essential that the court should make an approximate assessment of the extent of the detriment suffered by the claimant. Furthermore, the concept of advantage and disadvantage is an important one which allows the court considerable leeway in the exercise of its discretion. It is significant that the courts seem only to refer to reciprocal benefits in those cases which are in fact unsuccessful.

In the context of the case the expenditure on schooling was detrimental in the sense the Gilletts had adopted a higher standard of living which might not otherwise have been appropriate to their income had Mr Holt not made promises of future testamentary benefits.'

R Wells, 'The Element of Detriment in Proprietary Estoppel' [2001] 65 *Conv* 13

In *Watts v Storey* (1983) 134 NLJ 631 the claimant had given up a Rent Act-protected tenancy in his home town, to live with his grandmother and to take care of her. He claimed rights in her house based on proprietary estoppel. His claim was refused because he had not proved that he had suffered detriment as he had received benefits from making use of rent-free accommodation provided by his grandmother. He had suffered some detriment by virtue of his move to her house but this had been compensated.

Slade LJ held that on balance he had not suffered any detriment in financial or material terms.

In *Henry v Henry* [2010] UKPC 3 the claimant had cared for the deceased and in return she had promised him a share in a plot of land that she jointly owned with another. Whilst she was still alive he had cultivated the plot and he had cared for her but on her death she left her interest in the land to another. His claim had been rejected at first instance because the court found that he had benefited in two ways whilst the deceased was alive. He had lived on her property rent-free and he had been able to enjoy produce from the land which he cultivated. The Privy Council upheld his claim holding that it was possible both to suffer detriment as well as to reap some benefits from the promisor.

Post-judgment misconduct

Can misconduct by the claimant after the representation has been made be sufficient to prevent the equity arising in favour of the claimant?

The leading case on this issue is *Williams v Staite* [1979] Ch 291. The defendants had been given rights to occupy two cottages indefinitely. The cottages were bought by the claimant who challenged the defendants' right to enjoy the cottages because they had used a paddock which they knew was not their own and had even erected a stable on it. The claimant had been granted an injunction to prevent the defendants from using the paddock. The claimant then sought an order trying to regain possession of the cottage. His argument was that the defendants had lost their entitlement because of their inequitable conduct.

JUDGMENT

'Excessive use or bad behaviour towards the legal owner cannot bring an equity to an end or forfeit it. It may give rise to an action for damages for trespass or nuisance or to injunctions to restrain such behaviour, but I can see no ground on which the equity, once established, can be forfeited.'

Goff LJ

In this case the judge held that the rights had been acquired prior to the behaviour complained of and so the defendants' rights in the property could not be challenged as they had already crystallised.

However, if the rights have not yet been acquired under estoppel then misconduct of the claimant may become a relevant factor. Consider the facts of the following cases.

In *Brynowen Estates v Bourne* (1981) 131 NLJ 1212 the claimant had sought a declaration from the courts that she had rights in a caravan park, based on proprietary estoppel. The court found that she was unable to claim such a right because there was evidence that she had behaved in a most objectionable way herself. She had persistently sworn and made obscene gestures at visitors to the caravan park. This was held by the court to prevent any rights arising in favour of the claimant. The conduct of the claimant pre-estoppel claim was also relevant in *Gonthier v Orange Contract Scaffolding Ltd* [2003] EWCA Civ 873. Negotiations for a lease had taken place and in reliance on promises made the claimant had spent money on improving the property but no written agreement had been drawn up. When the claimant was asked to leave the property after negotiations broke down he claimed compensation based on proprietary estoppel. The court refused to make an order having found that a number of the invoices for work done were false.

Other remedies

The courts can combine remedies so that they order the transfer of land to the claimant but they can also order the claimant to compensate the defendant. This is an unusual award but is available because this is a right that is enforceable under equitable principles.

CASE EXAMPLE

Lim Teng Huan v Ang Swee Chuan [1992] 1 WLR 113

Two parties each had an interest in land because it had been conveyed jointly into the names of their fathers. One party (the defendant) decided to build on the land and he drafted an agreement whereby the defendant claimed the whole of the land in exchange for a transfer to the claimant of some land that he anticipated getting from the government. The house was completed and the defendant went into occupation without any complaint from the claimant. Later, the two argued and the claimant then claimed a half share of the property. The court held that the defendant was entitled to the whole of the property but that the claimant was also entitled to a sum by way of compensation.

The court has also been prepared to grant an easement by way of remedy where it has been appropriate. This award will only arise on specific facts where an easement is the appropriate remedy. It illustrates the flexibility of the remedy in proprietary estoppel compared with other areas of law such as the constructive trust.

CASE EXAMPLE

E R Ives Investment Ltd v High [1967] 2 QB 379

The claimant had been granted an easement arising through estoppel where he had resurfaced part of the land owned by his neighbour. He had been assured some time before that he would have a right of way.

An easement was also awarded in *Crabb v Aran District Council* [1976] and more recently in *Hoyl Group Ltd v Cromer Town Council* [2015]. It is often the most appropriate remedy where access to property is denied to the claimant who has been led to believe such rights have been promised by the defendant.

KEY FACTS

Remedies
1. The court has complete discretion in awarding a remedy.
2. The remedy should be one which as nearly as possible fulfils the parties' reasonable expectations raised by the representation given.
3. The grant of the freehold should only be made where that has been assured by the representor.
4. If monetary compensation is awarded it should be either the equivalent sum spent or equivalent to the increase in value of the property.
5. Misconduct by the claimant may result in the loss or reduction of rights.
6. Remedies may be combined so the defendant can be ordered to pay money to the claimant in exchange for rights in the property.

Lifetime right to occupy	May satisfy the equity but limited rights as no right to sell the property.	*Re Basham* (1986) *Inwards v Baker* (1965) *Greasley v Cooke* (1980)
Monetary compensation	Appropriate where financial detriment is fairly small and the lifetime right to occupy is inappropriate on the facts.	*Dodsworth v Dodsworth* (1973) *Campbell v Griffin* (2001) *Hussey v Palmer* (1972) *Re Sharpe* (1980) *Wayling v Jones* (1995) *Southwell v Blackburn* (2014)
Transfer of the legal estate	Must be promise of transfer of legal estate; requires a high standard of proof.	*Pascoe v Turner* (1979) *Dillwyn v Llewellyn* (1862) *Gillett v Holt* (2001) *Thorner v Major* (2009) *Bradbury v Taylor* (2012)
Easements	The promisee is led to believe that he/she has been granted a right of way by the promisor although it is not in writing and the promisee later acts in reliance on this.	*Hoyl Group Ltd v Cromer Town Council* (2015) *Crabb v Aran District Council* (1976)
No remedy where there has been misconduct	Rights will be upheld where the misconduct took place after the rights had been acquired.	*Williams v Staite* (1979) *Brynowen Estates v Bourne* (1981)

Table 7.2 Remedies that can be awarded in proprietary estoppel

7.4 Loss of rights under proprietary estoppel

Lack of clean hands

The remedies in equity are subject to the claimant behaving in an equitable manner as demonstrated by the decisions in *Brynowen Estates v Bourne* (1981) and *Gonthier v Orange Contract Scaffolding Ltd* (2003). If the defendant can prove lack of clean hands pre-estoppel claim then the rights will be defeated. Although, as shown in *Williams v Staite* (1979) misconduct will not be relevant if it occurs after a successful claim for rights under estoppel.

The argument would be that as the remedy is based on unconscionability, then it would cease to be unconscionable if the claimant himself has acted unconscionably.

Delay

Equitable remedies are also defeated where there is evidence of delay in bringing the action. This could be argued where the claimant has delayed in bringing his claim to the courts, however it is likely that in many cases there is bound to be delay because the claimant is enjoying undisturbed rights in land.

ACTIVITY

Applying the law

Freddie lives in Yorkshire and his elderly father, Jim, lives in Surrey. Jim is getting less and less mobile and recently twisted his ankle badly when he fell down on the path outside his front door. He asks Freddie if he would like to come and live in the old family home and to help him out when necessary. Freddie cannot make up his mind but Jim tells him that he will leave him his house in his will on his death if he will come and live with him. Freddie sells his own house and moves in.

After Jim's death Freddie finds that the house has been left to a charity. Advise Freddie.

ACTIVITY

Self-assessment questions

In what circumstances will the following benefits conferred on the claimant prevent estoppel from arising?

1. The defendant allows the claimant to live in the property rent-free.
2. The defendant's son is friendly with the claimant's son and he promises to pay for his school fees at an expensive public school. The claimant has two other sons.
3. The defendant allows the claimant who worked for him on his farm to join him on several social activities such as joining expensive shoots and going to game fairs.
4. The defendant allowed the claimant to live in property rent-free while the claimant cared for the defendant's elderly mother. The claimant did not receive any payment for the care that she provided.

7.5 The proprietary nature of a claim to proprietary estoppel

Personal or proprietary rights?

Personal rights only take effect as rights against a person, e.g. the landowner but proprietary rights will be binding against a third party.

If the court finds that the claimant has rights in land based on estoppel then those rights will be upheld. The problem is to decide whether estoppel rights are proprietary in nature and will then be binding on a purchaser or merely personal.

When the court in *Greasley v Cooke* (1980) granted the maid a right to live in the property for her lifetime, it was not clear whether her right to occupy the property would bind a third-party purchaser if the legal owner tried to sell the legal title. If the right is seen as a licence only, then the nature of a licence is that it is not a proprietary right so it will be personal only.

Winn LJ said in *E R Ives Investment Ltd v High* (1967): 'Estoppels arising from representations made by owners of land that rights exist affecting their land will, unless in form they are limited to the duration of the interest of the representor, bind successors in title.'

ACTIVITY

Applying the law

Gemma Smith has worked for Mrs Brown for many years and when Mrs Brown becomes seriously ill she stays on living in the house without payment and is treated as one of the family. She cares for the youngest child living at home and looks after the house. The brother of Mrs Brown tries to evict her after Mrs Brown's death. Gemma can successfully bring evidence that Mrs Brown promised her the right to live in the house on several occasions before she died. What will the nature of her rights be?

The Land Registration Act 2002 has clarified the position with regard to the nature of estoppel and has accepted that rights arising under proprietary estoppel were proprietary in nature and therefore were capable of binding third parties. Under s116 of the 2002 Act it is provided:

SECTION

's 116 It is hereby declared for the avoidance of doubt that, in relation to registered land, each of the following –

(a) an equity by estoppel, and
(b) a mere equity

has the effect from the time the equity arises as an interest capable of binding successors in title (subject to the rules about the effect of dispositions on priority).'

Rights in registered land will need to be registered unless the claimant has a right which can be claimed as an overriding interest.

The decision of *Lloyd v Dugdale* [2001] EWCA Civ 1754 has now clarified any doubt that there may have been surrounding the nature of rights under estoppel.

> 'Now that *Lloyd v Dugdale* has confirmed – in advance of section 116 LRA 2002 – that estoppel rights are proprietary, and that they can bind a purchaser of registered land as an interest that overrides through actual occupation, the path is clear and well lit for a claimant seeking to impeach the registered title that is to be so carefully protected under the LRA 2002.'
>
> M Dixon, 'Proprietary Estoppel, Third Parties and Constructive Trusts:
> A Taste for the Future? *Lloyd v Dugdale* [2001]
> EWCA Civ 1754' [2002] *Conv* 584

Can rights arising under proprietary estoppel be overreached?

Rights under proprietary estoppel can be subject to **overreaching**, so if the remedy takes the form of an equitable estate then such an estate can be overreached where the purchaser pays the purchase money to two trustees. Some rights arising under estoppel cannot be overreached, such as an easement or a lease. This is because such rights take effect in law. However, it was clear that the licence given to the son in *Inwards v Baker* could not be overreached if the property was sold by his father's executors.

This still leaves the issue of the status of estoppel in unregistered land. This is still subject to notice.

The effect is that third parties can be bound by these rights. The following two cases illustrate this point.

CASE EXAMPLE

Re Sharpe [1980] 1 WLR 219

The aunt's rights were held to be binding on the trustee in bankruptcy. She had contributed to the purchase of property by her nephew and the court had granted her a lifetime right to live rather than a right to a share in the property itself. Since these rights were binding, the trustee in bankruptcy was unable to sell to a third party.

CASE EXAMPLE

Voyce v Voyce (1991) 62 P & CR 290

The rights of one brother who had lived in his mother's house which had been promised to him over many years were held to be binding on his other brother who had received the legal title by way of gift. The rights under estoppel therefore were binding on a third-party donee.

ACTIVITY

Applying the law

Consider this situation and discuss whether there could be a successful claim for proprietary estoppel. If there is a claim for estoppel, what would be the appropriate remedy?

Jack Jones bought Laurel Villa ten years ago and became the registered owner. He travelled around the country and did not like to leave the property empty. He was visiting his cousin, Winnie, when she told him that her lease had come to an end. He asked her if she would like to come and live in his house. He told her that she could live there rent-free so long as she carried out repairs on the property and kept 'a bit of an eye on things' while he was away. She moved in and immediately started to work on the property, putting in double glazing because it was so cold in the house. This was quite expensive and cost her over £2,000. She also spent money on replacing the bathroom upstairs. Jack was away when she carried out this work and when he came home he said to her: 'Keep caring for the house and you can do anything that you want with the property.' Last week, he was away on business and he was involved in a fatal accident. Winnie wants to know if she can still remain in the house. Advise her.

It seems that this type of right can bind the legal owner so long as they have notice of the right, even before the court has granted the remedy.

SUMMARY

1. Where a person makes a representation to another that he has rights in land and the other person acts on it to his detriment the representor cannot later deny the claimant rights.

2. Under the modern doctrine of proprietary estoppel the claimant must prove three elements: a representation, reliance on that representation and detriment.

3. A representation can be active or passive but it must relate to rights in property.

4. A representation of rights under a will after the representor's death can be enforceable if the representee has acted on the assurance to his detriment relying on the representation.

5. Detriment can take a number of different forms including expenditure of money, incurring financial loss and suffering personal detriment by not taking advantage of opportunities or giving up time and effort to care for the representor.

6. The court has complete discretion in deciding what remedy to grant.

7. The remedy granted in proprietary estoppel must be proportional to the detriment suffered.

SAMPLE ESSAY QUESTION

Proprietary estoppel aims to address unjust enrichment in the context of real property and is an area of equity where the courts have consistently shown flexibility, proportionality and fairness.

Assess the accuracy of this statement.

Explain the doctrine of proprietary estoppel.

Consider the five *probanda* of *Willmott v Barber*.

Consider *Taylor Fashions Ltd v Liverpool Victoria Trustees Co Ltd*.

Examine the first element of the statement and its accuracy.

Give examples where the doctrine has sought to address unjust enrichment: e.g. *Dillwyn v Llewelyn*; *Crabb v Arun District Council*; *Jennings v Rice* and *Gillett v Holt*.

Consider how the courts assess unjust enrichment in the context of real property.

Consider limits on use of doctrine, e.g. *Cobbe v Yeoman's Row* (not in business context when formalities have not been adhered to); *Coombes v Smith* (no detriment suffered in a domestic context).

Compare *Thorner v Major*; *Gillett v Holt*; *Pascoe v Turner*.

Draw conclusions.

Consider whether the courts have shown:

flexibility, e.g. different contexts where the doctrine has been used *Crabb v Arun District Council*;

proportionality, e.g. in the context of remedies *Jennings v Rice*;

fairness, e.g. *Greasley v Cooke*.

Examples of each.

CONCLUSION

Further reading

Books

Dixon, M, 'Proprietary Estoppel and Formalities in Land Law and the Land Registration Act 2002: A Theory of Unconscionability' in E Cooke (ed.), *Modern Studies in Property Law* Vol 2 (Hart Publishing, 2013).

Stevens, J and Pearce, R, *Land Law* (5th edn, Sweet & Maxwell, 2013), p. 727.

Articles

Bray, J, 'Proprietary Estoppel: A New Chapter Dawns?' [2010] *DLJ* 175.

Carroll, E, '"The Assurances are Only Half the Story ..." Proprietary Estoppel and Testamentary Capacity in *James v James*' [2018] 2 *Conv* 192.

Cooke, E, 'Estoppel and the Protection of Expectations' (1997) 17 *LS* 258.

Dixon, M, 'Proprietary Estoppel: A Return to Principle?' [2009] 3 *Conv* 260.

Dixon, M, 'Defining and Confining Estoppel' (2010) 30 *LS* 408.

Gouriet, M and Thomas, J, 'Showing an Interest' [2014] 139 *Fam LJ* 5.

Hughes, R, '(I Can't get No) Satisfaction ... Proprietary Estoppel' [2015] PCB 25.

Lower, M, 'Liden v Burton: Proprietary Estoppel and the Family Home' [2018] *Conv* 84.

Mee, J, 'Proprietary Estoppel and Inheritance: "Enough is Enough"?' [2013] *Conv* 280.

McFarlane, B, and Robertson, A, 'Apocalypse Averted: Proprietary Estoppel in the House of Lords' (2009) 125 *LQR* 535.

Milne, P, 'Proprietary Estoppel in a Procrustean Bed' (1995) 58 *MLR* 412.

Shea, C, 'The Role of Knowledge in Proprietary Estoppel' *L & T Review* [2018] 22(4) 129.

Thompson, M, 'The Flexibility of Estoppel: *Jennings v Rice* [2003] P & CR 8' [2003] *Conv* 67.

Thompson, M P, 'Estoppel: A Return to Principle' [2001] 65 *Conv* 78.

Thompson, M P, 'Constructive Trusts, Estoppel and the Family Home' [2004] *Conv* 496.

Wells, R, 'The Element of Detriment in Proprietary Estoppel' [2001] 65 *Conv* 13.

Welstead, M, 'Proprietary Estoppel: A Flexible Familiar Equity' [1995] *Conv* 6.

8

Co-ownership

AIMS AND OBJECTIVES

After reading this chapter, you should be able to:

- Explain the different types of co-ownership of land
- Describe the key features of a joint tenancy
- Describe the key features of a tenancy in common
- Describe the key indicators of a tenancy in common in equity
- Discuss what is meant by severance, in particular the rules concerning severance under statute and at common law
- Explain the rights of a co-owner in land
- Describe the different ways that co-ownership can come to an end

8.1 The nature of co-ownership

Land is rarely owned by one single owner; it is much more likely that several different people will have an interest in a piece of land. Much of residential property ownership today comprises ownership of a family home. When property is owned by more than one person it is referred to as **concurrent ownership**.

The land then becomes subject to **co-ownership**. Co-ownership can only take place behind a trust of land, under the Trusts of Land and Appointment of Trustees Act 1996.

- **Legal title**: there will be co-ownership of the legal title if there is more than one owner of the land in law.
- **Equitable interests**: co-owners in equity share the equitable ownership of the land behind a trust.

8.2 Types of co-ownership

English law recognises two different types of co-ownership:

- the joint tenancy;
- tenancy in common.

Where land is co-owned in a joint tenancy, the co-owners are described as **joint tenants** and where land is co-owned in a tenancy in common they are described as **tenants in common**.

8.3 A joint tenancy

There are three key features of a joint tenancy:

1. The main feature is that the co-owners are each entitled to the whole of the co-owned land. However, they do not own individual shares of the land.
2. Another feature of the joint tenancy is the 'right of survivorship'.
3. Finally there can only be a joint tenancy if 'the four unities' are present.

ACTIVITY

Consider these examples:

a. Duncan and Deirdre are the joint tenants of Lilac Cottage. It is not appropriate to speak of them each owning a half of the cottage. If their friend Jackie comes to visit and they tell her that they are joint tenants, she may say 'Who really owns the cottage?' The proper answer is that Duncan owns the whole of the cottage and Deirdre owns the whole of the cottage at the same time. There is no part that they do not completely own but there is also no part each owns to the exclusion of the other.

b. Susie, Sally, Vicki and Stuart are all students at the University of Thameshire. They decide that they will all join together to buy a terraced house with four bedrooms at 45 Grange Road. They buy as joint tenants. Although there are four of them, they all own the whole of the house and even though they each have a separate bedroom, no one can claim one of the bedrooms as his or her own. The fact that they each have a separate bedroom is just a matter of convenience.

8.3.1 The 'four unities'

A joint tenancy will only exist if the four unities are present:

  i. unity of possession;
 ii. unity of interest;
iii. unity of title;
 iv. unity of time.

If any of these is missing, then there cannot be a joint tenancy of the land.

> **'Unity of possession'**
>
> All of the joint tenants must be equally entitled to possess the whole of the co-owned land. One joint tenant cannot exclude another from any part of the land.

In the example above, Sally cannot exclude Susie from her room in the house. If it were possible to do so, then it cannot be a joint tenancy.

ouster order
An order of the court preventing a person from entering property at all or within strict terms laid down by the order. Breach of the order will be seen as contempt of court. The order will be granted under the Family Law Act 1996

Unity of possession will be displaced in some circumstances, such as an **ouster order**.

> **'Unity of interest'**
> Each of the joint tenants must have the same interest in extent, nature and duration in the land. For example, there cannot be a joint tenancy between a person who has a freehold interest in the land and someone who has a leasehold interest.

In the earlier example, if one of the students, Stuart, purchases the property outright then he will own the freehold and if the others rent rooms in the property they will all have leasehold interests if each has exclusive occupation of his or her room. In this case there can no longer be a joint tenancy with the other students as there is no unity of interest.

Once property is owned as a joint tenancy at law, any attempt to deal in the title must be with the agreement of all the joint owners. So if there is a sale of the property or a mortgage is executed over the land it will only be effective if everyone agrees. If one person tries to mortgage his share then it may affect the share in equity but not at law.

Susie, Sally and Vicki buy a flat together as joint tenants. Sally is short of money and she attempts to mortgage the property on her own, by forging the signatures of the other two owners. This would not affect the co-ownership at law but it would affect her ownership in equity. She cannot mortgage the flat without the others' agreement. The same would apply if she tried to sell the land.

> **'Unity of title'**
> The joint tenants must derive their title to the land from the same document or alternatively where they have acquired title under adverse possession.

The purchase of 45 Grange Road would be by one conveyance or transfer which all four students – Susie, Sally, Vicki and Stuart – would sign. They would then derive title from this conveyance or transfer rather than from four separate documents.

> **'Unity of time'**
> The interests of all the joint tenants must vest at the same time.

If property has been left to Deirdre's mother for her lifetime and then to Duncan and Deirdre there is no unity of time between all three, because Deirdre and Duncan do not receive the title until after the death of Deirdre's mother, but there is unity of time between Duncan and Deirdre.

8.3.2 Survivorship

The key practical difference between a joint tenancy and a tenancy in common is that the principle of survivorship operates between **joint tenants**.

> 'It has been said that the right of survivorship (or *IUS ACCRESCENDI*) is the "grand and distinguishing" incident of joint tenancy. On the death of any one joint tenant the entire co-owned estate "survives to" the remaining joint tenant or tenants. Ultimately, in the manner of the medieval tontine, the surviving joint tenant becomes the sole owner – the winner takes all. This concentration of ownership was elegantly described by Blackstone … When two or more persons are seised of a joint estate … the entire tenancy upon the decease of any of them remains to the survivors, and at length to the last survivor … The interest of two joint tenants is not only equal or similar, but also is one and the same. One has not originally a distinct moiety from the other … but … each … has a concurrent interest in the whole; and therefore, on the death of his companion, the sole interest in the whole remains to the survivor.'
>
> K Gray and S F Gray, *Elements of Land Law*
> (5th edn, Oxford University Press, 2009), p. 914

CASE EXAMPLE

Solihull MBC v Hickin [2012] UKSC 39

Mr and Mrs Hickin rented property from Solihull Borough Council. Mr Hickin moved out leaving Mrs Hickin living there alone with her daughter. When she died the daughter claimed the right to take over the property. The Supreme Court held that the joint tenancy was still in existence and the father still had rights. The daughter could have taken over the property if both the father and the mother died. The Council could claim that the father had forfeited his right to the tenancy due to his absence.

This case reinforces the rule that a joint tenancy will always vest in the survivor or survivors of two or more joint tenants irrespective of whether they are actually occupying the property.

ACTIVITY

Applying the law

Duncan and Deirdre own Lilac Cottage as joint tenants. Consider whether Deidre has a claim if Duncan has an accident and dies.

Will your advice differ if Duncan has left his share in Lilac Cottage to his Uncle Edwin in his will?

The joint tenant who dies cannot therefore leave any interest in the land by will, nor will his or her interest pass under the rules of **intestacy**. This is because in the example above both Deirdre and Duncan are joint owners of the cottage but they do not 'own' anything that they can specifically say is his or her own. This means that they could not then leave specific property or a specific share to anyone. Deirdre will become sole owner of the property on Duncan's death. Your advice will not differ if Duncan has left his share in Lilac Cottage to his Uncle Edwin.

In the earlier example, if Sally and Susie are involved in a fatal accident, both their shares in 45 Grange Road will pass to the survivors, Vicki and Stuart. It would be irrelevant that Susie had made a will leaving all her property to the NSPCC because this part of the will would not take effect. Her share passes immediately on death and before the will takes effect.

The doctrine of survivorship in practice

1. It simplifies probate

On death, the estate vests in the survivor or survivors of the joint tenants. There is no need to vest the property in the survivor as the survivor is recognised in law as owning the title. This is a simple procedure that does not require action from the survivor and saves on costs. The effect is that the joint tenants do not have to deal with jointly owned property in their will; indeed, for many, who have few assets, the jointly held home is probably their main asset. The principle of survivorship will apply whether either has made a valid will or not.

2. It simplifies a purchase from joint tenants

As there is just one title vested in several co-owners, only one title needs to be investigated by a purchaser.

Historically, land could be subject to several different types of legal estate. This meant that in any sale of the land there was a risk of complications because there would be several titles to investigate. This was simplified by s 1 of the Law of Property Act 1925 which provided that there could only be two legal estates in land: the freehold and the leasehold.

3. It gives effect to the wishes of the majority on succession

Many couples fail to make provision by will for their property on their death, but if asked each would want the co-owner to benefit. The co-owner may be a spouse or a partner. The right of survivorship reflects this wish.

ACTIVITY

Applying the law

Tony and Guy live together. They have each contributed to the purchase of a house and own the legal estate as joint tenants. Tony has a fatal heart attack. He has not made a will.

Tony's two nephews are claiming a share under the rules of intestacy. Can Guy claim the house? Advise.

This is similar to the situation earlier where Deirdre and Duncan were living together as joint tenants and Duncan died. Deirdre became sole owner because she was the survivor of a joint tenancy. Likewise here Tony and Guy live together as joint tenants; irrespective of whether Tony has made a will or not leaving the property to the nephews Guy can claim the property for himself as the gift takes effect on the death of Tony.

8.3.3 Severance

Joint tenants can effectively separate their equitable interest from that of the other joint tenants by means of severance. Their interest in equity is then converted into a tenancy in common and the principle of survivorship will no longer operate.

Where a joint tenant does sever his share in equity, he will be entitled to a proportionate share of the property, depending upon the number of joint tenants. There can never be severance in law of the legal estate.

ACTIVITY

Self-assessment question

How can a joint tenant of land ensure that a gift in his will leaving his share to his sister will be effective?

In the earlier example where the property was owned by Susie, Sally, Vicki and Stuart, if Susie wants to sever her share then she can do so. There are rules as to how this will be done and if she follows the correct procedure the law then treats her share in equity as a separate share which can pass on her death. If Susie and Sally had a fatal accident and they both died Susie's share would pass under her will to the NSPCC whereas Sally's share would pass to the other joint tenants even if she had later made a will because she had not severed it during her lifetime.

KEY FACTS

Joint tenancies
1. No single owner can claim they own a separate share.
2. A joint tenancy cannot arise unless the 'four unities' are present: possession, interest, title and time.
3. The right of survivorship will operate in a joint tenancy.
4. It is possible to sever a joint tenancy in equity but never at law.
5. The effect of severance is such that the interest in equity will constitute a separate share.

8.4 Tenancy in common

In contrast to joint tenants, tenants in common are said to own an undivided share in land. This means that they actually have notional shares of the ownership of the land but they still cannot claim any specific physical division of the land to represent a separate share. Just as in the case of a joint tenancy, the students cannot say of their rooms in the house 'this is mine'.

However, the law will recognise that the tenant in common can deal in the share in a number of different ways during his lifetime as well as on death in a will. The tenant in common can sell or mortgage his share and, most significantly, leave it to someone in his will, and that provision will be effective. The shares of the tenants in common may be equal or unequal. In the earlier example, Duncan can argue that his share represents two-thirds and Deirdre has a share representing one-third.

8.4.1 The 'four unities'

The 'four unities' must be present before a joint tenancy can exist but in the case of a tenancy in common it is necessary for there to be unity of possession between the tenants. So, unlike a joint tenancy, unity of interest, title or time need not be present.

In practice, this means that each tenant in common must be entitled to possession of the whole. So if we refer back to the four students who purchase property together, none of the students can claim that he or she 'owns' his or her room. None of the students could be forced to allow others into his or her room. If Sally decided she did not like another student, for instance Stuart, she could not prevent him from entering her room. She could not successfully bring an action for trespass. He has as much right as Sally to be there.

If they were all tenants and each in a separate relationship of landlord and tenant then their rooms would be for them alone. They would each have a legal estate in the land and it would be exclusive to them, which means they could keep others out including the landlord.

Suppose that Sally and Stuart take separate leases of 20 Hill Road, Oxford. They may take them at the same time but they are tenants and they each have a separate legal estate in their part of the land. They are not joint tenants. This will allow them to keep the other out from their part of the property and they can be said to own a separate share of the land.

8.4.2 Survivorship

Tenancy in common
1. The major difference between a joint tenancy and a tenancy in common is that the principle of survivorship does not operate between tenants in common.
2. Each tenant in common can make arrangements in his will to leave his putative share in the property after his death.
3. Even if no will has been executed the share will pass to the nearest kin of the tenant in common under the rules of intestacy.
4. A tenant in common can deal in his share in a number of different ways such as taking out a mortgage.

In the example above, if Duncan and Deirdre held as tenants in common from the start then you could argue that they always held their shares separately and when one dies then the other's share would pass under the terms of his or her will or on intestacy and it would not automatically pass to the survivor.

In the earlier example Duncan and Deirdre owned the property as joint tenants. If on the other hand they held as tenants in common then you could argue that they held separate shares from the start. If they were tenants in common if, for instance, Duncan died then his share would pass under the terms of his will or on intestacy. It would not automatically pass to Deirdre.

8.5 Creation of co-ownership in land

In this section the legal title and equitable title in co-owned land will be considered separately. The key feature is that the legal title can only be owned as a joint tenancy whereas the equitable title may be owned as either a joint tenancy or as a tenancy in common.

8.5.1 The legal title

A person may acquire the legal title to land by means of a conveyance of the title to him followed by registration as the registered proprietor. If the legal title is registered in the name of more than one person then co-ownership of the legal title will arise.

The legal estate can only exist as a joint tenancy
Under the Law of Property Act 1925:

SECTION

's 1(6) A legal estate is not capable of subsisting or of being created in an undivided share in land.'

Under this section it is impossible for there to be a tenancy in common of the legal title of land. So co-ownership of the legal title must be in the form of a joint tenancy.

The legal estate cannot be severed
Under the Law of Property Act 1925:

SECTION

's 36(2) No severance of a joint tenancy of a legal estate, so as to create a tenancy in common in land, shall be permissible, whether by operation of law or otherwise, but this subsection does not affect the right of a joint tenant to release his interest to the other joint tenants, or the right to sever a joint tenancy in an equitable interest whether or not the legal estate is vested in the joint tenants.'

Under s 36 a joint tenancy of the legal title cannot be severed so there can never be a tenancy in common of the legal title.

There is a limit as to how many people can own the legal title at law

No more than four persons can hold the legal estate. Under the Law of Property Act 1925:

SECTION

's 34(2) Where, after the commencement of this Act, land is expressed to be conveyed to any persons in undivided shares and those persons are of full age, the conveyance shall (notwithstanding anything to the contrary in this Act) operate as if the land had been expressed to be conveyed to the grantees, or, if there are more than four grantees, to the four first named in the conveyance, as joint tenants [in trust for the persons interested in the land].'

This section provides that a maximum of four persons can be joint tenants of the legal title. If the legal title is conveyed to more than four people then it is the first four named on the conveyance who are *sui juris* and will become the joint tenants of the legal title. Anyone suffering from a disability in the eyes of the law is not *sui juris*, for example if they are under 18 or mentally incapable.

ACTIVITY

Applying the law

Five students – Sarah, Tara, Una, Vera and Wanda – jointly buy a house in Salisbury. Tara is only 17 and therefore cannot hold the legal title to land. Who will hold the legal title in the land?

Note here that as Tara is only aged 17 she cannot hold an estate in land so even though she is named second on the conveyance the legal title cannot pass to her. Therefore in this case the legal title will be held by Sarah, Una, Vera and Wanda. Tara will have a share in equity.

8.5.2 Co-ownership in equity

In equity the title can be held either as a joint tenancy or as a tenancy in common. This contrasts with the legal title which can only be held jointly. There is a common law presumption in favour of a joint tenancy in equity based on the equitable maxim 'equity follows the law'. However, there are circumstances which indicate a tenancy in common.

Solving the question: is it a joint tenancy or a tenancy in common?

There are a number of questions to address where the parties have not expressly stated whether they hold as joint tenants or tenants in common. Some depend on looking at the evidence at the time of such matters as their intentions; others consider the context of the purchase such as whether the purchase was for business purposes.

1. Intentions of the parties

The parties may expressly state on the conveyance of the property whether they own as joint tenants or a tenancy in common; any words used which suggest severance will indicate a tenancy in common. Thus there will be a tenancy in common if the conveyance includes such expressions as '**to be divided between**' (*Fisher v Wigg* (1700) 1 Salk 391), '**equally**' (*Lewen v Dodd* (1599) Cro Eli 443) and even '**in equal shares**' (*Payne v Webb* (1874) LR 19 Eq 26). The reason that this will imply a tenancy in common is because the law sees any suggestion of a share as implying a division between the owners.

However, where there is an express statement in the conveyance as to how the shares are to be held, that will be conclusive. In *Goodman v Gallant* [1986] Fam 106 the conveyance stated that the property was to be held 'upon trusts to sell … as joint tenants'. This was conclusive and it was irrelevant whether the contributions were unequal or whether there were other factors which would suggest a tenancy in common.

In *Pankhania v Chandegra* [2012] EWCA Civ 1438 property had been purchased in the joint names of two people, an aunt and her nephew. There had been an express declaration that they held as tenants in equal shares in equity. The aunt claimed successfully in the High Court that she owned the entire equitable interest in the house arguing that it had been the original intention at the time of purchase. This was overturned by the Court of Appeal who held that an express declaration of trust was conclusive for all purposes between the parties unless there was evidence of an underlying matter such as fraud, following the decision in *Goodman v Gallant* (1986). In *Taylor v Taylor* [2017] EWHC 1080 a father argued that he held four-fifths of jointly held property with his son. The property which comprised a hotel and campsite had been originally purchased by them as joint tenants but in 2013 they had severed the joint tenancy by written document declaring that they held in equal shares. The father argued that as they had not signed the original declaration of trust he would not be bound. The court held that under s 53(1)(b) all that was necessary was evidence in writing at a later date and both parties had later signed the notice to sever which was sufficient. The express declaration of trust remained binding.

Where there is no express declaration the law can imply either a joint tenancy or a tenancy in common. The law will favour a joint tenancy since equity follows the law but there might be some special reason why a tenancy in common may be implied.

Since *Stack v Dowden* (2007) there has been considerable focus on the form used by joint tenants to register property at the Land Registry. The form in use today is known as Form JO which has replaced the TR1 as used in *Stack v Dowden*. This is an optional form but if used by the parties has a box for the transferees to enter whether they are to hold the property on trust for themselves as joint tenants or on trust for themselves as tenants in common in equal shares or on some other trusts which are inserted on the form.

Baroness Hale urged the Land Registry in *Stack v Dowden* to review its practice to ensure that the box is always filled in by the parties.

In response to the comments of Lady Hale in *Stack v Dowden* (2007) a Practice Note was issued by the Law Society and the Land Registry on Joint Ownership (dated 14 January 2013) concerning the introduction of the new Land Registry Form JO. The form indicates whether the equitable title is to be held as a joint tenancy or tenancy in common. The declaration in the form will be conclusive as indicated above in *Goodman v Gallant* and confirmed in *Pankhania v Chandegra* (2012) and *Taylor v Taylor* [2017].

JUDGMENT

'[T]he Land Registry form which has been prescribed since 1998 is to be applauded. If its completion and execution by or on behalf of all joint proprietors were mandatory, the problem we now face would disappear. However, the form might then include an option for those who deliberately preferred not to commit themselves as to the beneficial interests at the outset and to rely on the principles discussed below. I say all this partly to urge the Land Registry further to review its practice, but mainly to illuminate the factual context in which transfers such as the one with which we are concerned were executed. In what circumstances should it be expected that, independently of the information required by the Land Registry forms, joint transferees would execute a declaration of trust?'

Baroness Hale

This form was not used in *Stack v Dowden* where a more ambiguous form was used (Form 19(JP)) which only asked one question 'can the survivor give a valid receipt for capital money arising on a disposition of the land?' The House of Lords was unable to conclude that this indicated that the parties intended to hold the property as joint tenants. It is anticipated that the new form JO will reduce litigation over whether jointly owned property is held as a joint tenancy or as a tenancy in common but until it is made compulsory there is still scope for disagreement as to the shares in equity of the jointly owned property.

2. Unequal contributions to the purchase price

Where parties have contributed unequally to the purchase price of land, it is implied that there is a tenancy in common. The shares will be proportionate to the size of their contributions. Of course, if they contributed equally, the presumption in the absence of other evidence will be that there was a joint tenancy. An express declaration as in *Goodman v Gallant* and *Taylor v Taylor* will override this.

3. Loan on mortgage

Where money is loaned by two or more mortgagees the interest that they take in the property will be held as tenants in common. This is the case even though they have taken the legal title as joint tenants.

4. Business partnerships

Where land has been purchased by persons as business partners the assumption is that they would not have wanted their relationship to be determined by survivorship, which is inappropriate in the business context. In this kind of relationship a tenancy in common will be implied. A joint tenancy would be inappropriate to a business relationship since the parties are often at arm's length. However, where the transfer of land in a business context expressly states that the purchasers are to hold as joint tenants in equity then this can take effect as a joint tenancy.

5. Individual business tenants

It will also apply where businessmen have taken a lease of premises together but for their individual purposes.

CASE EXAMPLE

Malayan Credit Ltd v Jack Chia-MPH Ltd [1986] AC 549 (PC)

Here, two business tenants took a lease. The terms were that they would jointly rent office space for five years. They paid rent and service charges in certain agreed proportions. The lease did not contain any words of severance. The court held that since they took the lease in the course of a partnership, they took as tenants in common.

'The argument is that, in the absence of an express agreement, persons who take as joint tenants at law hold as tenants in common in equity only in three classes of case:

first, where they have provided the purchase money in unequal shares; in this case they hold the beneficial interest in similar shares;
secondly, where the grant consists of a security for a loan and the grantees were equal or unequal contributors to the loan; again they would hold the beneficial interest in the same shares; and
thirdly, where they are partners and the subject matter of the grant is partnership property.'

Lord Brightman

He found in this case that there could be a tenancy in common for the following reasons:

1. The lease was clearly taken to serve the separate commercial interest of the defendant and the claimant.

2. Prior to the grant of the lease the parties had settled between themselves what space they would respectively occupy when the lease came to be granted. This was roughly 62 per cent to the defendant and 38 per cent to the claimant.

3. Prior to the grant of the lease, the parties had taken meticulous measurements of their respective allotted areas, and divided their liability for the rent and service charge in unequal shares in accordance with the respective areas that they would occupy.

4. Prior to the grant of the lease, the claimant was invoiced for a share of the deposit. After the grant of the leases, the defendant and the claimant paid the stamp duty and the survey fees in the same unequal shares.

5. As from the grant of the lease, the rent and the service charges were paid in the same unequal proportions.

Deciding whether there is a joint tenancy or a tenancy in common

	Joint tenancy	Tenancy in common
What is expressly or impliedly included in the conveyance? Has the Form JO been filled in?	The law favours a joint tenancy since equity follows the law. A statement in the agreement will be conclusive.	A tenancy in common will not be implied where the agreement is silent.
Are the contributions to the purchase price equal or unequal?	Equal contributions.	Unequal contributions.
Are the co-owners business partners?	Usually family arrangements.	Business partners.
Are the co-owners mortgagees?	If the agreement states it is a joint tenancy then it is irrelevant that there are two or more mortgagees.	Two or more mortgagees.
Have the parties taken a lease as individual business tenants?	Must be expressly stated to be a joint tenancy.	If business tenants take a lease together in the course of a business.

It is clear from the above that if the agreement states how the parties are to hold the property then it will be conclusive and other evidence is irrelevant but if the agreement is silent then the other factors will be material to the decision.

ACTIVITY

Quick quiz

Consider the following and decide whether the parties hold the land as joint tenants or as tenants in common:

1. Gillian purchased Holly Lodge with her two friends, Kim and Keith. The house cost £300,000 and they each contributed £100,000.
2. Gillian purchased Holly Lodge with her two friends, Kim and Keith. The house cost £250,000 and Gillian contributed £170,000 while the others contributed £40,000 each. The conveyance read 'The purchasers declare that they hold Holly Lodge as beneficial joint tenants.'
3. Kim and Keith are business partners in a small business as IT consultants. They buy a terraced house, 2 Microchip Road, Hendon, as their business premises.
4. Bella and Ishmael lend money to Kim and Keith to purchase 2 Microchip Road, Hendon.

8.6 Methods of severance of a joint tenancy

8.6.1 Meaning of 'severance'

It is possible for a joint tenant in equity to sever the tenancy and become a tenant in common in equity of his share. The size of the share will be the proportionate share as at the date of severance. For example, if there are three joint tenants the party who severs his share will be entitled to a one-third share when the property is sold. This does not affect the other joint tenants if there is more than one. Their shares will continue to be held under a joint tenancy.

What is the effect of this?

The interest will no longer be subject to the right of survivorship. The benefits that arise under the right of survivorship will be lost.

ACTIVITY

Applying the law

Consider the following situations:

1. Frederick buys a house with his friends, Robin and Daniel. They buy jointly in equal shares and it is held that they are joint tenants. Daniel has made a will leaving all his property, real and personal, to his sister Fiona. When Daniel dies can Fiona claim his share?
2. Four friends – George, Gerald, Gregory and Gary – buy Wintry Lodge as joint tenants. George severs his interest and now holds as a tenant in common. Consider what will be the position in equity if Gary has an accident and dies. He has made a will leaving all his property to his sister Geeta. Can Geeta claim his share? What is George's position?

It is important to remember that there can only be severance at equity it is not possible to sever at law. Decisions with regard to the legal estate can only be taken where all the owners at law have given their agreement.

In the first situation Fiona cannot claim under the will because Daniel has not severed during his lifetime and there can be severance by will. In the second situation George has severed and cannot take advantage of the right of survivorship. Gary has not severed during his lifetime so Geeta cannot benefit under his will.

8.6.2 Methods of severance under statute

Severance by written notice under the Law of Property Act 1925:

SECTION

's 36(2) ... no severance of a joint tenancy of a legal estate, so as to create a tenancy in common in land, shall be permissible, whether by operation of law or otherwise, but this subsection does not affect the right of a joint tenant to release his interest to the other joint tenants, or the right to sever a joint tenancy in an equitable interest whether or not the legal estate is vested in the joint tenants ... if any tenant desires to sever the joint tenancy in equity, he shall give to the other joint tenants a notice in writing of such desire or do such other acts or things as would, in the case of personal estate, have been effectual to sever the tenancy in equity.'

One key feature of severance is the need to give written notice to all the other joint tenants. This method is entirely unilateral, which means the joint tenant does not require the consent of the other joint tenants. The written notice does not need to be signed. The notice does not need to be in any particular form.

The Law of Property Act 1925 covers what constitutes proper service by post for the purposes of s 36(2):

SECTION

> 's 196(1) Any notice required or authorised by this Act to be served or given by this Act shall be in writing...
>
> (3) Any notice required or authorised by this Act to be served shall be sufficiently served if it is left at the last-known place of abode or business in the United Kingdom of the lessee, lessor, mortgagee, mortgagor, or other person to be served, or, in the case of a notice required or authorised to be served on a lessee or mortgagor is affixed or left for him on the land or any house or building comprised in the lease or mortgage...
>
> (4) Any notice required or authorised by this Act to be served shall also be sufficiently served, if it is sent by post in a registered letter addressed to the lessee, lessor, mortgagee, mortgagor, or other person to be served, by name, at the aforesaid place of abode or business, office, or counting-house, and if that letter is not returned ... undelivered; and that service shall be deemed to be made at the time at which the registered letter would in the ordinary course be delivered.'

The main difference between the two sections is that under s 196(3) where ordinary post is used then the notice will be properly served if it is left at one of two places: either the last place where the joint tenant was living or the last-known business address of the joint tenant.

Under s 196(4), where registered post is used then the letter should be sent to the last-known business address or home address of the joint tenant.

ACTIVITY

George, Gerald, Gregory and Gary, four law students, buy Wintry Lodge. They purchase as joint tenants. Suppose George decides that law is not for him and decides to leave Wintry Lodge and go travelling. He can write to Gerald, Gregory and Gary and that would be sufficient for him to sever his interest. If Gary says 'I am not happy about you leaving and I won't agree to you severing your interest', can George ignore this?

Advise George.

Gary cannot object because written severance is a unilateral act and does not depend on agreement with the other joint tenants.

Key case on severance by written notice

CASE EXAMPLE

Kinch v Bullard [1999] 1 WLR 423

A wife, who was terminally ill, decided to take action to sever the joint tenancy of the matrimonial home where she lived with her husband. The relationship had broken down and she was contemplating divorce proceedings. Her solicitors prepared a notice of severance and this was posted using ordinary post. The letter was delivered but the husband suffered a serious heart attack before he read it and went into hospital. The wife found the letter of severance at the home and decided to destroy it. The husband died a fortnight later, without reading the notice. Some five months after that, the wife herself died. The court had to decide whether the issue of proceedings by the wife was sufficient to sever the joint tenancy even though the husband had not had an opportunity to read the notice.

It was held that there had been sufficient severance under s 36(2) of the Law of Property Act 1925.

The case for the husband's estate relied on the meaning given to s 196(3) of the Law of Property Act 1925 which held that any notice would be sufficiently served if it was left at the last-known place of abode or business in the United Kingdom of the person to be served. It was applied to the facts of the case as follows:

| The last-known abode of the husband was the matrimonial home. | The notice was left at the house because it was placed in the letter box, even though it was later removed by the wife. | In these circumstances the notice had been duly 'served' in accordance with s 196(3). |

JUDGMENT

'The very purpose of sending a notice is to convey information, with legal consequences, on the addressee: it cannot be right that the sender of a notice can take positive steps to ensure that the notice does not come to the attention of the addressee after it has been statutorily deemed to have been served, and then to fall back on the statute to allege that service has none the less been effected.'

Neuberger J

Neuberger J also suggested that the notice of severance could have been withdrawn at any point preceding its postal delivery if the joint tenant had told the other joint tenant that she wished to do so. So the wife could have prevented service of the written notice if she had gone to the husband and told him that she no longer wished to sever. The letter then would have had no effect. Once a letter is in the postal system, it is very difficult to intercept it.

Severance may occur through the service of documents as part of an action through the courts.

CASE EXAMPLE

Quigley v Masterson [2011] EWHC 2529

An application to the Court of Protection by Mrs Masterson who jointly held a house with her former partner, Mr Pilkington, was held to sever the joint tenancy under s 36 LPA 1925. In the application she stated that she and Mr Pilkington each owned a 50 per cent share in the property. This allowed Mrs Quigley, Mr Pilkington's daughter, to claim his share in the property after his death.

Key issues to be considered in relation to severance

There will not be severance if the proposal to sever is merely part of proposals during negotiations. So if severance of the legal estate is proposed during negotiations for divorce as one of a number of alternatives in relation to jointly owned property, then the court will not accept that this is sufficient severance to satisfy s 36(2) of the Law of Property Act 1925. A number of cases have considered this point in the context of court proceedings particularly in the context of a divorce. Consider below the cases of *Gore & Snell v Carpenter, Harris v Goddard* and *Re Draper's Conveyance.* In each of these cases the court had to consider whether documents in the divorce proceedings had effected severance.

CASE EXAMPLE

Gore & Snell v Carpenter (1990) 60 P & CR 456

After the parties' marriage had broken down they started to negotiate a separation agreement. A clause of severance of the property was included with the divorce proposals but it was not separate from the other papers. The husband died during the negotiations over the agreement and the divorce. It was held that there had not been effective severance under s 36 of the 1925 Act and the property vested in the wife by survivorship.

'It is in my judgment, a question of intention and this applies also when it is a question of the fourth possible method of severance, namely the service of a notice under s 36(2) of the Law of Property Act 1925. It is argued for the executors that the proposed separation agreement put forward by Mr Carpenter amounted to such notice. It will be recalled that the paragraph I read expressly refers to severance, but that was only part of the deed and the deed was never accepted. It was put forward by Mr Carpenter, not in isolation but as part of the package of proposals, and was not intended, in my judgment, and therefore did not take effect as a notice under section 36(2).'

Judge Blackett-Ord

Severance will only be effective if the joint tenant manifests an intention of an immediate desire to sever his interest. It would not be sufficient to express an intention to sever sometime in the future.

CASE EXAMPLE

Harris v Goddard [1983] 1 WLR 1203

The husband and wife jointly owned the matrimonial home. When their relationship broke down, the wife issued divorce proceedings which included a request 'for such order with regard to their property as may be just', specifically referring to a transfer of property and settlement of the property. The husband was involved in a car crash and he died from injuries he sustained before the petition was heard.

There were opposing arguments as to whether there had been severance:

1. Counsel for the **executors for the husband** claimed that the joint tenancy had been severed by the service of the petition. The effect would be that half the property would pass with his estate.	2. Counsel for the **wife** argued that there had not been severance and that the husband's putative share would pass to the wife under the principle of survivorship.

The Court of Appeal held that there had been no severance because the wife had not shown an immediate intention to sever. 'A desire to sever must evince an intention to bring about the wanted result immediately' (Lawton LJ).

Notice must be served on **all** the joint tenants.

Note that **no specific form** is necessary for the notice. The notice can take any form so long as it clearly shows a wish to sever immediately. It can be contained in another document such as an application to court for an order concerning the property. Notice must be served on all the joint tenants, it is not sufficient to serve notice merely on one other joint tenant.

CASE EXAMPLE

Re Draper's Conveyance [1969] 1 Ch 486

An application for an order directing the sale of the matrimonial home with the proceeds to be distributed between the parties was held to be a written notice of severance. An order had been made, but had not been executed, when the husband died. It was held that there had been severance.

Harris v Goddard (1983) and *Re Draper's Conveyance* (1969) should be compared. Although both cases concerned applications to the court, *Harris v Goddard* did not show an immediate desire to sever the estate, but merely a request for the court to decide the issue, and this was not enough for severance.

ACTIVITY

Applying the law

1. Three art students – Anne, Barbara and Carol – live together in a small studio in Brighton which they own as joint tenants. Anne is offered a chance to study in Paris and she decides to leave. Over Christmas, she writes to Barbara, who is at home with her parents, telling her that she wants to sever her interest in the studio, but she does not write to Carol. Will this be sufficient service for severance under s 36 of the 1925 Act?
2. If Anne decides to sever her interest in the flat and writes to Barbara and Carol, addressing the letter to the flat in Brighton, will this be written severance?

Note in the first situation notice has only been served on one joint tenant so it will not be sufficient. In the second situation the fact that notice has been served by post would be sufficient for the law to conclude that there has been service even if the parties do not read the notice, as in the case of *Kinch v Bullard*.

Service of the notice can be by ordinary post **or** registered post. It will be sufficient to send a notice by registered post to either the other joint tenant's last-known abode or his place of business, even if he does not receive it. However, a notice sent by registered post to either of these addresses will be effective even if it is not delivered, unless it is expressly returned to the sender.

CASE EXAMPLE

Re 88 Berkeley Road NW9 [1971] Ch 648

Miss Goodwin and Miss Eldridge lived together at the same address, as joint tenants. Miss Goodwin decided to get married and served a notice of severance on Miss Eldridge by sending a registered letter to the address where they lived together. Miss Eldridge was away on holiday when the letter arrived, so Miss Goodwin signed a receipt for her own notice of severance. She died a few weeks later. Miss Eldridge contested that she had never received the notice.

The court held that service is effective when the letter is sent by registered post, even if the co-owner seeking to sever signs on behalf of the recipient to prove receipt of the notice.

This case shows us that the law treats severance by ordinary post in a different way from registered or recorded post or next day delivery. This has considerable impact on the outcome of a case where everything depends on the timing of severance such as *Kinch v Bullard*. Mary Percival discusses these points in the extract from her article below.

'The decision in *Kinch* echoes the earlier case of *Re 88 Berkeley Road* since it again raises the question of whether or not a written notice of severance from one joint tenant to another had been "given" as required by s 36(2) LPA 1925. This, in turn, requires consideration of what constitutes proper service of a notice under s 196 LPA 1925 – is it sufficient merely to leave it at the premises or must it be established that it was actually received by the addressee? In *Re 88 Berkeley Road* the court held that delivery at the last known address of the other joint tenant constituted service without the need to establish actual receipt. This decision would clearly have disposed of *Kinch* had it not been for the fact that the notice in *Re 88 Berkeley Road* was sent by recorded delivery and came under s 196(4) whereas the notice in *Kinch* went by ordinary first class post and so was covered by s 196(3). In the event Neuberger J refused to distinguish between these two methods of delivery and held that, as in *Re 88 Berkeley Road*, it was sufficient to establish that the notice sent by first class post had been delivered to the addressee's last known place of abode and there was no further necessity to show actual receipt by the addressee … A more difficult argument put forward by the defendants was that a notice should not be treated as properly given where it is the actual sender who picks it up and files or destroys it, as opposed, for example, to its having been eaten by the family dog. The judge saw here a possibility of abuse by a joint tenant who might post a notice of severance and then collect it on its arrival at the house thereby ensuring that it never came to the attention of the other joint tenant.'

M Percival, 'Severance by Written Notice:
A Matter of Delivery?' [1999] 63 *Conv* 61

KEY FACTS

Severance by written notice
1. Under s 36(2) of the Law of Property Act 1925, notice can be effected by serving notice in writing.
2. It is entirely unilateral and does not require consent from the other joint tenants.
3. Written notice will only be effective where the severance is to take effect immediately.
4. There is no written severance if the proposal to sever is simply part of other proposals and is not mentioned separately.
5. The notice must be served on all the joint tenants.
6. No specific form is necessary for the written notice.
7. Service of the notice can be by registered post or ordinary post if there is proof that it was actually served at the correct address.

8.6.3 Severance at common law under *Williams v Hensman* (1861) 1 J&H 546

JUDGMENT

'A joint tenancy may be severed in three ways: in the first place, an act of any one of the persons interested operating upon his own share may create a severance as to that share. The right of each joint tenant is a right by survivorship only in the event of no severance having taken place of the share which is claimed under the *ius accrescendi*. Each one is at liberty to dispose of his own interest in such manner as to sever it from the joint fund – losing, of course, at the same time, his own right of survivorship. Secondly a joint tenancy may be severed by mutual agreement. And in the third place, there may be severance by any course of dealing sufficient to intimate that the interests of all were mutually treated as constituting a tenancy in common. When the severance depends on an inference of this kind without any express act of severance, it will not suffice to rely on an intention, with respect to the particular share, declared only behind the backs of the other persons interested.'

Wood V C in *Williams v Hensman* (1861) 1 J&H 546 (70 ER 802)

Williams v Hensman (1861) suggests that there are three different ways that a joint tenancy can be severed at common law:

- severance by **conduct** (an act of any one of the persons interested **operating upon his own share**; e.g. joint tenant transfers his share to a third party; a transfer of the joint tenant's share in the land to another joint tenant);
- severance by **mutual agreement** (dependent on all the joint tenants being in agreement);
- severance by **mutual conduct** (this involves actual physical division of the land or a course of dealing leading to a physical division of the land).

8.6.4 Severance by conduct

There are several different ways that this can be put into effect.

An act of one party operating upon his share

The most obvious example would be sale of your share. The reason it severs the joint tenancy is because it destroys unity of title and all four unities are essential to a joint tenancy.

Janet, John and Sally purchase 3 Maiden Lane in London from Mr Rules, when they are students at Thameshire University. Sally's course ends after three years and she sells her share to Kevin. Janet and John each have one more year at university. Kevin will not have the same title as the others as his purchase derives from Sally and the others have purchased from Mr Rules.

Note that the legal title cannot be severed and although Sally has sold her equitable estate she will remain joint tenant of the legal estate. This means that when eventually the property is sold, Sally will have to consent to the sale of the property and Kevin will receive only a share in equity.

The formal commencement of litigation concerning a joint tenancy will be considered as an act operating upon one's share.

CASE EXAMPLE

Re Draper's Conveyance [1969] 1 Ch 486 [see above]

It was held that proceedings prior to the court order, such as the serving of the summons and the affidavit in this case, could constitute acting on one's share as well as severance under s 36(2) of the 1925 Act. It is important to see that the court order itself did not constitute the act; the order was merely putting into effect the request made to the court under the summons.

Another example of severance under this head would be by mortgaging his share in equity. It will also be severance where the tenant applies to court for an order directing sale of the jointly owned property. The position is the same even if the mortgage itself is fraudulent.

CASE EXAMPLE

First National Securities v Hegerty [1985] QB 850

A husband fraudulently forged his wife's signature when applying for a mortgage of the family home owned by them as joint tenants. He defaulted on the mortgage instalments but the court held that there had been severance at the time of the application and they then held as tenants in common. The important effect of this was that Mrs Hegerty's share was free of the mortgage.

The position is different where all the joint tenants join together to seek a mortgage over the property. As they are acting together, they will not be held to sever their interests.

Bankruptcy

A joint tenant's bankruptcy will also sever his interest which will then vest in his trustee in bankruptcy. This means that the trustee in bankruptcy takes over as if he is the owner of the property. It is irrelevant to the issue of severance that this is a hostile and involuntary act. Under the Insolvency Act 1986 the beneficial joint tenancy is severed on the making of the order of bankruptcy and the property is immediately vested in the trustee in bankruptcy. If, however, the debtor dies before the bankruptcy order is made the entire co-owned property will vest in the survivor or survivors and the creditors of the now deceased joint tenant have no claim against the property.

CASE EXAMPLE

Re Palmer Dec'd (A Debtor) [1994] Ch 314

A husband and wife jointly owned the family home. The husband died a debtor but no insolvency order had been made at the time of his death so the house passed to the wife under the rules of survivorship.

Under the Insolvency Act 1986 an insolvency order does not take effect until there has been an order of bankruptcy from the court. If the debtor who is a joint tenant dies without such an order being made, the whole of the property will vest in the other joint tenant under the doctrine of survivorship.

A gift of the property under a will is not seen as 'acting on one's share'.

If one joint tenant draws up a will and leaves his share to another, that will not be seen as acting on one's share. There will be no severance of the interest and the gift under the will does not take effect on death.

Transfer by one party to a third party

Here, there is an overlap with the previous section. The transfer of one's share to another will constitute an act of severance. This may be by way of gift or sale.

Severance by means of sale of a share

In Figure 8.1, **W**, **X**, **Y** and **Z** own the title of the property in law and in equity. **W** decides to sell his share and **A** agrees to buy. **W** will remain joint owner of the legal estate but **A** will now own a share in equity as tenant in common. **X**, **Y** and **Z** continue to own jointly in equity.

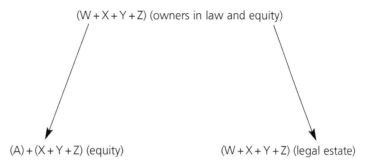

(W + X + Y + Z) (owners in law and equity)

(A) + (X + Y + Z) (equity)   (W + X + Y + Z) (legal estate)

Figure 8.1 Severance by means of sale of a share

If **Y** had an accident and died, his share would now pass to **X** and **Z**. **A** would not receive a share as **A** holds as a tenant in common.

If they all decide to sell after the death of **Y**, **A** will receive a quarter share, as **A**'s share will remain the same fraction as when he bought the property. The remaining purchase money will then be shared between **X** and **Z**. **W** will have to take part in the sale.

No decision on the legal estate can be taken without the agreement of **W** but **W** no longer has an interest in the equitable interest and will receive nothing back from the sale. **W** received the purchase price when he sold his interest to **A**.

If **W** decides to sell his share and **Y** says that he would like to buy the share, which is also an act of severance. Although there appear to be the same four unities present, unity of interest will no longer be present.

In Figure 8.2, **Y** holds one-quarter share as a tenant in common. However, he also holds as a joint tenant with **X** and **Z**.

W + X + Y + Z

(Y) + X + Y + Z

Figure 8.2 Severance by transfer of one joint tenant's share to another joint tenant

If **Z** had an accident and died, his share would then pass to **X** and **Y** but **Y**'s share as a tenant in common would not be affected.

If **X** and **Y** now decide to sell to **A**, the purchase price will be divided as follows. **Y** will receive one-quarter of the money as tenant in common and then **X** and **Y** will receive half of the remaining value. If the house was sold for £200,000 it would work out as follows. **Y** receives £50,000 and then the remaining £150,000 will be divided equally, giving **X** and **Y** £75,000 each.

Y will finally have £125,000 and **X** will have £75,000.

The law is prepared to consider even the contract for sale as constituting an act of transfer. If the contract for sale is itself specifically enforceable then the contract will be sufficient.

What constitutes 'acting on one's share'?
1. Sale destroys the four unities necessary for there to be a joint tenancy and severance is then effective for that share.
2. The formal start of litigation will be sufficient for severance.
3. Mortgaging one's share, even where there is no agreement from the other tenant.
4. The bankruptcy of one of the joint tenants will sever the share and the trustee in bankruptcy will become a tenant in common.
5. A gift of an interest under a joint tenancy in a will cannot be an act of severance sufficient to sever the joint tenancy.

8.6.5 Severance by mutual agreement

If severance relies on mutual agreement then there must be some contact and measure of agreement between the parties. Unlike severance under s 36(2) of the 1925 Act, this cannot be a unilateral act. The key feature here is the fact that the joint tenants act together and so an agreement can be inferred. The courts are not necessarily looking for an agreement that can be specifically enforced.

JUDGMENT

'The significance of an agreement is not that it binds the parties; but that it serves as an indication of a common intention to sever, something which it was indisputably within their power to do.'

Sir John Pennycuick in *Burgess v Rawnsley* [1975] Ch 429

If Cato and Peta, who have lived together for 12 years, decide to sever their joint tenancy, then the fact that they agree orally that one party will buy the other's share may be enough to imply an agreement. If the negotiations are inconclusive as to the decision to sell then there can be no severance under this head. So if Cato tries to persuade Peta to stay and not to sell her share to him, it is doubtful whether there is severance by mutual agreement.

The agreement would not be legally enforceable because it would not comply with s 2 of the Law of Property (Miscellaneous Provisions) Act 1989 which requires any contract for the sale of an interest in land (subject to certain very limited exceptions) to be in writing. It could still be effective as severance of the equitable estate preventing the doctrine of survivorship from applying if there is agreement.

Severance by mutual agreement was contested in the important case of *Burgess v Rawnsley* (1975).

CASE EXAMPLE

Burgess v Rawnsley [1975] Ch 429

Mrs Rawnsley met Mr Honick at a scripture rally in Trafalgar Square and, in spite of his rather unprepossessing looks ('He looked like a tramp', said Mrs Rawnsley), they formed a close relationship. Shortly after they met, they jointly purchased the property in which for some time he had been living as a tenant. The relationship did not last and Mrs Rawnsley agreed orally that she would sell her share to Mr Honick. However, she changed her mind about the price and asked for more money. Mr Honick died before the negotiations were finalised. The court considered whether there had been a severance of the joint tenancy. The main problem was that Mrs Rawnsley had decided not to proceed on the oral agreement.

<table>
<tr><td>

Arguments on behalf of Mrs Rawnsley:

1. no conduct is sufficient to sever a joint tenancy unless it is irrevocable;

2. the agreement was not in writing;

3. the agreement was revocable.

</td><td>

Arguments on behalf of Mr Honick's estate:

1. an oral agreement is capable of severing a joint tenancy;

2. even when an agreement is not specifically enforceable, it is capable of severing a joint tenancy;

3. even when an agreement is subsequently revoked, it is still evidence of 'mutual conduct' under *Williams v Hensman* (1861).

</td></tr>
</table>

The court upheld the arguments on behalf of Mr Honick's estate, which meant that half the value of the property passed with his estate to his daughter. If there had been no severance then Mrs Rawnsley could have claimed the whole of the property under the doctrine of survivorship.

'I think there was evidence that Mr Honick and Mrs Rawnsley did come to an agreement that he would buy her share for £750. That agreement was not in writing and it was not specifically enforceable. Yet it was sufficient to effect a severance. Even if there was not any firm agreement but only a course of dealing, it clearly evinced an intention by both parties that the property should henceforth be held in common and not jointly.'

Denning MR

This decision is seen as a very wide interpretation of what constitutes mutual agreement. Since it was decided over four decades ago there have been very few claims based on mutual agreement and none have been successful where severance has been claimed on the basis of an agreement which had subsequently been revoked.

In *Gore & Snell v Carpenter* (1990) discussed earlier, the agreement fell short of mutual agreement because there was no evidence of an agreement, merely agreement in principle. The couple jointly owned two houses. When their relationship broke down they discussed whether each party should own one of the two houses. When the husband later committed suicide and the issue was whether there had been common law severance. There had been discussions but there had never been agreement.

There is a direct contrast between this case and *Burgess v Rawnsley* (1975) where there had been agreement that Mrs Rawnsley would sell to Mr Honick but the price was not settled.

JUDGMENT

'Then was there a course of dealing? There were negotiations, as I have said, but negotiations are not the same thing as a course of dealing. A course of dealing is where over the years the parties have dealt with their interests in the property on the footing that they are interests in common and are not joint … But in the present case there were simply negotiations between the husband and wife and again there was no finality and there was no mutuality. For severance to be effected by a course of dealing all the joint tenants must be concerned in such a course and in the present case there is no evidence that Mrs Carpenter was committing herself to accepting a tenancy in common prior to the property division which would have been made in the divorce proceedings.'

Judge Blackett-Ord

In *Davis v Smith* [2011] EWCA Civ 1603 a couple S and M had mutually agreed to sever their interest in the former matrimonial home. There was correspondence between the solicitors of the parties as to how the proceeds of the sale would be divided between them. Before a notice of severance could be put into writing M unexpectedly died. The judge held that the joint tenancy had been severed either by mutual agreement between M and S or by the course of dealing between them following the principles from *Burgess v Rawnsley*. This was upheld by the Court of Appeal. The court looked at a range of evidence beyond the agreement to sell and divide the proceeds of sale which on its own would not have been sufficient.

Types of agreement that will sever the tenancy

- An agreement that contemplates severance expressly, as in *Burgess v Rawnsley* (1975), will be sufficient even if the exact terms such as price have not been agreed.
- An agreement during divorce proceedings about the division of property in specific terms, for example in equal shares.

Types of agreement that will not sever the joint tenancy

- An agreement by all the co-owners to sell or lease the property.
- An agreement that does not relate specifically to the ownership of the jointly owned land.

CASE EXAMPLE

Nielson-Jones v Fedden and Others [1975] Ch 222

After separation, the parties entered into negotiations about the ownership of their property. The negotiations were in very general terms and included a memorandum agreeing that the husband was to use his 'entire discretion ... to ... sell the matrimonial home and employ the proceeds realised to his new home ... in order to provide a home ... for himself to live in'. Although the husband had indicated his intention to sever the joint tenancy, he died before that was put into effect. It was held that the husband had nothing more than authority to sell the property on behalf of them both; it did not sever the tenancy.

'If, as I have held, the memorandum was not an assignment of Mrs Todd's interest in the proceeds of sale of the house to her husband, can it nevertheless be read as a severance of their joint beneficial interests: an agreement to the effect that each of them thereafter is to be solely entitled to his and her respective one half share in such proceeds? With the best will in the world, I find myself wholly unable to give the memorandum such a construction ... I think it is in fact rather easier to read the memorandum as an assignment than it is as a severance, so that as I cannot give it the first construction, almost a fortiori I cannot give it the second ... The question then is, can such a declaration – a unilateral declaration – ever be effective to sever a beneficial joint tenancy? It appears to me that in principle there is no conceivable ground for saying that it can. So far as I can see, such a mere unilateral declaration does not in any way shatter any one of the essential unities. Moreover if it did, it would appear that a wholly unconscionable amount of time and trouble has been wasted by conveyancers of old in framing elaborate assignments for the purpose of effecting a severance, when all that was required was a simple declaration.'

Walton J

8.6.6 Severance by mutual conduct

Severance may be effected 'by any course of dealing sufficient to intimate that the interests of all were mutually treated as constituting a tenancy in common' (Page-Wood V-C in *Williams v Hensman* (1861)).

The **key feature** here is that there must be a **course of conduct** that shows that the parties intended to treat their shares as separate and distinct. If this leads to an agreement then of course it will fall under 'mutual agreement'.

What amounts to a course of dealing sufficient for severance?

Long-term assumptions about ownership

The parties may have acted in such a way that although they purchased as joint tenants they have treated their shares as separate and distinct shares.

JUDGMENT

'A course of dealing is where over the years the parties have dealt with their interests in the property on the footing that they are interests in common and are not joint.'

Judge Blackett-Ord in *Gore & Snell v Carpenter* (1990) 60 P & CR 456

In this case there had been discussions about the ownership of jointly owned property but these had not been acted on and the status quo remained until the husband died. There was no evidence that the wife had committed herself to a tenancy in common.

Mutual wills

It is possible for two people to be bound by the terms of wills where they have been drawn up in identical terms and they intend them to take effect as mutual wills. The usual terms will be to leave property to each other and then to a third party on the death of the survivor. These mutual wills sever the joint tenancy and the doctrine of survivorship will not apply. This is an exception to the principle that there can be no severance of interests in a joint tenancy under a will. The second party is bound to leave the share from the deceased party in the way previously agreed because it is seen as a contract between the parties. The consideration is the forbearance of the first party not to change the terms of his will during his lifetime, which, of course, he would have been entitled to do.

ACTIVITY

Applying the law

Fred and Tina jointly own Grove Farm where they have lived all their life. They want to leave it to their nephew, Jonathan, and their niece, Jane, jointly on their death. They execute mutual wills leaving the farm to the survivor and then to Jonathan and Jane in equal shares. On Fred's death Tina meets Jeffrey and they marry. Tina has had second thoughts about leaving the property to Jane and Jonathan. Can Tina leave the Farm to Jeffrey?

Physical division of the property

Division of the property into separate units will not necessarily amount to a course of dealing leading to severance of the interests.

CASE EXAMPLE

Greenfield v Greenfield (1979) 38 P & CR 570

A house had been bought jointly by two married brothers. They then divided it up into two separate maisonettes where each brother lived with his wife. One brother died and his widow claimed to be entitled to his share of the property under his will. She argued that there had been severance through the physical division of the property. The court held that this was insufficient to constitute a 'course of dealing' and the share passed to the other brother under the doctrine of survivorship.

'The mere existence of separate maisonettes and of their separate occupation is not inconsistent with the continuation of a joint tenancy. The two can perfectly well exist together. The matter must be considered in the light of the evidence of the actual intentions of the parties.'

Fox J

Inconclusive negotiations over the property

Where the parties discuss severance but do not come to any conclusions then it could be sufficient evidence of a course of dealing for severance. The law is not conclusive because the judiciary is not in agreement over this.

In *Burgess v Rawnsley* (1975) Lord Denning held that the fact that there were discussions constituted severance under this head.

JUDGMENT

'It is sufficient if there is a course of dealing in which one party makes it clear to the other that he desires that their shares should no longer be held jointly but be held in common. I emphasise that it must be made clear to the other party ... Similarly it is sufficient if both parties enter on a course of dealing which evinces an intention by both of them that their shares shall henceforth be held in common and not jointly.'

Lord Denning

This view was not supported by the other judges in the case.

JUDGMENT

'I do not doubt myself that where one tenant negotiates with another for some rearrangement of interest, it may be possible to infer from the particular facts a common intention to sever even though the negotiations break down. Whether such inference can be drawn must I think depend upon the particular facts. In the present case the negotiations between Mr Honick and Mrs Rawnsley, if they can be properly described as negotiations at all, fall, it seems to me, far short of warranting an inference. One could not ascribe to joint tenants an intention to sever merely because one offers to buy out the other for £X and the other makes a counter-offer of £Y.'

Sir John Pennycuick

The commencement of litigation

If one of the parties decides to commence litigation over the shares in the property this will not constitute severance under this head but it could be sufficient under one of the other headings under *Williams v Hensman* (1861), for example 'acting on one's share'.

ACTIVITY

Applying the law

Consider the following examples and decide whether or not there has been severance of the equitable estate either under statute or under common law and explain why.

1. Gillian and Jack jointly own Honeysuckle Cottage. They have been living together for the past 15 years. Recently, they have begun to argue and Gillian consults a solicitor about how she can sever the equitable estate of the property since she does not want to press for sale immediately. A letter is delivered to Jack at the property but before he has a chance to read it Gillian intercepts it and destroys it.
2. Gillian, Jack and Helen live together in property which all three of them jointly own. Helen lives on the top floor of the property and converts it into a self-contained flat where she lives on her own.
3. Gillian, Jack, Helen and Kerry buy a house together. Jack wants to emigrate and Kerry orally agrees to buy his share. They drew up an informal agreement but Kerry felt that the price was too high and she telephoned Jack to tell him that. The following day, she was run over and killed by a bus.
4. Gillian and Jack buy a house and move in together. They live happily for ten years and then their relationship breaks down. Gillian finds out that she has a serious illness and decides to make her will and, not wishing Jack to inherit her estate; she leaves her property to her sister, Greta.
5. Helen and Ian got married and lived together for ten years in Chestnut Villa, a house that they jointly owned. Helen met James at a conference in June and she told Ian that she wanted to split up. In July she contacted a solicitor and he wrote to Ian, telling him that Helen wanted to get the property matters sorted out without any fuss and that included ownership of Chestnut Villa. They agreed some of the issues but before they had been finalised Ian had a fatal car crash and Helen is arguing that the interest in Chestnut Villa has not been severed.

8.6.7 Severance by operation of law

Forfeiture

A further means of severing a joint tenancy arises where one joint tenant kills a fellow joint tenant. This has the effect of severing the joint tenancy and through forfeiture the murderer is prevented from profiting from the unlawful killing.

Consider this example: Ralph and Rosie jointly own a house in Yorkshire. Ralph is a very jealous man and he believes that Rosie is having an affair. Rosie comes home late from work one evening and he threatens her with a kitchen knife and eventually loses his temper and plunges it into her back, thereby killing her. The doctrine of survivorship would result in the property passing to Ralph. The law views this as unfair and imposes severance, allowing Rosie's share to pass under her will or under the rules of intestacy if there is no will.

The effect, then, is that the legal estate is held on trust for the murderer and the victim's estate as tenants in common. So, here, the house in Yorkshire will be held on trust for Ralph and Rosie's estate in equal shares.

The Forfeiture Act 1982 gives the court the power to grant relief against forfeiture in cases of homicide other than murder:

'$s2(1)$ Where a court determines that the forfeiture rule precluded a person (in this section referred to as "the offender") who has unlawfully killed another from acquiring any interest in property ... the court may make an order under this section modifying the effect of that rule. (2) The court shall not make an order under this section modifying the effect of the forfeiture rule in any case unless it is satisfied that, having regard to the conduct of the offender and of the deceased and to such other circumstances as appear to the court to be material, the justice of the case requires the effect of the rule to be modified in that case.'

CASE EXAMPLE

Re K [1985] Ch 85

In this case the wife was convicted of the manslaughter of her husband. The facts of the case showed that she had been subjected to terrible abuse at his hands. The ordinary rules on joint tenancies would allow her to claim the entire estate but the rules on forfeiture prevented her from doing so and she would only have been able to claim a half-share. The court exercised its discretion and allowed her to claim the husband's half-share of the property and so inherit the entire interest.

The situation can become more complicated if there is more than one tenant involved. There has been a suggestion in an Australian case *Rasmanis v Jurewitsch* (1970) 70 SR (NSW) 407 that the innocent joint tenants should not be deprived of their share of the estate from the victim of the murder or manslaughter. In *Chadwick v Collinson* [2014] EWHC 3055 (Ch) the court refused to exercise its discretion in the defendant's favour allowing him to seek relief from forfeiture where he had killed his partner and son in spite of evidence that he was suffering from a mental health condition. The court held that in spite of his mental health condition he was still aware of his actions and their consequences.

Suppose that four postgraduate students Rosie, Ralph, Susie and Geoff all purchase property Rose Villa together. They jointly own Rose Villa. Ralph loses his temper and pushes Rosie against the kitchen window, which gives way, and she falls out on to the road below, suffering fatal injuries. Ralph is found guilty of manslaughter. The court would hold that Rosie's share should be held on trust for Susie and Geoff as joint tenants. Ralph should not be able to benefit from the share.

Application of constructive trust principles

'Increasingly, the view is taken that the forfeiture imposed on the killer is best justified in terms of the application of an equitable doctrine of constructive trust based on unjust enrichment. In other words, the killer is recognised as taking the entirety by survivorship but is, by reason of his misconduct, subjected to the full rigour of equitable control. He is made to hold the legal estate on a constructive trust for himself and the victim's estate in equal shares.'

K Gray and S F Gray, *Elements of Land Law*
(5th edn, Oxford University Press, 2009), p. 960

8.6.8 Severance by court order

Certain court orders can effectively sever an equitable joint tenancy. This occurs when the court has resolved issues between the parties usually during matrimonial cases. The order itself is seen to sever the interests, so if one of the parties dies before the property has been sold the law regards the interests as severed although they have not expressly put it into writing under s 36(2) LPA 1925.

8.6.9 Possible reform of severance

There is uncertainty over the different methods of severance. It is also felt that it should be possible to sever one's estate by will. For this reason, the question of severance was considered by the Law Commission in 1985. It looked at three options:

1. no substantive reform, but the incorporation of all methods of severance into a statutory provision;
2. the restriction of methods of severance to written notice;
3. the introduction of severance by will.

Possibly the most radical suggestion is the last point, which would allow severance on death through a provision in the will. This is discussed in the article below:

> 'This is a radical suggestion, which runs counter to the whole concept of joint tenancy with its right of survivorship. This right is its distinctive feature, and is why equity in general favours the less capricious tenancy in common. Thus the arguments in favour of introducing severance by will, must be carefully examined. The working paper mentions that in a matrimonial breakdown a spouse may be anxious to sever but unwilling to serve a notice and thereby aggravate negotiations over, for example, access to the children. The argument has a certain force, but the period during which such considerations hold sway should be quite short ... A more persuasive argument is that severance by will would prevent undesired devolution of property.
>
> The counter argument is two-fold:
>
> (i) it would be unfair to allow severance by will, and;
> (ii) difficult questions of construction would arise.
>
> The first argument is that a "rogue" beneficial joint tenant could secretly sever by will and then enjoy the possibility of the right of survivorship without any risk to his estate. If he survived his co-tenant, he would take all, and if he pre-deceased, his chosen beneficiaries would inherit his share. The other difficulty with severance by will is a practical one – the construction of the will.'
>
> L Tee, 'Severance Revisited' [1995] *Conv* 105

Eight years earlier, severance was discussed in a series of articles by Thompson and Pritchard. The main issue was whether the confirmed use of both joint tenancies and tenancies in common could be justified.

> 'In his recent article "Beneficial Joint Tenancies: A Case for Abolition?" [[1987] Conv 29] Mr Mark Thompson has reviewed a number of complications that can occur in law where land has been vested in co-owners as beneficial joint tenants. His suggested solution is to leave potential co-owners with just the one form, the tenancy in common, in respect of the beneficial interest in land. He also suggests that until legislation is effected to this end practitioners should urge clients to adopt that form of co-ownership. What he does not seem to make entirely clear is whether spouses and other co-purchasers should adopt a tenancy in equal shares or one according to their contributions, in so far as they may be at the outset calculable.

The mischiefs he envisages as justifying this radical solution are:

(i) problems when the marriage or other initial arrangement goes sour;
(ii) the uncertainties as to the manner in which severance may be effected;
(iii) the special problems arising when one co-owner is responsible for the death of another; and
(iv) the unpleasant surprise for severing co-owner that a severance will create equal beneficial shares, not resurrect the original contribution proportions.

Underlying all these mischiefs seems to be a belief that the parties have often, perhaps even usually, opted for joint tenancy without adequate advice. Is there any real evidence that this is so?

Against all this is the clear fact that many people are genuinely attracted to the survival aspects of joint tenancy. Not just married couples in the first romantic flush, wishing to demonstrate the full commitment of their mutual vows, but also unmarried siblings anxious to secure the smooth transmission of ownership as death overtakes each of them in their family home; or the father or mother in business with a child, wishing to effect just such a smooth transmission whether deaths do or do not occur in expected order.'

A M Pritchard, 'Beneficial Joint Tenancies: A Riposte' [1987] *Conv* 273

This article makes out a strong case for the retention of two forms of co-ownership in spite of the obvious difficulties. Professor Pritchard argues against the proposition put forward by Mark Thompson that there should be only one form of co-ownership, namely the tenancy in common, because for many the joint tenancy genuinely reflects the wishes of the parties. The conversion of all co-owned property into a tenancy in common would only respond to those relationships which break down or encounter problems. Over 20 years later this debate is still alive and common law severance as shown in *Davis v Smith* still has a role to play in severance of a jointly owned equitable estate in land.

8.7 The rights of co-owners in land

Co-owners of land have a number of rights. They arise under statute and also under common law and cover such rights as the right to occupy the land

8.7.1 The right of occupation of the co-owned land

Co-owners are entitled to occupy the land and they cannot exclude each other from the land or any part of it.

KEY FACTS

The right of occupation in co-owned land
1. A co-tenant can never legally exclude another co-tenant from his room and could not bring an action for trespass.
2. A co-owner not in occupation of the land through his/her own choice does not have an automatic right at common law to receive rent.
3. If a co-owner is excluded, e.g. through fear of violence from the other party, then rent will become payable by the co-owner in occupation.

CASE EXAMPLE

Dennis v MacDonald [1982] Fam 63

A wife was forced to leave the property she owned jointly with her husband because of his violence towards her. The court held that he should pay rent to her since he had remained in occupation. This was because she had been a deprived of her right to live in the property.

Exclusion does not have to be made through an order of the courts. Exclusion can cover the case where one party leaves the family home after the marriage has broken down.

CASE EXAMPLE

Re Pavlou (A Bankrupt) [1993] 1 WLR 1046

The issue arose as to whether rent should be paid by a wife in sole occupation of property but who had continued to pay the mortgage instalments and to make improvements to the property. The husband had left because the relationship had broken down. Where it is a matrimonial home and the marriage has broken down, the party who leaves the property will in most cases, be regarded as excluded from the family home, so that an occupation rent should be paid by the co-owner who remains. But that is not a rule of law; that is merely a statement of the prima facie conclusion to be drawn from the facts.

The rent is assessed as if it was an assessment of a fair rent assessed at the Rent Tribunal; half the cost of any repairs carried out by the sole occupier can be set off against the rent to be paid.

8.7.2 The right to claim rent received from the land

If the co-owner lets the property then the rent should be shared between the parties, whether or not a co-owner is in possession. The rights of a co-owner are quantified according to the size of their share in the property.

What if the profit is the consequence of one co-owner's work or expertise?

JUDGMENT

'For instance, one tenant employs his capital and industry in cultivating the whole of a piece of land, the subject of the tenancy, in a mode in which the money and labour expended greatly exceed the value of the rent or compensation for the mere occupation of the land; in raising hops for example, which is a very hazardous adventure. He takes the whole of the crops: and is he to be accountable for any of the profits in such a case, when it is clear that, if the speculation had been a losing one altogether, he could not have called for a moiety of the losses, as he would have been enabled to do had it not been cultivated by the mutual agreement of the co-tenants?'

Parke B in *Henderson v Eason* (1851) 17 QB 710

The main points raised in this judgment are that:

1. If one tenant does all the work then the logic is that he should be able to claim the profits.

2. If one tenant did all the work and made a loss then the other co-tenant could not be made to pay towards the loss, so why should the co-tenant get the profits?

3. The judge says that he who takes the risk should be able to claim the profit for himself.

When will the co-tenant have to account for profits made on account of his own work?

The co-tenant will be liable for any profits made that affect the value of the land. The type of case would be where mining has taken place and the land is reduced in value. The co-tenant is quarrying for Fuller's Earth which renders the land 10 per cent less valuable than it was before the work began, so he must account for part of the profit that he has made.

It does not matter that he did not try to prevent the other co-owners from also making a profit from the land.

8.7.3 Liability for repairs

Improvements

The rule is that there is no right to a contribution towards repairs and improvements from a co-tenant.

CASE EXAMPLE

Leigh v Dickeson (1884) 15 QBD 60

This case lays down the principle that the co-owner has no right to claim a contribution for the cost of repairs. A contribution can be claimed if there is an express or implied agreement that they should share the costs, or the work was requested by the co-tenant. Assessing the value of the contributions depends on whether the value of the property has increased or decreased.

If the co-tenant spends time and money on property but the actual increase in value is less than the costs involved, the co-tenant is limited to a claim on the increase in value of the property. If the property increase in value is far in excess of the value of the improvements, the co-tenant may be able to claim the value of the improvements as well as a share in the increased value of the property.

The right to receive compensation from a co-tenant may be an equity in the property itself which can even bind a third party if they buy with notice of such a right.

8.8 Termination of co-ownership

Co-ownership can be ended under the following circumstances:

Transfer of trust property to purchaser

Once the purchaser buys from the co-owners, the trust of land comes to an end and they cease to be co-owners of land. The rights of the beneficiaries will transfer to the proceeds of sale and the purchaser will be absolute owner.

Partition of trust property

If the co-owned property is effectively split between the co-owners so each has a legal estate carved out of the property, the co-ownership will come to an end. The property is then split into separate legal estates. This can only be done by deed under s 52 of the Law of Property Act 1925. There is provision for partition under s 7(1) of the Trusts of Land and Appointment of Trustees Act 1996 but it has been rarely used.

Property in hands of sole owner

Sometimes the joint tenants agree that one co-owner will release his share to the other co-owner. Under the Law of Property Act 1925:

SECTION

's 36(2) No severance of a joint tenancy of legal estate, so as to create a tenancy in common in land, shall be permissible, whether by operation of law or otherwise, but this subsection does not affect the right of a joint tenant to release his interest to the other joint tenants.'

For example, if three students – Sue, Andrew and Chris – share a house in Essex as joint tenants. Chris decides to go around the world and, although he contributed towards the purchase of the property, he says he does not want the responsibility of a house in England. He releases his share to Sue and Andrew. There remains a joint tenancy between Sue and Andrew in law and in equity. This is not a sale but merely a release whereby the co-owner loses all rights to the property.

Vesting in a sole owner

If one of two surviving joint tenants dies, leaving a sole survivor, the co-ownership is destroyed. This is the result of the doctrine of survivorship. There was a problem in any sale by a sole owner if the title was unregistered land. The purchaser would not be clear whether there had been severance of the title during the co-ownership.

Registered land

Rule 172 of the Land Registration Rules 2003 lays down that the Registrar can remove from the Register any names of a joint proprietor who has died, if the death certificate is produced. The registered owner has the right to deal as absolute owner.

Unregistered land

If the property has unregistered title and the property vests in a single joint tenant, there is always the chance that there had been severance in the lifetime of the tenant and so the property will pass as if it is a separate share in equity. Until 1964 there could be no conveyance by the sole surviving joint tenant of the co-owned property unless a second trustee was appointed.

Law of Property (Joint Tenants) Act 1964:

SECTION

's 1 ... the survivor of two or more joint tenants shall, in favour of a purchaser of the legal estate be deemed to be solely and beneficially interested if the conveyance to his purchaser includes a statement that he is so interested.'

The section will not apply in **two** circumstances:

1. A memorandum of severance signed by one of the joint tenants has been attached to the conveyance.

2. A bankruptcy order made against any of the joint tenants or a petition for such an order has been registered under the Land Charges Act 1925.

It will never apply to registered land.

The effect of s 1(1) of the Law of Property (Joint Tenants) Act 1964 is that the purchaser is allowed to assume that there had not been severance of the legal estate.

CASE EXAMPLE

Grindal v Hooper [1999] EGCS 150

A memorandum of severance had not been annexed to the conveyance as requested but it was effective notice under s36(2) of the Law of Property Act 1925. When the surviving co-owner sold the property there was no memorandum of severance. However, the purchaser knew the owner and was aware of the fact that there had been severance of the interests. The court held that there been severance and the fact that the purchaser had notice was sufficient for him to be fixed with notice. The purchaser was not deemed to be a purchaser in good faith sufficient for him to ignore the rights of the tenant in common.

CO-OWNERSHIP

SUMMARY

1. There are two types of co-ownership a joint tenancy and a tenancy in common.
2. The legal estate can only exist as a joint tenancy.
3. The key feature of a joint tenancy is the right of survivorship.
4. The key feature of a tenancy in common is that property can be dealt with separately and can be left under a will; the right of survivorship will not apply.
5. A joint tenancy in equity can be severed under statute or by common law.
6. There are three ways to sever at common law: acting on one's share, mutual agreement and mutual conduct.
7. Each co-owner has equal rights in land unless adjusted by the court.
8. Co-ownership can come to an end by sale to a purchaser, partition of the property or when the property vests in the hands of a single owner.

SAMPLE ESSAY QUESTION

The preservation of two forms of ownership no longer serves any useful purpose. A joint tenancy can so easily become a tenancy in common that it might as well be abolished. Discuss.

Explain the two forms of joint ownership in land:
- legal estate: can only exist as a joint tenancy;
- equitable estate: a joint tenancy or a tenancy in common.

Discuss the joint tenancy.

Key features: the right of survivorship. The advantages of the right of survivorship: simplifies probate; it simplifies purchases from joint tenants; it gives effect to the wishes of the majority on succession.

Discuss the tenancy in common.

Key features: no rights of survivorship but the ability to deal in the property, in particular the right to leave property on death.

Discuss the advantages of retaining the distinction.

Discuss severance of a joint tenancy.

Severance under statute s 36(1): discuss relevant case law. *Kinch v Bullard*; *Re 88 Berkeley Road*; *Re Draper's conveyance*; *Gore and Snell v Carpenter*.

Severance under common law: *Williams v Hensman* methods. Discuss the uncertainty of what constitutes mutual conduct and mutual agreement: consider *Burgess v Rawnsley*.

Discuss the proposition that it is easy to sever a joint tenancy.

Consider the possible reform of severance, i.e. only use statutory severance.

CONCLUSION

Further reading

Books

Gray, K and Gray, S F, *Elements of Land Law* (5th edn, Oxford University Press, 2009), pp. 914, 960.

Articles

Conway, H, 'Joint Tenancies, Negotiations and Consensual Severance *Saleeba v Wilke*' [2007] QSC 298 [2009] 73 *Conv* 67.

Dixon, M, 'The Never Ending Story of Co-ownership after *Stack v Dowden*' [2007] 71 *Conv* 456.

Gardner, S, 'Understanding *Goodman v Gallant*' [2015] *Conv* 199.

Hayton, D, 'Joint Tenancies: Severance' (note on *Burgess v Rawnsley* and *Nielson-Jones v Fedden*) [1976] *CLJ* 20.

Luther, P, '*Williams v Hensman* and the Uses of History' (1995) 15 *LS* 219.

Neild, S, 'To Sever or Not to Sever: The Effect of a Mortgage by One Joint Tenant' [2001] *Conv* 462.

Pawlowski, M and Brown, J, 'Joint Purchasers and the Presumption of Joint Beneficial Ownership – A Matter of Informed Choice' (2013) 27 *Trusts Law International 3*.

Percival, M, 'Severance by Written Notice: A Matter of Delivery?' (note on *Kinch v Bullard*) [1999] 63 *Conv* 61.

Pritchard, A M, 'Beneficial Joint Tenancies: A Riposte' [1987] *Conv* 273.

Tee, L, 'Severance Revisited' [1995] *Conv* 105.

Thompson, M, 'Beneficial Joint Tenancies: A Case for Abolition?' [1987] *Conv* 29.

Thompson, M, 'A Reply to Professor Pritchard' [1987] *Conv* 275.

9

Trusts of land

AIMS AND OBJECTIVES

After reading this chapter, you should be able to:

- Explain what is meant by a trust of land
- Describe the reasons for the introduction of the Trusts of Land and Appointment of Trustees Act 1996
- Assess the extent of the powers and duties of trustees of land
- Understand the nature of the duties of trustees of land
- Understand how the courts resolve disputes in a trust of land
- Describe the approach taken by the courts in relation to an application to court by a trustee in bankruptcy

9.1 Introduction

Whenever two or more people have interests in property, be it a house or a piece of land, their interests are held under a trust of land.

The rights could be either **concurrent** or **successive**. Different rules take effect, depending on the nature of the interest.

Concurrent rights

Where property is purchased by two or more people at the same time, their rights are said to be concurrent.

Felicia and John purchase Featherstone Castle together for £2,250,000. They have concurrent interests as their rights take effect at the same time (see Figure 9.1).

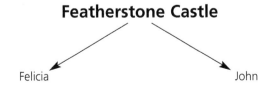

Figure 9.1 Concurrent rights

They hold the legal title for themselves on trust.

Successive interests

Where property is held by one or more persons for their lifetime with the property passing to one or more persons on their death, their rights are said to be successive.

Felicia is left Featherstone Castle by her godfather for her life and then for her son, Theodore. These interests are said to be successive as Theodore's rights do not come into effect until after Felicia's death (see Figure 9.2).

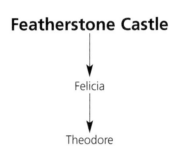

Figure 9.2 Successive interests

9.2 The old law

Today, all trusts of land are governed by the Trusts of Land and Appointment of Trustees Act 1996 (usually referred to as 'TOLATA') but it is useful to consider the traditional principles operating under the 1925 legislation which led to the passage of the 1996 Act. Before TOLATA 1996, where land was co-owned it took effect as either

- a trust for sale; or
- a strict settlement.

The trust for sale had many similarities with today's trust of land.

9.2.1 The strict settlement

This is a trust comprising land which gave effect to successive interests and is governed by the Settled Land Act 1925. Since 31 December 1996, no new strict settlements can be created. However, settlements in existence at the time TOLATA 1996 was passed were not abolished and are still governed by the Settled Land Act 1925. A significant number will continue for many years, so the law is still of some relevance.

The strict settlement came into existence in two circumstances:

1. where limited successive equitable interests were carved out of ownership of a legal estate in land;
2. where an absolute (as distinct from a limited) interest in land was conferred on a grantee who was subject to some disability, liability or contingency which qualified his capacity or entitlement to hold such an interest.

So **either** it applied where there were people entitled in succession to the property: **or** it applied where the beneficiary could not hold the land because of some disability or contingency.

KEY FACTS

Strict settlement
1. The person entitled to enjoy the property for his lifetime (the tenant for life) had all the powers of ownership which included the right to sell the property and the power to lease it.
2. The tenant for life also held all the powers of management over the property. So the trustees of a strict settlement had a reduced role.
3. If the tenant for life decided to sell the property he played the crucial role of receiving the purchase money from the purchaser.
4. The Settled Land Act 1925 introduced the principle that the tenant for life should be able to sell the land because land was being tied up for too long. (Capital was often needed to fund work on the property and the only way that could be raised was by selling some of the land.)
5. The rights of those with an interest in the property after the death of the tenant for life would have those rights transferred from the land itself to the purchase money provided that it is paid to two trustees. (This is the principle of overreaching.) If the money was not paid to two trustees then the rights in the property would not be transferred to rights in the purchase money but would remain as rights in the property.

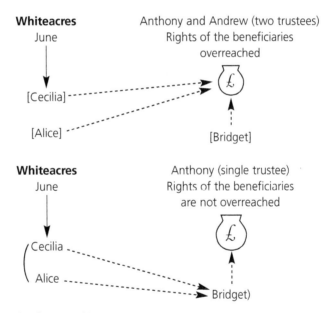

Figure 9.3 Example of overreaching

Can strict settlements still exist?

The right to create a strict settlement was abolished by s 2(1) of TOLATA 1996. However, strict settlements do continue to exist because under TOLATA 1996 those settlements that were in existence at the time of the Act were not abolished. The Settled Land Act 1925 will also apply where land within the settlement is resettled on new terms. A strict settlement will continue until it can be said that there is no more land or property within the settlement. If the land is sold but personal property remains in the settlement it is no longer a strict settlement under the Settled Land Act 1925 and it cannot be a trust of land. Under TOLATA 1996:

> 's 2(4) … Where at any time after the commencement of this Act there is in the case of any settlement which is a settlement for the purposes of the Settled Land Act 1925 no relevant property which is, or is deemed to be, subject to the settlement, the settlement permanently ceases at the time to be a settlement for the purposes of that Act.'

9.2.2 The trust for sale

Before 1996 a trust for sale arose in a number of situations under statute:

1. Where two or more concurrent interests were held in property they took effect as a trust for sale. It could arise expressly or it could be implied. Under s 36(1) of the Law of Property Act 1925 a trust for sale would be implied where there was a joint tenancy of the legal estate. It would not matter whether the equitable interests were enjoyed as a joint tenancy or a tenancy in common.

2. A trust for sale was always imposed where a person died intestate (i.e. without making a valid will).

3. The trust for sale was also imposed where interests were successive. Generally, this would only take effect if the settlor expressly stipulated this but the courts were also prepared to imply this into some provisions.

Where there is disagreement between the trustees of a trust for sale then the court would always order sale, as the main purpose of a trust for sale was sale of the property. This contrasts with the trust of land where sale is only one option for the trustees.

The doctrine of conversion: why rights in money, not rights in land?

Under a trust for sale the trustees had a duty to sell the land, and the doctrine of conversion reflects this principle.

One of the main criticisms of the trust for sale was that the beneficiaries would prefer to have rights in the land and not rights in the proceeds of sale. This was one of the reasons why the law was changed. The law should reflect the **expectations of the parties**.

The doctrine of conversion has been abolished under TOLATA 1996. All trusts for sale in existence on 1 January 1997 were automatically converted into trusts of land. Since 1996 **a trust for sale of land** will take effect as **a trust of land**.

It is still possible to create a trust of land that takes effect as if it is a trust for sale after January 1997 under s 4 of TOLATA 1996.

It is only possible where the trust has been created expressly and the settlor states in the trust instrument that the trust is to be a trust for sale. In this case the trustees will have a duty to sell the trust land immediately but there will be implied into the trust a power for the trustees to postpone sale.

Under s 4 of TOLATA 1996 this power to postpone cannot be excluded even where it is expressly excluded under the trust instrument.

9.3 Reform of the law

There were many problems in having two types of trusts of land according to whether the interests were concurrent or successive. There was a certain amount of overlap between the two and the use of the settlement was regarded as outmoded.

9.3.1 Criticism of the trust for sale

A trust for sale was implied into many cases of co-ownership. This was impracticable as the whole purpose of purchasing land was not to sell it and the purchasers wanted their rights to be rights in the land, not rights in the capital value.

9.3.2 Criticism of the strict settlement

The strict settlement had many drawbacks including the complicated method of creation. Two separate documents – the vesting deed and the trust instrument – had to be used in order to create a strict settlement. There was also a problem in the overlap of function between the tenant for life and the trustees.

9.4 Trusts of land

TOLATA 1996 introduced a new system of trusts for land which combined both strict settlements and trusts for sale and also bare trusts into one type of trust: the trust of land. The trust of land covers both successive ownership as well as concurrent ownership. Under the trust of land the trustees have dual powers of either selling or retaining the trust land. The most important feature is that there is no longer a duty to sell. A key feature of a trust of land is the interest in possession. Certain rights are given only to a beneficiary with an interest in possession. It means someone who has an immediate right to enjoy the property. Where someone has a successive interest he or she will not have an immediate right to enjoy property. An example would be where a house is left to a surviving widow for her life and then to the children. The children in this example do not have an interest in possession.

Consider these facts. Dennis leaves his house to Shona his wife for her life on his death and then to Fiona and Joss. After the death of Dennis, Shona can move in and enjoy the property. Fiona and Joss both have an equitable interest in the house but they do not have an interest in possession which means they do not have an immediate right to occupy the house.

9.4.1 Definition of a 'trust of land'

TOLATA 1996 provides that:

SECTION
....

's 1(1) (a) "Trust of land" means ... any trust of property which consists of or includes land, and
(b) "Trustees of land" means trustees of a trust of land.'

's 2 The reference in subsection (1)(a) to a trust –

(a) is to any description of trust (whether express, implied, resulting or constructive) including a trust for sale and a bare trust, and
(b) includes a trust created or arising, before the commencement of this Act.'

KEY FACTS
....

Trusts of Land
1. A trust of land includes all trusts of property which consist of or include land, so a trust of personal property which includes some land will be governed by the 1996 Act.
2. A trust of land includes any trust whether it is express, implied, resulting or constructive and includes a trust for sale under the old law and a bare trust.

3. The trustee of land has all the powers of absolute owner including the power to sell or retain the land.
4. Trusts of land include trusts such as all trusts for sale in existence when the 1996 Act came into force.
5. Strict settlements that were in existence when the 1996 Act was passed continue to exist as settlements and are not converted into trusts of land.
6. The doctrine of conversion has been abolished in relation to trusts for sale of land. Rights of the beneficiaries do not automatically attach to the proceeds of sale but are rights in the land itself.

ACTIVITY

Self-test questions

Consider the following examples and explain whether they give rise to a trust of land or not:

1. Margaret owns a racing stables in Newmarket. She lives in a small flat above the stables and has five horses at the moment all in training. She wants to leave the stables to her friend, Mike.
2. Orla owns five horses in training that she trains. They are in a stable owned by her friend, Daniel. She wants to leave the horses to her cousin, Finnian.
3. Lord Berkeley has a flat in London and a large estate in Yorkshire. He holds them under a settlement created by his father in 1980. Under the settlement they will pass to his eldest son.
4. Lord Rothermere creates a trust for sale of his flat in York, his estate in Lancashire and his collection of vintage cars in 1995.

All of the above will constitute a trust of land except (2) because Orla is leaving a trust of only personal property (five horses). In all the other examples the trust includes some land which brings them into the definition of a trust of land in s 1 TOLATA 1996.

9.5 Powers and duties of the trustees

9.5.1 General

The trustees of a trust of land have a number of important powers. Most significant of all is that they hold the power of an absolute owner. This potentially gives them rights to deal in the land which includes the power to sell, mortgage or lease the land.

The trustees have the powers of absolute owner
TOLATA 1996 provides that:

SECTION

's 6 For the purposes of exercising their functions as trustees, the trustees of land have in relation to the land subject to the trust all the powers of an absolute owner.'

This means that the trustees can treat the land as if they were the absolute owners; in other words, as if the land was their own. It is possible for these powers to be excluded when the trust is created. The trustees must act together so they must either act unanimously or not at all.

This is in direct contrast with the old law where the rights of trustees were carefully restricted. The powers were so restricted that it made it very difficult for the trustees to deal with the property at all.

9.5.2 Power to buy, lease and mortgage land

Under s6(3) of TOLATA 1996, as amended by the Trustee Act 2000, the trustees of land have the power to purchase freehold or leasehold land in the United Kingdom (previously only in England and Wales). This is important as it allows the trustees to invest in land either to provide accommodation for the beneficiaries or as an investment or for any other reason.

Under the old law the trustees had very limited power to acquire land unless it was expressly allowed in the trust instrument. They could not acquire land to provide accommodation for the beneficiaries and they could not purchase land if there was no existing land in the settlement. Their general powers to lease land were restricted to leases of under 50 years.

9.5.3 Power to partition the land

Under TOLATA 1996:

SECTION

's7 ... the trustees of land may, where beneficiaries of full age are absolutely entitled in undivided shares to land subject to the trust, partition the land, or any part of it.'

This section allows the trustees to divide the land up between the beneficiaries where the estate is large. It was available to trustees for sale before 1997.

Conditions to be satisfied for partition to take effect:

1. the beneficiaries must be of full age;
2. the beneficiaries must all consent;
3. the beneficiaries must be absolutely entitled.

This power can be expressly excluded under the trust instrument.

ACTIVITY

Applying the law

Claude and Jean-Francois are trustees of a trust comprising a large house on the seafront in Brighton. They hold the land on trust for two beneficiaries, Alexis and Olivier. The house has already been split into two self-contained flats which have been let in the past. Alexis and Olivier both want to live in the house but they do not want to live together.

Advise the trustees.

9.5.4 Power to force the beneficiaries to take a conveyance of the land

Under TOLATA 1996:

SECTION

's6(2) ... where in the case of any land subject to a trust of land each of the beneficiaries interested in the land is a person of full age and capacity who is absolutely entitled to the land, the powers conferred on the trustees by subsection (1) include the power to convey the land to the beneficiaries even though they have not required the trustees to do so.'

Conditions to be satisfied before the beneficiaries can be compelled to take a conveyance of the land:

a. the beneficiaries must be of full age and not under any legal disability;

b. the beneficiaries must be absolutely entitled.

The effect of this is that the trustees will cease to be trustees and the land will be held by the beneficiaries. If there is a sole beneficiary then he will simply become absolute owner, but where there are several beneficiaries then they will hold as trustees for themselves. It is not necessary under this section to get the beneficiaries to consent.

ACTIVITY

Delia and Charles are trustees of a trust in favour of their five nephews and nieces. All five are now over 18 and Delia and Charles decide that they would like to cease to have the responsibility of being trustees so they transfer the property to the nephews and nieces.

Advise them.

9.5.5 Power to delegate their powers in relation to the land

The trustees have extensive power to delegate any of these functions as a trustee (under TOLATA 1996):

SECTION

's 9(1) The trustees of land may, by power of attorney, delegate to any beneficiary or beneficiaries of full age and beneficially entitled to an interest **in possession** in land subject to the trust any of their functions as trustees which relate to land. . . .

(3) A power of attorney under subsection (1) shall be given by all the trustees jointly and (unless expressed to be irrevocable and to be given by way of security) may be revoked by any one or more of them; and such a power is revoked by the appointment as a trustee of a person other than those by whom it is given.

(4) Where a beneficiary to whom functions are delegated by a power of attorney under subsection (1) ceases to be a person beneficially entitled to an interest in possession in land subject to a trust –

(a) if the functions are delegated to him alone, the power is revoked,

(b) If the functions are delegated to him and to other beneficiaries to be exercised by them jointly (but not separately) the power is revoked if each of the other beneficiaries ceases to be so entitled.'

The trustees' duties in relation to delegation have been amended under the Trustee Delegation Act 1999 and a new s9A has been inserted into TOLATA 1996:

SECTION

's9A(1) The duty of care under section 1 of the Trustee Act 2000 applies to trustees of land in deciding whether to delegate any of their functions under section 9.'

The duty of care under the Trustee Act 2000 is a duty 'to exercise such care and skill as is reasonable in the circumstances'.

's 9A(6) A trustee of land is not liable for any act or default of the beneficiary, or beneficiaries, unless the trustee fails to comply with the duty of care in deciding to delegate any of the trustees' functions under section 9.'

The Law Commission had recommended that the trustees should be strictly liable for any acts or defaults after delegation but this was rejected, probably in order to encourage delegation.

The law draws a distinction between delegation, which can only be a unanimous decision between the trustees, and revocation, which can be carried out by a single trustee. Revocation also occurs when a new trustee is appointed and under s 9(4) when a beneficiary to whom functions are delegated by power of attorney ceases to be beneficially entitled.

The 1999 Act also imposes a duty on the trustees to review the delegation from time to time and to act where they think it is appropriate by revoking the delegation or by giving directions to the beneficiaries.

KEY FACTS

Delegation of trustees' functions
1. Delegation under TOLATA 1996 must be by power of attorney.
2. The trustees can delegate to a beneficiary any function if that beneficiary is of full age and is beneficially entitled to an interest in possession in the land.
3. Delegation of any function must be done collectively by all the trustees.
4. All the powers held by the trustees under s 6(1) of TOLATA 1996 can be delegated to the beneficiaries.
5. TOLATA 1996 does not allow the settlor to exclude the trustees' power to delegate.
6. The trustees are protected from liability for the defaults of the beneficiaries after delegation, so long as they took reasonable care in deciding to delegate the function.
7. The delegation of functions can be revoked by any one of the trustees and revocation is automatic if a new trustee is appointed or a beneficiary loses beneficial entitlement.

9.5.6 Duty to consult the beneficiaries

Under s 11 of TOLATA 1996 the trustees have a duty to consult the beneficiaries:

SECTION

's 11(1) The trustees of land shall in the exercise of any function relating to land subject to the trust:

    (a) so far is practicable, consult the beneficiaries of full age and beneficially entitled to an interest in possession in the land,

    (b) so far as consistent with the general interest of the trust, give effect to the wishes of those beneficiaries, or (in case of dispute) of the majority (according to the value of their combined interests).'

The trustees have no absolute duty, so they only need to consult **where it is practicable**. This means that where the beneficiaries cannot easily be contacted then the trustees have no obligation to seek them out. They do not have any obligation to act on the beneficiaries' suggestions or comments unless it is 'consistent with the general interest of the trust'. It is unclear whether the beneficiaries could control the trustees' decisions and what would be considered to be 'in the general interest of the trust'. However, the beneficiaries do have the right to sue the trustees where they have acted without consulting them or against the best interests of the trust and the court may grant an injunction. The duty to consult may be excluded or limited by express provision at the time the trust was created.

9.5.7 Duty to seek consents

Under s 10 of TOLATA 1996 the trustees have a duty to obtain the consent of a named individual, if required, before exercising some or all of their powers. Failure to obtain the required consent will expose the trustees to a potential breach of trust action and the purchaser's title may also be under threat. Not all settlors will require consent from a named person in a trust.

The trustees have some flexibility under s 10(1) of TOLATA 1996, if the disposition creating the trust requires the consent of more than two persons then the purchaser will be protected if the trustees obtain the consent of any two of them. Nevertheless, the trustees may still be vulnerable to an action for breach of trust.

Where under s 10(3) of TOLATA 1996 if the consent is required of anyone not of full age then it can be given by a parent with parental responsibility or a guardian.

Trustees have some protection under s 14 TOLATA 1996 as they can apply to the court for the removal of the requirement for consent.

9.6 Rights of the beneficiaries of a trust of land

9.6.1 General

The beneficiaries have a number of rights in connection with the land. These include:

- a right to occupy the land; and
- a right to be consulted about any sale.

Many of the rights reflect the old law but generally TOLATA 1996 extends the rights of the beneficiaries. The most significant change is that now the beneficiaries are seen as having rights in the property itself rather than rights in the proceeds of sale.

9.6.2 The right to occupy the trust property

Where joint tenants occupy land they have rights over the whole of the land which cannot be restricted by each other. Under common law they do not have to pay rent to each other where one of the joint tenants is out of occupation. The courts have only restricted the right of one co-owner to occupy the property in very exceptional circumstances.

CASE EXAMPLE

Chhokar v Chhokar [1984] FLR 313

While his wife was in hospital having a baby, the husband sold the matrimonial home to a friend. The wife had an equitable right in the property and was therefore a beneficiary under an implied trust. The purchaser was now owner of the property and should have had the right to live there. However, the court refused his right to occupy. If it had upheld his rights there would have been the unfortunate scenario of Mrs Chhokar being forced to live with her husband's friend.

'Why is it that a man who has bought a half-share in a house is told that he cannot live there? That he is a married man is entirely beside the point. If Mrs Chhokar can live there with her husband, why should not Mr Parmar be able to live there with his wife? It cannot, I think be argued that Mr Parmar had no right of occupation. Having a beneficial interest as tenant in common is generally understood to confer a right of occupancy, a view which has been affirmed in a series of cases including decisions of the House of Lords. These cases hold that a beneficial co-tenant, even where there is a trust, enjoys, by reason of that interest, a present right of occupation. Had it not been for that right of occupation, indeed, Mrs Chhokar would not have had any claim to remain in the house after her husband had sold it: she would instead have had to rely on a claim against him for a share in the price he received. It seems, therefore, that the acquisition of a beneficial interest by Mr Parmar should have been enough to confer on him a right of occupation. If the court was denying the existence of any such right, it was wrong.'

R Pearce, 'What Kind of Castle?' [1992] *DLJ* 153

TOLATA 1996 confers an express right on the beneficiaries to occupy trust property which was denied to the beneficiaries under a trust for sale unless the trust instrument expressly gave them such a right.

SECTION

's 12(1)   A beneficiary who is entitled to an interest in possession in land subject to a trust of land is entitled by reason of his interest to occupy the land at any time if at that time –

(a) the purposes of the trust include making the land available for his occupation (or for the occupation of beneficiaries of a class of which he is a member or of beneficiaries in general), or

(b) the land is held by the trustees so as to confer on a beneficiary a right to occupy land if it is either unavailable or unsuitable for occupation by him.

(2) Subsection (1) does not confer on a beneficiary a right to occupy land if it is either unavailable or unsuitable for occupation by him.

(3) This section is subject to section 13.'

(Section 13 allows the trustees to exclude or restrict the right of the beneficiaries to occupy the trust property.)

Under a trust for sale, the beneficiary did not have a right to occupy. He could be given permission to occupy but this was different in effect from the right to occupy. The courts gradually accepted that the beneficiary could expect to be able to occupy the trust land. This was admitted by Lord Denning in *Bull v Bull* (1955) but the significance is that the right had to be conferred, it was not a statutory right. Under TOLATA 1996 it is now a statutory right.

What makes land unavailable or unsuitable for occupation?

'Land is by its very nature almost always available and suitable for some sort of occupation. What then does "unavailable" mean? For example, is land unavailable if it is already occupied by tenants or licensees? Or is it only available if their rights of occupation cannot be terminated? Similar problems arise over "unsuitable".

Can land only be unsuitable for occupation by a beneficiary because of its condition, or may his personal circumstances render it unsuitable, quite apart from its condition? Inevitably trustees will form their own judgement as to whether or not land is unavailable or unsuitable for a particular beneficiary who requests occupation. In doing so, they will be carrying out much the same process as trustees carried out before the 1996 Act, when exercising their discretion whether or not to accede to the request of a beneficiary to go into occupation.... The crucial difference now is that paragraph (b) of section 12(1) and section 12(2) treat unavailability as objective criteria, depriving a beneficiary of an entitlement that he would otherwise have, and not as considerations for the exercise of a discretion.'

J G Ross Martyn, 'Co-owners and their Entitlement to Occupy their Land Before and After the Trusts of Land and Appointment of Trustees Act 1996: Theoretical Doubts are replaced by Practical Difficulties' [1997] *Conv* 254

The courts have found it difficult to define what is meant by 'unsuitable' under the 1996 Act because it is not defined within the legislation. The cases focus on what is the nature of the property. If it is to be used for residential purposes not all property will be suitable. The court also looks at the beneficiary and considers characteristics of that individual. So it may conclude that property may not be suitable for that particular person although it may have been suitable for someone else.

JUDGMENT

'There is no statutory definition or guidance as to what is meant by "unsuitable" in this context, and it would be rash indeed to attempt an exhaustive definition or explanation of its meaning. In the context of the present case it is, I think, enough to say that "unsuitability" for this purpose must involve a consideration not only of the general nature and physical characteristics of that particular property but also a consideration of the personal characteristics, circumstances and requirements of the particular beneficiary. This much is, I think, clear from the fact that the statutory expression is not simply "unsuitable for occupation" but "unsuitable for occupation *'by him'* ".'

Jonathan Parker LJ in *Chan Pui Chun v Leung Kam Ho* [2003] 1 FLR 23

In *Chan Pui Chun v Leung Kam Ho* (2003) the claimant argued that his girlfriend should move out of the house that they had jointly occupied when their relationship broke down. He argued that the house was unsuitable for her because it was too large for one person. She successfully argued that the original purpose of the trust was to give her a home and she needed a home whilst she studied for some examinations.

KEY FACTS

The right of occupation
1. The right is only conferred on a beneficiary with an interest in possession.
2. The right is absolute and can only be refused where there are two or more beneficiaries with a claim in the land.
3. It is possible for the trustees to restrict the right to occupy if the property is unsuitable or unavailable for a particular beneficiary.
4. The right to occupy will be conferred if that is the purpose of the trust.

ACTIVITY

Applying the law

Freda and Harry are trustees of a trust of land created in June 1999. The trust property comprises a bungalow in Sussex and a second-floor flat in London. Under the terms of the trust they hold the legal estate on trust for Jane for life with remainder to Sam in fee simple. Consider whether Jane or Sam have a right to occupy the property.

Would it make any difference if Jane was under a disability and there was no lift in the flat in London?

There may be other limits on the right to occupy. The trustees may have let the property to tenants or it may be commercial property and unsuitable for residential occupation.

The rights of the beneficiaries to occupy can be limited by s 13 of TOLATA 1996:

SECTION

's 13(1) ...Where two or more beneficiaries are (or apart from this subsection would be) entitled under section 12 to occupy land, the trustees of land may exclude or restrict the entitlement of any one or more (but not all) of them.

(2) Trustees may not...

　　(a) unreasonably exclude any beneficiary's entitlement to occupy land, or

　　(b) restrict any such entitlement to an unreasonable extent.

(3) The trustees of land may from time to time impose reasonable conditions on any beneficiary in relation to his occupation of land...

(5) The conditions which may be imposed on a beneficiary under subsection (3) include, in particular, conditions requiring him –

　　(a) to pay any outgoings or expenses in respect of the land, or

　　(b) to assume any other obligation in relation to the land or to any activity which is or is proposed to be conducted there...

(7) The powers conferred on trustees ... may not be exercised –

　　(a) so as to prevent any person who is in occupation of land ... from continuing to occupy the land,

　　(b) in a manner likely to result in any such person ceasing to occupy the land, unless he consents or the court has given approval.'

KEY FACTS

The exercise of the trustees' powers under s 13 of TOLATA 1996
1. The trustees can exclude the right of the beneficiary to occupy the trust property where there are two or more beneficiaries.
2. The trustees cannot exclude or restrict the occupation of all the beneficiaries.
3. The right to exclude the beneficiaries from the property must not be exercised unreasonably.
4. The trustee can never force a beneficiary already occupying trust land to cease to be in occupation unless he consents or the trustees have taken the issue to court.
5. The trustees have the power to impose reasonable terms such as the payment of compensation or outgoings on the property.
6. The beneficiary who remains in occupation of the property may be made to forego a benefit arising under the trust either money or in another form.

Under s13(4) TOLATA 1996 the trustees must take certain factors into account when deciding whether or not to exclude a beneficiary:

- What were the intentions of the person(s) who created the trust?
- What was the purpose for which the land was held?
- What are the individual circumstances and wishes of each beneficiary entitled to occupy the land?

The cases under the pre-1996 law may indicate to the court today whether the settlor intended the property to be used for the occupation of the beneficiaries or not.

CASE EXAMPLE

Barclay v Barclay [1970] 2 QB 677

One of five beneficiaries under a trust of a bungalow claimed the right to live in the property. The bungalow was left on trust with an instruction for the property to be sold after the death of the settlor and the proceeds to be divided between the five beneficiaries. The beneficiary had been living in the property during the testator's lifetime and wished to continue to live there.

The Court of Appeal held that the property should be sold. The beneficiary was refused the right to continue to live in the bungalow because the trust instrument clearly indicated a wish for immediate sale so the proceeds could be distributed between all the members of the family.

The law has always held that rent cannot be claimed by one party who decides not to occupy the trust property from the party who is in occupation. The position is different where a party is unable to claim the right to occupy the property. This principle has recently been considered in the courts.

CASE EXAMPLE

French v Barcham [2008] EWHC 1505

Mr and Mrs Barcham jointly owned a house as beneficial joint tenants. A bankruptcy order was made against Mr Barcham in 1994 which had the effect of vesting his half-share in his trustee in bankruptcy. In spite of this the couple remained living in the house until the trustee in bankruptcy applied for an order for sale in 2006. Whilst it was admitted that the property had been owned in equal shares by the couple the trustee in bankruptcy argued that the share of the wife should be reduced by a sum equivalent to rent payable whilst the couple remained in the property. This was refused at first instance on the basis that both parties were entitled to continue to occupy the property. The High Court reversed this decision holding that the trustee in bankruptcy was entitled to rent.

Blackburne J reviewed the discussion in Stack v Dowden concerning occupation rent and concluded that occupation rent can be payable where one party is denied the statutory right to occupation. The trustee in bankruptcy had no right to occupation but the husband had such a right and therefore the court was entitled to order rent from the wife.

By contrast in Davis v Jackson & Anor [2017] EWHC 698 (Ch) a property had been purchased by a couple in joint names but the couple were estranged and it was never intended that the husband should occupy the property. He later became bankrupt and the trustee in bankruptcy claimed that occupational rent should be paid by the wife for the use of the property. The court held that since the husband was never intended to live there the trustee in bankruptcy could not claim such a right as the law would not allow him to be in a better position than the husband.

One unusual approach used has been apportionment. The property is physically split into two or more parts. It will only be appropriate where the property is large enough to be split in this way.

CASE EXAMPLE

Rodway v Landy [2001] Ch 703

A medical partnership was wound up and the case turned on how the co-owned property should be dealt with. One party claimed immediate sale while the other sought partition so both could claim a separate share of the premises. This was so each could practise from separate parts of the building. The court applied s 13(1) of TOLATA 1996:

'Where two or more beneficiaries are (or apart from this subsection would be) entitled under section 12 to occupy land, the trustees of land may exclude or restrict the entitlement of any one or more (but not all) of them.'

It held that the trustees had the power here to divide the property between the partners and so each party would have access to just one part of the property. The trustees had the power to impose the cost of dividing the property on one party alone.

'I do not see why, in relation to a single building which lends itself to physical partition, the trustees could not exclude or restrict one beneficiary's entitlement to occupy one part and at the same time exclude or restrict the other beneficiary's entitlement to occupy the other part. Each part is land subjected to a trust of land and the beneficiaries are entitled to occupy that part until the entitlement of a beneficiary is excluded or restricted by the exercise of the power under s 13.'

Peter Gibson LJ

Some writers have questioned whether the legislative regime introduced under the 1996 Act has assisted beneficiaries. As seen above the sections incorporate a number of loopholes enabling the trustees to refuse the right to occupy.

'It is unfortunate that ss 12 and 13 passed through the entire legislative process without any comment or discussion. Sections 12 and 13 represent a judicious, though imperfect and problematic, innovation in statutory law in the context of trusts of land. The chameleon-like qualities of this right to occupy, accentuated by doctrinal incongruities and disparate dogma, raise the question whether the golden age of rights to occupy lay prior to 1997 and whether legislative prescription is a retrograde step. Commonwealth jurisdictions have not introduced the equivalent of ss 12 and 13 of the 1996 Act and retain the flexibility of the common law developing piecemeal by way of ad hoc developments without the constraints of legislative circumscription.'

S Pascoe 'Right to Occupy under a Trust of Land: Muddled Legislative Logic?' [2006] 70 *Conv* 54

9.6.3 The right to be consulted

SECTION

's 11(1) ... The trustees of land shall in the exercise of any function relating to land subject to the trust –

(a) so far as practicable, consult the beneficiaries of full age and beneficially entitled to an interest in possession in the land, and

(b) so far as consistent with the general interest of the trust, give effect to the wishes of those beneficiaries, or (in case of dispute) of the majority (according to the value of their combined interests).'

This section confers a general duty on the trustees to consult with the beneficiaries where they are of full age and are entitled to an interest in possession, before they exercise any function under TOLATA 1996. The importance here is that this provision applies to express trusts.

There was a similar power under the Law of Property Act 1925 (s 26) but it applied to implied trusts and did not automatically apply to express trusts. This is not an absolute duty.

Key words: 'so far as is practicable'. This means that the trustees would not have to take steps which were disproportionately expensive or complex to try to consult with a beneficiary who was difficult to find.

Key words: 'so far as consistent with the general interest of the trust … give effect to the wishes of those beneficiaries'. This means that they do not have to accept what the beneficiaries say, so long as they actually consult with them. If they choose to ignore their wishes the beneficiaries cannot take the issue to court unless they can contend that the trustees have gone against the general interest of the trust. An example would be a decision to sell the property. If the trustees go ahead with a sale at a time when property prices are falling then the beneficiaries may have an action against them if they had argued that the trustees should delay sale.

The right to consult can be expressly excluded under the trust. It will not apply to any trust for sale created before TOLATA 1996 came into force, unless the settlor is still alive and executes a deed to the effect that it is to apply.

ACTIVITY

Applying the law

Auntie Margie and Auntie Betty are trustees of a trust created in 1998. The property consists of a large flat in London and three holiday cottages in Deal in Kent. The beneficiaries are their three nephews, Tim, Jon and Malcolm and Malcolm's son Ben. The gift is as follows: to Tim, Jon and Malcolm for life with remainder to Ben. The trustees decide to sell all the property in Kent because they think it is unnecessary to keep these cottages. Tim objects because he likes to spend his holidays there.

Advise the trustees. Would it make any difference if the trust was created in 1995?

Consider here the exact nature of the duty imposed under s 11 TOLATA. There is no obligation to act on the beneficiaries' view unless it can be proved that their view is in the general interest of the trust.

KEY FACTS

Consultation with the beneficiaries
1. The trustees are under a duty to consult with the beneficiaries but only as far as is practicable.
2. The trustees must give effect to the wishes of the beneficiaries but only so far as is consistent with the general interests of the trust.
3. In cases of dispute between the beneficiaries, the trustees must give effect to the majority view according to the size of their shares.
4. The trustees only have to consult those beneficiaries who are of full age and who have an interest in possession of the land.

5. The duty to consult does not apply to trusts of land created before 1996 (old trusts for sale which were converted under the 1996 Act).
6. The duty to consult can be expressly excluded by the trust instrument itself.
7. The duty to consult can be suspended by order of the court.

9.6.4 The right to require that consents be obtained

Trustees are under a duty under s 10 of TOLATA 1996 to gain consents from individuals named by the settlor in the trust instrument. These could be beneficiaries or others who have no interest in the trust. This is a useful device for the settlor to ensure that his wishes are carried out.

Exclusion and restriction of powers

SECTION

's 8(1) Sections 6 and 7 do not apply in the case of a trust of land created by a disposition in so far as provision to the effect that they do not apply is made by the disposition.
(2) If the disposition creating such a trust makes provision requiring any consent to be obtained to the exercise of any power conferred by section 6 or 7 the power may not be exercised without that consent.
(3) Subsection (1) does not apply in the case of charitable, ecclesiastical or public trusts.
(4) Subsections (1) and (2) have effect subject to any enactment which prohibits or restricts the effect of provision of the description mentioned in them.'

Some argue that these sections re impose the so-called 'dead hand' of the settlor on the trust.

The effect on purchasers of the need to require consents

One problem for the purchaser could be that there are several consents to be obtained by the trustees and there may be disagreement amongst them as to whether or not to give their consent.

Under s 10(1) of TOLATA 1996 the purchaser for value only has to be satisfied that any two of the named persons have consented. The trustee could always be liable for an action against him by the beneficiary where the requisite consents have not been obtained so the trustees would be wise to ensure that the consents of all the beneficiaries have been sought.

ACTIVITY

Applying the law

Fred and George are trustees of a trust comprising two houses, Nos 2 and 3 Church Road. The trust instrument lays down that they must consult all the beneficiaries before they decide to sell, and get their consent. There are four beneficiaries and three agree but the fourth is on a year-long trip of a lifetime going round the world and is impossible to contact. If Fred and George sell No 2 Church Road to Greta can Greta get the title free of any rights of the beneficiaries?

Will the trustees be liable for breach of trust if the fourth beneficiary comes home and finds the property sold and says that he would have raised an objection to the sale?

The court has the power under s 10(3) to dispense with the consents which cannot be obtained because someone is away. So in this case the fact that one beneficiary is difficult to contact should absolve the trustees if they obtain permission from the court to dispense with consent. In any event Greta will obtain title to the property free from the beneficiaries' claim. This contrasts with the need to consult with the beneficiaries under s 11. Under that section the trustees are not under an absolute duty to consult, whereas under s 10 the need to obtain consent is absolute and can only be dispensed with by the court.

The court can also dispense with consent where it is unreasonably withheld.

9.6.5 The right to appoint trustees and to remove trustees

TOLATA 1996 expressly confers the right upon beneficiaries of a trust of land to select and also remove trustees. This is against general principles of the law of trusts where beneficiaries do not generally have this power unless expressly reserved for them by the settlor. These powers apply to trusts of land created after 1997.

SECTION

's 19(2)   The beneficiaries may give a direction or directions of either or both of the following descriptions –

(a)   a written direction to a trustee or trustees to retire from the trust, and

(b)   a written direction to the trustees or trustee for the time being … to appoint by writing to be a trustee or trustees the person or persons specified in the direction.'

Conditions to be satisfied:

1.   The beneficiaries must be of age and of full legal capacity.

2.   The beneficiaries must act unanimously.

3.   The appointment or removal of a trustee must be carried out in writing by all the trustees.

4.   This power is only given to the beneficiaries where the trust instrument does not nominate someone to carry out the function of nominating a trustee.

This provision gives the beneficiaries considerable control over who should act as trustee since the appointment of a trustee may be instrumental towards ensuring that the views of the beneficiaries are to be acted on. Of course, the major safeguard against this is that the decisions have to be taken unanimously. The issue is not one which can be subject to an application to the court under s 14 of TOLATA 1996.

These provisions apply to all trusts not just trusts of land so they also apply to any settlement which continues to be governed by the Settled Land Act 1925.

9.7 Resolution by the court of disputes in a trust of land

ACTIVITY

Applying the law

Consider the facts below and advise the trustees.

Annie, Benjie and Colin are trustees of land owned by their parents. The trust includes a large farm called Worley Edge Farm, a cottage by the sea in Cornwall and a house in Basingstoke. The beneficiaries under the trust are Annie's daughter, Fifi, who lives abroad; Benjie's two sons, Eddie and George (George is partially disabled and relies on a wheelchair); and Colin's three daughters, Hattie, Iris and Jill. Fifi wants all the property sold and the proceeds divided between the six of them. George wants to live in the cottage in Cornwall but it is difficult to access in a wheelchair and Jill wants to carry on living in the house in Basingstoke where she has been living for the past five years. Eddie would like to take control of the farm but he is only 19 and has no experience of farming. Annie and Colin are not speaking to each other as they are always having rows about who should have the right to live in each property.

The court has always had inherent jurisdiction to intervene in disputes over trusts of land. A statutory right existed under s 30 of the Law of Property Act 1925 for the parties to seek resolution of any dispute arising under a trust for sale by taking the matter to court. This was replaced by s 14 of TOLATA 1996:

SECTION

's 14(1) Any person who is a trustee of land or has an interest in property subject to a trust of land may make an application to the court for an order under this section.

(2) On an application for an order under this section the court may make any such order:

(a) relating to the exercise by the trustees of any of their functions (including an order relieving them of any obligation to obtain consent of, or to consult any person in connection with the exercise of any of their functions), or

(b) declaring the nature or extent of a person's interest in property subject to the trust as the court thinks fit.'

9.7.1 Who can make an application under s 14?

Key words: 'Any person who is trustee of land or has an interest in property.' These words suggest that a large number of persons will have sufficient interest to make an application to the court:

1. a trustee;

2. beneficiaries with interests in possession;

3. beneficiaries with an interest in the remainder;

4. a mortgagee;

5. a trustee in bankruptcy of a beneficiary;

6. (possibly) a creditor with a charge against the property of the beneficiary.

The trustees will only take the matter to court in a limited range of circumstances, for instance where they cannot agree or where they cannot get one of the required consents under s 8.

9.7.2 Matters to be considered by the court in deciding applications

The court can consider certain matters which are laid down in s 15 of TOLATA 1996 as being relevant to any decision that they take:

SECTION

's 15(1) The matters to which the court is to have regard in determining an application for an order under section 14 include –

(a) the intentions of the person or persons (if any) who created the trust,

(b) the purposes for which the property subject to the trust is held,

(c) the welfare of any minor who occupies or might reasonably be expected to occupy any land subject to the trust as his home, and

(d) the interests of any secured creditor of any beneficiary.'

a. The intentions of the person or persons who created the trust

The intentions of the settlor were relevant in deciding whether to postpone sale under a trust for sale.

In *Barclay v Barclay* (1970) a case discussed earlier the court ordered sale of the property in spite of the fact that one of the beneficiaries was living there. The reason was that the testator had expressly left instructions that the property should be sold and the proceeds divided between the beneficiaries. Sometimes there will be no clear intention expressed in the trust but the intention can be inferred from the overall circumstances.

b. The purposes for which the property subject to the trust is held

This was always a significant issue in any decision of the courts under s 30 of the Law of Property Act 1925. The courts looked specifically at the purpose behind the trust for sale and if the purpose had come to an end then the court would not direct that sale should be postponed.

CASE EXAMPLE

Re Buchanan-Wollaston's Conveyance [1939] Ch 738

Four residents of houses near the sea in Lowestoft, Suffolk, purchased land with the primary purpose of preventing development which would interfere with their view of the sea. They agreed among themselves that they would not sell the land except by unanimous consent. One of the four decided that he wanted to sell his own house and realise his share in the co-owned land. He made an application to the court, which refused his application for sale of the co-owned land since the main purpose of the trust still existed.

JUDGMENT

'The court of equity must look at all the circumstances of the case and consider whether or not, at the particular moment and in the particular circumstances when the application is made to it, it is right and proper that such an order be made.'

Sir Wilfred Greene MR

More recently the issues raised in *Re Buchanan-Wollaston's Conveyance* about the weight that the court should give to the wishes of the beneficiaries have been revisited in the case of *Finch and Others v Hall* [2013] All ER (D) 92.

CASE EXAMPLE

Finch and Others v Hall [2013] All ER (D) 92

Four siblings had been left property by their parents. The trust deed stated that all decisions should be made by a majority and further if the property was to be sold then all should be in agreement. One sibling wanted sale in 2012 which was supported by the agents and two of the other siblings. A fourth beneficiary, Peter Hall, did not want the sale to go ahead. The court held that Mr Hall was entitled to stop the sale. It also held that the Buchanan-Wollaston case gave the court discretion to order sale in accordance with the provisions of the underlying trust deed. However in view of the express term of the trust deed that no sale could be undertaken without the unanimous agreement of all the parties the court would not order sale under s 15 TOLATA 1996.

Where the property is purchased to provide a family home then the courts have been reluctant to order sale. *Chhokar v Chhokar* (1984) is an example of where the courts have not ordered sale because of the subsisting purpose which was to provide a home for the family. The position is different in cases of bankruptcy which is discussed below. In these cases the courts will generally order sale even where there are children although the sale may be delayed. We shall consider this later in the chapter.

Note the cases below, many of which are pre-TOLATA but are still regarded as having some relevance to current applications and see the different approaches of the court to a request for an order for sale. The court will always consider whether the original purpose of the trust still subsists.

CASE EXAMPLE

Bedson v Bedson [1965] 2 QB 666

Property had been purchased both as a matrimonial home for the parties and also as premises for the husband's business. The husband had paid the full price for the property but the property was conveyed to them both as beneficial joint tenants.

The court was impressed that there were two purposes. First, that the property was purchased as a matrimonial home and, second, as premises for the business.

Since the second purpose was still subsisting the court did not order sale. Denning MR: 'In considering whether an order for sale should be made, the court must undoubtedly have regard to these purposes. It will not allow one party to defeat them, or either of them, by arbitrarily insisting on sale.'

The most difficult decision is where a childless relationship ends and one party wishes to remain in the property while the other party wants the property to be sold. The court will then have to choose between the parties on the basis of other factors.

CASE EXAMPLE

Jones v Challenger [1961] 1 QB 176

A couple had purchased property as their matrimonial home. After they split up, the wife sought a sale of the property but the husband wanted to continue to live there. The courts decided that the property had been purchased as a matrimonial home for them both and since they had now divorced the purpose was at an end.

Even where there are secured creditors claiming that the property should be sold the courts have been prepared to delay sale where there are children living in the property. The case below is unusual because the courts have moved towards ordering sale where there are secured creditors in line with cases on bankruptcy even though an order for bankruptcy has not been made.

CASE EXAMPLE

Edwards v Lloyds TSB [2004] EWHC 1745 (Ch)

An order for sale which had been sought by the mortgagees was delayed for five years because the court accepted that the children of the relationship of the co-owners needed a home. The mortgagees owned over 50 per cent of the equity in the property.

c. The welfare of any minor who occupies or might reasonably be expected to occupy the trust land as his home

This section gives effect to the needs of the children of the parties who do not normally have rights in the property and would not have the right to make an application to the court under s 14 of TOLATA 1996.

In *Jones v Challenger* (1961) the courts were not prepared to delay sale because the underlying purpose, that is to provide a matrimonial home, had ended. Where there are children then that purpose is seen to subsist.

CASE EXAMPLE

Re Evers' Trust, Papps v Evers [1980] 1 WLR 1327

An application was made to sell property which had been purchased as a matrimonial home. The relationship had broken down but the wife continued to live there with the child of their relationship and two children of the wife's earlier marriage. The husband wanted the house to be sold. The court held that the purpose of the trust would continue until the child of the relationship reached the age of 18.

'[T]he irresistible inference from these facts is that, as the judge found, they purchased this property as a family home for themselves and the three children. It is difficult to imagine that the mother, then wholly responsible for two children, and partly responsible for the third, would have invested nearly all her capital in the purchase of this property if it was not to be available to her as a home for the children for the indefinite future. It is inconceivable that the father, when he agreed to this joint adventure, could have thought otherwise, or contemplated the possibility of an early sale without the consent of the mother. The underlying purpose of the trust was, therefore to provide a home for all five of them for the indefinite future.'

Ormrod LJ

Ormrod LJ highlighted the inferences that could be drawn in this case from the parties' conduct. These are basic common sense conclusions that can be drawn from the parties' behaviour when purchasing property and the courts are entitled to take them into account.

d. The interests of any secured creditors of any beneficiary

The court is here looking at the needs of secured creditors outside an application by the trustee in bankruptcy where different criteria apply. The court should balance their interests against the interests of the co-owner. An important point is that there is no indication in s 15 TOLATA as to how a court should go about balancing the different criteria laid down in the section. The court leans in favour of the creditor on the basis that he should not be kept out of his money indefinitely but there are several exceptions in the case law. *Mortgage Corporation v Shaire* (2001) and *Edwards v Lloyds TSB* (2004) are examples where the court has been prepared to postpone an order for sale claimed by a creditor.

CASE EXAMPLE

Mortgage Corporation v Silkin; Same v Shaire (2001) 80 P & CR 280

This case gives an indication of how the courts will apply the factors under s 15 of TOLATA 1996. An unmarried couple, Mr Fox and Mrs Shaire, purchased property in their joint names, to live in as their home. Their contributions were in unequal shares and it was found that the woman was entitled to a share of 75 per cent while the man could claim 25 per cent. Mr Fox took out a mortgage over the property without telling Mrs Shaire; indeed, he forged her name on the mortgage deed. After his death the loan was discovered and the mortgage company sought to enforce its security and sought an order from the court for sale. The court held that as a result of the forged signature Mrs Shaire's portion was not found to be subject to the mortgage. The court held that there should be an eventual sale of the property but subject to a delay while Mrs Shaire assessed the options for herself.

Under the old law, the court would only refuse to order sale in exceptional circumstances but as a result of TOLATA 1996 the court held that there had been a change in the law allowing the court to consider all the matters under s 15 equally, making the interests of the secured creditors just one of at least four matters which the court would have to consider. Mr Justice Neuberger then considered the overall effect of s 15:

> 'To my mind, for a number of reasons, Mr Asif is correct in his submission on behalf of Mrs Shaire that section 15 has changed the law. First, there is the rather trite point that, if there was no intention to change the law, it is hard to see why Parliament has set out in section 15(2) … the factors which have to be taken into account specifically albeit not exclusively, when the court is asked to exercise its jurisdiction to order a sale.'

Note that Neuberger J set out a list of reasons why he believed that the law had been changed as a result of s 15 of TOLATA 1996, including, among others, the observation above and the points below.

> 'To put it at its lowest, it does not seem to me unlikely that the legislature intended to relax its fetters on the way in which the court exercised its discretion in cases such as *Citro* [see below] and *Byrne* and so as to tip the balance somewhat more in favour of families and against banks and other chargees … All these factors, to my mind, when taken together point strongly to the conclusion that section 15 has changed the law. As a result of section 15 the court has much greater flexibility than heretofore, as to how it exercises its jurisdiction on an application for an order for sale on facts such as those in *Citro* and *Byrne*.'
>
> Neuberger J

It seems that under s 15 no one factor will be held to take priority over others. According to Neuberger J, the statute had listed the needs of the secured creditor as just one of the factors among others to be considered by the courts. It could not take priority in this case.

In the later case of *Bank of Ireland Home Mortgages Ltd v Bell* [2001] 2 All ER (Comm) 920 the court held that the interest of the secured creditors and whether or not they were entitled to their money was a powerful consideration. This reversed the view taken by the court in *Mortgage Corporation v Shaire* (2001) which held that the rights of the secured creditors would not rank above the other factors of s 15. The case concerned a husband who had forged his wife's signature on a mortgage deed. He worked abroad and when he got behind with the mortgage repayments the court ordered sale ignoring the needs of the son and the wife's ill-health. Sir Christopher Staughton observed that the bank was after all 'as much a beneficiary of the trust referred to as Mrs Bell'.

There are several more recent decisions which take a different view from *Shaire* and *Edwards* on similar facts. In *Edwards v Edwards and Royal Bank of Scotland* [2010] EWHC 652 the bank was seeking possession of the former matrimonial home of an older couple. Neither was in poor health and no children lived at home. Mrs Edwards had taken out a mortgage and had forged her husband's signature. When the bank sought repossession he claimed the right to remain in his own home. The claim was refused. Mr Edwards was in good health and had sufficient money to move. A similar view was taken in *Fred Perry*

Holdings v Genis [2015] 1 P & CR DG5 where the court ordered sale in favour of a secured creditor in spite of the fact that two children living in the property attended specialist Jewish schools which would not be possible if they left the area. It was said in the judgment by Master Price that 'the authorities demonstrated a recurring tension between [those] competing claims, but accepted that precedence was given to commercial interests and economic buoyancy rather than to the residential security of the family'.

Finally in *National Westminster Bank plc v Rushmer* [2010] EWHC 554 the court was not prepared to uphold the claim of the family even in the light of an application based on Article 8 of the ECHR which protects the right to family life. The judge was prepared to entertain the application and he held that it was important to take the effect of Article 8 into consideration but he did not find in favour of Mrs Rushmer. This was the first case taken by a secured creditor to consider the effect of the ECHR. The same point was taken in *Fred Perry Holdings v Genis* (2015) but again was unsuccessful.

Other matters for the court
These matters are not the only criteria for the court. The needs and preferences of the beneficiaries should also be considered in applications under s 12 for a right to occupy the property. There is no indication in the legislation as to how much weight is to be placed on each factor.

9.7.3 Disputes likely to come to court
Occupation of trust property
Where there are several beneficiaries then there are frequently disputes about occupation of the trust property. It may be impossible for all the beneficiaries to occupy at the same time so the trustees will have to give one preference.

Disputes over sale of trust property
This is a difficult problem which can seldom be resolved without one party feeling that they have been treated unfairly. These disputes will relate to unmarried couples and members of families as above where the Matrimonial Causes Act 1973 does not apply. The court will be guided by the needs of the parties and try to balance them, giving a result that will be the fairest in the circumstances. An example of this is the recent case of *Finch v Hall* (2014).

Applications by creditors for sale of the property
These will be initiated by those who have a charge over the property and their needs are listed under s 15 of TOLATA 1996.

Disputes over the need to consult the beneficiaries
The 1996 Act specifies that the beneficiaries should be consulted but where this is impracticable the need to consult can be dispensed with. However, beneficiaries may challenge what the trustees view as the type of circumstances which would make it impracticable to consult them if they have not been consulted.

The court has a very wide jurisdiction to make orders relating to the trust of land.

9.7.4 Applications by the trustee in bankruptcy
The court takes a different approach where there is an application by the trustee in bankruptcy. The court has to make such order as it thinks just, considering a number of factors.

The problem in these cases is that there are competing claims between the wife and children who want to retain the property and the creditors who are also keen to realise their asset.

The application may be made by the trustee in bankruptcy under s 14 TOLATA 1996 but the matters under s 15 no longer govern the issue as under s 15(4) the Act makes it clear that it is governed by matters listed in s 335A of the Insolvency Act 1986.

SECTION

's 335A (1) Any application by a trustee of a bankrupt's estate under s 14 of the Trusts of Land and Appointment of Trustees Act 1996 ... shall be made to the court having jurisdiction in relation to the bankruptcy.

(2) On such application the court shall make such order as it thinks just and reasonable having regard to:

(a) The interests of the bankrupt's creditors.

(b) Where the application concerns a dwelling-house which is or has been the home of the bankrupt, his spouse or former spouse, –

(i) the conduct of the spouse or former spouse in connection with the bankruptcy.

(ii) The needs and financial resources of the spouse or former spouse, and

(iii) The needs of any children.

(c) All the circumstances of the case other than the needs of the bankrupt.

(3) Where such an application is made at the end of the period of one year beginning with the first vesting under Chapter IV of this part of the bankrupt's estate in a trustee, the court shall assume, unless the circumstances are exceptional that the interests of the bankrupt's creditors outweigh all other considerations.'

What are 'exceptional' circumstances

Lawrence Collins J outlined what constitutes exceptional circumstances in the case of *Dean v Stout* (2004). He stated that typically, exceptional circumstances related to the personal circumstances of one of the owners such as a medical or mental condition. He was unwilling to categorise what constituted exceptional circumstances stating that it was for the court to make a value judgment after looking at all of the circumstances. He also held that 'exceptional' circumstances must be truly exceptional.

Compare these two cases:

CASE EXAMPLE

Re Citro (A Bankrupt) [1991] Ch 142

In this case the trustee in bankruptcy applied for sale of the family home. The wife applied for the sale to be deferred on the basis that the children were young and would be forced to move school in the event of sale. These were not seen as exceptional circumstances under s 335A of the Insolvency Act 1986.

'What then are exceptional circumstances? As the cases show, it is not uncommon for a wife with young children to be faced with eviction in circumstances where the realisation of her beneficial interest will not produce enough to buy a comparable home in the same neighbourhood, or indeed elsewhere. And if she has to move elsewhere, there may be problems over schooling and so forth. Such circumstances while engendering a natural sympathy in all who hear them, cannot be described as exceptional. They are melancholy consequences of debt and improvidence with which every civilised society has been familiar.'

Nourse LJ

Re Holliday [1981] Ch 405

Property was purchased as the matrimonial home in 1970, after the couple had three children. The wife had filed for divorce and almost immediately after she had applied for ancillary relief the husband had filed his own bankruptcy petition. The wife was without any capital of her own and the court found that she would need £26,000 in order to purchase property of similar quality. The court refused sale because it held that the circumstances in this case were exceptional as the husband had deliberately filed for bankruptcy to thwart the wife's efforts to gain ancillary relief.

> 'Of course the creditors are entitled to payment as soon as the debtor is in a position to pay them. They are entitled to payment forthwith; they have an unassailable right to be paid out of the assets of the debtor. But in my view, when one of those assets is an undivided share in land in respect of which the debtor's right to an immediate sale is not an absolute right, that is an asset in the bankruptcy which is liable to be affected by the interest of any other party interested in that land, and if there are reasons which seem to the court to be good reasons for saying that the trust for sale of the land should not be immediately enforced, then that is an asset of the bankruptcy which is not immediately available because it cannot be immediately realised for the benefit of the creditors.'

Buckley LJ

The rule in bankruptcy cases was laid down by Nourse LJ in *Re Citro* (1991) as shown above. It seems that in spite of the decision in *Re Holliday* (1981), it will be very rare for the court to postpone sale. The exceptional circumstances described in s 335A of the Insolvency Act include serious ill-health and specific conversion of the property for a disabled family member. Such exceptional circumstances arose in *Claughton v Charalamabous* [1999] 1 FLR 740, where the bankrupt's wife was seriously ill and had a much reduced life expectancy. Further the property had been specifically converted for her needs. Sale was postponed indefinitely.

In *Re Raval (a Bankrupt)* [1998] 2 FLR 718 the court postponed sale for a further year specifically to allow alternative accommodation to be found for a paranoid schizophrenic who had three children. In *Grant & Anor v Baker* [2016] EWHC 1782 (Ch) sale was also successfully postponed where the bankrupt's daughter rather than the bankrupt was shown to suffer from serious mental health problems. However, the length of time postponing sale was limited on appeal. The district judge at first instance postponed sale until such time as the daughter would no longer be living in the property, whereas on appeal Henderson J limited that time to just one year giving the family time to find suitable alternative accommodation. This suggests that where the courts are prepared to take into account ill-health as constituting 'exceptional circumstances' warranting a delay in sale, postponement will not be allowed beyond a further year. The decisions above were reflected in the decision on appeal by a High Court judge in *Pickard v Constable* [2017] EWHC where postponement was limited to one further year in spite of the poor health of the husband of the bankrupt.

CASE EXAMPLE

Barca v Mears [2005] 2 FLR 1 (Ch D)

The father of a child with special educational needs claimed that these were exceptional circumstances under s 335A of the Insolvency Act 1986. The child attended a special school and the father relied on Article 8 of the European Convention on Human Rights, arguing that his son's right to family life would be infringed. The court refused this claim, on the basis that the circumstances were not exceptional within the meaning of s335A.

'The eviction of the family from their home, an event that naturally ensues from the operation of the presumption of sale in s335A, could be considered to be an infringement of the right to respect of the home and family life under Article 8 if the presumption is given absolute priority without sufficient consideration being given to the Convention rights of the affected family ... In particular it may be incompatible with Convention rights to follow the approach taken by the majority in *re Citro* in drawing a distinction between what is exceptional, in the sense of being unusual, and what Nourse LJ refers to as the "usual melancholy consequences" of a bankruptcy. This approach leads to the conclusion that, however disastrous the consequences may be to family life, if they are of the usual kind then they cannot be relied on under section 335A; they will qualify as "exceptional" only if they are of an unusual kind, for example where a terminal illness is involved.'

Strauss QC

The judge concluded that in the ordinary run of cases the creditor's interests will outweigh all other interests, but left it open to a court to find there are exceptional circumstances in the case. Further, the application of the Convention will involve balancing the general interest of the community and the interests of the individual which is inherent in any application under the Convention.

Although *Barca v Mears* appeared to herald possible protection for a bankrupt's family against an application by the Trustee in Bankruptcy under the Human Rights Act 1998 it has not been as successful as anticipated. Under Article 8 (respect for private and family life) there is wide list of qualifying matters, including protection of the rights and freedoms of others who in the context of bankruptcy would be the creditors. So the court could justify failing to protect family life (evicting the bankrupt's family) by balancing the rights of the creditors to recovery of the money owed to them.

CASE EXAMPLE

Nicholls v Lan [2007] 1 FLR 744

The matrimonial home was owned jointly between husband and wife. After the husband was adjudicated bankrupt the trustee in bankruptcy sought an order for sale under s14 TOLATA 1996. Although the wife suffered from long-term schizophrenia and this was regarded as an exceptional circumstance the court at first instance and also on appeal held that the interests of the husband's creditors should prevail. An important factor here was that there were no children of the relationship. However an order for sale was postponed for 18 months.

Although it is a case that concerns public bodies, *Manchester City Council v Pinnock* [2011] 2 AC 104 has reopened the question of to what extent a court must consider the ECHR when making a decision on possession of property which is a family home. *Pinnock* concerned a possession order sought by a local authority. Although the order for possession was upheld by the Supreme Court Lord Neuberger in considering the issue raised a number of points:

'Any person at risk of being dispossessed of his home at the suit of a local authority should in principle have the right to raise the question of the proportionality of the measure, and to have it determined by an independent tribunal in the light of article 8, even if his right of occupation under domestic law has come to an end.'

He continued by observing that

> 'Although it cannot be described as a point of principle, it seems that the EurCtHR has also franked the view that it will only be in exceptional cases that article 8 proportionality would even arguably give a right to continued possession where the applicant has no right under domestic law to remain.'

These points were raised in a case concerning an application for an order for sale by a trustee in bankruptcy. In particular to what extent the court needed to apply the principle of proportionality when considering s 335A Insolvency Act 1996.

CASE EXAMPLE

Ford & Ford v John Alexander (Trustee in Bankruptcy) [2012] EWHC 266 (Ch)

Bankruptcy orders had been made against Mr and Mrs Ford and the trustee took proceedings for possession. Mr and Mrs Ford argued that it would be disproportionate to order a sale of their home in all the circumstances, and that there were "exceptional circumstances" (per s 335A(3)) why the statutory presumption that applies one year after first vesting should not apply. Their claim was based on Article 8 ECHR. They relied on a number of facts which included the limited amount that would be realised, medical conditions, the fact that they would not be accommodated by the local authority and the need to house their fish and terrapins. The District Judge granted an order for possession suspended for six weeks having found no exceptional circumstances.

They were refused permission to appeal by the High Court which held that the DJ had considered the facts of the case as if the law of proportionality was applicable to the case, and found it would not be disproportionate to order possession on the circumstances of the case.

However, he went on to consider the grounds of appeal in more detail, noting that all the bankruptcy cases that considered Article 8 pre-dated *Pinnock*. He found nothing in *Pinnock* of assistance to the Fords, it being a decision apparently limited to public bodies. He concluded that, notwithstanding the change in jurisprudence brought about by Pinnock, the wording of s 335A Insolvency Act 1986 provides:

> 'a necessary balance as between the rights of creditors and the respect for privacy and the home of the debtor. That balance serves the legitimate aim of protecting the rights and freedoms of others. I am therefore of the opinion that the requirements of section 335A satisfy the test of being necessary in a democratic society and are thus proportionate ... This was the conclusion in the pre Pinnock bankruptcy cases and I see no basis for ... a different conclusion.'

Nicholls v Lan and later cases shows that the suggestion in *Barca v Mears* that the Human Rights Act will make a significant difference in these applications was misplaced. As Martin Dixon commented:

> 'In *Nicholls v Lan* (2006) and *Ford v Alexander* (2012), the court found no incompatibility between the provisions of the Insolvency Act 1986 and the Convention, thus neutralising the concerns raised in *Barca*.
>
> M Dixon, Modern Land Law (9th edn, Routledge, 2014), p. 157

Dixon continues by concluding that *Barca* does concede that the convention *might* have an impact on the interpretation of s 335A and thus 'exceptional' does not mean 'nearly never'. He concludes that the Supreme Court made it clear in *Manchester City*

Council v Pinnock that it is *possible* that the enforcement of a proprietary claim such as the claim of a creditor under s 14 TOLATA could give way in the face of an Article 8 defence based on exceptional circumstances of the occupier.

9.7.5 Applications by secured creditors

Where an application is made by a creditor rather than by the trustee in bankruptcy the court will apply the Trusts of Land and the Appointment of Trustees Act 1996 s 15 and not s 335A of the Insolvency Act 1986.

As discussed earlier in *Mortgage Corporation v Shaire* (2001) Neuberger J held that the matters under s 15 ranked equally and the interests of the creditors was one of several factors to consider and their interests did not automatically rank higher than the other matters. However, later cases suggest that this has not consistently been applied and in more recent cases the court has tended to find in favour of the claimant creditor.

9.8 The protection of the purchaser

When a purchaser buys land from the trustees he wants to be sure that he purchases free of the rights of the beneficiaries under the trust.

If two trustees, Alice and Andrew, hold property, Willow House, on trust for Jack and Jim and Mr P wishes to buy the house, he does not want to have the worry that Jack and Jim will continue to have rights in the land. Overreaching allows Mr P to buy free from their rights as long as he follows the conditions laid down in the legislation.

The 1925 land law legislation tried to address the potential problems that can arise in this situation by trying to give the rights of each beneficiary protection but also allowing the purchasers to buy free of the rights of the beneficiaries, by introducing overreaching.

9.8.1 What does 'overreaching' mean?

1. The purchaser takes the legal estate free from any rights in the land if the correct procedure is followed.
2. The beneficiaries' rights are transferred from the land to the purchase money.

9.8.2 How does overreaching protect the purchaser?

1. The purchaser does not have to investigate the provisions of the trust.
2. The purchaser does not have to check whether the sale is in breach of trust.

Mr P could buy Willow House from trustees, Alice and Andrew, and the rights of the beneficiaries will transfer from the house itself to the purchase money. Mr P does not have to concern himself about these rights once the correct procedure has been followed.

9.8.3 Conditions necessary for overreaching

Under the Law of Property Act 1925:

SECTION

's 2(1) . . . A conveyance to a purchaser of a legal estate in land shall overreach any equitable interest or power affecting that estate, whether or not he has notice thereof, if – . . .

(ii) The conveyance is made by [trustees of land] and the equitable interest or power is at the date of the conveyance capable of being overreached by such trustees under the provisions of subsection 2 of this section or independently of that sub-section, and [the requirements of section 27 of this Act respecting the payment of capital money arising on such a conveyance] are complied with; . . .

(iv) The conveyance is made under an order of the court and the equitable interest or power is bound by such order, and any capital money arising from the transaction is paid into, or in accordance with the order of, the court.'

The conveyance must be made by trustees of land

The trustees of the land are the legal owners. All the trustees must join in the sale to pass ownership to the buyer, for example. If there are four trustees then all four must join in the sale even though overreaching can take place with only two trustees. A conveyance can include a mortgage and also a lease. If a sole trustee conveys the land to a purchaser then the rights of the beneficiaries are not overreached.

CASE EXAMPLE

Williams & Glyn's Bank v Boland [1981] AC 487

A house was registered in the sole name of a husband but the wife had made contributions which gave her rights in equity in the house. The husband therefore held the property on trust for them both. He mortgaged the property to Williams & Glyn's Bank, the mortgage being treated as a conveyance for the purposes of s2(1)(ii) of the Law of Property Act 1925. It was held that the bank was unable to overreach the rights of the wife because Mr Boland was the sole trustee. Her equitable rights would continue to attach to the land and would not transfer to the proceeds of sale. It gave her the right to continue living in the property.

The equitable interests must be capable of being overreached

There are some interests in land that are incapable of being overreached. The law draws a distinction between 'general' burdens and 'real' burdens:

General burdens

The key feature of a general burden is that it is an interest which is readily convertible into monetary terms. The types of rights which can be converted in this way are:

- the rights of joint tenants;
- the rights of tenants in common;
- the holder of a life interest;
- the holder of an interest in remainder;
- the rights behind a bare trust.

ACTIVITY

Applying the law

The nature of the rights of tenants in common behind a trust, is that their rights are to share proportionately to the amount that they put into the property. Suppose that Bert and Freda purchase property costing £200,000 and Freda puts in £50,000. If the property is sold and the purchase money is paid to two trustees then how much will Freda and Bert each receive?

The holder of a life interest will receive the cash equivalent of the share, which will be the income received from the share if invested. The problem here is assessing how long the person entitled to the share will live and that will have to be calculated on an actuarial basis.

Contrast real burdens which cannot easily be quantified in terms of money. In the words of Robert Walker LJ, these rights 'cannot sensibly shift from the land affected by it to the proceeds of sale' (*Birmingham Midshires Mortgage Services Ltd v Sabherwal* (2000) 80 P & CR 256).

'Real' burdens
These are:

- estate contracts;
- easements;
- restrictive covenants;
- rights of re-entry.

The key feature here is that these interests were always intended to be rights in the land, for example an easement. If you have a right of way over someone's land the right is only useful if you have the right to cross the land. If that was quantified into rights in money then much would depend on how often you used the right of way and for what purpose. The owner of the land which takes the benefit is probably far more interested in the way such a right enhances his enjoyment in the land.

In registered land these rights may be registrable as burdens on the Register and may also be rights capable of taking effect as overriding interests.

Capital money must be paid over as laid down in the Law of Property Act 1925
The purchaser must pay the money as prescribed under s 27 of the 1925 Act:

SECTION

's 27 Purchaser not to be concerned with the trusts of the proceeds of sale which are to be paid to two or more trustees or to a trust corporation...

(2) ...the proceeds of sale or other capital money shall not be paid to or applied by the direction of fewer than two persons as [trustees], except where the trustee is a trust corporation, but this subsection does not affect the right of a sole representative as such to give valid receipts for, or direct the application of, proceeds of sale or other capital money.'

This section has been strictly applied and it is irrelevant that there is only one trustee or that there is a provision in the trust instrument that expressly lays down that one trustee can receive the proceeds of sale.

The effect of s 27 is that the rights in the land are not overreached where only one trustee receives the capital monies.

Why have two trustees?
It has always been assumed that having two trustees is much safer for the beneficiaries and that their interests are much better protected. It is less likely that two trustees will misapply the money or take it for their own benefit. Case law suggests that this assumption is not necessarily correct.

CASE EXAMPLE

City of London Building Society v Flegg [1988] AC 54

A property was purchased jointly by a husband and wife. Contributions were made by the wife's parents, giving them equitable rights in the property. The husband and wife raised money on mortgage for their own purposes. The mortgage constituted a sale for the purposes of s 2(1) Law of Property Act 1925 and since there were two trustees the mother- and father-in-law found their rights overreached. Their rights transferred from rights in the property to rights in the purchase money. The problem was that the mortgagees had first claim on the purchase money and there was virtually nothing left after the debt owed by the daughter and son-in-law had been paid.

You will recall that the issue of fraud was discussed in *HSBC Bank v Dyche* (2009) discussed in Chapter 2. Unusually the judge set aside a sale and allowed a claimant to argue that his rights had not been overreached even where capital money had been paid to two trustees. The sale had been made in order to defeat the claimant's rights and in those circumstances the judge decided in his favour. The problem with this decision is that there is nothing in s 27 Law of Property Act 1925 which suggests that a sale must be in good faith in order to overreach an interest of a beneficiary.

Where no capital monies come into the hands of the trustees the overreaching provisions can still apply as seen in the case below also discussed earlier in Chapter 2

CASE EXAMPLE

State Bank of India v Sood [1997] Ch 276

The special issue in this case was whether the rights of the beneficiaries could be overreached where no capital monies passed hands so the case did not appear to come strictly within s 27 of the 1925 Act. Here, property was owned by two trustees but occupied by others, all of whom had interests in the property. It was mortgaged to a bank by the trustees. There was no advance of monies because the mortgage was raised as security for debts owed by a company owned by one of the two trustees. The bank tried to enforce its rights when one of the trustees was made bankrupt. Although s 27 of the 1925 Act did not apply, the Court of Appeal held that the principle of overreaching still applied. It can still apply even where no capital monies have actually been paid.

Exceptions to the 'two trustees' rule:

■ payment to a trust corporation;
■ payment to a sole personal representative.

9.8.4 Impact of overreaching on the purchaser

1. The purchaser takes the title free from any beneficial rights in the property, even where the beneficiaries are in occupation of the land.	3. The purchaser of trust land will not be responsible for applying the trust money.
2. The trustees are no longer trustees of land but they become trustees of the capital money.	4. Even overriding interests will be overreached if the conditions are complied with.

See *City of London Building Society v Flegg*. In that case, once the mortgage money was paid over to the two trustees, the rights of the beneficiaries immediately were transferred to the capital money.

9.8.5 The effect of s 16 of the Trusts of Land and Appointment of Trustees Act 1996 on purchasers

There is some possibility that TOLATA 1996 draws a distinction between a conveyance in good faith and one that is carried out *ultra vires*. The result would be that overreaching will not occur where a conveyance is not made in good faith. This would result in cases such as *City of London v Flegg* (1988) being decided differently today.

> 'The exclusion of subsections of s 16(2) and s 16(3) of TOLATA from registered land has created a new risk. It is currently assumed that a disposition by two trustees of land allows a purchaser to rely on ss 2 and 27 of the Act, as explained in *City of London Building Society v Flegg*. Flegg established that any overriding interests arising under a trust for sale of land would be overreached and cease to affect the land. This assumption is no longer valid, as explained above. An explanation of the state of the law after 1996 needs to begin with a consideration of the 1996 Act. The Act clearly operates upon the assumption that overreaching will continue after its passage ... The only question is, how extensive is overreaching to be? The drafting of s 16(2) and (3) suggests that those provisions are designed to prevent overreaching occurring. Thus the Act does not show any intention to abolish overreaching, but it does show an intention to curtail the operation of overreaching in some situations.'
>
> G Ferris and G Battersby, 'The Impact of the Trusts of Land and Appointment of Trustees Act 1996 on Purchasers of Registered Land' [1998] *Conv* 168

Trustees have the powers of absolute owner in relation to the trust property and can treat the land as if it were their own.	s 6 TOLATA 1996
Trustees have the power to partition the trust land if beneficiaries are of full age, all consent and all are absolutely entitled.	s 7 TOLATA 1996
Duty to gain consents of the beneficiaries where laid down in the trust instrument. Consent of two named individuals amongst a larger group will protect the sale to the purchaser but not the trustees from an action for breach of trust.	ss 8, 10 TOLATA 1996
Trustees have power to delegate their functions and will not be liable for defaults of the trustees to comply with the duty of care.	s 9 TOLATA 1996
Duty to consult with the beneficiaries of full age where practicable and must give effect to their wishes where consistent with the general interests of the trust.	s 11 TOLATA 1996
Power to exclude or restrict a beneficiary from their right to occupy under s 12 but not to exercise this power unreasonably.	s 13 TOLATA 1996
Power to make an application to court for an order to declare the interests or in relation to the exercise of their powers under TOLATA 1996. The court shall then consider certain matters laid down in s 15(1) in order to make their decision.	s 14(1) TOLATA 1996

Table 9.1 Powers and duties of the trustees under TOLATA 1996

9.8.6 Reform of the rules of overreaching

Many regarded the result of *City of London v Flegg* as unacceptable. The rules of overreaching were designed to protect the interests of beneficiaries under a trust by either protecting their right to remain in the property or transferring the right to the purchase money. It was assumed that the rights would therefore always be adequately protected. *Flegg* shows us that that view was incorrect and following the decision in *Flegg* the Law Commission considered ways that beneficiaries such as the Fleggs could have some protection from the law.

'Overreaching: Beneficiaries in Occupation' (Law Com No 188, 1989)

The Law Commission recognised the purpose of the 1925 Act which was to protect beneficiaries under trusts of land but also to protect the purchaser and to ensure that conveyancing was both simple and certain.

The main proposal of the Law Commission was that a conveyance of land should not overreach the interest of any beneficiary of full age and capacity who had a right to occupy the property and who was in actual occupation of it at the time of the conveyance **unless** that person had either expressly or impliedly consented to it.

This was a radical suggestion which represented a reversal of the doctrine of overreaching and was not universally welcomed; indeed there was considerable criticism mainly because it would then protect the beneficiary in occupation at the expense of the purchaser.

SUMMARY

1. A trust of land arises whenever two or more people have interests in land.

2. Such rights can be either successive or concurrent.

3. The trust of land replaces strict settlements and also trusts for sale although existing strict settlements can continue to exist.

4. Trustees have all the powers of the absolute owner including the power to lease and mortgage land.

5. Trustees have a duty to consult beneficiairies and a duty to seek consents if required under the trust deed.

6. Beneficiaries have the right to occupy the trust property if it is available and suitable for occupation but the rights of occupation may have conditions imposed by the trustees.

7. Disputes amongst the trustees or beneficiaries or anyone with an interest in the land can be resolved by the court which has a statutory duty to consider certain matters.

8. Where an application is made by the trustee in bankruptcy then the court must make an order for sale unless there are exceptional circumstances which are very narrowly construed.

9. The purchaser is protected from the rights of beneficiaries if the doctrine of overreaching applies.

SAMPLE ESSAY QUESTION

The introduction of the trust of land was a much needed reform. It strikes a balance between protecting the rights of beneficiaries behind the trust as well as protecting any purchaser who buys the trust property from the trustees. Discuss.

Define a trust of land.

Discuss the historical context of the Trusts of Land and Appointment of Trustees Act 1996.

Briefly define (i) strict settlement; and (ii) a trust for sale. Explain the problems of each.

How does the trust of land protect the beneficiary?

The beneficiary has a number of rights under a trust of land.

The duty of the trustee to consult when decisions are taken s 11 TOLATA.

Discuss the limitations placed on this duty: consultation is only necessary as far as is practicable . . . and so far as consistent with the general interests of the trust.

The duty of the trustee to seek consents from named beneficiaries under s 10 TOLATA. Discuss the absolute nature of this provision and the way it allows the settlor to retain some control over the trust. Can be dispensed with by the court and where consents are necessary from more than two people, only two consents are necessary.

Beneficiaries have a right to occupy under s 12 TOLATA although conditions can be imposed by the trustees.

Any dispute will be resolved by the court under s 14 looking at matters under s 15.

How does the trust of land protect the purchaser?

The doctrine of overreaching will protect the purchaser as the purchaser is not concerned with the beneficial interests behind the trust if the purchaser complies with the statutory requirements under s 27 LPA 1925. Explanation of the 'curtain principle'.

Consider the statutory requirements and the case law: *Williams and Glyn's Bank v Boland* (1981) and *City of London Building Society v Flegg* (1988). Critically analyse the apparent inequity of the two cases.

Has the trust of land succeeded in its aims?

Consider the lack of protection for the beneficiary in occupation where the capital monies of a second mortgage are paid over to two trustees, e.g. *City of London v Flegg*.

Consider Law Commission Report 188 on overreaching and discuss proposals; discuss the article written by Charles Harpum criticising the proposals.

Discuss other ways protection can be given to beneficiaries in occupation. Possible protection could be given if some powers of the trustees were limited, e.g. power to grant a second mortgage.

Conclude best protection will arise where the claimant owns the legal estate, e.g. *Stack v Dowden,* as all decisions concerning legal title must be taken jointly. This would have alerted the parties in *Flegg* of the second mortgage.

CONCLUSION

Further reading

Book

Dixon, M, *Modern Land Law* (9th edn, Routledge, 2014), p. 157.

Articles

Baker, A J, 'The Judicial Approach to "Exceptional Circumstances" in Bankruptcy: The Impact of the Human Rights Act 1998 [2010] *Conv* 352.

Cowan, D and Hunter, C, ' "Yeah but, No but", or Just "No"? Life after Pinnock and Powell' [2012] 15(3) *JHL* 58.

Dixon, M, 'Bankruptcy; Creditors; Peaceful Enjoyment of Possession; Right to Respect for Private and Family Life; Sale of Land; Special Educational Needs' [2005] 69 *Conv* 161.

Dixon, M, 'To Sell or Not to Sell: That is the question. The Irony of the Trusts of Land and Appointment of Trustees Act 1996' (2011) 70 *CLJ* 579.

Harpum, C, 'Overreaching, Trustees' Powers and the Reform of the 1925 Legislation' [1990] *CLJ* 277.

Massey, W, 'Trusts of Land and Appointment of Trustees Act 1996 and the Family Practitioner' [1997] *SJ* 1158.

Oldham, O, 'Overreaching where no Capital Monies Arise' [1997] *CLJ* 494.

Pascoe, S, 'Can a Joint Tenant Remain in Possession after the Other Joint Tenant has given Notice to Quit?' [2004] 68 *Conv* 370.

Pascoe, S, 'Right to Occupy under a Trust of Land: Muddled Legislative Logic?' [2006] 70 *Conv* 54.

Pawlowski, M, 'Ordering the Sale of the Family Home' [2007] 71 *Conv* 78.

Probert, R, 'Creditors and Section 15 of the Trusts of Land and Appointment of Trustees Act 1996: A Change in the Law' [2002] 66 *Conv* 315.

Ross Martyn, J G, 'Co-owners and their Entitlement to Occupy Land Before and After the Trusts of Land and Appointment of Trustees Act 1996: Theoretical Doubts are Replaced by Practical Difficulties' [1997] 61 *Conv* 254.

Law Commission Papers
'Cork Committee on Insolvency Law and Practice' (Cmnd 8558, 1982).
'Overreaching: Beneficiaries in Occupation' (Law Com No 188, 1989).

10

Easements

AIMS AND OBJECTIVES

After reading this chapter, you should be able to:

- Define an easement and describe the main characteristics under *Re Ellenborough Park* (1956)
- Compare easements with other rights in land, such as restrictive covenants, licences and *profits à prendre*
- Understand the rules governing the express and implied grant of an easement
- Explain how easements can be acquired under the rules of prescription
- Discuss the reform of easements introduced under the Land Registration Act 2002
- Explain the proposals for the reform of the law of easements

10.1 The characteristics of easements

Easements are important rights that allow one landowner to enjoy the land of another. They can bind successive landowners so it is important that the rules are clear as to what rights can constitute easements and also when such rights can arise. Easements have a number of key characteristics which were outlined in the key case *Re Ellenborough Park* [1956] discussed below.

10.1.1 Definition of an 'easement'

Although land may be owned at law by one person or more, it is possible that others will enjoy rights over that land. These are known as easements, or alternatively servitudes, and they consist of a right to use, or restrict the use of, the land of another person in some way, for example a right of way, a right to light and a right to water flowing through your neighbour's land.

A wide range of rights have been held to constitute easements. There is no closed or settled definition of the type of rights that can form the subject-matter of an easement.

Instead, there are four essential characteristics of easements and if any of these characteristics is missing then the right claimed will not be capable of existing as an easement. It is important that these characteristics are clear. Easements are very valuable rights and because easements can take effect at law the rights will pass to any future owner of the land of the claimant and will bind any owner of the servient land granting the rights.

10.1.2 The nature of an easement

The main characteristics of an easement are laid down in the following case:

CASE EXAMPLE

Re Ellenborough Park [1956] Ch 131

The owners of Ellenborough Park and surrounding land sold some of the land to property developers. The developers built on the land and sold various plots. On sale certain rights such as the right to enjoy the land, in particular the pleasure ground (Ellenborough Park) passed to the purchasers, subject to the payment of a fair and just proportion of the costs, charges and expenses of keeping the ground in good order and condition. The claimant who was the new owner of the Park tried to prevent the purchasers of the various plots from enjoying the use of the Park.

'The substantial question in this case, which we briefly indicated, is one of considerable interest and importance ... if the house owners are now entitled to an enforceable right in respect of the use and enjoyment of Ellenborough Park, that right must have the character and quality for an easement as understood by, and known to our law.'

Evershed MR

tenement
A plot of land

1. There must be a dominant and a servient tenement

The right must relate to two separate plots of land:

- The **dominant tenement** is the plot of land whose owner enjoys the right constituted as an easement.

- The **servient tenement** is the plot of land over which the easement is exercised or the land burdened by the easement (see Figure 10.1).

Dominant tenement

– owner enjoys the easement

Servient tenement

– owner bears the burden of the easement

Figure 10.1 The tenements in an easement

If the easement is a right of way then it is the land that is crossed that constitutes the servient land.

Hetty lives in Holly Cottage, next door to Rachael in Holly Lodge. Hetty likes to walk her two dogs on the common which adjoins Rachael's garden. She has no access to the common and has to walk to the village and then take the main footpath. This takes about 20 minutes. If she could cross Rachael's land then she could get to the common in about four minutes. If Rachael grants a right to Hetty to cross her land then Rachael's land would be the servient land and Hetty's land would be the dominant land (see Figure 10.2).

Dominant land	Servient land
Holly Cottage	Holly Lodge
Hetty enjoys the easement	Rachael's land bears the burden of the easement

Figure 10.2 Easement (right of way)

This demonstrates that an easement attaches to the **land** and not to a person. In order to have an easement, the owner must have an estate in land. Further an easement cannot exist independently of the land itself.

A licensee cannot have an easement over the licensor's land but a tenant under a lease can have an easement, even against land retained by his landlord. A public right of way is not an easement because there is no dominant tenement taking the benefit.

CASE EXAMPLE

London & Blenheim Estates Ltd v Ladbroke Retail Parks Ltd [1992] 1 WLR 1278
The claimant, who owned a part of a shopping centre, claimed that the right of customers to park on a central car park could exist as an easement. The claimant had not got an interest in land at the time when the easement was first claimed.

'An easement cannot exist as an incorporeal hereditament unless and until there are both a dominant and servient tenement in separate ownership. That never occurred in this case. Before the dominant tenement had been acquired as a dominant tenement the servient tenement had been disposed of. That, as it seems to me is fatal to the creation of the easement.'

Judge Paul Baker QC

2. *The easement must accommodate the dominant tenement*
This means that the right must be for the benefit of the land and not merely for the benefit of a person in his personal capacity. If the right can be said to be attached to land then it is assumed that it is for its benefit.

appurtenant
A right to become attached to a piece of land

The dominant and servient land do not have to adjoin each other or have a common boundary but they should be close enough to establish a connection between the two. There must be an element of **propinquity** which means nearness to another place.

JUDGMENT

'There can be no right of way over land in Kent **appurtenant** to an estate in Northumberland.'
Byles J in *Bailey v Stephens* (1862) 12 CB NS 91

There are three key issues here:

i. Can an easement for **business use** accommodate a dominant tenement?

ii. Can a purely **recreational right** exist as an easement?

iii. Can an easement with **significantly increased use** from that originally granted still exist as an easement?

i. Business use

Problems arise where it is claimed that the right is for the benefit of a business. Since the business is run by an individual, it is difficult to argue that the right takes effect as a right which benefits the land rather than the owner.

CASE EXAMPLE

Hill v Tupper (1863) 2 H & C 121

The claimant had a lease of an area that fronted on to a canal. He was given the sole and exclusive right to put pleasure boats on it. He claimed that this right was infringed when the defendant, who owned a small inn on the canal, also put boats on it. It was held that the right was no more than a licence as it did not enhance the enjoyment of the land but was merely incidental to the business run by the claimant and so the defendant had not infringed the claimant's rights.

JUDGMENT

'It is clear that what the plaintiff was trying to do was to set up, under the guise of an easement, a monopoly which had no normal connection with the ordinary use of the land, but which was merely an independent business enterprise. So, far from the right claimed subserving or accommodating the land, the land was but a convenient incident to the exercise of the right.'

Evershed MR

Compare this case:

CASE EXAMPLE

Moody v Steggles (1879) 12 Ch D 261

The issue was whether the right to fix a sign advertising a public house on the wall of a neighbouring property could exist as an easement. The question was whether the easement accommodated the land or merely the business use of the land. The court rather generously found that it could take effect as an easement.

JUDGMENT

'[T]he house can only be used by an occupant, and the occupant only uses the house for the business which he pursues, and therefore in some manner (direct or indirect) an easement is more or less connected with the mode in which the occupant of the house uses it.'

Fry J

It is not easy to explain the difference between these two cases. Dixon writes:

> 'It is not the commercial nature of the right granted that is important, but whether the commercial advantage endures as an aspect of the benefited estate or, in contrast, whether it is given to a person irrespective of whether he owns an estate in the land.'
>
> M Dixon, *Modern Land Law* (9th edn, Routledge, 2014), p. 292

ii. Recreational use

Historically, it was held that if the right was purely recreational it could not accommodate the land. The courts seem to take a very restricted view of what can constitute recreation. The main focus is on what the court regards as providing utility to the claimants. At first the right to walk was not seen as being of sufficient utility to the claimants but in *Re Ellenborough Park* Evershed saw that the right to 'walk at will' in the neighbouring gardens was of value to the owners of the properties surrounding the gardens.

The right 'must be a right of utility and benefit, and not one of mere recreation and amusement' as described by Baron Martin. In *Mounsey v Ismay* (1865) 3 H & C 486 the court refused to accept that the right claimed by the freemen and citizens of Carlisle to use land for annual horseracing on Ascension Day could exist as an easement. It failed because there was no obvious utility or benefit for the land, merely recreation and amusement.

CASE EXAMPLE

International Tea Stores Company v Hobbs [1903] 2 Ch 165

The use of the landlord's gardens for his own enjoyment could not exist as an easement because it was merely the right to walk at will. It did not appear specifically to increase the enjoyment of the land.

The decision in *Re Ellenborough Park* (1956) allows the possibility of an easement where it is purely for recreational or leisure purposes. The facts of this case (discussed above) allowed owners of houses use of an ornamental leisure park which adjoined their houses. It has to be connected with the dominant land. Lord Evershed discussed how the owners could **not** claim an easement if the right was one to enjoy the right to visit a zoological garden free of charge or to go to cricket matches at Lords cricket ground. This is because there is no real connection between the land and the right claimed.

JUDGMENT

'It is not fairly to be described as one of mere recreation or amusement, and is clearly beneficial to the premises to which it is attached.'

Lord Evershed

> 'The judicial animus against recreational easements has undoubtedly receded in recent times. It may be an index of a hedonistic (or even more health-conscious) age that it no longer seems inappropriate to acknowledge the easement character of certain recreational facilities annexed to dominant land. This is particularly the case where the claim of easement refers to a defined area over which a right of recreational enjoyment has been given not to the public but to limited number of lot holders.'
>
> K Gray and S F Gray, *Elements of Land Law* (5th edn, Oxford University Press, 2009), p. 612

The right to use land for recreational use has recently been extended by the Supreme Court in *Regency Villas Title Ltd v Diamond Resorts (Europe) Ltd* [2018] UKSC 57. This case concerned a claim by owners of timeshare properties which they argued carried legal rights to use adjoining sports facilities such as tennis and squash courts, a golf course, putting green and an outdoor swimming pool. These were all upheld including the right to use indoor facilities such as a sauna, a gym and snooker tables which had been upheld by the High Court but were rejected by the Court of Appeal. The point argued here was that the properties had been developed giving such rights to the owners and were intrinsic to their use. It is less likely that such rights would accrue if a mere licence to use recreational facilities was granted to a tenant who later purchased the property claiming such rights to be easements. The key question in *Regency Villas* was: what did people regard today as utility and benefit? Can we distinguish between walking in a garden as in *Re Ellenborough Park* and playing recreational sport? The judgment highlights the changing nature of easements over time.

The Supreme Court by a majority of four to one upheld all the recreational rights claimed without distinction thereby extending the definition of an easement to include a recreational right so long as it satisfies the requirements of *Re Ellenborough Park*. The Court of Appeal had accepted that recreational and sporting rights could take effect as easements but had drawn a distinction between the various rights. It had excluded certain indoor rights such as the use of the gym and snooker facilities. The Supreme Court rejected this rather narrow view and reinstated all the rights as easements. In the view of the Court there had been a 'single comprehensive right to use a complex of facilities as they evolved, not fixed as they existed at the time of the transfer'.

iii. Increased use of the easement
Once the easement is held to accommodate the land, an increase in the use of the land will not necessarily extinguish the easement.

CASE EXAMPLE

British Railways Board v Glass [1965] Ch 538

A farmer had the right 'to cross a railway crossing with all manner of cattle'. Many years later, the farmer gave a number of caravan owners the right to use his land. They all used the railway crossing. The number of caravans grew from six to thirty caravans, so the traffic using the line was quite considerable. However, the court held that so long as the nature of the use did not vary and was not excessive, the use of the railway crossing was within the terms of the initial grant.

If the use becomes excessive then the right can be challenged. The courts have had to determine what is the difference between increased use and excessive use.

CASE EXAMPLE

Jelbert v Davis [1968] 1 WLR 589

The owner of land, who was a farmer, had a right of way for agricultural use over a driveway which led to the main road. At first he used it for agricultural purposes only but later, he developed his land, creating a caravan park for 200 caravans and/or tents. The owner claimed that the caravan users all had a right to use the right of way across the neighbouring land.

'In my opinion a grant in these terms does not authorise an unlimited use of the way . . . It must not be used so as to interfere unreasonably with the use by those other persons, that is, with their use of it as they do now, or as they may do lawfully in the future . . . More generally, the true proposition is that no one of those entitled to the right of way must use it to an extent which is beyond anything which was contemplated at the time of the grant.'

Lord Denning

The courts continue to have a fairly restricted attitude to attempts to extend the enjoyment of an easement to customers of the claimant as shown in the case below.

CASE EXAMPLE

Greatorex v Newman [2008] EWCA Civ 1318

The owner of a bar had an easement for himself, his staff and trade customers over a passageway owned by the respondent Newman. He claimed that such a right extended to the users of the bar. The respondent complained that the customers made excessive noise as they left the public house at night and that the right to use the passageway was limited to trade customers, staff and the defendant.

The Court of Appeal refused to extend the easement to the retail customers. Although the retail customers could use the right of way in the case of fire or any emergency they had no general right to use the passageway.

3. The dominant and servient tenements must be owned or occupied by different persons

This means that the dominant and servient land must be either owned or occupied by different persons. It has long been accepted that you cannot have an easement over your own land. It may be possible to have a **quasi-easement** but that is not binding until it becomes a full easement. A quasi-easement is a right over one's own land that is not an easement but could be an easement if the two plots of land were owned by two different persons.

Can a tenant acquire an easement over the land owned by his landlord?

A tenant can acquire an easement over his landlord's land because although the dominant and servient lands are owned by the same person, they are occupied by different persons. The key feature here is the fact that the land is occupied by different people. It is also possible for a landlord to reserve an easement over the land that has been leased to a tenant. Without this the landlord may not have access across the tenant's land for the currency of the lease.

4 The easement must be capable of forming the subject-matter of a grant

There are several different aspects to this:

a. there must be a capable grantor and grantee;

b. the right itself must be sufficiently definite;

c. the right must be in the nature of an easement.

a.   **There must be a capable grantor and grantee.** A person can only grant an easement over land if he/she has a proprietary interest in that land. The grantor must be legally capable of making the grant. If a grantor has not got a legal estate in land then he/she cannot grant a legal easement. The grantee must also be capable of acquiring an easement. This means that it must be granted to a definite person or a definite body of persons. There could be no effective grant to a fluctuating group of persons, such as people living in a village. In this case the right granted will take effect as a local **customary right**. These are rights that a group can exercise over land; the group could be those living in a village or town. The rights can be the right to play sport or to hold a fair An easement can be held by either a leaseholder or a freeholder.

b.   **The right itself must be sufficiently definite.** It must not be too vague and uncertain. It must be clear to the grantee and the grantor the exact nature of the rights. Unless a right is clearly defined it will not be clear whether it has been exceeded or denied. There cannot be an easement of a good view or a prospect: *William Aldred's Case* (1610) 9 Co Rep 57. A challenge was made in *Re Ellenborough Park* (1956), by the owner of the park, that the right claimed was merely a right to walk at will over another's land. He argued that the right was too vague in nature. However, the judge found that it was quite different from a right to wander at will but a definitive right to enjoy the park as a garden which benefited the land owned by the original purchasers. Recently the decision in *Coventry v Lawrence* (No 1) [2014] contemplated that an easement could include a right to make noise. Such a right would be difficult to define with sufficient clarity, but nevertheless the Supreme Court did not see that to be an obstacle to its existence as an easement.

c.   **The right must be in the nature of an easement.**

JUDGMENT

'The categories of servitudes and easements must alter and expand with the changes that take place in the circumstances of mankind.'

Lord St Leonards in *Dyce v Lady James Hay* (1852) 1 Macq 305

This means that the right must be within the categories of rights already recognised as easements or very similar to such categories. The law recognises that the categories of easements are not closed, but nevertheless there must be justification before the courts are prepared to admit a new type of easement.

CASE EXAMPLE

Phipps v Pears [1965] 1 QB 76

The claimant based his case on an easement of protection against the weather. This was not a positive right but a negative right which prevented the neighbour from enjoying the property in such a way as to interfere with his neighbour's enjoyment of the property. He claimed damages for breach of the easement.

'If we were to stop a man pulling down his house, we would put a brake on desirable improvement. Every man is entitled to pull down his house if he likes. If it exposes your house to the weather, that is your misfortune. It is no wrong on his part.'

Lord Denning

The creation of new types of easements

There is a real problem in finding a balance between allowing new easements to keep abreast with developments and not rendering the land unsaleable because the land has burdensome limits placed upon it. As there is no exhaustive list of easements the court will entertain applications concerning a novel use of land. As can be seen from the cases below the applications meet varying degrees of success.

CASE EXAMPLE

Hunter v Canary Wharf [1997] AC 655

When the Canary Wharf tower was built, a number of people living in the neighbourhood found that it interfered with their television reception. They claimed that they had an easement in the nature of television reception. The court refused to accept that such a right could exist. One reason that influenced the judges was that it could impose an immense burden on a person wishing to build on their land. If such a right existed then Lord Hoffmann saw that there was a risk that the landowner could be sued by 'an indeterminate number of plaintiffs, each claiming compensation in a relatively modest amount'. In this case he thought that there were sufficient safeguards in the planning system to ensure that the rights of the people were not intentionally interfered with.

As mentioned earlier *Coventry & Ors v Lawrence* [2014] UKSC 13 considered the possibility of acquiring a right to affect neighbouring property by noise from stock car racing. The Supreme Court held that such a right could exist as an easement if it had been practised over a period of time although the right did not arise on the facts of this case.

The Court of Appeal in *The Supreme Court in Regency Villas v Diamond Resorts* [2018] extended the definition of easements to a range of recreational and sporting rights taking into account the greater emphasis on enjoyment of sport in daily life in the twenty-first century.

In *Dowty Boulton Paul Ltd v Wolverhampton Corp (No 2)* [1976] Ch 13 the right of visitors to a factory to use neighbouring land as an airfield in order to land their private aircraft was upheld.

The right to use lavatories on neighbouring premises belonging to another was upheld as an easement in *Miller v Emcer Products Ltd* [1956] Ch 304.

JUDGMENT

'In my judgment the right had all the requisite characteristics of an easement. There is no doubt as to what were intended to be the dominant and servient tenements respectively and the right was appurtenant to the former and calculated to enhance its beneficial use and enjoyment. It is true that during the times when the dominant owner exercised the right, the owner of the servient tenement would be excluded, but this in greater or lesser degree is a common feature of many easements (for example, rights of way) and does not amount to such an ouster of the servient owner's rights as was held by Upjohn J to be incompatible with a legal easement in *Copeland v Greenhalf*.'

Romer LJ

Re Ellenborough Park [1956] Ch 121

1. There must be a dominant and a servient tenement.
2. The easement must accommodate the dominant tenement.
3. The dominant tenement and the servient tenement must be owned or occupied by different people.
4. The easement must be capable of forming the subject-matter of a grant.
    i. There must be a capable grantee and grantor.
    ii. The right must be sufficiently definite.
    iii. The right must be in the nature of an easement.

10.2 Easements compared with other rights

Profits à prendre

A *profit à prendre* allows the grantee to take something from the land of his neighbour rather than simply use his neighbour's land. This could include crops, fruit and fish. The person granted a *profit* is also granted a licence to enter the land to take advantage of the right.

The main difference from an easement is that a *profit* can exist **without ownership of land**. So the right can be given to someone just for his/her own personal benefit.

Profits also differ from easements because they can be enjoyed by several persons at the same time, whereas an easement is enjoyed by a single landowner and those who derive a right from him. A *profit* may last indefinitely or for a fixed term.

Licences

There is a direct contrast between easements and licences:

■ Licences give someone personal permission to enter the land, whereas legal easements give someone a proprietary right in the land.

■ A licence can never bind a third-party purchaser, whereas a properly created legal easement can be binding on third parties.

■ There is also an important fundamental difference because a licensee can have exclusive enjoyment of the land while the licence lasts, whereas the grantee of an easement only has a right to use the land, not exclusive rights over the land.

■ Licences need not be created formally but easements can usually only exist in law if certain formalities, for example creation by deed, are complied with.

The type of right covered by licences is much more extensive than the right covered by an easement.

Restrictive covenants

Restrictive covenants restrict the owner's enjoyment of their own land:

■ There is an overlap between restrictive covenants and easements, in particular negative easements. Some case law has suggested that restrictive covenants are one type of negative easement.

- However, the main difference is that the burden in restrictive covenants can only pass in equity, whereas easements can exist in law or in equity.

- A restrictive covenant can only limit enjoyment of land, whereas an easement can both give positive rights over land and also restrict use of land in the case of a negative easement.

- The subject-matter of an easement is much more restricted than that of a restrictive covenant.

Public rights

Certain public rights are very similar to easements, such as a public right of way, but they differ because they are not reliant on the members of the public owning land or having rights in land. Public rights over a highway can be proprietary since they constitute overriding interests under Scheds 1 and 3 para 5 Land Registration Act 2002. There is no necessity for an express grant. The grant is not subject to any formalities. Under the Wildlife and Countryside Act 1981 the local authority has a duty to keep a definitive survey map of all public rights of way. Once a public right of way is included in such a map it is presumed that such a right of way exists and the presumption can only be rebutted by strong contrary evidence.

Natural rights

Natural rights differ from easements because they arise naturally and are not subject to a grant. The main right is the right of support. Until recently it was only a right of support for the land and never a right for any buildings on the land.

CASE EXAMPLE

Holbeck Hall Hotel v Scarborough Borough Council [2000] 2 All ER 705

In this case the court held that the servient owner may have to take steps to provide positive support for a building if he knows that there is a hazard which would affect his neighbour. The claimants owned a hotel which had been severely affected by a landslip. The local authority owned the land subject to the landslip and the claimants argued that they were responsible because they knew that the land had been subject to two landslips in previous years. Although the court upheld the principle that it could be liable, it did not find the local authority liable in this case because it could not have reasonably foreseen the extent of this landslip. The two previous landslips had been on a much smaller scale.

The court found that there was no difference between a nuisance on the land of the servient owner and the withdrawal of support for buildings of your neighbour.

ACTIVITY

Quick quiz

Consider the following and decide what kind of right arises in each case:

1. David agrees with his neighbour, George, that he can run pipes under his land when George builds a second house in his garden.
2. Fred and George move to a small cottage in a village in the Cotswolds. They discover that they have a right to walk across fields to the neighbouring village.

3. David moves into his new house and his solicitor tells him that he can cut wood on his neighbour's land.
4. George has discovered, after checking at the Land Registry, that his neighbour has a duty to keep the fence between them in good repair.
5. Fred has just been told by his solicitor that if he buys the house he wants in Kent he will be unable to run a business from the property.
6. Geraint is given permission to store some furniture in his friend's garage.

Easements	Profits à prendre	Restrictive covenants	Licences	Public rights	Natural rights
Subject to formalities; can exist in law and equity.	The holder has a proprietary interest in land.	Only exist in equity, never at law, except between the original parties.	Licensees do not gain proprietary rights.	No proprietary rights can be claimed.	Arise automatically and are incidental to ownership.
Must own a parcel of land.	No ownership of land necessary.	Ownership of land necessary.	The licensee does not need to own any land.	No ownership of land necessary.	Dependent on the ownership of land.
Subject-matter of an easement within strict limits.	Wide range of rights, e.g. right to fish or cut down timber.	Covers very broad range of rights.	Covers enjoyment of rights to enter and enjoy another's land.	Fairly restricted subject-matter. Mainly covers rights of way.	Fairly narrow in nature, e.g. right of support and the right to a flow of water.

Table 10.1 Easements and other rights compared

David (question (1)), Fred and George, (question (2)) and Geraint (question (6)) can all claim an easement. They should take effect in law and be binding on successive land-owners but it will depend on the way the rights were created. David (question (3)) can claim a *profit à prendre* as he wishes to take something from his neighbour's land. George (question (4)) may have the benefit of an easement as although it requires the servient owner to spend money if it is a fence it can constitute an exception as seen below. Fred (question 5) will be limited in running a business because his neighbour has a restrictive covenant over his land.

10.3 General principles of easements

1. Must not impose a positive burden on the servient owner such as the expenditure of money. The easement should be permissive rather than imposing a burden on the servient owner

An easement must not impose any expenditure of money or any positive action on the servient owner unless it has been agreed between the parties or constitutes one of the few exceptions, such as fencing (*Crow v Wood* (1971)).

For example, Rodney has a right of way over his neighbour Greg's land and the path goes through the orchard at the back. There is no requirement that the right of way is maintained, so long as it remains open. It is always possible that Greg and Rodney come to a separate agreement that Greg will mow the grass to allow Rodney to walk through with ease.

The position would be different if there was a deliberate attempt to interfere with the easement. If the right of way could not be used at all because the path was fenced off, then there could be a challenge.

CASE EXAMPLE

Duke of Westminster v Guild [1985] QB 688

It was held that a tenant's right to use drains running through his landlord's premises imposed no duty on the landlord to keep the drains in repair.

ACTIVITY

Applying the law

Tariq lives at 14 Meadow Rise and uses a short-cut through his neighbour Jane's garden. The right of way constitutes an easement because it has been properly granted to Tariq. What are Jane's obligations in relation to the easement enjoyed by Tariq? If Tariq finds the route muddy and uneven does Jane have an obligation to improve the quality of the road?

Jane's duty is permissive. She must allow Tariq to use her land as a short-cut but she has no obligation to improve the quality of the road.

There are a few very limited examples of easements that do impose a positive burden on the servient owner, for example fencing: this is the major exception to the rule. Fencing has been described as 'in the nature of a spurious easement' by Archibald J in *Lawrence v Jenkins* (1873) LR 8 QB 274. It has been upheld as an easement even though it may involve payment of money by the servient owner.

CASE EXAMPLE

Crow v Wood [1971] 1 QB 77

The court upheld both the right of the servient owner to use his neighbour's property but also the right to impose the burden of keeping a fence between the properties in repair.

2. *Must not exclude reasonable alternative user of the servient tenement*

a. The general principle is that the easement must never exclude the grantor from use of his land. Where use is in the nature of exclusive user, it can never exist as an easement. The key issues as identified recently in *Moncrieff v Jamieson* [2007] 1 WLR 2620 is that the grantor must not be deprived of possession and control of his land. Inevitably, however, there will be some limitation placed on the grantor's use of his land. It is a matter of striking a balance between this inevitable interference with enjoyment and upholding the grantee's rights.

b. There are specific types of easement involved here, for example storage and parking.

Storage

Consider the following two cases. It is difficult to justify the difference between the two decisions.

CASE EXAMPLE

Wright v Macadam [1949] 2 KB 744

A tenant was allowed to store her coal in a shed on the landlord's land. This was upheld as an easement although, on the facts, the landlord would not have had access to, or use of, the shed at all.

CASE EXAMPLE

Copeland v Greenhalf [1952] 1 Ch 488

The claimant owned an area of land opposite the defendant, who was a wheelwright. The defendant used some land of the claimant to store vehicles belonging to customers. This constituted almost permanent use by the defendant and it was held that it could not constitute an easement.

> 'I think that the right claimed goes wholly outside any normal idea of an easement that is, the right of the owner or the occupier of a dominant tenement over a servient tenement. This claim ... really amounts to a claim to a joint user of the land by the defendant. Practically the defendant is claiming the whole beneficial user of the strip of land on the southeast side of the track.'
>
> Upjohn J

The following extract from an article by Peter Luther considers the difficulty that lawyers have in reconciling the two cases *Wright v Macadam* and *Copeland v Greenhalf*. He suggests that it is *Copeland v Greenhalf* that is correctly decided.

> 'The case of *Copeland v Greenhalf* (1952) has puzzled students of land law for over forty years. It is usually taken as authority for the proposition that a claim to an easement will fail if it amounts, in effect, to a claim to exclusive possession of the servient land ... The issue remains alive largely because the central point of *Copeland v Greenhalf* – is whether it is possible to have an easement to park a car or other vehicle on someone else's land. Not only did *Copeland v Greenhalf* prove a hard case to analyse and justify, but it has also been pointed out by both judges and academics that the judgment of Upjohn J ignored at least one apparently contradictory case decided by a superior court namely *Wright v Macadam* (1949) in which the Court of Appeal had accepted that the right to store coal in a coal shed could be a valid legal easement – it has been suggested as a consequence that the case may have been decided *per incuriam* ...
>
> With the exception of a few problematic phrases ... the judgment of Upjohn J in *Copeland v Greenhalf* falls four square into the line of cases which simply stated that a claimed right must be sufficiently certain if it was to qualify as an easement ... All positive easements must involve doing something jointly with the owner of the land, but what was wrong with the defendant's claim in *Copeland v Greenhalf* was that it amounted, in the judge's view, to joint user for any purpose, or at any rate for too wide a range of purposes. On this analysis *Copeland v Greenhalf* is simply applying a well-established rule about certainty.'
>
> P Luther, 'Easements and Exclusive Possession' (1996) 16 *LS* 51

Luther shows here that it is possible to have an easement of storage where the owner may be denied use of the property temporarily. The real issue is what the landowner can still do on the land. If there is still space for him to store his goods or to use his land for parking, then the easement can exist, even if some rights are denied to the owner.

CASE EXAMPLE

Grigsby v Melville [1973] 1 All ER 385

The claimant had a right to unlimited storage within a cellar beneath his neighbour's property and it was held that this could not be an easement because it was a claim to beneficial ownership.

'A purchaser does not expect to find the vendor continuing to live mole-like beneath his drawing room floor.'

Brightman J

Parking

The right to park can seem like exclusive use of the land. This could mean that the owner of the land is prevented from any use of his own land. Permanent parking is similar to the claim to storage in *Wright v Macadam* (1949) and also *Copeland v Greenhalf* (1952).

The right to park has traditionally depended on extent of use and could not be upheld if it effectively deprived the landowner from using his land.

The following could indicate whether or not parking would give rise to an easement:

- parking limited to certain times of the day;
- parking anywhere in a general area of land (*London & Blenheim Estates Ltd v Ladbroke Retail Park* [1992] 1 WLR 1278).

Compare the following cases:

CASE EXAMPLE

London & Blenheim Estates Ltd v Ladbroke Retail Park [1992] 1 WLR 1278

The claimant owned a shopping centre and he claimed that the right for customers to park cars on a central car park could be an easement. Previously, a claim for parking could not generally be upheld because it would deprive the owner of his right to enjoy the land.

It was held that an easement could exist. It was seen as another form of storage and on the basis of *Wright v Macadam* (1949) it could be upheld as long as the claimant did not deprive the owner of any enjoyment of the land.

'That leaves the main point ... whether the right to park cars can exist at all as an easement. I would not regard it as a valid objection that charges are made, whether for the parking itself or for the general upkeep of the park. The essential question is one of degree. If the right granted in relation to the area over which it is to be exercisable is such that it would leave the servient owner without any reasonable use of the land, whether for parking or anything else, it could not be an easement though it might be some larger or different grant.'

Judge Paul Baker QC

CASE EXAMPLE

Batchelor v Marlow [2003] 1 WLR 764

The claimant sought the exclusive right to park six cars on a verge of land between 8.30 a.m. and 6.30 p.m., Monday to Friday. The area was only large enough to park six cars so the effect was that the owner of the land would not be able to park at all during those hours and could only use the area at weekends and for a limited time during the evening and at night. The High Court held that an easement could exist because the right was limited in time and did not therefore amount to total exclusion of the claimant. However the Court of Appeal rejected the claim as the right was too excessive, making any enjoyment by the owner of the servient land illusory.

'If one asks the simple question: "Would the applicant have any reasonable use of the land for parking?" the answer, I think, must be "No". He has no use at all during the whole of the time that parking space is likely to be needed. But if one asks the question whether the applicant has any reasonable use of the land for any other purpose the answer is even clearer. His right to use his land is curtailed altogether for intermittent periods throughout the week.'

Tuckey LJ

CASE EXAMPLE

Hair v Gillman (2000) 80 P & CR 108

The claimant argued that he had the right to park his single car on a forecourt which was big enough for four cars. The Court of Appeal upheld his right because it would not interfere with the owner's right to park a car on the forecourt at any time he wished. Chadwick LJ: 'The authorities fall between one side or another of an ill-defined line between rights in the nature of an easement and rights in the nature of an exclusive right to use or possess.'

More recently the House of Lords has reconsidered the law on parking in *Moncrieff v Jamieson* [2007] UKHL 42. The rules have been relaxed to some degree so it is no longer dependent on the issues that were seen as crucial in previous cases such as *Batchelor v Marlow*. The fact that the owner of the dominant tenement may be denied enjoyment of the parking space would not automatically prevent an easement from arising. This point was raised in *R Square Properties v Nissan Motors* [2014] (unreported) where it was held that a judge had been right to conclude that a company's exclusive right to use parking spaces on an industrial estate constituted an easement. The case was distinguishable from *Batchelor v Marlow* because the owner of the servient land had not been completely deprived of the reasonable use of the land by virtue of the company's exclusive right to park. However, where the sole use amounted to something more akin to possession then the law would not regard this as an easement. So if there was a lockable bar across the space and the claimant had the only set of keys to the bar this could never be an easement. These issues were discussed in the case of [2007] UKHL 42, which was an appeal from the Scottish Court of Session. The law on easements in Scotland is not exactly the same as that in England and Wales but there are similarities in the way the rules are applied.

CASE EXAMPLE

Moncrieff v Jamieson [2007] 1 WLR 2620

The Moncrieffs owned a property in Shetland called Da Store. The property had one boundary with the sea, two boundaries were owned by Mr Jamieson their neighbour and the other by a third party. Before they purchased Da Store there was no direct access to public roads and when the land had been purchased by the Moncrieff's predecessor's in title, a right of access over Mr Jamieson's land was included but there was no express grant of any other easement. The Moncrieffs had no other right of access so unless they had a right to park on Mr Jamieson's land the nearest parking was on the public road and involved walking through rough, open land in order to reach their house.

The Moncrieffs claimed a right to park as an ancillary right to the right of access.

The House of Lords granted the right to park to the Moncrieffs and accepted that where a claimant had vehicular access over the servient land it could also confer by implication a right of parking on the surrounding land.

The House of Lords also revisited the circumstances when the court would be prepared to grant a right to park even where this seriously interfered with use and enjoyment of the land by the dominant owner. Lord Scott criticised the test laid down in *London & Blenheim Estates* as applied in *Batchelor v Marlow* (Has the servient owner been left with any reasonable use of his land?) and substituted a new test. Has the servient owner retained possession and subject to the reasonable exercise of the right in question, 'control' of the servient land?

JUDGMENT

'I would for my part reject the test that asks whether the servient owner is left with any reasonable use of his land, and substitute for it a test which asks whether the servient owner retains possession and, subject to the reasonable exercise of the right in question, control of the servient land.'

Lord Scott

The effect of Lord Scott's test on future claims will be to allow a claim for an easement even where it involves very extensive use of the servient land. The easement will be rejected only if possession and control of the land are lost. The court will look at whether the claimant has acquired the right to control the land as if he owned the land. This test can pose problems as under it the right to park in an allocated space will be upheld and the right to store property on the servient land can also be upheld.

However, Lord Scott was at pains to explain how the servient owner continued to retain some control over the land. In the case of a parking space the owner could retain possession and control by deciding to build above or under the parking area or to place advertising hoardings on the adjacent walls.

It remains fairly difficult to distinguish between these cases. Michael Haley has commented as follows;

'There is little radical in the recognition that, in appropriate circumstances, a right to park can be implied into a right of access or be classified independently as an easement. Provided that the claimant is not asserting permanent and exclusive rights in relation to the entirety of the servient tenement, the authorities have made it clear that such an easement might exist. If, instead, the claim is inconsist-ent with the servient owner's estate in the land, it is properly to be viewed as a claim to a lease or a claim based upon adverse possession. The court is therefore, expected to balance the factual extent of the third party claim with legal notions of proprietorship. The difficulty lies with exclusionary rights which do not give the dominant owner exclusive possession and are based upon express permis-sion. These rights can only exist *in rem* if classified as easements. If not so catego-rised, they exist merely as revocable licences … The boundary between exclusive use as of right and exclusionary use that is merely incidental to the exercise of a particular right remains as elusive as ever.'

M Haley, 'Easements, Exclusionary Use and Elusive Principles: The Right to Park' [2008] *Conv* 244

Amy Goymour argued that this decision should be confined to cases where the facts are similar to those of *Moncrieff*, i.e. where the options to park are very limited. She suggests that the decision does not sit well with the life in a more urban landscape.

'The difference in approaches might become significant if one moves away from the extreme geography of Shetland. Following *Moncrieff*, when might the conveyance of an inner-city flat, together with vehicular access, impliedly include a valuable adja-cent parking right? In the interests of certainty, there is merit in the law being reluctant to intervene when the right has not been expressly negotiated or implied under other recognised doctrines. Accordingly, it would be desirable to confine *Moncrieff* to situations where it is impossible to park on the dominant land; and where the geographical terrain renders it at least very difficult to park on a nearby public road and then walk to the dominant tenement.'

A Goymour, 'Easements, Servitudes and the Right to Park' [2008] 67(1) *CLJ* 20

Cases following *Moncrieff* suggest that the stricter view taken in *Batchelor v Marlow* can still apply. Indeed as *Moncrieff* was decided on appeal from the Scottish courts the decision is *obiter*. In the two decisions below, the courts nevertheless came to the conclusion that an easement of parking arose even though there was only one parking space.

CASE EXAMPLE

Virdi v Chana [2008] EWHC 2901 (Ch)

In this case, which concerned an easement of parking over a very small space which allowed parking of one vehicle only, the judge applied the test from Batchelor rather Moncrieff and asked the question: would the owner of the tenement still have reasonable use of the land? The judge concluded that the owner of the servient tenement still had reasonable use of his land because the servient owner could still choose the surface material and plant around the parking space. This suggests that reasonable use is calculated broadly and is not limited to the area of land under use by the easement but looks at the total area of servient land. As a result it is possible to have an easement to park in a parking space provided that the servient owner has reasonable use of the rest of the tenement.

CASE EXAMPLE

Kettel v Bloomfold Ltd [2012] EWHC 1422

The applicant leaseholders applied for an injunction restraining the respondent landlord (B) from building on their car parking spaces. The leaseholders who lived in flats, had the benefit of using designated parking spaces under the terms of their leases. They sought an injunction preventing the landlord from building a block of flats on the site covering their parking spaces.

   The application was granted. The court held that the right to use the parking spaces could amount to an easement by the tenants even though at the time of use the landlords would not be able to park on the spaces themselves because they continued to have control over the space.

ACTIVITY

Quick quiz

Could an easement have arisen in the following circumstances?

1. Cleo lives in a remote Welsh cottage. She acquires a right of access over her neighbour Peter's land. She wants to park on his land overnight because it is more convenient to get to work. She has room to park on her own land.
2. Ellie has the right to park her car in Irfian's driveway. There is only room to park one car on the driveway. Her cottage is at the end of a long and muddy driveway owned by Irfian.

The Law Commission has considered the appropriate test for the characteristics of an easement in the recent Law Commission Report Law Com 186 and has suggested a test which is different both from the old test under *London & Blenheim Estates v Ladbroke Parks Ltd* (1992) (whether the landowner is left with any reasonable use of his land) and also *Moncrieff v Jamieson* (2007) (whether the landowner retains possession and control over the land).

   They propose: 'the best approach is to consider the scope and extent of the right that is created, and to ask whether it purports to confer a right with essential characteristics of an easement'. The question should be: 'What can the dominant owner do? Rather than what can the servient owner not do?'

10.4 The grant of easements

Easements can be granted in a number of different ways:

1. express grant or reservation;
2. implied grant or reservation;
3. prescription.

Easements can be created by means of either **grant** or **reservation**.

   A **grant** is made when one landowner, A, creates an easement over his land in favour of his neighbour, B.

If Peter lives next door to Henry, and Henry wants to use Peter's garden as a short-cut to get to the woods at the back of it, Peter must formally grant Henry an easement. This must be created by a deed, as the right of way is an interest in land. If the documents used were not in the form of a deed then only an equitable easement would be created. If a formal grant is not made the law may imply an easement but within very strict rules.

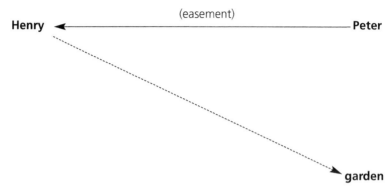

Figure 10.3 Creation of an easement by grant

A **reservation** arises when a landowner transfers part of his land to another but he keeps or reserves himself a right to use part of the land he has sold.

Peter has a huge garden and he decides to build a house in part of the garden, which he then sells to Henry. When the house is sold to Henry, Peter must expressly agree with him that he can continue to use a short-cut which runs from Peter's house through Henry's new garden.

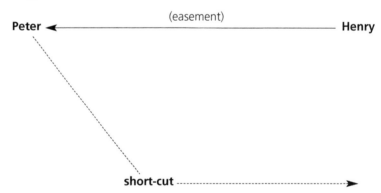

Figure 10.4 Creation of an easement by reservation

The courts have always viewed reservations with suspicion because the vendor is trying to reserve rights over the land he is selling. He is trying to hold rights over the land back from the purchaser for himself. The purchaser does not know the land as well as the seller so the purchaser could be said to be at a disadvantage. The overall principle is that the seller must not derogate from his conveyance. A principle which would prevent a seller from asserting rights which have not been expressly reserved except in very limited circumstances.

The only circumstances when the courts will imply a reservation are:

- in the case of **necessity**; or
- an **intended easement**.

These are both discussed later in the chapter.

10.4.1 Express grant

Two neighbouring landowners can expressly agree about rights to be exercised over the other's land. This may be incorporated into the formal documentation when land is either transferred as freehold or granted as leasehold. Alternatively, it can arise independently of the conveyance of the property. The creation of an express easement must always be recorded formally in a deed and will not take effect until it has been entered on the register. An oral grant of an easement will not take effect in law and would normally amount to no more than a licence.

If land owned by a single landowner is developed and houses are built on the land, each new house must have certain rights such as a right to drainage across the neighbouring land. The developer must consider how this is to be achieved. The right of drainage could be put into the transfer of each property. The grant will take effect in law.

Occasionally, easements are granted expressly under statute. These are made in favour of some of the privatised utilities that supply essential supplies such as gas or electricity. In these cases the easement will not accommodate the dominant tenement since there will not be a dominant tenement. These easements form an exception to the rule that easements only apply where there is a dominant and a servient tenement.

Consider the following example: George is a farmer in Dorset. The Secretary of State for Trade and Industry can apply to install electricity lines over or in his land. Compensation will be payable but George can be forced to accept this use of the land. The Secretary of State will not necessarily own any neighbouring land as a dominant tenement and so the use of George's land (the servient tenement) will carry the burden without the neighbouring land receiving the benefit.

In *Baker v Craggs* [2018] EWCA Civ 1126 it was confirmed that the grant of an easement was not a conveyance of a 'legal estate in land' within the meaning of s2 Law of Property Act 1925 and so was not capable of overreaching a right. The case concerned the sale of land which included the grant of a right of way to the defendant Mr Craggs. During a delay before he registered his title a second sale was made to the claimants purporting also to grant a right of way. A judge at first instance held that the rights of the defendant had been 'overreached' by the second sale. The Court of Appeal allowed the defendant's appeal holding that the defendant's right to an easement had not been overreached by the second sale.

10.4.2 Implied grant

Sometimes the grant of an easement will be implied or simply inferred in favour of a purchaser of land. These easements will take effect as legal easements. It is important to see that the rights that can be implied into the transfer must be capable of existing as an easement under the conditions in *Re Ellenborough Park* (1956).

Easements by implied grant can arise in the following ways:

1. necessity;
2. intended easements;
3. the rule in *Wheeldon v Burrows* (1879) 12 Ch D 31;
4. s62 of the Law of Property Act 1925.

1. Necessity

Easements of necessity usually arise where the land would be landlocked without the right which means no legal right of access. The courts will always imply an easement in these circumstances. The land must be genuinely landlocked.

If Rodney develops his garden and builds two houses at the bottom of his garden which are then bought by Charles and Karina they will be concerned how they are to gain access to and from their properties. If there is no mention of access in the conveyance and the only way that Charles and Karina can access their land is by using Rodney's drive the courts will not allow Charles and Karina to be landlocked but will imply into the transfer a right of access over Rodney's land.

The easement of necessity is strictly controlled. The dominant tenement must have no access at all. It is not enough merely to show that there is an alternative route but that it is simply inconvenient or a much longer way round. However, the route must be safe. There is no question of denying such a right where the alternative route would be dangerous, such as along the edge of a cliff. There is no reason why easements of necessity could not arise in the case of access to property for services but it is generally implied in relation to a right of way.

CASE EXAMPLE

Nickerson v Barraclough [1980] Ch 325

In this case it was held in that an easement of necessity can only arise on the sale of land where the dominant land is genuinely landlocked.

Access to Neighbouring Land Act 1992

A landowner may not be able to carry out essential repairs to his land without first gaining access to his neighbour's land. Without a right to enter the neighbouring land, the repairs could not be carried out. Under the Access to Neighbouring Land Act 1992 an access order can be claimed which allows the landowner to claim the right to go on his neighbour's land to carry out the repairs.

SECTION

'**Access orders**

s 1(1) A person –

(a) who, for the purpose of carrying out works to any land (the "dominant land"), desires to enter upon any adjoining land (the "servient land"), and

(b) who needs ... the consent of some other person to that entry, may make an application to the court for an order ...

(2) On application under this section, the court shall make an access order if, and only if, it is satisfied –

(a) that the works are reasonably necessary for the preservation of the whole or any part of the dominant land; and

(b) that they cannot be carried out, or would be substantially more difficult to carry out, without entry upon the servient land ...

(3) The court shall not make an access order in any case where it is satisfied that, were it to make such an order –

(a) the respondent or any other person would suffer interference with, or disturbance of, his use or enjoyment of the servient land, or

(b) the respondent, or any other person (whether of full age or capacity or not) in occupation of the whole or any part of the servient land, would suffer hardship.'

The Act defines basic preservation works in very precise terms. It includes repair or renewal of a building, clearance of drains, sewers or pipes, and cutting back or felling trees or shrubs (s 1(4)).

Once an order has been granted the courts can impose terms such as the date, hours and timing of any works and controlling who carries them out (s 2).

The important point to consider here is that the rights of the servient landowner are being severely infringed by forcing them to allow their neighbours or their neighbour's workmen to access the land. The strict controls that can be imposed by the court go some way towards alleviating this. The court can further require that compensation be paid to the servient owner.

ACTIVITY

Applying the law

Fred and Dan live next door to each other, with Fred's wall acting as the boundary between the two properties. The two neighbours have argued for years. Fred has no access to part of his roof except by going on to Dan's drive which runs down the side of it. There are no windows along that part of the wall and Fred would really like to put some in to allow extra light into the bedrooms adjoining the wall. One winter, violent storms cause several tiles to fall off Fred's roof. In order to mend the roof and to carry out the work to add the extra windows Fred must have access to Dan's land.

Advise Fred. Would the 1992 Act assist either of his claims?

In this situation the courts will grant rights of access for essential repairs to the roof but not for improvements such as putting windows into the wall between the properties. The court may impose conditions before granting the right to access Dan's land such as only working on certain days and between certain hours such as 9.00 a.m. and 5.00 p.m.

KEY FACTS

Access to Neighbouring Land Act 1992
1. An application may be made where someone needs to go on the land of a neighbour but he will not give his consent for him to do so.
2. The court will only make the order if the maintenance works must be carried out.
3. The order will only be made if there is no other way of accessing the land to do the work.
4. An access order is not an easement over the land; it is only the right to go on the land under the terms of the order.
5. An order will be refused where the court thinks that it will be unreasonable because the order will interfere with the landowner's enjoyment of his land.
6. It covers a wide variety of works including repair of a building, clearing drains and sewers, cutting back or removing a hedge or tree.
7. The order may include conditions such as the timing of the access and who will be responsible for the work.
8. The order is capable of registration and it can be binding on a successor in title for the length of the order if it has been correctly registered.

The rule in *Harris v Flower* (1904) 74 LJ Ch 127 prevents exploitation of an easement. If a landowner has built a house in his garden and an easement is implied to allow access to it, then it does not give him an automatic right to claim that right of way for a further house. The right of way is for that property alone. However all visitors to the new house will be able to use the right of way. The recent case of *Gore v Naheed* [2017] EWCA Civ 369 which revisited this rule decided that a right of way can only be used for the benefit of the dominant land, not for other plots. However, it was accepted by the court that a right of way can sometimes extend to the additional plot if that plot is used for purposes which are ancillary to the dominant tenement. It cannot be used for purposes quite separate from the dominant tenement.

CASE EXAMPLE

Das v Linden Mews Ltd [2002] EWCA Civ 590

Two owners of mews houses acquired land near to their houses for parking. They had a right of way over a private road for access to their houses but they also claimed a right of way to gain access to the area for parking. The Court of Appeal held that the claim was for an easement for a separate piece of land rather than an easement to accommodate their dominant tenement. The key issue was whether the use of the area to park was ancillary to the enjoyment of the mews houses or whether there was intrinsic enjoyment in the area of land itself. It was held that the benefit of access to the garden ground was not for better access to the houses but for the use of the garden ground itself as a car park and so could not exist as an easement.

Limitations on easements of necessity

An easement of necessity will only be implied if there would be no enjoyment of the land at all without such an easement.

CASE EXAMPLE

Union Lighterage Co v London Graving Dock Co [1902] 2 Ch 557

In this case tie-rods on the claimant's land had held in place the wooden walls of the appellant's dock for over 20 years. The right had not been expressly granted so the court had to consider whether or not the right had arisen under necessity.

'In my opinion an easement of necessity, such as is referred to, means an easement without which the property retained cannot be used at all, and not one merely necessary to the reasonable enjoyment of that property. In *Wheeldon v Burrows* the lights which were the subject of decision were certainly necessary to the enjoyment of the property retained, which was a workshop, yet there was held to be no reservation of it. So here it may be that the tie-rods which pass through the plaintiff's property are reasonably necessary to the enjoyment of the defendant's dock in its present condition; but the dock is capable of use without them, and I think that there cannot be implied any reservation in respect of them.'

Stirling J

'It has sometimes been suggested that implied easements of necessity rest ultimately on some freestanding rule of public policy which favours the efficient use of land resources. In the Court of Appeal (in *Nickerson v Barraclough*) Brightman LJ held that a way of necessity is not founded upon public policy at all but upon an implication from the circumstances. The Court of Appeal held that a way of necessity can exist only in association with a transfer of land and rests on the implication, drawn from the circumstances of the case, that unless some way is implied a parcel of land will be inaccessible.'

K Gray and S F Gray, Elements of Land Law (5th edn, Oxford University Press, 2009), p. 651

2. Intended easements

Easements may be implied in favour of a transferee in order to give effect to a common intention of the parties. The law is generally more generous in cases of intended easements than in cases of necessity.

There are two circumstances when an easement of common intention will be implied:

- if it is necessary for the enjoyment of a right that has been expressly granted;
- if it can be implied from the circumstances in which the grant was made.

The easements have been described as

> 'such easements as may be necessary to give effect to the common intention of the parties to a grant of real property, with reference to the manner or purposes in and for which the land granted … is to be used. But it is essential for this purpose that the parties should intend that the subject matter of the grant … should be used in some definite and particular manner. It is not enough that the subject of the grant … should be intended to be used in a manner which may or may not involve this definite and particular use.'
>
> (Lord Parker in *Pwllbach Colliery Company Ltd v Woodman* [1915] AC 634)

The key feature as seen in the case below is that the owner of the servient tenement was aware of the specific use to be made of the land at the time of the agreement. This must be more than general use such as access for the owner. The key feature in the case below is that the landlord was aware that Mr Wong intended to use the land as a restaurant.

CASE EXAMPLE

Wong v Beaumont Property Trust Ltd [1965] 1 QB 173

The claimant had taken over a lease from a tenant with the express purpose of using the premises as a Chinese restaurant. He covenanted to comply with the public health regulations and also not to create a nuisance and to control and eliminate all smells. This could only be fulfilled by installing a new ventilation system leading through the upstairs premises retained by the defendant landlord. It became necessary to pass a ventilation shaft through the landlord's property but he refused access to the tenant.

The Court of Appeal granted the tenant the right on the grounds of necessity although much of the reasoning was based on what the parties had intended at the start of the lease. It is likely as suggested by Martin Dixon in *Modern Land Law* 11th edition, p. 306 that such a decision today would have been made on the grounds of common intention because the land could still be used without the ventilation system though not for the purpose for which it was leased. When the tenant took the lease it was clear that it was for use as a restaurant and it was the common intention of the parties that the tenant should have all rights necessary to carry this out.

Stafford v Lee (1992) 65 P & CR 172

An area of woodland had been granted by deed of gift. The owners wanted to build a house on the land. They claimed that the builders had the right to use the access to deliver building materials. The owners of the access road claimed that the right of way was limited to the original use of the land, namely as a woodland. As the original grant envisaged that a house was intended on the land, their claim to an easement based on common intention was upheld and the builders were able to use the right of way to deliver materials.

More recently in *Donovan v Rana* [2014] EWCA Civ 99 the court reasserted the right of a claimant to rely on the principle of intended easement. Here land was sold for development and the parties were both aware of the need for there to be access across the servient land for pipes and the provision of other utilities. A claim for damages by the servient owner after a small plot of his land was dug up to facilitate the work was dismissed. The court held that the easement proposed was necessary to achieve the parties' expressly intended purpose. There was a similar decision in *Linvale Investments Ltd v Walker* [2016] 2 P & CR 12 where a court granted a declaration that a property had the benefit of a right of way over a pathway owned by another party, which led from the property's fire exits in a business park. The easement was necessary for the land to be used in the way contemplated by the parties, whose common intention was that the land be fully occupied to maximise profit.

3. *The rule in* Wheeldon v Burrows *(1879) 12 Ch D 31*

This category of implied easements is much more significant than easements of necessity or intended easements which are both comparatively rare in practice. The rule in *Wheeldon v Burrows* will only apply to **grants** of easements and cannot apply to **reservations**.

The rule will apply where land is sub-divided into two or more plots and sold to a purchaser. The purchaser X can claim the benefit of any rights in the nature of easements enjoyed by the seller Y before the sale. These rights are referred to as **quasi-easements** which are rights over one's own land that are not easements but could be if the land was divided into two separate plots and were owned by two different persons. X will now own the dominant land; and Y will retain the parcel of land taking the burden of the easement, referred to as the servient land. Y was the original owner of the whole plot. Once these quasi-easements take effect they are then converted under the rule in *Wheeldon v Burrows* into easements and can be enforced by the X . Where the seller Y divides the plot into two parcels and sells both to X and Z both purchasers can claim the rights over the land of the other which could have been claimed if the seller had retained one parcel of land.

Consider the following example. Rodney decides to develop his garden and builds a bungalow, 'The Retreat', for himself in the garden. He transfers his old house, 'Pear Tree House', to Simon. He usually used a route through his old garden to access the main road by way of a short-cut. The law will imply into the transfer of 'Pear Tree House' to Simon any right that Rodney exercised in his own favour, including the use of the short-cut.

When does the rule apply?
Lord Justice Thesiger explained that the rule will apply on the grant of part of a parcel of land by the landowner and as a result the new owner will be able to enjoy all the rights and privileges over the land that the previous owner had once enjoyed.

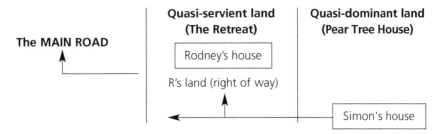

The MAIN ROAD

**Quasi-servient land
(The Retreat)**

Rodney's house

R's land (right of way)

**Quasi-dominant land
(Pear Tree House)**

Simon's house

Figure 10.5 Quasi-easement

JUDGMENT

'[O]n the grant by the owner of a tenement of part of that tenement as it is then used and enjoyed there will pass to the grantee all those continuous and apparent easements (by which, I mean quasi-easements), or in other words, all those easements which are necessary to the reasonable enjoyment of the property granted, and which have been and are at the time of the grant used by the owners of the entirety for the benefit of the part granted.'

Thesiger LJ in *Wheeldon v Burrows* (1879) 12 Ch D 31

The rule can apply whether the land is held freehold or leasehold and it will apply to rights which can take effect in law as well as rights which can take effect in equity only. So it will apply both where there has not been a formal grant of a lease to take effect in excess of three years and also where the grant is one of a contract to grant a lease which can take effect in equity.

In order to claim an implied easement under *Wheeldon v Burrows* (1879), it is necessary for the quasi-easement to be:

1. continuous and apparent;
2. necessary for the reasonable enjoyment of the property granted; and
3. in use by the owner at the time of the grant for the benefit of the part granted.

'Continuous and apparent' suggests that the quasi-easement has been enjoyed over a substantial period of time and which is discoverable or detectable on 'a careful inspection by a person ordinarily conversant with the subject'. The purchaser would be able to detect a right of way by a worn path through the servient land.

'Necessary' is not as strictly applied as in easements of necessity. It is possible to acquire a right of way under *Wheeldon v Burrows* (1879) where there is another form of access. However, the courts have sometimes taken a fairly strict approach to such claims.

In cases where the alternative route is considered to be dangerous or where it involves an excessive detour (*Millman v Ellis* (1995) 71 P & CR 158) the court will sanction an easement under the rule in *Wheeldon v Burrows*.

CASE EXAMPLE

Wheeler v J J Saunders [1996] Ch 19

The claimants purchased land which had two routes of access over the defendant's land. They claimed rights over both routes, relying on the rule in *Wheeldon v Burrows* (1879). The Court of Appeal refused their claim.

'Even to a novice in the law of easements, it seems clear that the class of easements implied in favour of a grantee is wider than easements of necessity. The question is how much

> wider? ... For my part I do not consider that the South entrance was necessary for the reasonable enjoyment of Kingdom Farm House. The East entrance would do just as well ... I would therefore hold that Dr and Mrs Wheeler acquired no right of way through the south entrance.'
>
> Staughton LJ

'In use at the time of grant' prevents old rights from being resurrected on the transfer of the land but it is broadly applied, so rights that have not been used in the previous six months will still be capable of passing under the rule.

Where the conditions are satisfied, the rule in *Wheeldon v Burrows* applies in a wide variety of situations, e.g.:

1. both freehold and leasehold transfer even including a sub-lease;
2. transfer on sale or a voluntary transfer or a devise;
3. a legal transfer (e.g. a sale) or a transfer taking effect in equity (e.g. a contract to sell the legal estate or a contract to create a lease);
4. the right can be expressly excluded but such exclusion must be clearly expressed.

Note the right can also apply where the seller divides his land and sells both parts.

The rule does not apply if it is inconsistent with the words of the express grant or contrary to the language of the conveyance.

4. Easements acquired under s 62 of the Law of Property Act 1925

SECTION

> 's 62(1) ... A Conveyance of land shall be deemed to include ... all buildings, erections, fixtures, commons, hedges, ditches, fences, ways, waters, watercourses, liberties, privileges, easements, rights, and advantages whatsoever, appertaining or reputed to appertain to the land, or any part thereof, or, at the time of conveyance, demised, occupied, or enjoyed with, or reputed or known as part and parcel of or appurtenant to the land or any part thereof. ...
>
> (2) ... A Conveyance of land, having houses or other buildings thereon, shall be deemed to include ... houses, or other buildings, all outhouses, erections, fixtures, cellars, areas, courts, courtyards, cisterns, sewers, gutters, drains, ways, passages, lights, water-courses, liberties, privileges, easements, rights and advantages whatsoever, appertaining or reputed to appertain to the land, houses or other buildings conveyed, or any part thereof, or, at the time of conveyance, demised, occupied, or enjoyed with, or reputed or known as part or parcel of or appurtenant to, the land, houses, or other buildings conveyed, or any of them, or any part thereof.'

Section 62 contains general words which can imply rights into the conveyance where they have not been specifically mentioned. This has a very dramatic effect on easements since rights which took effect as lesser rights, such as licences, could later become easements under this section. They would be implied into the conveyance transferring the estate in land and so the law can still hold that easements under s 62 are created by deed.

Reconsider the case of *Wright v Macadam* (1949), where the tenant gained the right to store coal in the shed of her landlord after her lease was renewed. The tenant had been granted a licence before the renewal of the lease. The new lease was a conveyance of a legal estate in land and so the previous licence to store coal became an easement implied into the conveyance under s 62.

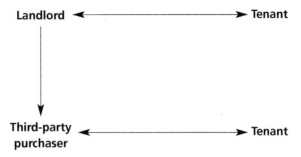

Figure 10.6 Licence taking effect as a legal easement

ACTIVITY

Applying the law

Alice rents a ground-floor flat from her landlord, Gervais. He lives on the top two floors but also has a garage and shed and a garden. Alice has a scooter and Gervais allows her to keep it in the shed in his garden.

1. Consider whether Alice has an easement over Gervais' property.
2. What will be the position if Alice's lease comes to an end and Gervais executes a new lease in her favour? Will she have any right to store her scooter on his land?
3. Will any rights that have passed to Alice remain enforceable if Gervais sells the land to his friend Gino?

The key issues under s 62 reflect the general law of easements. The right must be capable of existing as an easement as discussed below. It is also dependent on proof of a conveyance upon which s 62 can operate. The key question is whether or not there is a written document. A short lease which does not require a deed but has been created by a written document will convey rights whereas an oral lease would not qualify.

Consider the cases below where tenants could claim that rights that existed as licences became easements on the purchase of the freehold or the renewal of the lease.

CASE EXAMPLE

International Tea Stores Company v Hobbs [1903] 2 Ch 165

A landlord allowed his tenant to use a short-cut across his land. This existed as a licence. The landlord then sold the leased premises to the tenant. Later, it was held that the tenant had the right to use the short-cut as that had now taken effect as a legal easement which was enforceable against not just the landlord but any third-party purchaser.

CASE EXAMPLE

Goldberg v Edwards [1950] Ch 247

The claimants were tenants who had started using a means of access through the landlord's property before the lease was granted. This took the form of a licence which then became a legal easement on the conveyance of the formal lease.

Note that rights cannot be acquired under s 62 where the use before conveyance has been intermittent or infrequent.

Consider the facts of this case:

CASE EXAMPLE

Green v Ashco Horticulturist Ltd [1966] 1 WLR 889

A tenant claimed a right of way over the landlord's property. The claim was based on infrequent use and was found to be too intermittent to establish a right. The landlord had also laid down strict limits on the use of the right. This shows that the courts will not uphold a right which is a temporary or intermittent use and could not be the subject of a grant because of its uncertain nature.

Section 62 can have far-reaching and often unintended consequences and it can only be prevented from taking effect by inserting a contrary intention into the conveyance. The key feature of s 62 is that the use conferred under s 62 must be capable of grant. It must be the kind of right that could be implied into a conveyance. The right must benefit the land and not the claimant personally so business use use could not become an easement simply by use of this section.

The Law Commission has recently criticised the acquisition of rights in this way. They referred to this method of acquiring rights as 'a trap for the unwary' and also criticised the fact that the acquisition of such rights in this way could transform these rights into overriding rights and would not have to rely on registration for their legality. The Law Commission proposed that s 62 should no longer automatically transform rights such as licences into easements on conveyance.

It contrasts with the rule in *Wheeldon v Burrows* (1879) in a number of ways and takes effect often in different circumstances. One important difference is the fact that s 62 will only take effect where there has been prior diversity of occupation, whereas the rule in *Wheeldon v Burrows* takes effect where there has been unity of ownership and the owner is now intending to split the land into two, retaining part for himself. The rule in *Wheeldon v Burrows* does not require the conveyance of a legal estate which is essential for the application of s 62. There are several other key differences between the two rules.

s 62	Must be prior diversity of occupation.	Must be a conveyance of the property.	No specific requirements but must come within the definition of an easement.	Applies to easements and profits.
Rule in Wheeldon v Burrows	Applies to quasi-easements.	No conveyance is necessary, e.g. passes with a contract to grant a lease.	Requirements: Right must be continuous and apparent right must be reasonably necessary to the enjoyment of the property. Right must be 'in use' at time of sale.	Cannot apply to profits.

Table 10.2 Comparison between s 62 and the rule in *Wheeldon v Burrows* (1879)

10.4.3 Prescription

If a right is exercised over the land of another for a sufficiently long period of time then it is possible to claim that the use becomes a legal easement, even without an express grant from the landowner. The claim is subject to a number of conditions. This is a complex and controversial area of law and the Law Commission has recently recommended wholesale reform of the rules.

KEY FACTS

Easements claimed under prescription
1. The claim is based on a notional grant of the right.
2. It is based on continuous use and although it can still succeed if there is infrequent use, it will fail unless there is use at least once a year.
3. The claim cannot succeed if the use would be lawful under another rule, for example there could be no easement to use the highway in front of your house if this was already subject to a public right of way although a different use such as vehicular access might succeed.
4. An illegal right cannot be claimed as an easement. The courts have shown that they distinguish between a use that could be or could become lawful and a use that could never be lawful.
5. The right must be *nec vi, nec clam, nec precario*. The assertion of a right must not be claimed as a result of physical force; or exercised secretly (it must not be concealed) and it must not be based on permission given by the servient owner. Mere acquiescence by a landowner cannot prevent a user as of right arising.
6. The claim can only be maintained by one fee simple owner against another fee simple owner. A tenant cannot claim an easement against his landlord by prescription.
7. The right must satisfy the characteristics of an easement as laid down in *Re Ellenborough Park* (1956).

Easements can be acquired by prescription under:

a. common law;

b. the doctrine of lost modern grant;

c. the Prescription Act 1832.

a. Common law

The claimant has to show that the easement has been enjoyed not just for a long period of time but since time immemorial. It is extremely difficult to satisfy this test. The law holds that time immemorial starts in 1189! As proof of use since 1189 will be virtually impossible, the courts will accept use within living memory.

If the defendant can show that the claimant could not have enjoyed the right at any time since 1189 then the claim would be defeated, for example if there is proof that at any time the land was under common ownership then it would have been impossible to grant an easement and a claim under common law would be defeated.

CASE EXAMPLE

Duke of Norfolk v Arbuthnot (1880) 5 CPD 390

A claim under common law for the right to light for a church failed because there was proof that the church was built in 1380 and so after 1189.

ACTIVITY

Applying the law

Rodney lives next door to Graham and is claiming an easement by prescription under common law over a garden path against him. He can show that he has used a path over Graham's garden for the past 20 years, but Graham has evidence that Rodney's house was built in the garden of Graham's house and then sold to a Mr Makepiece in 1870.

Will his claim succeed under the rules of acquiring prescriptive rights under common law?

The problem for Rodney is that he is relying on a rule that can only support his claim if there is no evidence to suggest that the right **could not** have existed in 1189. If the house was built in the nineteenth century as suggested here then Rodney cannot argue that the right **may** have existed in 1189. His claim will fail under this principle but it may succeed under one of the other principles discussed below.

b. *The doctrine of lost modern grant*

As it is so difficult to prove that a right has been exercised since 1189, the law has allowed a much easier test to be applied. Claims are based on a legal fiction which suggests that a grant had been made at one time but the grant had been lost. A successful case today would generally show that there had been continuous use for 20 years. It can be any 20-year period. It will not be defeated by evidence that there has been no such grant but it will be defeated if there is evidence that no one could have made the grant, for example there was no one legally competent to make the grant, or again that the land had once been in common ownership.

CASE EXAMPLE

Tehidy Minerals Ltd v Norman [1971] 2 QB 528

It was held that even where there was evidence that no grant had ever been made, this would not prevent a right from arising under the doctrine.

c. *The Prescription Act 1832*

Claims under common law were so difficult to prove that the Prescription Act was introduced in 1832 to try to meet the difficulties. However, the Act passed was not very successful. This Act is popularly known as one of the 'worst drafted Acts' on the statute book. The 1832 Act tried to solve the problems that arise under common law prescription and the doctrine of lost modern grant.

Under the Act, the claimant must satisfy one of two periods of time in order to succeed:

1. The **short period**: 20 years' continuous and uninterrupted use immediately before the claim, 'next before some suit or action'. This can be defeated by the defendant if he can prove that the right was based on consent of the owner.

2. The **long period**: 40 years' continuous and uninterrupted use immediately before the claim, 'next before some suit or action'. This claim cannot be defeated even if there is proof that the right was granted with the consent of the landowner, unless the consent was given in writing.

The Act provides that no act of obstruction is deemed to be an interruption until it has been submitted to for a period of one year. In *Davies v Du Paver* [1953] 1 QB 184 the servient owner began to block the claimed easement with a fence. The plaintiff objected and his solicitor wrote a series of letters on his behalf over the next two months. The fence was completed early in August but proceedings were not commenced until late September the following year. It was held that there had not been submission or acquiescence to the interruption for the required year. The interruption must be hostile.

d. Some key issues in acquiring rights by prescription

The use of the land under prescription must be 'as of right'. This means that the use of the land by the claimant cannot be explained by any other reason such as permission given by the owner of the dominant tenement.

i. Without force [nec vi]

Force can cover a variety of situations such as physical force where the claimant makes threats to the landowner when using the land or more subtle force such as blatantly ignoring protestations by the landowner. A complex problem arises where the landowner has placed signs objecting to the use by the claimant which are then ignored. This could be interpreted as force. In *Winterburn v Bennett* [2016] EWCA Civ 482 the owners of a car park had erected signs which said 'private car park for use of club patrons only'. The premises had been used until 2010 as a private club. For a period of over 20 years customers and suppliers of a nearby fish and chip shop had used the car park ignoring the signs. The fish and chip shop owner sought to claim prescriptive rights. The Court of Appeal held that the mere presence of the signs clearly indicated the landowner's continuing objection to unauthorised parking. It was not necessary for them to take further steps such as physical obstruction or legal action. The use of the car park had not been 'as of right'.

ii. Without secrecy [nec clam]

The use must not be carried out secretly. An easement cannot be acquired by prescription where the claimant has only made use of the land secretly. So the claimant who only uses a short-cut at night when it is dark could not claim to have had use. The basis of the claim is that the servient owner is well aware of the use made by the dominant owner but does not take action to prevent the use.

> 'only when enjoyment has been open – that is to say, of such character that an ordinary owner of the land, diligent in the protection of his interests, would have, or must have taken to have, a reasonable opportunity of becoming aware of that enjoyment.'
>
> LJ Romer, *'Union Lighterage Co v London Graving Dock Co'* [1902] 2 Ch 557

iii. Without permission [nec precario]

The use must not be with the permission of the landowner. One of the key features of a prescriptive easement is that it cannot arise where permission to use the land has been given. The permission can be unilateral without an express acceptance. Recently the question has been raised as to what is the position when use has been permissive but the permission lapses. In *London Tara Hotel Ltd v Kensington Close Hotel Ltd* [2011] EWCA Civ 1356 the claimants had been given the right to use a service road. Permission was given in a written document and consideration of £1 was agreed. The owners of the servient land changed hands several times and no payment was ever made. The claimants argued that having used the road for over 20 years without permission then a prescriptive easement arose. The Court of Appeal upheld their claim. This contrasts with *Odey v Barber* [2008] 2 WLR 618 where permissive use had never been sought by the claimants but they were aware that they used a right of way with the permission of the servient owners, so an easement was refused on the basis that permission had been granted.

iv. Use must have been lawful

Long use will never give rise to an easement if it has arisen through unlawful use. The issue was raised in *Bakewell Management v Brandwood* [2004] 2 AC 519. The owner of a common argued that the users of a right of way across the common could not arise prescriptively because they were committing a criminal offence each time they crossed the common. The House of Lords drew a distinction between vehicular access which can be lawful in most circumstances and behaviour which could never be lawful under any circumstances. In this case, as it was only unlawful in the particular circumstances of the case (under statute it was a criminal offence to drive without lawful authority over common land which has been dedicated to public recreational use but in general circumstances driving over land in this way would have been lawful), the prescriptive right could be claimed.

v. The use must have been against the freehold owner of the land

Easements can never be acquired prescriptively against tenants even where they have a long lease. This rule has been criticised but there is no recommendation for change in the Law Commission Report. The rule is based on the reasoning behind prescriptive easements. They arise because the law is upholding a grant by the fee simple owner to the claimant of rights. The rule suggests that such rights cannot be granted by a tenant

e. Rights to light

The law treats the right to light slightly differently. Under s 3 Prescription Act 1832, 20 years of uninterrupted enjoyment will make the right absolute and indefeasible unless it was by written consent or agreement. The courts will ignore provisions within a written agreement concerning the development unless they expressly concern the grant of rights of light. So in *Salvage Wharf Ltd v G & S Brough Ltd* [2010] Ch 11 a building agreement which referred to previous rights to light did not prevent rights to light arising outside those expressly included in the agreement. In *CGIS City Plaza Shares 1 Ltd v Britel Fund Trustees Ltd* [2012] EWHC 1594 the court refused a claim for a right to light where it had been stated in the conveyance that the servient owner could build on the land which impliedly consented to interference with the right to light of the dominant owner.

Reform of easements of light

The Law Commission has made some recommendations in its final report, 'Rights to Light' (Law Com No 356) for reform of this area of law. The key recommendations are:

- a statutory notice procedure which would allow landowners to require their neighbours to tell them within a specified time if they intend to seek an injunction to protect their right to light, or to lose the potential for that remedy to be granted;
- a statutory test to clarify when courts may order damages to be paid rather than halting development or ordering demolition;
- an updated version of the procedure that allows landowners to prevent their neighbours from acquiring rights to light by prescription;
- amendment of the law governing where an unused right to light is treated as abandoned; and
- a power for the Lands Chamber of the Upper Tribunal to discharge or modify obsolete or unused rights to light.

It does not recommend that prescription should be abolished as a means of acquiring rights to light although it had made a provisional recommendation at an earlier stage.

These are all recommendations and it is for the government to implement the proposals.

KEY FACTS

The Prescription Act 1832
1. How long has the right been enjoyed?
2. Has the enjoyment of the right been interrupted and was it immediately before the claim?
3. Has the landowner given consent to the use of the right?
4. In what form was that permission given?

The Law Commission made a number of proposals in relation to prescriptive easements and *profits à prendre* in its report in 2011. The Law Commission does not propose the total abolition of prescriptive acquisition of easements. It recognises that there are some advantages in its retention but it does propose that there should be a new clearer statutory method of acquisition of easements by prescription. Therefore it proposed that the three existing ways of acquiring prescriptive rights should be abolished and replaced by a single statutory method.

ACTIVITY

Applying the law

Finn owns Blackaterry Cottage, situated in Devon one mile from the sea. His neighbours Orla and Daniel love to swim in the sea and swim all the year round. Orla uses a short cut from her house through the garden of Blackaterry Cottage. She has done this for many years. Finn has recently discussed this with a close friend who is a solicitor who tells him that as Orla has used the short cut for 19 years and one month she has nearly established rights in law over his land. In May he decides to lock the gate leading from Orla's property on to his land. She is away on holiday at the time but when she returns she writes a letter to Finn complaining about his action to which he does not respond. Finn then contacts his solicitors who write to Orla asserting his rights. Orla starts swimming in the local swimming pool but she so dislikes the chlorinated water that she wants to resume swimming in the sea. She finds that Finn often leaves the gate open and she has resumed using the short cut. Finn brings court proceedings in June the following year.

Can Orla claim that an easement has arisen by prescription in her favour? The key issues to consider here are first, the length of time of use, in particular, how long there has been a gap between the last use and the resumed use. Second, whether the use satisfies the three requirements of no force, no secrecy and no permissive use. Third, when the solicitor writes to Orla, is that sufficient for Finn to argue that he has asserted his rights for Orla to no longer use the path as of right?

Common law	Doctrine of lost modern grant	Prescription Act 1832
Acquired on proof of continuous use 'since time immemorial' (1189).	Continuous use during living memory or for at least 20 years.	Use for either 20 or 40 years immediately before the action is brought.
Can be rebutted if there is proof that the right could not have been acquired in 1189.	Rebuttal limited to showing that there was no person legally capable to make the grant.	Rebuttal can be made on proof that written permission was given or in some circumstances oral permission.
Takes effect as a legal easement.	Takes effect as a legal easement.	Takes effect as a legal easement.

Table 10.3 Different ways of acquiring rights under prescription

10.5 Legal and equitable easements

An easement or a *profit* can be either **legal** or **equitable**.

A legal easement arises when the required formalities have been complied with and it is created for a length of time equivalent to one of the two legal estates that can exist in land:

- a fee simple absolute in possession; or
- a term of years absolute in possession.

A legal easement must be created by **deed** under s 52 of the Law of Property Act 1925 because it creates an interest in land.

The deed must comply with s 1 of the Law of Property (Miscellaneous Provisions) Act 1989. If the deed does not comply with the necessary formalities then it will not take effect in law. An easement acquired prescriptively will not have a formal deed but as it is based on a fictitious deed it is still based on a deed. A contract to create a legal easement will take effect but only in equity.

An easement that is implied, for example under s 62 of the 1925 Act, is impliedly created by deed as the easement will be implied into the conveyance. Easements that arise through necessity, common intention and under the rule in *Wheeldon v Burrows* (1879) are also implied into the conveyance and will therefore take effect in law.

An equitable easement arises where either it fails to satisfy the formalities required for a legal easement or the period of time for the legal easement has not been satisfied, i.e. it is not for a fee simple absolute or for a leasehold. Such easements will be rare in practice.

Registered land

Where an easement exists in equity it must be entered on the Charges Register of the servient land where the land has registered title in order to be binding on any subsequent purchaser. The Land Registration Act 2002 changed the status of equitable easements which had previously been binding on a purchaser irrespective of whether they had been entered on the Register or not. This is illustrated by the case of *Chaudhary v Yavuz* [2011] EWCA 1314. The claimant Mr Chaudhary had built a metal staircase on land belonging to Mr Vijay in order to access his upper storey flat. Mr Vijay sold his land to Mr Yavuz who then denied Mr Chaudhary access.

The Court of Appeal held that Yavuz was not bound by the easement. It had not been registered by notice against the title to the servient land. Mr Chaudhary also argued that he had an overriding interest based on actual occupation under schedule 3 para 3 of the Land Registration Act 2002. This claim also failed. The Court of Appeal held that there was a difference between 'actual use' and 'actual occupation'. When the claimant was using the staircase he was making use of the easement as opposed to occupying the land belonging to the defendant.

Consider the comments below on this case:

> 'The crucial question arises in a case where: (i) the claimant has failed to register a pre-existing legal or equitable interest in land; and (ii) in contrast to the position in *Chaudhary* itself, the defendant purchaser *has* undertaken a new obligation to B. It is difficult to see why, if the purchaser has made such a promise, the result should change as a result of the claimant's failure to protect him or herself by the alternative means of registration.'
>
> B McFarlane, 'Eastenders, Neighbours and Upstairs Downstairs: *Chaudhary v Yavuz*' [2013] *Conv* 74

Where an easement arises impliedly, e.g. those under necessity or under the rule in *Wheeldon v Burrows* the law will protect these easements as 'overriding interests' under schedule 3 Land Registration Act 2002. This is not automatic as the easement must first satisfy the requirements of the schedule. It means that the easement will only be overriding if, for instance, it would have been obvious on a reasonably careful inspection of the land or it had been used within one year immediately prior to the transfer in question.

Unregistered land

Where title to land is unregistered the transfer of the title will trigger registration and so any easement will normally be entered onto the charges register at first registration. Where the title is unregistered and there is no trigger for registration, legal easements will be binding on the servient tenement but equitable easements will be subject to registration and will only be binding if they are entered on to the Land Charges Register.

ACTIVITY

Quick quiz

Consider the following and decide whether they give rise to a legal or equitable easement:

1. Josh wants to use Jaivin's garden as a short-cut to the shops. Jaivin is reluctant to commit himself to an indefinite easement so he grants an easement for Josh's life. Josh pays him £450 for the privilege.
2. Alvin lives next door to Ravi, who is his landlord. Alvin has no parking space in front of his house but he is told by Ravi that he can use his drive to park his car while his lease lasts.
3. Alvin lives next door to Ravi, who is his landlord. Alvin has no parking space in front of his house but Ravi agrees in writing that he will grant him the right to park his car in his drive while the lease lasts.

10.6 Extinguishment of easements

There are a limited number of ways that an easement will come to an end:

JUDGMENT

'A man cannot have an easement over his own land.'

Fry LJ in *Roe v Siddons* (1889) LR 22 QBD 224

Unity of ownership

If the fee simple of the dominant and servient land is owned by one person, any easements over the servient land will cease. If the fee simple of one piece of land is owned by one person who also owns a lease in the other plot of land, any easements will be suspended rather than extinguished. If the land is later owned by two different people, the easements will revive.

Release

The owner of the dominant tenement can release his rights over the servient tenement. The release should be carried out by deed. If the release is oral then equity may give this effect if there is evidence in support of the release such as acting to one's detriment.

CASE EXAMPLE

Waterlow v Barlow (1886) LR 2 Eq 514

The dominant owner gave written permission for his neighbour to raise the height of his wall and then tried to claim that his right to light was being affected. There had been an effective release of the easement.

Abandonment

Once the right has been acquired as a legal easement, failure to make use of the right will not cause the dominant land to lose the right. However, where there has been no use for over 20 years then abandonment can be presumed unless there was no occasion to use the right.

CASE EXAMPLE

Benn v Hardinge (1992) 66 P & CR 246

Non-use for 175 years was not enough to indicate an intention to abandon an easement as there had been no occasion to use the right of way involved because the owner had an alternative means of access to his property.

Compare this earlier case decided nearly 70 years before *Benn v Hardinge* was decided:

CASE EXAMPLE

Swan v Sinclair [1924] 1 Ch 254

The landowner had not used a right of way for 38 years. He assented to building works which would have prevented him permanently from exercising the right of way over his neighbour's land. It was held that the easement had been abandoned.

The case of *Walker v Bridgewood* [2006] NSWSC 149 decided in the New South Wales Supreme Court confirms that it is not just the English courts that support the view that abandonment of an easement does not automatically arise through non-use.

Change of circumstances

CASE EXAMPLE

Huckvale v Aegean Hotels Ltd (1989) 58 P & CR 163

It was accepted by Slade J that an easement can be extinguished by a change of circumstances because it no longer accommodates the dominant tenement. He thought it would be rare and in that case the right was not lost as there was a chance that it might benefit the dominant land again in the future:

'circumstances might have changed so drastically since the date of the original grant of an easement … that it would offend common sense and reality for the court to hold that an easement still subsisted. Nevertheless, I think the court could properly so hold only in a very clear case.'

Slade J

10.7 *Profits à prendre*

A *profit à prendre* allows an individual to take something from another's land. It is similar to an easement but an easement will not allow the claimant to take something from the land but merely to use the land temporarily.

It is created in the same way as an easement and can be either legal or equitable, according to whether it is created for the equivalent of one or two legal estates and according to the required formalities.

10.7.1 Types of *profits à prendre*

1. The right to graze cattle on the servient land (*profit à pasture*).
2. The right to fish and take away fish that have been caught (*profit à piscary*).
3. The right to take away and cut down wood (*profit à estovers*).

It is possible to hold a *profit* without owning adjoining neighbouring land or in many cases without owning any land at all intended to benefit. In these cases if the *profit* is to exist for a period longer than seven years it must be entered at the Land Registry with an independent title.

The holder of the *profit* does not acquire rights over the land and it cannot take effect if it conflicts with the landowner's rights of ownership. The *profit* can be held by a number of people. A *profit à prendre* may be granted indefinitely or for a fixed period of time.

KEY FACTS

The creation of *profits à prendre*
1. The owner of the servient land can grant a *profit à prendre* expressly by deed.
2. If no deed is used, it will take effect in equity.
3. A *profit à prendre* can arise impliedly but only under s 62 of the Law of Property Act 1925.
4. The rule in *Wheeldon v Burrows* does not apply to *profits à prendre*.
5. *Profits à prendre* can be acquired under the Prescription Act 1832.
6. The periods of time to be satisfied under prescription are 30 years and 60 years.
7. A *profit* will be lost through release or acquisition of the servient land or by abandonment.

10.8 Changes made by the Land Registration Act 2002

The Land Registration Act 2002 has reformed the law on easements in a number of ways. The 2002 Act is discussed in detail in Chapter 3.

10.8.1 Overriding interests: equitable easements

One of the main initiatives behind the 2002 Act was to try to limit the number of overriding interests that can exist in land.

Before the Land Registration Act 2002

Under s 70(1)(a) of the Land Registration Act 1925 (now repealed), legal easements were held to be overriding interests. If the claimant had failed to register a legal interest as a minor interest, it would still be binding on the third-party purchaser.

After *Celsteel Ltd v Alton House Holdings Ltd* [1985] 1 WLR 204 it was held that equitable easements could also have overriding status if they were exercised and enjoyed openly.

After the Land Registration Act 2002

The 2002 Act has reformed the law so that equitable easements can no longer be overriding under any circumstances.

An equitable easement will only be binding if it has been properly registered. If the land has an unregistered title, it will be lost unless it has been entered in the Land Charges Register. It will then have to be entered on the Register on first registration.

If an equitable easement is created after first registration, it will need to be protected. This is done by entering a burden on the register of title.

10.8.2 Overriding interests: legal interests

Legal easements continue to be overriding but in more limited circumstances:

1. All legal easements or *profits à prendre* will take effect as overriding interests against a first registration of title to the land under Sched 1 to the Land Registration Act 2002.

2. Under Sched 3 to the Land Registration Act 2002, a limited number of legal easements will continue to be overriding on a subsequent registration of title if they satisfy any of the following conditions:

   i. an easement that is within the actual knowledge of the person to whom the disposition is made; or

   ii. it would have been obvious on a reasonably careful inspection of the land over which the easement or profit is exercisable; or

   iii. if the easement has been used in the year preceding the disposition.

Under s 27(2)(d) of the 2002 Act, an easement or profit that has been expressly granted must be entered on the Register in order to take effect at law. It cannot be overriding because it is not yet effective at law and it cannot take effect in equity because equitable interests are no longer overriding. So the only types of easements that will be overriding on a subsequent disposition will be an easement that arises under an implied grant or by prescription.

There may be some problems over what the courts interpret as reasonably obvious on careful inspection of the land under the 2002 Act. 'Of course, there may be some interpretative difficulties over "obvious on a reasonably careful inspection", especially in relation to long-disused land where the "one year use" clause may not apply' (M Dixon, 'The Reform of Property Law and the Land Registration Act 2002: A Risk Assessment' [2003] 67 *Conv* 136).

ACTIVITY

Applying the law

Consider the following problems:

Question 1:
Windy Hollow and Windy Villa are two neighbouring cottages. Freda is tenant of Windy Hollow and Leila owns Windy Villa. Freda has been given the right to use a short-cut by her neighbour, Leila, who is also her landlord. In December 2003 Freda purchases the freehold of Windy Hollow from Leila.

1. Can Freda continue to use the short-cut?
2. If Freda is allowed to continue to use the short-cut will it be binding on any purchaser from Leila?

Question 2:

In 1983 Frank bought a house called Sturdy Manor. He liked to walk on the seashore which was several miles away but he could get to the sea much quicker by using a short-cut through his neighbour Geraint's land. Geraint ran a small market garden and owned 30 acres of land. Frank could easily get to the sea by the main road but it took much longer. Frank was sent abroad with his job for one year and so did not use the path. When he came back he decided to turn Sturdy Manor into a guest house and he created eight bedrooms. The guests started to use the short-cut to the sea. Geraint decided to sell the market garden to Harry in November 2006. Harry has put up a fence and neither Frank nor his guests have been able to use the path leading to the sea.

Consider whether Frank or his guests can continue to use the short-cut across Harry's land.

10.9 Reform of the law on easements and *profits*

There are many aspects of easements which are unsatisfactory, in particular the law on prescription.

In 1966 the Law Reform Committee reported on 'Easements: Acquisition of Easements and Profits by Prescription' (Cmnd 3100). It recommended that prescription should be abolished for both easements and *profits*. It also recommended that there should be one single period for acquiring rights prescriptively, which would be 12 years. This was not implemented.

The Law Commission report leading up to the 2002 Act ('Land Registration for the Twenty-First Century: A Consultative Document' (Law Com No 254, 1998)) also recommended that the law on prescription should be changed so that both common law prescription and prescription under the doctrine of lost modern grant should be abolished, so that only prescription under the 1832 Act would remain. These proposals were not implemented but other recommended reforms in relation to the overriding nature of easements were put into effect.

The most recent proposals for reform were included in the Law Commission consultation paper 'Easements, Covenants and *Profits à Prendre*' published in 2008 (Com 186), which was followed in 2011 by the publication of its final report: 'Making Land Work: Easements, Covenants and *Profits a Prendre*'. This report made a number of proposals; the most radical of all was the abolition of all existing forms of prescription to be replaced with one single statutory method of acquisition. It proposed abolition of the existing rules on the implied creation of an easement and replacing those rules with a single statutory rule based on what is necessary for the reasonable use of the land. The most significant effect of this would be to prevent easements arising by implication under s 62 Law of Property Act 1925. There were also proposals on extinguishment of easements so that an application could be made to a land tribunal to discharge or modify easements in the same way as exists for covenants. As mentioned above there are also proposals to reform easements arising under prescription. None of these proposals have been acted on by the government.

SUMMARY

1. An easement is a right in land enjoyed by one person over the land of another.
2. The essential characteristics of an easement are found in *Re Ellenborough Park*.
3. There must be a dominant and servient tenement.
4. The tenements must be owned by two different people.

5. The easement must accommodate the dominant tenement so it will not be an easement if it is for business use or purely recreational use. Where there is significant increase in the use of the land it will not necessarily extinguish the easement.

6. The easement must be capable of forming the subject-matter of a grant. There must be a capable grantor and grantee.

7. Easements must not impose a positive burden on the servient owner.

8. An easement must not exclude reasonable alternative use of the servient tenement.

9. Easements can be granted in a number of different ways: express grant, implied grant or reservation or by prescription.

10. Easements through express grant can only arise where the formalities are followed under s 52 LPA 1925.

11. Easements by implied grant can arise through necessity, intended easements, the rule in *Wheeldon v Burrows* or under s 62 LPA 1925.

12. Easements can be acquired under prescription in three different ways: common law, lost modern grant and under the 1832 Prescription Act.

SAMPLE ESSAY QUESTION

Has the time come to revisit *Re Ellenborough Park* and substitute a new definition of an easement?

Consider the definition of an easement and the use and benefit of easements to landowners. Consider the need for clarity as to extent of the right and when the right arises.

Outline the four essential characteristics of an easement as set out in *Re Ellenborough Park*.

There must be a dominant and servient tenement.

Discuss this requirement and explain that this is the fundamental point of an easement.

An easement exists for the benefit of one parcel of land for the enjoyment of a second parcel of land.

The dominant and servient tenements must be owned by two different people.

Explain that an easement is a right in another's land to enjoy the other person's land.

Discuss the Law Commission proposal that an easement can exist where the two tenements are owned by one person. The safeguard would lie in the fact that the dominant and servient tenements will be registered with separate title numbers.

The easement must accommodate the dominant tenement. The two tenements must be sufficiently close *Bailey v Stephens* (1831).

Explain the nature of this, i.e. that the right must benefit the land and not the person owning the land. Illustrate with conflicting case law, e.g. *Hill v Tupper* (1863) and *Moody v Steggles* (1879).

Consider the exclusion of certain rights, e.g. recreational rights and the modern view that such rights should not prevent a right from existing as an easement.

The easement must be capable of forming the subject matter of a grant. Note that this is a very large category and comprises many different aspects:

Discuss that there must be a capable grantor and grantee.

Discuss that the easement must be sufficiently certain. For example *Aldred's Case* (1610).

Discuss that easements must not involve a positive obligation, with some exceptions, e.g. fencing *Crow v Wood* (1971).

Discuss that for a right to be capable of being an easement it must not give the owner of the dominant tenement too extensive rights of occupation or control over the land. Discuss *Copeland v Greenhalf* (1952); *Wright v Macadam* (1949); parking cases, e.g. *London & Blenheim Estates Ltd v Ladbroke Retail Parks Ltd* (1992). Then discuss the decision in *Moncrieff v Jamieson* (2007). The problems here in extending rights to include rights that seem to undermine enjoyment of the owner of the servient tenement. Consider Lord Scott's definition in *Moncrieff* 'that rights claimed must not be inconsistent with the continued beneficial ownership of the servient land by the servient proprietor'.

Discuss if *Re Ellenborough Park* continues to serve a useful purpose.

Discuss the proposals by the Law Commission in relation to the ownership of the tenements by the same person but in different capacities.

Discuss the problems posed by the decision in *Moncrieff v Jamieson* and the need for clarity in how much use and occupation a dominant owner can have over the servient land before the right loses the characteristics of an easement.

CONCLUSION

Further reading

Books

Dixon, M, *Modern Land Law* (11th edn, Routledge, 2018), pp. 283–331.

Gaunt, J and Morgan, Hon Mr Justice, *Gale on Easements* (19th edn, Sweet & Maxwell, 2012).

Gray, K and Gray, S F, *Elements of Land Law* (5th edn, Oxford University Press, 2009) pp. 612, 651.

Articles

Battersby, G, 'More Thoughts on Easements under the Land Registration Act 2002' [2005] *Conv* 195.

Bray, J, '*Kent and anor v Kavanagh and anor*: s 62 Fills a Black Hole' [2006] *DLJ* 203.

Bray, J, 'More Than Just a Walk in the Park: A New View on Recreational Easements' [2017] *Conv* 418.

Bogusz, B, 'The Doctrine of Lost Modern Grant: Back to the Future or Time to Move On?' [2013] *Conv* 198.

Conway, H, ' "Out with the Old": Easements and Obsolescense' [2007] 71 *Conv* 87.

Dixon, M, 'The Reform of Property Law and the Land Registration Act 2002: A Risk Assessment' [2003] 67 *Conv* 136.

Dixon, M, 'Editorial Comments' [2012] *Conv* 1.

Douglas, S, 'Reforming Implied Easements' [2015] *LQR* 251.

Goymour, A, 'Easements, Servitudes and the Right to Park' [2008] 67(1) *CLJ* 20.

Haley, M, 'Easement, Exclusionary Use and Elusive Principles: The Right to Park' [2008] 72 *Conv* 244.

Lee, R and Stokes, M, 'Navigating the Boundaries' [2014] 1432 *EG* 46.

Luther, P, 'Easements and Exclusive Possession' (1996) 16 *LS* 51.

McFarlane, B, 'Eastenders, Neighbors and Upstairs Downstairs: *Chaudhary v Yavuz*' [2013] *Conv* 74.

Odell, P, 'Parking is such Sweet Sorrow Too' [2009] *JBL* 488.

Poulsom, M, 'Taking a View: The Protection of Prospects in England and Wales' [2018] *Conv* 133.

Pratt, N, 'Confrontation, Contentious Use and a West Yorkshire Chip Shop' [2016] *Conv* 414.

Romer, LJ, 'Union Lighterage Co v London Graving Dock Co' [1902] 2 *Ch* 557.

Spark, G, 'Easements of Parking and Storage: Are Easements Non-Possessory Interests in Land?' [2012] *Conv* 6.

Tee, L, 'Metamorphoses and s 62 of the Law of Property Act 1925' [1998] Conv 115.

West, J, '*Wheeldon v Burrows* Revisited' [1995] *Conv* 346.

Law Commission Reports

'Easements, Covenants and *Profits à Prendre*' (Law Com CP No 186, 2008).

'Making Land Work: Easements, Covenants and *Profits à Prendre*' (Law Com No 327, 2011).

'Rights to Light' (Law Com No 356, 2014).

11

Freehold covenants

AIMS AND OBJECTIVES

After reading this chapter, you should be able to:

- Define freehold covenants and their role in land ownership
- Distinguish between covenants at common law and covenants in equity
- Understand why the law does not uphold positive covenants
- Explain the consequences of a breach of a covenant
- Explain the way that covenants can be discharged or modified
- Describe the proposals for reform of the law on freehold covenants

Neighbours will often draw up agreements between themselves about the use each makes of his land. These will be personal obligations governed by the rules of contract. They have a considerable impact on the enjoyment of the land by both parties and they are quite independent of any rights and obligations which arise under planning law. Land law has long sought a way to make these agreements enforceable against third parties. These agreements often have a profound effect on the enjoyment of property, but unless they are enforceable against successors in title, the value of a covenant will be limited. It is the ability to be able to enforce these rights as a third party or against third parties that give covenants real value to successive landowners. If one landowner can prevent a neighbouring landowner from building on his land that will increase the enjoyment of the claimant for the present. However, if this right can be enforceable against anyone who lives at the property and by anyone who purchases the land from the claimant that will increase its amenity value enormously as it will reassure the purchaser that the land can never be used for building purposes.

11.1 The nature of a covenant

A covenant is an obligation entered into by deed which usually restricts the use of land for the benefit of another.

An example would be where Mr Ford covenants with Miss Carefree not to use his land for business purposes. Miss Carefree can sue for breach of the covenant if she finds that Mr Ford has set up a printing business in the barn adjoining his house.

- The agreement is made by deed between the covenantor (who carries the burden) and the covenantee (who carries the benefit).

- As the agreement can be enforced under the law of contract, the rules of privity will apply and this means that the covenant can only be enforced between the original parties and burdens cannot be imposed on third parties.

- As this is a contract, the original parties will continue to be bound even after they have left the property.

Covenants may be either **positive** or **negative** in nature and different rules will apply in each case.

- **Positive covenants**: burdens imposed on the covenantor to carry out a specific act, for example a covenant to repair a wall or to keep property in good repair.

- **Negative covenants**: these prohibit specified kinds of activity or development of the covenantor's land for the benefit of the covenantee's land, for example a covenant against any further development on the land.

ACTIVITY

Quick quiz

You own an area of land called Midsummer Meadows with a farmhouse called Midsummer Farm. Consider the following covenants and decide whether they are positive or negative:

a. to keep Midsummer Meadow as an open space;
b. to erect a fence along the boundary of Midsummer Meadow;
c. not to divide Midsummer Farm into flats;
d. not to let Midsummer Farm fall into disrepair.

In each case, ask the question 'Would the covenantor have to put his hand into his pocket in order to carry out the covenant?' In other words, does it cost money to comply with the covenant? Putting up a fence along the boundary of Midsummer Meadow and the maintenance of Midsummer Farm will cost money whereas maintaining an open space and agreeing not to divide a farm into flats will not cost money.

Covenants play a vital role in the development and use of land and rank alongside planning law as a means of regulating its use.

There are a number of questions to consider in relation to covenants: can they be enforced between the original parties and can they be enforced against or by successors in title?

The answers to these questions depend on whether they are enforceable at law or in equity. The enforceability of covenants was extended by equity after the decision of *Tulk v Moxhay* (1848) 2 Ph 774 but the effect was that only negative covenants could be enforced.

This is why in the law of freehold covenants one usually refers to restrictive covenants over land.

Common law and **equity** therefore treat covenants and the transfer of the benefits and burdens under them differently.

11.2 Covenants at law

The common law rules relating to covenants can be traced far back in history.

CASE EXAMPLE

The Prior's case (1368) YB 42 Edw III pl 14 fol 3A

This was one of the earliest recorded cases, in which it was held that a covenant may be enforceable against the covenantor by the covenantee even where the covenantor owns no land to be benefited. In this case, the covenant was for the covenantor to sing during the week in the chapel of the covenantee.

This is enforceable between the parties because it is a contract and so will be enforceable under the law of contract as opposed to property law. Covenants are enforceable under property law in order to protect the land of the landowner, whereas under contract law, it is the rights under the contract that the law protects.

In practice, the covenantor generally owns some land but it is more important that the covenantee owns some land to be benefited by the covenant.

11.2.1 Statutory methods of transmitting the benefit of a covenant at law

There is generally no difficulty in enforcing a covenant between the original parties but there are a number of statutory provisions which extend or restrict the category of person who may enforce the original covenant if they were not party to the original agreement.

1. **Section 56(1) of the Law of Property Act 1925**: this has the effect that a covenant will be enforceable by all persons who are named generically in the covenant, for example if X covenants with Y and all owners for the time being of Blackacre, the unnamed owner will be able to enforce the covenant even though he is not specifically mentioned in the conveyance. This section does not apply to future owners of the land, but only to persons who are in existence and identifiable at the date of the covenant. This has been a limitation on the use of s 56. A person who acquires a benefit under s 56 may then pass it on to his successors in title by annexation or assignment.

   Section 56 creates some special problems. It was considered in *White v Bijou Mansions Ltd* [1937] Ch 610 by Simonds J who said:

JUDGMENT

'[U]nder section 56 ... only that person can call it in aid who, although not named as a party to the conveyance or other instrument is yet a person to whom that conveyance or other instrument purports to grant something or with whom some agreement or covenant is purported to be made ... I interpret [s 56] as a section which can be called in aid only by a person in whose favour the grant purports to be made or with whom the covenant or agreement purports to be made.'

Simonds J in *White v Bijou Mansions Ltd* [1937] Ch 610

This section was pleaded in the following case:

CASE EXAMPLE

Amsprop Trading Ltd v Harris Distribution Ltd [1997] 2 All ER 990

A landlord sought to recover the cost of repairs from a sub-tenant. Under the lease the tenant was responsible for keeping the premises in good repair and agreed to allow the landlord to enter the premises to carry out such repairs if they had not been carried out. The tenant sublet the premises and the sublease was made on very similar terms to the head lease including reference to the superior landlord. In spite of these clauses the judge held that the superior landlord had no rights against the sub-tenant and could not use s 56 LPA 1925 in order to recover the costs of repair. In the absence of privity of estate or contract between the superior landlord and sub-tenant the landlord could not recover these costs directly from the sub-tenant. Neuberger J held that in order to enforce the covenant the landlord must show that it had been made on behalf of the sub-tenant and it clearly had not.

This shows that there are limits on the extent of s 56. The section can only be relied on where the covenant not only confers the benefit on the third party but that it can also be shown that he/she was intended to be parties.

2. The **Contracts (Rights of Third Parties) Act 1999** has made extensions to the rights of any third party to enforce a covenant entered into after May 2000. Covenants can now be enforced by anyone for whose benefit a party named in the deed was expressly contracted or was purportedly made for their benefit but they are not expressly referred to by name, for example if X covenants with Y so as to benefit the owners of Blackacre and Greenacre, the owners of the two properties can argue that they have the right to enforce the covenants. The value of relying on this statute is that under s 1(1) the person relying on the right does not have to be in existence at the time when the contract is entered into. Further the covenant does not have to touch and concern the land.

3. The benefit of a covenant which is not exclusively personal may always be assigned in writing as a chose in action under s 136 of the Law of Property Act 1925. Notice should be given to the covenantor.

4. **Section 78(1) of the Law of Property Act 1925** provides that a covenant 'relating to' any land of the covenantee is presumptively 'made with the covenantee and his successors in title and the persons deriving title under him or them, and shall have effect as if such successors and other persons were expressed'. This section has two main limitations: it only applies to covenants which relate to (or 'touch and concern') the covenantee's land and it can only apply to covenants that were entered into after 1925. Although this section was enacted in the 1925 Law of Property Act it took several decades before its full effect was understood by lawyers, claimants and the courts. It is almost as if those involved in this area of law could not believe that the transmission of the benefit of a covenant could be so simple.

11.2.2 The passing of the benefit at law

Property often changes hands frequently and so it is important to know whether a covenant will continue to benefit any or all purchasers from the covenantee.

If Freddie sells part of Blackacre to Alistair, and Alistair enters into a covenant (i) not to build on the land and (ii) to erect a fence around his plot, the benefit of this covenant may extend to Shane, who buys a further part of Blackacre from Freddie.

If Alistair then starts to build a bungalow in the garden of Blackacre, Shane can take action against Alistair who is liable both on the positive covenant (to build the fence) and also the negative covenant (not to build on the land).

If Shane wants to take action, certain conditions must be satisfied:

1. The covenant must touch and concern the land.
2. The covenantee must have a legal estate in the dominant land.
3. The transferee of the dominant land must also take a legal estate in that land.
4. There must have been an intention that the benefit should run.
5. The benefit of the covenant must have been annexed to the land either expressly or impliedly or under statute.

1. The covenant must 'touch and concern' the land

The key issue here is that the covenant must benefit the land. It must not be purely for the personal benefit of the covenantee, for example it must confer a benefit on you as landowner and not on you as an individual. An example would be a covenant preventing your neighbour from using his land for business purposes; this would be held to benefit the land.

CASE EXAMPLE

Smith and Snipes Hall Farm Ltd v River Douglas Catchment Board [1949] 2 KB 500

The covenant by the defendant River Douglas Catchment Board to improve and keep river banks in repair was held to have 'touched and concerned' the covenantee's land, which was flooded when repair was neglected, because ... 'it affects the value of the land per se and converts it from flooded meadows to land suitable for agriculture'.

In *P & A Swift Investments v Combined English Stores Group* [1989] AC 632 Lord Oliver of Aylmerton laid down a test to discover whether a covenant 'touches and concerns' the land:

1. The covenant must benefit the estate owner for the time being and it would cease to be of benefit to the covenantee if separated from the ownership of the benefited estate.

2. The covenant must affect the nature, quality, mode of use or value of the benefited land.

3. Even where (1) and (2) are satisfied, the covenant will not be regarded as 'touching and concerning the land' if the benefit is in some way expressed to be personal to the covenantee.

Although use of the land may usually be said to confer a benefit on the land itself it has been construed restrictively in some cases as seen below.

CASE EXAMPLE

Morrells of Oxford Ltd v Oxford United Football Club Ltd [2001] Ch 459

A covenant that:

> 'the vendors will not at any time hereafter permit any land or building erected thereon within half a mile radius of the land hereby conveyed which is in the ownership of the vendors at the date of this conveyance to be used as a brewery or club or licensed premises'

was held to operate as a personal covenant only. It was clear from the whole tenor of the agreement that it was intended to apply to the parties for the time being and not to extend to others.

CASE EXAMPLE

Hua Chiao Commercial Bank v Chiaphua Industries [1987] AC 99

It was held that a promise by the landlord to return a deposit paid as security for rent at the end of the lease was purely personal, and so the successor in title from the landlord had no obligation to return the deposit to the tenant at the end of the lease. This remained the personal responsibility of the original landlord.

ACTIVITY

Quick quiz

Do the following covenants touch and concern the land?
  The covenantor hereby agrees:

i.   not to keep a dog;
ii. to ensure that the hedges do not grow higher than six metres;
iii. not to use the land for any purposes associated with religion;
iv. not to build a greenhouse on the land.

Parts (i) and (iii) do not 'touch and concern' the land although (i) may be controversial. Parts (ii) and (iv) both affect the enjoyment of the land.

2. *The original covenantee must have a legal estate in the benefited land*

This would be either a fee simple absolute in possession (freehold) or a term of years absolute (leasehold) under s 1 of the Law of Property Act 1925.

3. *The successor in title of the original covenantee must have a legal estate in the benefited land*

Until 1926 it was assumed that the successor in title must have the same legal estate in land as the original covenantee. However, under s 78 of the 1925 Act, it is held that the legal estate held by the successor in title can be different. So the original covenantee can hold a fee simple absolute but the successor in title can be a leaseholder and still have the right to enforce the covenant at law. On the rare occasions that the covenant in question was made before 1925 then the assignee could not enforce it.

In *Smith and Snipes Hall Farm Ltd v River Douglas Catchment Board* (1949) the original covenantee sold his land to the first plaintiff who then leased the land to the second plaintiff. Under s 78, both the first and second plaintiffs were able to enforce the covenant. The court held that the effect of s 78 is that a covenant is enforceable on behalf of not only the original covenantee, but all successors in title and all persons deriving title from such successors.

The covenant will not run at law to someone who only holds an equitable estate in land. An example would be a person who had an interest in the land under a constructive trust.

4. *The benefit must have been intended to run with the benefited land*

The parties must intend that the benefit of the covenant is to run with the land. It had to be shown that the parties to the deed intended the covenant to be enforceable not only by the original covenantee but also by successors in title to the original covenantee.

5. *The benefit must have been annexed to the legal estate in land either expressly or impliedly*

It must be shown that the benefit was actually attached or 'annexed' to the land. This could either be expressly at the time of conveyance or assigned by a separate document. More recently the benefit of most covenants is deemed to pass impliedly under statute.

This caused problems before 1926 because the covenant had to be very specific in its wording in order to allow the benefit to pass to their successors. After 1925, such an intention is assumed by s 78 of the 1925 Act:

SECTION

's78 ... The covenant is deemed to be made with the covenantee and his successors in title and the persons deriving title under him.'

In *Smith and Snipes Hall Farm Ltd v River Douglas Catchment Board* (1949) Lord Denning said:

JUDGMENT

'The covenant of the Catchment Board in this case clearly relates to the land of the covenantees. It was a covenant to do work on the land for the benefit of the land. By the statute therefore, it is deemed to be made, not only with the original owner, but also with the purchasers of the land and their tenants as if they were expressed. Now if they were expressed, it would be clear that the covenant was made for their benefit; and they have sufficient interest to entitle them to enforce it because they have suffered the damage.'

Unless a covenant is phrased in such a way that it is only intended to bind the original covenantee, there is a statutory presumption that a covenant relating to any land of a covenantee 'shall be deemed to be made by the covenantee on behalf of himself, his successors in title and the persons deriving title under him or them'.

The benefit of both negative and also positive covenants can pass at common law, provided the criteria discussed above are satisfied. In *P & A Swift v Combined English Stores* (1989) a covenant was enforceable which concerned the provision of a surety for rent payable under a lease.

ACTIVITY

Applying the law

Consider the following situations and decide whether the successors of the original covenantee can sue at law on the running of the covenant at common law.

1. Mr and Mrs Brown purchased Blackacre which had a number of covenants in its favour including not 'to use the property for business purposes'. The title was registered in Mr Brown's name but Mrs Brown had contributed to the purchase. While Mr Brown is working in South America on a two-year contract, their neighbour starts to build industrial units. Mrs Brown believes this to be in breach of the covenant. Can she take action against the neighbour?
2. Mr White acquired a long leasehold of The Laurels in 1953 which he left to his grandson in 2000. The original covenantee, Mr Grey, had purchased The Laurels in 1950. Can Mr White's grandson sue on the covenant not to allow the garden of the property next door to become overgrown?
3. Mr Wong covenanted with Mr Wu not to alter the exterior of any of the buildings which he purchased in 1980. Will the benefit of this covenant run to Mr Wang when he buys the properties from Mr Wu in 2000?

11.2.3 The running of the burden at law

The general rule is that the burden of a covenant will never run at common law. So the purchaser from the covenantor will not be bound by any covenants which they agreed with the covenantee. The covenantor remains liable on the covenant even after sale of property.

If Mr Brown enters into a covenant with Mr Grey not to let the exterior of his house, Ivy Cottage, fall into disrepair, the burden of this covenant will not run at law. When

Mrs Green purchases Ivy Cottage from Mr Brown, she will not become liable for the positive covenant entered into by her predecessor in title, Mr Brown.

Mr Brown himself will remain liable if the exterior of the house begins to crack and needs to be painted so Mr Grey could always sue him as the original covenantor and Mr Brown, will remain liable throughout his life unless the covenant is eventually discharged.

CASE EXAMPLE

Austerberry v Corporation of Oldham (1885) 29 Ch D 750

The owners of a site of a road covenanted that they and their successors in title would make a road and keep it in repair. The road was sold to the defendants the Corporation of Oldham and it was held that the repair covenant could not be enforced against the successors in title to the original owners of the road.

It was held by Cotton LJ that the burden of a covenant cannot run at common law.

The explanation for this can be found in a more recent judgment of Lord Templeman in *Rhone v Stephens*.

JUDGMENT

'To enforce a positive covenant would be to enforce a personal obligation against a person who has not covenanted. To enforce negative covenants is only to treat the land as subject to a restriction.'

CASE EXAMPLE

Rhone v Stephens [1994] 2 AC 310

This case concerned the enforcement of a positive covenant entered into by a freehold owner agreeing 'to maintain to the reasonable satisfaction of the purchasers and their successors in title such part of the roof as lies above the property conveyed in wind and water tight condition'. Part of the roof of a house extended over an adjoining cottage. In 1960 the owner of the property divided it into two separate dwellings and the owner retained the house and sold the cottage. The covenant was included in the conveyance. Mr and Mrs Rhone who were now the owners of the cottage sought to enforce the covenant to repair their roof against the owner of the house (Mrs S) who was executrix of the previous owner, Mrs Barnard. Water had leaked through the roof over the cottage into one of the bedrooms.

This is an inconvenient rule, as shown by the facts of *Rhone v Stephens* (1994). It would be very valuable to enforce repairing covenants against your neighbour where properties are divided into two plots but there is some measure of overlap between the properties.

How can the rule be justified?

We can justify the rule because land may become burdened with endless covenants which then make it difficult to sell freely because of the costly burden of repairs to the covenantee's property. It is possible in the future that the rule in *Austerberry v Oldham Corporation* (1885) will be reversed. There have been several proposals by the Law Commission to allow the burden of positive covenants to run at law, for example in the Law Commission Report 'Transfer of Land: The Law of Positive and Restrictive Covenants' (Law Com No 127, 1984). The Law Commission proposed a new form of right called a 'land obligation' which could encompass both positive and negative obligations. This was never acted on.

The judge at first instance had found that the defendant was the owner of the roof and held that since the maintenance of the roof by the defendant was also to the benefit of her, she must pay for the necessary repairs.

The Court of Appeal allowed the defendant's appeal, holding that the disputed roof was owned by the plaintiffs, the burden of a positive covenant did not run with the land and the principle of mutual benefit and burden did not apply since the benefits to the defendant's property were minimal.

The House of Lords held that the original covenant to repair, being positive in nature, could not bind the defendant who was the original covenantor's successor in title at common law, under the rule in *Austerberry v Oldham Corporation* (1885).

Figure 11.1 Progress of *Rhone v Stephens* through the courts

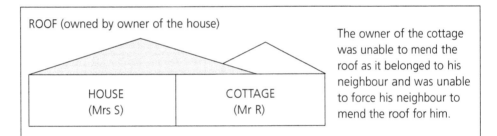

Figure 11.2 *Rhone v Stephens* (1994)

JUDGMENT

'Your Lordships were invited to overrule the decision of the Court of Appeal in the *Austerberry* case. To do so would destroy the distinction between law and equity and to convert the rule of equity into a rule of notice. It is plain from the articles, reports and papers to which we were referred that judicial legislation to overrule the *Austerberry* case would create a number of difficulties, anomalies and uncertainties and affect the rights and liabilities of people who have for over 100 years bought and sold land in the knowledge, imparted at an elementary stage to every student of the law of real property, that positive covenants, affecting freehold land are not directly enforceable except against the original covenantor.'

Lord Templeman in *Rhone v Stephens*

Possible reform: commonhold

Under the Commonhold and Leasehold Reform Act 2002, ownership of land can be held under a commonhold scheme. The land must be specified under a memorandum of commonhold association as land in relation to which the association can exercise certain functions. The commonhold community statement lays down the rights and duties of each owner of land. Within this statement will be the rules and regulations that apply to the landowners. The statement will lay down their rights and duties and these duties can be both positive and negative. Although it was expected that commonhold would mainly cover blocks of flats, it could also be used for communal ownership of gardens in towns and also the shared ownership of roads and communal gardens; there could be an association of just two members. This Act came into force in 2003 but very few commonhold schemes have been adopted and the problems of non-enforceability of positive covenants has not been solved by commonhold. Commonhold is considered in detail in Chapter 15.

The most recent Law Commission Consultation Paper in 2008 'Easements, Covenants and *Profits à Prendre'* has looked at proposals to deal with the problems that arise from the *Austerberry* rule. The Law Commission has returned to the 1984 Law Commission proposals proposing that 'land obligations' should be introduced. Again, this would be binding on successors in title and would cease to be enforceable by the original parties once the land had been sold. It also proposes that the land obligation would be capable of imposing positive obligations on successors in title. Land obligations would have to benefit the land and so would exclude personal covenants. Such rights would have to be expressly created between the parties and would need to be completed by registration. So the interest would need to be entered on the Register for the benefited land and there would also have to be a notice on the Register of the burdened land. There is an overlap with the system of enforceable rights under commonhold but the proposals by the Law Commission are far less complex and can be independently enforced by single landowners rather than as party to a commonhold scheme. Although commonhold may be appropriate where there are a number of landowners who wish to enforce rights the new land obligation would be far more effective for claimants such as Mr and Mrs Rhone in *Rhone v Stephens*.

11.2.4 Methods by which the rule in *Austerberry v Oldham Corporation* (1885) can be avoided

The rule in *Austerberry v Oldham Corporation* (1885) is inconvenient and over the years a number of methods have been used in order to try and avoid the effects of the rule.

- **Chains of indemnity covenants**: the original covenantor will remain liable on the original covenant. In practice, the original covenantor will take out an indemnity covenant with any purchaser in order to protect himself against subsequent breaches of covenant over which he will not have any control. Then, on a later sale, another indemnity covenant will be taken out with the new purchaser. The main disadvantage is that as the chain grows, it is likely that it may break. The original covenantor may have died or just cannot be found or may have become insolvent and so there is no point in suing. The only remedy is damages, which may not be appropriate as an injunction or specific performance forcing the covenantor to act or cease to act is generally a much more satisfactory remedy.

ACTIVITY

Quick quiz

Charlotte covenants with Kate not to allow the garden of her property, Mistletoe Cottage, to become overgrown and to plant new shrubs and plants every year. Charlotte moves away from the area selling the property to Lydia. Lydia does not like gardening and allows the garden to become overgrown with weeds and does not plant any new shrubs or plants. Has Kate any remedy against either Charlotte or Lydia?

The covenant cannot be enforced at law against the successor in title, Lydia, but Kate can enforce the covenant against Charlotte the original covenantor even though she has moved away and left the property. However her remedy would only be in damages.

It may also be possible to enforce the burden of the covenant by ensuring that each purchaser of the burdened land will covenant directly with the person who takes the benefit. This would be entered into at the time of purchase. The initial covenant would be in two separate parts:

i.   the covenant concerning the land;

ii. the covenant agreeing to impose the obligations on a successive purchaser.

In this way the covenantee has privity of contract with each owner of the property. However, this requires the covenant to be renewed at each sale.

- **A long lease**: this may be enlarged into a fee simple under s 153 of the Law of Property Act 1925. It is suggested that this will allow the freehold to be subject to the same covenants as those contained originally in the lease. The burden of leasehold covenants can run at law and in this case the leasehold rules continue to apply. This is rarely used as it is both cumbersome and artificial.

- **The rule in *Halsall v Brizell* [1957] Ch 169**: this is also known as the doctrine of mutual benefit and burden. This is a useful rule frequently used to enforce positive covenants. If a purchaser takes certain benefits under the conveyance then the purchaser cannot avoid the burdens of an associated covenant even where it imposes positive duties. In recent years it has been very strictly construed so it is only available within very strict criteria.

CASE EXAMPLE

In *Halsall v Brizell* [1957] Ch 169 an estate was developed, and each owner agreed by deed that they would contribute towards the upkeep of certain communally enjoyed benefits including the drive, the sewers and the repair of the sea wall. Since each owner had the right to enjoy the benefits, the court held that they had an obligation to contribute towards their upkeep. The rule holds that if you have the right to use your neighbour's drive or sewers then you have to bear some of the cost of upkeep, even where you are not the original covenantor. The rule appeared to allow widespread reliance on positive covenants since it could be very easy for most covenantees to prove that the covenantor derived a benefit over the covenantee's land where the parties shared certain facilities such as driveways.

In more recent cases this rule has been interpreted more narrowly. In *Rhone v Stephens* (1994) it was held that just because the deed conferred a benefit on a person, it did not mean that all the burdens imposed by that deed became enforceable. The burden must in some way relate to the benefit conferred. This will be so where the covenantor can make a choice between accepting the benefit and burden or rejecting the benefit and thereby being released from the burden. So in this case the fact that A's roof was supported by B's property which could be construed as a benefit did not entitle B to enforce a positive covenant to repair the roof made by A's predecessor in title because A had no choice between accepting and rejecting the benefit. There was no alternative but to accept the benefit of the support of the roof whereas the use of a driveway will usually be the covenantor's choice. In *Thamesmead v Allotey* an even narrower interpretation was given to the *Halsall v Brizell* rule. The court considered whether or not the covenantor's successor in title had chosen to enjoy the benefit of the covenant.

CASE EXAMPLE

Thamesmead Town v Allotey (2000) 79 P & CR 557

The defendant was relieved of maintenance costs in respect of certain facilities because they were the ones that he did not use and from which, therefore, he derived no benefit. Here, the owners had two distinct 'benefits'; a charge for the upkeep of roads and sewers and a separate charge for the maintenance of common parts, such as walkways, open spaces, etc. The claimant chose not to use pathways and footpaths in a London County Council estate and so escaped an obligation towards their upkeep. The charges for the use of sewers and of roads were upheld.

There has been criticism of the narrow view that seems to have limited the effect of the rule in *Halsall v Brizell* even further. The decision in *Thamesmead Town v Allotey* (2000) has set limits on the rule in *Halsall v Brizell*. It means that the rule of mutual benefit and burden only applies where there is not only a benefit conferred but also that the burden is closely linked to the benefit and if the defendant has chosen to enjoy the benefit. Kevin Gray comments:

> 'the law relating to the transmission of covenanted burdens between freeholders is left in a deeply unsatisfactory state and in *Thamesmead Town Ltd v Allotey* the Court of Appeal could only express a sense of urgency that the deficiency of the law be addressed by Parliament.'
>
> K Gray and S F Gray, *Elements of Land Law* (5th edn,
> Oxford University Press, 2009), p. 252

The rule in *Halsall v Brizell* continues to be a popular way to avoid the problems created by the rule in *Austerberry v Oldham* but it has been further restricted as seen in *Davies v Jones* [2009] EWCA 1164. In this case Andrew Morritt laid down three conditions which must first operate in order for the *Halsall v Brizell* rule to apply.

These conditions are derived from Lord Templeman's judgment in *Rhone v Stephens*.

1. The benefit and burden must be conferred in, or by the same transaction.
2. The receipt or enjoyment of the benefit must be relevant to the imposition of the burden in the sense that the former must be conditional on, or reciprocal to the latter.
3. The person on whom the burden is alleged to have been imposed must have, or have had, the opportunity of rejecting or disclaiming the benefit.

As pointed out by Bevan:

> '... *Davies* therefore represents a narrowing of the doctrine by making clear that it will not apply based alone upon an "understanding" between the parties however "clear" that may be in the view. What is required is a deed or other writing. This reflects a tightening, a constraining of the doctrine from its earlier, more flexible operation. ... Davies further establishes that the benefit and burden must be conferred in the same transaction. This requirement will be determined in most cases by construing the deed effecting the conveyance and associated documents. The second requirement that the benefit be "relevant to the imposition of the burden" has been held to be "a matter of substance rather than form". The effect of this is that the benefit does not need to be expressed in the deed to be conditional upon the burden, provided there is a clear and obvious link between the two. By far the

most uncertain aspect of the doctrine is the second factor identified, namely, the requirement of "relevance"; that the benefit and burden must be relevant, related, linked to one another....'

C Bevan, 'The Doctrine of Benefit and Burden: Reforming the Law of Covenants and the Numerus Clausus "Problem"' [2018] *CLJ* 80

CASE EXAMPLE

Wilkinson v Kerdene [2013] EWCA Civ 44

The owners of holiday bungalows in Cornwall argued that they should not have to contribute towards the maintenance of facilities such as access roads, footpaths and leisure facilities which had fallen into disrepair. They had agreed to contribute to these costs on purchase. The owners of the bungalows argued that as the repairs had not taken place they had no obligation to pay the sums sought by the new owners of the holiday complex. The Court of Appeal held that as the sums related to the provision of services some of which they continued to enjoy such as the use of the access roads then the sums must be payable. They upheld the principle of *Halsall v Brizell* because the payments related to rights in their favour which they continued to exercise.

CASE EXAMPLE

Elwood v Goodman [2014] Ch 442

A judge had rightly found that the purchasers of industrial units were liable to contribute to the cost of maintaining an adjacent road both in contract, under the terms of covenants in two transfers, and the principle of benefit and burden. He rejected an argument that the contribution should not be paid because the obligation to contribute had not been entered on the Register. It was held that this right did not have to be entered on the Register in order to make it enforceable.

The Court of Appeal did conclude that the purchasers were not liable to contribute to the cost of maintaining a post-transfer extension to the road over which no rights of way had been granted as there was no correlation between the burden of maintenance costs and the benefit of rights of way.

There are several other ways that a positive covenant can be enforced against a successor in title but as you can see from the examples below they are all complicated conveyancing devices.

- **Rights of re-entry**: the dominant owner can reserve a right of entry which will become exercisable upon a breach of a positive covenant.

- **The grant of a lease**: the land can always be leased rather than sold and then there is no difficulty in enforcing covenants against successors to the original covenantor.

- **A rent charge**: it is possible to annex a right of entry to a legal rent charge which is itself a legal interest in the land. In this way positive covenants to repair, even covenants to build and improve the land, can be enforced. The proprietor can enter the land where the covenants have not been observed and make good himself, charging the cost to the landowner. It is an ingenious device but only useful where lawyers can deal with the legal complexities, so making it an expensive option. **Note**: a rent charge is a right to claim a periodical sum of money from the owner of land which is not dependent on a landlord and tenant relationship.

Method of avoidance	How it works	Disadvantages
Chain of indemnity covenants	Dependent on the legal right to sue the original covenantor; depends on each owner taking out a covenant indemnifying them from loss arising from a breach of covenant.	The chain can easily break down; difficult always to locate the original owner; original owner may have become insolvent or have died.
A long lease	May be enlarged into a fee simple under s 153 of the LPA 1925.	Rarely used as a cumbersome method of ensuring that positive covenants are enforced.
The rule in *Halsall v Brizell*	Known as the doctrine of mutual benefit and burden; if you receive a benefit you must also bear the burden.	Interpreted narrowly so must relate to the benefit conferred, if no benefit can be proved then will be released from obligation: *Thamesmead Town v Allotey*.
Rights of re-entry	The dominant owner can reserve a right to re-enter the premises if there is a breach of covenant.	Legalistic and complicated.
The grant of a lease	Covenants can always be enforced within a lease and against successors in title.	It is easy to enforce the covenants but it relies on a method which forces you to accept leasehold ownership when you want to buy freehold.
A rent charge	Can annex a right of re-entry to a legal rent charge.	Complex and legalistic.

Table 11.1 Methods by which the rule in *Austerberry v Oldham Corporation* (1885) can be avoided

There has been considerable criticism of the position of the law on positive covenants since the decision in *Rhone v Stephens* (1994).

'In 1971 the Law Commission described the law on rights appurtenant to land as "illogical, uncertain, incomplete and inflexible" (Law Commission WP No 36 *Appurtenant Rights* (1971) paras 31–35). The incompleteness of the law was specifically attributed to the failure to make provision for the enforcement of the positive covenants relating to freehold land against successors in title to the original covenantor. The decision of the House of Lords in *Rhone v Stephens* [1994] has reaffirmed that incompleteness and has thereby underlined the need to revive the recommendations of the Law Commission and others on land obligations and common hold schemes.... Although the enforcement of positive covenants has been recommended in a series of reports over the past thirty years, Lord Templeman regarded it as inappropriate for the courts to overrule the *Austerberry* case, which had provided for the basis for transactions relating to the rights and liabilities of landowners for over 100 years. On the contrary, the potential problems of such judicial legislation together with the experience in relation to the enforcement of positive covenants between landlord and tenant, pointed to the clear need for Parliamentary legislation to deal with consequences ... Few would dissent from the view that in appropriate circumstances positive covenants should be capable of enforcement against successors in title to the original covenantor.'

N P Gravells, 'Enforcement of Positive Covenants Affecting Freehold
Land' (1994) 110 *LQR* 346

These problems highlighted here by Nigel Gravells were revisited by the Law Commission in 2008 which made a number of recommendations in its consultation paper: 'Easements, Covenants and *Profits à Prendre*' (Consultation Paper No 186). The recommendations are discussed later in this chapter.

There continue to be advantages of the covenantee suing at law rather than in equity and the reform of the rule in *Austerberry v Oldham* (1885) remains a continuing necessity. It is anticipated that the recent Law Commission Consultation Paper will be acted on by Parliament at some time in the future.

Advantages of the common law for the enforcement of covenants:

1. The claimant can claim damages as of right once the breach of the covenant has been proved.
2. The covenantor does not need to own land before a case can be brought by the claimant at common law.
3. The covenant can be either positive or negative to be enforceable at common law.

11.3 Covenants in equity

Common law clearly had a number of difficulties for a claimant seeking to enforce a covenant. During the nineteenth century equity stepped in to address these problems and it is the rules in equity that predominate the law on covenants today. However, enforcement in equity has its limitations as only negative covenants can be enforced, so the rules of equity could not assist Mr and Mrs Rhone.

The benefit
The benefit of a covenant will run in equity if the following conditions are satisfied:

1. The covenant is one that benefits and protects the dominant land so the covenant must be one that 'touches and concerns' the land.
2. The claimant has a legal or equitable estate in the land of the original covenantee. In equity this is very wide and under s78 LPA 1925 the claimant not only does not need to have the same estate as the original covenantee, but also any occupier may enforce the benefit of a restrictive covenant. This means an owner in equity can enforce a covenant in this way and it extends to other occupiers such as an adverse possessor.
3. It is also necessary to show that the benefit of the covenant has passed to the covenantee.

There are several ways in which the benefit can pass in equity and the different rules are complicated.

The benefit will pass through:

- annexation;
- assignment; or
- a building scheme.

11.3.1 Annexation
Annexation involves the 'nailing' of the covenant to land. The land itself must be clearly identified. Once the covenant is annexed either expressly or impliedly the benefit will pass in equity on each successive transfer of the land.

Annexation can be **express**, **implied** or **statutory**.

Express annexation

At common law, the question of annexation rested on the question of intention. The conveyance had to annex the covenant **expressly** or **impliedly**.

For example, a purchaser, Myrtle Brown, covenanted with a vendor, Pansy Green, so that the benefit was annexed to each and every part of the land that the seller retained. The law was strict about the way this was interpreted and much depended on the exact words used in the conveyance.

In *Re Ballard's Conveyance* [1937] Ch 473 it was held that there was no express annexation of a covenant which purportedly benefited the whole of an estate of 1,700 acres, although in *Wrotham Park Estate Co Ltd v Parkside Homes Ltd* [1974] 1 WLR 798 a less strict approach was taken, allowing a covenant to be annexed where it benefits a substantial part of the dominant tenement.

Earlier, in *Renals v Cowlishaw* (1878) 9 Ch D 125, a claim that a covenant had been expressly annexed to a piece of land was rejected because although the parties who could rely on the annexation were named there was no reference to the land which was intended to benefit on annexation.

The problem of deciphering whether the covenant has been annexed to a part of the land which is subsequently sold separately used to be addressed by interpreting the words of the conveyance and if the words 'to each and every part' of the covenantee's land had been used. These words could allow a broad interpretation to be taken of the passing of the benefit.

In *Marquess of Zetland v Driver* [1939] Ch 1 the Court of Appeal held that where a covenant was expressly annexed to any part or parts of the dominant land it would be enforceable by a subsequent purchaser of a part of the dominant land.

Implied annexation

It has also been held that a covenant can be **impliedly annexed** from surrounding circumstances, but the benefit of the covenant must be clearly referable to a defined piece of land and the parties must have intended that the benefit attach to the land and not to the covenantee personally.

Statutory annexation

Express and implied annexation of covenants has become far less important in conveyancing since s78 Law of Property Act was reinterpreted in such a way as to statutorily annex every covenant on the sale of land with only very limited exceptions.

This section reads as follows:

SECTION

's78(1) A covenant relating to any land of the covenantee shall be deemed to be made with the covenantee and his successors in title and the persons deriving title under him or them and shall have the effect as if such successors and other persons were expressed. For the purposes of this subsection in connection with covenants restrictive of the user of land "successors in title" shall be deemed to include the owners and occupiers for the time being of the land of the covenantee intended to be benefited.

(2) This section applies to covenants made after the commencement of this Act, but the repeal of section 58 of the Conveyancing Act 1881 does not affect the operation of covenants to which that section applied.'

The law on annexation of freehold covenants is now governed by the interpretation of this section in the following case:

CASE EXAMPLE

Federated Homes Ltd v Mill Lodge Properties Ltd [1980] 1 WLR 594

The case concerned the owners (Mackenzie Hill) of land which was divided into four plots. They obtained planning permission to build 1,250 houses on the site. The owners sold one plot (the 'blue site') to Mill Lodge Properties Ltd.

The conveyance contained the following covenant:

'the purchaser Mill Lodge hereby covenants with the vendor that ... in carrying out the development of the land the purchaser shall not build at a greater density than a total of 300 dwellings so as not to reduce the number of units which the vendor might eventually erect on the retained land under the existing planning consent'.

It was clear that the covenant was intended to benefit the 'adjoining or adjacent property retained' by the covenantee, although the terms of the covenant were not expressly annexed to the remaining plots of land. The owners sold two of the remaining plots of his land and they eventually came into the hands of the claimant. Mill Lodge (the covenantor) tried to build more than 300 houses on the 'blue site' and the question was whether the owners of the adjoining two sites had the benefit of the covenant which could stop Mill Lodge from building. For one plot there had been an express assignment of the covenant but for the other plot the conveyance had not referred to it.

Brightman LJ considered s78 of the 1925 Act and found three ways of interpreting the section:

1. It was simply a word-saving device aimed at reducing the length of legal documents. This was rejected.
2. The section only operated to annex a covenant if the document in some way showed that the land was intended to have the benefit of it.
3. The section effected annexation as long as the covenant touched and concerned the land of the covenantee and this applied whether or not it was apparent from the document or from surrounding circumstances.

He concluded that if a covenant touched and concerned the land then that covenant will run with the land for the benefit of his successors in title, persons deriving title under him or them and other owners and occupiers.

The section will allow covenants to be automatically annexed by virtue of s78 unless there is a contrary intention as discussed below. There is no necessity for the successors in title to be even aware that they have the benefit of such a covenant annexed to their land.

There are criticisms of this approach. They centre on the fact that Brightman LJ's decision seems to run contrary to all the previous decisions on the running of covenants. In particular, how could a section that had been on the statute book for over 50 years suddenly transform the whole law on restrictive covenants?

Consider the following comments:

'Annexation was always considered to be a matter of intention ... There is not a word in any earlier case to suggest that annexation could come about without the parties intending to bring it about, and the conventional rules had been accepted universally by practitioners until November 1979, whatever the date of the covenant. Further, it was repeatedly held, from *Renals v Cowlishaw* [(1879) LR 11 Ch D 866] onwards, that the presence of words referring to successors of the covenantee was not of itself sufficient to effect annexation. Such words had been added by the Conveyancing Act 1881 s 58 and still did not of themselves effect annexation, but the Court of Appeal concluded in the *Federated Homes* case, that the change of wording between s 58 of the Conveyancing Act 1881, and its successor s 78 of the Law of Property Act 1925, necessarily made this drastic change, a change unsuspected from 1926, when apparently it occurred, until the end of 1979 … The Act of 1925 was a consolidating Act and it would be decidedly odd if a change of such far-reaching importance was to be made by such an Act.'

> C H S Preston and G H Newsom, *Preston and Newsom's Restrictive Covenants affecting Freehold Land* (9th edn, Sweet & Maxwell, 2009), p. 17

Subsequent cases have considered the effect of the decision in *Federated Homes v Mill Lodge Properties Ltd* (1980) and revisited the effect of s 78 LPA 1925 and refined its use in the following ways:

1. *Roake v Chadha* [1984] 1 WLR 40: if **there is an express contrary intention** shown in the conveyance expressly restricting the passing of the benefit to successors in title then s 78 will not automatically annex a covenant to land. The wording in this case was that the covenant was expressed 'not to enure for the benefit of any owner or subsequent purchaser of the … estate unless the benefit of the covenant shall be expressly assigned'. It was held that the covenant did not relate to the land and was not therefore annexed to it. In *Holland Park Management v Hicks* [2013] EWHC 39 (Ch) a covenant which had used the words 'as only benefitting assigns' was not sufficient to show a contrary intention.

2. **The conveyance must be construed in the light of all the circumstances**: *Sainsbury (J) v Enfield London Borough Council* [1989] 1 WLR 590. In this case the covenants had been undertaken before the 1925 Act had been passed so the 1881 Conveyancing Act applied. It was accepted that the wording of the 1881 Act was far more narrow and could not allow the benefit of the covenants to automatically run.

3. *Crest Nicholson Ltd v McAllister* [2004] 1 WLR 2409: suggests that **annexation under s 78 will only be in respect of the land of the covenantee which is intended to be benefited**. The conveyance will need to be construed as a whole in order to identify what land is intended to be benefited. Land was sold off in separate plots by two brothers in Surrey between 1928 and 1936. Each conveyance included a covenant restricting the purchaser to not more than one house per plot but no land was specifically identified. A purchaser of land, Mr McAllister, tried to argue that covenants that had been entered into when land had originally been split into the separate parcels could be enforced by him. The judge found that the benefit of the covenant preventing building was only for the benefit of the original parties and had not been annexed to the land. He said:

JUDGMENT

'It may be a case where the parties to the instrument make clear their intention that land retained by the covenantee at the time of the conveyance effected by the transfer is to have the benefit of the covenant only for so long as it continues to be in ownership of the original covenantee and not after it has been sold on by the original covenantee.'

Chadwick LJ

He explains the potential ambiguity in the words 'the land of the covenantee intended to be benefited' and shows that it must mean, **first**, so much of the retained land as from time to time has not been sold off by the original covenantee; and, **second**, so much of the retained land has been sold off with the benefit of an express assignment but not as including, **third**, so much of the land as has been sold off without the benefit of an express assignment.

A useful comment is made in *Megarry & Wade* to explain Chadwick LJ's approach:

> 'Chadwick LJ was bolstered in his view by the desire to ensure that a person inspecting the register of title should be able to determine the benefited land by inspection of the register rather than having to engage in a wider search for the person entitled to enforce the covenant. Although this does not seem an overpowering argument, and one might argue that Chadwick LJ is wrong to equate the need for land to be easily identifiable with a requirement that this can be done only by words in the conveyance, this more limited interpretation must be regarded as definitive.'
>
> C Harpum, S Bridge and M Dixon (eds), *Megarry & Wade: The Law of Real Property* (8th edn, Sweet & Maxwell, 2012), p. 1410

More recently in *Bryant Homes Southern Ltd v Stein Management* [2016] EWHC 2435 it was held that a covenant registered at the land registry was enforceable against the vendor's successors in title where it touched and concerned the land in spite of the fact that the vendor had entered into a separate personal agreement to release the covenant, and in spite of the fact that the covenantee's successor in title retained only a part of the original land.

4. **Statutory annexation will not take place where it is clear that the covenants had only been intended to enable the original owner to have control whilst owner of the land**. *Sugarman v Porter* [2006] 2 P & CR 274 reinforces the reasoning in *Crest Nicholson*. Here land had been sold in separate parcels. The claimant had purchased directly from the original owner and sought a declaration that the benefit of a covenant limiting the number of houses to be built would not pass unless they were expressly assigned with the conveyance. The claimant wanted to build eight self-contained apartments. The court held that it was plain that the covenants had been intended to enable the original owner to have control so long as she was the owner of the land. Once she ceased to be owner of the land the benefit of the covenant ceased to be annexed to that land unless it was expressly assigned. As the land had all been sold and there was no express assignment, the benefit of the covenant could not be impliedly claimed.

ACTIVITY

Applying the law

Sandra owns a plot of land on which she builds herself a house. She divides the remaining land into two building plots, selling one to Tanya and the other to Ursula who each build themselves a house. When Sandra sells her house to Vera, Vera wants to know if she can claim the benefit of any covenants agreed between Sandra and Tanya and Ursula.

Advise Vera.

In your advice to Vera you would need to consider the exact wording of the original covenants. If the wording was such that it showed an intention to benefit each and every part of the land including the house sold to Vera and there was no intention shown to only benefit the parties at the time of the agreement then Vera can claim that the benefit has passed to her on purchase. You need to refer to Chadwick LJ's judgment in *Crest Nicholson* in your advice.

Note the case of *Small v Oliver & Saunders (Developments) Ltd* [2006] EWHC 1293 (Ch) which confirms that there is a presumption independent of s78 LPA 1925 that an annexed covenant endures for the benefit of each part of the original covenantee's land and is enforceable by several purchasers when the land is split up.

It is also dependent on the landowner owning land before sale that carries the benefit of the covenant and the purchaser must also own land after sale; the covenant cannot be assigned in isolation.

The impact of s78 in the context of restrictive covenants is even more wide ranging because of the inclusion of mere occupiers within its scope, so that a restrictive covenant may be enforced by a licensee of the dominant tenement.

11.3.2 Assignment

The decision of *Federated Homes v Mill Lodge Properties Ltd* (1980) has resulted in assignment also becoming far less important as a way of transferring the benefit of a covenant to successors in title of the original covenantee.

There may be reasons why the benefit of a covenant has not been annexed to the dominant land, for example the original covenant may provide that the benefit can only be passed by express assignment. In these cases the benefit must pass to a successor in title by express assignment.

The difference between **annexation** and **assignment** is that **assignment** will only take place when the land is transferred by a person who enjoys the benefit of the land. **Annexation** is effected the moment that the covenant is granted.

At common law, the assignment of a covenant must satisfy the requirements of s136 LPA 1925.

In equity, these conditions must be satisfied:

1. The covenant that is assigned must be capable of benefiting the dominant land.
2. The dominant land must be 'ascertainable' or 'certain'.
3. The assignment must have taken place contemporaneously with the transfer of the dominant land so that it is actually part of the transaction.

The effect of assignment is that the assignee is entitled to enforce the covenant against the covenantor or his successors in title if it is restrictive.

11.3.3 Building schemes

The third way that the benefit of a covenant may pass in equity is where land is under a building scheme. Every owner of the land carrying the benefit will be able to enforce the covenants if he can show that the benefit runs to him. He will be able to enforce against the other owners who in turn will be able to enforce against him. This is a separate way of proving that the benefit of a covenant has passed to a successor in title of a covenantee. There is a problem in most building schemes with the gradual sale of plots of land leaving no plot able to enforce as a covenantee but all owners of the other plots carrying the burden of the covenant. Where there is a building scheme special rules apply to address this issue.

What is a building scheme?

In *Elliston v Reacher* [1908] 2 Ch 374 a building scheme was defined as

> 'a local law for the area over which it extends and has the practical effect of rendering each purchaser and his successors in title subject to the restrictions and of conferring upon them the benefits of the scheme, as between themselves and all other purchasers and their respective successors in title.'

What this means is that each owner of property within the area gets the right to enforce the individual covenants as covenantees and they themselves are also subject to the covenants as covenantors.

Common vendor

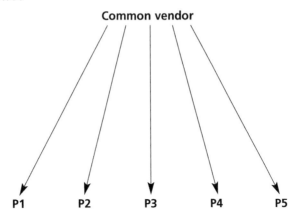

Figure 11.3 Purchasers from a common vendor

There were **four** requirements laid down in *Elliston v Reacher* (1908) before the covenants could be enforced:

1. Both the claimant and the defendant must have derived title from a common owner.
2. The common vendor must have laid out a definite scheme of development, prior to the sale of the plots now owned by the claimant and defendant.
3. There must have been an intention to impose not only on the purchasers of land within the development, but also on their successors in title, a scheme of mutually enforceable restrictions.
4. Every purchaser must have bought his land in full knowledge of the scheme, and with an intention to be bound by its mutually enforceable restrictions.

A **fifth** requirement was added in *Reid v Bickerstaff* (1909). The area to which the scheme extends must be clearly defined.

In more recent cases the courts have tended to relax these requirements. In *Baxter v Four Oaks Properties Ltd* [1965] 1 Ch 816 a building scheme was upheld although the vendor had not divided the property into lots but had left it to each purchaser to purchase a lot of the size required. Stamp J relaxed the requirements further in *Re Dolphins Conveyance* [1970] Ch 654. He held the requirements set down in earlier cases to be no more than indications of a common intention and they were based on the wider rule that there must simply be evidence of a common intention. He laid down the most important feature as being 'the common intention to lay down a local law involving reciprocal rights and obligations between several purchasers' and upheld a scheme where there was no common vendor and the land was not laid out in predetermined lots.

In *Jamaica Mutual Life Assurance Society v Hillsborough Ltd* [1989] 1 WLR 1101 the Privy Council upheld the need for just two requirements:

i. There must be an identifiable scheme.
ii. There must be a mutually perceived common intention.

Lord Jauncey said 'the essence of a scheme of development is reciprocity of obligations'.

The value of building schemes enables restrictive covenants to run which would otherwise be defeated either because one of the essential requirements of running the burden cannot be satisfied when the developers sells the last plot or, having sold the last plot, he has no interest in enforcing the covenants.

It also ensures that the benefit of the covenants imposed on other plots will automatically run to all successors of the original purchasers without the need for express annexation or for assignment.

Building schemes can also involve more than one developer so long as they have mutually enforceable obligations between them, e.g. two developers own adjoining fields. They decide to develop their fields building two houses each. The houses could then form part of a scheme of development in spite of the fact that the houses are built by two different people. It depends on whether the neighbours enter into an agreement that some obligations will be enforceable between the neighbours. If so, then the scheme of development will allow each owner of the new houses to enforce against the other owners.

In *Birdlip v Hunter* [2016] EWCA Civ 603 the claimants Mr and Mrs Hunter failed to establish that the right to enforce a covenant had passed to them under a building scheme. The developers Birdlip wanted to build two extra houses on a plot on which a single house had been built in about 1910 when a series of covenants had been imposed on the land. The relevant covenant: 'not to build more than one dwelling' was one of a number of restrictions imposed when the land was originally sold off by the common vendor. Surrounding land had also been sold off by the common vendor with similar (though not always identical) covenants. Birdlip had planning permission for its intended development, but the Hunters, whose land adjoined Birdlip's, objected to the development. For various reasons the Hunters could not rely on annexation nor on assignment. This left them with proving that there was a building scheme. There was some evidence of a scheme, such as the fact that between 1906 and 1914 the common vendor had sold off numbered plots each containing similar restrictions and evidence from plans at the time that the land had been split into lots. However, an obstacle for the Hunters was that the 1910 conveyance referred only in the most general terms to an 'agreement' preceding the conveyance and the conveyance plan identified only the plot being sold and gave no clue as to the geographical extent of any defined estate area. The Hunters failed because they could not show that at the time of the division of the land there had been a clear intention to establish a building scheme under which all the owners could enforce their rights.

A key feature of a building scheme continues to be whether there had been an initial scheme of development. This is illustrated in *Whitgift Homes v Stocks* [2001] EWCA Civ 1732 where a building scheme was rejected because although a building scheme may have been envisaged at the initial start of the development there was an underlying uncertainty about the extent of land that was covered by the scheme.

11.3.4 The running of the burden in equity

The key feature of covenants in equity is not the running of the benefit, which can of course run at common law, but the upholding of certain burdens in favour of successors in title. The rules can be traced back to the nineteenth century. It is significant that this was at a time when land was being developed particularly in the larger cities. This principle was initially introduced by the decision in *Tulk v Moxhay* (1848) 2 Ph 774 a case which concerns the development of a well-known part of London, Leicester Square.

CASE EXAMPLE

Tulk v Moxhay (1848) 2 Ph 774

The claimant sold an area of open land in Leicester Square to the covenantor who covenanted on behalf of himself, his heirs and assigns to keep the land 'in an open state, uncovered with any buildings, in neat and ornamental order'. The covenantor subsequently sold the land to the defendant who had notice of the covenants although it was not included in the conveyance. The defendant tried to build on the garden area in the centre of the square. An injunction was granted in favour of the claimant to prevent the defendant from building on the land.
Lord Cottenham LC asked the question:

JUDGMENT

'[W]hether a party shall be permitted to use the land in a manner inconsistent with the contract entered into by his vendor, and with notice of which he purchased. Of course, the price would be affected by the covenant, and nothing could be more inequitable than that the original purchaser should be able to sell the property the next day for a greater price, in consideration of the assignee being allowed to escape from the liability which he had himself undertaken.'

Lord Cottenham LC

The rule in Tulk v Moxhay

The principle established by Lord Cottenham LC is now known as 'the rule in *Tulk v Moxhay*'. The rule has gradually evolved over the years and its application is subject to **four** conditions:

1. **The covenant must be negative in nature.** The rule will not allow positive covenants to be enforced. The distinction was addressed in *Haywood v Brunswick Permanent Building Society* (1881) 8 QBD 403 which declared that the rule in *Tulk v Moxhay* would not apply to positive covenants. The issue of whether a covenant is positive or negative always involves a question of substance. Cotton LJ defined the positive covenant as 'requiring the covenantor to put his hand into his pocket'. Note the more recent case of *Norwich City Council of Further Education v McQuillin* (2009) where a college was claiming that certain covenants no longer applied to land that it owned. One of the covenants entered into by a predecessor in title was that the owners of the land would erect a wall or fence. This could not be enforced partly because it was a positive covenant and also because it was shown that it was never intended to bind future owners of the land because the wording was such that it was only to take effect for the benefit of the land whilst it remained unsold. More recently in *In Holland Park Management v Hicks* [2013] EWHC 39 (Ch) a covenant that required a neighbour to agree to any future planning application was held to be negative in nature since it could be construed as preventing future development if consent was withheld.

2. **The covenantee must, at the date of the covenant, have owned land benefited by the covenant which can be identified.** There can be no restrictive covenant where the covenantee does not own land. There cannot be a covenant 'in gross' as there can be at law. The well-known case of *LCC v Allen* [1914] 3 KB 642 illustrates this point. There was a covenant between the Council and a builder who agreed not to build on a certain plot of land but the Council never owned any land to be benefited

from the covenant. This requirement would cause difficulties for housing developments but for the special rules for building schemes. The area of land to benefit must also be sufficiently close to the land carrying the burden for the covenant to apply. 'Land at Clapham would be too remote and unable to carry a right to enforce ... covenants in respect of ... land at Hampstead' (*Kelly v Barrett* [1924] 2 Ch 379). The main exception to this rule is the scheme of development. There are also statutory exceptions where a local planning authority which could not argue that it owned any land specifically to benefit from a covenant could still have the power to enter into a covenant with a developer because it wanted to preserve the character of neighbouring land.

3. **The covenant must benefit the dominant tenement, i.e. it must 'touch and concern' the land.** The nature of the covenant must be such that it benefits the land itself and not the owner. A benefit in this context would be anything that affects either the value of the land or the method of its occupation or enjoyment.

4. **The burden of the covenant must have been intended to run with the land of the covenantor.** Since the Law of Property Act 1925, the effect of s 79 is such that it will be assumed that it will be intended that the burden of the covenant will run unless the contrary is expressed. *Morrells of Oxford Ltd v Oxford United Football Club Ltd* (2001) highlights that a contrary intention can be inferred from the difference in the wording of other covenants in the same deed. Morrells sought an injunction to enforce a restrictive covenant that was contained in a conveyance of land against the Oxford Football Club, which intended to use the land as a football stadium with leisure facilities. The covenant had been contained in a conveyance of 1962 and had prohibited the building of licensed premises within half a mile of the public house which had been the object of the original conveyance. The claimants relied on s 79 LPA 1925 and argued that the covenant could be presumed to bind successors in title to the land unless a contrary intention was expressed. The Court of Appeal held that to impose s 79 of the Act would be to read words into the instrument. Other covenants within the conveyance made it clear that successors should be bound, and the absence of such words in the clause in question showed a contrary intention. So the covenant relied on here was personal in nature and could not be enforced against successors in title.

11.3.5 Notice of the covenant

The burden of a covenant can pass in equity so long as all four requirements of the rule are satisfied and the purchaser has notice of it. The purchaser will have notice if the right has been registered correctly. Under the Land Registration Act 2002 s 29(1) the covenant will take effect as an interest requiring protection on the Register and must be entered by way of notice against the title of the covenantor's land. The notice will be entered on the Charges Register. This will usually be by an agreed notice but in the event of a dispute between the parties it may be by way of unilateral notice.

In unregistered land the covenant must be registered as a Class D II land charge entered on the Land Charges Register at Plymouth.

Note that failure to register will render the covenant unenforceable; this is even in cases where the purchaser has actual notice. So a purchaser would not be bound where he knows about a covenant before buying the property but when he checks the Register it has not been entered on the Register by the vendor.

ACTIVITY

Applying the law

Mr Brown owns Hazel Lodge which is a pre-fabricated house built in 1947. It has a large plot of land. He decides to knock down the house and build himself a new house and to split the land into two further plots which he intends to sell. They share a large lawn and each has a right to use it for recreation. Mrs Green buys Plot 1 and Miss Black buys Plot 2 and in each conveyance there are the following covenants:

- not to use the property for any trade, profession or business;
- not to allow the garden of the property to become overgrown;
- to contribute to the upkeep of the common lawn area.

Miss Black does not like the area and sells to Mr Wierd who runs a business as an acupuncturist from his house. He has let the garden become overgrown because he says he likes wild gardens. He is refusing to contribute to the upkeep of the lawn which is overrun by moles. Advise Mr Brown as to whether he has any rights against Mr Wierd.

11.4 Breach of covenants and the consequences

If a covenant is broken then the covenantee or his successors can claim a remedy.

In most cases the burden of the covenant will only run in equity so the remedy sought will lie in equity. This means that the remedy will be subject to equitable principles, for example the various maxims of equity, e.g. delay will defeat a claim. If the claimant has taken no action for years, the court will not award a remedy.

The remedy is also discretionary and the claimant may still find that even after the case against the defendant has been proved, he is without a remedy.

The court may also grant an order for specific performance in the case of a breach of a positive covenant.

The court generally has a choice of damages or an injunction. It will grant an injunction where the breach has not been carried out. It is up to the court to decide in each case on the facts how much to award in damages for the breach of an injunction (*Gafford v Graham* (1998) 77 P & CR 73).

Damages or an injunction?

The following questions will be asked:

1. Has there been a blatant disregard of the claimant's rights?
2. Is the injury to the claimant's legal rights small?
3. Can the damage be estimated in money and can it adequately be compensated by a small money payment?
4. Will it be oppressive to the defendant to grant an injunction?

The court can award damages in lieu of an injunction but will not do so unless there are exceptional circumstances. The circumstances in which such an award is made has recently been revisited in the case of *Coventry v Lawrence* [2014] UKSC 13. This is discussed below. The courts have rarely ordered the demolition of property where there has been a breach of covenant. This is in sharp contrast to cases where there has been an order for demolition of property where there has been a breach of planning regulations.

CASE EXAMPLE

Wakeham v Wood (1982) 43 P & CR 40 CA

The defendant had flagrantly breached a covenant against building in a way that would obstruct a view of the sea.

The Court of Appeal granted the plaintiffs a mandatory injunction to remove the building and Waller LJ expressed the opinion that the value of a view could not be expressed in monetary terms and therefore could not be compensated by a small money payment. (N.B. The building was a single room summer house.)

More recently the courts ordered the demolition of an extension to a house in breach of a restrictive covenant, *Mortimer v Bailey* [2005] 2 P & CR 9. This was in spite of the fact that the building had been completed and no attempt had been made to prevent the building by seeking an interim injunction.

CASE EXAMPLE

Wrotham Park Estates Co Ltd v Parkside Homes Ltd [1974] 1 WLR 798

A number of houses had been built in breach of a restrictive covenant. Brightman J refused to order a mandatory injunction to pull the houses down. Instead he awarded monetary compensation. He based his decision on the fact that people now lived in these houses. He said that to demolish the houses would be 'an unpardonable waste of much needed houses to direct that they be pulled down'. The amount awarded was based on what reasonably might have been expected for release of the covenant which amounted to 5 per cent of the defendant's profits on the houses which had been built.

It could however be argued that a more appropriate award would be to award damages on the basis of 'unjust enrichment'. This would be based on what the developer has gained from ignoring the covenant.

CASE EXAMPLE

Jaggard v Sawyer [1995] 1 WLR 269

Damages were awarded for breach of a covenant preventing building development on the land. The failure to award an injunction was explained by the court on the basis that in many cases there is no protection at all for proprietary rights and so the claimant must be contented with damages. The amount in this case was calculated on the basis of what sum the covenantee could have reasonably expected to receive for the release of the covenant.

The courts have frequently been reluctant to grant an injunction for the breach of a covenant and tend towards an award of damages. Cases where an injunction may be awarded are where there is a blatant and calculated disregard of the claimant's rights.

The principles guiding the courts as to whether or not to grant an injunction or award damages are taken from *Shelfer v City of London Electric Lighting Co* (1895). Smith LJ held that damages should be awarded instead of an injunction where:

i. the injury to the plaintiff's legal rights is small;

ii. it is capable of being estimated in monetary terms;

iii. it is one that can be adequately compensated by a small money payment;

iv. the case is one in which it would be oppressive to the defendant to grant an injunction – then damages in substitution for an injunction may be given.

The Supreme Court reviewed these criteria in the recent case of *Coventry v Lawrence* [2014] UKSC 13. Although this case concerned an easement and a nuisance claim the principles from the judgments in this case are also applicable to the law on restrictive covenants. Lord Neuberger reasserted that the court had discretion in such cases which should not be unduly fettered by the principles of *Shelfer*. He held that the prima facie position is that an injunction should be granted and it is for the defendant to show why it should not. He advocated the adoption of a more modified approach where: first, the application of the four tests should not be seen as a fetter on the court's discretion; second, where there are no additional relevant circumstances it must be right to refuse to grant an injunction where the four tests are satisfied; third, where the tests are not all satisfied it does not mean that an injunction must be granted. It is anticipated that the question of whether the grant of an injunction will be oppressive to the defendant will remain the key issue.

ACTIVITY

Applying the law

Three years ago, Ophelia purchased a large rectory with several acres of garden. The property had a restrictive covenant created in 1980 in favour of the owners of adjoining properties and their successors in title. The covenant prohibited building in the grounds of the Rectory. Last month, Ophelia obtained planning permission to build a block of flats in the orchard of the Rectory. The owners of the adjoining properties, Gertrude and Polonius, have both threatened to seek an injunction to prevent the building in breach of the covenant. Gertrude is concerned that the building will prevent her house and garden from having sunshine in the afternoon and evening. Her house does not get the benefit of a view of the surrounding countryside but she is able to enjoy views when she walks 100 metres down the road. This view will be lost when the flats are built.

Can Ophelia build the flats without fear from her neighbours claiming breach of covenant and what remedy will they be likely to get if they successfully sue for breach of covenant?

In this problem, consider whether the benefit of the covenant has passed to Gertrude and Polonius. Can you argue that it has been annexed to their titles? The burden cannot pass to Ophelia at common law but it can pass to her under the rules of equity under *Tulk v Moxhay* (1848). Consider whether the necessary conditions apply here.

11.5 Discharge and modification of restrictive covenants

There is no express limit for a covenant. It will continue to affect land until it is discharged or modified. However, it is clear that covenants will often cease to be relevant and may hinder the landowner's enjoyment of land rather than enhance it. It may be difficult to sell land which is bound by a number of covenants. The Law of Property Act 1925 includes special provision to cover modification and discharge of covenants.

11.5.1 Section 84 of the Law of Property Act 1925

An application to discharge or modify a restrictive covenant may be made to the Lands Tribunal under s 84 of the 1925 Act. The grounds include that the restrictive covenant impedes some reasonable use of the land and is contrary to the public interest. If the tribunal agrees to discharge or modify the covenant, compensation may be ordered to be paid.

The applicant must bring his case within the following statutory grounds:

1. **Obsolete**: 'that by reason of changes in the character of the property or the neighbourhood or other circumstances of the case ... the restriction ought to be deemed obsolete'.

2. **Obstruction**: 'that the continued existence thereof would impede [some reasonable user] of the land for public or private purposes ... or as the case may be, would unless modified so impede such user'.

3. **Agreement**: 'that the persons of full age and capacity for the time being or from time to time entitled to the benefit of the restriction, whether in respect of estates in fee simple or any lesser estates or interests in the property to which the benefit of the restriction is annexed, have agreed, either expressly or by implication, by their acts or omissions, to the same being discharged or modified'.

4. **No injury caused**: 'that the proposed discharge or modification will not injure the persons entitled to the benefit of the restriction'.

The fact that planning permission has already been granted for a development does not mean that the Lands Tribunal will automatically discharge a covenant.

A restrictive covenant cannot be enforced if the character of the neighbourhood has been so altered since the covenant was entered into that it is now of no value to the claimant and it would be inequitable and senseless to enforce it.

A restrictive covenant will automatically be extinguished once the burdened and benefited land comes into common ownership and occupation.

An application can be made for both freehold as well as leasehold land if it is a long lease of over 40 years and at least 25 have expired.

Once the terms of a restrictive covenant have been modified or the covenant has been discharged, this must be noted on the Register.

The Law Commission commented in 1984 on the complex nature of the provisions of s 84(1) and observed that they are unnecessarily complex and difficult to interpret. It proposed that when the Land Tribunal exercised its jurisdiction it should seek to give effect to the purpose for which the restriction or other interest in land was imposed. The Tribunal should be able to discharge or modify the restriction or interest on certain grounds including that modification would not cause substantial injury to the person entitled to the benefit of the restriction, or would allow the land to be put to a use that is in the public interest where there is no other appropriate land, and the person losing the right could be adequately compensated in money. The Law Commission also recommended that obsoleteness should cease to be a ground for discharge.

In the case of *Re Ben Lynch* [2016] UKUT 488 (LC) 23 November 2016, the objectors in this case applied for the modification of a restrictive covenant, following the grant of planning permission, under s 84 LPA 1925. The applicants wished to build more than one house on what would have been one of the original lots. The objectors were successful in resisting the modification on grounds s 84(1)(a) LPA 1925, i.e. it could not be shown to be obsolete but the restrictive covenant was modified under s 84(1)(aa) as impeding a reasonable use of the land, namely the implementation of a planning permission which is sufficiently controlled by conditions to adequately protect the amenity of the immediately neighbouring objectors.

11.6 Proposals for reform

'The Law Commission has been working away at the problems posed by restrictive covenants since 1967. In its reports on the Law of Positive and Restrictive Covenants in 1984 it proposed that restrictive covenants should be replaced by a system of land obligation. This obligation would have the characteristics that it would be a new interest in land capable of subsisting as a legal interest so that it bound the person who owned the land from time to time and benefited the owner for the time being of the dominant land ... although the current report is entitled "Obsolete Restrictive Covenants" the Law Commission does not limit its recommendations to them. There is no clear distinction between those which are obsolete and those which are not. They all require to be examined on a conveyance of the property and on title registration. The Registrar has no discretion to omit mention of them whether or not they may be considered obsolete. Application to the Lands Tribunal for discharge or modification is not a practical course of action in most cases and insurance against the possibility of claims is most often an expense which fortunately sees little return.'

H W Wilkinson, 'Nothing to Lose but your Fetters: Obsolete
Restrictive Covenants' [1992] *Conv* 2

11.6.1 What are the main problems with the law on restrictive covenants?

The 1984 Law Commission report on the law of positive and restrictive covenants outlines the main problems with the law at present:

'The burden of a restrictive covenant does not run at all at law, but it does run in equity if certain complicated criteria are met. The benefit by contrast runs at law and in equity but according to rules which are different. These rules are if anything more complicated than the rules about the burden and some of them are particularly technical and hard to grasp; as examples one may cite those about annexation and those about building schemes.'

Law Commission, 'Transfer of Land: The Law of Positive and
Restrictive Covenants' (Law Com No 127, 1984)

The thrust of its proposals is that covenants should be replaced by land obligations. These would be subject to rules similar to those applying to easements. The land obligation would take effect in law and would bind successors in title. The important difference would be that after sale the original parties would lose their contractual rights and obligations. This would destroy the present continuing contractual obligation of the original covenantor. Since the original covenantor loses any control over the property it has never made sense to force him to remain liable on the property that he once owned and over which he once entered into a covenant. The new scheme would make no distinction between positive and negative covenants.

The more recent consultation paper from the Law Commission 'Easements, Covenants and *Profits à Prendre*' (Consultation Paper No 186, March 2008) again proposed that restrictive covenants should become 'land obligations'. The land obligation must 'touch and concern' the land in the same way as restrictive covenants. They would include both positive and negative covenants and would rely on entry on the Register for their enforceability against both the covenantee's land and the convenantor's land. Once entered on the Register these obligations would bind all persons with any estate or interest in the land and the benefit would run with every part of the land and would pass when the land was later divided into parcels. Such obligations would take effect in law as opposed to equity and would therefore require an amendment of the Law of Property Act 1925. It also proposed that the original parties would cease to be able to enforce a covenant or be liable for a covenant once they had sold the land. Existing covenants would continue to take effect and would be subject to the old rules. A final report was published by the Law Commission in 2011. It included a draft Bill which proposed the introduction of land obligations and other proposals mentioned above.

There is far more optimism than previously that these proposals will become law over the next few years although the government has not yet acted on the proposals. The result would be a much clearer and simplified set of rules relating to the enforcement of covenants.

SUMMARY

1. A restrictive covenant is an obligation entered into by deed which affects the use and enjoyment of land of one landowner in favour of a third party.
2. The rules of covenants at law and in equity differ.
3. Common law will allow the benefit of a covenant to pass to another owner of a legal estate under certain conditions but will never allow the burden to pass.
4. There are a number of ways that exceptionally the burden of a covenant can be enforced at law, including the rule of mutual burden and benefit and the enlargement of the interest from a leasehold into a freehold and a chain of indemnity covenants.
5. The original covenantor will always remain liable for any burden under a covenant even after he has moved away from the property.
6. Under the rule in *Tulk v Moxhay* equity allows the burden of restrictive covenants to pass if certain conditions apply.
7. The benefit of a covenant can pass in equity either under annexation, assignment or a scheme of development if certain conditions apply.
8. The benefit of most covenants pass both at law and in equity under s 78 Law of Property Act 1925.
9. The remedy for breach of a restrictive covenant will be governed by equitable principles and damages may be more appropriate.
10. An application can be made to the Land Tribunal to modify or discharge a covenant that has become outdated.

SAMPLE ESSAY QUESTION

'For over 100 years it has been clear and accepted law that equity will enforce negative covenants against freehold land but has no power to enforce positive covenants against successors in title of the land … To enforce a positive covenant would be to enforce a personal obligation against a person who has not covenanted. To enforce a negative covenant is only to treat the land as subject to a restriction.'

Lord Templeman in *Rhone v Stephens* [1994] 2 AC 310

Critically discuss this description of the law of covenants.

> Definition of a covenant: a restrictive covenant is an obligation entered into by deed which affects the use and enjoyment of land of one landowner in favour of a third party.
>
> Difference between rules concerning covenants in law and in equity. The perceived problem in allowing burdens to run against a person who was not a party to the original covenant.

Covenants at law: brief discussion of the running of the benefit.

General discussion of the running of the burden at law and the strict rule under *Austerberry v Oldham Corporation* (1885).

Discuss modern attempt to modify the rule: *Rhone v Stephens*. Discuss facts.

Analyse judgment of Lord Templeman and discuss views and refusal to enforce the covenant.

Discuss ways of circumventing the rule in *Austerberry v Oldham Corporation*.

Rule in *Halsall v Brizell*: doctrine of benefit and burden.

Discuss limits on the rule as shown in *Thamesmead v Allotey*. Doctrine only available if:

i. there is a connection between the burden and the benefit taken by the successor in title to the covenantor;

ii. there must be an opportunity to choose whether to take the benefit or not.

Discuss the chain of indemnity covenants. Explain the drawbacks to the chain of indemnity covenants.

Discuss the other ways that the burden of a covenant may run: long leasehold.

Critically analyse the limits of all ways of circumventing the rule.

Discuss the running of burdens in equity.

State the rule in *Tulk v Moxhay* and explain its limitations.

Can never allow the burden of a positive covenant to run.

Discuss possible reform of the rule.

Law Commission proposals in 1984.

Discuss Law Commission recent proposals in 2008.

Enforcement of land obligations:

i. both positive and negative obligations will be enforceable;

ii. all land obligations will be entered on both registers;

iii. limitation on what rights could take effect as a land obligation.

CONCLUSION

Further reading

Books

Gray, K and Gray, S F, *Elements of Land Law* (5th edn, Oxford University Press, 2009) p. 252.

Preston, S and Newsom, G, *Restrictive Covenants affecting Freehold Land* (9th edn, Sweet & Maxwell, 1998).

Rainey, P, Walsh, M, Harrison, P and Dovar, D (eds), *Megarry's Manual of the Law of Real Property* (9th edn, Sweet & Maxwell, 2014).

Articles

Bannister, E and Jackson, D, 'Past their Sell-By Date?' [2006] 177 *PLJ* 16.

Bevan, C, 'The Doctrine of Benefit and Burden: Reforming the Law of Covenants and the Numerus Clausus "Problem"' [2018] 77(1) *CLJ* 72.

Cash, A, 'Freehold Covenants and the Potential Flaws in the Law Commission's 2011 Reform Proposals' [2017] 3 *Conv* 212.

Colby, A, 'Positive Thinking' [2013] 1314 *EG* 85.

Cooke, E, 'To Restate or Not to Restate? Old Wine, New Wineskins, Old Covenants, New Ideas' [2009] *Conv* 448.

Francis, A, 'Construing Covenant Chaos' [2007] 157(7259) *NLJ* 206.

Gravells, N P, 'Enforcement of Positive Covenants affecting Freehold Land' (note on *Rhone v Stephens*) (1994) 110 *LQR* 346.

Hayton, D, 'Revolution in Restrictive Covenant Law?' (1980) 43 *MLR* 445.

Kenny, P, 'Drafting and Enforcing Restrictive Covenants' [2006] 70 *Conv* 1.

Martin, J, 'Remedies for Breach of Restrictive Covenants' [1996] 60 *Conv* 329.

Nurston, G, 'Universal Annexation' (1981) 97 *LQR* 32.

Todd, P, 'Annexation after Federated Homes' [1985] *Conv* 177.

Turano, L, 's 79 Law of Property Act 1925' [2000] 64 *Conv* 377.

Walsh, E and Morris, C, 'Enforcing Positive Covenants: A Practical Perspective' [2015] 4 *Conv* 316.

Wilkinson, H W, 'Nothing to Lose but your Fetters: Obsolete Restrictive Covenants' [1992] *Conv* 2.

Williams, A, 'A Thorny Issue' [2014] 318 *PLJ* 26.

Law Commission Report

'Easements, Covenants and *Profits à Prendre*' (Law Com CP No 186, 2008).

12

Mortgages

AIMS AND OBJECTIVES

After reading this chapter, you should be able to:

- Explain what is meant by a mortgage
- Trace the development of mortgages through history
- Compare a mortgage and a charge
- Compare an equitable mortgage and a legal mortgage
- Describe the protection given to the mortgagor
- Describe the rights of the mortgagee
- Understand the basic principles of priority of mortgages

12.1 Introduction

A mortgage is one of the most important interests in land. In essence, a mortgage is a form of security interest in land which will guarantee the amount of a loan made so the mortgagee has confidence that he will be able to recover his money. Today, mortgages provide a means by which people are able to purchase their homes and raise cash for improvements and commercial ventures.

It is rare that a purchaser of property has sufficient capital to finance the purchase from savings. Most people will have to borrow funds but a mortgagee will be unwilling to lend money without a substantial security. The security will ensure that the mortgagee has an asset to claim if the mortgagor fails to repay the money borrowed.

Imagine two people, Darren and Anne, who wish to purchase a house together. Darren has been given £30,000 from his parents and was left £25,000 by his granny when she died last year. Anne has been saving from her job as a dental hygienist. She has saved £5,200 over three years. Together they have £60,200 which is enough for a deposit on a house but is far too little to purchase property. They see a house – 12 Station Terrace, with two bedrooms and a small garden – for £190,000, which they want to buy. They approach the Helping Hands Building Society which agrees to lend them the money. If Darren and Anne get into financial difficulties the Building

Society can sue them for the outstanding money that it has lent them. If the Building Society has a mortgage over the house in Station Terrace then it can recover its money from any monies received on the sale of the house.

12.1.1 Definition of a 'mortgage'

A mortgage is a transaction whereby property, either land or personal property, is given as security for the repayment of money borrowed. Normally the security used is real property, in particular a house, but it can also be personal property such as a valuable piece of jewellery.

CASE EXAMPLE

Bradley v Carritt [1903] AC 253

In this case the owner of shares in a tea company mortgaged the shares to raise capital.

12.1.2 What is a mortgage?

The borrower, called the **mortgagor**, grants the lender, called the **mortgagee**, a mortgage over his property. The effect of this is that the mortgagee has rights in the property which can be realised if the mortgagor defaults in repayment. If the borrower runs into debt and cannot repay the sum borrowed, the mortgagee has a number of remedies claiming possession of the property and forcing a sale and so recovering the sum borrowed from the proceeds of sale.

mortgagor
The borrower

mortgagee
The lender

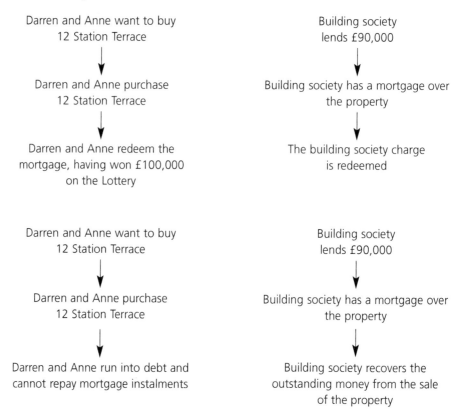

Figure 12.1 Recovery of sum borrowed under a mortgage

There is a difference between a mortgage and a charge. Under a mortgage the mortgagee gains rights in the property whereas under a charge the chargee only gets rights against the property. There is a subtle difference between the two.

A mortgage	A mortgage is a legal or equitable interest in land granted to the mortgagee as a security for the payment of a debt subject to the mortgagor's right of redemption.
A charge	A charge attaches to the land of the mortgagor and gives rights over the land but does not convey a legal or equitable interest in the mortgaged land to the chargee.

Table 12.1 The difference between a mortgage and a charge over property

The true value of the mortgage is the assurance that, in the event of the mortgagor having no money to repay the loan, there will be an asset which allows the mortgagee to claim rights over property and which will allow the mortgagee to realise the full amount that he has loaned. Without the asset the mortgagee carries the risk that the mortgagor will become insolvent before he has repaid the loan and then the mortgagee will become one of the creditors of the mortgagor and is unlikely to recover the whole of the sum lent.

The use of a mortgage also means that someone who needs money, either because they are setting up a new business or because they want to buy property, will be more likely to be able to persuade someone to lend them the money.

> 'The advantage of such real security is that, even if the borrower becomes insolvent, the lender, as a secured creditor, will take priority over the general unsecured creditors of the borrower and can demand that the specific property be sold and that the loan be repaid from the proceeds of sale.'
>
> N Gravells, *Land Law: Text and Materials* (4th edn, Sweet & Maxwell, 2012), p. 891

12.2 The development of mortgages at common law and in equity

12.2.1 Mortgages at common law

Historically the common law did not recognise a mortgage. Lending money at a fixed rate of interest was forbidden. The mortgagor's rights were not enforceable in common law courts. This often had a disastrous effect on the rights of the mortgagor. It is a fact of commercial life that a person running a business will want to borrow money at some stage, so other ways of raising capital arose.

The original mortgage took the form of a conveyance of the property. The mortgagee literally became the owner of the property and the mortgagor did not recover rights in the property until the loan had been repaid. At common law the mortgagee owned the property but the mortgagor had the chance to recover his property. This had to be on a particular day at a particular time, as stipulated in the contract. This was called the legal right to redeem and was based on the contractual agreement between the parties. If the mortgagor did not repay the money on the correct day, the property could be claimed by the mortgagee as his own. This could be worth much more than the actual sum owed.

An example of an early mortgage of land

Edwin wants to raise money on his property, The Old Manor, Broghampton, in Wessex. Felix lends money to Edwin on 12 January 1514. Edwin conveys his interest in The Old Manor to Felix and he agrees to re-convey the property back to Edwin on 11 January 1534.

On 11 January 1534 Edwin takes the full sum to Felix but he has left the country and is nowhere to be found.

On 12 January 1534 Felix now owns The Old Manor, without being encumbered by a mortgage in favour of Edwin. Edwin has now been dispossessed of his property and he has lost the chance to redeem the mortgage.

There was no point in Edwin taking the case to the common law courts because his rights would not be recognised. The only chance of recovering his property would have been to take the case to the courts of equity and to ask the King to use his discretion to recognise his rights in the property. The mortgage was one of the earliest rights recognised by equity and in many cases the mortgagor's right to repay the loan and thereby recover his land was upheld.

Under common law the mortgagor still has a contractual right to redeem the mortgage on the date agreed in the mortgage contract. However, the intervention of equity allowed the mortgagor to redeem the mortgage on a later date after the legal date for redemption has passed.

12.2.2 Mortgages in equity

The equity of redemption

The equity of redemption described the bundle of rights that a mortgagor retained in the property used for the security of the loan. These are rights recognised by equity but not common law. The rights go beyond the right to redeem the mortgage. Today the equity of redemption has become a separate proprietary right in property and has a value of its own and can be transferred to others or sold. The equity of redemption arises as soon as the mortgage is created.

The position at common law

Under the common law the mortgagee of capital would become the owner of the mortgagor's property subject to the mortgage. It gave the mortgagee rights, including the right to sell the property, and the mortgagee was also able to claim any income which arose from the property while the mortgage was in existence. These rights would last until the mortgagor repaid the mortgage.

Under the common law there was only one day on which repayment could take place and so discharge the mortgage from the land. Repayment had to be on the day laid down in the mortgage deed. This was called the 'legal date of redemption'. If there was a delay, the right to redeem was lost. So if the mortgagor was just one day late, the land was lost and yet the mortgagor was still liable for the debt.

Mortgagors felt aggrieved by the common law rule, especially when it was not their fault that they were unable to repay the loan. The mortgagor may have deliberately made himself unavailable for repayment. The result would be that the mortgagor lost his property although the amount borrowed might be worth just a fraction of the total value of the property.

12.2.3 The equitable right to redeem

What does this mean? The 'equitable right to redeem' allows the mortgagor to redeem after the legal date for repayment has passed. It is at the heart of the law on mortgages. It means that any mortgagor who fails to pay on the legal date for redemption retains the right to redeem. Therefore he could ignore the date set out in the mortgage deed and repay whenever it was convenient, so long as the legal date for redemption under the contract had passed. Equity would uphold the rights of the mortgagor to have the right to redeem his property at any time on any day. This remains one of the core features of a mortgage today.

Initially, this was only allowed in special circumstances:

1. The mortgagor was unable to repay because he had had an accident and physically was unable to repay the money.

2. The mortgagor was unable to repay because he had made a mistake about the date of repayment or who was owed the money.

3. The mortgagor could prove special hardship.

Later, redemption was allowed in all cases, whatever the circumstances, so long as the debt was repaid by the mortgagor. The right to redeem was a right in the property so it could be enforced against a third-party purchaser.

Gerald owned Limestone Hall. He needed to borrow some money to fund the marriage of his daughter, Ophelia. He borrowed some money from an acquaintance, Harold, and Limestone Hall was conveyed to Harold. The date for repayment was 10 April 1673. He failed to repay on 10 April but offered to repay on 24 May 1673. Equity recognised Gerald's right to repay on the later date and Gerald could recover his property.

If Harold sold his property to James then the rights of Gerald would be unaffected. Gerald could still redeem the property either on 10 April or later on 24 May since the right to redeem would be seen as a proprietary right in the property and James would have been bound so long as he had notice of Gerald's rights.

The legal right to redeem	Could only be exercised on the date stipulated in the mortgage deed.	A legal right arising under contract.	Exercisable as of right.	Arises on the legal date for redemption.
The equitable right to redeem	Could be exercised any time after the stipulated day for repayment.	A right recognised in equity.	Exercised on terms that are considered to be just by the courts of equity.	Arises after the contractual date for redemption has passed.

Table 12.2 The legal right to redeem and the equitable right to redeem compared

The legal date for redemption became less important since the mortgagor could rely on his rights in equity to allow redemption at any time. Later, the date stipulated as the legal date for redemption was always fixed very early, for example six months after the mortgage. Of course, there was no real expectation that the loan would be repaid on that date. Once this date was passed, the mortgagee had a right under contract to call in the loan and if the money was not forthcoming then he had the right to take proceedings. However, the mortgagor would not be worried as equity would protect him against a request for repayment on the date agreed in the mortgage deed.

Equity also allowed the mortgagor the right to any income derived from the property while the mortgagee was in occupation. This reduced the advantage for the mortgagee to occupy the property.

So the nature of a mortgage changed and the mortgagor would remain in the property and there was no question that the mortgagee would move into the property. The property was now seen simply as security for the loan.

What rights arise under the equity of redemption?

The equity of redemption arose as soon as the mortgage was created. It was itself a right in property and it could be dealt with in several ways:

1. It could be conveyed to another.

2. It could be leased.

3. It could be devised/left to someone by will.

4. It could even be mortgaged itself.

KEY FACTS

The development of mortgages in equity
1. Mortgages were initially not recognised at all by common law.
2. Early mortgages took the form of leases or conveyances of the fee simple to the mortgagee who took possession of the property.
3. At common law the loan could only be repaid on the specified day, called the legal date for redemption.
4. Failure to repay the loan on the date stipulated in the deed meant that the mortgagor lost all rights over the property.
5. Equity recognised the rights of the mortgagor to repay on a later date, called the equity of redemption.
6. Equity gave the mortgagor an equitable right to redeem which allowed him to redeem after the contractual date for repayment had passed.
7. The right was recognised as an interest in the property itself which could be sold, leased or left to someone by will.

12.3 The creation of mortgages

The law on mortgages can be defined into three distinct periods. The law before 1925, the law after 1925 and the law post-2002, reflecting changes made in the Land Registration Act 2002.

12.3.1 Before 1925

Before 1925, a legal mortgage of freehold land was created by conveying the fee simple estate to the mortgagee. This included a covenant for re-conveyance on redemption of the mortgage. The mortgagee then became legal owner of the mortgaged property. Eventually, equity accepted that the mortgagor retained the right to redeem after the date for repayment had passed.

12.3.2 Post-1925

Under s 85 of the Law of Property Act 1925, conveyance and re-conveyance were made impossible. Under the 1925 Act two methods for the creation of mortgages were recognised:

1. a **demise** for a term of years absolute, subject to a provision for cesser on redemption; or

2. a charge by deed expressed to be by way of legal mortgage.

Both types of mortgage had to be created by deed.

> **demise**
> The transfer of property to another by lease or under a will

1. **Demise for a term of years absolute**: this involved creating a long lease, usually for 3,000 years, over the land which would cease as soon as the loan was repaid. The mortgagee would not have the legal estate conveyed to him and the mortgagor was expressly given the right to remain in the property. The mortgagor had the right to take further mortgages which meant that there could be several mortgages over one property although the mortgagor might find it increasingly difficult to persuade anyone to lend him money, on the basis that the rights of a second mortgagee would be secondary to those of a first mortgagee.

2. **A charge by deed expressed to be by way of legal mortgage**: this is governed by s 87 of the 1925 Act. Under this form of mortgage there is no conveyance of any estate in the property to the mortgagee. The mortgagee merely gets a charge over the land giving him rights which attach to the property. However, the charge gives the mortgagee certain rights over the property as if he had an interest in it. The mortgagee has the right to enforce covenants and he is able to create tenancies. This became the main way of creating mortgages and the demise was rarely used.

The advantage of using the legal charge is that it is short and expressed in simple terms. It is now the only way to mortgage a registered title.

12.3.3 Post-2002

Under s 23(1)(a) of the Land Registration Act 2002 the only way that a mortgage of registered land can be created is by registered charge. The law on the creation of mortgages will eventually be substantially affected by the introduction of electronic conveyancing as envisaged in the Act under s 91. This is because the mortgage will come into legal effect at the same time as it is created. The introduction of the digital mortgage for remortgages by the Land Registry in 2018 is changing the way mortgages are registered. It removes the need for paper signatures and allows borrowers to sign a mortgage deed digitally online. Registration is still carried out by the Land Registry, but the actual creation of the mortgage is different. This system will eventually be used for all mortgages, including those obtained for a first purchase, and it will take the conveyancing process one step closer to electronic conveyancing.

Charges by way of legal mortgage must be created by deed to satisfy s 52 LPA 1925. The legal mortgage is regarded as a conveyance of land and will trigger the overreaching provisions, as seen in *City of London v Flegg* (1988). It must also state that it is intended to take effect as a charge by legal mortgage.

Under the 2002 Act the mortgage only takes effect in law when it is entered on to the title of the registered land.

SECTION

'...

's 27(1) If a disposition of a registered estate or registered charge is required to be completed by registration, it does not operate at law until the relevant registration requirements are met.

(2) In the case of a registered estate, the following are the dispositions which are required to be completed by registration – ...

(f) the grant of a legal charge.'

Failure to complete the legal charge by registration will have the effect that the mortgage will not take effect in law only in equity.

CASE EXAMPLE
....

Barclays Bank Plc v Zaroovabli [1997] 2 All ER 19

A bank failed to register a charge as required under law. Under the charge there was a prohibition on leases by the mortgagor. In spite of the prohibition the mortgagor granted a lease to a tenant for six months. The tenant then acquired a statutory tenancy under the Rent Act 1977.

The Court of Appeal held that the lease was binding on the bank and took priority. The bank had failed to register the charge when it had been created.

A different result was reached in *Halifax Plc v Curry Popeck (A Firm)* [2008] EWHC 1692. The case concerned two mortgages taken out over a single property, but because of the intervention of fraudsters were taken out over a strip of land of little value. The first mortgage made in favour of the Halifax Plc took effect as an estoppel in their favour as a result of the fraud. The loan was not properly registered as required by the 2002 Act. The second mortgage was in favour of the Bank of Scotland, but again it was only for the strip of land as opposed to the property. The repayments were not made and both Halifax Plc and the Bank of Scotland claimed priority. Usually a mortgage loses priority if it has not been registered but in this case the second mortgage was not a transaction for valuable consideration as required under s 29 and so Halifax Plc did not lose priority in spite of a failure to register.

12.3.4 Creating equitable mortgages

There are three main ways that an equitable mortgage can be created:

1. A **contract** to create a mortgage: equity will treat a contract to create a mortgage as an enforceable mortgage if it satisfies s 2 of the Law of Property (Miscellaneous Provisions) Act 1989:

SECTION

> 's 2 . . . A contract for sale or other disposition of an interest in land can only be made in writing by incorporating all the terms which the parties have expressly agreed in one document or, where contracts are exchanged, in each.'

This means that the contract to create a mortgage must be in writing. **Before 1989** it was possible to have an enforceable equitable mortgage where it was supported by some evidence in writing or there were acts of part-performance.

The document must:

- be in writing;
- be signed by both parties;
- contain all terms.

The parties may have accidentally created an equitable mortgage because they intended to create a legal mortgage by deed and they failed to satisfy the formalities necessary for a deed, such as having the signatures witnessed. An equitable mortgage will also arise where the mortgage has been created by deed but registration has not been formally completed at the Land Registry.

2. An equitable mortgage created by the **deposit of title deeds**: before 1989 it was possible to deposit title deeds in unregistered land with the lender and that would create a mortgage. This method had its merits as it was possible to create a short-term mortgage without having to comply with strict formalities. The intention to create a mortgage had to be proved.

CASE EXAMPLE

Russel v Russel (1783) 1 Bro CC 269

This case recognised this method of creating equitable mortgages. It was assumed that there could also be a mortgage by depositing a land certificate. The requirement for a written contract for the disposition of an interest in land under the 1989 Act should have made this method impossible but there was still some doubt after the Act was passed.

CASE EXAMPLE

United Bank of Kuwait v Sahib [1997] Ch 107

This case makes it clear that this type of mortgage cannot be created unless there is some writing which satisfies s 2 of the 1989 Act, otherwise this will be seen as an attempt to create a mortgage by unwritten contract. The 2002 Act has removed any doubt in relation to registered land because land certificates will no longer be used and without a certificate to deposit it would be impossible to create mortgages in this way as there would be no documentary proof of ownership of the land.

3. Mortgages of **equitable interests**: the mortgagor may only have an equitable estate in property because he is an equitable owner behind a trust. In such a case he can only create an equitable mortgage: 'the mortgagor can mortgage only that which he owns'. The mortgage is created by transferring the whole of the interest to the mortgagee with a provision for re-transfer of the interest once the debt has been repaid. There are formalities to be satisfied. The transfer must satisfy s 53(1)(c) of the Law of Property Act 1925 which requires that the transfer should be in writing. Failure to satisfy this requirement will result in the mortgage being void.

12.3.5 Equitable charges

An equitable charge is a completely informal way of creating a mortgage over property. There are no specific formalities to satisfy but there must be an intention to charge the property with a debt.

CASE EXAMPLE

National Provincial and Union Bank of England v Charnley [1924] 1 KB 431

This case upholds the need for there to be an intention for the property to be so charged for the charge to take effect.

Because of this uncertainty, it is rare to use an equitable charge in either a commercial or domestic mortgage. It is also vital that anyone holding an equitable charge or mortgage protects the right by registration.

ACTIVITY

Self-assessment questions

In the following examples, are the mortgages legal or equitable?

1. Kenneth is borrowing £20,000 from his friend, Donald. They draw up a document which creates a charge in favour of Donald over Kenneth's house, Clematis Cottage. Kenneth and Donald both sign the document.
2. Gloria runs a mail order company for dog accessories and wishes to raise money. She borrows money from her sister and the solicitor draws up the terms in a document which Gloria signs. The secretary agrees to sign also.
3. Selina has contributed to the purchase of Trimley House but she is not registered as owner. She wants to raise some cash to fund a trip around the world and she borrows from her friend Sally who signs a document which creates a charge in her favour over Trimley House. Selina's next-door neighbour signs the document.

Both examples in questions (1) and (2) could potentially be legal mortgages. However in example (1) the mortgage is not created by deed because there is no signature so although this is potentially a legal mortgage it can only take effect in equity. The secretary signs the document in example (2) so once this is entered on to the Register it can take effect in law. There cannot be a legal mortgage in example (3) because Selina is not the legal owner so any mortgage will take effect in equity only. The formalities required for s 53(1)(c) have been satisfied so this can take effect as a legal charge.

12.4 Protection for the mortgagor

The rights of the mortgagor are a combination of rights derived from the contract and rights arising because of the proprietary nature of the rights.

The mortgagor is protected under the law in a number of different ways:

1. the mortgagor retains **an equity of redemption**;
2. **no collateral advantages** for the mortgagee;
3. a mortgage will be set aside if it has been obtained through **undue influence** or **oppression**;
4. **unlawful credit bargains will not be recognised**.

12.4.1 The equity of redemption

This describes all the rights of the mortgagor that arise in the land as soon as the mortgage is executed. It includes the legal rights enforceable in the common law courts as well as the equitable rights arising in equity. It covers not just the right to redeem the mortgage, but also all that bundle of rights protecting the mortgagor from exploitation by the mortgagee. A mortgage cannot be made irredeemable and it cannot be limited by the terms of the mortgage deed so that it can only be redeemed by certain persons or for a limited time.

JUDGMENT

'[T]he mortgagor is entitled to get his property as free as he gave it, on payment of principal, interest, and costs, and provisions inconsistent with that right cannot be enforced. The equitable rules "once a mortgage always a mortgage", and that the mortgagee cannot impose any "clog or fetter on the equity of redemption" are merely concise statements of the same rules.'

Walker LJ in *Browne v Ryan* [1901] 2 LR 653

This principle extends to all types of transactions which can be described as mortgages. If the law regards the relationship as one of mortgagee and mortgagor then the court will protect the equity of redemption in a way that would not be accorded to an ordinary contractual relationship of debtor and creditor.

If the right to redeem is merely postponed then the mortgage will be upheld so long as there is still a genuine right to redeem.

CASE EXAMPLE

Knightsbridge Estates Trust Ltd v Byrne [1939] Ch 441

Redemption of a commercial mortgage was postponed for 40 years. The mortgagor argued that the period was unreasonable. In fact he wished to redeem the mortgage early in order to borrow the money at a cheaper rate from someone else. It was held that so long as the date of redemption is genuine and not a sham, it will be upheld. There were good reasons in the case why the date of redemption was postponed for so long (the rate of interest was reduced and also the repayments were spread over a long period of time to accommodate the mortgagor). These terms had been negotiated at arm's length and the judge held that there was no requirement for the mortgage to be reasonable.

'But equity does not reform mortgage transactions because they are unreasonable. It is concerned to see two things – one that the essential requirements of a mortgage transaction are observed, and the other that oppressive or unconscionable terms are not enforced. Subject to this, it does not, in our opinion, interfere.'

Sir Wilfred Greene MR

Compare the following cases:

CASE EXAMPLE

Fairclough v Swan Brewery Co Ltd [1912] AC 565

The date for redemption of a 20-year mortgage was postponed to just six weeks before the end of the mortgage term. The court upheld the claim by the mortgagor that he could redeem at an earlier date. The actual term made the right to redeem illusory.

The upholding of the right to redeem is applied very strictly by the courts even where, on the facts, it seems to be unfair.

A provision within a mortgage giving the mortgagee an option to purchase the property is void. The mere fact that such a provision has been included within the mortgage agreement is sufficient to raise the presumption that it offends the equitable right to redeem.

CASE EXAMPLE

Samuel v Jarrah Timber and Wood Paving Corporation Ltd [1904] AC 323

The mortgagee was given the option to purchase the property of the mortgagor within a year of the date of the loan secured by the mortgage. When the mortgagee sought to exercise this option, the mortgagor challenged on the basis that the term excluded the mortgagor's equity of redemption.

The House of Lords declared the term to be illegal and void. However, it was reluctant to do so. The agreement was negotiated fairly and at arm's length and the parties were both fully aware of the terms. The court was not able to change the rules but would have liked the opportunity to do so.

'Speaking for myself, I should not be sorry if your Lordships could see your way to modify it so as to prevent its being used as a means of evading a fair bargain come between persons dealing at arm's length and negotiating on equal terms. The directors of a trading company in search of financial assistance are certainly in a very different position from that of an impecunious landowner in the toils of a crafty money-lender.'

Lord Macnaghten

Where a mortgagee is granted an option to purchase in an agreement outside the mortgage then this will be upheld so the key issue in many cases is whether the term is within the mortgage. The court will decide whether an agreement is a mortgage by deciding on the substance of an agreement rather than the particular label or name given by the parties to the agreement. The courts have found that even where there appears to be two separate agreements it will be considered to be part of the mortgage whereas where it can be shown that the two agreements are separate the option to purchase will be upheld. The cases discussed below illustrate these points.

However, the principle that there must be no clog on the equity of redemption still persists in spite of some criticism by the judiciary.

JUDGMENT

'[T]he doctrine of a clog on the equity of redemption is, so it seems to me, an appendix to our law which no longer serves a useful purpose and would be better excised.'

Phillips MR in *Jones v Morgan* (2001)

CASE EXAMPLE

Lewis v Frank Love Ltd [1961] 1 WLR 261

An option to purchase the mortgaged property was included in a separate document but it was drawn up contemporaneously on the same day with the mortgage deed. The court held there to be a clog or fetter on the equity of redemption and refused to uphold the term.

You will note above that the fact that there were two documents was held to be less important and here the court regarded the agreement as one single and undivided contract rather than two distinct contracts.

CASE EXAMPLE

Jones v Morgan [2001] EWCA Civ 995

Morgan and his brother used some land as security for a loan from Jones. Morgan intended to develop this land. The loan was later varied and included a term whereby Morgan agreed to transfer to Jones a one-half interest in the property for which Jones did not pay any sum. When Morgan did not transfer the interest Jones claimed an order for specific performance. The Court of Appeal dismissed the claim partly on the grounds that the agreement was a clog on the equity of redemption. The fact that the agreement to transfer the share was made three years after the mortgage had been agreed did not prevent the provision from being viewed as part of the mortgage.

CASE EXAMPLE

Warmborough Ltd v Garmite Ltd [2003] EWCA Civ 1544

W sold land to G and left the purchase money on mortgage in favour of G with a provision at the time of purchase that W had an option to repurchase the land for the original sale price. G argued that the option to repurchase was 'a clog on the equity of redemption'. The court found that the substance of the transaction was a sale and purchase and not a mortgage and therefore the rule against 'clogs' did not apply and the sale could go ahead.

If the mortgagor agrees to sell the land to the mortgagee as a completely separate transaction then such a sale will be upheld.

12.4.2 The mortgagor is protected from the mortgagee gaining any collateral advantages

Equity developed other ways of protecting the mortgagor. If the mortgage deed contained a term which prevented the mortgagors from redeeming the mortgage for another reason, this term would be void.

There must be no clog or fetter on the mortgagor's equity of redemption.

The rights of the mortgagee were limited to the return of the loan, the interest and costs; and any attempt to get an extra benefit from the mortgagor was struck down by the courts.

However, the courts have been less strict on collateral terms in more recent years.

> 'it used to be thought that all collateral advantages bargained by a mortgagee were rigorously and automatically struck down by the courts. However modern courts have had less occasion (and probably less desire) to apply the same censure to mortgage terms and collateral advantages which would have attracted the displeasure of judges of an earlier generation. Distaste for the self-serving preferences of the grasping mortgagee – once considered more a feature of Victorian mortgage deeds than of today's standard form high street mortgage transaction – has long ago relaxed into a simple prohibition of those collateral advantages which are excessive and oppressive.'
>
> K Gray and S F Gray, *Elements of Land Law* (5th edn, Oxford University Press, 2009), p. 728

A collateral advantage which ceased when the mortgage was redeemed could be upheld. It was seen as a term of the contract and this did not affect the right of the mortgagor to redeem the loan.

CASE EXAMPLE

Biggs v Hoddinot [1898] 2 Ch 307

The property subject to the mortgage was a public house. The mortgage deed included a term that the mortgagors would buy all their beer from the lenders during the subsistence of the mortgage. The covenant was held to be separate from the term allowing the mortgagors to redeem the mortgage.

Compare the following case:

CASE EXAMPLE

Noakes & Co Ltd v Rice [1902] AC 24

The mortgage included a covenant to purchase beer from the lender even after the mortgage had been redeemed. The court refused to enforce the term after the mortgage had been redeemed, relying on the principle 'once a mortgage, always a mortgage and nothing but a mortgage'. The meaning of that is that the mortgagee shall not make any stipulation which will prevent a mortgagor, who has paid principal, interest and costs, from getting back his mortgaged property in the condition in which he parted with it.

The judge, Lord Davey added: 'When the mortgage is paid off the security is at an end, and, as the mortgagee is no longer kept out of his money, the remuneration to him for the use of his money is also at an end.'

CASE EXAMPLE

Bradley v Carritt [1903] AC 253

A similar decision was reached when the mortgagee stipulated that the mortgagor should continue to use the services of the mortgagee as tea broker even after the sum borrowed had been repaid. The House of Lords held this to be a fetter on the equity of redemption. However, there was a strong dissenting judgment from Lord Lindley:

'I cannot bring myself to believe that it is part of the law of this country that mortgagors and mortgagees cannot make what bargains they like with each other so long as such bargains are not inconsistent with the right of the mortgagor to redeem the property mortgaged by discharging the debt or obligation to secure which the mortgage was effected.'

The reason Lord Lindley dissented was because he thought that there was no connection between the right of the mortgagor to redeem the mortgage and the right of the mortgagee to enforce the covenant. There was no question in *Bradley v Carritt* (1903) that the mortgagor could not redeem the mortgage on the date stipulated. The term would simply be separate from the mortgage.

The courts later upheld the right to enforce the terms of the collateral agreement even after the mortgage had been repaid.

CASE EXAMPLE

Kreglinger v New Patagonia Meat and Cold Storage Co Ltd [1914] AC 25

The mortgagor agreed with the mortgagee that for five years their sheep skins would be offered to the mortgagee. When the mortgage was redeemed two years later, the mortgagor claimed that they were no longer bound to sell the skins to the mortgagees. The court upheld the original agreement. The mortgage was seen as a commercial transaction. The parties were negotiating at arm's length and neither party was put under any pressure so in this case there was no necessity for the court to intervene. The important issue was whether the term affected the mortgagor's right to redeem and whether the collateral agreement was outside the mortgage transaction.

Three principles emerge from Lord Parker's judgment in *Kreglinger v New Patagonia Meat and Cold Storage Co Ltd* (1914). A collateral advantage will be struck out in the following circumstances:

1. the term is unfair and unconscionable;
2. the term is in the nature of a penalty clogging the equity of redemption; or
3. the term is inconsistent with or repugnant to the contractual and equitable right to redeem.

CASE EXAMPLE

Re Petrol Filling Station, Vauxhall Bridge Road, London (1969) 20 P & CR 1

An agreement that the mortgagor, who was a garage owner, would purchase petrol from the lender, a petrol company, was held to be enforceable even after the repayment of the debt. Ungoed-Thomas held that the agreement to buy petrol from the mortgagees was separate from the loan and so did not present a fetter or clog on redemption.

It is not always as easy to separate the collateral advantage from the terms of the mortgage, as they may appear to be part and parcel of one transaction.

Modern cases and restraint of trade

The modern cases on collateral advantages are more likely to be challenged on the basis of restraint of trade which is a principle arising out of contract law rather than from the law on mortgages.

The law of contract has long held that an agreement which operates unreasonably in restraint of trade will be held to be void on the ground of public policy.

CASE EXAMPLE

Esso Petroleum Co Ltd v Harper's Garage (Stourport) Ltd [1968] AC 269

Under the terms of the mortgage deed over the mortgagor's garage the garage agreed to sell only the mortgagee's petrol for 21 years. The mortgage had to be redeemed over a period of 21 years. The court considered whether the term was in restraint of trade and held that it should be struck down because it was excessively long. If it had been for a shorter period of time, such as five years, it would have been upheld.

It is up to the court to decide whether an agreement takes effect as a mortgage or not.

Case	Decision	Comment
Biggs v Hoddinott (1898)	A collateral advantage can be upheld so long as it ends when the mortgage comes to an end.	The mortgagees could enjoy the additional advantage of the covenant as well as the repayment of the capital and the interest.
Noakes & Co v Rice (1902)	Any collateral terms in the mortgage deed must come to an end when the mortgage is redeemed, even if the mortgage allows them to continue.	'[O]nce a mortgage, always a mortgage and nothing but a mortgage' (Lord Davey).
Bradley v Carritt (1903)	A collateral advantage which continued after the mortgage ended was unenforceable.	In this case there was a strong dissenting judgment from Lord Lindley who thought the term should be upheld.
Kreglinger v New Patagonia Meat and Cold Storage Co Ltd (1914); see also *Re Petrol Filling Station, Vauxhall Bridge Road, London* (1969)	A collateral advantage lasting after the mortgage has been redeemed will be upheld if it is fair and does not clog the equity of redemption and is not inconsistent with the right to redeem the mortgage.	*Kreglinger* marked a turning point in the law on collateral advantages in mortgages because it allowed such terms to continue after the mortgage has been redeemed.

Table 12.3 Cases on whether collateral advantages can be upheld as part of the terms of a mortgage

12.4.3 A mortgage will be set aside if it has been obtained through undue influence or oppression

A mortgage can be set aside or the terms modified where there is evidence of undue influence or misrepresentation. A mortgagor can be pressurised by the mortgagee in such a way that the transaction that he enters is not from his own free will, for example the terms may be particularly favourable to the mortgagee because the mortgagor is so desperate for money that he is willing to accept very unfavourable terms.

What constitutes undue influence?

Equity has always sought to protect the weaker of two parties from oppression and from exploitation. In the context of a mortgage, equity will seek to intervene where the mortgage terms are oppressive. There are several important developments in this area.

Undue influence can be in **two different forms**:

1. **Actual** undue influence: this means that you could rely on evidence of actual undue influence or pressure put on the mortgagor by the mortgagee or a third party. Examples of this would be actual threats of violence from a husband towards a wife if she refused to agree to sign a mortgage deed.

2. **Presumed** undue influence: this means that the relationship of the parties is one where one party is assumed to be more powerful than the other and so they could easily take advantage of this position to put pressure on the other side in negotiations.

Undue influence was defined in *Bank of Credit and Commerce International SA v Aboody* [1990] 1 QB 923 as follows:

- **Class 1: actual undue influence.** This is where the claimant must prove that undue influence was actually exerted by the wrongdoer. In these cases there is no necessity to show that the transaction operated to the claimant's manifest disadvantage. This requirement was removed by *CIBC Mortgages v Pitt* [1994] 1 AC 200. However, it would add weight to the mortgagor's case if it were shown that the transaction was manifestly disadvantageous to the claimant.

- **Class 2: presumed undue influence.** This is where the claimant can show that there was a relationship of trust and confidence between the parties of such a nature that it is fair to presume that the trust and confidence of the claimant were abused. Once the claimant can establish the existence of the relationship of trust and confidence, the burden of proof then shifts to the alleged wrongdoer to rebut the presumption of undue influence, and to prove that the transaction was entered into freely.

Presumed undue influence can be further sub-divided into two groups:

- **Class 2A** covers **specific relationships**, for example solicitor and client, medical adviser and patient, and parent and child. It does not cover husband and wife. There may be equality between the parties or there may be inequality. It will depend on the particular relationship. These cases are relatively rare.

- **Class 2B** covers relationships where undue influence would **not automatically be presumed** from the nature of the relationship itself but may arise because **one party placed so much trust in the other** that the presumption would arise. Most of the cases that have arisen in recent years have been in this category.

These further definitions come from the judgment of Lord Browne-Wilkinson in *Barclays Bank v O'Brien* [1994] 1 AC 180 and also *Royal Bank of Scotland v Etridge (No 2)* [2001] UKHL 44 which are considered in detail below.

Class 1: actual undue influence	Claimant must prove that the wrongdoer actually exerted undue influence.	
Class 2: presumed undue influence	Claimant must prove that there was a relationship of trust between the parties.	*BCCI SA v Aboody* (1990)
Class 2A: relationships where undue influence is presumed	Relationship is one where undue influence is presumed because of the nature of the relationship itself, e.g. solicitor and client. Husband and wife are excluded from this group.	*Langton v Langton* [1995] 2 FLR 890 *Allcard v Skinner* (1887)
Class 2B: relationships where undue influence is presumed because of a specific relationship between the parties	Relationship itself does not give rise to undue influence but it can apply, depending on the actual relationship.	*Barclays Bank v O'Brien* (1994); *Royal Bank of Scotland v Etridge (No 2)* [2001]; *Thompson v Foy* [2009] (no undue influence by daughter over her mother)

Table 12.4 Different types of undue influence

ACTIVITY

Applying the law

Consider the following transactions and decide whether they are affected by undue influence and, if so, what type of undue influence applies:

1. Mr and Mrs Charlesworth own Langley Ridge, a large house in Hendon. They have one son, Ronald, who lives with them. He runs his own business, a specialist travel firm. Recently it has run into difficulties. He needs to raise some cash quickly and he asks his parents to stand surety for his debts. The mortgage company will only do so if it gets a charge over his parent's house; he tells his parents that the house is safe from the mortgage company.
2. Freddy Spendthrift persuades his partner, Alice Thrifty, to allow him to use her property as surety for a loan that he takes out with Barclays Bank. She does not want to do so but he says if she does not agree he will leave her, so, reluctantly, she agrees to what he asks.

There have been two landmark decisions which have clarified the law on what constitutes undue influence in a mortgage transaction. *Barclays Bank v O'Brien* [1994] 1 AC 180 and *Royal Bank of Scotland v Etridge (No 2)* [2001] UKHL 44. These cases also make it clear when a mortgage transaction will be tainted with undue influence and can therefore be set aside. It is a difficult area of law and usually depends on the individual facts of any case.

CASE EXAMPLE

Barclays Bank plc v O'Brien [1994] 1 AC 180

Mrs O'Brien signed a legal charge over the co-owned matrimonial home as security for her husband's debts. The bank did not explain the contents of the mortgage documents to her when they were signed and did not advise her to obtain independent legal advice and she did not read the documents before signing them. Mrs O'Brien relied on her husband's false representation that the security was limited to £60,000 and covered just a short-term loan for three weeks while the house was remortgaged. Once the overdraft exceeded the loan, the bank sought an order for possession of the property. Mrs O'Brien then sought to set aside the mortgage transaction on the ground that she signed the documents under undue influence and misrepresentation. It was held that the mortgage had been obtained either by her husband's misrepresentation or because of his undue influence over her and the court ordered it to be set aside.

Lord Browne-Wilkinson sought to bring the law up to date to show that there remains a need for the concept of undue influence even though there is a greater degree of equality between the sexes.

JUDGMENT

'although the concept of the ignorant wife leaving all financial decisions to the husband is outmoded, the practice does not yet coincide with the ideal. In a substantial proportion of marriages it is still the husband who has the business experience and the wife is willing to follow his advice without bringing a truly independent mind and will to bear on financial decisions. The number of recent cases in this field shows that in practice many wives are still subjected to, and yield to, undue influence by their husbands. Such wives can reasonably look to the law for some protection when their husbands have abused the trust and confidence reposed in them.'

In the cases that followed *O'Brien* a variety of approaches was taken by the court and it was clear that the law was still in need of clarification. Most of these difficulties are addressed by the later case of *Etridge* which has to a large extent now clarified the approach to be taken in cases of undue influence.

CASE EXAMPLE

Royal Bank of Scotland v Etridge (No 2) [2001] 3 WLR 102

The case concerned the rights of wives in eight different claims, who had each entered into charges over their matrimonial home. The principal judgment was given by Lord Nicholls.

Overall, the decision reduces the threshold for liability for mortgagees in a number of ways. Lord Nicholls highlighted several areas where liability may arise.

Summary of the main points raised by Lord Nicholls:

1. He accepted that undue influence is covered by a large number of situations wherever there is abuse as well as exploitation of trust and confidence, reliance or dependency reposed in another; there are no longer special categories of relationship; he concluded that the division of cases into Class 2A and Class 2B presumed undue influence was not useful.
2. An inference of undue influence can arise whatever the relationship.
3. In some relationships trust and confidence must be proven and in others it is assumed.
4. The burden of proof shifts to the other party where trust and confidence or dependency has been reposed in them and also that the transaction cannot readily be explained by their relationship.
5. In cases of actual undue influence there is no necessity to prove manifest disadvantage; where undue influence is inferred, then manifest disadvantage must be shown.

In order for a claim to be made, the claimant must prove actual or presumed undue influence. Further the bank will be put on inquiry whenever one person stands as a surety for another unless the surety is offered commercial advice. *Etridge* clarifies the point that it is the fact that one person is lending to another that is significant here and as a result the bank has a duty to inquire about the circumstances and whether undue influence played a part in the transaction.

Where a claimant relies on **presumed undue influence** then the first point that must be established is that there is a relationship of trust and confidence. Once this is established then the burden of proof will shift from the claimant or victim to the person alleged to have 'influenced' or pressurised the victim.

In order to discharge the burden of proof the alleged wrongdoer must explain the transaction and show that, in the circumstances, it would have taken place in any event and was not as a result of any pressure or persuasion. It must also be shown that the transaction was not manifestly disadvantageous to the victim.

Steps where victim wishes to rely on undue influence

Actual undue influence.	(i) No requirement to prove relationship of trust and confidence. (ii) Must prove facts of undue influence. Manifest disadvantage does not have to be proved. Victim can rely on the fact that he/she has entered into a transaction as a result of pressure or a threat.
Presumed undue influence Class A under *Barclays Bank v O'Brien*. Presumed undue influence Class B under *Barclays Bank v O'Brien*.	(i) Must prove relationship of trust and confidence. (ii) Once relationship proved burden of proof shifts to the 'influencer' who must prove that the transaction was not of manifest disadvantage.

Lord Nicholls considered the core duties that **a bank or any mortgagee will owe to the claimant** who enters into a transaction as surety for another and concluded as follows:

1. A bank or any financial institution lending money should take steps to ensure that the claimant receives legal advice by asking for the name of the claimant's legal adviser.
2. The meeting should contain certain core advice, for example the nature of the liability of someone standing as surety, the fact that their home is at risk and the wife should be urged to take legal advice and the name of the legal adviser should be given to the bank or building society.
3. Where the claimant is advised by a solicitor, the legal advice should also contain certain core elements such as the nature of the transaction and its implications and the seriousness of the risk and the fact that the wife has a choice in the matter.
4. The mortgagee has a duty to inform the solicitor of any concerns that it has over whether the consent is genuine.
5. The legal adviser can act for both the husband and also for the wife.
6. The bank will not be acting as the agent of the husband so it is assumed that the advice given is given properly.

JUDGMENT

'The furthest the bank can be expected to go is to take reasonable steps to satisfy itself that the wife has had brought home to her, in a meaningful way, the practical implications of the proposed transaction. This does not wholly eliminate the risk of undue influence or misrepresentation. But it does mean that a wife enters into a transaction with her eyes open so far as the basic elements of the transaction are concerned.'

Lord Nicholls

The effect of this decision could be that the risks are now carried by the solicitor rather than the lending institution which can now discharge its liability fairly easily. In *HSBC v Brown* [2015] EWHC 359 a mother had agreed to stand as surety for her son. The court refused to make an order for possession of her property because the bank had not properly communicated to her the reasons why she should receive legal advice so, although she had signed a certificate of execution, she had neither met with a solicitor nor received any advice explaining the financial risks involved with the loan.

ACTIVITY

Quick quiz

Consider the following situations and decide whether or not the claimant can argue undue influence:

1. Iman is married to Abu. They jointly own their home. Abu runs a retail business which has recently run into difficulties and persuades Iman to agree to stand as surety for him. They visit the bank, which agrees to lend the money if the wife agrees to act as surety. No separate advice is given to Iman nor was she advised to seek such advice.
2. In the same situation, would it make any difference if Iman was told to seek legal advice and she visited a solicitor? Iman could speak no English and the solicitor could not speak Urdu.
3. Would it make any difference if Iman and Abu took advice from the same solicitor?
4. Would it make any difference if Iman and Abu visited the bank together? Iman can speak English well. She appears nervous when they visit the bank. The bank tells her to seek independent legal advice.
5. In the same situation as in (1) above, but Iman is Abu's mother.

Effect of a successful plea of undue influence

In most cases a successful plea of undue influence will have the effect that the security offered by the mortgagor will be voided completely. This means that the mortgagee loses the right to claim the property as security. By way of contrast, in some cases only that part of the security will be voided over which the undue influence was operative, the rest of the property remains as security and the mortgagees can pursue their rights against it.

Suppose Emily and Richard jointly own a house with a small cottage attached. Richard owns a business in recycling plastic cartons. He and Emily visit the bank and he asks for a loan to extend his business. She agrees that the house can be used as security for the loan. She does not realise that the cottage is also to be used as security. She was not given separate advice and no one checked at the bank that she understood the position. She had agreed a mortgage over the house and understood the nature of the transaction but she did not realise that the cottage should be used also as security. Richard's business did not prosper and he was unable to repay the instalments on the loan. The bank can now claim that the house should be sold to satisfy the debt but even if the debt is still outstanding after its sale they cannot claim rights over the cottage.

The approach of the court in decisions since Etridge

Three cases decided following *Etridge* show that the courts are applying the guidelines laid down. In *Hewett v First Plus Financial Group plc* [2010] EWCA Civ 312 it was held that the failure of a husband to disclose to his wife that he was having an affair when he was requesting that she agree to grant a mortgage over the family home amounted to undue influence and was a breach of his duty of fairness and candour to her. He needed the money in order to pay off his credit card debts. Likewise in *Annulment Funding Co Ltd v Cowey* [2010] EWCA Civ 711 the court upheld the claim by one cohabitant S that the partner C had exerted undue influence over the other when he had persuaded her to act as joint chargee for a bridging loan. The charge against S was set aside. By way of contrast in *Davies v AIB Group Plc* [2012] EWHC 2178 a claimant was not successful in having her liability set aside on the basis of undue influence by her late husband. It was found that she was in possession of the relevant facts at the time of the loan. In this case the claimant had had legal advice in relation to the security.

Oppressive interest rates

The courts have jealously guarded their right to strike down any term in a mortgage transaction which operates in an oppressive or unconscionable manner. This is part of the court's inherent supervisory jurisdiction and is quite separate from any statutory provision protecting the mortgagor. The right has usually been exercised in relation to interest rates.

CASE EXAMPLE

Cityland and Property (Holdings) Ltd v Dabrah [1968] Ch 166

This case concerned an arrangement between two individuals. The claimant purchased property from the defendant at a price of £3,500. The claimant paid £600 in cash but the rest was to be raised by a mortgage granted by the defendant. However, the sum that the claimant agreed to repay represented a 57 per cent premium over the sum owed. Goff J held that this was an unlawful premium and used the court's inherent jurisdiction to declare this premium to be unconscionable and oppressive. The court then imposed a different rate of interest.

Compare the facts of the following case where the courts took a very different approach.

CASE EXAMPLE

Multiservice Bookbinding Ltd v Marden [1979] Ch 84

In this case the mortgage agreement between the parties included a term that linked the interest rates payable to the rate of exchange between the pound sterling and the Swiss franc. The amount payable by way of interest had increased so significantly that it now exceeded £133,000, whereas the original loan was for £36,000.

The claimants challenged on two grounds:

1. **Public policy**: the claimants argued that it was against public policy to have repayment of interest that was index linked. This was rejected by the court, although in previous cases it had been upheld. The reason the defendants wanted to index link the repayment of interest was to ensure that inflation would not affect the amount repaid.

2. **The terms were unconscionable and unreasonable**: Browne-Wilkinson J held that the claimant must show that the bargain was unfair and unconscionable and that it was not enough simply to show that it was unreasonable: 'one of the parties must have imposed the objectionable terms in a morally reprehensible manner ... in a way which affects his conscience'. The sort of example he cited was of taking advantage of a young, inexperienced or ignorant person or party.

Browne-Wilkinson J did not find that there were unconscionable and unfair terms in this case.

Why?
1. The company needed the money and the mortgagees were willing to lend it to them.
2. The company had the opportunity to refuse the terms laid down.
3. They had advice from an independent solicitor.
4. The mortgagee was not a professional money lender.
5. Although the terms were unfair, they were not unconscionable, so the court could not intervene.

JUDGMENT

'The parties made a bargain which the [claimants], who are business men, went into with their eyes open, with the benefit of independent advice, without any compelling necessity to accept a loan on these terms and without any sharp practice by the defendant. I cannot see that there was anything unfair or oppressive or morally reprehensible in such a bargain entered into in such circumstances.'

Browne-Wilkinson J

On the facts of this case there was no objection in principle to the parties agreeing to index link the mortgage repayments.

12.4.4 Statutory protection

The mortgagor may be protected against oppressive interest rates and charges under a number of different statutes and regulations, for example:

i.   the Consumer Credit Acts 1974 and 2006;
ii. the Financial Services and Markets Act 2000.

i. The mortgagor may be protected by the Consumer Credit Acts 1974, 2006

A mortgage may fall within the statutory controls imposed on any credit relationship. The mortgage may be regarded as a regulated credit agreement within the provisions of the Consumer Credit Act 1974 as amended by the Consumer Credit Act 2006. The effect of the Act on domestic mortgages may be limited because so many mortgages may be exempt. First mortgages of residential property remain exempt under the Act and are governed instead by the Financial Services and Markets Act 2000. The Act gives protection mainly to second mortgagors and other loans. The 1974 Act allowed even exempt agreements to be re-opened if they could be defined as **extortionate credit bargains**. This has now been replaced by a new definition of an 'unfair credit relationship'. Under the 2006 Act the court has even wider powers to make orders where the court determines that 'the relationship between creditor and the debtor arising out of the agreement ... is unfair to the debtor'. This is determined on a number of different grounds such as interest repayments. Where the court has power to intervene it may alter the terms of the agreement or set the agreement aside. In deciding whether to intervene the court has a statutory duty to consider 'all matters it thinks relevant (including matters relating to the creditor and matters relating to the debtor)'.

Suppose Penelope wants to raise £10,000 to put in double glazing on all the bedroom windows in her cottage, Wayfarers' Rest. She already has a first mortgage with the Thomson bank which is now unwilling to lend her any further money. The Dubious Money Co is willing to lend her the sum, subject to a very high rate of interest. This transaction will be covered by the 1974 and 2006 Acts.

The courts were reluctant to intervene and re-open a credit agreement under the 1974 Act unless the terms come within s 138 of the Consumer Credit Act 1974. This section included such matters as the relationship of the parties, the debtor's age, experience and business capacity and state of health. It could also look at the financial pressure put on the debtor and the nature of that pressure as well as factors that could affect the creditor such as the degree of risk accepted by the creditor and his relationship with the debtor.

JUDGMENT

'Under the Act the test is not whether the creditor has acted in a morally reprehensible manner, but whether one or other of the conditions of section 138(1) is fulfilled, although it may be thought that if either condition is fulfilled there is likely to be something morally reprehensible about the creditor's conduct.'

Edward Nugee QC in Davies v Directloans Ltd [1986] 1 WLR 823

CASE EXAMPLE

A Ketley Ltd v Scott [1980] CCLR 37

The defendants had been granted a loan by the claimant company. When they failed to repay, the defendants sought relief from the court, on the basis that the agreement was an extortionate credit agreement. However, although the rate of interest in this case was 48 per cent, it was not held to be extortionate under the Consumer Credit Act 1974.

Why?
1. The loan was arranged at very short notice for the completion of the purchase of property in favour of the defendants.
2. The documentation had been signed by the parties in great haste.
3. One of the defendants had not disclosed the fact that they had already charged the property to secure a bank overdraft, which amounted to deceit.
4. The defendants had known what they were doing and were in no way subjected by the claimants to pressure.

In 2016 the Mortgage Credit Directive came into force introducing a framework of conduct for mortgagees which was consistent with the rest of the EU. The framework applies to all mortgages whether first or second mortgages or for the purchase of buy-to-let property. These are now regulated by the Financial Conduct Authority. Mortgages are now outside the consumer credit regime and have their own framework of protection.

ii. The Financial Services and Markets Act 2000

The Financial Services and Markets Act 2000 gives extensive protection to many mortgagors where the mortgage has been entered into after 31 October 2004. The Act requires that a provider of a 'regulated mortgage contract' to ensure that the consumer is treated fairly and is not subject to excessive or hidden charges. Guidance as to what constitutes an excessive charge and on other matters comes from the *Financial Services Act Handbook* which indicates that an excessive charge is to be determined by having regard to charges for similar products or services on the market.

12.5 Rights of the mortgagee

The law protects the mortgagee or lender in a number of ways. It is important that the law offers the mortgagee protection because individuals or institutions would not lend money unless they felt they were properly protected. The right to sue on the contract may be of little value if the mortgagor is in financial difficulties and the mortgagee will want to look to the property to ensure that the money that has been lent can be recovered.

It is also important that these rights are not dependent on lengthy and expensive court proceedings.

The rights of the mortgagee can arise in three ways:

(i) from the agreement itself, or (ii) under the rules of equity, or (iii) under statute:

1. the right to sue on the covenant;
2. the right to possession;
3. the power of sale;
4. the right to appoint a receiver;
5. the right of foreclosure.

12.5.1 The right to sue on the covenant

The mortgage is a contract of loan between the mortgagee and the mortgagor so the mortgagee has an action on the mortgagor's express contractual promise to repay the sum borrowed. This arises as soon as the date fixed for repayment has arrived. The mortgagee has twelve years under s 20 Limitation Act 1980 in which to claim the debt as the right arises under the deed rather than under the ordinary rules of contract which would give a limitation period of six years. By contrast the time period for the recovery of any interests is limited to six years.

CASE EXAMPLE

Alliance & Leicester Plc v Slayford [2001] 1 All ER (Comm) 1

A successfully appealed against the dismissal of its application for leave to pursue a money judgment against the mortgagor H. A had pursued possession proceedings against the mortgagor but the wife had successfully argued that she had an overriding interest in the property and the possession proceedings had been adjourned. The judge had refused to allow A to amend its application to a money judgment on the grounds that it was an abuse of process. The Court of Appeal held that A was not prevented from pursuing a different remedy even where that might result in an application by the trustee in bankruptcy for sale of the property.

KEY FACTS

The right to sue on the covenant
1. The mortgage takes the form of a contractual agreement between the mortgagor and the mortgagee.
2. The agreement includes a term that the mortgagor will repay the money lent as well as any interest.
3. If the mortgagor fails to repay as agreed on the date stipulated in the contract, he is in breach of covenant.

4. The mortgagee can then take action against the mortgagor and the court will order payment.
5. The claim can be made even after the mortgagee has been unsuccessful in possession proceedings.
6. Failure to pay will allow the mortgagee to execute the sum against the property of the mortgagor and it can even lead to bankruptcy proceedings against the mortgagor (*Alliance & Leicester plc v Slayford* (2001)).
7. This is a personal action against the mortgagor and the mortgagee can recover any outstanding sums in this way if the value recovered from sale of the property is less than the sum lent.
8. The mortgagee has twelve years in which to pursue the recovery of debt.

12.5.2 The right to possession

The mortgagee usually has the right to possession of the mortgaged property. This is a right which arises as soon as the mortgage is made and is not dependent on default.

JUDGMENT

'[T]he right of a mortgagee to possession in the absence of some contract has nothing to do with default on the part of the mortgagor. The mortgagee may go into possession before the ink is dry on the mortgage unless there is something in the contract, express or by implication, whereby he has contracted himself out of that right. He has the right because he has a legal term of years in the property or its statutory equivalent.'

Harman J in *Four-Maids Ltd v Dudley Marshall (Properties) Ltd* [1957] Ch 317

Although this is the traditional right of the mortgagee and has been protected by law over the years it is likely today that there is the possibility that the mortgage itself may prevent the exercise of the right of possession. In some mortgages the mortgagee agrees not to take action to seek possession unless the mortgagor defaults on repayments or some other obligation. In these cases the mortgagor can rely on s 98 of the Law of Property Act 1925.

SECTION

's 98(1) A mortgagor for the time being entitled to the possession or receipt of the rents and profits of any land, as to which the mortgagee has not given notice of his intention to take possession or to enter into the receipt of the rents and profits thereof, may sue for such possession, or for the recovery of such rent and profits, or to prevent or recover damages in respect of any trespass or other wrong relative thereto.'

This section allows the **mortgagor** the right to possession rather than the mortgagee but if the mortgagor defaults on repayment or is in breach of the terms of the mortgage then the law will uphold the mortgagee's right to take possession without recourse to the courts.

The mortgagee can exercise his right to take possession so that he can let the property and therefore has the right to receive rents and profits to satisfy the sum owed. Alternatively, the right to take possession is the first step before the exercise of the power of sale. An order for possession can be delayed where the mortgagor believes that he can obtain a higher price if he sells the property himself.

In his judgment of *Target Home Loans v Clothier* [1994] 1 All ER 439, Lord Justice Nolan said:

JUDGMENT

'If the view is that the prospects of an early sale for the mortgagees as well as for Mr Clothier are best served by deferring an order for possession then it seems to me that that is a solid reason for making such an order but the deferment should be short.'

Where, however, the presence of the mortgagor would depress the sale, or perhaps the mortgagor would not co-operate in the sale of the property, the possession would not be deferred.

In most cases it is unlikely that the mortgagee will exercise the right to possess unless the mortgagor has defaulted on the mortgage. Once the mortgagee goes into possession the mortgagee owes a number of duties to the mortgagor.

A mortgagee in possession will be liable to account for any income that is generated by their possession.

CASE EXAMPLE

White v City of London Brewery (1889) 42 Ch D 237

A mortgagee had to account for the higher rents that he would have received if the property (a public house in London) had been let as a free house rather than a 'tied' public house.

The mortgagee will not have the same right to possession where the property is subject to a lease as there will be tenants in occupation of the property. Their legal rights will be binding for the duration of the lease.

The court's inherent jurisdiction to grant relief to the mortgagor

The court has always reserved to itself the right to adjourn proceedings concerning the mortgagee's claim for possession of the property. However, the adjournment is usually only for a short period.

CASE EXAMPLE

Birmingham Citizen's Permanent Building Society v Caunt [1962] Ch 883

The court observed that the power of the court to adjourn possession proceedings under its inherent jurisdiction merely allows the court to adjourn for a short time for the purpose of allowing the mortgagor a limited time to find the means to pay off the mortgagee.

Statutory controls on the right to possession

The mortgagor in a 'dwelling house' is protected in certain circumstances against an action for possession. Under s36(1) of the Administration of Justice Act 1970 (as amended by s8 of the Administration of Justice Act 1973) the mortgagor can apply for possession to be:

1. suspended;
2. adjourned; or
3. postponed by the court.

The Act was originally thought to have interfered with the inherent right of the mortgagee to take possession of the property.

Possession without a court order

CASE EXAMPLE

Ropaigealach v Barclays Bank [2000] QB 263

Here, the mortgagees took peaceful possession of the mortgaged property while it was standing empty, undergoing repairs. The mortgagors had fallen behind with their repayments but had not received notification of the imminent sale of the property. The house was sold at auction with vacant possession. The Court of Appeal held that the mortgagees had power to take possession in this way. The right to seek relief under s 36 could only arise where possession is sought by a court action. The mortgagee cannot take action in this way if there is anyone present or living in the property.

KEY FACTS

Statutory control on the right to possession
1. Is the property a dwelling house? This will depend on whether or not the property is being used as a dwelling house at the time when the order for possession is being sought. The fact that part is used as an office or a shop will still allow it to be regarded as a dwelling house.
2. The mortgagors are entitled under the mortgage deed or by some agreement between them and the mortgagees either: a. to pay the principal sum by instalments; or   b. to defer payment of it in whole or in part.
3. There is provision made for earlier payment in the event of any default by the mortgagor or a demand by the mortgagee.

Under the 1970 Administration of Justice Act (as amended by the 1973 Act) the court must be satisfied that there is a realistic chance of repayment of certain sums outstanding within a reasonable time. Under the 1973 Act these represent such amounts as the mortgagor would have expected to be required to pay if the mortgage had not contained a default clause rendering the entire mortgage monies payable in the event of any of the instalments falling into arrears. The 1973 Act prevented a potential problem from arising under the wording of the 1970 Act which had clearly not been foreseen by the draftsmen of the legislation. A default clause usually results in the mortgagor becoming immediately liable for the whole of the sum if he defaults on a repayment of the loan. The 1973 Act held that such clauses could be ignored when considering whether the court has the power to delay possession proceedings.

The following case considered what is meant by a 'default clause'.

CASE EXAMPLE

Habib Bank Ltd v Tailor [1982] 1 WLR 1218

The claimant had a bank overdraft which was secured by a mortgage against his house. He exceeded the overdraft limit and the bank then called in the loan on the basis that it was a term of the loan that the overdraft was repayable on demand. Mr Tailor argued that the demand for repayment in full was similar to a default clause and so his case was within s 8 of the 1973 Act. However, the court held that s 8 was not applicable to this type of loan because there was no question of the bank having the discretion to defer payment once the bank had demanded payment and, as the claimant could not repay the whole sum within a reasonable time, possession should be ordered.

In most cases if the mortgagor were suddenly to become liable for the whole sum, there would never be a realistic chance of repayment.

Exercise of the court's discretion:

1. The court cannot grant an open-ended postponement of possession orders. The court must lay down a precise period of time for repayment.

2. The court has power to delay proceedings to allow the mortgagor to sell the property himself. In *Royal Trust Co of Canada v Markham* [1975] 1 WLR 1416 the Court of Appeal held that the court has no jurisdiction to order suspension of possession proceedings indefinitely. So the Court of Appeal allowed a four-month adjournment in *Target Home Loans v Clothier* (1994) to give the mortgagor a chance to sell his property.

3. Applications could be granted under this section even where no sum has become due under the mortgage agreement (*Western Bank v Schindler* [1977] Ch 1). Here the bank was seeking clarification that it was entitled to possession of the property within a ten-year period, even though no sums of capital or interest were contractually due until ten years after the execution of the mortgage. It applies whenever the mortgagee seeks possession by a court order.

4. The position of the mortgagor should be looked at realistically to see whether there is a genuine prospect of repayment. The jurisdiction is exercised under the Act if it appears to the court that the mortgagor is likely to be able to 'within a reasonable period' pay any sums due under the mortgage. In the key case of *Cheltenham and Gloucester Building Society v Norgan* [1996] 1 All ER 449 guidelines were laid down as to how to approach these cases. This resulted in reducing the discretion given to judges in these cases and as a consequence reduced the prospect of recurring litigation in cases where the mortgagor had defaulted on a previous occasion.

There are many questions for the court to consider but the key issues are:

- How much of the mortgage term remains?
- How much can the mortgagor reasonably afford to pay both now and in the future?
- Why has the mortgagor been unable to pay and how long will this reason last? If the prospect for repayment was not reasonable, as in *Bristol and West Building Society v Ellis* (1996) 73 P & CR 158 (here, at the present rate of repayment it would take 98 years to pay off the arrears), an order for possession should be granted immediately.

In *Cheltenham & Gloucester Building Society v Norgan* (1996) the court was prepared to reschedule repayments over the whole of the remaining term of the mortgage. This represented a marked contrast with the previous attitude of the courts, which was to reschedule repayments over a very short period of time, normally no more than two years. Once rescheduled, however, the courts will rarely allow further applications to challenge possession.

JUDGMENT

'There is another factor which weighs strongly in favour of adopting the full term of the mortgage as the starting point for calculating a "reasonable period" for payment of arrears ... The parties have been before the court with depressing frequency over the years on applications to enforce, or further to suspend, the warrant of possession, while Mrs Norgan and her husband have struggled, sometimes with success and sometimes without, to meet whatever commitment was currently approved by the court. Cheltenham has ... added to its security the costs it has incurred in connection with all these attendances. It is an experience which brings home the disadvantages which both lender and borrower are liable to suffer.'

Waite LJ

Lord Justice Waite outlines here a real problem in allowing frequent applications to the court by the mortgagee because the costs automatically rise and thereby increase the sum owed. The approach in *Norgan*, which is to take a long-term view of the relationship between mortgagor and mortgagee, will always keep costs lower as court appearances are avoided as long as the mortgagor keeps to the terms of the repayment schedule.

Under s 91 of the 1925 Act, the court has the power to direct sale on such terms as it sees fit. It may make the order in spite of opposition from others. Often there will be a dispute between the mortgagor who may want to sell himself and the mortgagee who may also want to sell the property. In *Palk v Mortgage Services Funding plc* [1993] Ch 330 the mortgagors wanted an immediate sale to prevent incurring a larger debt, but the sale price of the property would not cover the value of the loan. The mortgagees wanted to delay sale and to let the property to tenants until the value of the property rose. The mortgagors were concerned that there would be an ever increasing debt. The court ordered immediate sale. Compare *Cheltenham & Gloucester plc v Krausz* [1997] 1 All ER 21 where the Court of Appeal refused to apply s 36, thus preventing an application under s 91. It held that the mortgagees could take possession and that this right is absolute. If the mortgagors seek to delay sale under s 36 then this depends on evidence that they have a reasonable chance of repaying the arrears. If there is no reasonable chance of that, the court cannot deny the mortgagees immediate possession of the property.

The court has no discretion to postpone proceedings indefinitely.	*Royal Trust Co of Canada v Markham* (1975)
The court has power to delay possession in order for the mortgagor to negotiate a private sale himself.	*Target Home Loans v Clothier* (1994)
The period for repayment must be 'reasonable'. There must be a realistic chance of the mortgagor being able to repay arrears. The courts may be prepared to reschedule the payment of mortgage arrears allowing a longer period of time for repayment.	*Cheltenham & Gloucester Building Society v Norgan* (1996) *Bristol & West Building Society v Ellis* (1996)
The mortgagor can apply to the court and the court may exercise its discretion even before any mortgage money has become due although this has not been upheld in every case.	*Western Bank Ltd v Schindler* (1977)
The court can order sale in favour of the mortgagor even where it would not fully discharge the debt under s 91 of the 1925 Act. However the mortgagor cannot resist an application by the mortgagee for possession under s 36 of the 1970 Act.	*Palk v Mortgage Services Funding plc* (1993) *Cheltenham & Gloucester Building Society v Krausz* (1997)

Table 12.5 The exercise of the court's discretion under s 36 of the 1970 Administration of Justice Act (s 8 of the 1973 Act)

The mortgagor's claim for peaceful enjoyment of his property under the Human Rights Act

There is a potential claim for a mortgagor who faces repossession from a mortgagee to claim his right to peaceful enjoyment of his property under Article 1 Protocol 1 of the Human Rights Act has been interfered with, as well as a claim under Article 8 'a right to respect for family life'. There have been few applications so far but those that have been heard have been defended under the qualification given in the Act that a claim can be defended by a legitimate right. In *Wood v United Kingdom* (1997) 24 EHRR CD 69, where an applicant challenged a repossession order, the courts commented that the mortgagee's claim to possession was necessary for the protection of the rights and freedoms of others, namely the mortgagee. In *Horsham Properties v Clarke and*

Beech [2009] 1 WLR 1255 (see discussion below) a claim under Article 1 Protocol 1 of the European Convention of Human Rights failed. Mortgagees had relied on their power to order sale without first relying on procedures to take possession thereby preventing the mortgagors from bringing a claim under the Administration of Justice Act 1970.

12.5.3 The power of sale

The power of sale arises in conjunction with the right to possession; this is covered under ss 101–107 of the Law of Property Act 1925. It can only arise if three conditions under s 101 are met:

1. the mortgage must be made by deed;
2. there must be no contrary provisions expressed in that deed; and
3. the mortgage monies must have become due.

Once **all the three conditions** are met, the power of sale arises. However, the power must also be exercisable and this occurs when any one of the three requirements laid down in s 103 of the 1925 Act is satisfied.

Note there is a difference between the power of sale arising and the power of sale becoming exercisable.

SECTION

's 103 Regulation of exercise of power of sale
A mortgagee shall not exercise the power of sale conferred by this Act unless and until –

(i) notice requiring payment of the mortgage money has been served on the mortgagor or one or more mortgagors, and default has been made in payment of the mortgage money, or of part thereof, for three months after such service; or

(ii) some interest under the mortgage is in arrear and unpaid for two months after becoming due; or

(iii) there has been a breach of some provision contained in the mortgage deed or in this Act, or in an enactment replaced by this Act, and on the part of the mortgagor, or of some person concurring in making the mortgage, to be observed or performed, other than and besides a covenant for payment of the mortgage money or interest thereon.'

Where sale by the mortgagee takes place, the purchaser will gain the legal estate and be entitled to register his title.

Duties of the mortgagee when exercising the power of sale:

- He owes the mortgagor a duty to take reasonable care to obtain a proper price for the mortgaged property.
- He does not have to:
  a. wait until the property market improves (*Cuckmere Brick Co Ltd v Mutual Finance Ltd* (1971);
  b. take into account persons other than the mortgagor, such as beneficiaries under a trust (*Parker-Tweedle v Dunbar Bank plc* [1991] Ch 26);
  c. sell immediately, and will not be liable for losses incurred if sale is postponed (*China and South Sea Bank Ltd v Tan Soon Gin* [1990] 1 AC 536);
  d. preserve a business until the sale of the property has taken place (*AIB Finance Ltd v Debtors* [1998] 2 All ER 929).

If there is a surplus when the property is sold, after the mortgage debt has been paid and any cost incurred with the sale, that sum must be passed to the mortgagor.

The mortgagee assumes the position of trustee over the proceeds of sale although he may not be regarded as a trustee during the sale. However, it is clear from the decision in *Cuckmere Brick Co Ltd* that the mortgagee does owe a duty of care to the mortgagor.

CASE EXAMPLE

Cuckmere Brick Co Ltd v Mutual Finance Ltd [1971] Ch 949

A repossessed property was sold through auction. The mortgagee failed to refer in the advertisements for the auction that the property had planning permission of which he had been fully aware. The property was sold at undervalue and the Court of Appeal held that the mortgagee's were liable in damages for the breach of its duty of care towards the mortgagors. The key issue here was that the mortgagees were fully aware of the planning permission. In cases where they were not aware there is no claim by the mortgagor. This would be a matter of fact.

The duty of care is also owed to any subsequent encumbrancer. In *Freeguard v Royal Bank of Scotland Plc* [2002] EWCA Civ 2509, F successfully claimed that she was owed a duty of care on the sale of property by the mortgagee although the mortgage had been between a previous owner of her property and the mortgagees. The court held that her interest in the property gave rise to a relationship with the mortgagees.

In *Horsham Properties Group Ltd v Clark and Beech* [2009] 1 WLR 1255 the mortgagee sold property to Horsham after the mortgagor defaulted on the mortgage. In law after the sale the mortgagors became trespassers in their own home. The effect of this was that the mortgagors could not reply on the Administration of Justice Act 1970 in order to apply to the court for relief from a claim for possession. The mortgagors then relied on Article 1 Protocol 1 of the European Convention of Human Rights claiming that their right to property had been infringed. This claim was rejected by the High Court. This case suggested that there was a loophole within the procedures for possession which would allow the mortgagee to claim possession and then sale without taking the case to court and thereby allowing the mortgagors a chance to claim protection under the Administration of Justice 1970. This loophole remains in spite of an attempt to address it by Parliament. A Private Member's Bill in 2009 failed to become law.

12.5.4 The right to appoint a receiver

This is a useful right and is another way of recovering the interest owed on the mortgage. The right to appoint a receiver is often included in the mortgage deed itself. If it is not provided in the mortgage deed then it can be made under s 101 of the 1925 Act. It arises in the same circumstances as the power of sale, that is the mortgage must be made by deed with no provision disallowing the appointment of a receiver and mortgage money must now have become due.

The receiver takes control of the mortgaged property and then sells it or manages it and uses the income from it to repay the loan. The receiver acts as agent of the mortgagor and the effect of this is that the mortgagor becomes solely liable for any acts or defaults of the receiver. However, the receiver owes a duty to the mortgagor to act 'with due diligence'.

CASE EXAMPLE

Medforth v Blake [2000] Ch 86

The receiver owes a duty in equity to the mortgagor and anyone else with an interest in the property to act in good faith. If the receiver decides to carry on the business of the mortgagor then he has a duty to act with due diligence and to conduct the business with reasonable competence.

12.5.5 The right of foreclosure

JUDGMENT

'As far as I am aware foreclosure actions are almost unheard of today and have been so for many years. Mortgagees prefer to exercise other remedies.'

Sir David Nicholls VC in *Palk v Mortgage Services Funding plc* [1993] Ch 330

Foreclosure allows the mortgagee to enforce his rights to possession of the property. The court can order that he can take over the entire ownership of the property irrespective of the size of the debt. Therefore any surplus left over after sale will remain with the mortgagee.

The Law Commission has recommended that foreclosure should be abolished and replaced with a remedy for the mortgagees to sell the property to themselves ('Transfer of Land – and Mortgages' (Law Com No 204, 1999)).

KEY FACTS

Foreclosure
1. This is regarded as a very draconian measure and it is rarely ordered today.
2. It can only be ordered by the court and if the court does order foreclosure, the mortgagee is entitled to the whole of the property; and that includes any excess over the actual sum lent and any interest that is outstanding. The mortgagor recovers nothing from the sale.
3. Any mortgagee of property can bring an action for foreclosure: s91(2) of the Law of Property Act 1925.
4. The effect of the action is to make the mortgagee owner of the property in law and in equity.
5. The right to foreclose arises any time after the legal right to redeem has been lost.
6. The mortgagee loses the right to seek any other order, so foreclosure is not advisable in cases of negative equity as the full loan will not be recoverable.
7. There are two steps in a foreclosure order: foreclosure *nisi* and foreclosure absolute. Under foreclosure *nisi* the mortgagor has a period of time (usually six months) to repay the mortgage and if he does so, the mortgage is discharged. The foreclosure absolute destroys the mortgagor's equity of redemption and transfers title to the mortgagee.
8. In rare cases a court will re-open a foreclosure order absolute. In *Campbell v Holyland* (1877) 7 Ch D 166 the case was re-opened three months after the foreclosure order had been granted.
9. The Law Commission has recommended that foreclosure should be abolished.

KEY FACTS

Rights of the mortgagee			
Action on the covenant in the contract	Arises once there is default on the terms of the agreement.		*Alliance & Leicester v Slayford* (2001)
Possession	Automatically arises when the mortgage is made.	s 36 of the Administration of Justice Act 1970 (s 8 of the Administration of Justice Act 1973)	*Target Home Loans Ltd v Clothier* (1994) *Four-Maids Ltd v Dudley Marshall (Properties) Ltd* (1957) *Cheltenham and Gloucester Building Society v Norgan* (1996)
Sale	Arises where the mortgage has been made by deed and the mortgage money has become due.	ss 101 and 103 of the Law of Property Act 1925	*AIB v Debtors* (1998) *Cuckmere Brick Co v Mutual Finance Ltd* (1971)
Appointment of a receiver	Where deed allows it, otherwise deed may imply such a power.	s 101 of the 1925 Act s 109 of the 1925 Act	*Medforth v Blake* (2000)
Foreclosure	Only arises by order of the court.		*Campbell v Holyland* (1877)

KEY FACTS

Rights of an equitable mortgagee under an equitable mortgage
1. The mortgagee does not hold the legal estate in land so the equitable mortgagee cannot claim possession of the legal estate.
2. The equitable mortgagee has the right to sue for the outstanding money in the same way as the legal mortgagee.
3. If the equitable mortgage was made by deed then there can be a power of sale once the conditions necessary are present. The property cannot be sold by the mortgagee himself.
4. A receiver can be appointed in the same circumstances as in a legal mortgage.
5. An equitable mortgagee has the power to foreclose.

ACTIVITY

Applying the law

Charlie and Grace have lived together for the past five years. They bought their house for £220,000 in 2005 with the aid of a mortgage provided by Easier Banking. They both had full-time jobs and they were both able to contribute towards the mortgage repayments. Grace loved to decorate the house and she started to buy expensive fittings and furniture. Grace left her job in 2012 when she took maternity leave. She unexpectedly had twin boys and has not returned to work. Charlie was made redundant in 2017 and has since found it difficult to repay the mortgage instalments. They are now over £40,000 in arrears and Easier Banking wants to repossess the property.

Advise Easier Banking on the steps that it should take in order to repossess the property. Has Easier Banking any other rights that it can exercise?

12.6 Priority of mortgages

If the mortgagor takes out a single mortgage then the question of priority does not arise. The mortgagee has the right to recover the outstanding sum and anything outstanding will belong to the mortgagor. However, there may be more than one mortgage and there may be insufficient funds to cover the outstanding amount.

The law lays down rules as to who is first in the queue to recover outstanding sums. The rules largely depend on three issues:

1. Are the mortgages legal or equitable?
2. Is the title to the land registered or unregistered?
3. When were the mortgages registered?

Legal mortgages of registered land depend on the date of registration, whereas equitable mortgages depend on date of creation. In *Barclays Bank v Zaroovabli* [1997] Ch 321 the failure to register a legal charge by the mortgagees resulted in the mortgagees losing priority to a legal lease over the land which took effect as an overriding right and therefore took priority.

Properly registered legal mortgages will take priority over all equitable mortgages created after the date of registration.

A mortgage will not take effect in law until it has been registered, so an unregistered legal mortgage will not take priority over a registered legal mortgage whatever the date of creation.

Under s 32 of the Land Registration Act 2002, an equitable charge should be protected by entry of a burden on the Register, but failure to do so may still allow the earlier charge to take priority because equitable charges have always been treated differently from legal charges and the date of creation has governed their priority.

SUMMARY

1. A mortgage is a contract between the mortgagee and mortgagor which gives the mortgagee both contractual as well as proprietary rights in the mortgaged land.
2. Historically a mortgage differed from a charge because under a mortgage the mortgagee could claim possession of the property whereas under a charge the chargee could only claim a charge over the property. All legal mortgages in registered land today take effect as charges.
3. Mortgagors are protected by the equity of redemption which includes all rights that a mortgagor can claim over the land.
4. The equitable right to redeem allows the mortgagor the right to redeem the mortgage even after the date for repayment has passed.
5. All legal mortgages must be entered on the Register in order to take effect as legal mortgages.
6. A mortgage can be set aside if it has been obtained through undue influence or oppression.
7. The mortgagee has a number of rights including the right to possess, the right of sale, the right to appoint a receiver, the right to foreclose and the right to sue on the covenant.
8. Legal mortgages once entered on the Register will always take priority over equitable mortgages but may lose priority to these interests if not properly entered on the Register.

SAMPLE ESSAY QUESTION

A homeowner who falls behind with mortgage repayments and, as a consequence, faces a possession claim has very little protection. Discuss.

> Define a mortgage.
>
> Discuss the relationship between the mortgagor and the mortgagee:
> - a relationship in contract;
> - the mortgagee gains proprietary rights in the property.
>
> Discuss the general protection given to mortgagors.
>
> The equity of redemption.

> Discuss the rights of mortgagees:
> - right to possession;
> - *Four-maids Ltd v Dudley Marshall*.

> Protection given to mortgagors against an order for possession by the mortgagees:
>
> - Administration of Justice Act 1970 s 36;
> - Administration of Justice Act 1973 s 8.
>
> Discuss *Cheltenham & Gloucester Building Society v Norgan*.
>
> Discuss the way the court applies the section: must be a realistic chance of repaying any sums due under the mortgage within a reasonable period; willingness of the court to reschedule over the whole of the remaining period of the mortgage.
>
> No indefinite postponement.
>
> s 91 Law of Property Act gives the mortgagor the right to sell the property.
>
> Discuss *Palk v Mortgage Services Funding* (1993).

> Discuss possible protection given to the mortgagor under the Human Rights Act 1998: Article 8 and Article 1 Protocol 1.
>
> Discuss the limited success of such claims.

> **CONCLUSION**

Further reading

Books

Dixon, M, *Modern Land Law* (9th edn, Routledge, 2014).

Gravells, N, *Land Law Text and Materials* (4th edn, Sweet & Maxwell, 2010), p. 891.

Gray, K and Gray, S F, *Elements of Land Law* (5th edn, Oxford University Press, 2009), p. 728.

Stevens, J and Pearce, R, *Land Law* (5th edn, Sweet & Maxwell, 2013), p. 637.

Articles

Andrews, G, 'Undue Influence: Where's the Disadvantage?' [2002] 66 *Conv* 457.

Capper, D, 'Undue Influence and Unconscionability' (1998) 114 *LQR* 479.

Dixon, M, 'Combating the Mortgagee's Right to Possession: New Hope for the Mortgagor in Chains?' (1998) 18 *LS* 279.

Dixon, M, 'Mortgages Duties and Commercial Transactions' [2006] *Conv* 278.

Greer, S, *Horsham Properties Group Ltd v Clark: Possession–Mortgagee's Right or Discretionary Remedy?* [2009] *Conv* 6 516.

Haley, M, 'Mortgage Default: Possession, Relief and Judicial Discretion' (1997) 17 *LS* 483.

Halladay, J, 'Recent Problems in Undue Influence' [2011] *DLR* 227.

Mujih, E, *Over Ten Years After Royal Bank of Scotland Plc v Etridge (No 2)*: Is the Law on Undue Influence in Guarantee Cases any Clearer? [2013] *ICCLR* 24(2) 57.

Neild and Hopkins (2013) 'Human Rights and Mortgage Repossession Beyond Property Law Using Article 8' 33 *LS* 431.

Thomas, S, 'Mortgages: Possession by Default' [1997] *Conv* 91.

Thompson, M P, 'Wives Sureties and Banks: *Royal Bank of Scotland v Etridge (No 2)* [2000] 4 All ER 449' [2002] 66 *Conv* 174.

13

Leases

AIMS AND OBJECTIVES

After reading this chapter, you should be able to:

- Identify the key characteristics of a lease
- Distinguish between exclusive possession and exclusive occupation
- Compare licences with leases
- Describe the different types of leases that can exist in law and explain how they can be created
- Explain the different covenants that may be expressly or impliedly included in a lease
- Describe how the law protects a landlord against breaches of covenant by a tenant
- Discuss the enforceability of covenants against third parties on assignment
- Explain how a lease might come to an end

If the purchase of freehold property is impossible or undesirable, taking a lease of property presents a solution. It has many advantages which make it an attractive alternative to owning freehold property. Leases are used for residential premises as well as for business premises and for many shops and also for agricultural land.

It has the advantage of being a very flexible relationship. The tenant of domestic accommodation is almost always protected from eviction in the very short term and the tenant has a legal estate which allows him to prevent anyone, including the landlord, from entering without his permission for the duration of the lease. However, the landlord is usually in a much stronger position than the tenant and can easily take advantage of him. The landlord may be tempted to argue that there is a licence rather than a lease knowing that a licence generally gives less protection to a licensee than the protection that a tenant might be able to claim. The law has always tried to protect the tenant from his potentially vulnerable position. This protection does not extend to licensees.

So, the first question to ask in a short-term holding of property is always: is this a tenancy or lease?

13.1 Characteristics of a lease

Under s 1(1)(b) of the Law of Property Act 1925 a lease or 'a term of years absolute' is a legal estate and is also a proprietary estate in land.

SECTION

's 1(1) … The only estates in land which are capable of subsisting or of being conveyed or created at law are:

(a) An estate in fee simple absolute in possession;

(b) A term of years absolute.'

The 'term of years absolute' as defined in the Law of Property Act 1925 is another term for a lease or tenancy. The terms are interchangeable. The real issue here is that the term of years absolute or lease creates a legal estate in land. In this way it is singled out as only one of two legal estates recognised in law. Historically the lease only created a personal right which arose in contract and could only give the tenant a right in damages rather than recovery of the land. Gradually the lease was recognised as a proprietary right which gave rise to recovery of the land rather than damages.

> Under the Land Registration Act 2002, a lease of over seven years now qualifies as a registrable interest and it must be compulsorily registered (under s 4 if granted out of an unregistered estate or under s 27 if it is granted out of a registered estate).

The lease will not take effect at law until it has been properly registered. Failure to register will result in the lease losing its status as a legal estate and it will only qualify as a mere contract to grant a legal lease.

> If the lease is for less than seven years, it does not require registration.

It does not matter how short the lease is in length, for example it can be for less than a year, it can be one month, but such a lease is still considered to be for a term of years absolute and will take effect in law.

A lease has always been difficult to define and there is still no adequate statutory definition even today. For a time there was a shift towards holding the intention of the parties as the real indicator of whether a lease or a licence existed. A lease was a lease if the parties intended it to be so.

Today, we are guided by the characteristics laid down in the following important case:

CASE EXAMPLE

Street v Mountford [1985] AC 809

Mr Street and Mrs Mountford entered into an agreement for furnished accommodation which was called a licence agreement. Mrs Mountford agreed to pay a sum of money each week described as a licence fee rather than rent. She was given exclusive possession of the premises. At the end of the agreement there was a statement as follows that the agreement … 'does not and is not intended to give me a tenancy protected under the Rent Acts'. After moving in Mrs Mountford applied to the Rent Tribunal for a fair rent to be assessed. Mr Street argued that she had a mere licence and therefore was outside the protection of the Rent Acts.

'The traditional view that the grant of exclusive possession for a term at a rent creates a tenancy is consistent with the elevation of a tenancy into an estate in land. The tenant possessing exclusive possession is able to exercise the rights of an owner of land, which is in the real sense his land albeit temporarily and subject to certain restrictions. A tenant armed with exclusive possession can keep out strangers and keep out the landlord unless the landlord is exercising limited rights reserved to him by the tenancy agreement to enter and view and repair.'

Lord Templeman

Lord Templeman laid down in *Street v Mountford* (1895) that there are three characteristics of a lease:

1. exclusive possession;
2. a determinate period;
3. for a rent or other consideration.

13.1.1 Exclusive possession

There has to be exclusive possession for a lease to exist. Lord Templeman held that exclusive possession was the conclusive feature of a lease. This means that the tenant has control over anyone who enters the premises and can exclude everyone, including the landlord. If someone occupying property does not have exclusive possession, they can only claim a licence which is a mere personal right.

JUDGMENT

'There can be no tenancy unless the occupier enjoys exclusive possession but an occupier who enjoys exclusive possession is not necessarily a tenant. He may be owner in fee simple, a trespasser, a mortgagee in possession, an object of charity or a service occupier.'

Lord Templeman in *Street v Mountford* (1985)

There will be no exclusive possession if:

1. The landlord is entitled to **move the occupier** at any time from one room to another. In *Westminster City Council v Clarke* [1992] 2 AC 288 there was held to be no exclusive possession in a council-run hostel for homeless persons who could not claim any particular room. Other rules included the provision that they might have to share with others, they had to be in their rooms by 11.00 p.m. and they could not have visitors after that time. In *Stewart v Watts* [2016] EWCA Civ 1247 the key question was whether residents of almshouses occupy as licensees, or as tenants. Mrs Watts was a resident in an almshouse and in 2014 she was served a notice to quit. In holding that she was a mere licensee, the Court of Appeal held that she had no exclusive

possession because the Charity who owned the almshouse could move her to another almshouse and visitors were not allowed to stay.

2. Someone merely has **exclusive occupation**, such as a hotel guest or a student in a university hall of residence or a resident in a nursing home (*Abbeyfield (Harpenden) Society Ltd v Woods* [1968] 1 WLR 374); the hotel guest has no right to exclude the hotel staff from the room. A note on the hotel room door 'do not disturb' is not exclusion of the hotel staff but merely a request that the staff do not access the room at that time. The request could be overridden in certain circumstances.

3. **Services are provided**, such as a housekeeper, the collection of rubbish and the cleaning of windows and also the cleaning of the flats themselves. In *Marcou v De Silvesa* (1986) 52 P & CR 2 the agreement required the landlord to provide services. The court considered whether this would require unlimited access to the premises. The type of services provided by the landlord was very limited, such as the removal of rubbish and laundering of linen, and did not need access to the flat. It is not the provision of services which prevents this from being a tenancy but the fact that the owner can enter at will. In *Huwyler v Ruddy* (1995) 28 HLR 550 services were provided by the claimant's brother for the defendant. They were very limited in nature and rarely took more than 20 minutes each week. However, Peter Gibson LJ found that even when the services were wound down to virtually nothing, the nature of the original contract was that the parties had an agreement for the provision of services and the defendant could claim the resumption of the services if he wished. The agreement was therefore a licence. If the provision of services is genuine then refusal of them will not allow the agreement to be seen as a lease.

4. Occupation of the premises is based on **employment** if it comes within the definition of a 'service occupancy'. This was defined in *Street v Mountford* (1985) as occupancy by a servant of his master's premises in order to perform his duties as a servant. Examples include farm workers and members of the armed forces. It is also accepted that the occupation would be for the better performance of the job. In *Norris v Checksfield* [1991] 1 WLR 1241 a coach mechanic was granted the use of a bungalow by his employer, located close to the depot. The Court of Appeal held that although he was found to have exclusive possession he was a service occupier and not a tenant.

5. **Purchasers were let into possession** of the premises prior to completion.

There may be exclusive possession **even if**:

1. The landlord retains **a set of keys**. In *Aslan v Murphy* [1990] 1 WLR 766 the owner retained a set of keys. This was seen as a pretence to prevent a tenancy arising. A landlord can retain keys but still have to request entry from the tenant if he wants to gain access.

2. There are a number of persons **sharing** the premises. This is because they may jointly occupy the premises. In *Antoniades v Villiers* [1990] 1 AC 417 it was held that there was a joint tenancy even though the owner had asked each of the two joint occupiers, who were an unmarried couple living together, to enter separate agreements with himself and each was described as a licence requiring them to separately undertake to pay half of the rent. There were also clauses reserving the right to the owner to occupy the flat with the couple or to introduce others. The House of Lords held these provisions to be a sham.

3. Premises are **provided by an employer**, so long as occupation is not required for the better performance of the tenant's job. In *Fachini v Bryson* [1952] 1 TLR 1386 the

assistant of an ice-cream manufacturer was allowed to live in a house in return for a sum of money paid weekly and this was found to be a tenancy even though the parties referred to it as a licence; the use of the premises did not improve the carrying out of the employee's duties.

4. **The grantor does not have an estate to support a lease**. In *Bruton v London & Quadrant Housing Trust* [1999] 3 WLR 150 the landlord had a mere licence but the landlord still had the right to create a lease in favour of the claimant.

5. If there are terms in the agreement that suggest that the occupier does not have exclusive possession which have been inserted as **a sham of pretence**. '[T]he court should, in my opinion, be astute to detect and frustrate sham devices and artificial transactions whose only object is to disguise the grant of a tenancy and to evade the Rent Acts' (Lord Templeman in *Street v Mountford* (1977)). In *Aslan v Murphy* (1990) the occupier occupied a small basement room and the agreement included a clause which said that the licensee had no right to use the room between 10.30 a.m. and 12.00 noon. The court found this to be a 'sham' or 'pretence'. The provision of services such as cleaning will normally prevent a lease arising unless the provision of services is a 'sham' or pretence'.

13.1.2 A determinate period
Commencement of the lease
If there is any uncertainty in the period, the tenancy will fail. This means that both the commencement and the duration must both be clear on the face of the lease. So even where the other terms of the lease are clear, such as the details of the rent and the length of the actual term, the lease will fail without a date of commencement (*Say v Smith* (1563) 1 Plowd 269).

Duration of the lease
The maximum date of duration must be certain at the date of commencement as shown below in *Lace v Chantler* (1944).

Consider the following cases:

CASE EXAMPLE

Lace v Chantler [1944] KB 368

A lease granted 'for the duration of the war' was held to be void. This was because at the time it was granted no one had any idea how long the Second World War would last and therefore no one had any idea when the lease would be certain to come to an end.

'The question immediately arises whether a tenancy for the duration of the war creates a good leasehold interest. In my opinion, it does not. A term created by a leasehold tenancy agreement must be expressed either with certainty ... or by reference to something which can, at the time when the lease takes effect, be looked to as a certain ascertainment of what the term is meant to be. In the present case the term was completely uncertain. It was impossible to say how long the tenancy would last.'

Lord Greene MR

Within a very short period after *Street v Mountford* had been decided this characteristic of a lease was challenged, although the challenge was not upheld for very long and within a few years the need for a certain period had been re-instated.

CASE EXAMPLE

Ashburn Anstalt v Arnold [1989] Ch 1

It was held that a term which allowed the occupiers of a shop to remain there rent-free until they provided the landlord with a quarter's notice was certain because in this case the term could be brought to an end by giving a quarter's notice and this was itself sufficiently certain.

'The arrangement could be brought to an end by both parties in circumstances which are free from uncertainty in the sense that there would be doubt whether the determining event had occurred. The vice of the uncertainty in relation to the duration of the term is that the parties do not know where they stand.'

Fox LJ

The problem with this decision is that there was no way of predicting when the quarter's notice would be given, so it was not possible to predict when the lease was going to end.

CASE EXAMPLE

Prudential Assurance Co Ltd v London Residuary Body [1992] 2 AC 386

The judgment in this case criticised the decision in *Ashburn Anstalt v Arnold* (1989) because it introduced an element of uncertainty into a key feature of a lease. It concerned the sale of a strip of land fronting a highway to the council which then leased it back to the owner for a period 'until the land is required by the council for the purposes of widening of the highway'. The council later assigned the reversion to the first defendants, who were not a highway authority and had no intention of widening the road at any time, and the tenancy was then assigned to the claimants who were still paying rent of £30 per annum for land now worth £10,000 per annum. The question was whether or not the agreement created a lease, and if it took effect as a lease could it be a valid lease of an indefinite term of years at a rent of £30 per annum and determinable only in the event of the freehold owners (the London Residuary Body) deciding to widen the road. Alternatively the freehold owners argued that the occupiers had a yearly tenancy with payment of periodic rent and terminable on giving half a year's notice.

If *Ashburn Anstalt v Arnold* was followed, the term would have been sufficiently certain because the defendants had the right to call for the determination of the lease. However, Lord Templeman overruled the earlier case because he viewed it as uncertain and he maintained that one of the hallmarks of a lease remained certainty of duration. He criticised the state of the law because in the *Prudential* case it produced a result that had not been intended by the parties.

Lord Browne-Wilkinson also gave judgment in this case, and also criticised the rule:

'This bizarre outcome results from the application of an ancient and technical rule of law which requires the maximum duration of a term of years to be ascertainable from the outset. No one has produced any satisfactory rationale for the genesis of this rule. No one has been able to point to any useful purpose that it serves at the present day ... for this house to depart from a rule relating to land law which has been established for many centuries might upset long established titles. I must therefore confine myself to expressing the hope that the Law Commission might look at the subject to see whether there is in fact any good reason now for maintaining a rule which operates to defeat contractually agreed arrangements between the parties.'

The lease may have been saved if the parties had included a maximum duration for the lease but had also included an event which would have allowed an early termination of the lease, for example a lease for 900 years but subject to termination by the landlord when the land was required for road widening. The courts would have accepted the 900 years as the maximum length of time that the lease could have lasted.

The rule today is that the maximum duration of the lease must be clear from the start of the lease.

The decision in *Prudential Assurance* has attracted criticism and support from academic writers. Compare the following views:

> 'The decision of the House of Lords in *Prudential Assurance Co Ltd v London Residuary Body* is welcome for its reassertion that the same certainty rule applies to fixed and to periodic terms. Leases had always required certainty of maximum duration at the outset. The choice by the House of Lords to reaffirm the traditional rule was the safe option in view of the danger of upsetting established titles. Any formal requirement, like that of prospective certainty of term, risks upsetting the intention of contracting parties. On balance, it has been argued, the result was not unjust, but if it was, escape routes were available. No need for reform of the law has been demonstrated.'
>
> P Sparkes, 'Certainty of Leasehold Terms' (1993) 109 *LQR* 93

Compare the view of Susan Bright, below, who is critical of the way that the court reacted to the potential uncertainty of the agreement between Prudential Assurance and London Residuary Body. She highlights the approach of Lord Browne-Wilkinson and shows that he thought the rule was ready for review. This approach is very topical in light of the recent decisions in *Berrisford* and *Walker* which are discussed below.

> 'It may well be that the indeterminate nature of the lease will become a problem over time. This will be where the parties contracted on the joint assumption that the terminating event would occur within a short period and allocated risks on this basis, but in fact the event does not occur. In *Lace*, if the war were still continuing after 50 years but the parties had only thought it would last for a couple of years and had agreed a fixed rent, it would clearly be unfair to the landlord that the tenancy could not be renegotiated. This is a contractual problem, not a property one, and should be met by being able to re-open the bargain. To prescribe the circumstances in which renegotiation would be permissible would be a difficult task, indeed this reflects many of the problems that the courts encounter in economic duress cases, in trying to distinguish those cases in which the contractual modification is sensible and reasonable, and those which are exploitative … As Lord Browne-Wilkinson observes in *Prudential Assurance*, the ancient and technical rule of law which requires the maximum duration of a term of years to be ascertainable from the outset is ripe for review … To recognise this does not mean that the rule should simply be abandoned. It is being used by the courts to free the landlord from a manifestly disadvantageous contractual arrangement.'
>
> S Bright, 'Uncertainty in Leases: Is it a Vice?' (1993) 13 *LS* 38

The outcome of the case was that the agreement was terminated but the actual outcome was rather different. The result was that the freeholder owners had a strip of land which they could not use for any other purpose. The owners of the shop lost the guaranteed frontage to the shop. It was thoroughly unsatisfactory as the above comments from various academics reflect.

The principle that a lease must have a certain term has been subjected to a challenge in the case of *Berrisford v Mexfield Housing Association* [2011] UKSC 52.

Mexfield was a housing co-operative who would help people in difficulties over mortgage repayments. It purchased property from people in mortgage arrears and then leased the property back to them on terms.

In an agreement with Ms Berrisford, the housing co-operative agreed that she was granted a tenancy from month to month which would be terminable by Ms Berrisford by giving one month's notice to quit and terminable by Mexfield only in certain circumstances which included arrears of rent, failure to perform or observe any of the stipulations, conditions or provisions contained in the agreement, if a member shall cease to be a member of the association or if a resolution is passed under the rules of the association.

Note that the effect of all these terms was that the length of the tenancy was uncertain as it was not clear from the outset when these terms would apply. Mexfield served a notice to quit on Ms Berrisford relying on her arrears of rent which she later paid. Mexfield sought to argue that the agreement was void because it was of uncertain duration and in that case the agreement was merely a monthly periodic tenancy and she could be given a notice to quit irrespective of whether she had breached any of the terms of the lease.

The Court of Appeal found for the Housing Association but the Supreme Court unanimously held that Ms Berrisford's appeal should be allowed.

The judgment took a very strange approach which has attracted criticism.

It held that the agreement was in fact certain because by a complicated route it was really an agreement to last for Ms Berrisford's life.

Why?

The Supreme Court held that the lease was uncertain but under common law any lease that was uncertain would be converted to a lease for life and then any lease for life would be converted into a lease for 90 years. By virtue of s 149(6) of the Law of Property Act 1925 the term would now be a tenancy for 90 years subject to the landlord's right to determine on the tenant's death.

One of the main reasons for criticism is that it distinguished between commercial leases and residential leases as commercial leases of uncertain length will always remain void as they could not be considered to be a lease for life as no individual is involved on whose life the lease could be based. This changes the law because prior to this the law on certainty of term applied equally to both. Note that this section would not have applied to the parties in the case of *Prudential Assurance v Co Ltd v London Residuary Body* [1992] 2 AC 386 because the parties involved were not individuals.

The Supreme Court called for legislation on this point to be considered.

Prior to the case of *Berrisford* the law had addressed the problem of uncertainty by allowing a term to be considered to be certain if the lease had a fixed maximum term but subject to the tenant's right to end it if an event agreed by both parties should occur. The attraction of this was that it retained an element of flexibility but the duration of the tenancy was regarded as certain. This remains a way of avoiding the problems of an uncertain term. For example, the lease has a maximum term of ten years but subject to early termination on a specified event such as when the war ends or should the land be required for road widening.

Berrisford was applied fairly narrowly in the subsequent case of *Hardy v Haselden* [2011] EWCA Civ 1387 where an oral lease on the terms 'as long as you want' was not held to be a lease for life. It also failed on the lack of formality as there was no written deed. More recently it was applied in *Southward Housing Co-operative Ltd v Walker* [2015] EWHC 1615 (Ch) and Hildyard J held that in this case a contractual tenancy arose. He concluded that in this case a lease for life could not arise because the parties had never intended a lease for life and *Mexfield* had left open the possibility that the rule could be disapplied where the parties' intentions and fundamental aspects of the agreement would be confounded by it. The decision in *Walker* has rendered the approach taken in *Mexfield* subject to a strict test, i.e. did the parties contemplate a lease for life when they entered into the agreement? It is highly unlikely that they would have contemplated such a result and so uncertain agreements will now rarely be saved in this way. In *Gilpin v Legg* [2017] EWHC 3220 (Ch) HHJ Matthews revisited the principles of *Berrisford*. The case concerned a number of beach huts which were situated in fields belonging to the landowner who had inherited them from his parents. On their death he issued licence agreements but some of the owners claimed periodic tenancies. The court reviewed the possibility that leases for life had arisen and in so doing cast some doubt as to whether the authorities on which *Berrisford* was based were in fact applicable in any event. In the light of this and the earlier judgment of *Walker* it is even less likely that uncertain terms will be saved in the future. Parliament may yet revisit the question of uncertainty of term and introduce some statutory control over the difficulties presented by the decision in *Prudential Assurance*.

Periodic tenancies

This certainty of term rule is difficult to apply to periodic tenancies because a periodic tenancy has no fixed maximum duration at its inception. The reason that it does not infringe the rule is that the length of the term is determined by the period with reference to which the rent payable is calculated.

For example, if the rent of £350 is paid per month then it will be a monthly tenancy. This will be implied even though it has not been specifically mentioned in the agreement. The tenancy could in fact last for many years.

So the law sees the periodic tenancy as a series of separate terms which then could be terminated at the end of each term. Each period is certain, so the term itself is certain.

13.1.3 For a rent

1. Rent is defined as the consideration paid to the landlord by the lessee in return for the use of the premises.

2. It will usually be in money but it can be in any form including benefits in kind.

3. It has historically been seen as an important feature of the landlord and tenant relationship. In more recent cases it has been accepted that you can have a lease without the payment of rent. In *Ashburn Anstalt v Arnold* (1989) Fox LJ stated:

   'In the circumstances I conclude that the reservation of a rent is not necessary for the creation of a tenancy. That conclusion involves no departure from Lord Templeman's proposition in *Street v Mountford* "if exclusive possession at a rent for a term does not constitute a tenancy then the distinction between a contractual tenancy and a contractual licence of land becomes wholly unidentifiable". We are saying only that we do not think that Lord Templeman was stating the quite different proposition that you cannot have a tenancy without a rent.'

   If rent is paid then it can be seen as an indicator of a lease.

4. In cases where no rent is payable, even where exclusive possession is enjoyed, it may suggest a licence. A man was held to be a licensee where he occupied agricultural land under an agreement with the council which allowed him to remain in occupation for the rest of the year without charge, and at his own risk (*Colchester Council v Smith* [1991] Ch 446).

5. If rent is to be payable then it must be certain at the commencement of the lease and the amount payable must be clear at the date for payment.

13.2 The distinction between a lease and a licence

The distinction between a lease and a licence remains a difficult issue but since the decision in *Street v Mountford* (1985) the three main indicators: exclusive possession; for a fixed or periodic term certain; in consideration of a premium or period payments outlined by Lord Templeman when applied together, will indicate a lease.

In *Street v Mountford* the agreement specified that the relationship between the parties was one of licence. Lord Templeman held that the issue would be determined by looking at the true nature of the agreement rather than the name given by the parties in the agreement:

JUDGMENT

'In the present case, the agreement dated 7 March 1983 professed an intention by both parties to create a licence and their belief that they had in fact created a licence … Both parties enjoyed freedom to contract or not and both parties exercised that freedom by contracting on the terms set forth in the written agreement and on no other terms. But the consequences in law of the agreement, once concluded, can only be determined by consideration of the effect of the agreement. If the agreement satisfied all the requirements of a tenancy, then the agreement produced a tenancy and the parties cannot alter the effect of the agreement by insisting that they only created a licence.'

In a later case, *Bruton v London & Quadrant Housing Trust* [2000] 1 AC 406, Lord Hoffmann said: 'the fact the parties use language more appropriate to a different kind of agreement, such as a licence, is irrelevant if upon its true construction it has the identifying characteristics of a lease'.

No exclusive possession	Exclusive possession	For a term	At a rent
No exclusive possession if the landlord is entitled to move the occupiers from room to room (*Westminster City Council v Clarke* (1992)).	There will be exclusive possession if the landlord retains sets of keys or provides services as a sham (*Aslan v Murphy* (1990)).	There must be no uncertainty in the period of the lease.	Any consideration paid to the landlord.
No exclusive possession if merely exclusive occupation such as a hotel guest (*Abbeyfield (Harpenden) Society Ltd v Woods* (1968)).	There may be exclusive possession even if the occupiers have entered separate agreements called licences (*Antoniades v Villiers* (1990)) and the owner reserves himself the right also to live in the property if this clause is not genuine.	The maximum date of duration must be certain at the start of the lease (*Lace v Chantler* (1944); *Prudential Assurance Co Ltd v London Residuary Body* (1992)).	Usually money but can be paid in kind.

No exclusive possession if services are provided to the employee by the employer for the better performance of his/her job (*Norris v Checksfield* (1991)).	There may be exclusive possession if the employer provides premises but it is not for the better performance of the employee's duties (*Fachini v Bryson* (1952)).	Periodic tenancies are saved as each period is determined by the period for which rent is payable.	It is possible to have a lease without rent (*Ashburn Anstalt v Arnold* (1989)).
There will be no exclusive possession if provision of services is genuine even if the services provided are relatively trivial and rejected by the occupant (*Huwyler v Ruddy* (1995)).	There may be exclusive possession and a tenancy for some purposes may arise even where the grantor does not have a legal estate to grant a lease (*Bruton v London & Quadrant Housing Trust* (1999)).		If rent is payable then it must be clearly stated in the terms of the lease.

Table 13.1 Key features indicating a lease or a licence

13.2.1 The significance of the lease/licence distinction in law

1. The tenant can assign his interest in land and the lease is enforceable against the original lessor. A licence is personal only – it cannot be assigned.

2. If the lessor transfers his interest in land, then the lease is capable of binding the transferee. A lease over seven years will be registrable but a lease under seven years will be overriding. A licence is not registrable whatever the length.

3. A licensee cannot claim statutory protection for security of tenure under the landlord and tenant legislation, for example the Rent Act 1977 or the Landlord and Tenant Act 1954 (business tenants only) although he has some protection under the Housing Act 1985.

4. Residential tenants under long leases may have the right to purchase the freehold. This is not available to a licensee.

5. Certain tenants have the right to enforce repairing and other covenants in the lease unavailable to licensees (Landlord and Tenant Act 1985).

6. The Protection from Eviction Act 1977 will protect licensees in domestic premises from immediate eviction as well as lessees so claiming a lease of residential premises will not be necessary in order to claim protection under this Act.

ACTIVITY

Applying the law

Mr Dodgy owns a number of flats in Cedar Mansions and lets them to a number of different people. Consider the following agreements and decide whether they take effect as licences or leases:

1. Lucy and Mary enter into an agreement with Mr Dodgy to occupy a flat in Cedar Mansions. The terms are that they will pay £300 each month. They will have clean sheets and regular cleaning of the premises provided by Mr Dodgy's aunt.

2. Nicki and Owen enter into an agreement with Mr Dodgy to occupy a one-bedroom flat in Cedar Mansions. They are to pay £400 per month. One of the terms included in the agreement was that Mr Dodgy reserves the right to move another person, including Mr Dodgy himself, into the flat at any time.
3. Mr Dodgy tells his niece Flora that she can have one of the flats for as long as she likes if she pays rent of £350 per month. The agreement is referred to as a lease.
4. Mr Dodgy allows his two nephews, Harry and George, who both work for an independent wine supplier, to live in the flat rent-free but they agree to supply him with two dozen cases of wine each month.
5. Mr and Mrs Bright move into the top-floor flat with their three children. They pay £500 in rent each month. Mr Dodgy retains a spare key and insists he must have constant access because the hot-water boiler for all the flats is in the roof and it is only accessible from the top-floor flat. The agreement is termed a licence.

13.3 Types of leases

There are many different types of leases. Some confer more rights on the tenant than others and some are very similar to contractual licences.

13.3.1 Fixed-term leases

A fixed-term lease is, as the name suggests, a lease where the exact duration is fixed at the outset of the lease. It can be for any period – a week or for 500 years – so long as the period is certain.

For example: to Anthony, a lease for six months of Windy Ridge, rent of £300 to be payable monthly. The lease will automatically determine after six months.

13.3.2 Periodic leases

A periodic tenancy is one that may continue indefinitely. It can last from week to week, month to month or from year to year. The length of the tenancy is determined according to the period for which rent is payable. If the period is for less than three years then the periodic tenancy will not require any formalities in spite of the fact that the tenancy may continue for a period well in excess of three years.

For example, Vishi takes a lease of a flat in Chelsea in July 1997. He is to pay rent of £800 each month. He likes the flat and remains there for many years. He is still there in July 2006. His tenancy has already lasted over nine years. The fact that it was not created by deed does not affect its validity even though it has lasted well in excess of three years.

Sometimes a periodic tenancy is implied because a property owner accepts rent paid on a periodic basis by a 'tenant at will' (discussed below).

13.3.3 Tenancy at will

A tenancy at will arises whenever a tenant, with the consent of the landlord, occupies or continues to occupy premises. The terms will be that the landlord can determine the tenancy whenever he wishes. Indeed either party can determine at any time. Rent will usually be payable but will not affect the existence of such a tenancy if it is not payable. However, once rent is paid and accepted on a regular basis then a periodic tenancy will be implied. It has been described as follows: 'The tenancy at will is not so much an estate as a relationship between landlord and tenant: there is no period for which the tenant is entitled to the land' (R J Smith, *Property Law Cases and Materials* (6th edn, Pearson, 2015), p. 501).

The agreement is very informal. Either party can determine at will. It will automatically determine on the death of either party. There is very little difference between the tenancy at will and the licence. The main difference lies in the fact that the tenant at will is able to claim against a stranger in trespass and the tenant at will can claim he has possession of the land. However, he has no proprietary right in the land, in the sense that the interest can be sub-let or assigned and the rights will not be binding on a third-party purchaser.

The tenancy at will may be expressly granted or it may arise by implication from the act of the parties.

The tenancy at will is very unusual today. It is most likely to be used where the parties are negotiating a relationship such as a legal lease. It has been said that such a tenancy 'can now serve only one legal purpose, and that is to protect the interests of an occupier during a period of transition' (Scarman LJ in *Heslop v Burns* [1974] 1 WLR 1241).

For example, Shelagh rented a flat in Mayfair for three years, on a fixed tenancy. She has found a house to buy in Fulham but it will not be available until July and her lease expired in March. The landlord agrees that she can continue to occupy the Mayfair flat on the same terms until July. Her status after March will be as a tenant at will.

CASE EXAMPLE

Javad v Mohammad Aqil [1991] 1 WLR 1007

The landowner was negotiating for a ten-year lease of premises and allowed the tenants into possession while negotiations were continuing, expecting that an agreement would soon be reached. Although the 'tenant' paid rent, the Court of Appeal held that there was no implied periodic tenancy but merely a tenancy at will.

JUDGMENT

'Where parties are negotiating the terms of a proposed lease, and the prospective tenant is let into possession or permitted to remain in possession in advance of, and in anticipation of, terms being agreed, the fact that the parties have not yet agreed terms will be a factor to be taken into account in ascertaining their intention. It will often be a weighty factor. Frequently in such cases a sum called "rent" is paid at once in accordance with the terms of the proposed lease: for example, quarterly in advance. But, depending on all the circumstances, parties are not to be supposed thereby to have agreed that the prospective tenant shall be a quarterly tenant. They cannot sensibly be taken to have agreed that he shall have a periodic tenancy, with all the consequences flowing from that.'

Nicholls LJ

A tenancy at will may be brought to an end by conversion into an implied periodic tenancy where rent is paid and accepted on a regular basis.

For instance, in the example above, where Shelagh remains in the flat in Mayfair, she may become an implied periodic tenant if the arrangement continues for some time and the rent is payable on a regular basis and accepted by the landlord.

13.3.4 Tenancy at sufferance

A tenancy at sufferance will arise where the tenant continues to occupy property but, unlike a tenancy at will, it is without the consent of the landlord. The rights of the tenant at sufferance do not extend to allowing him to maintain an action in trespass. If the landlord expressly refuses the tenant the right to remain, then the tenant becomes a trespasser subject to the protection afforded by the Protection from Eviction Act 1977.

CASE EXAMPLE

Remon v City of London Real Property Co Ltd [1921] 1 KB 49

A tenant remained in possession after a valid notice to quit had expired. The tenant claimed to be a tenant at sufferance but the court held that as the landlord had already taken action to endeavour to remove him from the premises, he could not be a tenant at sufferance.

'[T]enants at sufferance seem to have been confined to persons who held over without the assent or dissent of their landlords, and not to have included persons who held over wrongfully in spite of the active objection of their landlords.'

Scrutton LJ

The distinction between a tenancy at sufferance and a tenancy at will is whether the landlord accepts the fact that the tenant is holding over in which case it will be a tenancy at will but if he refuses the rent then it will take effect as a tenancy at sufferance. A tenancy at sufferance will be converted into a tenancy at will if the landlord accepts the tenant's occupation of the premises and can in turn become an implied tenancy.

13.3.5 Leases for life

If a lease is granted for someone's lifetime it will be uncertain. Therefore it offends against the rule that the maximum length of a lease must be certain. Under the Law of Property Act 1925:

SECTION

's 205(1)(xxvii) ... a term of years absolute does not include a lease for life or a lease which is determinable on the death of some named person.'

A lease for someone's life may be saved under s 149(6) of the 1925 Act:

SECTION

's 149(6) ... Any lease or underlease at a rent, or in consideration of a fine, for life or for lives or for any term of years determinable with life or lives, or on the marriage of the lessee, or any contract therefore ... shall take effect as a lease ... for a term of ninety years determinable after the death or marriage ... of the original lessee.'

This section only applies where rent is payable. If a lease for life is granted and no rent is payable then it cannot be a legal estate under s 1(1) of the 1925 Act and can only exist in equity under a trust of land as a life interest, if at all.

Where rent is payable then the lease is converted into one of 90 years but will be determinable on the death of the original lessee, with one month's notice.

For example, in 1986 Ronald grants a lease to Quentin for his life, at a yearly rent of £3,000. On Quentin's death in 2002 there are still over 74 years left to run but Ronald can determine the lease by giving notice to Quentin's successors in title.

Note the recent application of a lease for life under s149(6) LPA 1925 in the case of *Mexfield v Berrisford* (2011).

13.3.6 Perpetually renewable leases

The lease may contain a covenant for the tenant to renew the lease. There is then the prospect that the lease may be indefinitely renewable.

Under s145 and Sched 15, para 5 Law of Property Act 1922, such a lease can be automatically converted into a lease for 2,000 years. To many, this seems a very generous provision for a lease which at first sight simply appears to offend the rule against certainty of duration. The provision is subject to quite strict rules. It will only apply if, by the wording, it is shown that the intention of the parties is that it should be perpetually renewable.

CASE EXAMPLE

Caerphilly Concrete Products Ltd v Owen [1972] 1 WLR 372

The lease contained the following clause which provided for renewal: 'containing the like covenants and provisos as are herein contained (including an option to renew such lease for the further term of five years at the expiration thereof)'. The court considered whether this was a perpetually renewable lease.

Russell LJ: 'In the present case the brackets make it abundantly plain that the parties are explaining that "containing the like covenants and provisos" is a phrase intended to embrace an option.'

The court reluctantly found that this was a perpetually renewable lease and therefore had to be converted into a term of 2,000 years.

Compare the following judgment in *Marjorie Burnett Ltd v Barclay* (1981) 258 EG 642 where the court took a less generous approach:

JUDGMENT

'Here, the second lease would contain a covenant for a further seven years and a rent to be agreed, but the final words, requiring yet another covenant for renewal, could not possibly be included, because they were not part of the covenant for renewal. A point of equal force appeared to be that the notion of a 2000 year term was completely inimical to a lease containing a rent review every seven years.'

Nourse LJ

It was held in this case that the lease was not perpetually renewable and the tenant could only claim the right to renew the tenancy twice.

13.3.7 Tenancies by estoppel

A tenancy by estoppel operates where the landlord has no title to the land when a lease is granted. The landlord is trying to do something which in law he is unable to do. However, the tenant believes that he has a legal estate in land, with all the effects of holding a lease, and if the court denied him the lease it would have serious consequences.

JUDGMENT

'It is a fundamental principle of the common law that a grantor is not entitled to dispute the validity of his own grant and may not therefore disaffirm the title of his grantee.'

Goodtitle D Edwards v Bailey (1777) 2 Cowp 597

It makes no difference that the parties were aware that the landlord had a defective title. The doctrine still allows both parties to claim a tenancy by estoppel.

The principle can take effect on both the interest of the tenant and the interest of the landlord.

JUDGMENT

'If a landlord lets a tenant into possession under a lease, then, so long as the tenant remains in possession undisturbed by any adverse claim – then the tenant cannot dispute the landlord's title. Suppose the tenant (not having been disturbed) goes out of possession and the landlord sues the tenant on the covenant for rent or for breach of covenant to repair or to yield up in repair. The tenant cannot say to the landlord: "You are not the true owner of the property."'

Lord Denning

What the courts are saying here is that the tenant, having paid rent and accepted the terms of the lease, cannot turn around to the landlord and then argue that the agreement was not a tenancy.

The principle was discussed in a landmark decision in the law *Bruton v London & Quadrant Housing Trust*. This case has created an interesting but confusing issue in relation to leases. Under the principle of *nemo dat quod non habet* it is assumed that it is not possible to grant an estate in land greater than that held by the grantor. This is an important principle which applies in many areas of law, in particular the buying and selling of goods in commercial law. In *Bruton* an interest was granted that the courts found to be a lease even though the grantor only had a licence rather than a lease himself.

CASE EXAMPLE

Bruton v London & Quadrant Housing Trust [2000] 1 AC 406

The claimant argued that he held a lease from a charitable housing trust. He wanted to enforce the repair covenant under common law which he could not do unless he could claim that he was a tenant. The landlord, however, did not hold the freehold of the property but was itself merely a licensee. It claimed that the claimant could not enjoy the property as a tenant because a lease could not be granted by someone who did not hold a legal estate in land.

> The Court of Appeal accepted this argument and held that Bruton held as a licensee because the housing trust could not grant a lease where they did not themselves have a legal estate. The court applied the principle of *nemo dat quod non habet* (no one can grant what they do not own).

> The House of Lords rejected this argument. It based its judgment on whether or not the claimant had exclusive possession of the property. There was a significant term in the lease under which the occupier would 'permit the Trust or its Agents, Surveyors or Consultants to enter the property for the purpose of inspecting the state of repair, and cleanliness of the property or for any purpose connected at all reasonable hours of the day'.

Lord Hoffmann gave the principal judgment in the case:

> 'There is nothing to suggest the he [Mr Bruton] was to share possession with the trust, the council or anyone else. The trust did not retain such control over the premises as was incon-sistent with Mr Bruton having exclusive possession, as was the case in *Westminster City Council v Clarke* [1992]. The only rights which it reserved were for itself and the council to enter at certain times and for limited purposes.'

Lord Hoffmann then discussed how a tenancy can arise when the grantor did not have a legal estate in land himself. He looked at the juridical basis for a tenancy by estoppel.

> 'In fact, as the authorities show, it is not the estoppel which creates the tenancy. The estop-pel arises when one or other of the parties wants to deny one of the ordinary incidents or obligations of the tenancy on the ground that the landlord had no legal estate. The basis of the estoppel is that having entered into an agreement which constitutes a lease or tenancy, he cannot repudiate that incident or obligation.
>
> Thus it is the fact that the agreement between the parties constitutes a tenancy that gives rise to an estoppel and not the other way round. It therefore seems to me that the question of tenancy by estoppel does not arise in this case. The issue is simply whether the agreement is a tenancy. It is not whether either party is entitled to deny some obliga-tion or incident of the tenancy on the ground that the trust had no title.'

The effect of this judgment was that the claimant could enforce repairing covenants under the agreement. These would not have been available if he had been a licensee.

Lord Hoffmann in *Bruton* distinguishes between two types of lease. He refers to the proprietary lease with which we are all familiar and which was defined by Lord Templeman in *Street v Mountford* (1985). There is also a lease which can be a contractual state of affairs between landlord and tenant which is not proprietary in nature. This is not the lease envisaged in *Street v Mountford*.

This has been extensively criticised by a number of academics.

> 'To put it another way, apparently there is in English law the "normal" proprietary lease that has been with us for centuries and also the "non-proprietary lease" or "con-tractual tenancy" being a "lease" between the parties, but not a "lease" in a proprietary sense. It is an understatement to say it muddies the waters. The decision in Street itself is premised on the assumption that a lease is proprietary and that is why it must be distinguished from a licence! To take the ratio of Street and apply it to Bruton in the manner suggested by Lord Hoffmann does great violence not only to established prin-ciples of property law but goes against the very purpose of Lord Templeman's judg-ment in the earlier case. Exclusive possession signifies exclusive control in virtue of an estate in land granted by the landlord; exclusive occupation signifies exclusive control in virtue of other arrangements and it might be thought that the occupier in *Bruton* had the latter but not the former.'
>
> M Dixon, *Modern Land Law* (9th edn, Routledge, 2014) p. 226

This case has given rise to a separate group of tenancies called 'Bruton tenancies' which have some of the key characteristics of a tenancy and allow the tenant to enforce certain rights such as repairing obligations but are not proprietary and therefore not enforceable against a third party purchaser.

There have been two subsequent cases which both followed the reasoning of the House of Lords in *Bruton*; however in neither case were the claimants able to maintain their rights in property against third-party purchasers, although they were found to hold leases in the non-proprietary sense outlined by Lord Hoffmann.

CASE EXAMPLE

Kay v Lambeth Borough Council [2006] 2 AC 465

A housing trust had granted rights to the claimants. The claimants maintained that their rights were binding even after the housing trust had been evicted from the land. They argued that their rights amounted to leases and were binding on the council who had recovered the property from the trust. It was held by the House of Lords that once the trust had been evicted then any rights binding on them could no longer subsist since the rights were carved out of the original estate in land which had now ceased to exist.

This later decision seems to suggest that *Bruton* is a single decision decided on the facts of the case in an attempt to uphold the particular claim in *Bruton* on the facts of that case. *Kay* suggests that it will not be universally applied.

CASE EXAMPLE

London Borough of Islington v Green and O'Shea [2005] EWCA Civ 56

The facts of this case were not dissimilar from those of *Bruton v London Quadrant Housing Trust* (2000) and *Kay v Lambeth Borough Council* (2005). A housing association held a licence from Islington Borough Council which was terminable on 28 days' notice. The council eventually issued a notice to quit after the housing association had held the licence for over 16 years. It had permitted a number of persons to occupy the property, including the two defendants, Miss Green and Mr O'Shea. The council argued that the notice to quit terminated all rights, including those of licensees or tenants. However, Miss Green (who by now had vacated the property) and Mr O'Shea both argued that they held tenancies from the association which had been granted with full knowledge of the council.

Their arguments were rejected on the basis that the association had no authority to grant the proprietary interest or estate to the claimants. Indeed, the court went further to conclude that even if the association had sufficient estate in the property or had been clothed with the requisite authority as agent so as to grant a sub-tenancy binding on the council, this would still not have been binding on the council once the licence had been terminated.

These cases both decide that the lease which was accepted by the House of Lords in *Bruton* cannot be binding on third parties and can only take effect as a lease in limited circumstances.

What we must also conclude is that there will be a considerable difference in effect if there is a finding of a licence rather than a non-proprietary lease. For Mr Bruton, there was a right to enforce covenants in the agreement. Other rights could include rent control, security of tenure and rights of succession: all denied to a licensee.

> 'The danger here is that the courts may be forced to accept [albeit unwittingly] that this type of legislation, originally aimed at tenants in the orthodox sense, is now also available to other residential occupants enjoying personal rights against their immediate landlords. If the contractual licence has now become synonymous with the personal tenancy, this seems to be an inevitable consequence of the Bruton line of thinking.'
>
> M Pawlowski, 'The Bruton Tenancy: Clarity or More Confusion?' [2005] 69 *Conv* 262

Different types of lease			
Type of lease	How created	How determined	Key features
Fixed lease	Informally under three years. Only by deed over three years.	Notice to quit formally served.	Must be clear from the outset when it is to determine.
Periodic lease	Can be created informally if under three years.	By serving a notice to quit equivalent to the period of rent payment, e.g. one month for monthly tenancies.	Can last in excess of three years but can be created informally without the need for a deed or even writing.
Tenancy at will	A tenant continues in possession after a lease has ended with the consent of the landlord or anyone who enters into possession as a tenant but does not gain a proprietary interest.	By converting to an implied periodic tenancy or termination by either party at any time.	Very similar to a licence except that the tenant at will can bring an action for trespass.
Tenancy at sufferance	Arises where the landlord neither assents nor dissents to the presence of the tenant who continues to occupy after his lease has ended.	The landlord denies the tenant's right to be on the premises.	It covers a situation where the tenant simply continues to enjoy the premises. Rarely lasts for any length of time because once the landlord accepts rent it will be converted into an implied periodic tenancy.
Lease for life	Any lease that is granted to someone for his lifetime will fail unless it can be converted into a 90-year lease under s 149(6) LPA 1925.	Once converted, it can be determined by either party giving at least one month's notice.	Cannot be a legal lease as there is no certain term so will fail unless converted under s 149(6) of LPA 1922.
Perpetually renewable lease	A lease which includes a covenant to renew which itself can be renewed.	Unless it has been converted into a 2,000-year lease, under s 145 of LPA 1922 it will determine on the last day of the period of the lease, having allowed one renewal.	These are very strictly construed against allowing conversion into a 2,000-year lease. *Marjorie Barnett Ltd v Barclay* (1980)
Estoppel tenancy	A tenancy by estoppel operates where the landlord has no title to the land when the lease is granted.	Can be determined according to the terms of the lease agreed between the parties.	The fact that the court held there to be a tenancy allowed the tenant to enforce significant repairing covenants. These would have been denied to a licensee.

ACTIVITY

Quick quiz

Define:

1. a periodic tenancy;
2. a tenancy at will;
3. a tenancy at sufferance;
4. a lease for life;
5. a tenancy by estoppel.

13.4 The creation of a lease

13.4.1 Creation of a lease exceeding three years

The grant of a lease for a fixed term of more than three years must be by deed (s 52(1) of the Law of Property Act 1925). This means that it should be signed, witnessed and delivered (s 1 Law of Property (Miscellaneous Provisions) Act 1989). This Act reformed the law, replacing the need for a seal on a deed with the need for a witness. Further, if the lease is for seven years or more it will not take effect unless it has been registered under the Land Registration Act 2002.

However, a lease can exist where it is for a very short period, even under one year. The formalities for short leases are necessarily much less strict.

13.4.2 Creation of a lease for less than three years

A lease for not more than three years may be created by a simple oral or written agreement. However, there are certain requirements that must be satisfied:

- it must take effect in possession;
- it must be at the best rent which can be reasonably obtained without taking a fine or premium.

To take effect in possession means that the lease must begin at the date of grant and not at some date in the future. Even if the lease is for less than three years, it must be created by deed if it is to take effect in the future. If it is to take effect more than three months in the future it must be registered, however short it is. The law regards it as a future lease.

CASE EXAMPLE

Long v Tower Hamlets Borough Council [1996] 2 All ER 683

A lease was granted by the council to the claimants. This was confirmed by a letter which was dated 4 September, stating that the lease would take effect on 29 September. The judge held that this could not be a legal lease because it was to take effect in the future. This made it a future lease and it could only have been granted by deed.

13.4.3 Contracts to create a lease for more than three years: equitable leases

Circumstances where an equitable lease might arise:

1. defects in the grant or transfer of a legal lease;
2. failure to apply for substantive registration under the Land Registration Act 2002;

3. a contract to create or transfer a leasehold term;

4. a grant of a lease by the holder of an equitable estate.

Under (3), where the parties have entered into a contract for the grant of a lease for a term of more than three years but no deed is executed to create a legal lease, an equitable lease may arise on the basis of the contract.

- **Before 27 September 1989**: a contract to grant a lease for more than three years had to satisfy s 40 of the Law of Property Act 1925; this held that all leases had to be evidenced in writing. The doctrine of part-performance could also apply where there was no evidence in writing. This allowed a tenant who entered into possession on the basis of an oral contract to enjoy an equitable lease even though there was no written evidence of the new contract.

- **After 27 September 1989**: a contract to grant a lease for more than three years must satisfy s 2(1) of the Law of Property (Miscellaneous Provisions) Act 1989. Under this Act, the agreement must be in writing and it must incorporate all the terms the parties have expressly agreed and it must be signed by or on behalf of them. If the contract does not comply with the requirements of s 2(1), then there will be no equitable lease. The doctrine of part-performance no longer applies.

13.4.4 The doctrine of *Walsh v Lonsdale* (1882)

If a contract to grant a lease satisfies s 2(1) of the 1989 Act, then the lease may be enforceable in equity. The landlord may still be forced to grant the promised lease.

The reason why such a lease may be enforceable is on equitable principles: 'equity looks on that as done which ought to be done'. Equity will therefore treat it as if there is a lease in existence. The parties are treated as having a lease in equity from the date of the contract. It depends on whether or not the contract is specifically enforceable.

The doctrine highlights the conflict between equity and common law. The common law would not uphold the lease because equity will allow the lease to be enforceable because it is quite clear what the parties had intended.

The rule was first established in the case of *Walsh v Lonsdale* (1882) 2 De G & J 559. This concerned an agreement for a lease of a mill. It had been executed in writing but not under deed, as required by law. The agreement held that rent was to be paid annually in advance; the actual amount would vary according to the success of the mill. The tenant moved into the mill and started paying rent on a six-monthly basis in arrears. The landlord accepted this for 18 months and then, without notice, demanded rent in advance, which was challenged by the tenant.

Equitable lease	Legal lease
The act of entering the property and paying rent supported the written agreement.	The tenant had an implied lease because he had possession of the property and paid rent.
The agreement was a written agreement not enforceable at law for a lease of seven years with rent payable in advance.	The lease would be an annual tenancy because the rent was paid at six-monthly intervals.
The lease would be enforceable in equity under equitable principles.	As rent had been paid and accepted in arrears, the law presumed that it was a term in the legal lease and the landlord could not change to claiming rent in advance.

Table 13.2 Arguments in *Walsh v Lonsdale* (1882) for an equitable or legal lease

The courts applied the Judicature Acts which lay down that in the event of a conflict between equity and common law, equity should prevail. It meant that the lease was declared to be equitable. The landlord had distrained for the outstanding rent and this would have been illegal if the lease had been held to be legal.

(N.B. Distraining was a form of self-help remedy called distress. It allowed the landlord to come and take goods belonging to the tenant in satisfaction of the rent that was outstanding. This would not have been legal if the tenancy was a legal tenancy as the landlord could not claim the rent in advance in these cases.)

When will specific performance be available?

Equity will not automatically grant specific performance. Certain conditions must first exist:

1. The agreement must be subject to the payment of rent or consideration.
2. The agreement must be in writing in order to satisfy s 2(1) of the 1989 Act.
3. The claimant must satisfy the requirement for 'clean hands'. This means that he must not have acted in a fraudulent or otherwise dishonest way. However, where there has been an attempt to rectify a defect such as non-payment of rent then the courts will uphold the right of the claimant.

The doctrine of Walsh v Lonsdale *(1882) today*

This doctrine applies to a much wider range of issues than merely leases:

1. the grant of easements;
2. the grant of profits;
3. the grant of a mortgage.

13.4.5 Is a *Walsh v Lonsdale* (1882) lease as good as a legal lease?

The doctrine of *Walsh v Lonsdale* converts an informal lease into a lease that is enforceable on the same terms as the original agreement.

Does that mean that an equitable lease is as good as a legal lease?

1. **Effect of equitable leases against third parties.** If Jon grants a lease for five years to Ben in writing but not in the form of a deed then it will be enforceable as an equitable lease. If Jon sells to Sam then Sam will not be bound by the equitable lease unless he has notice of the lease and this depends on whether the lease has been registered. For unregistered land this would be as a Class C(iv) estate contract and for registered land it would be entered as a burden on the Charges Register. In registered land it may also take effect as an overriding interest which does not require protection but the tenant must be in occupation of the property. It arises under Sched 3 para 2 and is dependent on proof of an interest in land and actual occupation. Compare a legal lease which will be binding on any purchaser, and occupation will be irrelevant.
2. **Do the covenants run against the landlord?** If the lease exists in equity then the rights and duties will not run automatically on assignment of the lease. They will normally run against the landlord on assignment but not necessarily against the tenant.
3. Informally created rights may take effect in law under s 62 Law of Property Act 1925 when the land passes under a conveyance. However the section is dependent on a conveyance and there will be no conveyance under an equitable lease. This means

that implied easements will not automatically pass in equity, whereas at common law if the right satisfies the tests necessary for an easement then the right will pass at common law.

4. The parties are dependent on the availability of specific performance. As mentioned above, unlike the common law remedy of damages, specific performance is only available if certain conditions are satisfied.

ACTIVITY

Applying the law

Consider the following statement: 'It is often said that an agreement for a lease is as effective as a legal lease.'

Do you agree?

13.5 The terms in a lease

Both the landlord and the tenant have obligations under the lease. These are contractual obligations and may be expressly or impliedly included in the lease, for example if the lease itself is implied, such as an implied periodic tenancy, then the usual covenants will be implied into that lease. Usual covenants are covenants that will apply to all tenancies.

There are a number of covenants which are implied into every lease and most leases include a number of express covenants.

13.5.1 The landlord's covenants

A number of covenants can be implied into the lease both at common law and also under statute.

Implied covenants:

- a covenant to allow the tenant quiet enjoyment;

- a covenant that the landlord will not derogate from his grant;

- a covenant that the premises are fit for the purpose for which they are let or are habitable.

A covenant to allow the tenant quiet enjoyment

It is implied in every lease that the landlord shall allow the tenant quiet enjoyment of the premises let.

KEY FACTS

Quiet enjoyment
1. The tenant is guaranteed the right to enjoy the property without interference from anyone else claiming rights in the land, or anything interfering with enjoyment of the premises, such as the roof leaking, or even allowing other tenants to interfere with enjoyment because they make excessive noise.
2. If the tenant can prove that he has been subjected to harassment or to unlawful eviction, this will constitute a breach of quiet enjoyment. The removal of windows and doors in *Lavender v Betts* [1942] 2 All ER 72 was sufficient, as were persistent threats which resulted in the tenant leaving in *Kenny v Preen* [1963] 1 QB 499; and interfering with the supply of essential

services in *Perera v Vandiyar* [1953] 1 WLR 672, where the landlord was held to be in breach of the covenant when he allowed the gas and electricity supply to be cut off repeatedly. This would now constitute a criminal offence under the Protection from Eviction Act 1977 if it could be shown that the landlord did this with the intent to 'cause the occupier ... to give up the occupation of the premises ... or to refrain from exercising any right or pursuing any remedy in respect of the premises'. In *Timothy Taylor Ltd v Mayfair House Corp* [2016] a landlord carried out works which interfered with the tenant's business. The tenant ran an art gallery on the ground floor which became difficult to access when the landlord erected scaffolding and started building works on the upper floors. Although the landlord had reserved to himself the right to carry out these works the judge found that the tenant's right to quiet enjoyment had been breached since the landlord had not taken reasonable steps to minimise disturbance to the tenant.

3. The extent of the covenant: it does not extend to the condition of the property at the start of the lease. In *Southwark LBC v Mills* [1999] 3 WLR 939 the tenants in a block of flats owned by the council complained about the excessive noise from neighbouring flats. It was attributable to the poor quality of the soundproofing rather than the tenants themselves. The House of Lords did not find the council to be in breach because the soundproofing was in place at the start of the tenancy.

4. If the breach merely causes inconvenience rather than genuine interference then that will not amount to a breach. In *Browne v Flower* [1911] 1 Ch 219 the tenant complained because an external staircase erected by the landlord allowed the other tenants to look through the windows of the leased premises. No breach of quiet enjoyment was found.

5. Breaches by third parties: the landlord may be liable to the tenant where the breach is committed by a third party who acts with the authorisation of the landlord but not for anyone acting in excess of the landlord's grant. So the landlord will not be liable for acts of other tenants unless they are acting in an unlawful manner.

6. Remedies: it is possible for the tenant to repudiate his lease but it is much more usual for damages or an injunction to be awarded.

A covenant that the landlord will not derogate from his grant

The general principle is that 'you must not take away that which you have given'. So the landlord cannot take away from the tenant any rights that have been granted under the lease. There is an overlap with the covenant for quiet enjoyment but under this covenant it is possible to claim a breach where there is no physical interference with the premises.

KEY FACTS

Non-derogation from the grant
1. The character of the premises must not be changed by the landlord so that they cannot be used for the purposes of the tenancy. In *Aldin v Latimer Clark Muirhead & Co* [1894] 2 Ch 437 premises had been let to a timber merchant. The premises had a natural flow of air necessary for his business. This came from a neighbouring property also owned by the landlord. When the landlord blocked this up by building on the land it was held to be a derogation from the grant. In *Harmer v Jumbil (Nigeria) Tin Areas Ltd* [1921] 1 Ch 200 the tenant took a lease of land to store explosives. The landlord allowed the adjoining land to be used for mining operations which endangered the explosives that had been stored and the tenant was in danger of losing his licence. This was held to be a derogation from the grant.
2. The tenant cannot claim if the landlord did not know about the tenant's intended use for the land. It must interfere with the use so as to make it impossible to use the land for the purpose at all. If it can be still used for the purpose but it is just more expensive or inconvenient, an injunction is less likely to be granted.

A covenant that the premises are fit for the purpose that they are let or are habitable

1. There is no general warranty of fitness for purpose. This principle was repeated in *Southwark LBC v Mills* (1999). The general rule is that of *caveat emptor*: 'fraud apart there is no law against letting a tumble down house' Erle J in *Robbins v Jones* (1863) 15 CB (NS) 221.

2. If the premises are furnished, the common law implies a condition of fitness for habitation (*Smith v Marrable* (1843) 11 M & W 5). If the covenant is broken, the tenant has the right to leave immediately, without giving notice to the landlord. The covenant is very limited in scope as it only applies to residential premises at the start of the lease. Only the tenant can sue, which excludes members of his family or visitors.

3. Duty of care under contract: the landlord may be liable in contract for breach of an implied term. In *Liverpool City Council v Irwin* [1977] AC 239 a local council was found to be in breach of its contractual duty where it failed to keep certain common areas in a block of flats free from rubbish and debris.

4. Negligence: this is wider in ambit as it can introduce liability to members of the tenant's family and visitors to the premises. However, such claims are limited to defects which arise whilst the tenant is in occupation not defects which are present at the start of the tenancy, as decided in *Cavalier v Pope* [1906] AC 428.

5. Under s 8 of the Landlord and Tenant Act 1985, if a house is let for human habitation at a low rent then there is an implied condition that it is fit for human habitation at the beginning of the tenancy and an implied undertaking that the landlord will maintain the premises in this condition throughout the tenancy. This rarely applies as the rent must be below £80 per year in London and £52 elsewhere, which is so low that very few, if any tenants could rely on this statute, a fact that has been criticised frequently by the judiciary. It was introduced in 1957 and at the time would apply to a large number of tenancies, but now, nearly 70 years later, it has lost any genuine relevance to most tenants. There are other restrictions on the use of the section: it cannot be used where the premises cannot be rendered fit for human habitation at reasonable expense.

6. Under s 11 of the Landlord and Tenant Act 1985, certain covenants relating to repair and maintenance are impliedly undertaken by the landlord in a lease of a dwelling house for a term of less than seven years. The landlord must keep in repair the structure and exterior of the dwelling house as well as drains, gutterings and external pipes and also maintain the installations of the building, supplying water, gas sanitation, including basins, baths etc., and also for space heating and heating water. There will be a breach here if the landlord cuts off the supply of electricity or gas. It is limited in effect. It would not extend to such matters as condensation. In *Quick v Taff Ely BC* [1986] QB 809 it was held that excess condensation was caused by faulty design rather than disrepair. 'Disrepair is related to the physical condition of whatever has to be repaired and not to questions of lack of amenity or inefficiency' (Dillon LJ). Repair does not include any improvement of the property and the extent of the duty is affected by the age, character and prospective life of the property. It also requires the tenant to serve notice on the landlord of the relevant defect and no liability will arise until this is done.

7. Under s 4 of the Defective Premises Act 1972 the landlord has a statutory duty 'to take reasonable care to prevent personal injury or damage to property to which may be caused by defects in the state of the demised premises'. The Act only covers defects for which the landlord would normally carry liability.

8. The tenant has a number of remedies for breach of repairing covenants, such as claiming damages or an order for specific performance. The tenant also has the right to a limited measure of self-help. In *Lee-Parker v Izzet* [1971] 1 WLR 1688 the court held that the tenant has the right to carry out the repairs himself and then set off the value from his rent. In *Hussein v Mehlman* [1992] 2 EFLR 87 the court held that in serious cases where the landlord has failed to repair the tenant can simply treat the lease as terminated on the grounds of breach of a fundamental term.

Express covenants

Most leases will contain a wide range of covenants by the landlord in respect of such matters as repair, insurance, maintenance of the common parts and also allowing the tenant the option for renewal of the terms. In shorter leases the landlord will generally undertake to carry out more structural repairs. In longer leases the responsibility will fall on the shoulders of the tenant.

13.5.2 Implied covenants of the tenant

There are a number of tenant's obligations implied under law. These are called the 'usual covenants' and include the following:

1. **The tenant's covenant to pay rent**: it is possible to have a tenancy without the payment of rent so this is not implied automatically into every lease but it would usually be implied into most leases.

2. **The tenant's covenant to pay rates and other taxes on the premises**: these include any rates or taxes for which the landlord is not responsible.

3. **The tenant's liability for damage**: the tenant must not commit voluntary waste which means he must not commit an act or omission which alters the state of the premises. This would include changing the nature of the premises by carrying out internal work such as knocking down walls and taking out windows. The rules vary according to whether it is a weekly, monthly or yearly tenancy. Generally, all tenants must not carry out acts of voluntary waste but some tenants are responsible for permissive waste as well. This includes failing to act when it is clear that the premises are falling into disrepair.

4. **A duty to allow the landlord in to view the premises**: the landlord has no automatic right of entry to the tenant's premises but the tenant must allow him to enter at a pre-arranged time if the landlord is under a duty to repair the premises.

The tenant may also have expressly agreed certain covenants in the lease itself:

- payment of rent;
- not to assign, sub-let or part with possession.

These covenants can be either:

- absolute: not to sub-let at all; or
- qualified: to sub-let only with the consent of the landlord.

The tenant can seek permission from the landlord where there is an absolute covenant against assignment but cannot take action if the landlord refuses. In a qualified covenant the landlord can refuse permission only if the refusal is reasonable: s 19 of the Landlord and Tenant Act 1927.

Section 1 of the Landlord and Tenant Act 1988 ensures that any request from the tenant to assign is dealt with quickly. The landlord has a duty to give consent unless it is reasonable to refuse to do so. The reasons for refusal must be given and if consent is given but subject to conditions then those conditions must be given. The tenant does have the power to create a licence which is often a way around the problem of gaining consent.

The courts regard an objection that is in some way related to the proposed assignee or to the use that he intends to make of the premises as an acceptable reason for withholding consent.

Refusal of consent must not come within the restrictions imposed by any of these statutes:

- s 24 of the Race Relations Act 1976;
- s 31 of the Sex Discrimination Act 1975;
- ss 22 and 23 of the Disability Discrimination Act 1995.

In the case of *International Drilling Fluids Ltd v Louisville Investments (Uxbridge) Ltd* [1986] Ch 513 Balcombe LJ laid down a number of principles which guide the court on what constitutes unreasonable refusal of consent by the landlord. First, he laid down that the purpose of such covenants was to protect the lessor from having his premises used or occupied in an undesirable way, or by an undesirable tenant or assignee. Second, a landlord cannot refuse his consent to an assignment on grounds which have nothing to do with the relationship of landlord and tenant. Third, the onus of proof that consent is unreasonably being withheld lies with the tenant. He also said it was not necessary for the landlord to prove that withholding of consent was justified. More recently in *Ashworth Frazer Ltd v Gloucester City Council* [2011] 1 WLR 2180 the House of Lords reviewed the principles laid down in *International Drilling Fluids* and concluded that the decision as to what constitutes the unreasonable refusal of consent should not be determined according to strict rules and, according to Lord Bingham, the court should decide the issue of reasonableness on a 'broad and common sense meaning'. However the landlord cannot refuse to give consent on grounds that have nothing to do with the landlord and tenant relationship.

A number of amendments were made to the rules on assignment and sub-letting in the Landlord and Tenant (Covenants) Act 1995 but these rules only apply to tenancies granted after January 1996. It allows the parties to expressly negotiate the terms on which the tenant will be allowed to sub-let and the ordinary rules of refusal of consent will not apply.

ACTIVITY

Applying the law

Consider the following examples and advise whether there has been a breach of covenant by the landlord:

1. Janice has taken the tenancy of a flat in a block of 12 flats called Fabulous Mansions. She likes the flat but has become very annoyed because every night she can hear the television of her neighbours. The block was built in 1972.
2. Kerry has taken a ground-floor flat in Fabulous Mansions. She liked the fact that it was on the ground floor but now she has discovered that it is very damp and frequently there is heavy condensation running down the walls.
3. Lara has another flat in the block. She pays a very low rent. She has recently discovered that the bath has a large crack which had been covered up with Polyfilla.

All three tenants have complained about the frequent build-up of rubbish around the front door. The landlord, Mr Sleasy, has not replied to the complaints but they recently heard him shouting at one of the other tenants, saying that if she did not stop her complaints he would make sure she really did have a cause for complaint. They are now feeling very worried about their position and have come to you for advice.

13.6 The determination of leases

Leases can be determined in a variety of ways but once a lease is determined the effect is that the tenant ceases to have an estate in land.

13.6.1 The effect of determination

When a lease is determined the tenant will no longer have an estate in land. The landlord will be entitled to recover the land immediately and the tenant will no longer have exclusive possession of the property.

If there is a joint tenancy it will be determined even if only one tenant gives notice. This contrasts with the need for agreement for all positive dealings with a joint tenancy such as the exercise of a break clause by joint tenants as shown in *Hounslow London Borough Council v Pilling* [1993] 1 WLR 1242.

JUDGMENT

'[A]ll positive dealings with a joint tenancy require the concurrence of all joint tenants if they are to be effective.'

Bridge LJ in *Hammersmith LBC v Monk* [1992] 1 AC 478

This has been interpreted to mean that if one periodic tenant indicates that he does not want the lease to continue then it will be determined, because a joint tenancy relies on agreement of all the parties. In one case *Hammersmith LBC v Monk* it was held that one joint tenant could terminate a joint tenancy without the knowledge or agreement of the other.

CASE EXAMPLE

Hammersmith LBC v Monk [1992] 1 AC 478

A couple took a periodic tenancy of a council flat. After some time, the relationship broke down and the woman moved out. The council said that it would not re-house her unless she ended the tenancy she already held with it. The House of Lords held that she was able unilaterally to end the tenancy and so the council could claim back the tenancy and she could be re-housed.

This was a fair decision because if the woman had to get her former partner's agreement he might refuse and she could not exert any pressure on him to do so.

This decision has been affirmed in the subsequent case of *London Borough of Harrow v Qazi* [2003] UKHL 43, and in *Sims v Dacurum Borough Council* [2014] UKSC 63 it was held that this was not contrary to the European Convention on Human Rights because the rights of the remaining occupiers are adequately protected by the possibility of raising a proportionality defence.

13.6.2 Ways of determining a lease

Leases can be brought to an end in a number of different ways. Many of the old common law means of ending a lease have been affected by the large number of statutory provisions which have been passed to protect tenants (see Figure 13.1).

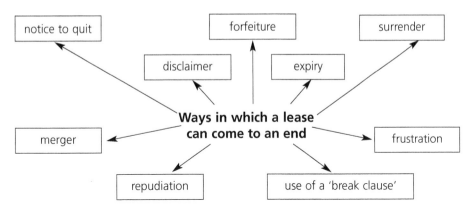

Figure 13.1 Termination of leases and licences

There are nine ways in which a lease can come to an end at common law:

1. **Notice to quit**: either party can serve on the other a notice to quit which will indicate that they no longer wish the tenancy to continue. Generally, the length of notice required is the same length as the period of the tenancy. The wider implications of eviction were raised in the case of *McDonald v McDonald* [2016] UKSC 28 where in a complicated set of facts parents of an adult child with mental health difficulties were forced to make an order to evict her when the parents fell behind with the mortgage over the property which they rented to her. An argument was made on behalf of the adult child that if she were evicted her Article 8 rights under the UCHR would be violated. This was a case concerning private individuals and on that basis the court rejected the application and one could conclude it goes much further.

2. **Forfeiture**: if the tenant is in breach of any covenants in the lease then the landlord may be entitled to forfeit the lease; the landlord has to decide whether the lease is continuing or whether he wishes to treat it as forfeited.

3. **Surrender**: a lease can be determined by the surrender of the interest of the tenant to his immediate landlord. If the interest is expressly surrendered then it must be contained in a deed in order to comply with s 52(1) of the Law of Property Act 1925. In some cases the law implies surrender by the tenant. An example would be where the tenant gives up possession of the land subject to the tenancy. The doctrine of estoppel would come into operation if the tenant then contested the surrender and claimed to have the property returned to him. However, there must truly be surrender, so if there is an uncompleted contract by the tenant to purchase the reversion of the lease, but it is not completed, there is no surrender by operation of law.

4. **Disclaimer**: a right to disclaim the lease usually arises under the lease itself or under statute. The most usual examples under statute occur when the trustees in bankruptcy and liquidators of companies disclaim what is termed 'onerous property' which they may have taken over in their role. The tenant would then be released from the tenant's obligations.

5. **Expiry**: a fixed-term lease or tenancy will automatically end when the term comes to an end.

forfeiture

Loss of an interest in land as a result of breach of a covenant

6. **Merger**: if the tenant acquires the landlord's freehold interest then the tenancy will immediately come to an end.

7. **A 'break clause'**: some leases may contain a clause which allows one party or even both parties to determine the lease on notice before the term expires.

8. **Frustration**: where frustration operates on the lease it destroys the whole basis of the agreement and so the tenancy comes to an end.

9. **Repudiation**: if there is a breach by either side that is sufficiently serious then the courts may allow the other party to repudiate the contract.

ACTIVITY

Quick Quiz

Jamil has a periodic tenancy in which he pays rent of £150 every month.
   How can he bring this tenancy to an end?

If the tenant is in breach of a covenant there are several possible remedies. There is a difference between breach for non-payment of rent and breach of other covenants.

13.7 Remedies of the landlord

13.7.1 Distress

The ancient right of distress is no longer available for non-payment of rent for residential premises. This involved the landlord selling goods belonging to the tenant. The landlord, or more often a bailiff, used to go to the premises and take the equivalent value of goods to the outstanding amount owed in rent. Some items could not be seized, such as clothes and bedding. It continues to be available for commercial leases.

13.7.2 Forfeiture

Forfeiture entitles the landlord to forfeit the lease before the agreed term has expired and is generally used as a remedy for non-payment of rent but it can also be used for other breaches of covenant. This is a very important remedy for the landlord, giving him the right to re-enter the premises and recover the lease, but it has severe consequences for the tenant.

When can forfeiture be exercised?

Forfeiture is only available where there is an express term in the lease giving the landlord the right of re-entry if the tenant fails to perform his obligations under the lease, such as payment of rent or a service charge.

In exercising forfeiture the landlord must take possession of the premises and he has two options:

- physical re-entry;
- service of proceedings against the tenant.

Today, physical re-entry is not encouraged, even where it is peaceable, and in residential premises it is not permissible for the landlord to re-enter without a court order s2 Protection from Eviction Act 1977.

In *Billson v Residential Apartments Ltd* [1992] 1 AC 494 a tenant had undertaken extensive work on the property in breach of covenant. The landlord peaceably re-entered the vacant property and changed the locks and served notice on the tenant. The tenant did not object at the time but objected later and sought relief from forfeiture. The House of Lords held that a tenant whose property has been forfeited by peaceful re-entry without a court order can apply for relief from forfeiture, i.e. restoration of the lease. The application for relief should be made as soon as possible as when the court decides whether to grant relief from forfeiture any delay in particular that of the tenant will be taken into account.

The tenant then has a reasonable time to try to remedy the breach. In the words of Lord Justice Slade in *Expert Clothing Service & Sales v Hillgate House Ltd* it is to give the tenants one last chance to remedy the breach of covenant.

Forfeiture may affect the rights of third parties such as sub-tenants or mortgagees and they have the right to seek relief from the courts, e.g. as forfeiture of the lease will mean that the sublease will automatically come to an end, the sub-tenant can ask the court to vest the tenancy in him/her thus becoming the tenant of the landlord.

There are different rules according to whether forfeiture is being exercised for non-payment of rent or for a breach of any other covenant.

Forfeiture for non-payment of rent

Where rent is overdue, the landlord must formally demand payment of the rent unless it is already six months overdue before exercising forfeiture either by peaceable re-entry or a court order. The tenant then has the right to seek relief which will usually be heard in the County Court. Where the landlord has re-entered the property the High Court can grant discretionary relief under its inherent jurisdiction. The tenant must pay the rent arrears and the landlord's costs of forfeiture. The County Court also has the right to grant relief under the County Courts Act 1984.

Forfeiture for breach of covenants other than to pay rent

The procedure for the breach of covenants other than the covenant to pay rent is started by the service of a s 146 notice which must contain certain key information. For example, which breach is relied on and a request that the breach be remedied if possible and a requirement that compensation for the breach must be paid to the landlord.

Other breaches of covenants

KEY FACTS

The s 146 notice
1. The tenant must be in breach of a covenant other than for non-payment of rent.
2. The tenant must then be given the chance to remedy the breach or to apply for relief from forfeiture.
3. The notice will not be valid unless it specifies the breach.
4. It must require the tenant to remedy the breach if it is capable of being remedied.
5. It must require the tenant to pay compensation for the breach.

Under s 146 of the Law of Property Act 1925, a notice must be served on the tenant. Circumstances which do not invalidate a s 146 notice:

1. If the landlord does not want compensation and this is left out of the notice, the notice will still be effective.

CASE EXAMPLE

Rugby School (Governors) v Tannahill [1935] 1 KB 87

Premises owned by the school had been used for prostitution and the school did not want to enforce compensation against the tenant. It was held that the school did not have to require payment of compensation from the profits made.

2. If the breaches cannot be remedied then it will not invalidate the notice if the requirement to remedy them is left out: in *Rugby School (Governors) v Tannahill* (1935) it was held that the breach of a negative covenant was incapable of remedy. In this case the covenant was not to use the premises for illegal or immoral purposes. It is not always clear whether a breach can be remedied within a reasonable time.

CASE EXAMPLE

Expert Clothing Service & Sales Ltd v Hillgate House Ltd [1986] Ch 340

The covenant was to build premises within a limited time. This had not been done but the court held that it was still possible to remedy the breach by performing the covenant out of time. The court drew a distinction between positive covenants and negative covenants and held that it would be rare for positive covenants to be incapable of remedy.

Compare the following case where the court held that it was not possible to remedy the breach.

CASE EXAMPLE

Scala House and District Property Co Ltd v Forbes [1974] QB 575

Where there had been breach of a covenant not to assign or sub-let the premises then it was held to be impossible to remedy such a breach. Russell LJ considered what was the position once the tenant had ceased to be in breach and held that the landlord was still able to pursue forfeiture proceedings and the tenant was able to attempt to seek relief.

Section 168 of the Commonhold and Leasehold Reform Act 2002 provides that in the case of a long lease of a dwelling a landlord may not serve a notice under s 146 of the 1925 Act unless:

- the landlord has made an application to the leasehold valuation tribunal for determination of whether the breach of covenant has occurred, unless the issue has been referred to arbitration or the court;
- the tribunal has decided that a breach has occurred; or
- the tenant has admitted the breach.

Breach of repairing covenants
The Leasehold Property (Repairs) Act 1938 provides relief for tenants who are in breach of the repairing covenants.

KEY FACTS

The 1938 Act
1. The lease must be a lease for a term of seven years or more, not being an agricultural lease.
2. There must be at least three years left to run.
3. The landlord must serve a s 146 notice on the tenant relating to a breach of covenant to keep the premises in repair.
4. The tenant must have 28 days to serve a counter-notice.
5. If the tenant serves a counter-notice then the landlord cannot take further proceedings to re-enter the premises without the leave of the court.
6. If the landlord has already carried out the repairs (because he cannot wait for the tenant to act) then the court has no jurisdiction to pursue the tenant for damages. In *SEDAC Investments Ltd v Tanner* [1982] 1 WLR 1342 it was held that where the landlord had already carried out repairs then he lost his right to pursue the tenant under the repairing covenant. However, more recent cases, for example *Jervis v Harris* [1996] Ch 195, have allowed the landlord to claim the cost of the repairs from the tenant, otherwise this would restrict the rights of the landlord. 'The short answer to the question is that the tenant's liability to reimburse the landlord for his expenditure on repairs is not a liability in damages for breach of his repairing covenant [at all]. The landlord's claim sounds in debt not damages; and it is not a claim to compensation for breach of the tenant's covenant to repair, but the reimbursement of sums actually spent by the landlord in carrying out repairs himself.' Millett LJ in *Jervis v Harris* (1996)

Relief from forfeiture

In most cases where the breach has been remedied the court will grant relief. The key issues influencing the court will be: the value of the premises compared to the effects of the breach; the nature and type of breach; whether there were any previous breaches by the tenant; the nature of the breach, e.g. was it deliberate or innocent? In *Magnic Ltd v Ul-Hassan* [2015] a tenant who had continued to trade in spite of the fact it was in breach of conditions of the lease was granted relief from forfeiture as in the court's view this was not a deliberate breach. By contrast, in *Freifield v West Kensington Court Ltd* [2015] EWCA Civ 806 the court granted relief in spite of finding that the breach by the tenant had been deliberate. The tenant had breached a subletting clause and the landlord used this as an opportunity to claim forfeiture because he recognised an opportunity to recover the property and receive a windfall profit. In granting relief the Court of Appeal accepted that the subletting by the tenant had been a deliberate breach but the court balanced that against the value of the property and the damage done by the breach which was relatively small. As a consequence the tenant was entitled to sell the head lease.

Waiver

Once a breach of covenant has occurred, the landlord must decide whether to forfeit the lease or treat it as continuing. If he treats it as continuing or waives the breach, the landlord cannot later attempt to forfeit the lease unless the breach is a continuing breach.

In *Matthews v Smallwood* [1910] it was held that the landlord will lose the right to claim forfeiture if it is deemed that he has waived this right by accepting rent or even sending a demand for rent, but there will be no waiver if the landlord is unaware that a breach of covenant has taken place. If, for instance, the tenant has breached the implied condition to keep the property in good repair and the landlord receives and retains rent after there has been damage caused by the tenant the receipt of rent will not be a waiver unless the landlord is expressly aware of the breach.

However, if the landlord is aware of the circumstances of the breach, then even if the waiver is a mistake as in the case of *Central Estates (Belgravia) v Woolgar (No 2)* [1972] 1 WLR 1048 forfeiture cannot take place. In this case the tenants had been convicted for keeping a brothel therefore the landlord instructed the agents not to accept any rent. However, something went wrong and a demand for rent was sent out. According to Lord Denning this constituted a waiver of their right even though it had been carried out by the agents of the landlord.

Relief available to a tenant under s 146(2)	Relief denied to a tenant under s 146(2)
The period prior to possession proceedings. The right to apply for relief arises as soon as the notice is served on the tenant.	Where final judgment has been given and it has not been appealed and is fully executed.
Where judgment has been given but has not been executed.	Where the tenant has delayed in seeking relief.
In *Billson* the right to relief remains available after the landlord had exercised peaceable re-entry without court order.	

Table 13.3 Relief available or denied to a tenant under s 146(2)

The court will not grant relief for trivial breaches; for example, where there is a covenant against keeping pets and the tenant keeps a hamster in the kitchen, the court is unlikely to grant forfeiture to the landlord even though there has been a breach of a covenant.

Reform

The Law Commission has proposed reform of the law on forfeiture in 1985 and also in 1994 and 1998. In its 'Report on Forfeiture of Tenancies' (Law Com No 142, 1985) the Commission's main criticisms of the system were that it was unjust and no longer had any coherence:

1. The system tried to incorporate two sets of rules – one for non-payment of rent and one for other breaches.
2. There was no protection for anyone who derived title from the tenant, such as a sub-tenant or mortgagee.
3. There was uncertainty over whether the landlord was going to exercise his discretion and waive the breach.
4. There was always the possibility that the court would exercise its discretion and reinstate the lease following forfeiture.

As a result, in 1995 a draft Bill was proposed, to contain the following provisions:

1. No distinction to be made between non-payment of rent and other breaches.

2. Every tenancy would remain in force until the court made a termination order that fixed the date on which the tenancy should end.

3. Termination would be granted on a wide range of grounds and it would no longer depend on whether there was provision for termination in the lease.

4. The court would have the discretion either to grant the termination as requested or to make a remedial order which required the tenant to take remedial action within a timescale.

The Bill met with considerable opposition and has yet to be introduced into Parliament, although there are a number of changes made under the Commonhold and Leasehold Reform Act 2002 which have some impact on forfeiture.

More recently the law Commission has introduced a report entitled 'Termination of Tenancies for Tenant Default' (Law Com No 303, 2006). The Law Commission argues that the law on forfeiture is long overdue for reform. It suggests that the law should be replaced by a statutory scheme. The key features of this scheme would be the 'termination action'. This will either be 'summary termination action' or a 'termination claim', 'tenant default' which would be strictly defined and protection for those persons with an interest in the land such as mortgagees and sub-tenants. In spite of support from academics and practitioners they have not been adopted by the government.

13.7.3 Specific performance
The court has power to order specific performance by the tenant of any covenant in a lease but has shown reluctance to do so, for example it is unwilling to order specific performance of a covenant to repair.

13.7.4 Injunction
The court has the power to grant an injunction against the tenant to prevent a breach of covenant but rarely uses it.

13.7.5 Damages
Damages may be awarded but only for a breach of a covenant other than non-payment of rent. They are assessed on a contractual basis.

ACTIVITY

Applying the law

Mohammed rents a flat in Blackpool. His lease is for five years and includes a clause requiring him to keep the flat in good repair. The landlord has recently visited the flat and has noticed that the windows, which face directly on to the sea, are in a very poor state of repair. Mohammed has refused to undertake the work. He has now been served with a notice to quit and has left.

What remedies can the landlord seek against Mohammed?

13.8 Enforceability of covenants against third parties on assignment
The enforceability of covenants between the parties has so far depended on the question of what is expressly and what is impliedly covered in the lease. The next issue is whether a third party who receives the property by assignment is able to enforce the covenants against either the original landlord or an assignee.

13.8.1 Privity of estate and privity of contract

In leasehold covenants it is important to distinguish between

- privity of estate; and
- privity of contract.

Between the two parties to a lease there is usually both privity of contract and privity of estate. If one decides to assign his interest then there will no longer be privity of contract between the assignor and the new tenant T1 but there will still be privity of estate.

Privity of **contract**

Figure 13.2 Privity of contract in a lease

In Figure 13.2 the landlord (L) has negotiated the lease with the tenant (T) and together they have privity of contract.

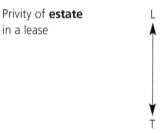

Privity of **estate**
in a lease

Figure 13.3 Privity of estate in a lease

In Figure 13.3 the landlord (L) has negotiated the lease with the tenant (T) and there is privity of estate as well as privity of contract.

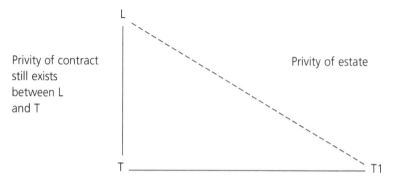

Privity of contract
still exists
between L
and T

Privity of estate

Figure 13.4 Privity on assignment of a lease by the tenant

In Figure 13.4 the lease has been assigned to T1. T1 now has privity of estate with L but not privity of contract, as T1 has not negotiated directly with L.

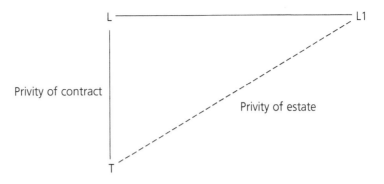

Figure 13.5 Privity of assignment of a lease by the landlord

In Figure 13.5 there is privity of estate between L1 and T but only privity of contract between L and T.

KEY FACTS

The nature of privity between a landlord and tenant
1. Privity of contract only exists between persons who are parties to a contract.
2. Privity of estate exists between the persons who are the current landlord and tenant.
3. Privity of estate only lasts while the parties are either landlord or tenant.
4. Privity of contract lasts while the parties are bound by the contract, so can last beyond their relationship as landlord and tenant.

It is always possible for a tenant to sub-let to a sub-tenant and there will then be privity of contract and estate between the sub-tenant and the lessee. There is no privity either of contract or of estate between the landlord and the sub-tenant.

There have been some important recent changes in this area of law under the Landlord and Tenant (Covenants) Act 1995. This applies to any tenancy granted after 1 January 1996. The old law applies to tenancies already in existence at that date.

13.8.2 The pre-1996 law on assignment of covenants

Before the 1995 Act was passed, the question of whether the benefit or burden of a covenant passed depended on:

1. whether there was privity of estate between the parties; and

2. whether the covenant 'touched and concerned the land'.

The covenant may confer a benefit on one side and a burden on the other side. The law relating to the running of burdens and benefits has already been explored in relation to freehold covenants.

Suppose Asif takes a tenancy of Flat 4, Elgin Mansions and expressly agrees that:

1. He will keep the interior of the flat in a good state of repair.

2. He will not keep a dog.

3. He will not assign or sub-let without the landlord's permission.

The landlord expressly agrees that he will keep the exterior of the property in a good state of repair and impliedly agrees that:

1. He will grant the tenant quiet enjoyment.
2. He will not derogate from the grant of the lease.

The landlord takes the burden of keeping the exterior in good repair and the tenant takes the benefit. Under the rules applicable to freehold covenants the burden will not run unless the covenant 'touches and concerns the land'. This is an old rule derived from *Spencer's Case* (1583) 5 Co Rep 16a which holds that the only covenants that can run at common law are those that touch and concern the land.

The test today is one laid down by Lord Oliver in *P & A Swift v Combined English Stores Group plc* [1989] AC 632:

1. Could the covenant benefit any owner of an estate in the land, as opposed to the particular original tenant?
2. Does the covenant affect the nature, quality, mode of user or value of the land?
3. Is the covenant expressed to be personal?

The issue of what constitutes 'touching and concerning' the land arises in a variety of situations in law including freehold covenants and leasehold covenants. Land law is primarily concerned with protecting owners of land and not individuals so, where a covenant is essentially for an individual then the law will not uphold the right. The definition given in the following case is useful both for freehold and leasehold covenants.

CASE EXAMPLE

P & A Swift v Combined English Stores Group plc [1989] AC 632

The lessee, A, in this case had in turn granted a sub-lease to B. B was actually connected with C who had entered into a covenant with A concerning the performance of certain covenants by B. When the reversion of the lease was assigned to D there was nothing expressly mentioned about the covenant of C in the assignment. B failed to pay the rent due and went into liquidation. The question was whether the landlord, D, could sue for the outstanding amount. It was held that the covenant undertaken by C was one that touched and concerned the land and could therefore run to D who could in turn enforce it.

If the covenant touches and concerns the land then it can be enforced by the assignee of a lease (T1) **or** it can be enforced against the assignee T1 and either can enforce against the landlord, L.

Under the old law, one of the difficulties was that the original tenant could still be liable under the principles of privity of contract even after he had assigned the lease. This meant that there was always the possibility that the tenant to whom he had assigned would default on the rent and then the original tenant would become liable himself for the outstanding amount.

The position of the landlord: benefit of covenants

Under s 141 of the 1925 Act, on assignment of the reversion the landlord has the right to sue on all the covenants that have reference to the subject-matter of the lease, in other words covenants that touch and concern the land. This section only applies to leases granted before 1996.

The position of the landlord: burden of covenants

Under s 142 of the 1925 Act, on assignment of the reversion, the burden of any covenant which has reference to the subject-matter of the lease passes. The burden passes whether or not there is privity of estate. This section only applies to leases granted before 1996.

The law is slightly different for an equitable lease. The benefits and burdens did not automatically run to the tenant since he did not have a legal estate in land.

The right to enforce a covenant may be expressly assigned under an equitable lease but the burden would not and only the original tenant would be liable for a breach of a covenant.

ACTIVITY

Quick quiz

Consider the following covenants and decide whether they 'touch and concern the land':

1. covenant by T not to keep a pet at the premises;
2. covenant by T to keep the property in good repair;
3. covenant by T to pay rent;
4. covenant by T not to allow any trees to grow over six feet;
5. covenant by L to renew the lease;
6. covenant by L not to open a garage within two miles of the garage leased to T;
7. covenant by L to ensure that the property is supplied with gas and electricity.

13.8.3 The post-1996 law on assignment of covenants

The Landlord and Tenant (Covenants) Act 1995 (LTCA 1995) applies to all leases, whether they are legal or equitable, made after 1 January 1996.

The tenant is automatically released from the burden of leasehold covenants on assignment of the tenancy although he may be asked to guarantee performance of the covenant of the next assignee.	s 5 LTCA 1995
The tenant may be asked to enter into an authorised guarantee agreement as a condition to an assignment of the lease. The tenant guarantees the performance of the covenants by the assignee. If the new tenant (T1) himself assigns to T2 then T is released but T1 may have to enter into an authorised guarantee agreement.	s 16 LTCA 1995
The original landlord is not released automatically from the burdens of leasehold covenants but may serve notice for release.	s 8 LTCA 1995
The rule that covenants must touch and concern the land or have reference to the subject-matter of the lease is abolished.	s 2 LTCA 1995
The benefit and burdens of the lease will automatically pass to the assignees of the lease and the reversion unless they are expressed to be personal or held not to be binding on the assignor.	s 7 LTCA 1995 s 3 LTCA 1995
The transfer of the benefit of a covenant to an assignee of the landlord does not deprive the assignor of the right to sue in respect of breaches occurring before the assignment.	s 24 LTCA 1995

Table 13.4 Main provisions of the 1995 Act

In relation to commercial leases there is an extension to s 19 of the Landlord and Tenant Act 1927 under s 22 of LTCA 1995. This allows a measure of control for the landlord over assignments of the lease by the tenant. The law allows the landlord the right to withhold consent in specified circumstances. The new provisions allow the parties to enter into an agreement specifying the circumstances in which the landlord may withhold consent; for example, the landlord can request that the new tenant shall provide certain financial guarantees before the assignment is made.

ACTIVITY

Applying the law

Consider the following situation:

Some years ago Alison wanted to set up her own business as a beauty consultant. She saw the ideal premises in November 1995 and took a lease for ten years. The lease contained covenants not to assign or sub-let without the landlord's consent in writing, to keep the premises in good repair and not to use them for illegal or immoral purposes. There was a forfeiture clause.

In 2000 Alison decided that she wanted a change of scene and she assigned the lease to Angela, without gaining the landlord's consent. Angela has been using the premises as an agency for 'escorts for businessmen'. The landlord has recently found this out and when he visited the premises he found that it was in a very poor state of repair.

Advise the landlord on what can be done about the breaches of covenant.

The Landlord and Tenant Act 1988 introduced a number of changes to assist the tenant seeking permission to assign. The Act requires the landlord to respond to the tenant 'within a reasonable time'. The landlord is required to give reasons for the refusal, in writing. The Act places the burden of proof on the landlord, who must move that his decision was reasonable.

SUMMARY

1. A lease is a legal estate in land.
2. It gives both contractual and proprietary rights to the claimant.
3. All legal leases must be created by deed unless for less than three years.
4. Leases over seven years in length must be registered in order to take effect at law.
5. The characteristics of a lease are the payment of rent, a fixed term and exclusive possession of the premises.
6. The law will imply a number of covenants into a lease in favour of the tenant including a covenant to allow the tenant quiet enjoyment, that the landlord will not derogate from his grant and a covenant that the premises are fit for the purpose for which they are let or are habitable.
7. The tenant can rely on a number of statutory provisions in relation to the repair and maintenance of the premises.
8. The law will imply a number of covenants into the lease in favour of the landlord such as the tenant's covenant to pay rent and taxes and to be liable for certain damage that occurs to the premises.
9. Leases can be determined in one of nine ways including forfeiture, surrender, repudiation and expiry.
10. The law will allow certain covenants to be enforced against third parties. The law differs according to whether or not the lease was created before or after 1996.

SAMPLE ESSAY QUESTION

'There can be no tenancy unless the occupier enjoys exclusive possession; but an occupier who enjoys exclusive possession is not necessarily a tenant' (Lord Templeman).
   Explain this statement and decide to what extent you agree with it.

Discuss the definition of a lease and the significance of claiming a lease rather than a licence:
   i. a lease is an interest in land;
   ii. a lease gives security of tenure;
   iii. a lease gives rise to rights to pursue some statutory protection for rent and right to remain in the premises.

Discuss the case of *Street v Mountford* and the key features of a lease:
• exclusive possession;
• for a term;
• at a rent.
Briefly mention the need for rent and the need for a term.

Discuss exclusive possession: define 'the right to use, occupy and enjoy the premises to the exclusion of all others including the landlord' as set out by Lord Templeman.

Discuss cases where no exclusive possession was found but instead exclusive occupation:
• *Westminster City Council v Clarke* (1992): occupants of rooms in a council run hostel for men could be moved from room to room.
• Hotel guests and residents in a nursing home *Abbeyfield (Harpenden) Society Ltd v Woods* (1968).
• Where services are provided such as a housekeeper, collection of rubbish, provision of meals.

Discuss cases where exclusive possession was found:
• Landlord retained a set of keys.
• Premises provided by an employer if not provided for the better performance of duties.
• There were terms that appeared to be a 'sham' or 'pretence'. Apparent provision of services but not provided by the landlord *Aslan v Murphy* (1990).

```
┌─────────────────────────────────────────────────────────────┐
│   ┌─────────────────────────────────────────────────────┐   │
│   │  Discuss Lord Templeman's quote.                     │   │
│   │                                                       │   │
│   │  Is this true?                                        │   │
│   │                                                       │   │
│   │  Case law suggests that exclusive possession is the   │   │
│   │  key feature of a tenancy. The name given to the      │   │
│   │  agreement is irrelevant and the courts will look at  │   │
│   │  the true nature of the agreement.                    │   │
│   └─────────────────────────────────────────────────────┘   │
│                              │                                │
│   ┌─────────────────────────────────────────────────────┐   │
│   │                    CONCLUSION                         │   │
│   └─────────────────────────────────────────────────────┘   │
└─────────────────────────────────────────────────────────────┘
```

Further reading

Books
Dixon, M, *Modern Land Law* (9th edn, Routledge, 2014), p. 248.
Smith, R, *Property Law Cases and Materials* (6th edn, Pearson, 2015), p. 501.

Articles
Baker, A, 'Bruton Licensees in Possession and a Fiction of Title' [2014] *Conv* 495.
Bright, S, 'Beyond Sham and into Pretence' [1991] 11 *OJLS* 138.
Bright, S, 'The Uncertainty of Certainty in Leases' (2012) 128 *LQR* 337.
Davey, M, 'Privity of Contract and Leases: Reform at Last' (1996) 59 *MLR* 78.
Dixon, M, 'The Non-Proprietary Lease: The Rise of the Feudal Phoenix' [2000] *CLJ* 25.
Harrison, P and Bernard, C, 'Implications of the Mexfield Ruling for Housing Co-Operatives' [2015] 19(4) *L & T R* 148.
Hill, J, 'Intention and the Creation of Proprietary Rights: Are Leases Different?' (1996) 16 *LS* 200.
Hinojosa, J P, 'On Property, Leases, Licences, Horses and Carts: Revisiting Bruton v London & Quadrant Housing' [2005] 69 *Conv* 114.
Pascoe, S, 'Periodic Tenancies Subject to a Fetter on the Tenant – Doctrinal Dilemmas' [2018] *Conv* 119.
Pawlowski, M, 'The Bruton Tenancy: Clarity or More Confusion?' [2005] 69 *Conv* 262.
Pawlowski, M, 'Equity's Jurisdiction to Relieve Against Forfeiture of Leases – An Historical Perspective' [2014] *Denning LJ* 149.
Sparkes, P, 'Certainty of Leasehold Terms' (1993) 109 *LQR* 93.
Street, R, 'Coach and Horses Trip Cancelled? Rent Act after *Street v Mountford*' [1985] 45 *Conv* 328.
Walter, P, 'The Landlord and Tenant (Covenants) Act 1995: A Legislative Folly' [1996] 60 *Conv* 432.

Law Commission Reports
'Renting Homes: The Final Report' (Law Com No 297, May 2006).
'Distress for Rent' (Law Com WP No 97, May 1986).
'Landlord and Tenant: Distress for Rent' (Law Com No 194, February 1991).
'Forfeiture of Leases' (Law Com No 142, 1986).
'Landlord and Tenant: Privity of Contract and Estate: Duration of Liability of Parties to Leases' (Law Com WP No 95, March 1986).

14

Adverse possession

AIMS AND OBJECTIVES

After reading this chapter, you should be able to:

- Explain what is meant by adverse possession
- Describe what is meant by 'factual possession'
- Describe what is meant by 'intention to possess'
- Explain the effect on the doctrine of adverse possession of the LRA 2002 and how adverse possessory rights might be acquired under the Act today
- Explain the effect of the Human Rights Act 1998 on the doctrine of adverse possession
  - Give reasons in favour and against the recognition of the doctrine of adverse possession

14.1 Introduction

Once a purchaser has purchased property according to the legal formalities and rules, his rights are recognised by the law as the legal owner. This should mean that the purchaser should be assured that the only way the legal estate will pass into the hands of another is if he takes the initiative by selling the property or dealing in it in some way.

Some examples would include:

1. giving the property to another during your lifetime;
2. leaving it to someone under your will;
3. mortgaging the property;
4. creating a legal lease over the property.

So, for example, if you do not repay the sum borrowed under the mortgage, the mortgagee (the lender) has the right to take possession of the property.

However, that is not the full story, as in certain circumstances someone who might be regarded as a mere trespasser with no legal right to be on the property can simply lay claim to rights of possession over the land belonging to another if he satisfies certain conditions. The trespasser merely has to satisfy the conditions and will not have to pay consideration to the landowner. The landowner will lose all rights to the property.

14.1.1 Long use of the land

JUDGMENT

'Those who go to sleep on their claims should not be assisted by the courts in recovering their property.'

RB Policies at *Lloyd's v Butler* [1950] 1 KB 76

The law has long recognised the rights of others to take over your property if you, as owner, do not assert ownership over a long period of time. We can own personal property such as a valuable painting and leave it in a bank vault for years and it will not undermine ownership. Land is treated differently. It has long been held that land is too valuable simply to ignore it.

Therefore the law recognised the rights of others to come and take over the property, and, if they treated it as their own for a long period of time they could then claim it for themselves. The law refers to those persons as 'squatters'. They are strictly trespassers until they satisfy the conditions required to claim the title.

Before the Land Registration Act 2002 was passed all claims to land by squatters, both registered and unregistered, was governed by Section 15(1) of the Limitation Act 1980 which provides that:

SECTION

'[N]o action shall be brought by any person to recover any land after the expiration of 12 years from the date on which the right of action accrued to him, or if first accrued to some person through whom he claims, to that person.'

It means that once 12 years have elapsed the squatter who satisfies the other conditions could argue that he now has rights in the property because he has treated it as if it were his own for over 12 years and the paper title owner has not objected. Today this section only applies to land with unregistered title, but even where land has registered title there is still recognition that a squatter has the right to seek registration of the title if he can prove he has had possession of the land for a long enough period of time.

14.1.2 Why allow adverse possession at all?

1. It appears to be very harsh on someone who occupies land for a long period of time and improves it, only to find that his claim cannot be upheld. This view is not held by everyone.
2. Land is a valuable asset and it should not be withdrawn from the market and removed from general circulation. Land must remain marketable.
3. The law should protect defendants from stale claims by landowners.

Martin Dockray argued strongly in 1985 in favour of upholding adverse possession. One of his arguments was that it helps to encourage better care of natural resources.

'It is arguable that it is in the public interest to promote the full use of neglected natural resources and that it is desirable that a fixed time limit should exist to encourage the improvement and development of land which might otherwise lie abandoned or under exploited for many years. For example, someone may have abandoned land many years ago and someone else may have started to use the land – possibly for limited purposes at first – and eventually taken possession of it … if the occupant is perpetually barred from dealing with the land as owner, there is a danger that the property will not be utilised to best advantage. This seems highly undesirable.'

M Dockray, 'Why Do We need Adverse Possession?' [1985] *Conv* 272

These arguments have not been supported by everyone. Indeed, the doctrine of adverse possession has been criticised by many, including the Law Commission. These criticisms are now reflected in the extensive changes to the law on adverse possession brought about by the Land Registration Act 2002.

14.1.3 The Land Registration Act 2002

To allow others to assert claims over your land does not seem fair to the landowner with the paper title who has paid for property and believes that it is still his own. One of the recommendations of the Law Commission ('Land Registration for the Twenty-First Century: A Consultative Document' (Law Com No 254, 1998)) was to modify the rules on adverse possession. As a result, it is far more difficult for anyone to try to claim property of another as their own, simply through long use and enjoyment. Adverse possession runs counter to the spirit of land registration. Since the Registrar is guaranteeing the title once it has been entered on the Register it is contrary to this underlying principle to allow title to be lost through adverse possession.

Under the Land Registration Act 2002, the paper title owner of property with registered title is much better protected from squatters trying to assert rights of ownership over his property. However, the possibility of losing title remains although there are now built-in safeguards in the system to prevent this. The 'paper title owner' is the owner at law of the property. If it has registered title he will be registered on the Proprietorship Register at the Land Registry.

The paper title owner has to be notified by the Land Registry before the squatter can try to register his rights. This notification then puts the paper title owner on notice that the squatter is trying to gain rights in his land. He will then try to take action to ensure that the squatter is evicted. It is anticipated that there will be far fewer successful claims to adverse possession as a result of the 2002 Act.

14.1.4 The meaning of 'adverse possession'

'Adverse possession' means that rights of ownership in land are acquired by simply taking possession of the land. No money passes hands and there is no formal conveyance.

The claimant must satisfy **three** main requirements before the rights are gained in the land:

1. He must show that he had **factual possession** of the land.
2. He must show that he had the necessary **intention to possess the land sufficient** to defeat the interests of the owner.
3. Both factual possession and intention to possess must have been exercised **over a sufficient length of time**.

The **three** elements to prove are:

- factual possession;
- intention to possess;
- sufficient length of time.

14.2 Factual possession

The claimant must take physical possession of the land. Time will only begin to run against the paper title owner from the date that the paper title owner was dispossessed or discontinued possession and the claimant took possession.

> 'In respect of unregistered land in England and Wales the basis of title to land is possession. Possession of land by itself gives a title to the land good against the whole world except a person with a better right to possession. If X takes possession of A's land, X has a title which will avail against all save A; a title acquired by wrong is still a title. X has a fee simple, and so has A; but all titles are relative, and so although X's fee is good A's is better. If, however, A fails to take steps to recover the land in due time, his claim will be barred by limitation, and X's fee, freed from the superior claims of A's fee, will be good against all the world.'
>
> P Rainey, M Walsh, P Harrison and D Dovar (eds), *Megarry's Manual of the Law of Real Property* (9th edn, Sweet & Maxwell, 2014), pp. 482–483

14.2.1 What constitutes factual possession?

There are certain consistent features required in factual possession:

1. The claimant must intend to **exclude all others** including the paper title owner.
2. The claimant must be in factual possession for an **unbroken period of time**.
3. The factual possession must be **openly exercised**.
4. The factual possession must be **adverse to the paper title owner**.

1. The claimant must intend to exclude all others

Physical control of the property depends on the type of property involved. If it is a very small area of land, then very clear evidence of physical control is necessary. In these cases other evidence is needed. If the adverse possessor puts up signs which attempt to exclude trespassers then the signs will be evidence of factual possession. Fencing constitutes the most conclusive proof of possession and shows an intention to exclude all others but it is not always possible to fence all the boundaries of a very large area 'Enclosure is the strongest possible evidence of adverse possession' (Cockburn CJ in *Seddon v Smith* (1877) 36 LT 68).

CASE EXAMPLE

Red House Farms (Thornden) Ltd v Catchpole [1977] 2 EGLR 125

The area claimed to be adversely possessed was very large and shooting wildfowl was held to be a sufficient act of possession because that was the only purpose for which the land could be used. Fencing would be impossible.

CASE EXAMPLE

Powell v McFarlane (1979) 38 P & CR 452

A claim for adverse possession was made on behalf of a boy of 14. He had kept a cow, which he named Kashla, on a large open space. The boy used the land as his own in the following ways:

- he cut and took a hay-crop;

446

ADVERSE POSSESSION

- he superficially repaired the boundary fences;
- he cut back brambles and cut down trees, including a large number of Christmas trees;
- he put in his cow and several goats and later more cows to graze;
- he put in a rudimentary water supply;
- he also did some shooting over the land.

Although there were numerous acts, Slade J thought that the acts themselves were equivocal and could be interpreted as mere temporary use rather than showing an intention to possess. The acts were seen as occasional acts rather than acts of someone treating the land as his own. They were not sufficient to support a claim for adverse possession as he thought they did not show that the boy intended to possess the land for himself:

'In the case of open land, absolute physical control is normally impracticable, if only because it is generally impossible to secure every part of a boundary so as to prevent intrusion ... everything must depend on the particular circumstances, but broadly, I think what must be shown as constituting factual possession is that the alleged possessor has been dealing with the land in question as an occupying owner might have been expected to deal with it and that no-one else has done so.'

Slade J

Slade J accepted that the whole area did not need to be fenced but when he analysed the facts in support of factual possession in this case, he found that they could simply establish temporary enjoyment of the property rather than indicate that he was treating the land as his own.

This is seen as a harsh decision and mainly rested on the fact that Slade J did not think that a boy of 14 years old could form the intention to treat land as his own. However many of the acts of the boy were acts that were consistent with land ownership such as the repair of the boundary fence.

CASE EXAMPLE

Buckinghamshire County Council v Moran [1990] Ch 623

Land had been acquired by Bucks County Council because it wanted to construct a road diversion. However, although it fenced the land from the road, the boundaries to several properties were left open. The adverse possessor had cultivated a piece of the land owned by the Council which was next to his garden. His successor in title fenced it and also put in a gate which he had both chained and padlocked. This was considered to be very clear evidence of factual possession. The property had been occupied by several different owners each of whom had continued to cultivate the land, and eventually Mr Moran bought it. The Council wrote a letter to him complaining about the actions taken and disputing the rights of the adverse possessor. The court found that Moran had 'complete and exclusive physical control' of the land belonging to the Council.

Compare the cases of *Moran* and *Powell v MacFarlane*. The approach of the court seems far more lenient in *Moran*. The difference probably rests on the fact that Mr Moran had a gate into the extended garden and he alone had a key allowing entry which was seen as unequivocal acts of enclosure.

A key feature of the claim in *Moran v Bucks County Council* was the fact that Mr Moran and his predecessors had treated the land as their own. This was supported in the later case of *Dyer v Terry* [2013] EWHC 209 where the court differentiated between acts which could constitute factual possession, such as cultivating the land and treating it as part of the claimant's garden and land, creating an area for parking by laying hardcore, but not more trivial acts such as tidying an area of land.

There have been several more recent cases concerning factual possession where it was not possible to enclose the land and these are discussed below. The key issue is whether or not the claimant is treating the land as if he were the owner. Use will vary according to the nature of the land.

CASE EXAMPLE

Roberts v Swangrove Estates Ltd [2007] EWHC 513 (Ch)

The Crown Estates Commissioner successfully claimed rights over the foreshore based on fishing and the grant of fishing rights and shooting rights to others and also periodic dredging of the river bed. It was held that cumulatively all these acts could constitute factual possession.

CASE EXAMPLE

Port of London Authority v Ashmore [2010] EWCA Civ 30

In a similar case the claimant Mr Ashmore had moored a boat on the Thames since 1983 and he now claimed rights over the river bed. During the day the boat would either be floating in the water or it came to rest on the riverbank. One issue before the court was whether this could constitute factual possession since the boat was for the most part floating on the river rather than lying on the river bed. The judge concluded that there was factual possession. He said that factual possession depended on the 'nature of the land and the manner in which land of that nature is commonly used or enjoyed'. It was not necessary to show physical presence every minute of the day. There was little more that Mr Ashmore could sensibly have done in his use of the land. This view was upheld by the Court of Appeal since it had been accepted by the Authority that it is possible, in appropriate circumstances, to acquire title by adverse possession of the foreshore and river bed by reason of mooring.

2. *The factual possession must be for an unbroken period of time*

If one person dies or sells the property, it is important that there should be no break in the claim to adverse possession over the land.

Adverse possessory rights can be left by will or pass under intestacy; they can also pass with the conveyance of the legal title to the rest of the land.

CASE EXAMPLE

Buckinghamshire County Council v Moran [1990] Ch 623

The property changed hands several times before eventually it came into the hands of Mr Moran; the adverse possession claim over the additional land passed each time with the purchase. However, there were no breaks in the possession of the property.

If there is any break in the period of possession, the limitation period ceases to run. It does not prevent the limitation period from starting again if the squatter shows the necessary intent.

ACTIVITY

Applying the law

Ashwin has taken possession of a strip of land which belongs to his neighbour, Imran. The strip borders his garden. He cultivates it for six years and then sells his property to John, who ignores the strip. John then becomes aware that Ashwin has been cultivating it and he starts to work on it. Advise John whether he can bring an action for adverse possession.

Note that in this case the action will depend on the length of time that John has been cultivating the land after Ashwin. As discussed later in the chapter it will also depend on whether the land has registered or unregistered title.

3. *The factual possession must be openly exercised*

It must be possible for the paper title owner to find out about the presence of the squatters and if they deliberately conceal themselves when the paper title owner visits the property then time would not run. If the paper title owner sees squatters in possession then he would be expected to take action to evict them and if he does not then he could not expect the law to protect him. 'This requirement of transparency or visibility ensures that the paper title owner is given every opportunity of challenging the possession before it can mature as a threat to his own title' (K Gray and S F Gray, *Elements of Land Law* (5th edn, Oxford University Press, 2009), p. 1180).

It does not matter, however, that the paper title owner is unaware of the fact that the squatter has taken possession. It is just important that it would be clear if the owner visited the property. If the paper title owner chooses not to visit the property then he/she misses a valuable opportunity to find out about the squatters and the law is not very sympathetic.

4. *The factual possession must be adverse to the paper title owner*

Occupation of the land with the permission of the owner or under some lawful right is not adverse. So where occupation is under a **licence** or even a **lease**, that is not adverse to the owner as it is permissive use and the time in occupation cannot be used as evidence of adverse possession.

It is different in cases where the claimant previously had permission to possess the land but that permission has now lapsed or been refused; he can show that the position has now changed and the possession is now adverse to the owner because the lawful permission has been withdrawn.

It may also be possible to argue that the terms of the original licence were different from the rights that you are seeking to exercise.

Contrast the following cases:

CASE EXAMPLE

Pye (JA) (Oxford) Ltd v Graham [2001] Ch 804

Pye owned a number of fields adjoining a farm owned by the Graham family. At first the Grahams used the fields under a written licence granted by Pye in 1984. The Grahams requested that those licences be extended in 1986 but the request was not answered. The Grahams continued to use the land from 1986 until 1997 when Mr Graham registered a caution against the property based on his rights under adverse possession. Pye challenged this, arguing that the Grahams had not gained rights under adverse possession. The High Court found in favour of the Grahams but the judgment was reversed by the Court of Appeal. The House of Lords upheld the decision of Neuberger J in the High Court and held that the Grahams had established adverse possessory rights over the land.

JA Pye (Oxford) Ltd v Graham
1. The judgment of the Court of Appeal: according to the judges Graham did not show sufficient intention to possess the land. The fact that he had requested further licences suggested that he understood that the land belonged to Pye and therefore he could not use the land without Pye's permission. He admitted that he would have been willing to pay for the use of the land under licence if a further licence had been granted.
2. The House of Lords reversed this decision on the basis that the licences were never granted and so Graham was in factual possession of the land from 1986. Further, he had sufficient intention because at all times he intended to show an intention to use the land for his own benefit. At all times he intended to possess the land for himself. It was argued on behalf of Pye that Graham had been willing to pay for the land and therefore there could be no adverse possession but this was not accepted by the House of Lords. The fact that the land was still used by the squatter proved a continuing intention to treat the land as his own.

Where permissive use is granted by licence then the licensee does not have to accept the licence in order for it to be binding. As seen in the case below if the licensee remains silent after being offered a licence by the licensor then the law assumes that the licensee has accepted the licence.

CASE EXAMPLE

BP Properties Ltd v Buckler (1987) 55 P & CR 337

Mrs Buckler had lived in the property for a long period of time believing it to be her own, although this was not true and she was squatting on the land. The paper title owner expressly granted her a licence to occupy the land. The licence was sent by letter addressed to Mrs Buckler, who was the squatter. She ignored the letter and continued to live in the property. The question was whether she became a licensee when she ignored the letters that were sent to her.

JUDGMENT

'The nature of Mrs Buckler's possession after receipt of the letters cannot be decided just by looking at what was locked up in her own mind. It must depend even more, on this aspect of the case, on the position as seen from the standpoint of the person with the paper title ... The rule that "possession is not adverse if it can be referred to a lawful title" applies even if the person in possession did not know of the lawful title; the lawful title would still preclude the person with the paper title from evicting the person in possession. So far as Mrs Buckler was concerned, even though she did not "accept" the terms of the letters, BP Properties Ltd would in the absence of any repudiation by her of the two letters, have been bound to treat her as in possession as licensee on the terms of the letters.'

Dillon LJ

The interesting effect of this is that if BP Properties had wanted to evict Mrs Buckler, it could not do so without first determining her licence, as she was lawfully in the property. She was not a trespasser. In any ordinary case of a squatter then the landowner can simply go to court and claim the land because the squatter is a trespasser. Of course, in a bare licence a licensor can determine the licence at any time subject to the Protection from Eviction Act 1977. Under s 5 of this Act it is held that anyone in residential accommodation must be given at least one month's notice before being evicted from the property. In *Smith and Others v Molyneux* [2016] UKPC 35 the Privy Council, overturning the decision of the Easter Caribbean Court of Appeal and applying *BP Properties Limited v Buckler* (1987) 55 P&CR 337, held that it was sufficient for the paper owner of land to give unilateral permission to a squatter to preserve his title, and that it was sufficient evidence of such permission having been given to prove that the paper owner had made clear to the squatter the circumstances in which he would have to leave the land even if nothing was said expressly about permission in the meantime. It was emphasised that this did not constitute a return to the doctrine of implied licence.

In *Allen v Matthews* [2007] EWCA Civ 216 a person who had been given permission to use a yard for storage far exceeded the permission given in both degree and nature and so could be said to be in adverse possession although he appeared to be there under a lawful right.

If the claimant believes he has permission to be on the land then that will be fatal to his claim. A claim was defeated in *Clowes Development v Walters* [2006] 1 P & CR 1 where the claimant believed that he held a licence from the landowner. The claim is always based on an intention to possess for oneself and this must rest on any claimant proving that he intended to exclusively possess the land.

The decision in *BP Properties v Buckler* was recently approved by the Privy Council in *Smith v Molyneux* [2016] UKPC 35. Where the court concluded that it was sufficient for the paper title owner of land to give unilateral permission to a squatter to preserve his title.

The doctrine of implied licence

Before the Limitation Act 1980 was passed it was possible for an owner to use this doctrine to defend claims. The paper title owner could argue that the land was left unused for a period of time but that he had a clear use in mind for the future and so the squatter could not claim rights over the land because he had an 'implied licence' from the owner. The squatter could show clear evidence of both factual possession and an intention to treat the land as his own but the claim would be rejected because the use made by the squatter did not interfere with the future use of the land.

In his judgment of *Leigh v Jack* (1879–80) LR 5 Ex D 264, Lord Justice Bramwell said:

JUDGMENT

'In order to defeat a title by dispossessing the former owner, acts must be done which are inconsistent with his enjoyment of the soil for the purposes for which he intended to use it: that is not the case here, where the intention of the plaintiff ... was not either to build upon or cultivate the land, but to devote it at some future time to public purposes.'

Bramwell LJ

CASE EXAMPLE

Wallis's Cayton Holiday Camp v Shell-Mex and BP [1975] QB 94

In this case Lord Denning upheld the principle that where the land was occupied by a squatter and the paper title owner had no plans for its immediate use, that occupation could be said to be with licence. In this case the licence would not be given expressly by the owner. Schedule 1, para 8(4) to the Limitation Act 1980 removed the doctrine of implied licence.

SECTION

'For the purpose of determining whether a person occupying any land is in adverse possession of the land it shall not be assumed by implication of law that his occupation is by permission of the person entitled to the land merely by virtue of the fact that his occupation is not inconsistent with the latter's present or future enjoyment of the land.'

The county council tried to argue the doctrine of implied licence in *Buckinghamshire County Council v Moran* (1990) but this was rejected.

KEY FACTS

Factual possession
1. Acts constituting factual possession will vary according to the type of land.
2. The consistent features of adverse possession are that the claimant must openly exclude all others in a way that is adverse to the paper title owner for an unbroken period of time.
3. Where the area claimed is small then acts constituting factual possession must be very clear.
4. Fencing is very good evidence of factual possession.
5. Some acts, such as grazing animals on open land, are equivocal and may not be sufficient to support a claim for adverse possession.
6. The doctrine of implied licence has been removed by the Limitation Act 1980.
7. The grant of a legal right to be on the land will be contrary to the claim for adverse possession.

14.3 The intention to possess

The squatter must prove that at all times he had the intention to treat the land as his own.

JUDGMENT

'[T]he intention, in one's own name and on one's own behalf, to exclude the world at large, including the owner with the paper title ... so far as is reasonably practicable and so far as the processes of the law will allow.'

Slade J in *Powell v McFarlane* (1979) 38 P & CR 452

14.3.1 Proving intention to possess

The squatter must make it clear to the world that he intends to possess the land. He must show *animus possidendi*. The court will look at the conduct of the claimant and decide whether that is indicative of intention. Of course, it is very easy for the claimant to give evidence that he had the intention to possess the land at a later date but proof of intention at the time of occupying the land may be more difficult.

The court needs evidence that the claimant regarded the land as belonging to him.

JUDGMENT

'The position, however, is quite different from a case where the question is whether a trespasser has acquired possession. In such a situation the courts will, in my judgment, require clear and affirmative evidence that the trespasser, claiming that he has acquired possession, not only had the requisite intention to possess, but made such intention clear to the world.'

Slade J in *Powell v McFarlane* (1979)

Slade J considered the way that the boy treated the land and decided that his treatment of the land did not prove that he intended to own the land. He was influenced by the boy's age and the fact that he appeared to use the land simply for convenience rather than with the firm intention that the land should become his own. In his view the boy could only form an intention to possess when he got older because by then he had started his own business and he treated the land as part of the land for that business. The problem was that there was not sufficient time to satisfy the 12 year period necessary for adverse possession.

The squatter need only prove an intention to possess and not necessarily an intention to acquire the property

ACTIVITY

Applying the law

Richard and Joanna bought a cottage bordering on land owned by the council. At the back of their property there is no fence or hedge and they can walk straight on to the open land. They have a very small garden and, being keen supporters of the organic movement, they want to grow their own vegetables. They decide to use a strip of land to grow potatoes and other vegetables. Gradually, they take in a further strip of the council land to extend their vegetable patch. The council mows the grass on the rest of the land but the strip is ignored. Consider whether Richard and Joanna have the required intention to acquire rights over the property?

In *JA Pye (Oxford) Ltd v Graham* (2001) the House of Lords held that the Grahams had the necessary intention because they showed that they maintained the land and used it as their own along with the rest of their farm property:

JUDGMENT

'[T]here has always both in Roman law and in common law, been a requirement to show an intention to possess in addition to objective acts of physical possession. Such intention may be, and frequently is, deduced from the physical acts themselves. But there is no doubt in my judgment that there are two separate elements in legal possession. So far as English law is concerned intention as a separate element is obviously necessary. Suppose a case where A is found to be in occupation of a locked house. He may be there as a squatter, as an overnight trespasser, or as a friend looking after the house of the paper title owner during his absence on holiday. The acts done by A in any given period do not tell you whether there is legal possession. If A is there as a squatter he intends to stay as long as he can for his own benefit: his intention is an intention to possess. But if he only intends to trespass for the night or has expressly agreed to look after the house for his friend he does not have possession. It is not the nature of the acts which A does but the intention with which he does them which determines whether or not he is in possession.'

Lord Browne-Wilkinson

Lord Browne-Wilkinson shows that mere presence on property can have several different implications and does not necessarily mean that someone is there with an intention to possess the property and yet in all cases they may treat the property in the same way.

14.3.2 Conduct indicating an intention to possess

Any conduct that indicates a clear intention to possess will be enough. In many cases the evidence establishing an intention to possess will be the same as the evidence that establishes factual possession.

These are some examples of intention to possess:

Notices

If the squatter moves in and then puts up notices which say 'Keep out – private property' this will be evidence of an intention to possess. However, the notices must be enforced and if the notices are put up but people continue to enter and use the land it will not be evidence of intention to possess.

For example, Russell has started to cultivate an area of land that borders his garden and which is owned by the council. He plants vegetables and around the boundaries which do not border his property he plants shrubs and bushes. People often walk on the land, believing it to be public property. After 18 months Russell decides to erect two notices at either end of the strip, indicating that it is private property. The next week, he sees a party of walkers on the strip. If he ignores them then the notices cannot be claimed as evidence of intention to possess but if he goes out and argues with them and asks them to leave then the notices could constitute very good evidence of intention to possess.

Fences and locked gates

In *Buckinghamshire County Council v Moran* (1990) the fact that the squatter had put up fencing and a gate and had then locked the gate was sufficient for the claimant to show an intention to possess. This was also evidence in support of a claim for factual possession. The court was also persuaded by the evidence that the squatter had started to cultivate the land, putting in bulbs and rose bushes.

In *Pye v Graham* the claimant Mr Graham held a key for one of the fields over which he was claiming rights and a representative from Pye could only look at the field from a nearby road.

Changing the locks

CASE EXAMPLE

Lambeth LBC v Blackburn (2001) 33 HLR 74

If the squatter changes the locks of the property there is clear evidence that he intends to treat it as his own and to exclude the paper title owner from the land. The claimant in this case was a tenant of a council property. He admitted that he had intended only to possess the property for himself until the council successfully evicted him. However, he had changed the locks of the property and this was accepted as clear evidence that he intended to treat it as his own and to exclude the paper title owner from the land.

The claimant can show intention to possess based on intention for the present.

Slade LJ held in *Moran* that the required mental element need not involve an intention to 'exclude the owner of the paper title in all future circumstances'.

Acts of adverse possession	Case
Notices 'Keep out – private property'	
Fences and locked gates	*Buckinghamshire County Council v Moran* (1990)
Changing the locks	*Lambeth LBC v Blackburn* (2001)

Table 14.1 Examples of acts disclosing an intention to possess

Some examples of acts disclosing no intention to possess:

Transient and trivial acts

If the acts are transient, they cannot be sufficient evidence. Most of the acts carried out by the claimant in *Powell v McFarlane* (1979) were considered by the courts to be transient.

CASE EXAMPLE

Tecbild v Chamberlain (1969) 20 P & CR 633

The acts relied on were all relatively trivial and included tethering horses and grazing goats and also allowing children to play on the land. Whenever the children and animals were away from the land it would be impossible to know that they had an intention to possess the property.

In *Dyer v Terry* [2013] EWHC 209 the claimant relied on mowing the grass and picking up litter which was deemed to be insufficient to constitute factual possession.

Fencing

Even fencing can be equivocal. It is always possible that the intention to own the land is lacking. A fence can be put up to keep the public out and may not be evidence of an intention to possess.

CASE EXAMPLE

Fruin v Fruin [1983] Court of Appeal transcript 448

The claim of the squatter was unsuccessful because, although a fence was erected, it was put up chiefly for the purpose of keeping in a senile member of the family who wandered away from the house from time to time, rather than with the intention of acquiring rights over the land.

A similar view was taken in *Inglewood v Baker* [2002] EWCA Civ 1733 where it was held that a fence erected around a piece of woodland was there primarily to keep sheep in rather than to keep others including the true owner out.

By way of contrast Millet LJ held in *Minchinton* discussed below that in some cases a fence can be equivocal and serve two purposes. It can keep others out as well as keeping animals or people in.

CASE EXAMPLE

Hounslow Borough Council v Minchinton (1997) 74 P & CR 221

The claimants had extended the end of their own garden into land owned by the council. They not only cultivated the area but also put up a fence to keep their dog in. The council argued that the fence had been put up in order to keep the dogs in rather than to keep others out. Millet LJ held that a fence can have two purposes in this case it was both for keeping their dog in, and also for excluding others.

Age of the claimant

Considerable weight was placed on the fact that the claimant was relatively young in *Powell v McFarlane* (1979). This does not mean that a young person, even a child, could not have an intention to possess but it does mean that a much higher standard of proof of intention will be required for a child.

Equivocal acts

Some acts are equivocal: this means that they could be interpreted in at least two ways. They could be referable to an intention to possess and equally they could be evidence of present enjoyment with no thought about a future intention to possess. Where they have more than one interpretation, the courts are going to require very clear evidence that they are referable to the acquisition of rights to the land.

In *Powell v McFarlane* (1979) Slade J decided that the acts carried out by the boy were not sufficiently compelling evidence of his intention to acquire rights in the land rather than just present enjoyment. This view has been subject to criticism since it appears to place a very heavy burden indeed on the adverse possessor.

Acts of the adverse possessor	Case
Trivial acts such as children playing on the land; occasional grazing of animals.	*Powell v McFarlane* (1979) *Tecbild v Chamberlain* (1969) *Dyer v Terry* (2013)
Fencing without the intention of keeping the public out.	*Fruin v Fruin* (1983) *Inglewood v Baker* (2002), but compare *London Borough of Hounslow v Minchinton* (1997)
Age of the claimant: the younger the claimant, the harder it is to show intention.	*Powell v McFarlane* (1979)
Equivocal acts cannot easily support an intention to possess.	*Powell v McFarlane* (1979)

Table 14.2 Acts disclosing no intention to possess

14.4 Possession for sufficient length of time

The squatter cannot acquire rights over land until he has occupied the land for a sufficient length of time. The law was earlier governed by the Limitation Act 1980. The Land Registration Act 2002 now applies different periods of time for land with registered title, so the Limitation Act 1980 is no longer used **except in relation to claims of adverse possession over land with unregistered title**.

14.4.1 The Limitation Act 1980

SECTION

's 5 **Time limit for actions founded on simple contract**
An action founded on simple contract shall not be brought after the expiration of six years from the date on which the cause of action accrued.'

This section may apply where land is subject to contract and there has been an exchange of contracts and there is an error on the face of the contract or the landlord is suing for outstanding rent from a tenant.

> 's 15(1) **Time limit for actions to recover land**
> No action shall be brought by any person to recover any land after the expiration of twelve years from the date on which the right of action accrued to him or, if it first accrued to some person through whom he claims, to that person.'

The key issue here is to decide when the right to bring the action arises. There are two conditions to consider:

1. If 12 years have passed, the paper title owner loses his right to recover his land.
2. The 12 years runs from the time when the right of action arose. This would be when the paper title owner is dispossessed and the squatter takes possession. The paper title owner could have discontinued use of the land sometime previously but the right of action for the squatter only arises when he takes possession.

So, today, if a squatter takes control of unregistered land, he must show that he has the requisite factual possession and intention to possess the land for **12 years** under the Limitation Act 1980. If these are proved then the paper title owner's rights will be defeated and the squatter can claim superior title and can make an application to the Land Registry to be entered on the Register as owner of the property.

In *Mitchell v Watkinson* [2013] EWHC 2266 the court held that where the claim was made under the law pre-2002, the squatter acquired title once the relevant limitation period had expired.

In these circumstances even if the squatter accepted an offer of a lawful right to be on the land such as a licence or a lease after the limitation period had expired title would not be defeated.

14.4.2 The Land Registration Act 2002

This Act radically changed the rules on adverse possession in relation to registered land. Under the 2002 Act no period of limitation under s 15 of the Limitation Act 1980 shall apply to a registered estate in land.

The 2002 Act has radically affected claims of adverse possession in relation to registered land. The registered title owner can no longer be said to 'lose title' under the rules of adverse possession.

SECTION

> 's 96(1) No period of limitation under section 15 of the Limitation Act 1980 . . . shall run against any person, other than a chargee, in relation to an estate in land or rentcharge the title to which is registered.'

Under the 2002 Act there is provision for a squatter to apply to the Registrar to be registered as proprietor of a registered estate if he has been adverse possession of that estate for ten years.

SECTION

> 'Schedule 6, paragraph 1(1) A person may apply to the registrar to be registered as the proprietor of a registered estate in land if he has been in adverse possession of the estate for the period of ten years ending on the date of the application.'

Proof of adverse possession will be on the established rules. Notification of the application is given to the paper title owner and also others with an interest in the land:

SECTION

'Schedule 6, paragraph 2(1) The registrar must give notice of an application under paragraph 1 to:

(a) the proprietor of the estate to which the application relates,

(b) the proprietor of any registered charge on the estate,

(c) where the estate is leasehold, the proprietor of any superior registered estate,

(d) any person who is registered in accordance with rules as a person to be notified under this paragraph, and

(e) such other persons as rules may provide.'

Proof will be on the same basis as in unregistered land and based on the old law. The two elements required are:

- evidence of factual possession;
- evidence of an intention to possess.

This is the first step in an application for registration of rights.

The Registry will serve notice on interested persons at the address registered at the Land Registry. There is no duty on the Registrar to check whether the notice has reached these persons. It is clearly sensible for the owner to notify the Registrar of any change of address otherwise the notification will not be received and the chance to object will be lost.

The registered proprietor and all others upon whom notice is served have a period of 65 business days in which to respond to the squatter's application by counter-notice. If there is no response, the squatter is entitled to be registered as the proprietor of the estate.

If the registered proprietor does object, the squatter's application to be registered will be rejected unless one of three exceptions applies. The squatter will have lost the opportunity to be registered. However, if the squatter remains on the land and the paper title owner does not evict him then he has a second attempt to register.

SECTION

'Schedule 6, paragraph 5(1) ... the applicant is only entitled to be registered as the new proprietor of the estate if any of the following conditions is met.

(2) The first condition is that –

(a) it would be unconscionable because of an equity by estoppel for the registered proprietor to seek to dispossess the applicant, and

(b) the circumstances are such that the applicant ought to be registered as proprietor

(3) The second condition is that the applicant is for some reason entitled to be registered as the proprietor of the estate.

(4) The third condition is that –

(a) the land to which the application relates is adjacent to land belonging to the applicant,

(b) the exact line of the boundary between the two has not been determined under rules under section 60,

(c) for at least ten years of the period of adverse possession ending on the date of the application, the applicant (or any predecessor in title) reasonably believed that the land to which the application relates belonged to him, and

(d) the estate to which the application relates was registered more than one year prior to the date of the application.'

If any of these three conditions applies then the squatter can apply to be registered but he must still satisfy all the requirements of adverse possession:

1. **Estoppel**: the squatter will rely on the fact that the registered proprietor made a representation to him and he has acted in reliance on that representation to his detriment. Under the rules of estoppel the proprietor is then estopped from going back on his representation. The Registrar could then register the squatter as proprietor but the 2002 Act envisaged other forms of relief being given. Under s 110(4) the Registrar is given the power to make any order that the High Court could make in the exercise of its equitable jurisdiction.

2. The Registrar may register the applicant if he is entitled to be registered as the proprietor of the estate **for some other reason**. This covers situations such as where the squatter has rights under intestacy or a valid will of the deceased proprietor.

3. **Boundary disputes**: many of the claims for rights under adverse possession concern boundary disputes. Under the 2002 Act, if the squatter reasonably believed the disputed land to be his own for the last ten years and the estate to which the application relates was registered more than one year prior to the date of the application, then the squatter is entitled to be registered if he can satisfy the requirements of both factual possession and also an intention to possess. One of the problems under this exception is defining what constitutes a reasonable belief. In *Zarb v Parry* [2011] EWCA Civ 1306 a squatter P claimed rights over land of his neighbour Z. The judge at first instance upheld the squatter's claim over a strip of land that ran between the two properties. Z claimed that his predecessor in title had given permission to P's predecessor in title. He also claimed that factual possession had been bought to an end during the ten-year period. The Court of Appeal held that in order for this claim to succeed the paper title owners had to bring the adverse possessor's exclusive possession to an end which in this case he had failed to do. Finally a claim that P did not hold the belief that he owned the strip throughout the ten-year period was rejected. The Court of Appeal held that P's belief was reasonable. In the later case of *IAM Group Plc v Chowdrey* [2012] EWCA Civ 505 the court took the view that there must be a ten-year belief by the squatter that the land belongs to him rather than showing that such a belief had continued up until the institution of proceedings. In this case the claimant, a tenant, had been using rooms that were in fact part of another property and had claimed that they belonged to him when he later purchased the property. The paper title owner argued that his solicitors must have known that they did not belong to him when the land was purchased. The Court of Appeal rejected this and held that it is the belief of the claimant that matters not that of his solicitor.

   The problem that every claimant under this exception must overcome is that as soon as the claimant challenges the other party on a boundary dispute then the belief that it belongs to him is much harder to prove. However, the decision in *Chowdrey* has kept open the possibility of a claim based on the reasonable belief of the claimant even where a dispute arises before the case comes to court as indeed it is likely to do.

If any of these conditions applies, the squatter can apply to be registered immediately and so acquire rights in less than 12 years but if none of them applies then the registered proprietor must take action to evict the squatter.

Although the squatter may make a further application any time over the following two years he will be prevented from doing so if any of the following conditions apply:

1. he is a defendant in proceedings which involve asserting a right to possession of the land;

2. judgment for possession of the land has been given against him in the last two years; or

3. he has been evicted from the land pursuant to a judgment for possession.

So the 2002 Act has added a further stage to the claim for adverse possession and has given the paper title owner the right to be notified of the claims of the adverse possessor.

The 2002 Act is trying to prevent the unnecessary waste of time and money of both the squatter and the paper title owner in repeated applications to be registered as proprietor of the property, most of which will be unsuccessful. However, there is also provision under the Act to allow the adverse possessor to gain rights over the land where justice so permits.

SECTION

'Schedule 6, paragraph 9 ... (1) Where a person is registered as the proprietor of an estate in land in pursuance of an application under this Schedule, the title by virtue of adverse possession which he had at the time of the application is extinguished.

(2) Subject to sub-paragraph (3) the registration of a person under this Schedule as the proprietor of an estate in land does not affect the priority of any interest affecting the estate.

(3) Subject to sub-paragraph (4) where a person is registered under this schedule as the proprietor of an estate the estate is vested in him free of any registered charge affecting the estate immediately before his registration.'

In any case, if the squatter is then registered as proprietor, he will take the land subject to any interests affecting the estate.

Rectification of the Register in cases of adverse possession

Where a squatter has been in adverse possession of land for over ten years the squatter has the right to apply to the Registrar in order to be registered as proprietor of the land. Such an application will only be successful if the squatter can prove the requisite elements of adverse possession, i.e. intention to possess and factual possession for the requisite length of time. If the Registrar later finds out that the claimant squatter has not satisfied these requirements then the registered proprietor who has lost title can claim that the Register should be rectified in his favour. In *Baxter v Mannion* [2011] EWCA Civ 120 Baxter claimed rights under adverse possession over a field where he grazed horses without permission of the landowner. He later attempted to register his rights at the Land Registry and the paper title owner Mr Mannion failed to object. This was as a result of illness and family issues. Mr Baxter was then registered as owner of the field. Mr Mannion later challenged the registration arguing that Baxter had not satisfied the requirements of adverse possession and sought rectification of the Register. The court held that failure to satisfy the requirements of adverse possession was a 'mistake' within the Land Registration Act 2002 Sched 4 which permitted the alteration of the Register by the Registrar.

Step 1	After ten years the squatter writes to the Land Registry, applying to be registered as owner of the property.
Step 2	The registered proprietor has 65 days to object to the squatter's application.
Step 3	a. If the paper title owner does not object, the squatter is entitled to be registered as owner. b. If the paper title owner objects, the squatter's application is rejected unless one of **three** exceptions applies.
Step 4	The Registrar considers whether the squatter's application comes within one of the following exceptions: a. estoppel; b. the squatter is legally entitled to the land; c. there is a boundary dispute. If the Registrar is satisfied that one of these circumstances exist, then the squatter is entitled to be registered.
Step 5	If the Registrar rejects the squatter's application to be registered, the paper title owner has two years to evict the squatter. If no action is taken then the squatter will have another chance to apply to be registered as proprietor. In this case the paper title owner will not be given an opportunity to defend the application.

Table 14.3 Steps in acquiring adverse possession rights under the Land Registration Act 2002

KEY FACTS

Adverse possession under the 2002 Act
1. The paper title owner of property will no longer 'lose' title once the limitation period has run against him.
2. An adverse possessor must apply to become owner of the land.
3. The paper title owner has notice of the application.
4. The adverse possessor cannot be registered as owner if the paper title owner or anyone else with an interest objects, except in three circumstances.
5. The three exceptions are: a. estoppel; b. the adverse possessor is for some other reason entitled to the land; c. a boundary dispute.
6. If none of these applies, the registered proprietor has two years to evict the squatter from the land.
7. If no action is taken to evict the squatter, he will have the chance to re-apply to be registered.

The 2002 Act protects any 12-year period of adverse possession which the squatter can prove was acquired before the Land Registration Act 2002 came into force.

14.5 Adverse possession in leasehold property

The principles of adverse possession apply to leasehold property in a similar way to that of freehold. A squatter can acquire the ownership of property held under a tenancy by way of adverse possession. However where the land is subject to a tenancy the rights of the squatter as against the freehold owner will not start to run until the lease has expired. The position can be considered both from the viewpoint of the squatter over leasehold property and from the viewpoint of the tenant and the freehold owner

14.5.1 The tenant as the squatter

If the tenant wishes to claim adverse possession against his landlord then time will only run when his lawful right to be there has run its course. So time will only run when the lease has expired and the tenant does not pay rent or acknowledge the landlord's title.

CASE EXAMPLE

Hayward v Chaloner [1968] 1 QB 107

The right to claim adverse possessory rights only arises when the relationship of landlord and tenant ceases. Here, the rector of a parish had been given a smallholding. He paid rent but after a while, as a result of the generosity of the landowner, he stopped paying anything. The rector then claimed that he had acquired rights under adverse possession because he was no longer there under a lawful agreement.

If the tenant claims adverse possession against other land belonging to the landlord then it will be presumed that he is there lawfully as an extension of his tenancy.

14.5.2 Adverse possession against tenants

It is much harder for someone to claim adverse possession against leasehold property than it is against freehold property because the squatter has to claim against both the tenant as well as the freeholder and so he must satisfy two limitation periods. However, there has been doubt as to whether the squatter has the right to remain in the property for the duration of the lease.

The law traditionally differed as to whether the title is unregistered or registered.

Leases of unregistered land

Once the squatter has taken possession then the question arises whether the tenant still has the right to surrender the lease to the landlord or whether the squatter can claim the right to enjoy the land until the lease ends. The landlord may be concerned as to what the squatter will do with the property while he is in possession.

CASE EXAMPLE

Fairweather v St Marylebone Property Co Ltd [1963] AC 510

A lease had been granted in 1894 for 99 years. Squatters took possession when there were still over 40 years of the lease left to run. The tenant sought to surrender the lease to his landlord in 1959. If the application was unsuccessful the landlord would have to wait until the lease expired in 1993 which was over 30 years away. The House of Lords held the surrender to be effective as the tenant still had a relationship with the landlord and the rights which were extinguished by the Limitation Act were those with the squatter himself. In other words, the tenant still had sufficient interest in the lease to surrender it.

The decision is difficult to justify but it is still upheld in relation to adverse possessory rights against tenants of unregistered land and will be unaffected by the 2002 Act.

It is clear that the squatter cannot claim that time has run against the freehold owner of the property. Time will only run when the lease has reverted to the freehold owner.

Registered leases

The law is different where the tenancy is in registered land. Once time has run against the tenant, the squatter has the right to be registered as the owner of the leasehold property. This means that once the squatter has registered title, the tenant can no longer surrender the lease as he owns nothing to surrender. This is obviously problematic for the freeholder who now no longer can claim rent and cannot enter the property until the term has ended.

CASE EXAMPLE

Spectrum Investments Co v Holmes [1981] 1 WLR 221

The squatter had applied for registration. He had been in adverse possession for 12 years. The Land Registry registered the squatter with possessory title and that replaced the tenant's title. This was even noted on the landlord's title. After registration had taken place, the tenant tried to surrender his title to the landlord. The judge held that there had been registration of the interest which prevented the tenant from surrendering the tenancy. The squatter had the right to the property until the lease came to an end and the landlord was subject to the squatter's rights as new tenant of the property.

In this case the surrender was attempted by the tenant after the registration had taken place but it was not clear if there could be an effective surrender before registration of the squatter's interests.

CASE EXAMPLE

Central London Commercial Estates Ltd v Kato Kagaku Ltd [1998] 4 All ER 948

Here, the squatter had not yet been registered as owner of the leasehold interest. However, the limitation period had run out and the squatter had the right to apply for registration. The judge held that the tenant had also lost the right to surrender the lease to the landlord. The tenant now held the lease on trust for the squatter.

The law is different under the 2002 Act as the tenant and the landlord will both have to be notified before there can be an application for registration. This allows the freehold owner the chance to object to the registration of the squatter and may allow time to bring the lease to an end before the interest is then extinguished.

14.5.3 Adverse possession against a trustee's title

This is governed by the rule that the trustee's title to trust land is never extinguished by reason of a stranger's adverse possession until the rights of all the trust beneficiaries have been barred.

Adverse possession against a trust
1. The trustee can never acquire adverse possessory rights against trust land himself.
2. The beneficiaries cannot acquire adverse possessory rights against each other where the property is co-owned.
3. Where land is held in succession the rights of one beneficiary can be barred, for example the tenant for life, but the rights of the remainderman will not be affected.

ACTIVITY

Applying the law

Uncle Alan created a trust over his land. He appoints Tricia and Tim as trustees to hold his house in the Lake District on trust for Alex and Fran for life with remainder to Abigale in fee simple absolute. Simon went into adverse possession of the land 12½ years ago.

Advise Tricia and Tim.

Would it make any difference to your answer if Alex and Fran had died two years before the expiry of the limitation period?

14.6 The nature of the rights in adverse possession

The nature of the rights of a squatter will vary according to whether the land is held with registered or unregistered title.

14.6.1 Unregistered land

If adverse possession is successful, the paper title owner is prevented from suing and his title is effectively extinguished after 12 years. No steps need be taken by the squatter.

Any rights in existence against the title will continue to be effective as the squatter will not be a *bona fide* purchaser for value of the land.

14.6.2 Registered land

Before the 2002 Act the paper title owner was deemed to hold the estate on trust for the squatter once time had run against him. Under the Act the law is different as the registered title owner does not lose title just because someone takes possession of the land for a fixed period of time (s 96).

SECTION

's 96 ... no period of limitation under section 15 of the Limitation Act 1980 ... shall run against any person, other than a chargee, in relation to an estate in land or rentcharge the title to which is registered.'

The squatter can only successfully obtain rights where he successfully applies to the Registrar for registration. However, this process is carried out only after the paper title owner has been notified and has a chance to register any objections to the registration.

14.7 Recovery of possession by the paper title owner

In unregistered land and in registered land before the 2002 Act it was very important that proceedings were initiated before time had run against the paper title owner. As seen above, the law held that the adverse possessor had acquired rights once he had satisfied the requirements for the requisite number of years (pre-2002 it was 12 years for both registered and unregistered land). It is still the case in unregistered land that once the squatter can show that he has adversely possessed the land for 12 years he can claim the land for himself. The paper title owner must stop time running. This can be in one of two ways: first, by giving the squatter permission to enjoy the land through a licence or lease; or, second, by bringing court action against the squatter. Asserting one's rights orally or by a letter will never be enough.

CASE EXAMPLE

Mount Carmel Investments v Peter Thurlow Ltd [1988] 1 WLR 1078

Here, it was held that merely to send a letter demanding return of the property was insufficient to stop time running against the paper title owner. The only way to stop time from running was to start legal proceedings to recover possession.

In registered land under the provisions in the Land Registration Act 2002 it is still important that the paper title owner takes action to evict the squatter even when the application to register has been rejected because the paper title owner has objected to the registration. If he takes no action to evict the squatter, he can re-apply to be registered in two years' time and in this case the paper title owner will not be notified of the application.

Where the squatter formally acknowledges the landowner's title then time will stop running. Such acknowledgement must be in writing and not merely an oral discussion between the parties.

14.8 Adverse possession and the Human Rights Act 1998

The nature of a claim in adverse possession is such that it can be seen to be in contravention of a person's right to peaceful enjoyment of their property under Art 1, Protocol 1 of the European Convention on Human Rights. However, the courts were initially reluctant to make a ruling on whether adverse possession does challenge basic human rights of the landowner.

The European Court of Human Rights has had one significant opportunity to rule on the issue of human rights in connection with adverse possession and the law has now been clarified by the Grand Chamber of the European Court of Human Rights. The issue was initially raised in *JA Pye (Oxford) Ltd v Graham* (2001). Both the judge at first instance and the Court of Appeal considered the effects of the human rights legislation on adverse possession: the House of Lords did not consider the issue in any detail because it was decided that the Human Rights Act 1998 did not have retrospective effect and therefore as the claim was brought prior to 2 October 2000 (when the 1998 Act took effect) it could not apply to the facts. However, the issue was referred to the European Court of Human Rights and has been finally considered by the Grand Chamber.

CASE EXAMPLE

JA Pye (Oxford) Ltd v Graham [2001] Ch 804

'A frequent justification for limitation periods generally is that people should not be able to sit on their rights indefinitely, and that is a proposition to which at least in general nobody could take exception. However, if as in the present case the owner of land has no immediate use for it and is content to let another person trespass on the land for the time being, it is hard to see what principle of justice entitles the trespasser to acquire the land for nothing from the owner simply because he has been permitted to remain there for 12 years. To say that in such circumstances the owner who has sat on his rights should therefore be deprived of his land appears to me to be illogical and disproportionate. Illogical because the only reason that the owner can be said to have sat on his rights is because of the existence of the 12 year limitation period in the first place; if no limitation period existed he would be entitled to claim possession whenever he actually wanted the land.'

Neuberger J, sitting in the High Court

The judge is here challenging the whole justification for adverse possession and arguing that simply because a landowner does not use his land for a period of time it does not then make any difference to the nature of his ownership of the legal title.

'I believe the result is disproportionate because, particularly in a climate of increasing awareness of human rights including the right to enjoy one's own property, it does seem draconian to the owner and a windfall for the squatter that, just because the owner has taken no steps to evict a squatter for 12 years, the owner should lose 25 hectares of land to the squatter with no compensation whatsoever.'

In this part of the judgment, although Neuberger J did not directly rule on the human rights issue, he does suggest that the loss of land through adverse possession presents a direct challenge to the whole principle of the right to enjoy one's own property under human rights legislation.

The Court of Appeal also looked at the issue of the impact of the human rights legislation on the facts of the case. The case for Pye was based partly on s3 of the 1998 Act which holds that legislation must be interpreted in such a way as to be compatible with Convention rights. The court did not think that s3 applied in this case.

'the parties focused on one point, namely the impact of section 3 of the 1998 Act on the interpretation of the relevant provisions of the 1980 Act ... My conclusions on the section 3 point are ... as follows ... Section 3 does not affect the case. The only Convention right relied on (the protection of property in Article 1 of the First Protocol) does not impinge on the relevant provisions of the 1980 Act. Those provisions do not deprive a person of his possessions or interfere with his peaceful enjoyment of them. They deprive a person of his right of access to the courts for the purpose of recovering property if he has delayed the institution of his legal proceedings for 12 years or more after he has been dispossessed of his land by another person who has been in adverse possession of it for at least that period. The extinction of the title of the claimant in those circumstances is not a deprivation of possessions or a confiscatory measure for which the payment of compensation would be appropriate.'

Mummery LJ, in the Court of Appeal

Keene LJ, who also sat in the Court of Appeal, was much stronger in his argument that the human rights legislation did not challenge the claimant's rights in this case:

'It has not been suggested in these proceedings that the 12 year limitation period provided for by the English law on actions to recover land is itself incompatible with the
Convention. In any event the Strasbourg jurisprudence recognises a margin of appreciation for national legislatures in determining such periods, which exist in most if not all
European jurisdictions in some shape or form. There is therefore no reason to conclude
that s 15 of the Limitation Act 1980 is incompatible with Convention rights ... What this
demonstrates is that the argument about confiscation or deprivation of property rights
without compensation has little to commend it. It was accepted on behalf of the appel-
lants that if this court finds that the respondents had satisfied the requirements of
English law as to adverse possession for 12 years, then no breach of the Convention
would result ... To my mind, that means that the arguments based on the Human Rights
Act add very little, if anything, to the submissions which relate to the pre-Human Rights
Act law.

Keene LJ, in the Court of Appeal

In the House of Lords, Browne-Wilkinson LJ did not consider the human rights issues in the
case because under the 1998 Act the case must be initiated after the Act was in force and the
case had been brought before the 1998 Act came into force.

CASE EXAMPLE

JA Pye (Oxford) Ltd v United Kingdom [2005] 3 EGLR 1

Pye Ltd pursued a claim in the European Court of Human Rights, arguing that its human rights
had been violated under Art 1 of the First Protocol and so it was entitled to compensation for
the loss of its land. The court found that there had been a violation of its rights because, under
the provisions of the Land Registration Act 1925 and the Limitation Act 1980, it had been
deprived of the right to enjoy its property. However, it accepted that there was some justification of the rules on adverse possession and the rules had been substantially modified under
the Land Registration Act 2002. Nevertheless, in this case, since the old rules applied, the decision had been disproportionately harsh. The applicant company had not only been deprived of
its property but had received no monetary compensation for its loss. The court pointed to the
fact that there was no procedural protection for the landowner, in particular the landowner
had no way of knowing that the loss of his title was imminent. The court therefore found
against the United Kingdom government, although only on a very narrow margin of four votes
to three, and had to compensate the applicant for the loss of its land. The government in turn
appealed against this finding.

The Grand Chamber of the European Court of Human Rights reversed this decision, again
by a relatively narrow margin of ten votes to seven, finding that the law applying to the claimants in Pye, i.e. the Land Registration Act 1925, was not a violation of the Convention. They
found that the existence of a 12-year limitation period for actions for the recovery of land as
such pursued a legitimate aim in the general interest. They noted that very little action on the
part of the applicant companies would have stopped time running. The evidence was that if
the applicant companies had asked for rent, or some other form of payment, in respect of the
Grahams' occupation of the land, it would have been forthcoming and the possession would
no longer have been adverse. They also commented that the legislation in place at the time
was within the state's margin of appreciation, unless they gave rise to results which were so
anomalous as to render the legislation unacceptable.

It would seem that this decision which upheld both the Land Registration Act 2002 as
well as the earlier law on adverse possession to be compatible with human rights has

now put an end to any potential claims from the landowner that a successful claim from a squatter is contrary to his human rights. As Kevin Gray comments:

> 'With the Grand Chamber's decision in *Pye* an aggravated passage in the history of adverse possession law is now beginning to recede into the distance. Whatever misgivings any members of the Grand Chamber may have had about the operation of the Land Registration Act 1925, there was broad agreement that heightened safeguards for registered proprietors introduced by its successor legislation have both strengthened the protection of registered titles and rendered the new law of adverse possession of registered land compliant with the Convention standard of "peaceful enjoyment" of possessions.'
>
> K Gray and S F Gray, *Elements of Land Law* (5th edn, Oxford University Press, 2009), p. 1169

However, following *Pye v UK* there has been one further attempt to challenge loss of title on the grounds of human rights.

CASE EXAMPLE

Ofulue v Bossert [2009] Ch 1

The case concerned property purchased by Mr Ofulue in 1976. Soon after purchase he went to live in Nigeria. The Bosserts (a father and daughter) went to live as squatters in the property in 1981, which was in a poor state of repair, having been allowed in by a former tenant. Mr Ofulue returned to the UK from time to time but did not pursue proceedings against the Bosserts and on each occasion returned to Nigeria. In 1992 the Bosserts offered to purchase the property. Again possession proceedings were not pursued. In 2000 and 2003 possession proceedings were finally issued against the Bosserts but the judge at first instance held that time had already run against Mr Ofulue. Mr Ofulue appealed claiming that his human rights under Article 1 Protocol 1 ECHR had been violated. The Court of Appeal applied *Pye v UK* and held that it should be followed unless there were exceptional reasons for not following it. There were no such reasons here. Mr Ofulue's rights under Article 1 Protocol 1 had not been violated.

14.9 Adverse possession and the criminal law

The Legal Aid, Sentencing and Punishment of Offenders Act 2012 s 144 makes trespassing in a residential building a criminal offence. The Act became law in October 2012 and there have been a number of prosecutions under the Act. The Act only makes it a criminal offence for trespass in residential buildings and not commercial buildings.

SECTION

's 144 **Offence of squatting in a residential building**

(1) A person commits an offence if —

    (a) the person is in a residential building as a trespasser having entered it as a trespasser,

    (b) the person knows or ought to know that he or she is a trespasser, and

    (c) the person is living in the building or intends to live there for any period.

(2) The offence is not committed by a person holding over after the end of a lease or licence (even if the person leaves and re-enters the building).

(3) For the purposes of this section –

(a) "building" includes any structure or part of a structure (including a temporary or moveable structure), and

(b) a building is "residential" if it is designed or adapted, before the time of entry, for use as a place to live.

(4) For the purposes of this section the fact that a person derives title from a trespasser, or has the permission of a trespasser, does not prevent the person from being a trespasser.

(5) A person convicted of an offence under this section is liable on summary conviction to imprisonment for a term not exceeding 51 weeks or a fine not exceeding level 5 on the standard scale (or both).

(6) In relation to an offence committed before the commencement of section 281(5) of the Criminal Justice Act 2003, the reference in subsection (5) to 51 weeks is to be read as a reference to 6 months.

(7) For the purposes of subsection (1)(a) it is irrelevant whether the person entered the building as a trespasser before or after the commencement of this section.

(8) In section 17 of the Police and Criminal Evidence Act 1984 (entry for purpose of arrest etc) –

(a) in subsection (1)(c), after sub-paragraph (v) insert –

"(vi) section 144 of the Legal Aid, Sentencing and Punishment of Offenders Act 2012 (squatting in a residential building);"

(b) in subsection (3), for "or (iv)" substitute ", (iv) or (vi)".

(9) In Schedule 10 to the Criminal Justice and Public Order Act 1994 (consequential amendments), omit paragraph 53(b).'

This new offence has raised the question as to whether an application can be made by a squatter to be registered as owner of the property if the application is based on a criminal offence. The question has been addressed in *Best v Chief Land Registrar* [2015] EWCA Civ 17. Mr Best applied to be registered owner of property which he had treated as his own since 2001. He had satisfied the requirements of adverse possession but since LASPO 2012 had come into effect he was committing a criminal offence whilst in the property. The Court of Appeal had to resolve the conflict that arose between those exercising their rights under the law of adverse possession and claiming their right to register under the 2002 LRA and that of relying on behaviour which now constituted a criminal act.

The court concluded that a claim for adverse possession was unaffected by s 144 LASPO 2012 and there were no public policy concerns which should override the normal operation of the rules of adverse possession.

JUDGMENT

'in my judgment ... Parliament did not intend that s 144 or the policy considerations which underlie it should have any bearing upon the operation of the law of adverse possession. Parliament is not lightly to be taken to have legislated with the intention of producing such capricious and arbitrary effects upon a carefully crafted and comprehensive statutory regime such as that contained in the LRA.'

Sales LJ

SUMMARY

1. Adverse possession allows a claimant to acquire rights through long use of land and proof of factual possession and intention to possess.

2. Factual possession is proved by showing that the claimant has physical control of the property.

3. Factual possession must be for an unbroken period of time.

4. If there is permissive use of land under a lease or a licence adverse possession will not arise.

5. The squatter must prove that at all times he intended to possess the land.

6. The squatter will acquire rights in unregistered land after 12 years if he can prove factual possession and intention to possess.

7. In registered land the squatter can only acquire rights after applying to be registered as title owner.

8. The landowner is given a chance to object to the application of the squatter.

9. The landowner cannot challenge loss of his land through adverse possession on the grounds of violation of his human rights.

SAMPLE ESSAY QUESTION

The 2002 Land Registration Act has effectively removed the possibility that individuals can successfully claim land under the doctrine of adverse possession.
   Do you agree with this view?

> Explain what is meant by adverse possession.
>
> Discuss the Law Commission report (Law Com No 271) and criticisms of the doctrine.

> Discuss the law pre-2002.
>
> Explain how a squatter may acquire rights.
>
> Explain factual possession; examples from case law *Bucks CC v Moran*. Compare *Powell v MacFarlane*. Explain intention to possess: *Pye Ltd v Graham*. Intention to possess not intention to own.

Discuss regime post-2002: explain that even where factual possession and intention to possess is proved the squatter must apply to the Land Registry to be registered as owner of the property.

Explain steps in application:

Step 1: squatter applies to be registered.

Step 2: Registrar notifies landowner and anyone with interest in the property that an application has been made; a counter-notice can be served and the application will be rejected except in three cases.

Step 3: the squatter can argue that his case comes within one of the three exceptional cases.

Step 4: if there has been an objection but the squatter remains in the property and the landowner does not evict him he can re-apply to be registered and the landowner will not be notified.

Discuss the safeguards built into the new system allowing the landowner to be notified of the application.

Discuss cases where the squatter may be successful (e.g. estoppel claims, boundary disputes).

CONCLUSION

Further reading

Books

Gray, K and Gray, S F, *Elements of Land Law* (5th edn, Oxford University Press, 2009), pp. 1169, 1180.

Rainey, P, Walsh, M, Harrison, P and Dovar, D (eds), *Megarry's Manual of the Law of Real Property* (9th edn, Sweet & Maxwell, 2014), pp. 482–483.

Articles

Colby, A, 'No Adverse Effects' [2015] 1508 *EG* 107.

Cooke, E, 'Adverse Possession; Electronic Conveyancing; Land Registration; Overriding Interests; Title to Land' [2002] *Conv* 11.

Dixon, M, 'Bringing Home Another's Rights' [2001] 65 *Conv* 276.

Dixon, M, 'Human Rights and Adverse Possession: The Final Nail' [2008] 74 *Conv* 160.

Dockray, M, 'Why do We need Adverse Possession?' [1985] *Conv* 272.

Fox, D M, 'Adverse Possession under the Land Registration Act 1925' [2008] 67(3) *CLJ* 474.

Griffiths, G, 'An Important Question of Principle: Reality and Rectification in Registered Land' [2011] *Conv* 331.

Hickey, R, 'The *Best* Outcome: The Application of Schedule 6 and the Reinforcement of Adverse Possession Policy under the Land Registration Act 2002' [2017] *Conv* 223.

Milne, P, 'Mistaken Belief and Adverse Possession: Mistaken Interpretation? IAM Group Plc v Chowdrey' [2012] 4 *Conv* 342.

Pawlowski, M and Brown J, 'Adverse Possdession and the Transmissibility of Possessory Rights – The Dark Side of Land Registration' [2017] *Conv* 116.

Radley-Gardner, O and Harpum, C, 'Adverse Possession and the Intention to Possess: A Reply' [2001] *Conv* 155.

Rhys, O, 'Adverse Possession, Human Rights and Judicial Heresy' [2002] *Conv* 470.

Tee, L, 'Adverse Possession and the Intention to Possess' [2000] 64 *Conv* 113.

Tee, L, 'Adverse Possession and the Intention to Possess: A Rejoinder' [2002] 66 *Conv* 50.

15

Commonhold

AIMS AND OBJECTIVES

After reading this chapter, you should be able to:

- Explain what is meant by commonhold
- Explain why commonhold was introduced
- Discuss the main elements involved in a commonhold association
- Explain what is meant by a community statement
- Describe how commonhold comes to an end

15.1 Introduction

This is a relatively new concept in land. It provides a structure for managing land where property is held for group occupation, such as flats or units on an industrial estate. The problem in the past has been how to manage those areas common to all, for example the road over which everyone passes to his own unit on the industrial estate or the stairs which are used by all the owners in a block of flats. These areas present problems, for example they need maintenance which can be costly and it is not always clear who should be responsible to pay for these costs. The lack of enforceability of positive covenants has made this particularly difficult to address.

The Law Commission considered the issue in 1984 (Law Com No 127) and proposed that there should be a new type of obligation called a **land obligation** which would be enforceable between neighbours.

The essence of its proposals was that there should be two types of obligations:

1. **neighbour obligations**; and
2. **development obligations**.

Neighbour obligations would be similar to positive and negative covenants between freeholders.

Development obligations would be reciprocal obligations within areas of multiple occupation, such as blocks of flats.

These original ideas are incorporated into the new legislation but the actual changes made are far more radical and are modelled on concepts used in many countries, in particular North America and Australia. (In North America such properties are known as condominiums.)

The issues were revisited by the Law Commission and the 'Commonhold and Leasehold Reform: Draft Bill and Consultation Paper' was introduced in 2000. However, for a number of reasons it did not immediately become law, only gaining royal assent in May 2002.

The Commonhold and Leasehold Reform Act 2002 lays down a radically new statutory scheme concerning how these areas are to be managed. It applies only to land with registered title. The basis of the new legislation is that although individuals will own their flats and separate units as unit-holders, the common areas will be owned by what are called **commonhold associations**. Ownership by the commonhold associations will be freehold and there is no provision for combined leasehold and freehold or continued leasehold ownership.

The commonhold association will be a company limited by guarantee that is controlled by the unit-holders. It will have several roles, including the administration of the common parts as well as the overseeing of the individual units. The commonhold association will be bound by a community statement. The statement can be changed to adapt to changes in circumstances of the community. The community will be controlled by its members through the commonhold association in general meeting. The directors of the association may be either members elected from their own number or professionals or other outsiders appointed by the members to run the community on behalf of the association. When a member sells his unit the purchaser will buy into the association. It is always possible to end the association and voluntarily to liquidate the commonhold association. However, there must be a majority in favour of terminating provisions. It is a flexible form of land holding and can be used even where there are only a small number of units, for example three or four flats in a block would qualify.

This is a form of landholding for freehold owners of land and it goes some way towards counteracting the difficulties of enforcing positive rights between owners of freehold land and the problems in forcing landlords to carry out repairs on communal areas of property such as flats.

The community statement defines the roles and duties of the commonhold association and the individual unit-holders. The statements will vary from one unit to another, according to their own particular needs.

> 'A commonhold is a community of linked freehold estates with mutual interests and obligations. It is a community formed to share facilities and undertake repair and maintenance of common parts. The community of interest (which is a consequence of commonhold) cannot tolerate other forms of estate within commonhold whether these are standard freehold or pre-existing leasehold. As a consequence, the site of the proposed commonhold has to be "legally cleared" of existing leasehold interests so that there only remains the freehold fee simple which can then be the basis to establish the commonhold on the freehold land by what is (essentially) a second registration of title. The existing freehold title is thereby transformed into a freehold estate in commonhold land.'
>
> D N Clarke, 'The Enactment of Commonhold: Problems, Principles and Perspectives' [2002] 66 *Conv* 349

15.2 The legislation

In the Commonhold and Leasehold Reform Act 2002:

SECTION

'*s*1 **The definition of commonhold land**

(1) Land is commonhold land if –

    (a) the freehold estate in the land is registered as a freehold estate in commonhold land,

    (b) the land is specified in the memorandum of association of a commonhold association as land in relation to which the association is to exercise functions, and

    (c) a commonhold community statement makes provision for rights and duties of the commonhold association and unit-holders (whether or not the statement has come into force).'

Initially, these three conditions must be satisfied before the 2002 Act will apply. It will not apply where the land has unregistered title. However, under s 2 it is possible to come within the provisions and to register if the applicant purchased with unregistered title and has applied to register, the title now being subject to compulsory registration.

Under s 3(1), an application under s 2 may not be made in respect of a freehold estate in land without the consent of anyone who:

- is the registered proprietor of the freehold estate in the whole or part of the land;

- is the registered proprietor of a leasehold estate in the whole or part of the land granted for a term of more than 21 years;

- is the registered proprietor of a charge over the whole or part of the land; or

- falls within any other class of person which may be prescribed.

It should be noted that there is no possibility of the land being partly held as commonhold and partly held as freehold. This makes it impossible to have a 'flying commonhold'. This would be a commonhold of a group of flats existing above other freehold land. It would not make sense for different rules to apply where property is held in such close proximity. Thus, commonhold now allows positive obligations to be enforced within the commonhold.

This section is important because under commonhold all existing charges are extinguished and this must involve agreement from everyone. There may be problems where the development is large or where there are large numbers of long leaseholders. Commonhold cannot exist without reciprocity and so every member must have the same rights and the same duties as everyone else.

SECTION

'*s*7 **Registration without unit-holders**

(1) This section applies where –

    (a) a freehold estate in land is registered as a freehold estate in commonhold land in pursuance of an application under section 2 and

    (b) the application is not accompanied by a statement under section 9(1)(b).

(2) On registration

    (a) the applicant shall continue to be registered as the proprietor of the freehold estate in the commonhold land, and;

    (b) The rights and duties conferred and imposed by the commonhold community statement shall not come into force (subject to section 8(2)(b)).

(3) Where after registration a person other than the applicant becomes entitled to be registered as the proprietor of the freehold estate in one or more, but not all, of the commonhold units –

(a) the commonhold association shall be entitled to be registered as the proprietor of the freehold estate in the common parts,
(b) the Registrar shall register the commonhold association in accordance with paragraph (a) (without an application being made),
(c) the right and duties conferred and imposed by the commonhold community statement shall come into force,
(d) any lease of the whole or part of the commonhold land shall be extinguished by virtue of this section.'

Section 7 covers new developments. It is envisaged that developers will see the advantages of commonhold and, before selling off the parts of the development, the developer will incorporate the commonhold association and also prepare the community statement. Once he has done this he will apply for registration of the land as commonhold and for this he will need to support his application with documentation. It is assumed that the developer owns the land because the application must be made by the registered proprietor of the freehold estate.

ACTIVITY

Applying the law

Bernard owns 'Developments for All'. He purchases a dilapidated house set in four acres of land. He intends to turn it into a number of luxury flats. He decides that he will sell off the flats as commonhold.

Describe the various steps that he must take before the flats can be sold as commonhold.

SECTION

's9 **Registration with unit-holders**
(1) This section applies to a freehold estate in commonhold land if –

(a) it is registered as a freehold estate in commonhold land in pursuance of an application under section 2, and
(b) the application is accompanied by a statement by the applicant requesting that this section should apply.

(2) A statement under subsection (1)(b) must include a list of the commonhold units giving in relation to each one the prescribed details of the proposed initial unit-holder or joint unit-holders.
(3) On registration –

(a) the commonhold association shall be entitled to be registered as the proprietor of the freehold estate in the common parts.'

This section covers registration where there are existing unit-holders and it then allows long leaseholders to have their property converted into commonhold. So here we contrast the situation under s7, where the developers will not know who is going to form the association, and s9, where the names of the association holders already exist and a statement covers them all. The commonhold will then come into effect as soon as registration has been completed. The conversion of existing groups of long leaseholders into commonhold will depend on how easy it will be to get everyone's agreement. The application for conversion cannot be made unless everyone involved consents. It has already been commented by Peter Smith in his 2004 article 'The Purity of Commonhold' (68 Conv 194), that 'the prospect of one or two capricious or recalcitrant long lessees holding up a conversion from long leasehold to commonhold is unappealing'. It has meant that the move to commonhold from existing leasehold ownership has been slow.

ACTIVITY

Self-assessment question

Canary Towers is a block of flats with eight long leaseholders. The freehold is owned by Frederick. If they decide to convert then every leaseholder must agree to the conversion as well as Frederick. What is the position if one of the leaseholders decides he does not want to agree to the conversion to commonhold?

Under s 7(3)(d), all leases will be converted into commonhold. The effect of this may be that some tenants will actually lose their leases.

ACTIVITY

Applying the law

Imagine Sue owns a long lease of a large mansion flat in Maida Vale. In order to meet some of the rising costs, she lets out her spare bedroom to Carrie who has a sub-lease of one year from Sue. If Sue and the other long leaseholders decide to convert to commonhold, Carrie will lose her rights and her lease will have been extinguished. Are there provisions for compensation under s 10 of the 2002 Act and to whom will the responsibility for payment fall?

This presents a challenge to the existing landlord and tenant legislation.

> 'In the case of a developer wishing to refurbish (say) a block of ten flats of which nine are vacant but one of which has a tenant (with some form of security of tenure) it does seem that the developer could proceed to apply (quite properly) for registration of the commonhold ignoring the existence of that tenant who does not need to consent to the registration. The developer would proceed to refurbish the other nine flats. On the sale of the first flat as a commonhold unit, the tenancy is extinguished. Is the developer then able to take possession proceedings to remove the tenant and refurbish the last flat? The 2002 Act is quite clear. The lease is extinguished. A court faced with a claim for possession of such a flat will be forced to consider the relevant earlier legislation providing for security of tenure in the light of the extinguishment of that tenancy under the 2002 Act.'
>
> D N Clarke, 'The Enactment of Commonhold: Problems, Principles and Perspectives' [2002] 66 *Conv* 349

The association

The association is dependent on unit-holders and under Sched 3, para 7 to the 2002 Act a person is entitled to be entered on the register of members once he becomes a unit-holder. Without ownership of a unit, someone is not entitled to become a member of the association. The association takes the form of a private company limited by guarantee.

The management of the association is dealt with under ss 35–36. One key feature is that all members of the association must be given a chance to vote.

Commonhold community statement

The commonhold community statement is described in s 38. This lays down very specific requirements of the statement. It must make provision:

- requiring the directors of the commonhold association to make an annual estimate of the income required to be raised from unit-holders to meet the expenses of the association;
- enabling the directors of the commonhold association to make estimates from time to time of income required to be raised from unit-holders in addition to the annual estimate.

Section 31 covers the matters covered by the community statement and includes under s 31(5), in particular, a duty –

- to pay money;
- to undertake works;
- to grant access;
- to give notice;
- to refrain from entering into transactions of a specified kind in relation to a commonhold unit;
- to refrain from using the whole or part of a commonhold unit for a specified purpose or for anything other than a specified purpose.

Other matters covered are to refrain from causing nuisance or annoyance and to refrain from specified behaviour.

The legislation is fairly detailed about the ambit of the statement and the duties that will be covered by commonhold.

Restrictions on dealing with the commonhold property

There are some restrictions on the way an owner of commonhold can deal with the unit that he owns. The property can be sold in the normal way but the new owner must accept the association and the responsibilities of commonhold. However, there is a restriction on leasing property under s 17 which prevents leases from being created unless they are within the section. This limits leases to the length prescribed by regulations which will be under seven years.

Termination of commonhold

Commonhold can be brought to an end through voluntary winding-up under ss 43–49 of the 2002 Act. The reasons may be because the commonholders want to be freed from the association or because the property is unsuitable for commonhold.

Under s 43 it is necessary to have the agreement of over 80 per cent of the members of the association. There must be a termination statement and everyone must be in agreement if the application is to go directly to the Registrar. The termination statement must include such details as the association's proposals for dealing with the land and distributing the association's assets. If only 80 per cent agree then the matter must go to the court under s 45, which will determine the terms on which the application may be made and the content of the statement. There are of course 20 per cent of the unit-holders who do not want to terminate the commonhold.

Termination by the court

If the association is in debt and unable to meet those debts then an application must be made to the court, which can order under s 51 that another association takes over, called the 'successor commonhold association'.

15.3 Comments on the nature of commonhold

Commonhold is a new approach to community property holding. It at last allows freeholders the right to enforce positive obligations among themselves. It has advantages over a landlord taking responsibility for these obligations because the interests of the unit-holders will be identical, whereas the interest of the landlord will never be the same as those of the tenants.

There are a number of disadvantages:

1. The unit-holder does not have complete freedom to deal with the unit. The most important restriction is in connection with the length of leases which may be created in the commonhold unit.

2. There is an expectation that all unit-holders will carry out their duties. This is unlikely to be the case and the 2002 Act does not deal with enforcement adequately. There is no sanction for the breach of obligation, particularly where those breaches are persistent.

3. There is no statutory system for resolution of disputes. There should be a tribunal established with the sole responsibility of dealing with disputes rather than putting the responsibility on to the Lands Tribunal.

4. There is a potential problem with insolvency if the association is wound-up with no replacement. It may deter mortgagees who may not be prepared to lend where there is an outstanding doubt about the future of the association if it is wound up.

'Commonhold is not the final answer to the problem of freehold covenants. That awaits the introduction of land obligations, commonhold only solves the problem of positive obligations within the commonhold community. Commonhold is no more than the framework for community living.'

D N Clarke, 'The Enactment of Commonhold: Problems, Principles and Perspectives' [2002] 66 *Conv* 349

The provisions of the Commonhold and Leasehold Reform Act 2002 have been gradually brought into force. Some provisions were introduced in November 2004 and February 2005, while most remaining provisions were brought into force in 2006.

The introduction of commonhold has not been an unqualified success. There has been a lack of engagement and very few registered commonholds. The Law commission commented in its 'Report on Easements, Covenants and *Profits à Prendre*' that there had been a low level of take-up and at February 2008 only 14 commonholds had been registered. The Report continues 'We understand that the Ministry of Justice considers this to be disappointing and that it will be consulting on ways to improve the commonhold legislation and to promote the take up of commonhold in due course.'

The commitment to the company and the need for a detailed statement from the members adds a layer of duties that most homeowners do not wish to engage with. Some of the homeowners must agree to be Company Directors which many will not want to do.

Smith suggests in a recent article that the recommendations of the Irish Law Reform Commission for 'Multi-Unit Developments' may have been more appropriate. The Irish system, if introduced, would be based on the long leasehold which was disapproved of in consultation before the 2002 Act in England. Smith admits that the long lease in Ireland is more suited to addressing the problem of maintenance of common areas than in England because in Ireland the long leases are much longer, often hundreds of years long. The key difference perhaps is that under the system proposed in Ireland new developments would have to transfer the freehold registered title to an owner's management company before any unit transfer could take place, whereas in England it is optional ('Apartment Ownership: The Irish Reform Package' [2009] *Conv* 21).

The Law Commission consultation on 'Easements and Restrictive Covenants' (Law Com No 186) has re-opened the debate on the best way to address reciprocal obligations between neighbouring landowners. There is room for the debate to revisit the law on commonhold to see if with some adaption it would be received with more enthusiasm.

ACTIVITY

Applying the law

You are approached by Dan, who is a property developer. He wants to purchase a run-down convalescent home and turn it into luxury flats. He asks you what are the advantages of adopting commonhold for the flats.

Advise Dan.

SUMMARY

1. Commonhold ownership is a scheme of land ownership which allows communal areas of land to be managed.

2. Commonhold combines freehold ownership of individual units and freehold ownership of communal areas through a commonhold association.

3. The commonhold association is a company limited by guarantee and will be bound by a community statement.

4. The community statement will govern the duties of the association.

5. Commonhold can be terminated by voluntary winding-up or through a court order.

Further reading

Books
Aldridge, T, *Commonhold Law* (Sweet & Maxwell, 2002).
Clarke, D, *Clarke on Commonhold* (Jordans Publishing, 2002).
Cowan, G and Driscoll, J, *Commonhold: Law and Practice* (The Law Society, 2005).

Articles
Clarke, D N, 'Commonhold: A Prospect of Promise' (1995) 58 *MLR* 486.
Clarke, D N, 'The Enactment of Commonhold: Problems, Principles and Perspectives' [2002] 66 *Conv* 349.
Crabb, L, 'The Commonhold Association as You like It' [1998] 62 *Conv* 283.
Danskin, D, 'Lenders have Fears' [2005] 0524 *EG* 17.
Dowden, M, 'Very Little Appetite for a Change in Tenure' [2009] 0917 *EG* 98.

Driscoll, J A, 'Modern Response to an Age-Old Question' [2008] 0827 *EG* 108.

Driscoll, J A, 'Whatever Happened to Commonhold?' [2008] 158(7333) *NLJ* 1137.

Kenny, P H, 'Commonhold: At Last?' [2001] 65 *Conv* 1.

Roberts, N, 'Commonhold: A New Property Term – But No Property in a Term!' [2002] 66 *Conv* 341.

Smith, P F, 'The Purity of Commonholds' [2004] 68 *Conv* 194.

Smith, P F, 'Apartment Ownership: The Irish Reform Package' [2009] 73 *Conv* 21.

Law Commission Reports

'Commonhold and Leasehold Reform: Draft Bill and Consultation Paper' (Law Com No 4843, 2000).

Glossary of legal terminology

accretion
additions to land bordering water

appurtenant
a right to become attached to a piece of land

beneficiary
a person who has an interest in the trust property in equity but does not own the legal title

bona fide
means 'in good faith'

cestui que trust
means a beneficiary under a trust

collateral contract
a separate contract that is not part of the substantive contract, enforceable as a separate agreement

common law
was the system of law after the Norman Conquest which was a combination of law initiated centrally and local laws

corporeal hereditaments
these are rights that have some real or tangible quality

deed
A document which has been drawn up to satisfy certain prescribed formalities. These formalities depend on the date at which the deed was executed

demise
a transfer of property to another by lease or under a will

diluvion
reductions to land bordering water

easements
an easement is a right over the land of another

encumbrance
means a right that attaches to the title of land

express trust
a trust which is expressly created by the settlor

fixture
anything that has become so attached to the land that it forms part of the land

forfeiture
loss of an interest in land as a result of breach of a covenant

franchise
an estate in land which entitles the claimant to claim a privilege over the land such as the right to hold an annual fair on the land

gazumping
the acceptance of a higher price by the seller from a new purchaser having accepted an offer from another purchaser before contracts have been exchanged

gazundering
the withdrawal of an offer to purchase property by the purchaser and substituted with an offer of a lower price

implied trust
a trust which arises because of circumstances and not through the express intention of the settlor

incorporeal hereditaments
these are intangible rights in land

incumbrance
means a right that attaches to the title of land

inter vivos
means a trust created during a lifetime, as opposed to one created in a will, taking effect on death

intestacy
where there is no will or no valid will on someone's death and his property passes under statutory rules of intestacy which lay down a list of relatives to inherit on someone's death

lease
one of two legal estates in land which gives the tenant exclusive possession of the property but for a limited time

mortgagee
the lender

mortgage
security for money lent usually in the form of land

mortgagor
the borrower

option to purchase
the right given to a purchaser to call on the seller to sell the land within the stipulated period at a pre-agreed price

ouster order
An order of the court preventing a person from entering property at all or within

strict terms laid down by the order. Breach of the order will be seen as contempt of court. The order will be granted under the Family Law Act 1996

personalty
personal property such as money or jewellery

prescription
acquisition of an easement by a claimant through long use

probate
the court's authority given to someone to deal in a deceased person's estate

profit à prendre
a right to take from land belonging to another produce or soil, e.g. the right to collect apples or timber

proprietary estoppel
based on the principle that if a person acts to his detriment in reliance on the belief or promise that he will get rights in land owned by another, the court will uphold his claim

realty
real property or another name for land

rentcharge
the right to claim a money payment from land that is neither a mortgage nor rent from a lease

representation
A person who makes a representation to another that he has rights in property cannot later deny those rights where the representation has been acted upon. The person who relies on the representation must prove that he has acted to his detriment

restrictive covenants
a covenant is an agreement in a deed between the covenantor and the covenantee imposing positive or negative obligations on the covenantor

specific performance
an equitable remedy granted by the court ordering one side of a bargain to carry out his obligations

tenement
a plot of land

tenure
an exchange of land holding for the performances of services to the superior lord

trust
the transfer of property to a trustee who holds the legal title for the benefit of a third party

writ
a formal document used initially in court proceedings without which a claimant had no access to the courts if he wished to claim a remedy

Index

Page numbers in *italics* denote tables, those in **bold** denote figures.